D1598045

CRIME AND FORGIVENESS

CRIME AND FORGIVENESS

Christianizing Execution in Medieval Europe

ADRIANO PROSPERI

Translated by Jeremy Carden

The Belknap Press of Harvard University Press
CAMBRIDGE, MASSACHUSETTS
LONDON, ENGLAND
2020

First printing

Originally published in Italian as *Delitto e perdono: La pena di morte
nell'orizzonte mentale dell'Europa cristiana, XIV–XVIII secolo,
Nuova edizione riveduta,* Piccola Biblioteca Einaudi Storia.
Copyright © 2013 and 2016 by Giulio Einaudi editore, s. p.a., Torino.

Library of Congress Cataloging-in-Publication Data
Names: Prosperi, Adriano, author. | Carden, Jeremy, translator.
Title: Crime and forgiveness : Christianizing execution in medieval Europe /
Adriano Prosperi ; translated by Jeremy Carden.
Other titles: Delitto e perdono. English
Description: First. | Cambridge, Massachusetts :
Harvard University Press, 2020. | Includes index.
Identifiers: LCCN 2019044040 | ISBN 9780674659841 (hardcover)
Subjects: LCSH: Capital punishment—Europe—History. | Capital
Punishment—Religious aspects—Catholic Church—History. | Capital
Punishment—Religious aspects—Christianity—History.
Classification: LCC HV8699.E85 P7613 2019 | DDC 364.66094/0902—dc23
LC record available at https://lccn.loc.gov/2019044040

CONTENTS

PREFACE TO THE
ENGLISH-LANGUAGE EDITION

This book recounts the way in which a religion born from the preaching of Jesus of Nazareth, a Jew who was condemned to death and crucified, legitimized the death penalty for over a millennium. But actually it did much more than that: it transformed capital punishment into a great public ritual and made the condemned person a figure of Christ, that is, someone willing to accept death in order to save humanity. The person who had been condemned to death for their crimes was expected to offer an example of a Christian death, declaring remorse for what they had done. In some penal systems, like the English one, the condemned had to give a last speech to the crowd, describing their misdeeds and exhorting the audience not to follow their example.

After the display of remorse and the plea for forgiveness, members of religious associations or Protestant pastors handed over the prisoner to the executioner and his assistants, who sometimes simply proceeded with the hanging or beheading, but very often had the task of making the prisoner suffer through mutilation, hot irons, and other forms of atrocious suffering that might last for a whole day. Among them was the breaking wheel, envisaged, like all the other terrible forms of punitive torture, by Charles V's penal Constitution of 1532. All of this took place in the presence of the crowd and with the blessing of one or more churchmen: Catholic chaplains, Protestant pastors, members of associations specialized in comforting the condemned. They were the ones who, in the preceding days, had prepared the prisoner to meet their death, persuading them that if they expressed remorse and asked for forgiveness, their soul would live forever in the bliss of heaven.

This religious legitimation of violence on the scaffold was for a long time one of the contradictions of human history: not the only one, but certainly one of the biggest in Western Christian culture and one of the most widespread in the world. This book, though long, offers just a rough idea of the many forms taken by this fundamental model. I have been able to do no more than give a brief account of a vast body of documentation relating to a large number of intellectual constructs and institutions extending all over the

Christian West. Testimony to these practices and events can be found in architectural monuments, in artistic and literary creations, in poetic, musical, and theatrical compositions. If the Italian tradition occupies a bigger place in my account, it is because the "Misericordie"—associations of men and women set up to comfort the condemned and bury their bodies—were founded in Italian cities. Starting in the fifteenth century, the model branched out from there throughout the Christian world and beyond. The discovery of America, contacts with the East and with Islam, and the shattering of the unity of the Western Church in the age of the Reformation multiplied its proliferation, which was split and reflected as in the fragments of a mirror. The Anglo-Saxon readers to whom this translation is addressed will recognize in it certain aspects of their own legal and religious traditions.

But this historical study also has the ambition of being more than just a straightforward description. From an anthropological point of view, I consider the "scapegoat" theory proposed by Sir James Frazer and later picked up on by René Girard to be valid: the condemned person is like the goat on which the Jewish priest laid his hands during Yom Kippur, transferring to it all the sins of the people before shooing it off into the desert. The community concentrated all the evil that afflicted it, and that had been expressed in the violence of the crime, on the condemned criminal. By eliminating the criminal, the community purified itself and eliminated the evil, but at the same time asked the prisoner to accept full responsibility and to forgive their executioners. But as the condemned person is a human being and not an animal, the contradiction between the Gospel message of forgiveness and fraternity and the supreme violence of legally taking someone's life was resolved with the distinction between body and soul: the soul has a life of its own, survives the death of the body, and lives forever in another dimension. When, in eighteenth-century European cultures, there began to be a crisis of faith regarding the existence of the soul and the Christian afterlife, the religious foundations of capital punishment started to crumble as well, and the death penalty was first abolished by the grand duke of Tuscany, Peter Leopold, in 1786. This was preceded, in 1782, by the abolition of the ecclesiastical Inquisition—the disarming of the religious court.

The division between the life of the body and the life of the soul is being reproposed today by the forms of warfare waged by fringe groups of so-called radical Islam. What makes the threat difficult to counter is the religious conviction of the terrorists, who believe that by becoming human bombs and blowing themselves up in order to kill as many people as possible, they will earn the prize of martyrs—a place in paradise. The instinct for self-preservation that acts as a brake on the killers and terrorists of our cultures cannot be relied upon in their case. And yet similar phenomena can be found in European Christianity's past: those who killed God's enemies (heretics, infidels, Jews, rebels) were guaranteed the reward of eternal beatitude.

So does radical Islam rest on ancient beliefs that are destined to fade away? Maybe. But one thing is certain: religion has an inerasable capacity to exert a grip on human minds and bring about great upheavals. The bond between religion and pain, and between injustice and death, is deep and hard to erase. It is part of what Kant called the "crooked timber" of humanity. There is no guarantee that our own past will not come back to life, even though it may take unexpected forms.

PREFACE

The death penalty is a reality that has been with us for a long, long time: interminable, continually reemerging, perhaps inerasable. It is a complex reality, a cultural fact: as historian Louis Gernet observed, "if the act of putting a criminal to death were only a practical solution to the problem of legal responsibility, and nothing more than the brutal manifestation of a quasi-instinctive passion, then our tour through the garden of punishments would hardly merit any interest, even the interest of the curious."[1] The model of "semantic study" he proposed in his great *thèse* a century ago remains a landmark study for anyone interested in exploring this subject.[2] And a scholar who drew on it when recounting the history of capital punishment in the ancient world has written that "few things help more in understanding the most deeply held religious convictions of a people, their remotest psychological needs, their most deeply concealed anxieties, their conception of civil coexistence than how they choose to apply the death sentence."[3]

Despite the periodic resurgence of good intentions, new and not so new campaigns on the part of abolitionists, and the recent UN "moratorium" on the death penalty, legalized killing continues to be practiced around the world. It is a fact, however, that the practice is slowly diminishing. The 2013 report of the Hands Off Cain league listed forty nations where the death penalty still exists, just one of which—Belarus—is in Europe. It is still practiced in some US states. The continent where the largest number of executions takes place is Asia. In its largest nation, China, total executions fell by around 50 percent in five years. The trend is one of a slow, and perhaps irreversible, decline.

But whatever the trend, this book is not another of the many attempts to offer a complete overview of the issue: a final all-encompassing study can wait until the whole of humankind has turned its back on the death penalty and the past will be addressed in an effort to understand it. Instead, this work sets out to analyze the complexity of the bonds forged by a whole culture with the condemned in flesh and blood, making them central figures of its symbolic universe. To do this, it is necessary to bear in mind the liminal condition of a person who is sentenced to death by the justice system. The bridge linking the living and the dead is an actual human being, someone who, though they are still alive, already belongs to the world of the dead as the result of a court sentence. It is a condition that only apparently resembles that of a terminally ill person, a figure familiar to our present because it embodies a condition experientially similar in some way to a futureless present. The figure of the condemned has specific features that are entirely different regarding their relationship with others: their death cannot be blamed on an impersonal cause. Nature or fate do not come into it: rather, it is their fellow human beings, in a word us, who, through the mechanisms of a law and a power that represent us, or even simply by being part of a more or less inherited and shared history, culture, and tradition, carry the responsibility for their death. This sense of co-responsibility enables us to understand the accumulated sediment of guilty feelings that rise to the surface in the dreams and visions with which the history of superstitions and the literature of miracles are so rich. The purpose of this book is to try to understand the cost of the investment that medieval Christian culture had to make in order to habitually maintain reconciled relationships with the thought and the concrete figures of those dying by way of legal channels.

The history that will be the focus of our attention belongs to the age of the Christianization of death as punishment. Springing from the rootstock of the Jewish Bible, the culture of European Christianity had to come to terms not only with the prohibition against killing laid down in the fifth commandment of the Bible, but above all with some fundamental Gospel teachings, such as nonviolence and forgiveness. All this has posed a problem for a religion that, in order to spread and survive over time, reached agreements and compromises with laws, customs, forces, and traditions of every kind—to the point that Christian culture itself acquired a special, reserved power among the powers of the earth. In this journey, a religion promising the way, the truth, and the life has had to draw on particularly elaborate cultural resources in order to legitimate the death penalty as a legal practice. Hence the great richness of theoretical argumentation and practical solutions whereby legal homicide found its place in the most eminent sites of the Christian city and was transformed into a powerful instrument of religious emotions.

In the course of research that has occupied me intermittently for many years, I have become indebted to many people. Acknowledging them all would take too long. But I must at least mention Pier Cesare Bori, the friend who suggested the theme to me way back in 1982. I am only sorry not to have been able to show him the finished work.

CRIME AND FORGIVENESS

Introduction

Justice—Revenge or Reconciliation?

ON THE NIGHT between the first and second of May 2011, US president Barack Obama made an unscheduled appearance on television to announce, to the nation and the world, the death of Osama bin Laden. His first words were: "Justice has been done." The news brought jubilation in the United States; in Europe it was greeted initially with amazement and uncertainty, and then with increasingly less veiled criticism, especially in Italy. While from one end of the States to the other, all the "good people" of America took to the streets to celebrate the elimination of an "evil monster," as Jeff Jacoby wrote in his opinion piece in the *Boston Globe*, the Jesuit Federico Lombardi, the head of the Vatican press office, remarked sternly that "a Christian never rejoices in a man's death." After days of embarrassed comments and reluctant approval, a long report from the United States appeared in the pages of the Italian daily *la Repubblica*, in which Vittorio Zucconi endeavored to show that no other course of action had been possible in this particular case because the hypothesis of arrest and a fair legal process was not feasible.[1] Various reasons lay behind these decidedly lukewarm reactions, some linked to immediate circumstances: in Italy, for instance, the news overshadowed another much-awaited event, the celebration of the announcement of the beatification of Pope John Paul II in Saint Peter's Square. But in general a deep resistance was emerging that went beyond the known political and cultural reservations about the "imperial justice" of the United States—the US tendency to legitimate acts of war around the world with the notion that justice is a special mission of American democracy.[2] The occasion had brought to the surface a different culture of justice that did not share the idea of revenge as the right of the wronged with respect to the wrongdoer. This may appear odd to those who know that the same core of Christian ideas and practices holds sway on both sides of the Atlantic. And the link between justice and war has been familiar for millennia, with the war fought against an external enemy and the war against those breaking the law from

· 1 ·

within being regarded as different sides of the same battle. Nor is there any shortage of examples in European history, ancient and more recent, of religious celebrations being held following the death of enemies: a case in point is the solemn Te Deum celebrated in Rome after the massacre of Protestants on Saint Bartholomew's Night in 1572. And yet the fact remains that the killing of Osama bin Laden brought to light a gulf between sensibilities and behavior.

The episode brought out once again an ancient dilemma that has long troubled the conscience of our age: What to do with the vanquished enemy? In terms of relations of force, the question was expressed with lucid clarity by Niccolò Machiavelli in his *Discourses on Livy,* at the point where he wonders how to "deal with a divided city," whether by eliminating the defeated enemy or by seeking pacification. Machiavelli examined the three possible solutions open to his Prince: to physically eliminate his adversaries ("kill them"), remove them ("expel them from the city"), or come to a peace agreement in exchange for a promise not to rebel ("make peace ... and to undertake not to attack").[3] Machiavelli advised against the third possibility: memories of blood spilled in the past would render fragile any peace achieved through the use of force. The way in which the practice of power has followed this rule requires no illustration. But in the twentieth century, with two world wars and the outbreak of ideological, social, and ethnic conflicts in the decolonized world, the issue resurfaced in quantitatively and qualitatively different terms, demanding fresh consideration: the politically and socially divided city that needed to be dealt with and healed was now the size of the globalized world. And here the expulsion and physical elimination of the vanquished enemy entail different general problems from those faced by the Italian Renaissance city-state. Nor can we neglect the fact that the democratic constitutions and principles of freedom widespread in the world make it difficult to openly resort to the violence that was typical of the absolute powers of other epochs. Where, however, the power setup and the distraction or consensus of public opinion permit it, ethnic minorities and defeated opposition groups are still hit hard, or subjected to full-blown acts of genocide, or forced to embark on large-scale mass migrations. Then come the difficult phases of healing—of coexistence and memory. In the post–World War II world there is a past that does not pass—that of the Holocaust, of genocides, and of large-scale massacres. Here the justice of the courts has left vast open wounds. Questions are asked about whether it is possible to achieve pacification through forms of collective re-elaboration of the causes of laceration. And there is reflection about the events in South Africa, a state that emerged from a regime of separation and racial subordination, and experienced the work of the Truth and Reconciliation Commission.

But the reactions to the physical elimination of Osama bin Laden brought out substantively opposing views about the function of justice: vengeance or reconciliation, physical elimination of the wicked person or a punishment leaving scope for repentance and moral regeneration. The scales of justice have always oscillated between these extremes—periodically returning, in the search for adequate retribution for the crime, to the principle of an eye for an eye.[4] It is an ancient fracture line within a common cultural root: that of the classical, Jewish, and Christian code that has dominated our culture for millennia. The death penalty was inscribed here from the very beginning under the sign of the sacred.[5] In the Letter of Paul to the Romans, the key text of the Christian idea of justice, punishment is the exercising of divine vengeance on the part of the earthly authorities instituted by God (Rom. 12:19 and 13:1). And in the Jewish Bible cited by Saint Paul, God says: "Vengeance is mine, I will repay" (Deut. 32:35). In ancient Greece the term used for justice was τιμωρία, the primary meaning of which was "vengeance." It was through the mouth of Socrates that Plato, in *Protagoras,* distinguished legal punishment from vengeance: and this has been signaled as "one of the most momentous discoveries ever made by humanity."[6] Set against each other are two interpretations of a common idea of justice: whether it should be vengeance or forgiveness. This is a specific feature of the Christian tradition regarding justice—or rather, a Christian way of articulating an original characteristic of the idea of justice, which in itself contains two different and opposing impulses in Christian culture. On the one hand there is the "good news" (Gospel), which is higher than the law, and on the other hand, submission to the laws and powers of this world. On one side lies the faith of forgiveness, which annuls the biblical punishment of lapidation for adultery, and proposes, in the Lord's Prayer, the rule of mutual forgiveness between God and human beings; on the other, there is the Christian Church's deference to political power deemed to be of divine origin: "There is no authority except from God" ("Non est enim potestas nisi a Deo"; Rom. 13:1–2). The idea taken as a point of departure, then, is that two different plants developed from the same Christian root. But was that root really identical?

Nor is this the only, or indeed the most important, question posed by what has been identified as a Christian nexus. The administration of criminal justice and the resort to the death penalty in Christian cultures must come to terms with a primary issue—namely, that the Christian god was embodied, according to believers, in a human being who was sentenced to an infamous death and represented as a criminal, crucified between two thieves. Over the centuries, the crucifix thus became the fundamental symbol of the Christian religion in every place of worship and devotion. Not long before it acquired the form of the "suffering cross," Saint Anselm of Canterbury offered, in the eleventh century, the interpretation of the incarnation and death of Christ as atonement for Original Sin: and since then the doctrine of satisfaction necessary for wrongdoing has provided the ideal foundation for the penal strategies of the West.[7] During the whole long age in which the death penalty was celebrated as a public spectacle, the Christian cross figured at the center of that grand and cruel festival.

That the most terrible punishment contained a marked festival element was noted by Friedrich Nietzsche in a passage from *On the Genealogy of Morals* that has had a long and persistent influence: Edgar Wind drew on and emphasized it in an article he published in 1938, when, as an exile in London, he worked to rebuild the library of the Warburg Institute.[8] Wind recalled Nietzsche's observation while he was studying English anthropological literature. Reading Frazer's monumental work, he came across the section on the figure of the scapegoat and the sacrifice of the criminal as a substitute of the "divine sovereign" that had to die for the good of his people. According to Wind, two elements helped to pinpoint in those remote folkloristic practices the origins of certain aspects of capital punishment: on one hand the features of a collective feast, on the other the superstitious belief regarding the special power of the condemned person's remains. As the encyclopedic repertoire of German superstitions specified, under the entry "Hanged" *(Hingerichtete)*, the greater the misdeeds of the criminal the more powerful their mortal remains were considered to be. The memory of these origins had already been lost when the Romans made use of crucifixion to punish criminals: but the symbol of the cross itself, that of the wheel, or the rituals of the dismemberment of bodies, observed Wind, referred to a symbolic order of the cosmos; so if Jesus of Nazareth had been put to death without resorting to the cross, maybe Christians would not have elevated the instrument of death to be the sacred symbol of that power.

The issues touched on by Wind in the wake of Nietzsche appeared increasingly on the horizon of historical studies about capital punishment. The justifications offered by the legal culture of the time—namely, that the atrocity of the executions was aimed at terrorizing would-be criminals—do not sufficiently explain the carnivalesque qualities surrounding the ancient execution rituals. In the very long historic path of the system of crimes and punishments, the ritual of the scaffold has gradually erased those elements, replacing them with the seriousness and sadness of a pedagogy of moral and social discipline: only the norms of criminal law and the impersonal, bureaucratic violence of power have remained evident. To paraphrase a celebrated remark, one might say that killing a person legally has only with time become the pure and simple killing of a person. Meanwhile, in the course of that long evolution the ancient criminal God had to make way for the Christian God who died as a criminal, whose image has long offered a religious legitimation of the punishment: so long in fact that even Hitler, in 1941, shied away from removing the crucifix from the wall of the place where executions were carried out.[9] In today's ever smaller and more crowded world, the need to base the rules of justice on universal principles must take account of the problems relating to persistent differences in cultures. Perhaps this is the reason for the intensification of efforts to explore the Western tradition that, in the name of a religion of forgiveness and nonviolence associated with a God who died on the cross, has legitimated for centuries the right to kill and to exact vengeance.

❧ I ❧

Thou Shalt Not Kill

IS IT LEGITIMATE and right to kill other human beings? If so, when and in what circumstances? The legacy of the Bible has taken different forms in Mediterranean cultures, diverging between the Christian and Islamic traditions. Among the most evident differences is the Christian abandonment of the practice of stoning adulteresses, a punishment that still exists in Islam. On the other hand, both traditions embraced the interpretation of the biblical commandment "Thou shalt not kill" as referring to the sphere of private behavior alone. The rule does not hold for public powers, which can impose killing as a norm of criminal justice and in the event of war. This has been justified on the grounds of the biblical dictate, or on that of the natural law of people. The death penalty continues to be habitually practiced in various parts of the world and is a feature of the historic past of the majority of our societies. Even where it is no longer part of criminal law it persists in the cultural tradition and mentality of societies, because the fact that it once existed holds out the possibility that it could return. Its cultural roots are so deep that attempts have often been made to elaborate general theories referring to a natural or symbolic root that would enable us to understand why we feel the necessity to kill: the explanations oscillate between the naturalistic and the psychological. It is talked about as a natural and non-eliminable fact of the human species, whereby *Homo sapiens* is also necessarily *Homo necans.* The legacy of a very long past weighs upon our present in the everyday use of the Italian language. Deriving from the word *giustizia,* "justice," is the verb *giustiziare,* "to execute," a synonym for the infliction of capital punishment. Cultural memory speaks through a repository of ideas and images that we continue to draw upon in the heated controversies that regularly flare up over the legitimacy or otherwise of the death penalty. The plane of historic knowledge offers overarching descriptions and general historic-anthropological interpretations devoted to myths and rituals in the ancient

Greek and Roman world: for the Western Christian tradition the abundance of available sources has yielded an array of analytical investigations of the history of social practices, norms, and doctrines. But little has been said and done to understand the historic relationship between capital punishment and the sphere of the sacred in Christian cultures. That the relationship exists is undeniable: the quantum of religion emerging from the sources is so evident that every study of the premodern history of European judicial rituals has had to signal the religious aura of the punishment as a recurrent feature. There have been plenty of theoretical suggestions and general theses as to how this tie formed and developed in the history of Western Christianity. For instance, on the basis of a comparative study of the history of religions, Sir James Frazer argued that the condemned individual is the "scapegoat" onto which the whole community offloads everything bad that has to be eliminated. René Girard later grafted a theological-philosophical reflection in the typical style of twentieth-century French culture onto the research findings of the English anthropological tradition. He suggested that the Jesus of the Gospels, and the Jewish and Christian foundations of the West, should be credited with having made the death sentence an object of shame, and with having stimulated intolerance of it—albeit one which, he admits, took two thousand years to manifest itself. But ultimately, what are two thousand years "on the scale of peoples and civilizations"?[1]

In this book I will try to avoid the risks inherent to general theories by following the arduous and tricky path of historic sources. The subject of this work is the history of the Christianization of capital punishment that took place in the course of the long European Middle Ages, a process that will be reconstructed by investigating the traces offered by Italian history. But it cannot be ignored that the timeless duration of the practice and its continual reappearance in human societies offer an argument to those who uphold its legitimacy. Right at the beginning of the eighteenth century, a French observer wrote that the custom of performing elaborate ceremonies when taking men to their death was so ancient that no possible change could be envisaged in the immediate future.[2] He could not have imagined that not long afterward another Frenchman, citizen Guillotin, would lend his name to the instrument that marked the passage from the ancient artisanal ritual to the machine age. And this was soon after solemn declarations made as a preamble to the revolutionary constitutions of the United States of America and France affirmed the natural right to life as the first and most important of human rights. That did not stop death sentences from being passed, nor did it put an end to the devising of ceremonies and rites. Human beings still continue to be killed today as a result of legal decisions that vary in form from country to country, and their deaths take place for the most part in a ritual framework of symbols and messages. It is a question of justifying what is happening, not just in the eyes of society, but first of all in those of the person who is going to be executed. The purpose of the framework is to highlight the significance of what is being done: the choice of methods draws on elements lying deep within cultures. Two examples will help to give an idea of some of these variants.

In the absence of reliable official data, it is estimated that in China several thousand people are sentenced to death each year. The European Parliament, when it requested a moratorium on the death penalty in 2007, indicated that at least 5,000 of the 5,420 officially known executions in the world—91 percent—were carried out in China. A number of cases were publicized in that country on a special television channel designed to measure the degree of social consensus for the justice system and to send pointed signals to would-be criminals. From November 18, 2006, and for some five years thereafter, the Henan Legal Channel aired a talk show called *Interviews before Execution,* watched on average by 40 percent of the province's one hundred million inhabitants. The program was conducted by a journalist called Ding Yu, so beautiful and coldly pitiless that she was dubbed the "Beauty with the Beasts." Every Monday morning, Ding Yu interviewed a criminal due to be shot within a week after having been found guilty of violent homicide. During the interview, and again at the end, the journalist declared that the sentence was just and that she felt no sympathy whatsoever. Indeed, the interviewees were described as "excrement," treated with hate and contempt as enemies of the country, and told to their faces that society as a whole would benefit from their execution. In one case that attracted a particularly large audience, that of Bao Ronting, a homosexual who had murdered his mother, Ding Yu said she felt awkward about his proximity (homosexuality still being a taboo subject in China). In her every action, the journalist displayed her lack of pity for the murderer, expressing scorn and loathing, and egging on the audience to do likewise. But she also said that she had been thanked on various occasions for having listened to them, because they had many things in their hearts. There was no one in prison they felt willing to open up to, while they wanted to "talk about past events."[3]

The death penalty also exists in some US states, where the execution rituals have many variants but a shared basic structure: the sentence must be carried out by a mechanical or chemical agent triggered by an apparatus that gives the executioner an impersonal identity. Following the definitive sentence, a human being becomes a "dead man walking."[4] His address is the prison's "death row," where he lives out the time given to him by his lawyers' efforts to obtain a review of the sentence or a pardon from the state governor. Permission to watch the condemned person die is granted to a select few—members of the murderer's family and the victim's family. Hateful and loving looks are balanced by a state power without feelings and by a justice whose impartiality is symbolized by the blindfold covering the eyes of its symbolic figure—a blindfold that also covers the eyes of the prisoner at the moment of execution. Because the sentence is not carried out in public, death remains a private matter for the person who is to die, and he or she can just say a few final words to those present. A trace does remain, however, of the long past of Christian culture: alongside the condemned person stands a member of their religious confession, to comfort them with the words and rituals envisaged by the particular faith.

These are two examples that give an idea of the importance of rituals as an expression of the foundations of the judicial system in force and of the idea of justice on which it is based. The way in which the condemned person is shown and made to talk is fully part of the process. Both in the Chinese region of Henan and in the US state of Louisiana, the person about to die wants to be heard, wants to leave some testimony of themselves, of what they would like to be remembered about them—a plea for forgiveness, in the majority of cases a declaration of innocence, but at any rate always a final living act, an appeal to the memory of others. Even claiming responsibility for the crime can, if necessary, be a way of not having lived in vain. This primary need into which the final residue of the natural instinct for self-preservation and survival is channeled has had to be taken into account by all the cultures that have practiced capital punishment, whether to deny it or, more often, to exploit its efficacy for the legitimation of power. And in the way they have bent it to such ends they have appealed to the deep sentiments of their tradition.

The majority of the historic forms of power have conceived and justified legal killing. But each culture has practiced it in their own way. This has not prevented all kinds of justifications being invoked for the act of killing. Long before Enlightenment culture reached the point of affirming, in the name of reason, that every human being possessed the right to life, religions had proposed it in the name of a higher divine authority. The Tables of the Law that the Jewish people received from Moses included the commandment "Thou shalt not kill." It should be noted that the fundamental authority invoked since then in all the texts was a passage from the prophet Ezekiel (33:11), where we read that the living God of the Jewish Bible does not want the death of the wicked but their conversion. It is worth bearing this word in mind—we will come across it often. The Christian religion started from here in order to attain a higher level: that of the duty to forgive wrongdoings and love one's enemies. And yet Christian cultures, no differently from all the others, used to resort to the death penalty, and indeed often still do. During the age in which power was conceived as the fruit of a divine investiture they did so by searching, according to circumstances, for legitimation in the sacred Hebrew-Christian texts. The inexhaustible repertoire of biblical passages supplied sufficient arguments to silence any calls for moderation and forgiveness. But the primary path to legitimating the death penalty was first embarked upon by Saint Thomas Aquinas, when he distinguished Christian precepts from the norms of natural law: on the basis of this distinction, animals could be killed to feed oneself, enemies to defend oneself, and wrongdoers to ensure the health of society. His key argument was that the part is subordinate to the whole, the imperfect to the perfect, the single person to the community. Thus, a tainted limb of the social body can—and indeed must—be cut off. Admittedly a Gospel parable did say that the wicked should be allowed to live and be reserved for divine justice, just as the owner of the field ordered his slaves not to remove the weeds from the midst of the wheat, but to leave it to him to destroy them by fire at harvest time: but if the bad seed could be pulled out without damaging the good, why not go ahead and eliminate it straight away? And so the Gospel prohibition lost all its efficacy, paving the way for that same parable to be used to legitimate death at the stake in the struggle against the "bad seed" of the heretics. But there is a more general, anthropological argument that justifies capital punishment for Thomas Aquinas: by committing the crime, the wicked person ("malus homo") loses all human dignity and becomes a beast. So killing them could be for the good, just as killing a beast is.[5] Abhorring the culprit as someone who had forgone the dignity of being human thus acquired the dignity of a theological argument. From then on the dehumanization of the condemned would remain a commonplace in crime reports, as it would in the erudite language of jurists.

Even after the publication and circulation of the work of Cesare Beccaria, the position officially maintained by Catholic doctrine was that the death penalty was universal, and therefore natural.[6] But the most effective argument, and the one still officially advanced by the Catholic Church today, was that of the division of tasks between religious and political power. In recent discussions about the death penalty it has often been pointed out that one of the last European nations to abolish it was presided over by the Catholic pope. The *Catechism of the Catholic Church,* formulated on the basis of a project drawn up by a commission headed by Cardinal Joseph Ratzinger, later Pope Benedict XVI, pointed out, at no. 2266 of the 1992 version, that the traditional teaching of the Church recognized the right and the duty of the legitimate public authority to inflict punishments proportionate to the gravity of the crime, without excluding, in extremely serious cases, "recourse to the death penalty" (2267). Such rights and duties are analogous, according to the *Catechism,* to those "holding legitimate authority . . . to repel by armed force aggressors against the civil community." To some readers this analogy seemed questionable. Indeed, the text of the *Catechism* was reworked in the new edition promulgated with the apostolic letter of August 15, 1997, where the issue is formulated as follows: "Assuming that the guilty party's identity and responsibility have been fully determined, the traditional teaching of the Church does not exclude recourse to the death penalty, if this is the only possible way of effectively defending human lives against the unjust aggressor." These formal changes reveal the uneasiness of the Church toward its tradition and its increasing distance from the arguments that had been used to legitimate the death penalty. This uneasiness grows all the stronger together with the embarrassment of legitimating the right to kill while holding up the slogan of the defense of human life in order to combat the practice of abortion.[7] It is no accident that, on November 30, 2011, an international conference held in Rome to celebrate the anniversary of the first abolition of the death penalty in the world, that of the grand duke of Tuscany in 1786, was greeted by the reigning pope with words expressing his encouragement for initiatives "to eliminate the death penalty."[8]

There is a profound tie linking Christian cultures to the death penalty. The God they worship took human form and was condemned to death. For centuries justice was administered in his name in European societies. And the crucifix very soon became a habitual presence wherever people were judged and sentenced, whether to console the condemned or to legitimate those sending them to their death. In the history of modern France a provision of the king made it obligatory to display the religious symbol in courts of justice, offering defense lawyers a ready opportunity to point to it as historic proof of the gravity of judicial errors.[9]

The question that arises is this: What was that crucifix doing in court? Who had brought it there and why? Just asking a question like this prompts the realization that the death penalty as it developed in the history of European societies would be incomprehensible if one did not take account of the contribution of Christianity. As Hans Kelsen had occasion to write, "one of the most important elements of Christian religion is the idea that justice is an essential quality of God."[10] Not for nothing does the historic tradition of Western Christianity encompass not only the legitimation of capital punishment but also its contestation. There is a celebrated statement which, by common consensus, is considered one of the noblest expressions of Christian culture: "To kill a man is not to defend a doctrine; it is to kill a man." It was written by Sebastian Castellio, the sixteenth-century Savoyard humanist who raised his voice in protest against the execution in Geneva of the Spanish physician Michael Servetus, who was condemned for heresy. It was the culmination of a denunciation of the practice of sending people to their deaths for heresy that had run through the reforming currents of Christianity in the sixteenth century, starting with the writings of Erasmus before then being channeled into the paths of the radical Reformation. Albeit under a pseudonym, a vehement contestation by Antonio Brucioli had circulated in print, in which the author stressed "how great is the impiety of those who kill the Lord's servants on the pretext that they are heretics," also recalling that "Christ came not to condemn anyone, but to save."[11] Yet such views remained marginal, and those who held them often paid the penalty with their lives. And it was above all to affirm ideas that legalized killing continued to be practiced, accompanied, moreover, by the infliction of particularly cruel torture and suffering.

A Starting Point: Cesare Beccaria

ALMOST AT THE END of the age of capital punishment, Cesare Beccaria wrote *On Crimes and Punishments,* where for the first time the very foundations of the death penalty were criticized and contrasted with another form of punishment that would take hold and become a new and long-lasting paradigm. It was the beginning of another history, which saw, as Franco Venturi wrote, "the birth of a new way of feeling and thinking" that would run up against the legacy of a past that was still alive in Beccaria's time.[1] Beccaria was keenly aware of this. In his home city of Milan, the "Nobilissima Confraternita"—the "Most Noble Confraternity"—which, under the protection and symbols of Saint John the Baptist directed the spectacle of death through justice, was still fully active. Beccaria apparently possessed a copy of its "ledger"—the list of condemned assisted by the *confratelli* between 1471 and 1760.[2] From this he would have gleaned not only the statistical data and the details of crimes and punishments but above all an idea of the tie that had bound together capital punishment and official religion for centuries. And so, knowing full well that he would stir a storm of controversy, he took pains in his preface to the reader to present himself in the most innocuous and beguiling manner possible. He acknowledged the merits of religion profusely and expressed himself in deferential tones. Divine revelation was cited as the first and most important source "from which the principles of morals and politics that guide men are drawn." He praised the first of the "three separate classes of virtue and vice," the religious one, as being superior to them all, because "it is revealed directly by God and is sustained by Him." It was an acknowledgment with an ulterior motive: to leave it in the background, immobile and eternal, so that "political virtue" and "natural virtue" could be detached from it and given their own independent status. Beccaria writes: "Not everything commanded by revelation is commanded by natural law; nor is everything commanded by natural law commanded by the purely social law."[3] Like the strategy employed by the Horatii warrior in dealing with the three Curiatii, as told by Livy, Beccaria kept divine and natural justice at a distance: "Divine justice and natural justice are both essentially unchanging and constant . . . but human or political justice, being nothing but a relation between an action and the varying state of society, can vary according to how necessary or useful that action is to society."[4] What remained before him was just the changeable field of politics, which he addressed by moving to the firm ground of the criterion of utility. But in analyzing the key question of the magnitude of punishments—involving nothing less than graduating the scales of justice—his voice rose on a crucial point: the difference between crime and sin, and the impossibility of penetrating the hidden depths of hearts to measure the gravity of sins.

> Lastly, some men have thought that the gravity of the sin plays a role in measuring the degree of criminality of an action. The fallaciousness of this opinion will be obvious to an impartial student of the true relations among men, and between God and man. . . . The gravity of a sin depends on the inscrutable malice of the heart, which finite beings cannot know without special revelation. How, then, could it be used as a guide for the punishment of crimes? If such a thing were tried, men could punish when God pardons and pardon when God punishes. If men can run counter to the Almighty by blaspheming against Him, then they can do so also by punishing on His behalf.[5]

The allusion to those who had taken it upon themselves to replace God on earth was transparent. The body professing to pursue hidden thoughts was an important institution that in Catholic Europe had established its jurisdiction over sins of belief and thought, punishing them as crimes: the ecclesiastical Inquisition. Beccaria devoted chapter 39, "Of a particular kind of crime," to it. Here, in the shape of a meticulous declaration of the limits of his argument, is a resonant denunciation of the horrors of the Inquisition and of the intolerable error of treating sins as crimes:

> The reader of these pages will observe that I have said nothing about a particular sort of crime which once covered Europe with human blood and raised those sorry pyres whose flames were fed with the bodies of living men. These were times when the blind mob enjoyed the pleasing spectacle and sweet harmony of hearing muffled and cha-

otic groans issuing from swirling black smoke—smoke of human limbs, together with the cracking of charring bones and the frying of still-quivering organs. But reasonable men will see that neither the place, the time nor the present subject-matter allow me to discuss the nature of such a crime. . . . My topic is solely those crimes which arise from human nature and the social compact, and not those sins whose punishments, even in this life, ought to be regulated by principles other than those of a limited philosophy.[6]

Beccaria's attempt to distinguish his subject from what theologians dealt with did not save him from a fiercely aggressive attack by the Vallombrosan monk Ferdinando Facchinei, and the condemnation of the Church, which placed his work in the Index of Prohibited Books. It was not easy to suddenly loosen the knot that for centuries had bound together revealed religion, positive law, and political power. The idea that human justice should be linked to divine justice had been the foundation of every discussion about it: and it is still possible today to find someone declaring, at the end of a disheartened analysis of the absence of justice in the world, that "the key recommendation for justice in the future" is that of "a human justice wrought in the image of divine justice."[7]

In the erudite world, reconciling capital punishment with the idea of divine justice had not been difficult before Beccaria either. Anyone casting an eye on crimes and punishments in Europe during the ancien régime will see the robust certainties of criminal lawyers and theologians: a significant sample can be found in the celebrated Book V of the *Sententiae receptae,* published in 1568 by Giulio Claro.[8] And yet those witnessing, out of duty or choice, the torments and scenes of human butchery paraded as the work of justice must often have been struck and upset by what they saw. The question of whether capital punishment really was just had in fact been posed even before Cesare Beccaria found suitable arguments and a useful context for criticizing it openly. No one put it more clearly than an English magistrate, then undersheriff of London, who, in a small book that appeared in Leuven in 1516, made so bold as to declare that "it's altogether unjust to take someone's life for taking money." According to Thomas More, "nothing in the world that fortune can bestow can be put on a par with a human life." More also pointed out that even the harsh

Mosaic law punished theft with a fine rather than with death, before adding: "Let us not think that in his new law of mercy, where he rules us as a father rules his children, God has given us greater licence to be cruel to one another."[9] Behind More was Erasmus, who attentively supervised the printing and circulation of the book.[10] The key point of More's reasoning was the absolute value of the commandment that prohibited killing. And so, according to him, even if an agreement between men allowed killing on the basis of certain rules, as effectively happened with the laws of States, that agreement was just a way of not obeying divine commandments. His view remained marginal, however, covered by the literary form of the invention and description of imaginary countries, in the face of a theological and judicial literature intent on legitimating the use of power and rejecting criticism and protest as heretical or subversive. But his argument would leave something of a mark not just in the tradition of utopias but also in the culture of legal practitioners. A treatise that enjoyed wide circulation and considerable publishing success, the *Sylva nuptialis* of Giovanni Nevizzano da Asti, printed for the first time shortly after *Utopia,* specifically directed readers to More's work, in the context of a radical critique of the death penalty that reaffirmed the full value of God's commandment not to kill. To this Nevizzano added a significant consideration: killing a wicked person ("homo malus"), in his view, was even more serious than killing a good one, because that person's soul was damned for all eternity.[11] The message of More's *Utopia* thus fell on the particularly sensitive Christian ground of the fate of the individual soul. But the criticism of capital punishment was also rooted in a humanist culture that was capable of keeping its distance from the present in the name of a restored antiquity: it was thanks to the tools of philology and history that a highly authoritative jurist like Andrea Alciato expressed an extremely harsh judgment on the indiscriminate and frequent resort to capital punishment practiced in his time. In his opinion, it amounted to full-scale slaughter ("mera carnificina"), which had nothing to do with genuine Roman law as practiced in pagan Rome. On the contrary, a greater knowledge of the reality of ancient times might suggest an important reform of the system of punishments: rather than inflicting capital punishment, the ancient Romans preferred to deport the condemned to Sardinia, to a life sentence of forced labor in the mines. It was an example deserving of reflection: if the ancients were imitated, rather than resorting so extensively to hangings, beheadings, burnings, and mutilations on the flimsy grounds of some city statute, the deterrent effect would yield a useful public outcome, and an effective brake would be placed on criminality. In Alciato's view, the comment made by Caesar and reported by Sallust, to the effect that death is a relief from suffering and not a torment, was not to be forgotten.[12] It can be seen here that if Christian evangelism offered ways of contesting the recourse to capital punishment, humanist culture did so too. Alciato's suggestions greatly anticipated the alternatives to capital punishment that Beccaria would propose two centuries later. The lesson in methodology that Alciato gave to future historians of the penal system should not be neglected either: it was by reflecting on the semantics of punishments, as Louis Gernet would do, that one could move beyond the description of the "torture garden." Thanks to that remote ancient world the jurist was able to keep his distance from the religious nature of the death penalty in his time.

The circulation of ideas like these is hard to document, because such opinions were considered heretical and dangerous. But this form of humanistic rationality, and its religious grounding in evangelism and in Erasmus's rejection of violence, survived in the culture of the radical heretics.

There was also a more immediate and elementary rejection of the death penalty, that of spectators who, when they witnessed the human butchery practiced by justice, asked if it was right to put other human beings to death. Those doubts and those feelings of rejection must have been widespread among those who, out of Christian devotion, carried out the compassionate work of assisting the condemned in their final hours. Father Giacinto Manara, a Jesuit active in Bologna in the seventeenth century and whom we shall encounter again, referred to these doubts and criticisms in order to confute them:

> Some . . . did not greatly approve of the death [sentence] so often given by justice to the guilty, and were amazed to see that men raised with such difficulty by fathers, with such care and anxiety by mothers, and raised with great hard work through to adulthood, should then,

in an instant, either be strung up on the gallows with a noose, or be-headed, or cut into pieces, or bound to the wheel, or burnt. And they were doubtful if it was right, in particular that judges made so many die, and so frequently, as those miserable beings could be castigated—so they said—in a painful and lasting way, without taking away their lives.[13]

The idea of a punishment that was "painful and lasting" but not capital therefore preexisted the work of Beccaria. These anonymous voices gathered together by the Jesuit express an instinctive feeling of people who, in thinking like parents, step out for a moment from the role assumed in the service of the Church and the State: they are like a profound choral lament arising from the experience of life and daring to cast doubt for a moment on the legitimacy of such extreme punishment. In the reader's eyes they evoke the spectacle of execution: hangings, beheadings, burnings, quarterings, the terrible torture of the wheel (where every bone in a living body was crushed by running a heavy iron wheel over it). These were some of the most common methods of inflicting cruelty on the condemned, who were put to death in different ways depending not only on their crimes but also on their social extraction. While burning was the punishment for witches, heretics, and sodomites, beheading was distinguished from hanging because the sword was used for blood crimes and for those of noble birth. The thief's lot was the infamous gallows, a one-branch tree that had replaced the cross since the time of the Roman emperor Constantine.

There was, then, plenty to stir horror, repugnance, and a crisis of conscience in onlookers, especially among those engaged in trying to convince the condemned to accept their fate. And this was precisely the case about which we are speaking: those words had been uttered within a small gathering of the devout in a Bolognese oratory where efforts were made to comfort the condemned and prepare them for death. In publishing them, however, Giacinto Manara did not intend to make them his own. Nothing could have been further from his intentions than criticizing the death penalty. Anyone trying to do so in Italy at that time would have been taking a huge personal risk. Only the radical sects of the Reformation age had dared to deny the lawfulness of the power to kill: and they had paid dearly for their audacity. In fact, Manara reported the opinions only in order to confute them. Part of his job was to dispel any doubt about the usefulness and law-fulness of capital punishment: those assisting the condemned had to be very clear in their minds about the arguments to set against any protests or complaints. His confutation gives an idea of the Church's position at that time. Manara's reasoning followed a solid, ancient tradition. While Saint Thomas had referred to the universal consensus regarding the justness of capital punishment, Manara attached an annotation made by the great jurist Baldus de Ubaldis on a regulation in Roman law, inviting judges not "to make overly fine distinctions" when dealing with a crime: the offender had to be punished "because the public good demands it." If someone were to raise the Fifth Commandment, adding to it the parable of the weeds among the wheat (Matt. 13:24–30) to demonstrate that God did not wish to see sinners die, no account should be taken of them: the crucial passage for Manara was chapter 13 of the Letter of Paul to the Romans, in which the apostle guaranteed the docility of Christians toward imperial power, and legitimated power—any power—as deriving from God: capital punishment was legitimate because it was inflicted "with the authority of the Almighty God, deriving from it in its principles, as the Apostle Paul teaches when writing to the Romans."[14]

A fundamental text for the history of the birth of the Christian Church was thus mixed together with Roman legal regulations, establishing precise limits on the validity of the evangelical precepts: even the principle of reciprocal forgiveness between the children of the heavenly Lord as a condition for enjoying the remission of sins, as found in the most popular Christian prayer, the *Pater noster,* which the condemned had to recite as they went to their execution.

The dialogue on the death penalty that acquired written form in Manara's writings had as its framework a holy Christian space and as its interlocutors people who had devoted themselves to the task of consoling those about to die with the promise of divine forgiveness. Those same people, according to Manara, should not entertain any doubts about the necessity and legitimacy of capital punishment, an instrument that was required in order to ensure the "public good." The knot linking forgiveness and vengeance was bound tight by the goal of social control: anyone wishing to untie it appeared to the Jesuit to be a danger to the established order of society. The picture we have here seems to prefigure the Dostoyevskian terms of the "legend of the Great Inquisitor," where the voice of the ecclesiastical authority acting as a guarantor of social order silences the evangelical word of Christ. Yet those expressions of Christian piety and criticism of capital punishment that Manara claimed to have listened to really did express the original impulse inspiring the members of those confraternities. The interweaving of forgiveness and vengeance that was habitual to them is what we shall seek to analyze.

❧ 3 ❧

The Law of Forgiveness, the Reality of Vengeance

"VENGEANCE IS MINE, I will repay," says the biblical God, and the powers of Christian Europe, who had the monopoly on vengeance, exercised it in his name. The death penalty was widely practiced in Europe's past for a period of time stretching back to the ancient Mediterranean world and the Germanic cultures: the advent of Christianity as the exclusive religion of the long European Middle Ages did not erase this reality. The use of execution as the habitual instrument of a terrifying justice became particularly intense precisely in the period in which modern nation-states took shape and became established on Christian foundations—roughly the fourteenth to the eighteenth century.

In this age, capital punishment—also known as "vengeance" *(vindicta)*—was a regular and vivid occurrence in Italian and European cities. The rule of vengeance governed all social relations, and did not arise from a spontaneous drive or vindictive impulse: in the times we are speaking of, as has rightly been noted, "the law of blood vengeance imposed itself as a duty." And so, in the words of a fifteenth-century commemorative song, "though the child lying in the cradle / is yet unable to speak / He will have to avenge his father."[1] It was a moral and legal, or reciprocal, obligation binding people with the thread of honor and the voice of blood, to the point of delineating a system where gestures and behaviors obeyed unwritten but very clear rules. A study into the motives lying behind the offenses described in the pardon requests addressed to the king of France shows that in the majority of cases the crime stemmed from some previously received wrong, an affront that had to be cleansed with blood.[2] "Strictly speaking, vengeance is the inflicting of punishment to satisfy anger," wrote Francesco da Buti in his commentary on the *Divine Comedy*.[3] Not for nothing did Dante himself, whose family

· 21 ·

had experienced the violent death of his father's cousin, Geri del Bello, represent him in the poem as an angry soul on account of the failure to avenge him, which hung over the entire family as a disgrace (*Inferno* XXIX, 31–56). The rule of private vendetta was rooted deeply in custom, and traditionally envisaged in communal statutes. It can still be found in the Florentine statutes of 1415, though by that time there was a discernible and growing tendency in moral treatises and *ricordanze* to eliminate the practice in favor of reconciliation or at least of peaceful mediation by the public judicial authorities.[4] But it would live on for a long time in custom: it was the duty-bound way of reacting to an offense or some form of damage, not just concerning the family and one's name, but even before that, the community, the sovereign, and before all else, God. The judge's death sentence fell upon the rebel, the traitor, and above all the heretic. In the sixteenth century Andrea Alciato drew on the tradition of "divine vengeance" for the condemnation of followers of heretical doctrines (but added a sly critical observation that in the primitive church heretics were left to divine vengeance, not to that of the ecclesiastical powers).[5] Actually, as an eminent Spanish legal historian has noted, people hardly ever turned to judicial institutions to report a crime or to collaborate with the judge in punishing the culprit: private vengeance was the rule.[6] And even the penal justice of the ancien régime was called vengeance. Execution was the extreme form of such vengeance. Killing was only one and, certainly not the most painful, aspect of the punishment, to which were added a number of "aggravations." There was the moral violence of being displayed in public, either alive or dead. And there were the mutilations carried out along the route of the procession of justice or in the public square: the tongue ripped from the mouth of the blasphemer or heretic, the hand cut from the arm of the thief or killer, red-hot pincers to claw the body of the condemned, which became the terrain for translating the Gospel precept—to cut off the part of the body that causes the sin (Matt. 5:30)—into reality. The culprit would already have suffered judicial torture during the trial and now had to face an even more painful and distressing ordeal. The private aspect of vengeance was combined with the public one. Unlike what happens today when the death penalty is carried out in some US states, where relatives of the victims are invited to enjoy the show, at that time justice as vengeance was collective and public. Every time historians have tried to recount what Johan Huizinga described as "the violent tenor of life" in the autumn of the Middle Ages, terms like "theater" and "spectacle" appear:[7] it was a spectacle designed to educate many through the suffering of one. It came at the end, and at the culmination, of legal elaborations, political strategies, and judicial practices in which the life of medieval Western European cities found expression. It is no accident that historical research in these fields has yielded particularly rich findings.[8]

Here we will restrict ourselves to examining just the tip of the iceberg, the moment when the condemned person was put to death and the execution organized as a public spectacle. It was here that the reality of vengeance was engaged by the invitation to forgive expressed in the word of Christ, which had guaranteed the divine remission of sins to those who forgave the debts of their fellow human beings (Matt. 6:12–15), and had extended the biblical prohibition against killing to every form of hostility (Matt. 5:21–24). The most popular and widespread prayer in the Christian world, the Lord's Prayer, reminded all Christians of the obligation to forgive if they wanted to be forgiven. That short sentence—"forgive us our trespasses as we forgive those who trespass against us"—has disturbed or brought peace to innumerable human beings over the course of history, and has set large and complicated processes into motion. The interpretation of its real meaning has tested not only people's intelligence but also their willingness to establish fraternal relations with other human beings in the name of belonging to a family of which the father is God. That adverb—"as"—lay at the center of the problem: of all the testimony we might mention, that of Friar Girolamo Savonarola will suffice. According to the famous preacher of penitence, who was also an active practitioner of the priestly ministry of confession, some penitents declined to say this part of the prayer because they were unwilling to forgive their enemies and feared that reciting the words was equivalent to pronouncing the sentence of their own damnation. The same phenomenon occurred in the German Protestant churches, where the *Pater noster,* precisely because it appeared in the Gospels, had become the prayer par excellence, to the exclusion of all others.[9]

In the Hebrew Bible and in the New Testament, Hans Kelsen wrote, two different notions emerge and engage with each other: on one hand, the idea of justice as retribution, known as the law of "an eye for an eye," and on the other, that of fraternal love and forgiveness.[10] The premises of both notions of justice—of love and of retribution—lay, in Kelsen's view, in Judaism. But in the preaching of Jesus of Nazareth, love and forgiveness is prevalent. It is in the Judeo-Christian tradition, according to Kelsen, that the intertwining and the conflict between the messianic idea of a justice to be achieved on earth (with the final judgment of God and the resurrection of the dead), and the shifting into the afterlife of justice as retribution for good and evil committed in life on earth, took root. On the one hand, then, there was the development of a conservative function of religion, if what prevailed was the idea that the individual soul would find just retribution only in the after-life; on the other hand, the expectation of the resurrection of the body and of the final judgment gave rise to a revolutionary function.

Similarly revolutionary was the idea of a general remission of debts and sins that emerges in the Gospels: here, it has been observed, Jesus communicated with his listeners in the context of the meanings of the language and of Jewish tradition of his time: an age in which the jubilee and the remission of debts had not yet become Church institutions.[11] Within Jesus's Jewish horizons the form assumed by the need to erase or redeem one's sins was that of the jubilee. As described in chapter 25 of Leviticus, the jubilee meant the reconciliation and recomposition of the whole of society, the liberation from debts, the return of everyone to their own family and their own property, the pacification of nature, the suspension of ordinary cares—feeding and clothing oneself, and so on. It was to be announced on the "day of expiation," meaning that regeneration required a rite of forgiveness of involuntary wrongs and compensation for wrongdoings (with voluntary wrongdoings remaining subject to legal judgment and punishment). The connection between expiation and remission documented in the Dead Sea Scrolls belongs to the mental horizon of Judaism at the time of Jesus. Here, with the prophet Isaiah, human conversion and divine forgiveness were bound to the idea of a restored justice and the prospect of eschatological hope. The general remission of the *Pater noster* is understood therefore as a passage of purification and expiation linked to the announcement of the imminent advent of the Kingdom of God: a God who was the father of his people, similar to those sovereigns of the ancient East who at the beginning of their reign granted an amnesty to their subjects and suspended the ordinary law to restore a higher justice. The eschatological and messianic nature of this notion remained in the background as a latent possibility, while the advent of the realm of justice and happiness was moved to beyond death and beyond the earthly world, the administration of which was entrusted in the meantime to political and religious powers presenting themselves as having been appointed by God. As we have seen, Saul of Tarsus's interpretation of the faith he proclaimed (after becoming the Apostle Paul) stressed its nonsubversive nature: slaves were to remain subject to their masters, women to their husbands: "Let every person be subject to the governing authorities; for there is no authority except from God" (Rom. 13:1). The Kingdom of God was put off to another time and another dimension: above all, it was not to be a human endeavor. Loyalty to Roman power, and a disassociation from and rejection of the messianic tensions simmering among the Jewish people, characterized his preaching. It is here that the regulatory function of the bond uniting the idea of justice with the notion of the "immortal soul" started. Meanwhile, the remission of sins was channeled into the sacrament of penitence and the practice of confession. The Fourth Lateran Council in 1215 approved the canon *Omnis utriusque sexus* promoted by Pope Innocent III; from then on the individual and secret confession of one's sins was established as an obligation for all Christians. As for the messianic idea of the restoration of human society through the canceling of debts and the general forgiveness of the jubilee, it preserved a deep root: the strength of the widespread sentiment of hope and the desire for renewal expressed in it came to the fore in the response to the great pardon of 1300, instituted by Pope Boniface VIII, which exceeded all expectations.

And it was exactly around 1300 that we encounter the representation of a scene that enables us to open the historical file on the relationship between the death sentence and Christian forgiveness.

ৠ 4 ঽ

The Murderer's Confession

"I THERE WAS LIKE a friar that confesses / a base assassin, who, on being planted, / calls him again, that death may be delayed" (*Inferno* XIX, 49–51). This is how Dante Alighieri describes the character of himself as a pilgrim in the afterlife, while bent over the soul of Pope Nicholas III (Giovanni Orsini), who has been buried head down. In this case too, the "like" is for Dante the cornerstone of the other world: the infernal punishment is drawn from the punishment practiced by the justice of the time. It was called *propagginatura*. In the language of peasant farmers, it denoted the operation whereby the branch of a vine or bush was pulled down and buried so as to produce a new plant. Likewise, the murderer asphyxiated in a ditch could aspire to a new life: confession opened the gates of heaven. It is barely necessary to recall the essential premises of this scenario, which are at least three in number: the personal and secret confession of sins to a priest, which was regulated and rendered obligatory by Pope Innocent III in the *Omnis utriusque sexus* decree of the Fourth Lateran Council (1215); the establishment and spread of the mendicant religious orders, delegated by the pope to perform the key functions of the religious government of peoples: preaching, administering the sacraments, and guarding against heretics; and the definitive affirmation of a vision of the other world structured in the three spheres of hell, paradise, and the crucial third place, purgatory, which introduced the dimension of time and of reparative punishment in the eternity of the kingdom of heaven, with the corollary of the immediate individual judgment of the dead person's soul without awaiting the universal judgment at the end of time.

Returning to the episode in Dante, what did the poet draw on for the elements in this scene? As far as Pope Nicholas III is concerned, a polemical prophecy that was circulating at the time and originated in the heretical movement of the Fraticelli (Spiritual Franciscans) condemned and described him as being surrounded precisely by the "cubs" cited by Dante. As for the scene of the confessor monk, he was an institutional presence in Italian cities of the time: envisaged by city statutes, a chaplain was generally entrusted with the task of administering religious services. The Florentine statutes of the early fourteenth century made provision for an experienced and reputable priest to be available day and night in the prison of the "Stinche" to visit prisoners and administer sacraments to them.[1] But Dante might have witnessed that scene in Pisa, where he spent a considerable length of time during Henry VII's visit. In Pisa as in Florence, the punishments for crimes were regulated by statutes: executions were performed outside the city walls so as not to contaminate with evil the blessed ground within them. We do not know of murderers being buried alive and headfirst in those years. But we do know with certainty that the condemned were assisted by a priest, and that their bodies were buried in consecrated ground: when this did not happen, it was because particularly execrable crimes or diabolic figures were involved, which had to be totally eliminated. Such was the case of Masina, a woman from Livorno, who in 1364 was condemned to be burned alive on a boat left to drift on the current of the river Arno.[2] It was an exceptional case, about which we know nothing else, and an extreme form of punishment designed to completely consume the evil. But right up to the last moment before the punishment was carried out, religious assistance was available, offering the possibility of confession. In Pisa the title of governor of the city jail was reserved for the chaplain. A Pia Casa della Misericordia was active there, presided over by a committee elected in 1305 following a joint initiative of the bishop and the city authorities: this body was responsible for aiding the *derelitti*—those who, either because they were outsiders or for some specific reason, could not count on other people or on the usual city institutions. It responded to situations of emergency, such as burying the bodies of the executed or providing comfort and the sacraments to prisoners. In the Pia Casa della Misericordia the secular power of the city authorities was combined with the authority of the bishop, who had the right to exercise a traditional power of intercession in judicial practices.[3] At the beginning of the fourteenth century, the governors of the Pia Casa requested and obtained from the bishop the appointment of a priest to confess prisoners and to administer the sacraments of the Eucharist and the Last Rites to those about to be executed;[4] the governors subsequently also asked the city authorities to build a chapel in the prison, where the priest could officiate the sacred rites.[5] A Confraternita di San Giovanni Decollato (Confraternity of Saint John the Baptist) is also reported to have existed in Pisa from 1329.[6] Carlo Gambacorta, the son of Pietro, who was captured while trying to wrestle back dominion over Pisa, found out that he was to be executed when he received "the commandment of the soul" ("lo chomandamento dell'anima") the evening before.[7] The expression, which would become commonplace in Italian cities, was a warning to prepare for death and to immediately attend to the sacraments. This particular case is exemplary. And historical events in Pisa offer us another example of how the intervention of the charitable lay associations limited the forms of execration and ignominy inflicted on the bodies of the condemned: when, in 1356, Holy Roman Emperor Charles IV sentenced six citizens to death to put an end to feuding between opposing factions, his order—that the bodies should remain on public display for three days—was modified after the Misericordia successfully pleaded to have the period of exposition reduced to just one hour.[8] Episodes like this give an idea of the role that city magistracies and lay associations were recognized as having in the Italy of the time in what was a key function of power—namely, capital punishment.

But the most mysterious and important part of Dante's scene is the one describing the gesture of the condemned man and the monk's reply: Why could the person who was paying with his life for a crime ask the churchman for confession right up to the very last instant? Confessing those who had been condemned to death was not a habitual practice in Christian Europe. It had long been a matter of discussion. Indeed, at the beginning of the fourteenth century, as the dramatic crisis of the clash between the papacy and the French monarchy unfolded, the Italian practice of granting the sacraments to the condemned was at odds with that of France, as we shall see. But the issue had a long history behind it: to start with, it presupposed that it was in the priest's power to remit sins in the name of God—that is, to perform a divine act by virtue of a power delegated to him by the Church. That power had been questioned by some. Peter Abelard, for example, had contested the soundness of the thesis that Christ had granted the power to bind and to loosen not just to the apostles but to all their successors, and had strongly criticized the exercising of ecclesiastical authority itself: What value could unjust excommunications and equally unjust and arbitrary remissions have before God? But Abelard's objections had been deemed heretical at the

Council of Sens (1140), and the "papal legislation on consciences" had continued its march.[9]

The rules were further fixed in the age of the papal revolution. The doctrinal battle was accompanied by a wide-ranging and complex reshaping of the system of tribunals and of the rules of justice.[10] A major part of this was the marked ecclesiastical shift toward the obligatory resort to private and secret sacramental confession, which would be ratified and generalized by the decree of the Fourth Lateran Council. It is certainly no coincidence that this was decided in the same context that saw the prohibition of trial by ordeal, a form of justice that left it up to direct intervention from God, in the shape of miraculous signs, to decide whether the accused should be condemned or absolved. What disappeared here was a form of trial based on a test that the accused or his representative had to undergo before the community. It was replaced by the trial as a process of searching for the truth, where a judge looked for clues and evidence, and tortured the accused in order to extract a confession of wrongdoing from the secret place of the heart. The secret nature of confession also became established; controlled by the ecclesiastical authorities, it contrasted with the tradition of the public confession of well-known sins, a practice that then gradually died out. The move toward the inquisitorial trial was a very significant change, which prevailed despite the doubts and opposition of jurists and the persistence of traditional ways of administering justice.[11] This type of trial ended up becoming the model for the proceedings of secular courts as well. The ecclesiastical inquisitorial trial as defined by papal documents in the twelfth and thirteenth centuries stemmed from the search for an effective way of acting against prelates guilty of excesses that encouraged heresies: to correct concubinary priests, murderers of bishops, illegality in the conferral of benefices, and so on, a procedure was invoked that did not wait for complaints to be lodged by other parties, or for proof to be exhibited, but made it possible to pursue in court those rumored to have committed blatant excesses. A type of justice developed from this that was aimed at imposing obedience on the ecclesiastical body as a whole, launching a harsh offensive against doctrinal dissent, with heresy being understood as the refusal to obey ecclesiastical authority:[12] and it was precisely in the definition of the crime of heresy that the issue of forgiveness was posed. Against the backdrop of the ferocious campaign against the Albigensians, a decision had to be made about how to treat heretics who, having fallen into error and been condemned to death, repented and pleaded for forgiveness. When Pope Alexander IV was asked by the inquisitors of Toulouse whether the life of repenters could be spared, or if they could at least be granted the sacraments of forgiveness and the Eucharist, he reiterated that the death penalty should certainly be inflicted on those defined as *relapsi*, thus reviving and hardening a category of crime originating during the persecution carried out by the Roman emperors. They were not, however, to be denied the sacraments of penance and the Eucharist. The papal letter was included in Book VI of the Decretals and became the canon of reference on the subject of religious forgiveness associated with the death sentence.[13] Admittedly, on a theoretical level there was the opinion of Saint Thomas, favorable to sparing the relapsed heretic's earthly life.[14] But the tough papal version of the norm was the one stuck to by the tribunals of the ecclesiastic Inquisition: it was a law permitting the heretic's property and goods to be confiscated and for the heretic to be put to death repentant and forgiven. Indeed, it is among the instructions drawn up for the tribunals that we first find the proposed union between condemnation and forgiveness—a model that would prove very successful and long-lived. Its distinguishing features are therefore worth considering for a moment. According to the *Directorium Inquisitorium,* the manual prepared for the judges of the medieval Inquisition by the Catalan Dominican Nicholas Eymerich, not only could the sacraments be granted to repentant heretics, but everything possible should be done to obtain their repentance. To this end the inquisitor and the bishop should turn to people trusted by the heretic and get them to convince the accused to renounce their heresies and think about the salvation of their souls: gentle, insistent persuasion such as to induce them to return to orthodox doctrine so they could be given the sacraments of penance and the Eucharist. This goal had to be achieved before proceeding with the death sentence, which was to be left entirely to the secular authorities, thus avoiding any possible contact with the holiness of ecclesiastical times, spaces, and persons. The same procedure was to be followed with the simple (non-relapsed) heretic. In such cases the work of persuasion was entrusted to groups of ten or twelve men, including laypeople, who were versed in law and theology and capable of adequately presenting orthodox doctrine and confuting heresies. There was to be no time limit on the process of persuasion, and the heretics were not simply to be handed over for execution even if they requested it (to avoid making them martyrs). Even while the pyre was being lit, the execution was to be halted if there were signs of repentance.[15]

Extant Inquisition proceedings show that this dialogue in the prisons and on the threshold of the scaffold was sought insistently for centuries. The authorities wanted to obtain the result of repentance so as to move on to the ritual of forgiveness and the readmission of the heretic into the ecclesiastical communion. The preferred practice at the time was to give the task of persuasion to members of religious orders, partly because of their theological competence and greater ability to argue against heretical doctrines. But in the meantime the pages of Eymerich's work reveal the beginnings, wholly within the ecclesiastic discipline and the tribunals of the Inquisition, of the harmonization between forgiveness and vengeance: it was the Church, through the words of its pontiff and of the intellectual and inquisitorial Dominican avant-garde, that placed the salvation of the soul and death on the scaffold alongside each other as two parts of the same sentence. The pivotal locus for this was to be the secret confession of sins to the priest, according to the form laid down by the canon of the Fourth Lateran Council. But it was precisely here that the Church's proposal would run into the resistance of political powers anxious to exercise their right to oversee and to punish. Their reasons were analogous to the ones that had prompted the papacy to devise the complex organization of its tribunals: it was a question of maintaining discipline over their subjects and punishing crime and rebellion. The nascent national monarchies could not quietly accept the confession of the condemned: to do so would be to acknowledge that those punished for their crimes could however be forgiven by the Church, and that the God to whom all the Christian powers referred was an executor of the decrees of the Church and of those alone. The issue had remote origins: the establishment of the Church in the heart of the Roman Empire had seen the elaboration of doctrines and practices of lasting efficacy. And it is to them that we must now turn our attention.

$\mathscr{H}$ 5 $\mathscr{F}$

The Earthly City, the Right to Kill, and the Ecclesiastical Power to Intercede

THE FIRST GENERATIONS of Christians were sustained by the messianic and eschatological prospect of the announced and imminent "Kingdom of God." Following the abandonment of messianism as the expectation of general renewal and the advent of divine justice, another perspective opened up, individual and no longer collective, regarding the survival of the soul after the death of the body. In a passage that would long remain at the center of theological speculation, Saint Paul wrote about the transformation of the mortal body into the incorruptible body of the dweller in the Kingdom of God (1 Cor. 15:35ff.). If to this victory of the mystical perspective that shifted the wait for perfect justice to beyond death we add the historic path that made the Christian sect the dominant religion in the Roman Empire, we have an idea of the function that Christianity was gearing up to assume in its dealings with the State—a function that found expression in a word that dominated in the "passions of the martyrs": soul. This is the word indicating the grounds on which the Christians rejected the cult of the emperor and were prepared to face the penalty of death.

The poignant description of "Saturus's vision" in the *Passio Sanctarum Perpetuae et Foelicitatis* gives an idea of how the members of the wandering Christian churches in the hostile empire imagined the journey of the soul: "We had suffered, . . . and we departed from the flesh and we began to be carried towards the east by four angels. . . . And when we were freed from this world, we saw a great light, and I said to Perpetua (for she was at my side): 'This is what the Lord promised us: we have received the promise.'"[1] Faith that the reward awaiting him was the eternal happiness of the soul enabled the martyr Carpus to smile as he was pierced with nails. And to those who asked him why he was smiling, he replied: "I have seen the glory of the Lord, and I am gladdened ... we bear everything. I fix my gaze upon he who sits to judge without error."[2] Standing in opposition to the earthly tribunal that torments and kills the body is the infallible tribunal of God that rewards the soul. These are potent images indeed, transmitted by the memory of the Church and capable of inspiring similar behavior hundreds and thousands of years later.

The history of justice, as an idea and as praxis, was profoundly transformed. Being condemned to death held no fear for those who believed that, through it, they were earning an eternal reward, citizenship in a realm incomparably superior to the earthly one of the Roman Empire. From then on the memory of the martyrs would remain a solid point of reference in Christian apologetics. But it was the divarication between body and soul, between citizenship of the transient earthly empire and that of the divine kingdom of heaven, that would characterize the idea of the administration of justice even when the reins of power were in Christian hands. Thanks to the notion and the representation of the soul, the religion of forgiveness ended up elaborating a model different from that of retributive justice—the justice of an eye for an eye or that of Roman penal law. In the Christian state, that of the Roman Empire and those of the Roman-barbarian kingdoms of Western Europe, the boundaries of the Christian community extended until they were identical with state boundaries. And the Church authorities—the bishops—performed a function that increasingly took the place of the political magistracies, carving out a dual power: to intercede with regard to the sentences of secular courts and to administer a special justice in relation to wrongdoings that undermined what was entailed in being a member of the community of the baptized.

This is not the place to examine the development of early Christianity and the building of the Christian community. The violent conflict with the imperial religion left traces in Christian martyrology of a willingness to forgive mixed up with the idea of an action, in history, of the God of justice, capable of reaching out and punishing the persecutors: this is what emerges from the *De mortibus persecutorum* of Lactantius. Forgiveness or punishment was the alternative posed in the meantime within the early community of the baptized with regard to the "traitors"—those who, at the time of the persecution under Diocletian, handed over the holy Scriptures to the imperial authorities. And it is here that we encounter the origins of the practice of confession and of the measures of expiation imposed on anyone who broke the baptismal bond of community. The Church as a community of redeemed thus developed the first rudiments of a discipline with legal norms and forms of punishment.

But it was when the Christian Church emerged victorious that the question of justice ceased to be a theoretical issue and became the business of a body of bishops invested with powers of government within the State structure. A situation was created in which the task of judging and punishing acquired religious features, churches became places of refuge, and bishops exercised powers of intercession as a matter of course. Saint Ambrose claimed to have successfully interceded with Emperor Theodosius I to secure the release of many people facing sentences ranging from prison to exile and the death penalty.[3] It is worth stopping here a moment to consider the figure and work of Augustine of Hippo, because his conceptual framework of Christianity's relationship with the earthly political order remained a fixed point in the history of the centuries that followed. And it remained so in the shape his thinking took after the previously persecuted new religion became the dominant one in the Roman Empire. Until then Augustine had firmly upheld the principle of the necessary link between faith and liberty, but after the shift in the balance of forces he found that there was a positive side to coercion. His Letter to the Donatist Vincentius, which offers evidence of this change, deserves to be read with special attention by anyone drawn to the tragic face of history. Here Augustine recounts how he arrived at his discovery: "My first feeling about it was that no one was to be forced into the unity of Christ, but that we should act by speaking, fight by debating, and prevail by our reasoning, for fear of making pretended Catholics out of those whom we knew as open heretics."

But he was then prompted to reflect on the example of his own home city: previously it had been entirely favorable toward the Donatists, but then, fearing imperial sanctions, had changed opinion so radically that "one could believe it had never existed there at all." The primary agent of the change had been fear. What was in itself a morally negative agent had provoked a positive change. There was thus reason to think again about the efficacy of power and the positive aspects of imposing faith by force. In his view, the vast majority of those Donatists held superficial convictions and were passively following a habit. Others were indifferent, or else had allowed themselves to be taken in by the propaganda of the heretics. Fear had pushed them to seriously rethink the question of the truth. And so people had been forced to learn more about it and to correct their superficial convictions, finally discovering the truth and embracing it unreservedly. Plunged into a state of anxiety by the imperial laws, they had recognized their previous errors and finally become convinced of the truth of the Catholic Church. The sovereign power had therefore done well to act with threats and the use of force. It was a shocking discovery, of which Augustine was the first to grasp the seriousness: that collective behavior is guided by needs and not ideas. The heroic age of the minorities of converts and martyrs was over. Christianity had become the dominant religion. The form it took, in the beliefs of the population and in shared convictions, would from now on be determined by the choices of those in power.

Hence Augustine's reconsideration of his own personal convictions about the free choice of conscience: for the mature Augustine, the discovery of the positive value of the *stimulus terroris* in the experience of the African churches after AD 400 paved the way for the theorization of the resort to educative violence, to the principle of tough love. A true friend is not the one who always treats you gently: God can be terrifying, but acts for the good of his children. Do the Scriptures themselves not demonstrate it? Here Augustine turns to the Gospel parable of the wedding banquet (Luke 14:23). There are the guests, to whom the message of salvation is addressed: but there are many empty places, and at a certain point the master orders his servants to go out and invite and urge anyone they meet to come and take part in the banquet. If some are doubtful or resist, they are to be compelled to enter *(Cogite intrare)*. That is what the Christian emperor had done when he used the force of his laws to compel the Donatists to abandon their heresy and to enter the true Church. The evangelical idea of a message of salvation that goes beyond the confines of Judaism and becomes universal gives rise, in Augustine's interpretation, to the theorization of the good use of violence. It was an example destined to be followed: the interpretation of the Scriptures changes according to context, adapts to the times, provides answers that illuminate and support necessary choices. It was in this way that the parable of the wedding banquet took on a normative value in the Western Christian tradition. The sovereign power became the good father of a family who had to use force to constrain those who were outside the true Church, or who had drifted away due to bad choices, to enter it. The principle was formulated by turning on its head, with the obligation of forced participation, the evangelical announcement of a wedding party open to everyone. And it provided the foundations, in the following centuries, for the doctrine of the legitimate resort to constriction and to the Christian use of violence in dealing with heretics and the faithless. But in reality Augustine had made a discovery that would cast its shadow far beyond the history of Christian theology: that of the relationship between political power and the views of the majority. The behavior and convictions of entire societies can be profoundly changed by a central will endowed with effective means.[4] Hence the conviction that the good of others can be achieved by force—something less reassuring than the "group confident of its powers to absorb the world without losing its identity" spoken of by the leading historian of Augustine, Peter Brown.[5] There was also the security of a divine plan legible in the history of the whole human race: a history that Augustine felt the need to rebuild on theological grounds when the world order guaranteed by the Roman Empire appeared to have been shaken to its very foundations and was no longer able on its own to absorb the whole world beneath the wings of the Church. In the treatise *De civitate Dei,* written after Alaric and his Goths had taken and sacked Rome on August 24, 410, the story of humanity was reconstructed in genealogical form starting from the postulate of a single progenitor, the biblical Adam: one man, whose companion was fashioned from his body "so that the human race might derive entirely from the one man" (XII, 22). The principle of the genealogical unity of the human species became allied with the idea of religious unity. And unity was built at the price of coercion and through the discrimination of rivals: pagans, heretics, Jews.

In the African context in which Augustine was operating, the weakness and often the absence of the Roman State gave bishops a particularly important role: the wish to preserve religious unity was indistinguishable from the defense of the political unity of the empire. From AD 380 onward, Christianity was considered the sole legitimate religion. Since the time of Constantine, bishops had had the faculty to exercise judicial functions, and in civil cases litigants could choose their court *(Audientia episcopalis)* in preference to that of the provincial governor.[6] And if we also add that celebrated bishops like Ambrose and Gregory had received legal training and performed civil functions before becoming bishops, we have an idea of what has rightly been defined as "a radical transformation."[7] The interweaving between State justice and Church justice became further complicated with the introduction of punitive state measures in defense of orthodoxy. The Theodosian Code of 438 gathered together laws upholding discrimination and punishing, with varying degrees of severity, religious acts and behavior that had become illegal; it codified a series of punishments that had been promulgated at different times and that lacked coherence. But the subsequent evolution of the system of punishments found here the foundations for a whole system of collaboration between political and ecclesiastical authorities in the exercising of repression. It was for this reason that the Theodosian Code became the focus of attention in the sixteenth century, when efforts were made to trace the foundations of religious intolerance and of State intervention with regard to the punishment of heretics. An important fact here is that the death penalty, already envisaged for black magic, was extended and used to punish pagan sacrifices and even Manichaean leaders.[8] This is how the first capital sentences came to be introduced, like that of the Spanish heretic Priscillian, executed in Trier in 385. It marked the victory of intolerance: a religion in power struck against dissenters by sending them to their deaths. And because the bishop alone had the means to inform the authorities of who was not in communion with the Church, a system of control sprang up that would lead to important developments. What had happened to the faith of forgiveness? A faint trace can be discerned in the distinction between the ecclesiastical powers of the bishop, on the one hand, and the state power of the functionary, on the other: the bishop had the right to intercede, calling for clemency toward the condemned, whereas the imperial officials had the duty to apply the punishment. These were the rules of the game, this is how the parts were divided up in a play with a forgone conclusion.

There was an example in AD 414, when the imperial vicar for Africa, Macedonius, received a letter from Augustine, bishop of Hippo, requesting that some condemned men be spared. In his reply, Macedonius asked Augustine if he really thought it was his duty as a priest ("officium sacerdotii") to ask for clemency for the guilty and if he expected the magistrates to be duty-bound to grant it. Could such an interpretation be based on religion ("ex religione descendere")? Was it not perhaps true that according to the Christian religion God forbade the falling into sin and did not give sinners the possibility to repent after the first fall? It was the first time that sin and crime were placed on the two dishes of the scales. The comparison was imposed by the far-from-clear distinction between the two authorities, that of the bishop and that of the imperial vicar. To acknowledge the bishop's right to place limits on the imperial vicar was to attribute greater power to the Church than to the State: but Macedonius's objections were not put in terms of a distinction that would become possible only many centuries later. Instead, the question here was to what extent the imperial vicar had to obey the precepts of the religion pointed out to him by his bishop without failing in his duty. For this reason Macedonius declared his total deference toward the bishop and religion, adding that having to be strict in sentencing was a burden for him as well. But severity was necessary: being soft on crime encouraged others to become criminals. In any case, religion also demanded that sinners be treated with severity: indeed, the perpetrator of a sin was condemned to the same degree as one who approved of it. By leaving the guilty unpunished, one became their accomplice. It was therefore necessary to conclude that the intercession of the bishop did not fall within the principles of the religion to which the whole empire was faithful.

The argument seemed to be deliberately designed to force the bishop to come to terms with himself. After all he was the one fighting the heretics, he was the theologian of the severity of God the judge, the moralist meditating on the corruption of human nature. And in Africa the struggle against the Donatists and the Circumcellions required the firm hand of an inflexible ecclesiastical authority guided by strict criteria that, in the face of the opposing threats of schisms and radical sectarianisms, were valid for everyone. Augustine replied with a long letter in which he reaffirmed the religious obligation to intercede on behalf of the condemned, but also distinguished the field of the magistrate from that of the bishop: crimes on one hand, sins on the other. That did not mean that bishops did not perform a judicial activity as well: they were responsible for punishing sinners, because without severity there was no law. Macedonius himself, as a Christian, had found himself in the position of interceding with a bishop to lighten a punishment given to a sinner. Here was the demonstration of the indispensable link between punishment and intercession. But the bishop had acted against the sin with a severe sentence—not a simple correction, a *correptio*. The punishment of the crime by the emperor's vicar was another thing. The sovereign power exercised by the judge and the resort to the executioner fell within the economy of a discipline of society thanks to which the good could live among the bad without concern. The connection between punishment and compassionate intervention formed part of the normal functioning of society. To forgive did not mean to condone the crime or wrongdoing. Jesus did not condemn the adulteress: yet anyone who was without sin could do so. But forgiving the guilty woman did not mean approving of her wrongdoing. And here Augustine wrote at length about the key texts of a religion of mildness and forgiveness. Pagan authors were invited to contribute as well. The God the father who forgives those who forgive others (Matt. 6:12–15), who opens the door to those who knock (Matt. 7:7–8), and the Christ who does not condemn the adulteress and forbids others to do so, can be reconciled with the wisdom of a Seneca whom Augustine believed to be in line with Saint Paul. Later, in another letter to Macedonius, Augustine substantiated the Christian notion of the "neighbor" and the religious idea of universal fraternity by turning to the celebrated phrase of Terence: "Homo sum, humani nil a me alienum puto" (I am a human being. Nothing human can be alien to me). It gave an idea of the relationship between bishops and magistrates in which the right to punish was softened by the request for leniency as an act reserved for bishops. The Christian magistrate was therefore no longer obliged to forgive, and the subversive effects of the model proposed by Jesus were eliminated: the punishments, both of sinners by the bishop and of criminals by the magistrate, were right; but intercessions were also right and appropriate. On this ideal ground proposed by Augustine, punishments were accompanied by the benefit of forgiveness, as welcome the latter as were just the former.

As Peter Brown has noted, the bishop's practice of intervening in judicial affairs in late antiquity was distinguished from that of the modern ecclesiastical Inquisition, above all by Protestant authors of the seventeenth century.[9] The great Reformation movement had been started by an Augustinian monk who took to its extreme consequences the conception of the separation between the city of God and the earthly city theorized by the bishop of Hippo. In a drawing by sixteenth-century German sculptor Peter Vischer, Luther's "discovery of the Gospel" is represented by the female figure of conscience, who, turning her back on the Roman papacy in ruins, entrusts herself to the sovereign as the sole executor of the divine plan of justice.[10] The Reformation—that is, the return to the form of the primitive Church—thus meant the cancellation of ecclesiastical power. But in the world of late antiquity the reality had been very different: the jurists of the Reformation age, from Andrea Alciato to François Baudouin, carefully examined the texts and history of Roman laws on religion and heresy, describing the landscape that opened up before those who looked at it above the walls erected by the ecclesiastical body—those walls that Luther, in his most violent and popular piece of writing, said he wanted to tear down. It was a landscape in which it was possible to see the gradual emergence of the religious bond as the one that was most fundamental to the unity of the empire, guaranteed by the emperor in person, but also, and increasingly so, by the widespread presence of the Christian religion and its network of bishops. In that empire the power of the bishops had become crucial for the functioning of laws. Here the recourse to religious coercion was the other side of a system where political ties had loosened. In the Africa of Augustine the imperial authority relied solely on the Church and the landowning aristocracy. When it came to administering justice, the power of the bishop was inevitably the decisive one. Reserving the right to intercede was also necessary to provide guidance to the imperial judges and prevent the excessive use of violence and terror. Bishops and imperial functionaries were still divided by a "thin wall of principle": that of the resort to the death penalty. Only in principle, however. Putting the heretic Priscillian to death on charges of magic and obscene practices had sent a decisive signal. The inclusion of capital punishment among the range of instruments for ensuring religious unity was a fact. Bishops like Augustine tried to contain its use within precise quantitative and qualitative limits, intervening at a practical level on behalf of the condemned, and on the theoretical plane clarifying the ecclesiastical point of view. In theory reference was made to the evangelical principle of forgiveness and leniency. But even the language of the bishops recorded impalpable changes in the climate of the times. Augustine resorted to oxymora to include severity in the field of charity: "Misericordia puniens" was preferable to "crudelitas parcens": a person who allows a child to play with a venomous snake without intervening is cruel. And referring to the fraternal duty to "correct" the brother who makes a mistake, he introduced a terminological variant that substantially altered the original meaning of the Gospel passage: he spoke of "ecclesiastica correptio" to define the exercising of the bishop's power to judge and condemn. The reality of resorting to coercion was thus legitimated and covered by the Gospel model, just as, in the same period, the parable of the wedding banquet was invoked to cover the use of force to con-

vert non-Christians ("compelle intrare"). A last formal distinction remained between the "correptio" of the bishops and imperial justice: the bishop's sentence stopped short of the death penalty. Unlike that of the imperial
vicar, the punishment imposed by the bishop allowed the sinner to live and
to learn to "live well." The use of "discipline" should not extend as far as
killing, because the punished would not have any possibility of benefiting
from it. But this did not mean that it was anti-Christian to kill: the judge
and the soldier had to kill in order to perform their office. The dividing wall
of principle was therefore full of cracks and breaches.

When Saint Augustine wrote to the proconsul Donatus in 408, asking
for clemency toward the Donatist rebels condemned to death, he made use of
that right. But it was a division of roles: magistrates had the task of being severe, bishops that of "tempering" severity with intercession.[11] They are expressions that would become rooted in the solemn and atemporal language
of the ecclesiastical tradition. The sentences of the ecclesiastical Inquisition,
for instance, entrusted the "secular branch" with the task of putting heretics
to death, while at the same time urging that it should "temper" its severity.
The principle of resorting to punitive violence was not in question. Indeed,
the extension of the punishments of common criminals to heretics was based
on the same arguments. Men of the Church had the task of proffering sentiments of mercy and moderation. But this did not mean casting doubt on the
system of punishments and the mechanism of retributive justice that put the
guilty to death. The virtue of mercy could ease the burden of sin carried by
every Christian: Saint Ambrose reminded the clergy and the Christian emperor that to spare a person who had been condemned to death was to release
oneself from the chain of guilt and to obtain forgiveness for one's sins.[12] But
anyone thinking that divine forgiveness for a whole life lived badly could be
readily obtained with that formula of the *Pater noster* must have been disil-
lusioned by Saint Augustine in some of the most severe pages of his greatest
work. Here, in confirming the eternity of punishments in hell, in opposition
to the doctrines of Origen, he sought to warn those who thought they could
easily secure divine forgiveness in exchange for forgiving their enemies. He
put it in terms that would have a very long and bleak echo amid the prison
population and those awaiting execution: "Yet we are not on this account to
suppose that every wicked man who has not changed his life for the good, or
even for the better, will be received into everlasting habitations."[13]

❧ 6 ❧

Bodies and Souls: Conflicts and Power Plays

THE DIVISION BETWEEN the two powers had taken place under the influence of the hegemony of the sacred power of the Church, which was in a position to dictate the rules to the political authorities insofar as it held the right to open or close the doors of God's kingdom. The distinction between earthly Rome and celestial Jerusalem corresponded to the one between body and soul; this parallel drawn by theology was pertinent to the concrete historic forms of the administration of justice into which the doctrine of the immortality of the soul in Western Christianity translated. In AD 494 Pope Gelasius established the distinction between the areas of competence: spiritual power relating to eternity and the salvation of souls was to be reserved for the Church, whereas the State was to hold temporal power, exercising it in the limited human time of life on earth. For the former the cross, for the latter the sword.[1] Effectively, what the Church and the bishops gained from the alliance with the empire was "a formidable power arrangement"; in exchange, the State acquired "a religious, sacred aura" as befitted a reality desired and blessed by God.[2] The recourse to the power of the sword by political authority thus received religious legitimation. The language of symbols spelled it out explicitly: the cross ended up with a central function in the loci of State violence, from military insignia to scaffolds. But the division of tasks created two different forms of rhetoric: that of forgiveness, the preserve of the Church, and of rigor, which belonged to the empire. In the age of the Hohenstaufen emperors, "rigor iustitiae" was still extolled as a special quality of the sovereign, with forgiveness being considered a fault, a sign of weakness of political power.[3]

In the meantime, as the case of Saint Augustine demonstrates, bishops were gradually exercising a power that became all the more effective as that of the imperial authorities weakened. When the Roman Empire collapsed, it was the Church, as institution and as culture, that performed a role of mediation with the new political and cultural realities of the barbarian peoples. Monarchic power, defined as a "divine service" (ministerium Dei), relied on the assistance of the bishops. The whole ecclesiastic hierarchy had a specific place in the administration of justice, which, as François Bougard has said, involved recognition of the clergy's "function as social regulator": an important example of this occurred when, in the imperial decree following the coronation of Charlemagne in AD 800, the new emperor condemned the pope's accusers to death for high treason. The pope, for his part, interceded for them, obtaining the commutation of the punishment into exile.[4] The legacy of Roman law left its mark in the drawing up of the ecclesiastical regulations for governing the Christian body: and as this coincided with the whole of society, infractions of the social order were considered and punished as religious crimes.

In this case, too, the new needs had to come to terms with existing reality in order to achieve lasting compromises. And if the legal patrimony of the Roman tradition appeared in Justinian's compilation already re-elaborated and adjusted to suit the Christian religion, now exclusive and obligatory, what unfolded in the Roman-barbarian kingdoms was the encounter between the Christianity imposed on the population with the baptism of sovereigns and the pre-Christian religious traditions, dominated especially by the rules of justice and the forms of punishments. That subject lies largely outside the scope of this book, but it needs to be taken into account in order to understand the interwoven threads created in the course of the Middle Ages between the rules of the Church and the forms of judicial administration, especially where the Germanic world and the Latin world came into contact and engaged with each other. Capital punishment lay at the center of this history right from the time when Tacitus wrote his great anthropological work about Germany. And it is worth recalling the opening words of Cesare Beccaria's celebrated work in order to understand the scenario facing the author as he searched for the origins of the criminal laws in force in his time: these derived, according to him, from "a few odd remnants of the laws of an ancient conquering race codified twelve hundred years ago by a prince ruling at Constantinople, and since jumbled together with the customs of the Lombards."[5] His horizon was filled above all by the Roman legal tradition that still held sway in Europe, but he did not neglect the importance of the traditions of the German peoples. These would be the focus of interest of the historic school of law, which, in the romantic and nationalistic nineteenth century, explored legal customs and popular traditions as expressions of a long-lived folklore and pre-Christian religion. In early twentieth-century Germany that legacy was brought together in a study by Karl von Amira, whose systematic reading of early German capital punishments presented them as sharing a sacred nature. For each of the ritual forms of execution it was possible to reconstruct the fundamental religious significance: an offer of human sacrifices to the specific deity that had been offended by the crime. The law of the Frisians provided that those guilty of sacrilege were to be drowned or suffocated in sand as an expiatory offering made to the water gods; heads were hung from trees to appease plant deities, while the sacrifice for the sun god was the agonizing death of the victim by the wheel.[6] The theme lent itself to a neo-pagan and racist twist with the Third Reich. But it is a matter of fact that the spread of Christianity had to come to terms with these kinds of practices. Adam of Bremen relates the fate of a Christian missionary named Wolfred who arrived in Sweden from England in 1030; after he destroyed an image of Thor, he was killed and his mutilated body thrown into a marsh. The story is lent credence by discoveries made at archeological digs in Denmark, the Netherlands, and Ireland, which have uncovered hundreds of blindfolded corpses with signs of torture well preserved by the marshy nature of the ancient execution sites.[7]

It was on different foundations, then, and in the face of deep-rooted resistances and traditions, that the Church formulated its canonic provisions regarding punishments for those guilty of publicly known misdeeds that broke the bond with the community of the baptized. In order to enable the guilty to make amends for their wrongdoings, to be punished, and to reenter the community, the sacramental channels of participation in the life of the ecclesiastical community had to be regulated.

To obtain forgiveness it was necessary to go through confession. And here we must remember the long process through which the culprit's request for forgiveness—an expression of contrition and a desire to reenter the communion of the Church—had been becoming institutionalized in confession as a sacred act: sacrament is the word that literally indicated a mystery, that of the special blessing of divine grace through the mediation of a minister. All these words—"confession," "pardon," "forgiveness," "minister"— came into being in the sphere of religion but were then transferred to the power to judge as an attribute of the sovereign. We will encounter them from now on as a key phase of the system of justice, that of the Church and that of the State. It is here that the original nature of the system came to the fore, the point where the sacred power of the Church and political power overlapped and became interwoven. Before the formalization of the obligation of private sacramental confession, relations with those who committed a crime and in so doing broke the communion of the Church used to be regulated through public confession and a plea for forgiveness directed at the members and the authorities of the ecclesiastical community: the example of Emperor Theodosius I, denied admittance to Milan Cathedral by Ambrose for the massacre of Thessalonica, is memorable. The pattern was repeated by Emperor Louis the Pious in 833, when he prostrated himself before the altar in the abbey of Saint-Médard de Soissons, and, before the bishop and the people, listed his violations of the *Ordinatio imperii,* which he had sworn to observe.[8]

A publicly known crime required punishment and amends. The confession of a secret sin was another matter, and the repentant sinner could be privately forgiven. A clear distinction was in force, then, between a crime and a secret sin: the latter was left to private confession and the contrition of the sinner, while the former required public penance. The experiment of the perfect life in the monastic communities reflects here the general orientation of the medieval Christian societies: John Cassian's institutes were very strict with wrongdoers, with exclusion from participation in the Eucharistic Communion and expulsion. In the life of individual Christians the norms established in the penitential books envisaged extremely severe punishments. Exclusion from the communion of the faithful was the fundamental punishment: and Communion was the same thing as the body of Christ, which in turn was the Church itself.[9] The wrongdoer could not participate in the sacraments for the duration of the penance, which could last for a very long time indeed, even for life. Centuries would elapse before the punishments were mitigated and it became possible to obtain forgiveness by paying tariff penance in money. But in the meantime there arose the problem of the relations between ecclesiastical punishments and those of secular justice. In the penal procedures of the Roman-barbarian kingdoms the most frequent punishment for crimes such as theft and murder was the death penalty. The system of ecclesiastical punishments for the readmission of the guilty person within the community was impotent in the face of a punishment that left no time for making amends and for rehabilitation. Could the condemned be readmitted to the communion before execution? If this was not done, the conviction of the temporal judge turned into an eternal one: the death of the body became the death of the soul as well. The two cities, the earthly and the celestial, ended up being subject to the same law, and the God of justice was forced to ratify the sentences of the earthly judges. Could the gates of heaven be opened to the souls of thieves and murderers or not? The matter was debated in councils of bishops in medieval Europe.

A record of such debate can be found in the deliberations of the synod of Reims in AD 630. A canon approved on this occasion stated that the communion was to be broken with any murderer who acted without the extenuating circumstance of legitimate defense. However, it also envisaged that if the culprit expressed remorse, the "viaticum of Communion" could be granted prior to execution.[10] In reality, though, things must have been quite different, because the diocesan statutes promulgated by the bishop of Reims, Sonnatius, in that same year contain an impassioned protest against the practice of denying the sacramental viaticum to the condemned. This was very serious, said the bishop, because it denied the hope and assistance necessary to face death; and the silence of the ecclesiastical authorities, who should have ensured that the canonic norms were respected, appeared all the more culpable.[11]

So not only was readmission to the communion denied to those condemned to death, but it was done with the connivance of the clergy. Surrounding those who were being sent to their deaths at the gallows we can glimpse a context of common loathing sanctioned by the breaking of the ecclesiastical communion and the withdrawal of the priest from the gallows. Nor was eternal malediction of the soul enough: the body had to be treated likewise. Christian burial was not similar to that of the Jews, nor to what was practiced by the Romans: Christians viewed death not as the end of existence, but as a temporary passage while awaiting the resurrection of the body. Saint Paul's words on this point (1 Cor. 15) suggest the extent to which the physical aspects of resurrection impassioned the early Christians. Dying was like sleeping, dozing off, resting. "Their flesh rests in hope," wrote Saint Augustine about the saints.[12] For this reason burial had to take place in consecrated ground; and the life did not abandon the burial area. Indeed, the tomb became the center of particular feasts and events that Augustine sought to regulate. But those who died outside the communion of the baptized did not have the right to burial in consecrated ground. This norm would remain fixed in European Christianity until very recent times: the emblematic case was that of the bodies of newborn children who died without having been baptized, who were long denied burial in consecrated ground.[13] But in medieval society the bodies of criminals were subjected to a far more severe interdiction.

An idea of what was involved can be gleaned from the wording of the curse recorded in the *Liber de synodalibus causis* of Regino of Prüm: the wrongdoer was to be buried in the donkey cemetery. Their tomb would be together with dogs and donkeys and their corpse would be devoured by wolves. Another formula specifically concerned the fate of the various parts of the body.[14] Ritual malediction was a form of exorcism of the evil power of a body that incarnated something demonical. And this signals to us the density of meaning associated with the execration of the wrongdoer: taking shape around them was the threat of obscure forces, which had to be fought off because they were conspiring against Christians. In the vying to combat these occult dangers could be measured the power of pope and king alike, both endowed with a divine mandate and both alarmed by the threat posed by enemies who, in rebelling against their power, endangered the collective body of Christianity and the similarly sacred body of the State.[15]

The norm attested by Regino did not come into being without resistance. This can be seen from the canons approved at the important synod of German bishops in Mainz in AD 847. They discussed what to do with the bodies of those condemned to death. Could they be buried in churches? And besides the bodies, there was the problem of their souls. Was it permissible to celebrate masses and offer intercessory prayers for them? The two issues were connected. In giving an affirmative answer to those two questions, the approved canon provided a long and complex explanation that is revealing of the difficulty in convincing those who were in doubt or disagreed. The case of those condemned to death is compared to that of the dying who receive absolution from sins and communion: If it was permissible to grant Communion to someone who confessed on their deathbed, why could it not also be given to those who were paying for their sins with death? And all the biblical and Gospel passages that would recur continually in the history of the problem were brought together here. The promise made to the good thief on the cross was recalled as an assurance that penitence is possible right up until the last moment.[16] Note that the question started here as an exploration of the general problem of the penance to assign to the infirm who were in danger of dying: because such people were not in a position to perform the penance requested for their sins, they would only be asked for a sincere confession in return for absolution.[17]

So the fate of the bodies and souls of the condemned remained problematic. One thing was evident to the ecclesiastical authorities: blocking the administration of the sacrament of penance to the condemned was a way of rendering the salvation of their souls impossible. The fact that the canon approved at Mainz was reiterated at the following Council of Worms in 868 is a clue to the continuing existence of the problem and the ecclesiastical body's commitment to solving it.[18] The sovereign could exercise the power of issuing the death sentence, but he was asked to acknowledge ecclesiastical jurisdiction over the future life of the soul. Final judgment was thus passed on the fundamental point over which there were conflicts and transactions between the two powers of the Christian world: the surest way of condemning someone to hell was to deny them readmission into the ecclesiastical communion and prayers in suffrage for the soul. This basically meant denial of participation in the sacraments of penance and of the Eucharist. Things would become even more evident beginning around the middle of the eleventh century, when the "refounding" of the Eucharistic dogma would give realistic meaning to the expression "body of Christ": from then on, the Host, when consecrated, "became one with the historic body of Christ," while the Church remained the "mystic body."[19] And the attempts to render executive in heaven the sentence passed on earth would accompany, like background noise, sometimes barely perceptible, at others clear and distinct, the history of the administration of justice in Christian countries. Those efforts rested on the bedrock of convictions that were widespread in Christian and not just in secular culture: that the culprit of a crime deserved eternal punishment, almost a transcription in heaven of an earthly sentence. There was no place here for the distinction between crime and sin. And doubts concerning the irremediable damnation of those sentenced to death would often arise not only in the minds of those about to meet that fate, but also in the views of the churchmen called upon to confess them.[20] Only in the long period of medieval Christianity would that attitude change, though the principle whereby someone who died in the act of committing a crime—a theft, a murder—was damned without question remained untouched. Even remorse on the scaffold was not in itself considered sufficient: the death of the condemned is certainly a torment—wrote the Dominican Saint Antoninus of Florence (Antonio Pierozzi) in the fifteenth century—but if it is punishment for an evil spell, and if the culprit expresses contrition only out of fear of pain, then their soul will certainly end up in hell.[21] The condemned knew this as well: a pseudo-Augustinian saying circulated in the halls of justice to the effect that of a hundred condemned, barely one was saved. In Christian Europe, and then in the Roman Catholic part of it, the criterion that a thief or murderer who died in the very act of committing the crime was to be considered reprobate for all time, and the body could not therefore be buried in hallowed ground, would be upheld for centuries.

However remote it might seem from the literal meaning of the *Pater noster,* this system represents the mature form of the construction of a Christian society subject to a power delegated by God. The demonstration of this is the long resistance of European sovereigns and their judges—but also of many theologians—to allowing the condemned access to the sacraments of confession and Communion.

Here there arises an issue that for a very long period of time—some thousand years—was destined to leave a great mark on the relations between ecclesiastical and secular powers regarding how to treat those who were condemned to death.

ꕔ 7 ꕔ

Confession and Communion for the Condemned: A Rift between Church and State

IT WAS PREDICTABLE that the secular courts and European sovereigns would end up being opposed to each other, as shown by the precedents in the acts of the German synods in the High Middle Ages. However, the conflict did not come to light until the declining phase of what has been described as the papal revolution, the rigorous affirmation of the supremacy of the Roman pontiff over every other power, pursued through the regulatory endeavors of popes from Gregory VII to Boniface VIII.[1] The contrasts that arose in the fourteenth century between the papacy and the French monarchy marked the first episode in the long history of strife between the papacy and European territorial states over the right to punish and forgive as the locus for ascertaining sovereignty. The contending parties faced off on the new foundations created by the papacy with the assertion of its power over every other earthly authority: a revolutionary affirmation given substance by a rapidly growing system of courts and a sophisticated legal culture capable of mastering a wide range of issues. The two powers—the papacy and the states—shared a common problem: how to impose obedience on their peoples, defend themselves from enemies, and combat the danger of subversion. Roman law, by now a subject of study in universities, provided a category of offense that took rapid hold and proved very long-lived: the political crime of lèse-majesté.[2]

Francesco Carrara, an eminent nineteenth-century Italian Catholic penologist, famously refused to discuss this type of crime in his course on penal law. For him it was not a theme in the history of law but simply an instrument of power, a juridical monster in its adaptability to a wide variety of deeds. Anything that sounded like disobedience to laws could be classified as lèse-majesté, and it obviously included any kind of plot or conspiracy against the sovereign. The sphere of power cloaked itself with the religious sacredness of divine investiture: so if disobedience to Church precepts and doctrines was classifiable as the crime of divine lèse-majesté, that which concerned the sovereign also came under the same name. The king of France, for example, was endowed with sacred power and priestly dignity by virtue of being anointed with oil from a sacred ampulla from which there derived, so it was claimed, the thaumaturgic power to heal scrofula. In exercising his regality he was the vicar of Christ, according to a conception that had matured by the fifteenth century: for this he was exhorted to combine the divine virtues of mercy and justice, punishing with death those who offended his majesty and rewarding with a pardon suppliants who invoked him.[3]

Trials became a political affair: those held in France can be viewed in tandem with the simultaneous development of ecclesiastical trials for the crime of heresy. At the beginning of the fourteenth century, the celebrated case of the Templars saw the authorities of the king of France and of the pope vying with each other in the resort to the criminal category of lèse-majesté. The inquisitorial procedure, involving the most savage forms of judicial torture, made its appearance here. This was the new face of justice, also found in cases of trials for violent crimes and theft. The establishment of total power over the life and thoughts of subjects took place under the influence of suspicion and the desire to know. The battle against enemies undermining the structure of the "respublica christiana" appeared difficult: it required a degree of multifaceted control impossible to achieve with the means available at the time. Hence the importance of preventive measures: the exemplary punishment of the criminal in the form of a public ceremony was one of these.

But above all it was necessary to examine people's consciences and to bring out what was hidden there. And it was here that two different and conflicting conceptions of confession stood at odds, both in practice and in the doctrines of the age. At the heart of the issue was the secret, that which remains hidden and immune to the gaze and to knowledge. It could be the secret giving solemnity to the sovereign's acts or the priest's prayers, but it could also be the secret covering misdeeds, revealed only to the ear of the confessor or to the investigation (inquisitio) of the judge. The widespread attention to the secret as the intimate repository of the conscience marked the historic commencement of a very important process: the development of the interior space as the preserve and refuge of the modern individual. But that hidden sphere also stoked a desire to know about and to govern people's inner lives. According to an adage widely cited by medieval canonists, the Church did not judge secret matters. God alone could enter into the human heart and decipher its content. The issue arose when, during the eleventh to thirteenth centuries, a new notion of penance gradually took shape. Penance began to be viewed no longer as an exercise performed by the Christian, but as a sacrament of Church membership, concentrated entirely in oral confession to the priest holding the sacramental power of absolution.[4]

It was around the question of the secret that the norms and strategies of the different kinds of courts set up in this period were measured. What I called the two opposing rhetorics of forgiveness and severity that distinguished the power of the Church and the power of the sovereign were becoming entangled from the time when, with the Gregorian Reform, ecclesiastical justice developed various branches and courts, and its remit was extended to include the pursuit of heresy and the disciplining of morals. This soon resulted in the establishment of a model of administering justice as an instrument of collective control and discipline, which the secular authorities quickly accepted and made their own. For the Church, justice ranged from confession (the sacrament of secret listening and the remission of sins) to inquisition (the investigation and trial of heretics and rebels in public courts), but the vast and complex landscape of courts elaborated by the juridical and theological knowledge of the Western Christian Church, as reconstructed by Paolo Prodi, was nonetheless traversed and gradually modified by tensions relating to the problem of conserving a system of power that felt threatened by any form of dissent or rebellion, and also considered itself appointed by God to procure the salvation of the Christian people. Hence the erosion of respect for the secrecy of the confession of sins.

The evolution that followed resembles in some respects that of the complex court structures of large modern democracies, where, in the name of exception, the guarantees of respect for individual rights have been placed to one side.[5] Effectively, while private confession furnished consciences according to the moral and theological categories of the institution, there began to be a tendency to transfer the hidden into the realm of the external forum. There was somehow a natural tension between the two fields; the power to judge could not really respect the secret repository of the individual conscience, paving the way for attempts to reveal the hidden and take hold of secret thoughts by persuasion or torture. When the threat of dissent and heresy shook the walls of ecclesiastical power, the boundary was quickly crossed, with the transformation of the norm of "evangelical correction" and charitable admonition (Matt. 18:15–18) into forms of constriction (what Saint Augustine had called "correptio"). "Evangelical denunciation" thus became "denunciatio iudicialis privata."[6] The sense of danger prompted a forcing of the rules and the introduction of norms for situations of emergency. As Jacques Chiffoleau has shown in a fundamental essay, it was in the context of the fight against heresy that wide breaches were opened up in the wall separating the secret of the confession from formal knowledge of the crime and its persecution in the external forum: and so, in the *Directorium* for inquisitors drawn up under the supervision of Raymond of Peñafort, confessors were invited to become "full-blown investigators or collaborators of the bishops in the struggle against dissidents."[7] We can understand, then, how a certain Auda from the Pyrenean village of Montaillou found herself brought before the inquisitor to be interrogated about some doubts she had about whether Christ was really present in the Host. She had expressed those doubts to her friend Ermengarda, who talked about them with her confessor.[8]

In the face of these developments in ecclesiastical justice, something of the ancient tradition of public penance for known crimes remained in place in the judicial procedures of the secular powers. French judges in the fourteenth century, for example, demanded public amends and refused to allow the condemned to receive the secret sacramental confession. So there was a conflict between two different realities, denoted in Italian by the word *confessione* and in French by two different terms: confession before the executioner *(aveu)* and in the presence of the confessor *(confession)*. In the French judicial system it was common practice to wait for the final confession of the condemned: in 1323 the knight Guillaume de Leans made his final declarations in several stages, the final one while climbing up "the ladder to Nicolas, the executioner").[9] The system remained unvaried when trials were held in courts of ecclesiastical jurisdiction. In 1357 Michelet de Terreblay, sentenced to death for theft by the judges of the abbey of Saint-Martin-des-Champs, confessed "on the gallows" to murder as well. He was brought down so his sentence could be increased, and then hanged.[10] A conflict arose here between the papacy and temporal sovereigns about how to treat those who were condemned to death for their crimes. Try to imagine things from the point of view of the condemned: the "perfido assassino" (perhaps) seen by Dante in early fourteenth-century Pisa calls the confessor as he is about to be buried head down. The priest immediately steps up close, hears his confession, and absolves him. In those same years in Paris, a woman named Marion de la Court was condemned by the royal court of Châtelet to die in the same manner. As she was being lowered into the grave, she indicated her wish to confess. They pulled her out and she confessed to a series of small thefts. But that confession was made to the judge, not the confessor, and what she said went on record.[11] The difference was substantive: French judicial practice made the public confession of crimes obligatory and excluded the condemned from the sacraments—and this represented an exceptional case in the eyes of the ecclesiastical authorities.[12]

The ritual of public confession had deep roots in Christian penitential practice. In front of the gallows the condemned had a final opportunity to tell the truth and lighten the burden of their conscience before appearing in front of the divine court. But the papal monarchy objected: to deny the sacraments to someone who, having expressed remorse, was readying themselves for death, entailed a denial of the power of the keys. And so, precisely in the period when the king of France had brought the papacy to Avignon, the new pope, Clement V, the Frenchman Bertrand de Got, found himself constrained to protest against the French ritual of justice: a decretal of 1317 contested the right of judges to refuse the sacrament of penance and the Eucharist. There was no shortage of theological arguments in favor of denying the Eucharist: to hang someone who had received it was tantamount to hanging Christ himself, according to Alain de Lille.[13] Justifying the denial of sacramental confession was more difficult, hence Clement V's protest: his decretal ordered judges, on pain of ecclesiastic censure, to allow condemned prisoners at least to receive the sacrament of penance before being executed.[14] But nothing came of it, and the traditional practice continued. The issue resurfaced at the end of the century: the knight Philippe de Mézières, a tireless champion of crusades who became a trusted advisor to King Charles V of France, proposed in a petition to the sovereign that those condemned to death should be allowed to receive the sacraments; but Charles V, on the advice of the chancellor Pierre d'Orgemont, declared that as long as he remained on the throne the ancient custom would remain in place.[15] Something changed when Jean Gerson added his authoritative voice to Mézières's plea. The renowned chancellor of the University of Paris submitted an appeal to the king on behalf of the condemned, calling on him to respect the truths of faith, as examined and certified by theologians: these included the fundamental obligation to confess one's mortal sins.[16] Every Christian, wrote Gerson, had to respect that obligation after baptism, and no earthly authority held the power to exempt them from it. Consequently, laws and edicts designed to impede the penitent sinner from confessing were without value and should not be observed.

But why was confession not granted to the condemned? Gerson explained it like this: If the condemned confessed to the priest secretly and in private, judges lost a useful opportunity to publicly hear revelations about possible accomplices and other crimes. So be it, responded Gerson, one must resign oneself to the will of God, who evidently does not want to leave everything to the judges on earth.

> If someone were to say that many crimes which would otherwise remain hidden are discovered thanks to the final confession, one can reply that this reason does not justify the transgression or obstruction of divine law: and it must also be said that God does not wish all misdeeds to be punished in this world, because otherwise nothing would remain for him to judge in the other one.[17]

The passage is significant for several reasons. Proceeding in step with the establishment of aural confession was the gradual overlapping of crime and sin. The ancient public confession of crimes before the community was dying out as a practice, together with the associated punishments and amends: or rather, it divided into two, over which the Church and the State established their respective powers. The sacramental tribunal of the former retained the power to absolve every misdeed in secret, while the lay courts of the sovereign claimed the right to continue using public confession. This had a wider justification than the one indicated by Gerson, because it transferred to royal power the symbolic value of performing justice by exhibiting a repentant culprit. In any case, the public declaration of the condemned had an undoubted judicial usefulness. Evidently, many crimes were only discovered with the final confession, when the condemned, before the gallows, freed their consciences by telling the truth after having tried at length to save themselves by telling lies. This is what normally happened before the court of Châtelet in Paris, as shown by fourteenth-century criminal records. The accused would initially confess to their crimes only in part, adding fresh details and disclosing further misdeeds with each successive act of torture, and calling on God and the Madonna to be their witnesses, to whom they commended their souls. But before the gallows, with all hope lost, many previously concealed crimes were then often revealed. A knight's groom named Guillaume de Bruc, once he had been dragged to the gallows, made a public confession listing over forty thefts he had kept quiet about until then.[18] By contrast, sacramental confession was liable to hide these final revelations by consigning them to the ear of the priest. The struggle over confession was therefore a struggle between powers for access to the symbolic value of justice, but also to the secret knowledge of the condemned. A related but clearly distinct issue was the granting of the Eucharist. In this case the protracted resistance on the part of State courts was sometimes justified with physiological arguments such as the physical presence of Christ in the body of the condemned, but was essentially grounded in the wish to confirm with divine condemnation the justness of decisions taken by earthly judges. It appeared an evident contradiction to readmit to the communion of the Christian body a person who was at the same time being expelled and eliminated by society.

The French experience saw an open clash between the powers of the Church and the State. But it also saw the affirmation of the salvation of souls as a supreme duty, a principle upheld with all his authoritativeness by the chancellor Gerson, who had no hesitation in threatening opponents with damnation. According to him, anyone, prince or judge, who used their power to deny confession to someone, stained themselves with a mortal sin and was condemned to punishment in hell. So, concluded Gerson, judges could consider themselves warned, and now knew the danger to which they were exposing themselves. If they chose not to believe his words, then they should at least have the foresight to seek counsel from those who knew the precepts of Christian law. The harsh tones of his injunction were followed by softer ones of compassion: the wretched condemned should not be subjected to further afflictions besides the ones they already had to suffer. Threatened by desperation about the condition they found themselves in, they could only be helped to die in a Christian way by the exhortations of a good confessor. Finally, Gerson sought to stir a sense of national pride: consider, he wrote, that there are countries like Lombardy where the Christian religion is not honored as it is in France, and which nonetheless do not adopt a custom as harsh, unreasonable, and unjust toward the condemned ("un costume si dure, si desraisonnable et si injuste") as the French one.

A royal edict of February 12, 1397, permitted those condemned to death to receive confession. Pierre de Craon had a stone cross erected near the gallows in Paris, where Minorite friars could hear the confession of the condemned.[19] But who knows how real a concession this was? The stone cross, like other similar monuments, sacralized the gallows in the very moment in which it made publicly verifiable the act of repentance of the condemned person, thereby maintaining something of the ancient confession before the community. When, in 1409, the treasurer and *grand maître* of France, Jean de Montago, was sentenced to death on charges of lèse-majesté and tortured unremittingly until he made a full confession of everything he had been accused of, he arrived at the gallows with a wooden cross in his hands and showing signs of great devotion, moving onlookers to tears. But he does not seem to have been allowed confession. And his final words were immediately reported to the judges.[20]

❧ 8 ❧

Buried with Donkeys

THE DISPUTE BETWEEN the papacy and the French judges was about the confession of the condemned—in other words, the fate of their souls. But in the background was still the fate of the body, a key issue in the history of the death penalty: the body was the sphere of punishment, the locus of many different torments preceding death, and the object of scorn following it. The importance of the final burial of the body in consecrated ground was in signaling the dead person's peace with Christ and the reconciliation between the condemned and the community. By looking at what became of the body, we can try to trace the specific quality of capital punishment in the long Middle Ages.

When a condemned person was executed, an irrevocable transformation took place, from the living into the dead. Until that moment, everything still seemed possible. A miracle was the solution imagined by legends that, for centuries, embellished with ex-votos the sanctuaries of saints and above all of the Madonna. In the absence of direct intervention by God or his saints, hopes were placed in the outcome of pleas for a pardon, in the intercession of powerful earthly protectors, in the benevolence of the sovereign, and, finally, in the impersonal bureaucratic convolutions of modern state powers: many channels of mercy that could lead to the materialization of a messenger bearing news of salvation. Medieval society found other solutions, thanks to the widespread presence of powers and places sacred to a God who lived materially among the living and could, through his grace, suspend or even cancel the sentence of death: and so, along the path to the gallows the procession of justice might encounter a priest offering the consecrated Host to someone about to die; or a prince of the Church, a cardinal; or again, the open door of a church offering the possibility of refuge. Innumerable fantasies were fueled by the feverish thoughts of a convicted prisoner awaiting a sentence feared but strenuously denied by the living person's consciousness.

There were those who imagined it would suffice to declare a willingness to marry a prostitute, or to become an executioner, in order to avoid death. And there was always the hope of a miracle: the relics of the saints, special prayers, magic-religious formulas, the protection of a divine lawyer. Finally, when all seemed lost, there was still a chance the executioner might miss with his axe blow, or that the hangman's rope might break—signs of God's judgment, which, having vanished from the legal system, reappeared and spoke once more to the crowd. All these things belong or belonged to the final hopes of the person about to die. Every now and then, those hopes came true: in the nineteenth century, while Victor Hugo was addressing the theme of a condemned man's final day, in Russia another writer, Fyodor Dostoyevsky, personally experienced the profound trauma of having his sentence suspended at the last moment and transformed into a long spell of imprisonment in the "house of the dead"—Siberia.

But in the majority of cases the sentence was carried out, and someone who a moment before had been living and breathing was transformed into a dead body. Killed by a deliberate act of violence, permitted and often desired by their fellow human beings. The sense of collective responsibility was gradually attenuated by the impersonality of the bureaucratic machine. Nowadays, impersonal executioners press buttons or, in bringing death to the living, resort to chemical agents, electricity, or poison. The distance between those who act and those on the receiving end is of the same kind as that which modern cultures introduced between dominant nations and colonial peoples, between the thinking subject and bodily functions—nourish it, evacuate it, make it breathe and vegetate without the participation of the mind. Even killing animals does not today have any of the qualities it once did, when the butcher's cleaver fell onto the ox's neck, or the sharp spike penetrated into the pig's throat and its long, unmistakable, piercing cry could be heard from a distance: other animals, sensing death and smelling the odor of blood, struggled frantically to escape, squealing and protesting. For many centuries the condemned were like beasts taken to slaughter. And the task of punishing them was an art, or at least a trade, with its own techniques and tariffs. Alongside the other trades and arts—the weaver, the painter, and so on—there was that of the executioner: in the German cities this was inherited, well paid, and socially important, albeit lumped among the "infamous" trades—butchers, tanners—by virtue of their shared proximity to the dead bodies of humans or animals.[1] There was, however, no executioner's art in Italian cities. Instead the role was a punishment, an alternative occasionally offered to someone who had been condemned—an "infamous" figure, "partially reintegrated thanks to their willingness to perform acts of ordinary ferocity on a daily basis."[2]

But for centuries the task of bringing about death involved laborious manual operations carried out directly on the body: and increases in sentences often made it a legal requirement that some prisoners should have their hands cut off, their tongue torn out, or their body branded with hot irons. "The end of the Middle Ages," wrote Johan Huizinga, "was an intoxicating time when painful justice and judicial cruelty were in full bloom."[3] The study of city chronicles to investigate the rituals of justice actually involved in Italian cities has shown that during the fourteenth century the additional punishments inflicted on bodies preceded the putting to death, and that only in exceptional circumstance were the heads exhibited on pikes: instead, the practice of quartering bodies following execution was a fifteenth-century innovation.[4] Some concrete examples will be given in due course. But we need to pause here for a moment to consider the relationship between the crowd that watched and often took part in those cruel and atrocious operations, and the memory of those put to death: they were impossible to forget, even if one wished to do so. Their blood had marked the path of the ritual procession of justice, their bodies were there, lacerated, hanging from the gallows, or quartered and fixed with butcher's hooks to the places where they had lived and committed their crime, with the statutes of many cities prohibiting the removal of the corpses.[5]

Therein lay a problem. The threatening shadow of a hostile ghost would appear on dark nights. And it would not be alone. The dead person, execrated and lacerated, violently expelled from the community of the living, would not disappear from the world, but would return, in the company of all the other prematurely dead, envious of those still enjoying the "dolce lome" (Dante, *Inferno* X, 69)—"sweet light." A common trope in Germanic folklore was that of the "Wild Hunt," also known as the "Furious Host": it spoke of ranks of dead roaming the earth, attacking the living to take revenge for an existence cut short by violence. Prominent among them were the hanged, who rode wildly through the night with a rope around their necks; and with them were those who had committed suicide, and children who had died without baptism.[6] Christianizing these beliefs required the invention of Saint Hubertus, a hunter saint who gave up hunting to become a heavenly mediator and savior of souls.[7] The fear that those who had died on the gallows would return to seek vengeance undoubtedly formed part of the universal paradigm of fear of the dead and of their envy for the existence of the living. At Trinity College Cambridge in 1932–1933, James G. Frazer delivered a series of celebrated lectures about the discovery of this paradigm in which he linked the universal fear of the dead to "the almost universal belief in the survival of the human spirit."[8] The data he gathered about the customs, beliefs, and expedients used to avoid the threatening return of the dead to the land of the living was not limited to the so-called primitive cultures of Africa and Asia, but extended in some cases to episodes in the European Middle Ages. What is striking about his survey is the number of remedies used to render the spirit of the dead harmless: decapitation, mutilation, the barrier of fire or water, complete destruction of the body.[9] And yet few have picked up on Frazer's suggestion.[10] The body that has attracted the interest of scholars of the medieval world has been only that of power, or rather, of powers, material and immaterial: the body of sovereigns, popes, or saints. It is in relation to these that the opposite and combined processes of the fragmentation of the physical unity of the material body of the individual and of the mental projection of the indivisible unity of the mystic body of power have been studied: the personal soul as a double of the body, the dynasty as the immaterial body of the sovereign. The bodies of the executed and the treatment of their remains have generally escaped attention—materials of a history of violence and abjection, to be forgotten. Those who did take an interest did so only to search, in the tangible remains of the condemned, for proof of a different destiny, of a natural predestination to crime: Cesare Lombroso, the founder of criminal anthropology as a science, collected the skulls of executed criminals in Alessandria, in order to study them together with many others and to find experimental data about the shape of the criminal's skull.[11]

The fact is that lives cut short by violence leave a feeling of horror in their wake, a special variant of the fear of the dead: it is as if the doors of the abyss hidden behind the colorful scene of life were to open. Those doors have to be shut, eliminating in any way possible those who have forced them open. This is borne out by the history of the forms of defense adopted in the face of another category of those who die by violence: suicides. On the symbolic plane, in Christian cultures their souls were considered to be excluded from the community linking the living and the dead: damned by God and confined in hell by widespread consensus more than by ecclesiastical decree. The curse extended to their bodies, which were seen as a source of corruption. The ritual symbolism of exclusion took different forms, but all were inspired by the principle of preventing any possible return among the living: enclosed in barrels and entrusted to the current of a river, buried with a stake run through the body, and so on. A constant was the refusal of a religious funeral, and of the reciting of any prayers or psalms. One special form of execration of the suicide, intended to keep alive fear and horror, involved subjecting the corpse to degrading rituals: for example, dragging it through the streets face down, displaying it on the gallows in the square and then dumping it among the rubbish. In the eighteenth century, besides being considered a religious crime, suicide began to be deemed a political one as well, an abandoning of one's obligations to the family and to the sovereign.[12] The fate of suicides thus seemed similar to that of criminals. Their crime fell within the category of treason, because they had betrayed themselves ("felo de se"),[13] a criminal category that, after first appearing in thirteenth-century England, would become established during a later age, revealing a wider scope when dealing with the problem of heresy.

But there is a deeper link between the two categories: the shared feeling of desperation. Persons who kill themselves despairs of the providence of God, refuses the gift of life, curses themselves and the whole of reality; a person who is condemned to death despairs of eternal salvation, weighed down by crimes and wrongdoings that earthly judgment, anticipating the judgment of God, declares to be unpardonable. This is what Bernardine of Siena said in sermons to his fellow citizens in Piazza del Campo in 1427, to encourage them to join the Compagnia della Morte: "Just think, when someone is sent to be executed, how much comfort they give him, and who perhaps, without it, would die in despair; and thanks to their help, he bears death patiently."[14] Actually, the despair of the suicide and that of the condemned were very often one and the same, because the terror inspired by death on the gallows and the suffering accompanying it was such as to drive many to take their own lives. Many clues indicate how obsessive fear about that type of death weighed heavily on the minds of prisoners. As we will see, those providing religious assistance to the condemned generally had to make sure they were constantly present at the prisoner's side during the night between sentencing and execution: one of their goals was to prevent suicide. In the provisions for the death penalty in German cities of the fifteenth century there is talk of the need for solid blocks of wood or even for a human presence alongside the condemned during the night preceding execution, to stop them from killing themselves; and it was for this reason, too, that they were allowed to drink copious amounts of wine or beer, so they could be dragged drunk but still alive to the gallows.[15]

A condemned prisoner was abruptly thrust into a condition we might define as terminal, the same term used for the experience faced nowadays by those whose doctors deliver the news of imminent death. In earlier ages the condemned was also a "terminal" living person: the sentence contained the date of death and the suffering that was to precede it. This plunged them into the abyss of despair that was the typical sentiment of the suicide. In the moral economy of Christianity, despair was a very serious sin: Hope was one of the three theological virtues. And denying hope was like denying faith or rebelling against the bond of love that should unite human creatures with the Creator and hold together the members of the Church. The image of Despair painted by Giotto in the Scrovegni Chapel (Plate 1) has the appearance of a suicide, the specular antithesis of spotless and trusting Hope; the figure of a demon harpooning the soul of the dying person shows the end awaiting the suicide.[16] Despairing and laden with hatred, the dead who had fallen into the arms of the devil were destined to loom over the living with all the threatening influence of their hostility. And so, as the condemned was put in the position of dying in despair like the suicide, it was necessary to comfort them, according to Bernardine, who was thinking of the fate of the soul. The nightmare of the avenging spirit of those who died a violent death on the gallows had to be kept away.

But decisions also had to be made about what to do with the executed person's body. Few aspects of material culture have been so important in the history of preindustrial societies as those regarding the burial of corpses. And in the everyday life of Western Christian societies during the long Middle Ages this was a problem that occupied minds in a special way.

The Christian culture of death inherited that of ancient Egypt, as has been demonstrated very clearly by the art historian Erwin Panofsky. Reconstructing the history of funerary sculpture in the Christian West, he placed

Egyptian culture at the origin of the evolution that led all the way to Bernini. The two cultures were linked by a shared contrast between a brief and painful earthly existence and survival in the afterlife like real life. The image offered by the medieval West is effectively like that of ancient Egypt: a society of the living at the service of the dead. Naturally, every attempt to enclose within a specific past age a subject like that of the human attitude toward the dead must come to terms with the very nature of a relationship that, as Panofsky rightly points out, lends itself like no other to the tenacious coexistence of "rationally incompatible beliefs," thanks to the incoercible force of "prelogical, one might almost say, metalogical, feelings," capable of stubbornly surviving even "in periods of advanced civilization."[17] Concealed behind rites and devotions apparently dedicated to honoring the memory of the dead there is often a sentiment of fear designed to exorcise the danger of the vengeful return of the "living dead." This feeling occurred particularly in cases of deaths on the gallows. What is involved here are lives suddenly and cruelly cut short as a result of collective responsibility—or at least with the contribution, and often the collaboration, of entire communities—and for this reason destined to weigh as threatening presences on the consciences of those remaining after them. We must take account of the weight of these fears if we wish to better understand the cultural investment necessary to pacify the hostile shadows of those put to death, and to forge a lasting peace with them. The history of the practices that took place around the execution site and the figures of the condemned is a constant demonstration of this looming fear of the return of the dead. Around the body and limbs of the condemned there hovers the sense of a special surviving energy, the legacy of a life that has not completed its natural course. The world of magical practices and of beliefs was long pervaded by it: as we will see more clearly further on, in the records of ecclesiastical trials for magic and superstition, we encounter what looks like a fixed repetition of invariably identical practices, where those corporeal remains are the ingredients of formulas and preparations destined to procure health, love, and riches. But for now let us focus on that body and on the way in which, in the long history of executions in the medieval West, steps were taken to prevent it from returning to threaten the living.

Still today, according to an Amnesty International report, "the condemned do not recover their identity even after execution: they are buried in the prison field, a place called the criminals' cemetery, and the hundreds of stone crosses carry no name and surname, but a matriculation number instead."[18] The vestiges of a long history surface in this contemporary fact. The first problem posed by the condemned for those sending them to their death has always been that of the body. What should be done with it? Remove life from it, of course. But execution is not a straightforward killing. It is an extreme punishment, after which the condemned escape forever from the power that kills them. Before death, their bodies are the instrument for making them suffer. The tortures inflicted to extract confessions of crimes and the names of accomplices are followed by further torment and suffering, depending on the gravity of the crime. But in ancient times it was not just a totting up of the compensation in suffering that the condemned had to pay for their crimes that determined the complex and atrocious execution procedure. Along the route to the gallows, their body would undergo a series of treatments dictated by an apparent logic of retribution, behind which, however, there lay another less explicit logic: severing thieving or murderous hands, just like the further fragmentations of limbs culminating in quartering and the display of the quarters in separate places were necessary procedures to destroy the unity of the body and erase for good the idea that the body might ever awaken from the sleep of the dead. Contrasting with their case is the desire for survival that prompted testators to request monumental tombs with depictions of the dead as sleepers; moving in the same direction are the stories of bodies discovered miraculously intact in their tomb, a demonstration of the supernatural nature of the dead, be they saints or vampires. For this reason, too, the death sentence was generally accompanied by the refusal of burial. Bodies torn into various parts, and then attached to butcher's hooks; or reduced to ashes and dispersed in the waters of rivers; or again, left to the mercy of animals who, by eating them, totally erased their humanity—all these operations relate to rituals of degradation and execration common to many peoples in different ages.

It does seem possible, however, to identify one specific feature characterizing the act of putting someone to death in compliance with a law, or at any rate in the name of justice: the authority that decides to carry out the death penalty resorts to the visibility of the act in order to legitimate it. This requires a public moment, the parading of the condemned, the making it known that the person is going to be or has been killed. To this end, use is made of the means of communication offered by the technology and culture of the age. A sovereign power may have its victims eliminated in the secrecy of the night and of the prison, but in the end the corpses will be publicly displayed. A power wishing to gain popular consensus will instead show the whole path of the condemned from the prison to the gallows, and will circulate infamous images. Only criminal regimes with complete disregard for the law, such as the military dictatorships or totalitarian systems of the twentieth century, hid the mass elimination of their victims in darkness, trying to eliminate their bodies in order to deceive public opinion. In imperial Rome, executions normally took place in prison without any popular control; but the corpses were then displayed on the Gemonian Stairs leading down from the Capitoline Hill, to publicly announce the elimination of a member of the community and to request consensus after the event, manifested in the form of a posthumous lynching. What remained of the corpse was then thrown into the Tiber.[19] In the vast array of execution methods offered up by Roman history, one fundamental point in common was denial of the right to a final burial of the body: only in exceptional cases might the authorities graciously suspend this interdiction.[20]

The final act was charged with significance. Nor could it be otherwise: nothing is casual about what is done to a human body by other human beings. We find this also in the culture of Christian Europe, marked by the recurrence of the form of extreme execration that consisted in denying burial to the condemned. Such privation was above all painful: there is a profound relationship between burial and the end of life that has left echoes in the myths and rites of many cultures. The suffering of the spirit that dwelt in the body is prolonged indefinitely, as it is left to roam unsatisfied in the place where the unburied corpse lies. From the drama of Antigone to the prayer of the hanged in François Villon's *Ballade des pendus,* culture has given voice to feelings that the condemned themselves expressed every time they had the opportunity. The extreme harshness of being condemned to remain unburied has left deep roots in folklore. The fear of the dead has always found a special hold here: and the miracle stories of the medieval Christian tradition show how the search for heavenly protection was stimulated. Without burial there was no peace for the dead: this was the belief long before Christianity, and this is what continued to be believed with the new religion. Among the punishments inflicted on the condemned to death, an especially infamous characteristic was the execration of the body, which, unburied and torn apart, was displayed on the gallows and then thrown outside the city walls and left to the dogs. Corresponding to it was the folkloristic image of the person condemned to death being forced to wander without peace together with other members of a furious army. The instinctive sentiment of fear of the dead here became fear of the vengeance of the dead, directed toward those who had cooperated in their violent end. "They have this persuasion," a Jesuit wrote to his superiors in the sixteenth century, "that the souls of the executed will come to disturb those who accompanied them to their death."[21] And a jurist of the time cited a popular proverb that warned against taking bodies down from the gallows after execution: "He who unhangs the hanged will be hung by the hanged."[22]

Even the clergy who heard the confessions of the condemned were not immune to these fears. One of the *exempla* gathered by Caesarius of Heisterbach tells the story of a murderer who threatened the priest on the threshold of the gallows, saying he would return to visit him after he was dead. Thirty days later, he did, and as a sign of his visit, left the priest with a paralyzed hand that had to be amputated.[23] He did not kill him because the priest had previously got him to sign a commitment to that effect.

Also for those condemned to the gallows, once the definitive, irreversible passage had occurred, culture as the symbolic embodiment of reality resumed its hold and dealt with the final treatment of the remains of what had been a human being. The remains were disturbing in two ways: in addition to the natural fear of the dead, there was a special reason for imagining a desire for vengeance, a curse emanating from the remains against those who had taken the life. The corpse is the primary incarnation of the idea of death: a linguistic trace has remained in German, where the body of the dead person has represented also symbolically the very idea of death (*der Tod,* Death). But the body of the condemned person, scorned and torn to pieces as decreed by the law, was a doubly malign presence: for the memory of the evil done by them and for that done to them. Execrable and execrated, all that was asked was that it should disappear forever from the earth and society where it had lived. The elimination of the body of the condemned is the fundamental step normally found in the rituals of the death sentence: thrown by the ancient Athenians into the ravine *(barathron),*[24] by the Romans into the Tiber, and by the inhabitants of medieval cities outside the city walls, the body was equated to trash with acts signifying the separation and dishonorable elimination of the condemned from the society of the living.

The bodies of the executed did not return to the earth. The boundary dividing the human being from other animal species was erased in their case. Unburied, thrown into a river or the sea, they were food for fish or dogs. Only special considerations placed limits in some cultures on one or another of these forms of body disposal. One example can traditionally be found in the culture of coastal populations, where fear of committing cannibalism prompted a ban on eating fish when there was the suspicion that they had fed on human flesh—a prohibition formalized in both Christian and Islamic religious norms.[25] Even when it came to capital punishment, Christians treated Jews as nonpersons, as animals: in Basel, during the homonymous council, two thieves were sent to their death in different ways: one was beheaded; the other, because he was a Jew, was strung up by his feet next to a large dog that bit him repeatedly.[26]

But the persistence of practices of execration in the transition from ancient culture to the medieval Christian one should not hide the existence of profound differences. Hand in hand with the advent of Christianity went a regulating of access to burial that was charged with new symbolic meanings. If the Jewish religion from which it derived had laid down funeral regulations with great care, Christianity soon set about specifying how and why care should be taken in attending to the dead. The expectation of the resurrection of the body and of eternal life in the kingdom of heaven that appeared in the Jewish Bible with the Book of Maccabees was the resounding good news of the preachers of the new religion. Hence the special care devoted to tombs where Christians were considered to be sleeping while awaiting Christ's return. This is how tombs came to invade places of worship, and the devotion of the relics of saints began. On the other hand, strict rules limited the right of the dead to be buried in the holy ground occupied by those destined for resurrection. The unity of the community of believers embraced the living and the dead; but it also barred access to a Christian burial to those who did not belong to that community. Ecclesiastical legislation was always at pains to establish the categories of exclusion. On one hand, the example of Sophocles's Antigone was used to recall that the pagans also attributed supreme value to the duty of burying the dead; but on the other, all the categories that did not have the right to be buried in the holy ground of the Christians were carefully indicated: Jews, pagans, heretics, despisers of the sacraments, suicides, newborn babies who died without baptism. In Rome during the modern age, the Congregation of the Inquisition had to conduct thorough inquiries to ascertain whether foreigners who died there had converted to Catholicism or not: where they were buried depended on it.[27] The remarkable thing, however, is that among these categories of the excluded there was no mention of those who died on the gallows.[28]

The executioner could torture and lacerate the body, and resort to the most atrocious forms of execration and vilification: these were the rules for symbolically affirming the expulsion of the condemned from membership of the human species. The Christian ecclesiastical ritual envisaged degradation for priests condemned to death. It was a particular aspect of the more general need for the symbolization of the descent of that body beneath the threshold of humanity: a threshold set very high, in a culture dominated by the idea of the human being as the image of God. But burial was not prohibited because of it.

At first sight all this seems very remote. The fate of human bodies is dictated by other customs and requirements. Behind us is the legacy of a cemetery culture regulated by norms of public hygiene in a difficult balance with ties of affection and memory: but above all there is the void left by millions of bodies eliminated in the crematorium ovens of the Holocaust, a point of no return in the history of humankind. And so the distant past reappears in isolated fragments, in the remains of ancient and solemn symbolic buildings. This is shown by a recent episode involving relations between Italy and the United States.

On July 22, 1997, the Italian newspapers were full of the news that, in the prison of Greensville, Virginia, the countdown had begun to the execution of Joseph O'Dell. Meanwhile, in Virginia, people were amazed to read that the Italian mayor of Palermo, Leoluca Orlando, had gone to see the governor of Virginia and had tried to visit O'Dell in prison. The request for a pardon and an appeal to the Supreme Court came to nothing. The execution took place as scheduled. But immediately afterward O'Dell's body was flown to Palermo, where it was buried in the municipal cemetery, in the presence of his wife and of Sister Helen Prejean, the author of a best seller about capital punishment in America and the leading light of a project to offer religious assistance to the condemned. In a short speech at the cemetery, the American nun declared that Palermo was "home to the most compassionate and justice-loving people in the whole world." A reporter noted that Joseph O'Dell's body rested alongside that of Stefano Bontade, a well-known member of the Mafia.

Where had the mayor of Palermo gotten the idea of offering honorary citizenship to the dead man in the world of the dead? And why did that idea go down so well in Italy, and cause amazement or indifference in the United States?

Among the things forgotten over time is the memory of the centuries in which the death penalty was practiced by the courts of the various local powers in Italy. In that period, the question of what to do with the bodies of the condemned had been important, and had yielded elaborate solutions. To piece together this story, we need to embark on a journey that will take us to various cities, small and large, and not only in Italy. But let's begin with Rome.

❧ 9 ❧

A Special Burial Place

IN THE HEART of ancient Rome, between the Theater of Marcellus and the Imperial Fora, is a place sacred to the dead of the Christian world: not the martyrs of the Colosseum, but a special category of the dead, those killed by an executioner. Their cemetery is named after and lies under the protection of a special patron, Saint John the Baptist—a very popular saint in the Christian tradition and to whom the primary centers of social life in medieval cities, the monumental baptisteries, were dedicated. But the figure that set Jews on their way to a new life by immersing them in the waters of the river Jordan appears here with another attribute, relating not to life but to death: his name is San Giovanni Decollato (Saint John the Beheaded), the eponymous saint of the homonymous confraternity. The burial place is in via di San Giovanni Decollato. Turning your back on the marble symbols of pagan Rome, you find yourself suddenly plunged into the most Catholic and Counter-Reformist climate of devotion imaginable. A short external staircase leads to the main entrance of the church dedicated to Saint John the Baptist. On the left of the façade a smaller door gives access to the premises of the archconfraternity that lends its name to the street: two small marble plaques on each side of the door bear an identical bas-relief image of a curly-haired, bearded virile head sitting in a bowl. Inside, the chapel is decorated with frescoes by sixteenth-century Mannerist painters narrating the events of the saint's death. From here you enter an open cloister, where, beneath the cobbled paving, are the graves of the *confratelli*. Like all other brotherhoods of the faithful, this too had the privilege of gathering its dead members together in consecrated ground. It was recognition of the function of burial as a work of Christian charity, which became so important that it was added to the end of the evangelical list of actions by which a Christian could acquire merit in the eyes of God. But as we shall see, the case of the Roman brotherhood was of a special kind.

Burying the dead has long been considered a task of the civil administration, regulated and controlled by public authorities. In Western culture, mourning is a private affair, as are choices about funeral rites, whether religious or not. The generally accepted principle of keeping the space of the living clearly distinct from that of the dead is the outcome of a fairly recent change dating from the eighteenth to nineteenth century. The process that, in compliance with hygiene regulations, led to the establishment of suburban cemeteries and the now-customary division between the dead and the living did not start until the eighteenth century. But the application of such rules encountered the resistance, in the Italian states, of an ancient and deep-rooted tradition, one that still speaks to us today from the tombs of churches and convents, and means that the ancient term *camposanto* has also survived alongside the definition of the "cemetery." The sanctity of the place and the sanctity of the deceased are interwoven in this tradition, which took shape at the historic beginnings of the Christian church: faith in resurrection became bound up then with the conviction that the bodies of martyrs possessed a protective and redemptive power. In them, the power of death had been defeated, and they were awaiting resurrection in order to be reunited with the souls that already sat in heaven "at the right hand of God." Saint Augustine had to intervene to regulate the behavior of the faithful, the feasts and the rites that took place near the tombs (the *laetitia*). The bringing of those bodies back into urban spaces and the sites of sacred rituals was the most evident sign of the break with pagan culture. There was no longer a clear-cut division between the spaces of the living and the spaces of the dead, but a continual circulation of the living in the places of the dead: the bodies of the deceased no longer offered testimony of the brevity of life and a stimulus to enjoy the pleasures of existence while there was still time. More alive than the living, they were the promise of future rebirth and a protective presence to whom one could turn. Hence the spread of relics, present in the altar where the consecration of the Eucharist took place and offered up to the veneration of the faithful. The chance discovery of the underground Rome of the catacombs at the end of the sixteenth century was a stirring event for a religious capital enjoying a strong revival, and provided a crucial argument to give fresh impetus to the international tourism of pilgrimages: but it also offered an opportunity to supply the new churches of the Tridentine parishes and those of the non-European countries with fragments of the bodies of saints, or of bodies presumed to be such.

In Christian language, death was called the sleep of the just. And efforts were made to sleep that sleep as close as possible to saints and their relics. Materially and symbolically reunited with those of saints, beneath the vault of the church or in the cloister of a consecrated site, the bodies awaited the day of resurrection and invited the living to pray for them, so that the suffering of expiation might be abbreviated and the purifying flame of the "place of purgatory" moderated and finally extinguished. Faith in the resurrection was accompanied by fear of the judgment of God. For this reason the protection of powerful patrons and their intercession with the heavenly judge was sought. How the resurrection of bodies could come about was a question that taxed the faithful for centuries; but one point remained constant in the proposals advanced by theologians—the certainty of the return of the limbs to the unity of a living body.[1]

The revival of cities in Western Europe was marked by a new religious disciplining of graves. They were once again housed within the urban environment, placed alongside cathedrals in spaces consecrated as holy ground, which was sometimes materially brought back from places in Palestine associated with the life of Jesus *(camposanti)*. From this time on, the question of the burial rites of the dead was posed in new terms: the presence of the dead alongside the living was the sign that the two societies constituting the reality of the Church, one formed by those still wandering on earth, the other by those who, at rest, contemplated the glory of God, had been recomposed and were at peace.[2] Just like many other social issues and problems, burying the dead was for centuries the principal task of associations and collective bodies: the confraternities. The bond of Christian brotherhood, initially formed by various monasteries united in prayer to the common Father of Christians, became characterized from the beginning of the thirteenth century onward by lay or clerical associations that, under the spiritual protection of a monastery, devoted themselves to assisting the poor and to burying the dead.[3] Their activity was regulated by the list of works of mercy, the genuine constitutional text of medieval Christian societies. Matthew 25 lists five of them, all concerning forms of fraternity and help for the living: feeding the hungry, giving the thirsty something to drink, offering shelter to pilgrims, clothing the naked, and visiting the sick and those in prison. But alongside and even more important than these was burial of the dead, which emerged as the fundamental work of Christian mercy. The sixth work *(mortuus sepellitur)*, which first appeared in a twelfth-century liturgy, can be found in the fourteenth century in the iconography of Giotto's bas-reliefs on the Campanile in Florence, and became ever more prevalent in later testimony.[4] Centuries later, another great artist, Piero della Francesca, in the panel painting commissioned by the Confraternita della Misericordia di Sansepolcro in 1445, depicted men and women under the broad protective cloak of the Madonna, and placed the representation of the burial of Christ in the center (Plate 8).[5] Burial of the dead was the task of the many Misericordia associations set up throughout medieval Christian Europe. This did not take place without opposition: the clergy demanded the exclusive right to the profitable business of conducting the funerals. In Rome, for example, a corporation of clergy, the Romana Fraternitas, appealed to the pope in 1237 against the lay brotherhoods.

The fear of death played a special part in Christian culture: after death the human soul had to face the judgment of God that had replaced the universal judgment expected imminently by the early Christians. Divine judgment might result in condemnation to an eternity of suffering if the dying person had not had time to repent and perform penance on earth. Hence the absolute necessity felt by everyone to be able to count on the mutual assistance of a company of *confratelli,* but also to profit from the death of others to meditate upon their sins, prepare themselves for judgment, and acquire merit in the eyes of God. What amounted to a kind of insurance policy evolved in the chapters of the lay confraternities, offering protection against the danger of dying without the rites of prayer and spiritual assistance. Participation in the burial rites of fellow brothers was one of the most important duties of these lay associations, inspired at the start by the exemplary model of monastic life. Burying the bodies of *confratelli* in the consecrated compound of the confraternity church meant they could enjoy the spiritual benefits of the masses and good works of the devout association of which they were members, just as the living members benefited from the protection of the souls of the just, positioned at the right hand of God and able to act as patrons. The living and the dead were linked by a bond that went beyond death—this was the promise inscribed in the statutes of the confraternities.

But what was so singular about the Confraternita di San Giovanni Decollato is that their *camposanto* did not just provide a resting place for members of the confraternity, as occurred habitually for every other devout association. It also took in the bodies of those who died on the gallows: beneath the feet of modern-day visitors are the bodies of those who were condemned to death in centuries past. Not all of them though. There would be no point looking for the remains of Giordano Bruno, who was burnt at the stake. Nor those of heretics or common criminals. For the body to be buried in holy ground, as the site run by the confraternity was, the condemned needed to have displayed remorse and paid for their misdeeds before dying. That is why not everyone who was executed was granted the privilege of being buried in the *camposanto,* or of being remembered in the masses for the dead to which the confraternity devoted the majority of their available income and the money they collected.

But in the meantime, it must be noted that a solid connection had been established between the sacrament of confession and burial in holy ground. Gerson's observation was correct then: compared to France, criminal justice took a different course in Italian cities, where the condemned could confess right up until the moment of execution, and their body could be spared the mockery of infamous display and "asinine" burial. How and why did this use to happen?

To answer this question we must examine the long history of the Misericordia confraternities. To a large extent it is a peculiarly Italian history, traces of which can still be seen today in the country's customs and institutions.

❧ 10 ❧

The Criminals' Crusade

IN HIS COMMENTARY on the *Divine Comedy,* Benvenuto da Imola recounts that Saint Francis of Assisi, on the point of death, said that "he wanted no other coffin for his body" than bare earth. And when asked by his monks where he wished to be buried, he replied: "ad Carnarium." The *carnaio* was the spot outside Assisi where the corpses of the condemned were dumped. That is where his body was buried, and it was on that spot, Benvenuto also relates, that a large, magnificent church, soon to become a magnet for pilgrims, was erected.[1]

Together with lepers in life and the condemned in death—the two categories excluded by definition, shunned and viewed with horror by the community. But things gradually changed, thanks also to the model offered by Saint Francis. Toward the middle of the fourteenth century, the Misericordia Maggiore di Bergamo, a lay association founded in 1265 by the Dominican Pinamonte da Brembate, began to set aside alms to help those in jail for debt and to bury prisoners who died there. Among the association's papers are payment orders for cowls, to be used by those who carried a cross and processed in front of the condemned as they made their way to the gallows.[2] In the space of little more than a century a profound change had taken place. A new work of mercy had been added, fraternity with the most despised category of human being: prisoners who had been condemned to death. This involved being close to them as they went to the gallows, and then burying them afterward. These were two aspects of the same work, consisting of redeeming them from loathing and rejection by opening for them the doors of membership to the community and treating their bodies accordingly. These were no longer thrown into the *carnaio* together with the carcasses of animals, but buried like those of other Christians. The practice did not just concern Bergamo. Many lay confraternities with a similar mission trace their origins—real or presumed—to around that same period in the middle of the fourteenth century. Real or presumed, because when tackling the history of the lay confraternities it is not easy to navigate through the mists of devout traditions to find the point where their work first commenced. On one thing all the confraternities were in agreement, irrespective of denomination or partisan loyalties: the need to root their origins in a very remote founding episode. It was the normal form of thought in a culture that measured nobility in terms of its ancientness. The dates proposed by the tradition of the confraternities tended to go back as far as possible. There were oral traditions, and there was often an evolutionary process whereby more generic and undefined charitable initiatives had led only with time to specialization around the sites and victims of justice: prisons and gallows. When annalistic counts of executions began to be kept in the fifteenth century, the lists ventured into the past as far as the year 1000. But already in that time the present was functioning as a magnifying lens, projecting the prestige achieved by the institution into a solemn founding moment. Historians who have investigated the first documentary traces left by the work of simple devotees— statutes, lists of *confratelli,* religious bequests, lives of saints—have actually reached the threshold of the mid-fourteenth century.

But the question that interests us here is why was it *then* that the fate of the condemned began to be viewed as a particular problem.

To answer this we need to look at the age of crisis of Italy's cities, dominated as it was by factional conflict and culminating in the great plague of the Black Death of 1348. Those years were marked by increasingly widespread social unrest, lacerating political conflicts, and a halt in general economic development: the examination of skeletons found in graves of the time has revealed signs of undernourishment and malnutrition that existed well before the onslaught of the plague. Donations for devout causes fell sharply.[3] The preaching and the religious movements of the time reflected the disquiet and bleak outlook of the Italian cities during the "Babylonian captivity" of the Church, marked by the transfer of the papal see to Avignon. In Italian cities of the time the prisons filled up with insolvent debtors, and obsessive fears about the threat posed by thieves and robbers hung over the trading of merchants and everyday life in general. Tensions between the wealth of the churches and clergy, and the shocking presence of the poor, prompted revolts and heretical protest. It was against this background that the preaching of the mendicant orders proposed the devout message of imitating the figure of Christ as a poor, suffering man. But there were also other reasons the function of the rituals of justice was exalted: reasons of power. The sentence of condemnation was pronounced by an authority acting in the name of God. And it was in the fourteenth century, as we have seen, that a battle without quarter began between the papacy and the king of France over who should exercise the sacred power of the sovereign-priest and embody the living image of Justice. In the previous century the decrees of the Fourth Lateran Council of Pope Innocent III had laid the foundations of papal theocracy and built a system in which the only alternative was between obedience and rebellion. So it became an obligation to swear obedience not only to members of the ecclesiastical body but also to all those in positions of public power. Anyone who did not obey was a heretic, guilty of the crime of lèse-majesté. But if the authority of the pope was like the light of the sun illuminating all the other celestial bodies, that of the temporal sovereigns also aspired to the same status. While imperial authority (*sacrum imperium,* as Frederick I called it) slid into crisis, the large European monarchies took its place. Completing the revolution that had begun during the previous century, at the start of the fourteenth century Boniface VIII propounded the image of the Church as the mystic body and the pope as God's representative on earth. Philip IV the Handsome responded by attributing sacred powers to the monarchy and by making his France the "holy land," the "mystic bride" of the king.[4] Consequently, all the rituals relating to the manifestation of power as the exercising of justice on earth received new attention and assumed a sacred guise. In addition to jurists, who began circulating ancient Roman models once again, simple Christians, together with their preachers and prophets, began to direct their resources toward justice.

It was then that the Misericordie that had sprung up in the Italian cities started to deal more closely with the problems of those who ended up in prison for debt, but also of those who went to their deaths on the gallows. Above all, the wave of the pauper movements brought to the fore a lay population animated by the desire to imitate the model of a poor and suffering Christ, and to search for his presence in the world of the marginalized and excluded. The contestation of a rich and powerful Church and the wish to personally read and interpret the Gospel message fueled heretical tendencies. But in the meantime the new mendicant orders were established, and their preaching provided stimulus for the devout lay confraternities. The desire to reform society with a return to the practicing of Christian values was channeled into local associations stimulated and linked by the network of new religious orders, which provided spiritual guidance.

From this sprang what for a long time would be the dominant theme of the statutory norms of the lay confraternities: peace, solidarity, and devotion to healing conflicts starting from a personal commitment to observing Christian precepts and the choice of special forms of mortification and penitence. A special role was played by the confraternities born out of the great penitential movement started in 1260 by Ranieri Fasani, a layman from Perugia—called the movement of the "disciplined," because, either naked or clad in sackcloth, they devoted themselves in public or in their churches to the ritual of self-flagellation. According to the rules of these associations, peace was an absolute value, to be preserved in every possible way in the internal dealings of what, not by chance, was called a "fraternity," but also to render triumphant in the life of the city at large. This was the purpose of their self-surveillance, with the mortification of the senses, the flagellation of the body, the frequency of the sacraments and in particular of confession. The micro-society of the confraternity had to obey rules that protected internal peace, resolving disputes between *confratelli,* correcting those who erred, expelling the incorrigible. In order to ensure that their fellow citizens might also enjoy peace—the white-clad figure representing the symbol of good government itself in Ambrogio Lorenzetti's fresco in Palazzo Pubblico in Siena—the brothers undertook to pacify litigants and offer fraternal assistance to the poor, sick, imprisoned, or condemned: actively performing works of mercy was seen as the way to restore peace and solidarity to society.

The echo of that original inspiration also reverberated for a long time in the wording of later statutes. "Since we knew how great the virtue of peace is and how much we need it . . ." invoked the statutes of the Compagnia di San Giovanni Battista della Morte of Modena, which presented the image of a universe where "the heavenly father ordered the planets, the sun and the moon and the stars and the other wonderful things visible to us, that all might be embraced and bound together by peace."[5] When statutes were reformed, it was "for the greater benefit of souls, and for its greater peace" (that is, of the confraternity).[6] The performing of charitable works stemmed from the desire to address problems of urban life by putting the Gospel teachings into practice: the poor, the hungry, the sick, and the imprisoned were to be viewed as figures of Christ. What was done for them was as if it had been done for Christ in person.

The urban nature of these movements can be seen in the need felt for precise norms in regulating the relationship with the dead. That is why Christian burial was added to the list of works of mercy. As has been observed, the gradual moving away from the natural forces imagined to be active in nonurban places translated into forms of marginalization of social groups and the loosening of ties between the living and the dead: city statutes were increasingly specific in laying down rules for funeral rites, placing limits especially on forms of mourning and on the presence of females.[7] The Jesus of the Gospels had said nothing about burying the dead, nor about consoling the condemned. But the original graft of medieval society onto the rootstock of the works of charity indicated in the Gospel of Matthew was precisely this. The lowest and most despised of all the dead were those who had been executed. Violently cast out from the city, put to death on a gallows that in very early times was generally outside the city walls, their bodies were left there, together with lepers and other threatening presences of a non-Christianized natural world, while in the city those of the deceased rested inside churches or in cemeteries where sacred soil brought back from Palestine in crusader ships was scattered—the *camposanti*.

Let us go back now to Bergamo, and the trail branching from there toward the other cities of central-northern Italy. Here we encounter a very popular and effective preacher of penitence named Venturino de Apibus, better known as Venturino of Bergamo. After entering the Dominican order, Fra Venturino became a preacher, building up a great following with a visionary oratory that scourged vices and invoked the advent of a new religious and social order where there was no longer any place for crimes, and where the problem of violence was resolved once and for all. In the context of the conflicts within an urban world undergoing rapid social evolution, Fra Venturino's work was distinguished by his calls for "penitence, peace, and mercy," made in the course of a journey that, in 1334, took him across Italy from Bergamo to Milan, Lodi, Mantua, Ferrara, Bologna, and down to Rome.

During his travels, Fra Venturino stirred up a vast penitential movement animated by highly effective preaching and his own personal example, as he sought in particular to resolve conflicts and obtain the release of the incarcerated. The dominant problem of the time in city life was the unchecked spread of social and political violence, the result of rapid social changes brought about by the ongoing commercial revolution and by the bloody disputes between political factions. Against this backdrop Fra Venturino launched his proposal for a crusade. After the previous waves of pious movements had led to the loss of many shepherds and adolescents *(fanciulli)* in the endeavor, the friar now proposed to take the worst men of every city, the criminals, to the walls of Jerusalem. They might not be able to capture the holy city, but they would in any case wash away their misdeeds with their blood by sacrificing themselves in the undertaking, and in so doing would also free Christian society from the evil embodied in their errant lives.

Venturino calculated that the number of *peiores homines* infesting Christian society amounted to around fifty thousand men. And so a new movement was born, known as the movement "of the dove" after the emblem emblazoned on the white attire of its members: a symbol of the Spirit that descended upon Venturino while he preached, but also of pacification and general liberation from violence. Prison gates opened miraculously— so legend says—and conflict was transformed into fraternization and forgiveness. It was not the first time that the dream of a fraternal and forgiving city appeared on the horizons of the medieval city. The violence of the political struggles and the lacerating consequences of social change had already produced movements of reaction championing a return to an evangelical peace between Christians, embodied in the fraternal associations. The members of the one that had been formed in Perugia by Ranieri Fasani in 1260 were known popularly as the *battuti* (the "beaten" or "flogged"), due to their practice of whipping themselves as a sign of remorse and penitence: these *battuti* were white or black, depending on the color of the habits they wore during the ritual of penitence. Their associations performed various kinds of charitable work.

Venturino's idea of a crusade was the visionary and failed outcome of his special concern for a particular human condition that had grown detached from the categories of the infirm and the imprisoned. These groups, moreover, were already the object of the traditional works of mercy in Bergamo: the members of the "consorzio di Santa Caterina" had included in their rule (1280) a commitment to visit the imprisoned and those who were poor and sick, and to offer alms for them.[8] Venturino—recounts the "legend" of his life—was also particularly struck by the condition of the imprisoned and ill, and was quick to visit them: like a searcher of alms, he was anxious to harvest the spiritual reward that those figures could bestow in the economy of Christian charity. To this he added the practice of associating himself with the rituals of justice, following the condemned to the place of execution, exhorting them to bear their suffering and death in memory of the Passion of Christ, and inviting them to believe firmly in God's mercy.[9] Even before he began calling for a crusade—arousing the suspicion and hostility of the papal court, and leading to a summons to Avignon to be put on trial—Venturino had reawakened with his preaching the spirit of the *disciplinati* movement, providing them with a new goal. Confraternities of *disciplinati* sprang up in rapid succession along the path he took, devoting themselves to a special form of penitence: being present at the *giustizie,* the executions. In the space of a few years there was increasing evidence of the spread of a movement that sought to offer tangible signs of a fraternal presence no longer just in hospitals but also in prisons and beneath the gallows. In fact, leaving the undoubted effectiveness of Venturino's preaching to one side, the movement that took shape in the genesis of associations linked to the functioning of the death penalty is not reducible to a single figure. We are in the presence of a devotional wave that ran up against and modified previous arrangements and preexisting ways of handling the emergencies of city life—poverty, illness, and death, known generally as the *misericordie.*[10]

A trickle of notary documents—private attestations, bequests—was transformed over time into the statutes of confraternities, where the new work of mercy stood out as the most important work: the years straddling the Black Death proved to be the decisive phase for the identification of the condemned as the person representing the most forlorn condition, the one with the greatest need of comfort. As the chronicler Matteo Villani recounts, the plague and the devastating wave of mortality had the unpredictable effect of stimulating a plethora of pious bequests for charitable works. This prompted an extraordinary drive to found hospitals as places for healing the body and the soul.[11]

The plague, preannouncing a very rapid death, certainly played a part in establishing a special symbolization of the condemned as an exemplary type of the human condition. Following their last moments, praying for them, and being at their side appeared to be the most meaningful way of meditating upon and preparing for a condemnation that hung over human nature and that could surprise anyone quite suddenly, leaving no time for contrition, confession, or stipulating in a will what amends to make. The theme of death as a curse that struck without warning, and left no time to prepare, materialized a few years after Venturino's preaching campaign and his crusade to rid society of its violent elements. In 1347 a Genoese ship fleeing Jaffa brought with it the bacillus of the bubonic plague. In the space of just a few months, the epidemic struck down a large proportion of the population in Europe. From then on the specter of the Black Death became an ordinary presence in European societies: it drew on all their resources, made it necessary to reconsider all the rules of shared coexistence, and became part of people's darkest nightmares. Particularly shocking was the speed with which the body was transformed; from the living being came the corpse as a truth that dispelled every illusion. And this is when the problem of burying the bodies became acute. The Modenese chronicler Tommasino Lancellotti noted that "no one could be found who was willing to bury the dead." So three lay confraternities took on the task, "and as they carried the men off for burial they scourged themselves so they were all bloody, and sang *laude,* praying to God to stop the pestilence."[12]

In the decades after 1348 the practice of being present at executions emerged as the most important form of devotion for the Battuti confraternities, in an area stretching from the vast region of northern Italy then called Lombardy to the cities and towns in the center of the peninsula. Fra Venturino's visionary dream was not fulfilled. Society continued to be violent, and the gibbet—the tree of the cross with just one arm—was a sign erected as a guarantee for wayfarers and merchants on trade and pilgrim routes; it was reassuring to see the bodies of brigands and plunderers hanging there, as Ambrogio Lorenzetti suggested by depicting inactive gibbets as evidence of a lack of security and bad government. But the popular movements that sprang up and spread like wildfire from town to town, calling for mercy and peace, periodically brought with them a demand for prisons to be opened and conflicts laid to rest. When the march of the *Battuti bianchi* that started in the spring of 1399 arrived in Pistoia, it was thanks to their pleas for mercy that two people who had been condemned to death were pardoned and an infamous painting was erased from the façade of the Palazzo Comunale.[13] Effectively, those who ended up in city jails and those taken for execution were no longer abandoned. Confraternities sprang up one after another, with men and women devoting themselves to the new work of mercy, that of escorting and accompanying the condemned to death on their final journey. There is the risk that such a choice might appear "natural," so familiar has the centuries-old practice become in Christian cultures. But we need to look far back in time to when it made its first timid appearance to appreciate just how new and unprecedented was the determination of those ordinary people—merchants, artisans, widows, notaries—to accompany thieves or murderers on their final journey and to pray for them while they suffered torture and faced their last moments of life.

So it was no accident that this special kind of charitable work intensified in the years around the middle of the fourteenth century. In a process remarkable for its speed, a network of lay confraternities engaged in this new activity developed, covering large and small cities across central northern Italy. The dates are clustered around the middle of the century. Not all of them are entirely reliable—due to wavering memories and to a devout emulation that led to the shifting of dates as far into the past as possible and to the choice of symbolically resonant anniversaries—but they paint an overall picture of the rapid spread of a new form of devotion. There are some solid reference coordinates. A careful investigation of notary sources has ascertained that the devout society of Santa Maria della Morte in Bologna, characterized precisely by the unusual and special work of accompanying the condemned *(qui vadunt ad iusticiam),* was founded on July 13, 1336.[14] The indulgence granted to the devout by Brother Giovanni, bishop of Bisignano, on May 15, 1356, speaks of assistance given to the poor in the confraternity's hospital and to those who died after being condemned by the commune of Bologna. In both cases the task of the *confratelli* was to bury the bodies in their church with pious fervor.[15] The year 1338 is the date indicated by tradition for the start of the comforting carried out by the Confraternita di Santa Maria della Misericordia in Sansepolcro.[16] The Florentine confraternity of San Giovanni Battista known as "dei Neri" dated its origins to 1347, even though in its record of executions burials "outside Porta all Croce" appear to start in 1356.[17]

Many other associations were founded in the same period. The Confraternita di Santa Maria della Giustizia in Verona and the Confraternita di San Giovanni Evangelista della Morte in Padua were providing assistance to the condemned before 1362.[18] The latter moved into the middle of the city from the outlying Camposanto area in 1363, taking as its main task the provision of assistance to prisoners and the condemned.[19] In Ferrara the Compagnia di Santa Maria Annunziata or "dei Battuti neri," founded on August 5, 1366, after breaking away from the Battuti bianchi, devoted itself "to justice, to accompanying those who are condemned to death . . . with discipline, litanies, *laude,* and silence."[20] In Modena the establishment of the Confraternita di San Giovanni Battista detta della Morte "was intended to relate"—as one of its members, bishop Giuliano Sabbatini, who was also its first historian, put it in 1755—to April 11, 1372, an evocative date, as the day fell on the second Sunday after Easter, commonly known as "Misericordia Domini."[21] That day a group of young people in the city founded the Ospedale della Morte and devoted themselves to the "well-being of the souls of those who were executed in the Commune, having seen that neither their souls nor their bodies were attended to or buried."[22] Active in Venice from the middle of the fourteenth century, in the church of Santa Maria delle Grazie e di San Fantin, was the Scuola di San Girolamo, joined, at a later date, by the Scuola di Santa Maria della Giustizia.[23] The list could go on. The spread of these confraternities was linked to the powerful channels of communication provided by the religious orders that acted as their patrons, generally Franciscans and Dominicans but also Benedictines (in Modena), and, increasingly, after the middle of the sixteenth century, the Jesuits as well. They were the ones who tuned in to and gave shape to the new needs of urban societies, encouraging laypeople, both men and women, to respond to social and political violence with an appeal to peace and forgiveness. The sight of penitents clad in habits, faces covered, and following the procession of the condemned person increasingly became the norm for the procedures known as *giustizie,* but also, more exactly, *vendette* ("vindictae"). The singing of psalms and *laude* accompanied the final journey of the condemned, transformed by religious intercession from their real state as a common criminal or political adversary into a figure of a contrite sinner, if not a martyr. It was a move toward disciplined and contrition-filled forms of a ritual, which, however, for a long time retained traces of the original loathing and buffoonish humiliation of the condemned. In Bologna, as late as 1448, a certain Baldassarre Canetoli, found guilty of murdering Annibale Bentivogli, was sent to the gallows "sitting backward on a donkey, forced to hold the tail of the donkey with his hand" and wearing the "miter of disgrace" on his head.[24]

When, in the following century, a periodic revision and reform of statutes was deemed necessary in accordance with the typical rhythms of the confraternities, elapsed time was alluded to in complaints about decadence and practices that had fallen into disuse: it was the "great interval of time," as the Modenese *confratelli* wrote, that made reform of the rules indispensable. "Modern new ways, and holy customs of good living" were required: this led, on June 24, 1452, to the reform of the ancient statutes so as to "place the neck under the gentle yoke of Christ."[25] As we shall see, an important change took place then in the history of comforting that concerned not only the forms of charitable work but also the setup of the confraternities and their place in Italy's cities and states. There were mergers and concentrations: in Venice, the Scuola di San Girolamo and the Scuola di Santa Maria della Giustizia joined forces in 1458 and became popularly known as the Scuola "dei Picai"—that is, "of the hanged." Above all, there was a substantive change in the function of comforting and the social position of those who practiced it. But before that change took place, there had been time for the "ancient forms" of mercy to leave some very evocative models and memories.

11

"I Received His Head into My Hands"

WE KNOW ALMOST NOTHING about Niccolò di Toldo da Perugia; like thousands sent to die on the gallows, all that remains is the name. So fleeting did he seem, and for so long, that his historic existence was doubted. His story could easily have remained a confused blur among the many who died at the executioner's hands. Yet he was destined to become an unforgettable case, an inspiration for centuries to those who worked to provide Christian aid to the condemned. This is thanks to a letter written by Caterina Benincasa (1347–1380), better known as Saint Catherine of Siena, to Raymond of Capua.[1] In it is the account of the execution of a man Catherine does not name, but who is indicated by the caption of the letter as being from Perugia, and to whom the saint's biographer, Tommaso Caffarani, ascribes the name Niccolò di Toldo. It is a celebrated document, worth summarizing in brief.

The man is condemned. Catherine visits, comforts, and consoles him. He makes confession and readies himself "very well" for what awaits him. But he gets her to promise that she will be by his side at the moment of the execution. And that is what happened. In the morning, before the execution bell rang, Catherine went to see him and they heard the Mass together. The man received Holy Communion, which he had not taken for a very long time. However, he continued to fear "not being strong at the final moment." But divine goodness came to his aid, seducing him with a great desire to join together with Catherine in God. A wedding of blood: Catherine was waiting for it as well. She relates to Father Raimondo that while "his head was resting on my breast," she could smell the fragrance of his blood, in which she sensed the fragrance of her own blood, which she was waiting to "shed for my gentle Spouse Jesus." Sensing Niccolò's growing fear, Catherine comforted him: the mystical wedding was approaching, she said, and he would go to it "bathed in the sweet blood of God's Son." And she promised: "I shall wait for you at the place of execution." The fear left Niccolò, and he exulted and called the place of execution "holy." He said: "When I think that you will be waiting for me there, it will seem a thousand years until I get there." The moment arrived: Catherine went to the place of execution, and, before Niccolò arrived, laid her "neck out on the block." Around her was a "a great crowd of people," but she saw no one:

> Then he arrived like a meek lamb, and when he saw me he began to laugh and wanted me to make the sign of the cross on him. When he had received the sign I said, "Down for the wedding, my dear brother, for soon you will be in everlasting life!" He knelt down very meekly; I placed his neck [on the block] and bent down and reminded him of the blood of the Lamb. His mouth said nothing but "Gesù!" and "Caterina!" and as he said this, I received his head into my hands.

Blood gushed from the severed head onto Catherine's gown. The fragrance of that blood became associated for her with a vision: she saw Christ's side opening and receiving the man's blood in his own blood. God also received his soul, saved "only through grace and mercy." At the moment of death the man cast a final gaze in her direction: "He turned as does a bride when, having reached her husband's threshold, she turns her head and looks back, nods to those who have attended her, and so expresses her thanks." The brutal reality of execution is transfigured into the rite of marriage: the people who have followed the execution procession become the members of the train accompanying the bride—who here is the soul of the dying man, the bride of Christ through the union of his blood with that of the "God-Man." It is the apotheosis of a love story:[2] a love that not only conquers death but is completed precisely in the act of death, which, in the Christian interpretation, is the passage to real life. Here *eros* and *thanatos* are no longer those conflictual drives of human existence revealed by an entire literary tradition and interpreted by depth psychology. Their conflict is transformed into an alliance, thanks to the two conditions created by Christianity: the promise of eternal life and the guarantee offered by the death of Christ as the sacrificial lamb. Death is the apotheosis of love. The impulse of death becomes an impulse toward the true life of a love that will last for eternity. It is in the very moment of the execution, says Catherine, that the union of divinity and humanity in Christ is rendered evident. "Then was seen the God-Man as one sees the brilliance of the sun. [His side] was open and received blood into his own blood—received a flame of holy desire (which grace had given and hidden in this soul) into the flame of his own divine charity." Through the Communion of blood with the Passion of Christ, the two lovers are bound together forever by an indissoluble tie: their love becomes part of and a manifestation of divine love.

A necessary premise for understanding the language used by Catherine is the idea of the blood tie uniting all Christians with Christ. In her time blood occupied a central place in the conception of God, and consequently in the relationship between human beings. The theological doctrine definitively established by the Fourth Lateran Council in 1215 ended centuries of theological disputes and elevated the divine blood of the Communion sacrament to the place at the top occupied until then by the water of baptism. This had a number of consequences. The division between Christians and Jews was strongly exacerbated, with a tendency to transform the sense of religious difference into racial difference.[3] But it was in female mysticism that the theme of the "holy feast" of Communion had a special resonance associated with the close relationship between women and food, and likewise between women, the body, and sexuality.[4] The desire for Eucharistic food was an impelling need for mystic women, which ran up against the resistance and suspicion of a Church that placed limits on frequent Communion. It has been said that with Catherine of Siena the Eucharistic realism of devotion to the Holy Blood "reaches the level of atrocity."[5] In the execution scene, she touched the zenith of the mysticism of the marriage of blood and death, by evoking the presence of Christ receiving the blood of the condemned man in his own thanks to the mediation of the loving, comforting woman. What appeared to her on the gallows in Siena was a figural repetition of the sacrifice of Christ on the Cross.

It is a shocking story, and the embarrassment of the devout and the resistance of scholars to accepting its historical reality is understandable. Did that event on the gallows in Siena really take place, or was it a mystical vision? The episode of Niccolò di Toldo does not in fact feature much in the iconography of Catherine's miracles. A certain embarrassment can also be discerned in the hagiographic literature relating to her: one stern critic cast doubt on the credibility of the story due to the absence of convincing documentary evidence.[6] In his view, the letter contained no proof that the person involved was Niccolò di Toldo. Perhaps Catherine was speaking about another condemned man, who might have been the Florentine poet Benci, or Giannozzo Sacchetti, who corresponded with her and was executed in Florence in 1379. And perhaps the events never actually happened, but were a mental construction. Historic truth versus devout fable, then. But a solid and thorough documentary investigation by a great historian of the Dominican Order, Antoine Dondaine,[7] has reconstructed the real scene beyond all possible doubt. Thanks to him, it can now be summarized as follows: Niccolò di Toldo really did exist, and died on the executioner's block in Siena in Catherine's arms. A native of Perugia but active in Siena, he was arrested on June 4, 1375, on the charge of conducting seditious political activities in the city. He was at the center of brief but intense negotiations between the city and the papacy: the Apostolic Nuncio to Tuscany Gérard du Puy intervened to try to get the trial dropped and to secure the release of Niccolò, who was suspected by the Sienese government of secretly supporting the pro-papal faction. At the time, Italian cities with weak governments were continually in danger of being overthrown by adversaries who linked up with outside powers. But Du Puy's intervention failed, as attested by a letter he wrote on June 13, and Niccolò was sentenced to death. While in prison awaiting execution, alone and desperate, he received a visit from Catherine. This was recounted by a witness during the process of canonization that took place between 1412 and 1416: the name of the witness was Tommaso di Antonio, who claimed to have been in the same cell as Niccolò. From his story it transpires that the meeting with Catherine left Toldo serene and as meek as a lamb ready for sacrifice. Catherine was also present at the execution. Niccolò died like a martyr saint and Catherine received his head in her hands. Another witness at the process of beatification, the Dominican Simone Neri da Cortona, recalled that at that time many prisoners went to their deaths in despair, without even being able to receive confession.[8] Catherine spent the night before the execution with them, offering prayers to Christ, comforting them, and exhorting them to have hope. In this way she softened their spirit, so much so that they requested a priest and confessed their sins with great contrition. When the time came for their execution, she joined them in the procession and knelt below the gallows, collecting their blood on her white gown.[9]

The scene described in Saint Catherine's letter is charged with extraordinary mystic overtones. It interprets and renews in an original way Christ's commandment to love, set in opposition to the pursuit of justice as vendetta. Like Saint Francis of Assisi kissing the leper, embracing the condemned prisoner proposed an interpretation of the principle of Christian love that was destined to leave a lasting impression. One male, the other female, the story of their fortunes offers two examples of the relationship between the charismatic testimony of the great model and the forms in which the need to reinterpret the Gospel precept was then put into practice by imitators of both sexes.

Moreover, Catherine herself can be seen as an imitator: before creating a tradition herself, the Sienese saint was one of many women who threw themselves into that new work of mercy, embracing it with enthusiasm and bringing to the scene of violence and death that was the gallows an empathic presence, thereby identifying in some way with the saintly women of the Passion story.

It is a presence that already emerges from the traces left by the preaching of Venturino of Bergamo. He stimulated devotion in Bologna for Saint Martha as a model of female virtue, and his following included women from every social class. A clear sign of the chords he struck are the bequests made in women's wills to the "company of justice."[10] After all, it was up to women to attend to bodies in the key phases of life and death: taking care of the newborn and the dead, and performing the functions of reproduction and nourishment, pertained to the female sphere. The fact that women took an active part in the devout confraternities that sprang up around the rituals of justice should come as no surprise. Only with time did the tendency to raise the social level of the composition of these bodies give male members an exclusive role increasingly associated with power and violence. Dying and putting to death became more and more a male affair: the presence of women at the gallows dwindled, and female participation in the life of the companies of justice became vague and secondary—when, that is, it did not fade away completely. The same downward trajectory in the role of women also characterized the regulation of the forms that funeral mourning could take in cities: it was considered necessary to avoid or limit as much as possible any loud manifestations of lament. And the ways in which women occupied the limelight at the gallows must also have been deemed excessive. In the confraternities of mercy, as long as these associations retained their "broad" (larga) form—that is, without any particular social discriminants regarding membership—the sphere effectively open to women was that of prayer and of participation in the spiritual benefits, together with assisting in hospitals. There were also cases where women were entrusted with visiting the sick and the poor in prison.[11] It was a question of guaranteeing salvation and the forgiveness of one's sins by participating in the sacraments, performing works of mercy, and benefiting from the indulgences issued by the ecclesiastical authorities. Men and women, bound by a community tie, obtained the assurance of burial when they died and the spiritual benefits of suffrage masses. In the images of them that we can see, they are gathered in indistinct groups—sculpted in church marbles, on tombstones, or in the miniatures of confraternity statutes (Plate 16). Sometimes chroniclers and notaries drew pictures of them in the margins of execution records. In these images the individual disappears, and what dominates is the group, faces humbly concealed by hoods and bodies clad in long white or black habits depending on the local tradition. In general, they were confraternities of *disciplinati:* the symbol of the "disciplines" accompanied and identified the majority of the companies of justice. Women were traditionally excluded from practices of self-flagellation. The search for the perfection of evangelical life took on particularly intense forms among them, arousing suspicion and condemnation in an ecclesiastical world that saw women as vehicles for the presence of the devil. The charge of heresy was always liable to be leveled against movements such as the Beghards. In Cologne, Germany, the Alexians (Alexianerbrüder), who had done charitable works and helped the poor and dying since the thirteenth century, were brushed by it. Later we also find them engaged in helping those who had been sentenced to death. The female presence in the history of these companies was transferred symbolically into the figure of the Madonna, an image epitomizing pain and involvement in death by execution but also the capacity to forgive. It was to the Madonna that the confraternity members who attended *giustizie—*executions—offered up their prayers and *laude.*

Saint Catherine was therefore an imitator of a model of mercy that was taking root in the society of her time. But she was also an effective promoter of it, albeit within quite specific limits. We will no longer encounter women at the gallows, if not as victims. But the Niccolò di Toldo episode exercised a suggestive influence due to the circulation of Catherine's letters, which was intense during the manuscript age and then enjoyed extraordinary success following the invention of the printing press. Not for nothing were her letters among the first texts to appear in the pocket-size format launched by Aldo Manuzio in 1500. Following her model, other Catherines entered the history of comforting the condemned: they did so more circumspectly, without the vigorous energy of the Sienese saint, contributing with their prayers and through mystic participation in the practices associated with executions—also because men had taken over the function of comforting. The model proposed by Catherine of Siena with her letter can be glimpsed as an underlying motif behind them. Take Caterina Vigri, for example, otherwise known as Saint Catherine of Bologna. In the fifteenth-century life of the saint by Illuminata Bembo, we read that she managed, through her good work, to resolve the case of a man facing execution in Ferrara who not only refused all religious comfort but "called on the devil for help." Catherine, who was in the convent of Ferrara at the time (she later moved to Bologna, where she died in 1463), was stricken by "inestimable sadness." She remained "in adoration" for the whole day, and in the evening asked her abbess for permission to spend the night in prayer. And that is what she did. She passed the night "praying and weeping." In the morning, while she continued to pray in the nuns' choir, "she heard the voice of Christ coming from the sacrament and saying: 'I cannot deny you: I wish the soul to be a gift for you and to be saved thanks to you.'" Indeed, the condemned man "confessed with great contrition." And as they led him off to execution astride a donkey, he called out to people urging them to heed his example: "Pray, all of you, learn from a sinner like me and change your lives, and forgive me, a wretched abuser."[12]

The key figure in this episode is a woman who remained within the walls of her convent, having no contact with the condemned man and relying on prayer alone to save him. The spiritual change of heart in the condemned man takes place, not through transgression of the rules of justice out of love, but by a miracle. Other women were quietly present behind the work of the men of the confraternities. A tangle of confraternities also lay behind the third Catherine we must mention here: the beatified mystic Saint Catherine of Genoa (Caterina Fieschi). A Compagnia della Misericordia "de redemption et succurre miseris" had been founded in her home city of Genoa, and provided assistance to the condemned from 1455.[13] The life of the saint, who married and remained a layperson, relates the story of a heated dispute with a monk. She denied he had the right to attribute to himself a more meritorious state than the one granted by "his love" of Christ.[14] It was through the filter of her personality that the work of a Genoese notary named Ettore Vernazza, the secret protagonist of a proliferation of new or renewed devout associations and a figure whom we will meet again, took shape. As with the other two mystics, the dominant theme of Caterina Fieschi's meditation was the love of God. Her great lesson was that certain works of mercy had to be done "only out of love for God and for the charity and health of one's neighbor," and not in order "to be considered good by the people of the world." In the shadow of Caterina Vigri's convent in Ferrara or in Caterina Fieschi's secluded existence, a religious inspiration was nurtured that coincided only in part with the institutionalization of assistance that was under way in the cities. And there was a perceived risk of a growth in power and social prestige such as to distort the sense of the work itself, which, it was felt, should be about helping the most desperate and neglected segments of society—secretly, without ostentation, and purely out of love for, and in the name of, a merciful God.

We will see in due course how that devout intent had significant outcomes thanks to the mediation of men like Ettore Vernazza. But naturally, behind the work of devout laypeople—men and women—we need to bear in mind the animating and inspiring role played by preachers from the two great religious orders, the Franciscans and the Dominicans, traditionally active in promoting their organizational models and spiritual motifs. Their voices from the pulpit drew attention to the merits of meditating upon death and the spectacle of other people's deaths. In the same years in which the two Catherines were practicing a religion of divine love and fraternal help, Fra Girolamo Savonarola was inviting his listeners to learn a new art, that of dying well: "So, take this as your rule," Savonarola said to Florentines, "go frequently to see the dead buried; go often to the graveyard, look often on those near death; make it your practice, if you know that one of your relatives or a friend or some other person is dying, to stay by them to see them die, and then go to see them buried."[15]

This brings us to the historic change that had occurred, and that is directly measurable in the composition of the confraternities. In Ferrara, where the episode involving Caterina Vigri took place, and in the Bologna that served as a backdrop for the painter Giulio Morina's representation of it, the *largha* confraternities, open to people of all backgrounds and comprising both men and women, had been superseded by *stretta* (narrow) ones for men only, selected according to their education and standing, and charged by the city authorities with the task of managing the execution rituals. It was a structural change that brought with it a different way of conceiving of comforting and rendering it effective. But before dealing with this new phase in the history of the confraternities, it would perhaps be useful to look more closely at how justice took its course in an Italian city of the time.

12

Factional Conflict and Mob Justice
in the Late Middle Ages

DURING THE FOURTEENTH CENTURY, the documents of some confraternities began to list names of condemned people and donations from the devout, but the public sphere of criminal justice offered little space for these figures with their talk of peace and forgiveness. Criminal justice was administered in a context dominated by other protagonists and other voices. Building up a picture of justice in this period is not a simple task. Not because of any shortage of documents or studies: there are a great many sources dealing with the history of justice in medieval Europe. What is more, a great deal of research has been done to analyze the laws and rules applied at one time or another, or to describe the judging powers, the men who formed part of them, and their cultural background. The history of the system of punishments has been tackled above all by jurists, interested in the laws in force at the time and keen to learn more about the gradual development of a legal culture and an idea of justice that would give form and regulation to national entities and European concord. But there were a great many legal norms in that age, and judicial practices varied from one place, authority, and person to another: there was the law of the Church, which had acquired great expertise in this field with the establishment and development of canonic law and the system of Roman tribunals; there was the university culture of jurists, who studied Roman law with a view to applying it to the needs of public authorities; and in society at large there were periodic "reforms" of the statutes of collective bodies and associations, whereas in civil suits and interpersonal disputes the weight of unwritten custom continued to be decisive.[1] However, in the arena of justice, when capital punishment was involved, there came into play many factors unregulated by norms—violence and spectacle, political passion, and the tumult of factional conflicts. On the one hand were the narrow horizons of everyday life and of what went on in castles, villages, or cities—in close proximity to the one judging and punishing—where all it took was a call to arms and a shout of "death to the Ghibellines" to spark collective violence.[2] On the other hand were the mental horizons, the struggle between good and evil. Evil was embodied by political enemies, constantly suspected of betrayal and of being in cahoots with external foes, or by heretics, who, as betrayers of the faith, represented the most serious form of the crime of lèse-majesté, the ancient criminal category rediscovered and adapted to the needs of power. The difference between the reality of what happened within the walls of the city, or in the villages and hamlets subject to it, and the continually reworked statutes that were purportedly in force was like the difference between the battle of Waterloo as seen through the eyes of Stendhal's hero Fabrizio del Dongo and as described in a handbook of military strategy. The collective participation of the urban populace, who gathered together and watched, commented on, and intervened, had a crucial influence on the course of events. In this context the ferocious struggle between factions often took the form of execution rituals determined "a furor di popolo"—by the furor of the people—though it was a furor not without its own rules.

Let us take a random example of the functioning of criminal justice from late fourteenth-century Florence. It was a troubled period in the city's life, what with internal conflicts and external wars. The political struggle raging within what was an embryonic but rapidly growing regional power was dressed up with names borrowed from the factions of the great German feudal families: the Guelphs and the Ghibellines. These names endured for centuries, legitimating violence and revolts, the settling of scores, and summary executions "a furor di popolo." The administration of justice was in the hands of a communal power that formally invoked the empire but in practice, and often by right as well, recognized no other superior authority.[3] In the Guelph comune, to be labeled a "Ghibelline" was to be considered an enemy of the city, and as such the term lent itself to being used by those in power to attack their adversaries.[4]

Leaving cumbersome statutory norms to one side, it is worth taking advantage of the view offered by a city chronicler to get a firsthand and turbulent picture of acts of political and judicial violence.

Florence, Monday, January 13, 1381. The anonymous author of a Florentine chronicle of the age opens his account of events that have occurred
in the city "in modern times" with the story of "how Messer Giorgio freed
Scatiza and died."[5] During the night a large group of armed men—around
four hundred, according to the chronicler—attacked the Palazzo dei Capitani
di Parte Guelfa and freed a prisoner, a shearer by trade, known by his nick-
name "lo Scatizza." He had been condemned for treason, on the grounds
that he was in league with Bernabò Visconti, the ruler of Milan, against the
government of Florence. Just a few years earlier, in 1378, a popular revolt
had overthrown the anti-magnate faction, which had moved closer to the
Milanese power of the Visconti and had waged the War of the Eight Saints
against the pope.[6] The victorious side raised the flag of anti-Ghibellinism
and accused adversaries of plotting with external powers—that is, of being
traitors. But the struggle was bitter, due to the conflict between the nobles
and the *popolo minuto,* hence the violent liberation of Scatizza.

The following morning, the *capitano del popolo* went to the Signori of
the comune and handed over the baton, which in the European world at that
time was generally recognized to be the symbol of the judge's office. Given
the attack he had suffered, he wanted to leave his post and return to his home
city of Imola (the appointment of the magistrate who administered justice
generally fell to someone from outside the city). The Signori debated the
matter, accepting the need for strong action: there was "great unrest" in the
city. Everyone was talking about the incident, and "great suspicion" reigned.
The government's decision arrived on Thursday: the baton was returned to
the *capitano* and he was given powers to punish those responsible. The acknowledged leader of the expedition, Giorgio Scali, was arrested that same
afternoon, and beheaded the following morning. In the meantime, on the
Thursday afternoon, a man called Simone di Biagio had been killed: his body
had been dragged through the streets of Florence by a gang of boys (*fanciulli*), who cut off his hands and played football with them. It was an execution regulated by a noninstitutional ritual of justice that the chronicler took
to be entirely legitimate and did not bother to explain. He merely describes
the victim's body, lacerated and derided by the *fanciulli* as it was hauled
through the dust and mud along the route customarily used for execution
rituals in the city. Such displays of public loathing and death by locals
whipped up into a fury had been seen in Florence before.[7] A central role in

them was played by the adolescent *fanciulli*—an age group seen as irresponsible and innocent, and therefore given special tasks serving justice. Not many years earlier, in March 1343, "some boys devoted to spiritual practices" had established the initial core of the Compagnia di Santa Maria della Croce al Tempio in Florence, with illuminations and the "singing of various *laude*."[8] Boys were also expected to perform collective acts of devotion and execration, an aspect generally neglected by those who have projected anachronistic images of a unilateral innocence onto the childhood and adolescence of this age.[9] These groups of boys committed acts of violence that did not spare the living, even less so the corpses of the dead. Simone di Biagio's fate is a case in point.

At the end of that week in January 1381, throngs of men armed with swords and shouting "Viva Parte Guelfa" had run throughout the city without encountering resistance. Compared to the violence of the previous century, the warring factions now covered themselves with "the legitimating cloak of the old and united *parte guelfa*."[10] The phase of unrest had ended with a troubled Sunday: two men, Messer Donato de Richo and an armorer named Feo, were arrested at the instigation of the populace, who wanted them put to death immediately. They were decapitated on Monday morning, while tumultuous crowds brought uproar to the city by demonstrating in the streets with banners and flags of the *parte guelfa*. It was the height of a political and social clash between the *Arti maggiori* and the *Arti minori*, the *popolo grasso* and the *popolo minuto*. In the background loomed the external threat of Milan, ruled by the Visconti family, offering a handy pretext for charges of treason, one of the crimes that, together with barratry, gave legal weight to the showdown between the struggling factions.[11]

Internal political and social violence and the threats posed by foreign powers fueled suspicion and conflict. The city chronicle gives accounts of almost daily vengeance killings, and military skirmishes in the surrounding countryside. There were long lists of citizens who were subject to measures of banishment and confinement. The vendetta of bandits was feared, and so people often rushed to close the doors of their workshops and the magistrates closed those of the city. With a climate like this, the execution procedure was simplified: in mid-February, orders were given that a number of people suspected of wanting to sack and burn the city were to be hunted down and put to death on the spot, or even dismembered ("cut them to pieces"). This was to be done "without ringing bells or reading out sentences."[12] For Saturday, February 22, the chronicler was able to describe a peaceful day as an exceptional occurrence: "The city rested, arms were set down, and the guilds plied their trades, and everyone did so safely." The calm was relative, though. As if internal and external political strife were not enough, there was the inquisitor, too, who for his own part dealt with capturing and burning heretics. In 1327 Cecco d'Ascoli died by burning after being condemned as an astrologer, and the city periodically witnessed other similar spectacles.[13] The most frequent, though not the only, victims were the so-called Fraticelli, proponents of a radical interpretation of Franciscan poverty. For instance, on October 25, 1384, a heretic named Niccolò dall'Occhio was sentenced to death by the inquisitor and burnt at the stake, despite opposition from the bishop and the contrary views of jurists.

But the anonymous chronicler's attention seems to have been drawn above all to the executions that concluded stories of violence and hatred among citizens. His descriptions of these offer a glimpse of rituals involving horrific violence. Such was the execution of Busecchino da San Frediano, guilty of having killed Scarlatto di Nuto. Busecchino had fled the scene of the murder, but was chased and captured by one of Scarlatto's relatives. The killing incensed the city, because Scarlatto was universally liked as a "good man." The priors therefore gave the *podestà* license to mete out "whatever justice he wished." He did just that: Busecchino was stripped naked, tied to a stake on a cart, and taken through the streets of the city, while the executioner tortured every part of his body with pincers. First his right hand was cut off, then, in front of Scarlatto's house, the left one came off too. The severed hands were then attached to the man's neck. This ritual of going through the city streets would remain a typical feature of the Florentine model of execution for centuries. It was part of a representation of justice as something concerted and participatory, a kind of inverted triumph. Having reached the spot where Scarlatto had been killed, Busecchino was dragged down from the cart and buried head first in a ditch with water in it, a form of execution known as *propagginatura*. But when they pulled him out he was still alive, because there was not much water in the ditch. So the process was repeated. When he was finally dead, a chain was put around his neck, and the body was hauled off to the gallows and strung up, with the order that it not be removed, "as an example to other malefactors."[14] Finally, six days later, at the entreaties of relatives, the dead man's body was taken down and buried. The chronicle does not say whether Busecchino received any form of religious assistance. Nor is there any mention of it in other cases of capital sentences handed out for crimes of treason, like that of Battista da San Miniato and Francesco known as Bernacchiola, sent to their deaths respectively on October 16 and 17, 1391, after enduring the path of torment through the streets of the city; or that of Pagoletto, who ended his days on October 23, "dragged, buried head first, and then hanged."[15] A faint indication of assistance can be found only in the account of the execution of Tommaso di messer Guccio Gucci, on January 17, 1393, which is also the most precise and detailed one. Tommaso, in jail for debt, had had one of his elder brothers killed in order to force his younger brothers to get him released from prison. It was a particularly heinous crime, stirring a wave of collective loathing and repugnance for a person who had betrayed his own family—the primary social body—severing what everyone considered to be the most sacred bond in a political body consisting of an association of families. The crime was discovered, and the sentence of death inevitable. When the officer of justice ordered the bells to be rung and the banner of justice to be raised, the whole city crowded into the square to hear the public reading of the sentence. The condemned man was paraded through the streets, though they were so packed that the customary route had to be altered a bit. At a certain point he tried to escape, but was recaptured, put back in prison, and then killed that evening "a furor" in the middle of the street, "without anyone there saying to him: 'Commend yourself to God.'"[16]

The extraordinary fact, according to the chronicler, was that the ferocity of an execution carried out at the instigation of the people had made everyone forget the duty to convince the victim to ask for God's forgiveness. And yet the Compagnia di Santa Maria della Croce al Tempio already existed at that time in Florence. Some information about its origins (collected and written down afresh from papers damaged by the flood of the river Arno on September 13, 1557) indicate that it was founded in 1343. Its mission was to "get some prisoners released from jail through their implorations, and to bury their dead, and others, out of love for God."[17] The practice of burying the condemned would appear to have started in 1356, at the initiative of "some of the most fervent," who undertook "to bury poor, abandoned executed criminals at their own expense." A horrific and dramatic narrative regarding the first case they handled was passed down from one generation to the next at that time: It seems that on April 28, 1356, while the body of a hanged man was being taken off to be buried, a "black, frenzied" horse charged headlong at the coffin bearers, who abandoned their burden in the middle of the street. It was deemed to be the devil, who wanted to prevent the man from being buried in holy ground. One man was so afraid that he wanted to give up on this work of mercy before it had even gotten under way, but "he was told [that] with more solicitude and care it had to be done, because the devil liked it not a bit." How much truth there is in this story is hard to say. The fact is that the chronicler's account of the Tommaso Gucci case does not specifically mention the presence of *confratelli*. The words that accompanied the condemned to their deaths along the route of infamy through the city were recorded as a collective voice. We do not know what the onlookers shouted. But one thing is certain: rather than being passive spectators, they were the choral voice of a great theatrical performance. The condemned prisoner was the focus and butt of the unleashed passions of a multitude animated by feelings that were almost always of loathing. Only exceptionally could the voice of religion be heard. "Commending oneself to God" was the obligation of the condemned, who was reminded of it by those present. If they did not do so, it was a sign of total hatred and rejection. The *confratelli* of the company devoted to this special work of mercy had the task of retrieving and burying the corpses if and when they were allowed to do so. Their prayers and acts of penance remained in the background of a crowd that filled the streets and squares for the ritual of blood and death.

This model of crowd justice has three components: betrayal, real or supposed; a crowd that punished the "traitor," subjecting the body to various forms of scorn and execration; and a final act performed by *fanciulli*, who reduced the body parts to shapeless, neutral things—by playing football with the dismembered limbs, for instance. In the vicissitudes of the city's government and the factional struggles for power, episodes of this kind were sparked just as soon as someone cried out "treachery," had the bells of the *palazzo comunale* rung, and incited the crowd to chase and capture the traitor. Similar cases are also recorded in the chronicles of cities in Romagna, where the conflict between Guelphs and Ghibellines raged on until well into the sixteenth century. In Forlí, the barber Andrea Bernardi known as Novacula recounted the acts of bloodshed that occurred all the time in the city's conflicts, and that took the form of executions "a furor di popolo." Here is one from 1495. The city bell rings out to summon the populace, who rush to congregate. The cry goes up to "hunt down and kill" the traitors. Chases ensue, as fugitives try to get out of the city. One person hides "in a bridal chest": he is a priest, Don Domenico da Lugo, accused of treachery toward Giacomo Feo, the governor of the city's fortress. Don Domenico is seized, bound by his feet to the tail of a horse, dragged into the square, and hit in the face with a sword. His throat is then cut with a "bread knife." He just has time to join his hands together in a sign of "contrition," before he is finished off with stab wounds and blows from sticks, and attached to an iron rod with his chest slit open like "pig lard." Nothing suggests he received any religious comforting. Yet at this time there were a number of companies of Battuti active in the city. No fewer than seven, each in a different color, took part in the Corpus Domini procession in 1485, parading large theatrical machines: the tree of life, the seven mortal sins, and saints ranging from Saint Francis to Simon of Trent.[18] The black Battuti were the ones who attended to burying those who had been killed, without distinguishing between the executed and the victims of political violence. They retrieved and buried the body of Count Cesare Riario, killed to cries of "freedom, freedom" on April 14, 1488, and put on display in a window of the *palazzo pubblico*.[19] But the functions they performed appear fairly uncertain: besides consolation and burial duties, they also seem to have assisted the executioner. In the case of Don Domenico the black Battuti came by night to take down the body, but they did not bury it: instead, they hung it up by the gate leading out toward Ravenna, where it remained until the end of the month; other Battuti dealt with the head, which, detached from the body, was displayed on a spike on the tower of the Palazzo del Popolo until March 1497, when it fell off.[20] And yet there was no lack of public displays of piety. When another priest, Don Antonio, known as "Pavagliote," was rushed off to his death for being a traitor, the populace displayed "great joy" because he managed to recite some prayers before he died.[21]

Popular piety was particularly evident when the person condemned was a heretic. This is illustrated in a chronicle written by an anonymous member of the Fraticelli sect in 1389, when the Fraticello Michele da Calci was put to death. It is an exceptional document, revealing how, during the ritual procession to the gallows, the crowd and the condemned man could engage in a singular dialogue.[22] The cloak of anonymity covers here a companion in faith of the heretic. His narrative is a martyrology giving voice to the convictions of the Fraticelli. What makes it unique is that it does not record Michele's final words or confessions from the gallows. Instead, it focuses on the discussion he had with the crowd as he made his way to the gallows, exchanges between an individual and a collective interlocutor that commented on and reproached him, trying to shape the story in the desired direction. Fra Michele, said the anonymous writer, walked with his head bowed, reciting the Office, to the extent that "he seemed one of the martyrs."

"And everyone, feeling compassion for him, said: 'You should not wish to die!'" He said: "I want to die for Christ." "Ah, you are not dying for Christ!" And he replied: "For the truth." The crowd said: "But you don't believe in God!" To which he responded: "I believe in God, and in the Virgin Mary, and in the Holy Church." "Miserable wretch, you have the devil upon you, tugging at you." And he said: "May God watch over me."

He raised his lowered eyes a first time when, as the proconsul's bell rang, a member of the sect mingling with the crowd (probably the author of the chronicle) said to him: "Brother Michele, pray to God for us." And he replied: "Go, Christian Catholics, you who are blessed."

And he raised them again, when, in front of the foundations of Santa Reparata, someone said to him: "What a fool you are, you must believe in the pope." To which Michele sarcastically replied: "You've turned this pope of yours into God. . . . These popes of yours have really sorted you out!"

The crowd commented in wonder: "He's going to his death cheerfully!"

But individual voices also stood out among the murmurings. One of the spectators accompanied him for a stretch longer than the range of a crossbow bolt, and accused him of being a "martyr of the devil." There are overtones of theological doctrine here (they would surface once again before the gallows when heretics were put to death in the age of the Reformation and the religious wars): a martyr of the devil who was a master of pride, because he wanted to "know more than many masters"—for example, more than his master Father Luca—even though, compared to his fellow brother, he barely knew how to read. And Michele responded: "Master Luca knows that having lots of money is against his rule, yet he doesn't give it up!"

Another person used a subtle doctrinal argument, asking him whether he was not in fact committing suicide. And did this not mean that he had despaired, and was thereby condemned to damnation? Michele replied: "I am not killing myself, it is they who are killing me." The other man answered: "Because you want it yourself." "So as not to go against the truth," said Michele. But his questioner continued to press him: "Saint Peter denied it!" Michele: "And he was sorry for it." The other man insisted: "If Saint Peter were here, he would deny it." Michele: "He wouldn't, and if he did, he would be wrong."

The route ended in the places that took their name from the execution ritual: having gone through the Porta alla Giustizia (Execution Gate), and arriving at the Prato alla Giustizia (Field of Execution), they passed in front of the church of Santa Maria al Tempio. This was the headquarters of the Confraternity of the Battuti Neri, known as the Croce al Tempio and also, colloquially, as the church "dei Neri." But the church door was barred, a deliberate move, noted the anonymous writer, "so it seemed he did not believe in Christ." The Church would not allow him in to receive the sacraments, because he was regarded as an impenitent heretic, and the *confratelli* wanted nothing to do with him either alive or dead. And in fact, after the wooden "hut" was lit and Michele burnt to death, the remains of his body were gathered up in a sheet and buried by some young men in a hole near the execution site.

His case is that of an outspoken critic of the rich and powerful Church, and he was viewed with curiosity and some sympathy by the crowd. It was not an isolated episode. Chronicles recount other stories of crowds who were incensed by inquisitorial monks and protested about sentences. In Bologna in 1299, cries of "Death to the inquisitor" went up in the city square against the capital sentence handed out to a man named Bompietro, tried on charges of Cathar heresy. Political passions and social conflicts triggered a collective ferocity that was without equal when it came to people being condemned for their religious convictions. The advance of the inquisition pursued by the preaching orders during the communal period in Italy was like the mixing together of a river's waters with a current of a different color—disliked and opposed, accused of arbitrariness and abuses of power.[23] In their work the monks could count on the favor of the pope and on the economic and political relations the city communes had with the power of the Church. But the river of justice of the Italian cities had in the meantime become channeled within the banks of the inquisitorial model of the written trial, combined with the traditional accusatorial model: a secret procedure, the use of torture, confession. And the thirteenth century had seen the gradual emergence of a political dimension of the city as a collective subject, and as an entity with a duty to preserve the peace.[24] A process of mass pedagogy conducted by means of preaching and the use of images had also commenced: it was a question of promoting a notion of justice as an ideal of coexistence and as an instrument for protecting the lives and property of citizens.

The proliferation of images in churches, on the façades of buildings, or in places associated with the government of the medieval city speak of a society that mirrored itself on an everyday basis in positive models and severe warnings: the image of justice in the seats of power was intended to reassure those who feared theft or assault.[25] In the fresco of Good Government in Siena, the severed head in the lap of the allegorical figure of Justice, or the bodies hanging from gallows, provided reassurance to citizens and merchants of the safety of everyday life and of trade routes. Besides physically being put to death, criminals received the additional punishment of infamous memory: images about them would appear on the façade of the *palazzo pubblico,* while their houses were razed to the ground and their names materially erased. It was against this backdrop that the volunteers of the Battuti confraternities endeavored to carry out their work.

13

"Holy Justice": The Turning Point of the Fifteenth Century

THE HISTORY OF THE CONFRATERNITIES is one of entangled relations and conflicts between movements inspired by the wish to put Gospel precepts into practice and the attempts by the political and ecclesiastical powers to control and channel that impulse. Studying the dense network of urban confraternities in one of the great Italian capitals, sixteenth-century Genoa, Edoardo Grendi traces their origin to the moment when the "popular and quarrelsome spirit of neighborhood and street communities" coalesced into associations. The Tridentine Church soon intervened, as it was keen to subject them to the bishop's power, which was at odds with the political powers.[1] Previously these associations had been guided and urged on by members of the religious orders, especially the Franciscans and Dominicans, who shaped their forms of organization and charitable practices through preaching and administration of the sacraments. It was in such preaching that we see comforting of the condemned emerging and taking precedence over all other work, and where at the same time we find an urgent plea for the pacification of political conflicts. The Disciplinati movement had affirmed the idea that only a profound and collective religious renewal, inspired by penitence and peace, could solve the problems of violence: white robes, crosses, and flagellation as a public ritual of penitence became established features of confraternal associations, which occupied a separate place in the panorama of devotion and urban sociality, and escaped the periodic pruning of popular society's luxuriant vegetation. This was also because the political usefulness of work intended to promote peace among citizens and a sense of unity in tackling social emergencies was immediately evident. In place of the factional strife and political violence that produced division and conflict, the preaching of the monks and the spiritual guidance of the confraternities that had sprung up in their churches offered a model of fraternal unity among all Christians. According to the popular preacher Friar Bernardine of Siena, it was a capital sin to take sides, even if this went undeclared and remained hidden in an individual's heart. Indeed, it was not a sin like all the others, but "the worst sin one can have."[2] From it came all the evils of the world: "theft, usury, betrayal, lustful acts, robbery, wars, and such like." Bernardine had been shocked by the factional conflict that had stained the cities of "Lombardy"—the Po Valley—with blood. For him, the theme of justice was bound up with that of peace. It was against this background that he exhorted his fellow citizens to support and appreciate the work of the Compagnia della Morte, dedicated in Siena, as almost everywhere, to Saint John the Baptist.

The path that opened up at this point led to a rearrangement in the forms of charity and assistance for the condemned. In the meantime, confraternities had become established almost all over the peninsula, and had forged close ties with the new powers that had replaced the associative communal setup. The original manifestations of Christian fraternity with the condemned changed in response to the need for religious legitimation of recently established and insecure powers. This gave rise to the spectacular forms taken by executions, which became the theatrical setting where obedience and fear were instilled into the spectators. Those in power had to combine the traditional functions of social control performed by exemplary punishments with medieval Christianity's key idea of the providence and mercy of God. In this changed context, the task of the confraternities was at once more necessary and more difficult. New forms of organization and different ways of selecting members accompanied a reworking of the rules of behavior and a reflection on which arguments to use when comforting. This challenge was addressed by a network of associations with a widespread presence in the cities and towns of northern and central Italy, and which had specialized in providing assistance to the condemned.

In the late fifteenth and early sixteenth centuries, the founding of new confraternities and the reorganization of old ones continued apace by way of imitation and dissemination. A network of specialist associations covered Italy. The spontaneous spread of existing confraternities was a response to the spread of a new sensibility. The situation faced by the condemned summed up the essential features of a dramatically urgent problem: the threat of sudden death tested the value of religious resources in a context marked by the crisis of ecclesiastical institutions and a growing need for Church reform and the renewal of religious life. The origins of the companies of justice had been rooted in the social and political crisis of the fourteenth century and the experience of mass mortality in the years of the plague; now, at the end of the fifteenth century, the first Italian wars and recurrent epidemics prompted groups of citizens to address the problems of assistance in hospitals and prisons.

If we look at the spread of charitable activities associated with public executions, we will see that by the middle of the fifteenth century the map of such work was not just limited to the "Lombardy" discussed by Jean Gerson, though that area was heavily represented: even just a rough list shows that all the major cities and many smaller ones had confraternal associations that provided religious assistance to those facing execution. Among the most important cities were Milan, Venice, Mantua, Modena, Ferrara, Padua, Florence, and Siena, where devout congregations of volunteers were ready at a moment's notice to hasten to the prisons or to the gallows dressed in a habit and cloak bearing their symbol, singing psalms and *laude* in order to be close to those referred to, with delicate circumlocution, as "the afflicted" or "the patient." Adding to the important work carried out by preachers from the religious orders, the confraternities spread to the main towns around the cities: and besides the spoken word from the pulpit, there was the written word of devotional texts and statutes that were circulating and reaching audiences even before the age of printing.

The company of Bologna stands out among these associations for the wealth of surviving documentation. It was also one of the oldest. Here, as we have seen, the origins of the Compagnia dei Battuti, devoted to comforting the condemned, dated back to the mid-fourteenth century. The company's church had been built around that time: a site had been chosen on the northern edge of the city, near the marketplace where executions were performed. It was to this church, dedicated to Saint John the Baptist, that the *confratelli* took the bodies of the executed for burial. The granting of special indulgences by the ecclesiastical authorities encouraged the devotion of citizens, who left bequests for the celebration of masses and to secure the release of the poor from prison. Originally the devout work essentially consisted of following the condemned on their final journey and then ensuring that the body was buried in the confraternity's church. The sources do not indicate if any more elaborate form of assistance was provided, involving spiritual comforting and encouraging the prisoner to remain steadfast in the face of suffering and death, in memory of Christ's Passion. According to the "legend" of the life of Venturino of Bergamo, this is precisely what the Dominican did: apparently Venturino used to accompany the condemned on their final walk, urging them to accept their suffering and death, reminding them of the Passion of Christ, and exhorting them to believe firmly in divine mercy.[3] However, bearing in mind that the *Legend* was written in the following century, when the Bolognese confraternity, as we shall see, had also developed and refined the practice of comforting the condemned, it can reasonably be supposed that the author was projecting onto the past something that had taken form only subsequently, according to a typical anachronism of devotion.

At any rate, there is no doubt that by the middle of the fourteenth century, the duty to give the executed a Christian burial had gained ground in the work of the city's charitable confraternities. The response of the city had been positive: a register of 1393 lists 394 names, prevalently of craftsmen. In Bologna in that period the guilds played a key role in the communal government, which was defined, even formally, as the government "of the people and the guilds."[4] From the very beginning, the duties of the Battuti in Bologna included the provision of assistance in hospitals as well as in prisons and for the condemned. But in the course of the fifteenth century, as the city's political constitution changed and a form of signorial government emerged, the company also underwent a process of social selection and specialization. While the number of executions in the city increased on average by nine to thirteen each year—a sign of a reinforcement of personal power—the office of comforting the condemned became more sought after and important.[5] From an indulgence granted by Bishop Niccolò Albergati in 1418, it can be seen that saving the souls of the condemned formed the kernel of the work done by the *confratelli*. The care they provided was described by the bishop as "solicita et charitativa": at the center of their rites was the Virgin Mary, celebrated in their *laude*.[6] Immediately after the restoration and enlargement of the hospital (1427–1428), the company obtained the privilege of housing the image of the Madonna di San Luca on the days of the Minor Rogations, when it was brought to the city from the shrine: it was a fertility rite that had a precedent in the Florentine procession of the Madonna dell'Impruneta. In the solemn processions from the shrine to the city and back again, the confraternity also had right of precedence over all the others.[7] Being granted such a prestigious role in what was a very important civic ritual offers a clue to the special preeminence that the confraternity had acquired. It cultivated a special devotion to the blood of Christ and the suffering of the Passion, a typical feature of these associations: the remembrance of the spilling of Christ's precious blood was evoked in the prayer they said while undergoing the penitential exercise of flagellation.[8] Such devotion was somehow a familiar aspect of these contexts. The mysticism of the blood of Saint Catherine comes to mind here. From when Innocent III had established the doctrine of the real presence of Christ in the consecrated Host (at the Fourth Lateran Council), the preachers of the mendicant orders had worked hard to root the devotion of the Corpus Christi in popular culture. The theme of the suffering, wounded Christ had become interwoven with the mysticism of blood and the adoration of the Host, further complicated by tinges of an anti-Jewish polemic in the blossoming of devotions and manifestations of religious fervor. The creation of the Monti di Pietà, or institutional pawnbrokers, that characterized the late fifteenth century in Italy was a particular aspect of the work of the Franciscan order in the anti-Jewish battle raging at the time, especially in the Iberian Peninsula. In a university city like Bologna, the theological dispute with Judaism surfaced in theological pamphlets and in preaching. It had an impact on the artistic patronage of the lay confraternities, which were under the spiritual guidance of members of the religious orders. While the Confraternita dei Battuti della Morte was beginning its work in Bologna, in Urbino, under the dominion of Federico da Montefeltro, the Confraternita del Corpus Domini commissioned the Florentine artist Paolo Uccello to produce a large altarpiece. Between 1465 and 1468 Uccello completed the predella, depicting the story of the miracle of the blood that came out of a Host stolen by a Jew. And in the city the commitment to providing assistance to the dying and condemned also began in earnest: a Fraternita di Santa Maria della Misericordia was active here from the middle of the fourteenth century, and the condemned were attended to by the Compagnia di San Giuseppe (founded by a Franciscan monk at the beginning of the sixteenth century) and a Compagnia della Morte.[9] But it is through the story of the confraternity in

Bologna, thanks to the wealth of surviving documentation, that we can best trace the development of comforting practices for the condemned.

Here, in 1436, a *stretta* group was set up within the *larga* company, with the former focusing on spiritual perfection and the latter being left to run the hospital.[10] The members of the Oratorio di Santa Maria della Morte undertook, "according to their ability, [to] live under the gentle yoke of Jesus Christ, and to lead a good and honest life for the well-being of their souls." This entailed meetings in the oratory on every festive occasion, reciting of the Office, and ritual flagellation or "disciplining" with ropes; these featured on their emblems and still help us today to identify the campanile of their church near Piazza Maggiore. Monthly confession and receiving Communion on the five key feast days of the liturgical year were steps in a path of perfecting in which one fundamental aspect related to the care devoted to the "way of reconciling" brothers who were in conflict with each other. This particularly concerned reconciliation with those sent to their death on the gallows. "Reconciled" thanks to the sacraments, these people were all to be "accompanied by our company to holy justice."[11] The expression "holy justice" is worth bearing in mind: what it amounts to is the exaltation of capital punishment—*giustizia*—insofar as it is a maker of saints. The structure of the Compagnia dell'Ospedale di Santa Maria della Morte was gradually being organized around this function. The statutes of the School of Comforters—a special group within the company—drawn up by the jurisconsult Cristoforo Pensabene in 1556 were incorporated into the general codification of the Compagnia dell'Ospedale of 1562, which documented its rise within Bolognese society: the white habit of the brothers who are gathered together under the pale blue cloak of the Virgin Mary in the telling image that opens the parchment codex was worn at that time by counts, knights, and doctors, members of the ruling orders of the papal city.[12] For the admission of new *confratelli* the doors were flung open only to "nobles, and the sons of gentlemen," with the rector's assent being all that sufficed. It was much more difficult for anyone else. The *confratelli* had to prepare themselves to comfort the condemned by attending Sunday meetings given over to "reasoning about spiritual matters." They were guided in this by the censor, tasked with prohibiting any discussion that carried even the faintest whiff of heresy. The author of the comforters' new statutory norms, Cristoforo Pensabene, knew all too well how sensitive the issue was:

at the age of nineteen he had secretly renounced heretical doctrines, before subsequently becoming an important member of the Bolognese Church.[13] The university city, home also to an important Dominican study center, had for years felt the effects of the activities conducted by the Roman congregation of the Holy Office: maintaining social order was by now bound up with the struggle against doctrinal dissent. In this framework, comforting the condemned became a high and sensitive office, the exclusive and secret task of the confraternity members: "good and diligent fishermen of souls," they had the duty to stay with the condemned person throughout the night preceding execution, convincing them to "patiently submit to the punishment" in order to save their soul. Secrecy, a solemn awareness of the delicacy and importance of their work, left a permanent mark on the self-consciousness of a body that now felt itself to be socially and culturally selected.

In the course of its long history the restricted group of the Oratorio was known as the "School of Comforters." The Greek-Byzantine word used in the Republic of Venice to denote the confraternities took on the meaning— better suited to the context of university study—of a place for reflection, meditation, and reading (of the statutes, but increasingly also of a literature comprising accounts of the practice and handbooks of theoretical instructions). There was scope here for pictorial and sculptural expressions of devotion. The Passion of Christ, the Redemption, and the miracles of the Virgin as the mother of mercy turned into visual homilies and meditative themes addressing a fundamental question that, as we shall see, dominated the thought and methods of the School: How and why was it possible for the most brutal of criminals to attain eternal salvation in exchange for an eleventh-hour repentance and acceptance of execution as an act of penance? They document a new historic phase, during which these companies now appeared to be definitively geared in to performing a function of recognized importance and noteworthy prestige. These increasingly dense documentary traces permit us to follow their work at close hand, offering clues to understanding the start of this specialization, which brought to an end the unity of charitable work for all ill and dying members of the community. And finally, in 1540, the names and surnames of the executed began to be recorded, together with those who comforted them: a glorious memory for the School, which was considered desirable to project onto the past as well. The first person to do this was Giovanni Martino Galasso, a *merzaro* (haberdasher) by trade.[14]

The development of other city companies of the same kind reveals common features with specific differences. The model of this special work of mercy spread to many small cities and towns, of which there was a dense network in Romagna. One example is Faenza, where a Confraternita di Santa Maria delle Grazie was active: in 1422 the members of its chapters, "when fate required that, God forbid, some person was to be executed . . . , had to order some [brothers] to stay the night comforting him in the holy faith and in the patience of Christ." After the night had passed, they had to turn up in the morning to accompany the condemned to the gallows, dressed in their cowls, holding the cross before them, and saying prayers "in a low voice."[15] In the sixteenth century the evolution of this special work of mercy in Faenza was caught up in the turmoil of the hunt for Lutheran heresy, leading to a restructuring. In Lombardy a model was provided by the Milanese confraternity of San Giovanni Decollato (known as "alle case rotte"), which sprang from the Disciplinati. There is evidence that a confraternity of "Disciplini bianchi" dedicated to Santa Maria della Morte was actively engaged in works of mercy around the middle of the fourteenth century. In its first statutes of 1380, the fundamental task that the lay brothers and sisters undertook to perform was that of accompanying and comforting those condemned to death.[16] Assisting the condemned, and undertaking to bury their bodies, confirmed by the statutes of 1396, was greatly appreciated by the city authorities: in 1395, Duke Gian Galeazzo Visconti ordered that the whole city should solemnly celebrate them on August 29, the annual feast of Saint John the Baptist.[17] In 1421 the archbishop granted permission to build and consecrate the cemetery next to their church, where the *confratelli* and the executed were buried. When the confraternity decided to keep a written record of executions, the brother dealing with it was only actually able, using previous notes, to go back to 1471; in the various surviving drafts, the list of the condemned covers, with some breaks, the period from 1471 until 1784, when Emperor Joseph II issued a decree suppressing the confraternity.[18] A chronicle-style register also exists, providing information about executed prisoners and punishments between 1552 and 1611.[19] In the Lombard area, there began to spring up new charitable confraternities such as Santa Maria del Sole in Lodi, which was established in 1551 to offer assistance to the imprisoned and condemned.[20] In this second phase of the history of the Milanese confraternity, a substantive change took place in its composition: following the disappearance of women from its membership, nobles became the dominant social group. Charles Borromeo's intervention was decisive in this; according to his biographer, Giovan Pietro Giussani, Borromeo wanted to give nobles the opportunity "to engage very fruitfully in works of great charity and mercy."[21] The revision of the statutes of what was called the association "of consolation of Saint John" formalized the decisive change that had taken place: the new reformed regulations of 1589 saw the nomination of the king of Spain and the governor of Milan as "born protectors," and the chapters of 1590 recorded a social composition dominated by gentlemen and high officials.

In Venice in 1562 the Confraternita di San Fantin lost its archive to a fire that destroyed the *mariegola* (book of statutes) and the minutes of meetings containing descriptions of "many wonderful orders regarding the government and administration of this School."[22] This and other vicissitudes impacted on the original lists of executions. But when, in 1806, Angelo Maria Bianchi, the last "degàn di mezz'anno" (one of the two people responsible for looking after the keys to the alms box), undertook to reconstruct the list of those who had been executed, he was able to use an old register beginning in 1412, probably the year in which this special form of accounting actually began.[23]

In Florence the relationship between the *larga* and the *stretta* companies evolved very similarly, in form and over time, to the confraternity in Bologna. The Florentine institution was founded toward the middle of the fourteenth century, as we have seen. According to the Neri's own tradition, it took place in 1343 and was attributed to the initiative of "some men of youthful age" concerned above all in obtaining the liberation of prisoners.[24] The practice of burying the bodies of the executed only began some years later: this was an important new development, as demonstrated by the story of the sudden appearance of the black horse and the abandoning of the coffin in the street. The confraternity's subsequent growth followed the course of Florence's development as a state, and was marked by increasing specialization in the management of executions, the fundamental ritual in the administration of justice. It was a collective ritual that unfolded in the streets and squares of the city, along a strictly determined route marked by the emblems of the company, at the end of which the condemned came to the place of execution. In compliance with Florentine statutes, this had to be situated at least one thousand *braccia*—approximately 640 yards—outside the city gates. Over time the Neri became the orchestrators and officiants of this great urban ritual.[25] During the fifteenth century the restricted group of the Neri became established within the Compagnia di Santa Maria della Croce al Tempio, their special task being to comfort the condemned. In the constitutions of 1488, the oldest ones to have come down to us, the origins of the Neri are dated to 1423, with the first chapters being approved on January 27, 1442. They were drawn up—according to the constitutions—after reflecting upon their design "among themselves, and with other spiritual and devout persons." The date of 1423 is borne out by the annotation regarding the first case dealt with by the confraternity members: "Dolfo d'Antonio, cotton beater from the community of San Piero. He was beheaded at the podestà's orders on October 14, and buried in the aforementioned San Piero. He was the first to be attended by the Battuti, that is, by our members with black attire, and there were ten of them."[26]

The formal ratification of the chapters in 1442 took place in the company's hospital, when Pope Eugene IV was in Florence, and they were first reformed on October 26, 1488.[27] The fact that one of the company's members at this time was Lorenzo de' Medici denotes a measure of the social prestige enjoyed by the confraternity. The first chapter of this revised version states that the purpose of the company was to act "for the solace and benefit of those whose lives end by violent death and execution, to comfort them so they are acquiescent, to conduct them onto the path of truth, and for the wellbeing of their souls; the exercising of these principles include all the works of mercy." This was the way to prepare for the "final judgment," by responding to the Gospel invitation. Evangelical inspiration and the model of the apostolic Church formed the mental horizons of those who made such a choice. The periodic reading of some or all of the chapters at the end of the regular monthly meetings (known as *tornate*) was intended to keep alive the sense of the choice made by the *confratelli* and the fervor of the company's origins. This was the wish of the *stretta* group that had formed within the Compagnia Grande del Tempio. Subsequent versions, or *riformanze,* of the chapters provide specific indications regarding the selection of members and forms of governance: there were seven elective offices, in line with the model outlined by the Acts of the Apostles. The chaplain had the duty "to confess and comfort, and to have Mass said in the rector's chapel to administer Holy Communion to them," to give a blessing to the "afflicted," and to provide for their spiritual needs to the end with the help of the sacraments and perhaps a last-minute reconciliation.[28] The mode and form of participation at executions was laid out very specifically: according to the statutes, this was "their work, and the most necessary one exercised in our congregation, and it is the main reason why it was ordered."[29] Initially comprising twelve members, then twenty-four, in 1442 the maximum number was fixed at fifty, with a distinction between the twelve leading notables ("experienced and able in three leading offices of the city") and thirty-eight members of the guilds, "all secular laypeople": the numbers were carefully gauged to ensure the preeminence of a power elite over a more broadly popular body. When Lorenzo de' Medici took part in the reform of the articles, he did so "with complete authority."[30] Granted special indulgences by Pope Eugene IV and special approval from the archbishop, these statutes were then once again "revised, corrected, and pronounced" in 1586, retaining the *stretta* setup of the company established in the fifteenth century: the number of members was not to exceed fifty, twelve of whom were to be *benifitiati*—members of families that had been part of the Signoria or had occupied the post of gonfalonier of justice.[31] But by this time the confraternity's nature as a devout body had become overshadowed by that of something resembling a magistracy: according to the description of the Florentine magistracies found in a "summary" by the Florentine notary and playwright Giovan Maria Cecchi (1518–1587),

these [Neri] do not recite any office, or do things that confraternities like the Battuti do . . . , but, in the guise of a magistrate, hear cases. And what is of greatest charity is that they comfort all those who are sentenced to death by Justice. . . . The Bargello family takes the culprit to the chapel. . . . The men of this company stay near to and comfort him, and bit by bit prepare him for confession and for death. So they stay with him all night . . . and accompany him right up until he dies, and, when dead, they bury him.[32]

With the fifteenth century well under way, then, the confraternity began to take on a visible presence in the rituals of justice. The members' distinctive black habits and cowls earned them the familiar name of "Neri," or "Blacks," which already found its way into the articles of 1488. The hospital and church of the Tempio where they met, and from which they took their official name, were situated outside the so-called Porta della Giustizia, where executions were carried out in that age and where, in a later period, the bodies of the condemned were buried in a plot of land made available by the commune.[33] The articles stipulated that "at an early hour" in the evening before the execution, two *confratelli* chosen by lot were to go to the prison wearing their habits, so as to be present when the prisoner "received the commandment of the soul." From then on they were not to leave the prisoner, "comforting and urging acceptance" until the beginning of confession. At this point they were to remain silent, "strictly commending him to the Lord." Immediately afterward they were to comfort him "both spiritually and bodily," giving him, for instance, some good white wine to drink. Then, together with other *confratelli,* they had to recite the seven penitential psalms, "with the litanies and orations, and spoken and silent prayers." After this the governor of the company, or someone delegated by him, was to approach the "afflicted" and deliver a sermon, "encouraging him to bear with good spirit the torment prepared to correct his errors." The governor also had to assure the condemned that they would not be abandoned right up to and after the end, because even after death they would help the dead person's soul with masses "and other offices for the dead."[34]

In the patchwork composition of the city's confraternities, the one called "dei Neri" by antonomasia earned a special place for itself. This is reflected in the judgment of Benedetto Varchi, who, in his history of Florence, cursorily describes the city's seventy-three confraternities, dividing them up into those made up of "boys" (with merely liturgical functions) and those formed by men, for the most part devoted "to pleasing themselves and others," though some also did charitable works and performed acts of devotion and penitence. But the "Blacks" received a separate description: Varchi calls it "the renowned company of the Temple, called [the company] of the Blacks," and describes its activities with a particular tone of respect: "The men . . . after the commandment of the soul is given to someone who is to be executed, go to comfort him all night long, and accompany him the next day like the Battuti, *tavoletta* in hand, continuing to comfort him and commending his soul right up until the last moment."[35]

The growing importance of Florence as the political capital of a nascent Tuscan territorial state, and as a dynamic trading and banking center with increasingly close ties with the great international court of papal Rome, was the driving force behind the spread of this special confraternity. As Florentine power advanced through Tuscany so too did the model of the Compagnia dei Neri. After Florence conquered Pisa, a Compagnia di Santa Maria delle Grazie, also known as the Fraternita dei Fiorentini, was established in the coastal city: the statutes of 1466 envisaged a membership comprising equal numbers of Florentines and Pisans, and determined that the assistance for the condemned was to be along similar lines to those taking root in Florence.[36] The Florentine company's influence extended to nearby Prato as well. Active here in 1502 was a Confraternita di San Giovanni Decollato, the task of which was to "comfort in faith and hope" those condemned to death during the night before their execution, to accompany them to the place of execution, hoisting the banner of the cross. Its members commended the souls of the executed to God and buried their bodies in specially designated places in their church, celebrating annual masses in remembrance of their souls.[37] The network covering the territory of the Tuscan regional state revitalized ancient oratories, like the fourteenth-century one in Cascina, where a large fresco serving as a reminder of the judgment of the divine court can still be seen today. And it led to a flourishing of Battuti companies in all the main towns and cities, dedicated to local saints in addition to John the Baptist. In Cortona, for example, toward the middle of the sixteenth century, an oratory of San Rocco e Onofrio was engaged in the "pious task of mercy for the imprisoned and for those condemned to the ultimate torment."[38] In San Miniato the confraternity of justice was founded in 1512, in step with the territorial expansion of the Florentine state toward Pisa and the sea; it was dedicated to Saint Peter Martyr and Saint John the Baptist.[39] In Castrocaro, in Tuscan Romagna, the construction, at Cosimo I's behest, of the fortress of Terra del Sole provided the occasion for founding a company of justice named after Saint Joseph—a typical instance of religious support for the judicial activities of the magistracies, especially in border areas.[40] But the Florentine confraternity's real conquest took place outside Tuscany, when it became the model for the Roman company of San Giovanni Decollato: it was the conquest of papal Rome that provided the strongest impetus for the spread of this devotion. It should be remembered that the Florentine company, and the one in Bologna, were pointed to as models for the Sienese by the most celebrated Franciscan preacher of the fifteenth century, Bernardine of Siena, in the course of sermons delivered in Piazza del Campo in Siena in 1427. Bernardine urged the Sienese to support and appreciate the work of the Compagnia della Morte, dedicated to Saint John the Baptist, which had just been established in Siena as an offshoot of the ancient Misericordia: "I remind you of your company of death, which, for the love of God, you should not allow to fade away. And no one should be ashamed to be part of it, though you have not considered how perfect it is."[41] Shame is a sentiment often evoked in the history of the gradual advance of companies of this kind in Italian cities: it stemmed from the perceived diminishment of rank hanging over those who lowered themselves by performing tasks considered degrading for members of the dominant orders and their aristocratic models of life. One needs only think of the contact with the bodies of the executed and the parts cut off from them and thrown to the dogs. Conscious of this, Bernardine invited his listeners to consider the nobility of saving souls in order to overcome their haughty reluctance to take care of the bodies:

> I would furthermore say to you that you should give emphasis to the Company of Death. Oh, if you were only to think of how salutary a thing it is for the souls of those executed by the commune. If you think upon this a little, you will say that it is true. I hear that you are building here outside the gate a beautiful chapel so that the blood of those beheaded may not be spilt, and that the dogs may not lick it up. I say that you do well indeed.[42]

Note that, for the popular preacher, Christian mercy should not interfere with city justice. Though he reaffirmed the evangelical precept of forgiveness ("Love is forgiving. Do you forgive? No? Then God will not forgive you") and invited his audience to help those in prison, Bernardine made it clear that charity should not impede the workings of justice: "If he deserves death, let justice, which is holy and good, and one of the main things that keeps the city in a good state, take its course."[43]

The company founded in Siena was dedicated to Saint John the Baptist, in line with the prevailing devotional model. It was initially based at the Badia Nuova, before moving to Pantaneto. One characteristic feature that it maintained for a long time was a membership comprising many common people: the register of *confratelli* compiled from 1518 onward includes weavers, builders, porters, and cobblers, and there was a list of *consorelle* too.[44] The fifteenth-century inventories refer to large crucifixes "to carry before justice," *tavolette* "to give peace," that is, to present to the condemned during the ritual, *libricioli* of lauds and litanies to recite, and the very core of the company's devotion, the book of chapters.[45] And it is here, in the prayers, that the strong tie between works of mercy and the political identity of an imperial city is revealed: prayers were offered for the "temporal state"— namely, for the Most Serene Emperor and for the city of Siena loyal to him; divine protection was invoked for the crops—"all the fruits above and below the earth"; and prayers were said "for all prisoners," with the addition of a "special prayer . . . for those in the hands of the infidels." Liberation was invoked for all of them, if such was the will of God: divine providence would decide whether that freedom might be useful "for the wellbeing of their souls." If not, prayers were offered that they might be given "true and perfect patience."[46] The confraternity's devotions were generally directed toward the needy, those in prison or hospital, and to the burial of the dead. Above all else prayers were offered up for the "holy peace," that God might bestow it not just on the devout company but on the entire city, rooting it "in our minds and in our hearts" but above all in the hearts of citizens and those in government": they were the ones who had the duty to maintain peace in "the city and the *contado,* and instil reason in the old and young."[47] In the background here it seems possible to see the candid female figure of Peace painted by Ambrogio Lorenzetti in the fresco of Good Government. Peace and justice dominated the city horizons of the Sienese *confratelli.* And in their prayers for the salvation of souls, the eternal fate of company members was present together with that of those "who have gone along the path of justice, for whom we have the obligation to pray, if, for some sin of theirs they were taken to some punishment in Purgatory." It is worth reading the interesting exchange between the prior of the company and the new member about to enter it, to understand how the principal work of mercy had become the one relating to the condemned:

PRIOR: Dear and devoted brother, the Prior and these other leading brothers ask what you are seeking.

BROTHER: The mercy of God and the peace of this holy and devout company.

PRIOR: You had and received the mercy of God when you had the water of Holy Baptism, and you will have and receive the peace of this holy and devout company when you observe these holy and devout chapters.

The obligations were these: first of all, the *confratello* had to attend Mass in the company's church and make the required offering. But above all he had to be willing to respond to the summons to funerals and executions *(giustizie)*. When the call was sent out by the sacrestans, he had "to spend the night in the prison with that wretch"; and if it was not his turn for the nighttime duty, he had to be ready, wherever he was, to kneel and pray as soon as he heard the sound of the bell of justice; immediately afterward, he was to don the company's habit and "accompany him [the condemned] to the place of execution and remain until the soul separated from the body."[48] The prestige of the company in Sienese society was recognized by the city authorities: the fifteenth-century reform of the statutes took place under the supervision of three citizens appointed by the consistory magistrate.[49] And the early seventeenth-century statutes contain a decree issued by Bishop Camillo Borghese recognizing the traditional privilege they had to "honor with torches and by wearing sackcloth" the relic of the arm of Saint John the Baptist when it was displayed in public on the day of Pentecost.[50]

From the trunk of the Florentine model that had prompted Bernardine to speak out in favor of the Sienese company sprang the Roman company of Saint John the Baptist. More will be said about this later. But in the meantime, surveying a densely populated Italian landscape of associations, we can list, without any pretense to completeness, some other parallel paths of the same form of mercy.

The case of the Confraternita di San Giovanni Evangelisti della Morte in Padua was similar to the one in Bologna. Having moved into the city in 1363, it devoted itself principally to assisting the condemned.[51] The text of the oldest statutes, dating to the mid-fifteenth century, bears testimony to the association's convictions and the tasks they undertook. As generally happened, the statutes formed the bedrock for a kind of devotion that penetrated deep into the minds of the *confratelli,* as they were ritually read aloud, usually during confraternity meetings. The statutes offered guidance for the thoughts and behavior of members. As regards the aims of the group in Padua, the job of assisting the condemned was given particular emphasis. Two members of the company were responsible for "going, on the night before the day of execution, to visit and comfort them and stay with them until justice is done." All the company members, men and women, had to collectively undertake to accompany the condemned to their deaths; and when the end came, "when the soul is separated from the body, that body is to be taken to the cemetery of our church and buried."[52] So by this time, besides the obligation for everyone to be present in the procession to the gallows, an important addition had been made: two members had the special task of going, at the command of the superiors, to console the condemned and prepare them for death during the night preceding execution.

Some fifty years later, new statutes plunged the reader into a climate of intense meditation about the misfortunes of life, replete with biblical psalms and references to Boethius's *De consolatione philosophiae.* They had been revised by Bishop Pietro Barozzi, a figure known for his work in running the diocese. He had an austere conception of the episcopal office, but participated actively in the intellectual life of his time. A trace of this can be found in a short treatise on the art of dying well that was influenced by the activities of the confraternity.[53] In accordance with the new statutes, the *confratelli* had to take "primary and particular care to console, accompany, and bury those who will be condemned to death by justice," and to keep them company on "the evening and through the night and that part of the day in which they are to be executed," so as to alleviate the "agony of the expectancy of violent death." Besides the obligations regarding their moral personal conduct, the sacraments, upholding peace and mutual concord among members, there was now a reflection on the importance and significance of comforting the condemned. There are two deaths, says the text, that of the body and that of the soul. Company members were thus to undertake to "console and accompany those who are put to death publicly and violently for their misdeeds and so as to teach others through their execution."[54] A legitimation of capital punishment can be found here: it is useful "to teach others," besides being valuable for the *confratelli*—they will receive the grace of God.

In the kingdom of heaven, comforting is of higher value than any other good work: this was the thinking intended to help overcome disgust for something considered repugnant and socially degrading: the duty to "console, accompany, and bury those who will be condemned to death by justice" is "most base and abhorrent, and of extreme distaste." They are signs of a raising of social barriers in a body that had already taken measures during the fifteenth century to explicitly bar people "of no condition" from admission to the company.[55] Baseness, disgust, abhorrence—sentiments that often surface in the documents of these associations. They are reminiscent of an act that made a big impression on Christian culture: Saint Francis kissing a leper, the figure of exclusion par excellence. Compared to the leper—obliged to live outside the city walls, avoided by everyone, and considered guilty of terrible sins for having been marked by God in such a manner—the impurity of someone who had been condemned to death might have appeared less dangerous. It should be remembered though that Christ's death had also been "very ugly" and that the precious opportunity offered by executions therefore needed to be grasped. The procedure to follow was described in meticulous detail: the names of all the *confratelli* were to be put into one of two bags, depending on whether they could read or not. When the warden was informed of an impending execution, he took one name out of each bag and gave the order to keep the condemned person company during the evening and night, "and that part of the day on which he is to be executed." In the meantime, the last supper of the "wretch" was prepared, at the company's expense. This was considered very important: the Bible recommends giving good wine to "those in bitter distress" (Prov. 31:6–7)—a necessary measure, because, as the statutes warn, those experiencing the agony of waiting to die would not be in a state to listen to the comforters without that help. And then begins the longest chapter, the one in which the duties of the *confratelli* chosen for the task are laid out. First of all, they must have clear in their minds which arguments to put to the condemned so they will accept what awaits them as penance for their sins, thereby avoiding the punishments of purgatory. For this reason the condemned must demonstrate their contrition by frequently reciting the Hail Mary and the Lord's Prayer, and kissing crucifixes and beating their chest. But above all the comforters were to urge the "delinquent" to make a general confession—and they had to be helped and taught how to do this.

When the time came for the execution, the *confratelli* followed the condemned person, wearing the company's robe and walking in line behind the cross, and then knelt in a circle around the gallows. In the evening they were to recover the body for burial in the most appropriate place, unless, that is, it was destined for anatomical dissection. But before doing that they had to collect the severed hands and gouged-out eyes in a box in order to bury them. It was a gruesome task, involving a degrading relationship with a "most base" humanity, but was carried out in the interests of a pedagogic function: to teach the people. Notations like this crop up frequently, and are indicative of socially elevated contexts, of the dominant noble orders. But aside from the social filter, what can also be glimpsed is the miserable living conditions in the prisons, the filth of the cells and of their human occupants, the disgust and repugnance felt by those who chose to put themselves in direct contact with the results of the ruthless butchery inflicted on human bodies— which then had to be recomposed with care, collecting any bits left scattered on the street, thus preventing them from being used for the magical or curative purposes that made them so precious and sought after.

However mean, degrading, and disgusting the task was, the response of those devoted to charitable deeds was extraordinarily positive, and quickly led to the spread of this kind of confraternity in many Italian towns and cities. The question that inevitably springs to mind is what prompted so many people to want to carry out this work of mercy. The answer can be found in the statutes, the book containing the rules and convictions affirmed by the founders and those who came after them, and which was devoutly read and meditated upon during regular meetings. One randomly chosen example are the statutes of 1479 of the Compagnia della Pietà, active in Viterbo. Here, emphasis is laid not just on the moral and religious obligations of the members, but also on the significance and religious foundations of the practice of comforting. The *confratelli* were bound by a series of regulations: assiduous attendance of the sacraments, exercises of personal penitence (ritual self-disciplining in private was fundamental), and works of charity toward the sick and the dead. They were expected to go to confession and take Communion each month. The moral rigor of each individual's behavior was carefully monitored, and any shortcomings could be reported in the company's meetings. On these occasions a kind of public confession took place that recalls the monastic model of the chapter of sins. A detailed set of rules concerned mercy as the provision of help and assistance for the body and soul of the sick in hospital and of the condemned. Both categories were to be prompted to confess their sins: the rules laid down by the Fourth Lateran Council for the sick were thus extended to the dying. It was necessary to attend to all the needs of the infirm, especially if they were poor. When there were outbreaks of plague, or even in the event of dangerous illnesses, the *confratelli* had to undertake not to abandon the dying. The bodies of the dead then had to be washed and prepared for burial, and ritually accompanied by *confratelli* dressed in black and carrying candles. Everyone, even the poor, were to receive this attention; the names of the dead were then to be remembered in masses for their souls. The job to be done "when someone is executed" was an extension of the compassion afforded to the sick and dying. But a special undertaking of the Compagnia della Pietà emerges here, one regulated with detailed norms covering each hour of the night before an execution. The rectors had to ensure that, from the evening of the sentence until the morning of the execution, successive shifts of two *confratelli* stayed with the condemned person, keeping him "company and comforting and consoling him 'iusta posse' to good patience." The first shift (or *muta*) ran from the evening until midnight; the second one, comprising two *confratelli* and a priest, then took over for the rest of the night. Their task was to combat the temptations of the condemned, encouraging them to remain strong, with the help of appropriate food ("sugar and other confections, and good wine to comfort them," all at the company's expense). In particular they were to suggest meditation on the evangelical beatitude closest to the condemned's condition, that of the persecuted for the sake of righteousness ("Beati qui persecutiones patiuntur propter iustitiam"). It is a singular line of argument, which alone shows how the company interpreted its role in the execution ritual. The condemned was someone who suffered persecution in the name of justice, and for this reason could aspire to be counted among the blessed. The voice of the company did not identify with the sentence of condemnation, as the one in Padua did. The nocturnal comforting culminated in confession. And here pains were taken to specify that the confessor was not allowed to request a fee or accept an offering. The usual practice of payment in money or in offerings for the sacraments was firmly rejected.

The third shift of *confratelli* took over in the morning. Their job was to take the condemned to Mass, during which they received Communion. At the third toll of the commune's bell, announcing the execution, a fourth *muta* of brothers took up position on each side of the prisoner, holding a cross to which the condemned was expected to commend his soul. Then the sentence was read out and the procession set off, singing litanies: all the members were obliged to be present, wearing their ritual attire—failure to do so incurred heavy punishment. One of the rectors had to hold the cross and get the condemned to kiss it. The procession sometimes went to a large cross, the usual site for executions, or continued along the road toward Rome as far as the Torre di San Michele. But right until the end the company had to guarantee the presence of some of its members and of a priest, who comforted the condemned without interruption. All the *confratelli* were then required to be present for the subsequent burial ritual. This too was an obligation that had to be strictly observed, and no absence was considered justified if not notified and demonstrated in advance. Failure to comply led to severe punishment: "because the whole company is based on this chapter."[56]

Two key reasons underpinned this acute consciousness of the importance of conducting the ritual correctly and smoothly. On the one hand was the relationship of exchange between the saving of the condemned person's soul and those of the comforters. Gaining a soul was the most meritorious work that could possibly be done: accumulating merits like these gave the *confratelli* who invested their labor some capital to present to God's tribunal on their own behalf. But on the other hand, the merit also concerned the earthly city for which the work was carried out. Ensuring that the execution ritual took place in such a way as to offer up on the gallows a repentant and penitent figure contributed to the compactness and harmony of the social body. The awareness of this bond with the city community can be seen in the final chapter, concerning the obligation of the *confratelli* to ensure "public union": and it was for this reason that they were not allowed to participate in secret factional meetings that posed a threat to "public peace." For the same reason they had to immediately pass on to the city's governor any information that might help to suppress unrest and punish the fomenters. If there was any danger of a revolt, the company's members were duty-bound to place themselves unhesitatingly at the service of the governor and to go to his palace, ready to support and defend him.

These statutes speak a language different from that of the communal *misericordie* associations, whose charitable endeavors took as many forms as there were conditions of need and affliction, and were pursued with the proceeds from hospitals and burials, with company members gaining in terms of spiritual enrichment and the net profit of investment in their own eternal salvation. A phase began in which assisting at executions brought social recognition and a role in public life: the corpse of a person who died penitent and reconciled was accepted into the blessed place of Christians awaiting the resurrection. The fracture was healed thanks to the condemned's "good death." The collective body of society knitted together again. The raison d'être of the company of justice was to ensure the preservation of good order, even at the cost of getting its men to defend the palace of power—something not at odds with the figural transformation of the condemned criminal or rebel into a martyr to be beatified.

The extent to which the function of the religious arm of power was taking shape in the development of the companies of justice can be seen in the case of the ones active in the state of the Este family in the Po Valley. The company in Modena was named after Saint John the Baptist, and its origin, as we saw, dates to 1372. Its original function was to offer fraternal aid and to assist the poor, but in the middle of the fifteenth century, more precisely in 1452, with a "reform" later consolidated by the revision of the chapters in 1482, it began to specialize in offering assistance to the condemned.[57] The city's "large square," where the scaffold tower stood, became the place where the rituals of punishment were performed. Here the *confratelli* went to work to ensure everything took place in due fashion, and that, at the end, the remains of the bodies and the hangman's ropes were carefully collected together, as attested by the detailed list of the executed kept for the years between 1593 and 1826.[58]

Features and practices such as these can be found in the development of many other companies arising out of the Disciplinati movement. A case in point is the Confraternita dei Disciplinati di Sant'Andrea in Perugia, where the movement began. The first constitutions of 1374 indicate that it had penitential goals, besides providing mutual assistance among members, especially in the event of death: everyone had the duty to "honor the dead," to be present at the burial of other *confratelli*, and to have masses said for the members' souls.[59] But a deliberation of the priors of the commune dated 1459 reveals that its new name, as of two years earlier, was "fraternita della Giustizia" (fraternity of justice). Its members accompanied the condemned to the execution site, comforting them and doing everything necessary to bring about their conversion ("circha conversionem animarum")—a word worth bearing in mind, as we will come across it continually from now on. The commune allocated funds to purchase black cloaks and hoods for members of the fraternity, and drapes to cover the bodies of the condemned and gather up their heads afterward. It also undertook to buy candles for the saint's annual feast day. The model provided by the Compagnia dei Neri in Florence was followed in Perugia, "always a diligent imitator of the wise institutions of the Florentine Republic."[60] There are traces of the Perugian confraternity's work in a record of the executed beginning in 1525, and in the printed constitutions of 1538, which indicate, among other things, that the confraternity handled the purchase of everything required for executions, and looked after the implements of justice.[61]

The confraternity of Santa Maria Annunziata (or of the Battuti Neri) in Ferrara evolved in the same way. Founded on August 5, 1366, it was "reformed" in the first half of the fifteenth century.[62] But here, in contrast to the trading city of Modena, there was the marked imprint of a sovereign dynasty. A document dating to its most ancient phase is a ritual in parchment from the fourteenth century, still housed in the confraternity's archive: on it can be read the Latin orations of the burial liturgy, and some *laude* in the vernacular. On one page is a trace of a later use: a few words in modern handwriting, with a signature and date: "I die willingly, because I die in the grace of God, Angelo de Angeli, 1633."[63] It is a dramatic document, inserted amid the ornate capital letters of the liturgical formulas, bearing testimony to the final moment of comforting, when the condemned man was asked to formally declare his wish to die penitent and converted. Imagine the anxiety of the comforter, grabbing whatever writing material came to hand. But by that time, more careful and accurate recording of the names of the condemned and the outcome of comforting practices had long since become established practice. The Ferrara company was the first to start keeping a regular record of the executed as a function directly connected to the power of the Este signoria. The confraternal custom of keeping track of the names of the dead buried in their cemeteries, so they could be remembered in prayers and masses, was an ancient practice of monastic origin. In the case of the companies of justice, something substantively different was grafted onto that tradition. And from then on the habit spread of recording the key details of executions—traces can be found scattered among the documentary sources of the confraternities. But it was around the second half of the fifteenth century that it acquired systematic form. The oldest and best-known examples are those of Bologna, Venice, Ferrara, and Florence, but over time others were drawn up by confraternities as they were set up.[64] They were the account books of a special form of trade: it is no accident that a person who performed comforting duties was known at the time as a "merchant of heaven."[65] The measure of success was the number of condemned who died showing all the signs of a religious conversion, and who received the sacraments. For this reason, the key items of information in the "execution" records were: the name of the individual; the date and, possibly, the mode of execution; and finally, whether or not the signs of a Christian death had been manifested. Other details might sometimes be added if the crime had been particularly brutal, or if the execution involved any spectacular and dramatic moments. These additional notes are what attracted the interest of readers and collectors in later times, due to the peculiar fascination that violent crime has always exercised. However, the compilers only focused on the evil in order to stress the good: the conversion, on the point of death, of a hardened criminal, a stubborn heretic, a Jew, or a Muslim was the demonstration of just how precious the work of the comforters was.

Despite their limits, they are the only remaining sources regarding the majority of the people who ended up on the gallows in Italy while this model of assistance lasted. What is more, the compilers often attempted to supplement their lists with names and cases from previous centuries, gleaned from sources that no longer exist. Thronging these pages is the army of the executed dead in the cities of Italy from the eleventh century onward: the one that peopled the mythological nightmare of the Wild Hunt, or Furious Army. But it was precisely the work of the *confratelli* of the "good death" that exorcised the fury of those who died without peace.

The importance of these lists has been greatly neglected until now. But they are the richest series of criminal statistics existing in the world. Only a few German cities—Nuremberg, for instance—have anything similar. The need to record and document names, crimes, and the circumstances of deaths on the scaffold took root in Italy in the same period that saw the spread of the practice of keeping baptism records, which endowed Italian cities with the great legacy of the most ancient sources of personal data. There was, then, a new need for detailed quantification not just of those entering the Christian community through baptism, but also of those leaving the earthly world due to the decision of a judge. We are far removed here from the ancient tradition of the necrologies of the monasteries laicized in the books of the dead normally kept by the confraternities. In place of that traditional link between living and dead through the periodic celebration of remembrance masses to commend souls to God's heavenly tribunal, a new concern now emerged, that of recording the efficacy of the tribunal of the terrestrial prince in administering his justice. It is this second aspect that comes to the fore in the case of the company of Santa Maria Annunziata in Ferrara. One of the duties of members listed in the first statutes, dating to 1366, was to accompany the condemned with "litanies, lauds, oration, and silence."[66] But a special register, introduced by ritual Latin formulas, kept an orderly record of condemned prisoners from 1441 onward, with information about their crimes and annotations regarding any signs of final remorse. The original manuscript, lost in the twentieth century, was compiled from 1488 onward by the *confratello* Antonio Bonacossi.[67] Subsequently continued by other copyists, it spawned a long series. It was one of the first fruits of what gradually became a habitual practice for the companies of justice, depositing within their archives a detailed chronicle of executions, or at least a list of the names of the condemned. The religious goal of ensuring that the condemned expressed remorse for what they had done and received the sacraments remained the fundamental one. But the prestige acquired by the companies of justice shows that a special relationship had been established between them and the public powers. The positive outcome of executions was entrusted to their intervention, in the sense that the comforters were expected to transform the condemned person—the "patient"—into a model of Christian death, which involved accepting punishment as an opportunity for penitence and expiation. If the condemned yielded meekly to the persuasions of the *confratelli* and "converted," the watching crowd no longer saw a loathed and despised criminal going to their death, but a genuine Christian martyr destined to find a place in the glory of heaven. If, instead, the condemned refused comfort and the sacraments, public execration was guaranteed: their lost soul was cursed by everyone, their body scorned and left unburied. What was played out on the gallows was the triumph of power, all the more effective as behind the sentence of the prince or commune it was possible to see the hand of God punishing or saving.

The Ferrara register does not just describe events with words: in one particularly sensational case, the codex features a brightly colored drawing. This is not a quick sketch illustrating a hanging or beheading, as can sometimes be found in the margins of trial records or city chronicles: it is a pictorial representation of a theatrical scene, a snapshot of a great public ritual. In the center, on the scaffold erected between the cathedral and the Palazzo Comunale, we see the condemned man walking toward the executioner, accompanied by a *confratello* holding a crucifix, while other members of the company pray at the feet of the scaffold. The setting for all this is the city square, between the buildings symbolizing the powers of the prince and the bishop. In Ferrara, as in Bologna and other cities, executions were no longer held on the edges of the city, outside the walls, but in the central square, in full view of crowds summoned by the town crier and drawn by the emotion of an extraordinary spectacle, which they could watch without any sense of guilt because the Church granted special indulgences to anyone who witnessed executions and prayed for the souls of the condemned. The choice of place is revelatory of how the nature of executions, and in particular the function of the companies of justice, had changed.

But if for the School of Comforters in nearby Bologna lists of this kind were primarily intended as a record of the successes and failures of comforting, only secondarily becoming repertoires of various crimes, the Ferrara one is an official annalistic register of the death sentences handed out by sovereign justice. The list was kept by successive hands, but retained the same style almost right up to the end of the Este family's dominion in 1577. The company's chronicler undertook to draw up and continually update the official list of the "malefactores et delinquentes" condemned to death by the "summa iustitia" of the sovereign. It was a stern but also providential justice, because everyone was offered the religious comfort of the confraternity—everyone who was Christian of course. In Ferrara, as in many other Italian cities, the population included Jews as well. But if a Jew was condemned to death the *confratelli* did not feel bound to record them, nor to attempt to convert them, as generally happened elsewhere: here the comforting of the Jews was practiced by their own community. The case of Isepo known as

Todeschino is exemplary in this respect. Hanged on April 29, 1544, "he was comforted by his fellow Jews": thanks to the special regime of ducal protection under which the Jews lived in Ferrara, a Jewish confraternity of mercy, the Gemilut Hasadim, had been set up in the city, and was active at least from 1517.[68] This offers an important clue to understanding the reasons for the transformation and spread of this type of confraternity. But before moving on to this, we need to describe some of the common features of their work, generally referred to as "the service."

14

The Service

IN THE COURSE OF the fifteenth century the noisy, furious, unbridled violence we saw in the Florentine chronicles disappeared from the spectacle of capital punishment in Italian cities. Increasingly we find accounts that stress the composure of the ritual and the solemn tones of devotion. In the meantime the chapters of the confraternities of justice drew up regulations for the work they undertook, and it is worth outlining a few distinguishing features.

The work was referred to as "the service," and it involved helping condemned prisoners face up to their impending death without falling into despair. As we read in the sixteenth-century statutes of the Compagnia della Morte di Siena, the task of the *confratelli* was to "pull back from pernicious despair those who are sentenced by justice to violent death by hanging, decapitation, burning, or other torment . . . and to bring them to hope, remorse, and contrition, so that such violent deaths might take place in peace and in tranquility of mind [. . . and] that the sinner might convert."[1]

There was a secret part and a public part. The former was carried out in the confines of a chapel on the premises of the confraternity: the place known as the *conforteria*. The latter was played out on the route through the city from the chapel to the gallows, and took place before the eyes of a public drawn not only by powerful curiosity but also by pressing invitations from the authorities and by promises of spiritual rewards (indulgences).

For the comforters, the condemned person was the "afflicted" one, "the patient." These were the names that the instructions for comforters invited them to use when addressing the prisoner handed over to them by the jailers. The vocabulary of the companies of justice was rich in allusive and elusive expressions like these. The prisoner awaiting death, in a state of maximum affliction, was in their eyes a person in the balance, the subject of a risky experiment that might fail at any time. This is what they had to think and see.

The experiment was called conversion. The word, one of the most important in the history of Christian language, had, as was often the case, a Jewish source. A conscious, explicit source: of the various passages expressing the same concept, the one recorded most often in the sources of their devotion was a sentence from the prophet Ezekiel, which in the Vulgate read: "Vivo ego, dicit Dominus Deus, nolo mortem peccatoris sed ut convertatur impius a via sua et vivat" (33:11). Conversion here meant a change of direction by a person who avoids death, remains alive, and undertakes to live in a different way. The translation in the Jerusalem Bible is: "As I live, says the Lord God, I have no pleasure in the death of the wicked, but that the wicked turn from their ways and live." But in the use made of it in the confraternities of justice, the meaning was completely distorted: the condemned had no possibility of changing their ways or of living. They were about to be deprived of their life; in its place, in exchange for repentance and sacramental forgiveness, was the promise of eternal life in the hereafter. The living God of the Bible had become the impassive administrator of a kingdom of the dead, recording with notarial precision the deeds drawn up by his priests. Changing direction and abandoning the wrong path consisted of a mental act of remorse, more or less intense, more or less genuine and profound, but legally valid—even if there was no real repentance and the person doing it was prompted solely by a fear of hell—if manifested with the formalities of the rite of sacramental confession. It was in this context that the final choice of the condemned was made: and here lay the great risk of the task undertaken by the generous, solicitous volunteers of the confraternities. The person about to die could become a soul in heaven or a cursed spirit, a prisoner of Satan forever. And if that happened, the final judgment then reiterated, confirmed, and underscored the one made at the beginning, when the criminal act or heretical conviction had been defined in the judge's sentence as the fruit of a sudden demoniacal possession. But what the *confratelli* set out to do was to prevent at all cost the victory of evil and the eternal loss of a soul. How to achieve this was the object of preparatory exercises, analysis of previous cases, readings, and meditations. There was just one preliminary condition stipulated by all the statutes and by a vast theological and moral literature: the ritual and moral purification of the *confratelli* so as to be fit for an extraordinary mission. In order to prepare for the "service" they had to confess, pray, lead an honest life, and be at peace among themselves. The job

of the internal authorities was to check that this was the case, and to intervene as required to resolve disputes and punish noncompliance. We are informed of this by the statutes, which for a long time were the key point of
reference, with individual chapters being read and meditated upon in confraternity meetings. As for what went on in the actual dealings with the "patients," detailed reports only began to be kept over time. At the beginning,
between the fifteenth and sixteenth century, all that sufficed was a cursory
note in the confraternity lists to record that an execution had taken place,
occasionally supplemented by a brief description of the crime and the
punishment.

The secret part of the "service" began when the prior of the company received notification that a prisoner was due to be put to death. This normally occurred in the evening, and sometimes deep into the night. The time
available was generally very limited—a few hours, those of the night preceding the execution, or the ones between a morning and an afternoon execution. Only in special cases involving heretics were the comforters given
all the time they needed to obtain conversion. And it was only from the late
sixteenth century onward, in the Spanish domains, that a norm was introduced into Charles V's criminal constitution (the "Carolina") establishing
that three days were to separate the sentence and the execution. But anyway,
having been notified of the impending execution, the rector or governor of
the confraternity informed the *confratelli* and summoned the comforters to
be used. According to the statutes they were to be divided into successive
shifts in order to manage the difficult task of being at the condemned person's side throughout the night. The statutes of the Compagnia di San
Giovanni Battista in Modena drawn up in 1482–1483 (the earliest remaining
ones) talk of the election of four comforters, "those who are most suited to
comforting that particular person": they were to work in pairs and swap over
at midnight.[2]

The statutes of the Bolognese *conforteria* adopted the same system,
though the shifts were organized in advance and the composition of the pair-
ings followed the pattern used in artisan workshops: a master and a pupil.[3]
Substitutes were also on hand to step in if for some serious reason the designated comforters were unable to attend. The first master-pupil pair were
to take up position and wait for the "patient" in a chapel inside the prison.
Other pairs readied themselves for the second part of the night. The model

drawn up by the *confratelli* of the Compagnia dei Neri in Florence was similar. The statutes of 1488 mention two "evening brothers," and four more who were to take over in due course, so as to "give some rest to those who had been there all night."[4] But what they had to do, and how they were to behave in dealing with the condemned prisoner from the very first moment of contact and through all the successive phases, would be developed into detailed instructions at a later stage. This is how a late instruction for members of the Compagnia dei Neri explained what the comforters should do when they first encountered the person they were to console:

> The comforter . . . will greet him by saying: "May the Lord God be with you," or other such words, and expressing sorrow for the state in which he finds himself, will endeavor, be he meek or obstinate, to relate to him with the utmost charity and gentleness, and to win his confidence, both with words and with works, to the point of embracing him if needs be, and even of kissing his hands and feet, giving demonstration that all which is said and done is without any self-interest or passion, but is only done out of charity and zealous concern for his soul.[5]

To establish a fraternal relationship and win the trust and confidence of the prisoner plunged into desperation by news of their impending death, it was necessary above all that the persons who presented themselves should appear completely different from the one who had condemned them. The habit and hood, the signs of the cross, the litanies, and the prayers signaled and announced this diversity. But the confraternity, generally speaking, enjoyed great prestige and authoritativeness, and this might lead the condemned to play their final cards by imploring the comforters to mediate on their behalf. All the more reason, then, to avoid any risk of seeming to be instruments of the court and allies of the executioner—a risk that was all the stronger because in reality comforters and punitive machinery were two sides of the same system. Great care was therefore always given to distinguishing places and responsibilities: the statutes and the whole literature of regulations and advice were at pains to specify that any confusion of roles had to be avoided from the very start. For example, it was important that the prisoner be informed of the sentence by officials of justice and that the comforters would only arrive after that, and in a different room.

The comforters' task was to lead the condemned away from the raw feelings of despair, protest, and grief that their lives and relationships were being cut short, directing their thoughts instead toward the salvation of their soul. This was the most important and delicate phase: the key considerations here were which arguments to choose, how to relate to the prisoner, and what kinds of words to use. They prepared for the challenge by reading and meditating upon the chapters of the confraternity's rules in periodic meetings, deepening their grasp of issues by drawing on one text or another from a vast literature. The comforter needed to be able to relate to people from very different social and cultural backgrounds, and to quickly focus the thoughts of their charges on the imminence of their fate, pointing out, over and beyond the sentence of the earthly judge, the other imminent judgment on which the eternal outcome of their soul depended.

To get the "patients" to listen to them, and to win their trust, the *confratelli* did have something to offer: it was in their power to make sure that messages and letters reached family members, to make a note of their final wishes, and to promise help for those who were going to lose the protection of a child, a father, or a husband. Moreover, though it was the norm never to remotely suggest the possibility of the sentence being amended, the condemned was not to be denied the faculty to confess the whole truth about actions and crimes for which they were held responsible. This was a very delicate point. The comforters might learn important secrets—or at least that is what was thought by people who would often crowd around the comforters' chapel and for whom the prestige of the confraternity grew as a consequence. The nighttime conversations might bring to light a truth very different from the one contained in the confessions made to the judge, often extracted under pain of torture and the fear of further torture. Such conditions of duress led to admissions of crimes that had never been committed and above all to attempts to pin them on others, with the naming of accomplices that prompted fresh arrests and further torture. The condemned could now atone for what they had done to others, and lighten the burden of their conscience. The comforter had to make a note of this "unburdening of the conscience" and report it to the judges—once again treading a fine line between collaborating with the judges and the executioner and offering spiritual assistance to the "patient" to enable them to carry out the reparation that was the third phase of the sacrament of penance.

The companies of justice also had to take account of what was expected of them from the city's powers that be. The aim of public execution rituals was to educate the people with terror, showing spectators the consequences of disobeying the law. The harsh punishment was not in itself enough: the condemned also needed to be heard calling on people to repent, and acknowledging that the sentence was both right and providential. What greater legitimacy could there be for those who exercised the power of life and death? In exchange the condemned received some benefit. The importance of a death that was not dishonorable—for example, by the sword rather than by hanging—cannot be ignored, or the offer of being strangled before burning at the stake. The condemned could also be blackmailed with the promise that vengeance would not be exacted on their relatives or property. All this could be negotiated behind the scenes of the spectacle. The price was summed up in a single word: conversion. This is what was asked of the condemned, what was sought from them right until the last. Conversion entailed the transformation of the cursed, diabolic being about to be expelled from life into a repentant sinner if not even into a martyr ready to ascend into heaven. This result was pursued with careful preparation and an extraordinary investment of individuals' energies and means of persuasion. It was necessary to curb the desperation of those who were being informed of their imminent end, to counter and overcome their defense strategies, and transform the pain of loss into hope for the glorious life of the soul. At the center of all this lay the word "justice"—and the justice that took away life was the same one that could open the door to another and more real existence.

The comforters were not always successful, but their methods did help to conceal in the secrecy of the night and the confines of their chapels the most dramatic moments of the relationship with the doomed person, and to suffocate in the whisper of prayers the despairing cries of those who saw themselves destined for an unbearable fate. For those who felt they were victims of an unjust sentence, there remained a final threat: an appeal before what was by definition the supreme court, that of universal judgment in the Valley of Josaphat. On January 14, 1673, in Bologna, the counterfeiter Paolo Cantelli known as Lievra was taken to the gallows. On the way, while passing the palace of the cardinal legate, he shouted out: "Cardinal Palavicini, see you in the Valley of Josaphat." Mention of the Valley of Josaphat was greatly feared, a sign that earthly justice's claim to be governed by God was not all

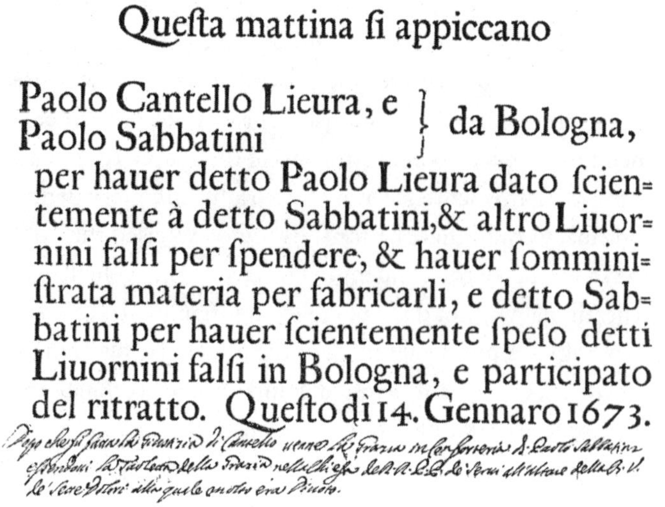
Queſta mattina ſi appiccano

Paolo Cantello Lieura, e
Paolo Sabbatini } da Bologna,

per hauer detto Paolo Lieura dato ſcientemente à detto Sabbatini,& altro Liuornini falſi per ſpendere, & hauer ſommini-
ſtrata materia per fabricarli, e detto Sabbatini per hauer ſcientemente ſpeſo detti
Liuornini falſi in Bologna, e participato
del ritratto. Queſto dì 14. Gennaro 1673.

[illegible]

FIGURE 14.1. "Hanging this morning." Notice hung in the piazza in Bologna on March 14, 1673, on the occasion of the execution of Paolo Cantelli (known as Lievra) with the handwritten granting of pardon, conceded to the second condemned man, Paolo Sabbadini. BOLOGNA: BIBLIOTECA ARCIVESCOVILE.

that firmly established in the minds of the powerful. Pallavicini must also have been quite unsettled by it, given that he decided to pardon Lievra's accomplice, Paolo Sabbadini (the official story was that it was a reward for the condemned man's special devotion to the Blessed Virgin Mary's Seven Sorrows during the night).[6] It was a citation that cropped up frequently at gallows around the world. In Germany, in order to silence the condemned, they had to stiffen the sentence.[7]

If and when the outcome was positive—that is, if the condemned resigned themselves and accepted the sentence as a divine decree—the next step was sacramental confession. This was generally with the company's chaplain, but might also be heard by another priest who enjoyed the confidence of the condemned person. At this point they might receive physical sustenance—food and drink, though in moderation, enough to restore the strength of people sorely tried by detention, often by judicial torture, but above all by the violent emotional shock of the sentence. "Above all, give him something to drink," warned one of the many concise handbooks in the vast literature on the subject. But, it added, "take care not to get him inebriated with excessive drink."[8] This was entirely different from the Germanic tradition of the condemned person's last supper, where the abundance of food and alcohol seems like a ritual celebration of human sacrifice. The expenses listed in the Italian confraternities' account books were fairly low. Provision was also made for some firewood to keep warm in the cold winter nights.

The relief of having the shackles removed was the reward for achieving harmony between the comforters and the "afflicted." Mass was celebrated at dawn, and Holy Communion was allowed. Right until the end a priest had to stand near the prisoner, ready to "reconcile" or absolve them from any belatedly remembered sins. The condemned was given plenary absolution "in articulo mortis," which meant that any kind of misdeed could be absolved by any confessor, without considering the canonic regulations that reserved certain more serious sins for the bishop or even the pontiff. The condemned was not, however, granted the viaticum of the dying, the sacrament generally called the "extreme unction." It was something that the condemned greatly desired and often requested: there was in that complex and mysterious rite a powerful promise of protection that concerned all the body's senses. For those steeling themselves for excruciatingly painful punishments by seeking help in short prayers, the protection of saints, and magic formulas, the sacramental rite of unction must have appeared more important than any other help the Church could give. The theoretical debate among theologians and canonists on the recourse to this sacrament continued for a long time, but in practice it was always denied. The fundamental point was that although the condemned person was about to die, their body was generally healthy and so one could not apply to it what remained a sacrament for the sick. An eighteenth-century law expert from Padua, Giovanni Chieregati, summed up the issue in a treatise on the sacraments with a particularly extensive section on extreme unction—almost half of the entire work—an indication of how the theme of dying had come to command attention in the ecclesiastical culture of the Counter-Reformation. As always, it took the form of the presentation of various previous cases: sticking in general to the principle that what was due to those about to die from ill health did not apply to the condemned—because although they were on the point of leaving this world, they were not sick—there were still possible exceptions that opened the door to the variety of cases. Extreme unction could be granted, for example, if the condemned was also feverish or suffered from a serious illness. The other case was that of a person who, having been subjected to the torment of the wheel, survived despite the "'horrida confractio" of every bone.[9]

On the other hand, the sacrament of penance was resorted to repeatedly. Confessions, reiterated several times, served to reconcile the "patient" and to give them the peace of mind of forgiveness for each and every misdeed. In their case, as in that of the comfort offered to any dying person, there were special indulgences as well, the heavenly protection of saints and the Virgin, the objects that carried promises of blessings and particular help.

Then came the second, public, phase, as the darkness of the night in the chapel gave way to the light of day outside. Generally in the morning (though sometimes in the late afternoon) the bell of the Palazzo Pubblico rang to announce that an execution was about to take place. A crowd would gather at the execution site, drawn by curiosity, encouraged by the authorities, and attracted by the spiritual rewards of ecclesiastical indulgence. By now the site was hardly ever outside the city walls—that was where something impure or cursed took place. There would often be a return to those sites in the seventeenth and eighteenth centuries, when, in response to a new urban sensibility, death would be shielded from the public gaze. But in the central phase of this history, it was in the very heart of the city, in the square, between the seat of power and the city's main church, that the executioner erected the platform, raised the gallows, positioned the block—and where, together with his assistants, he awaited the arrival of the prisoner. The condemned emerged from the cell or from the confraternity chapel where they had spent the preceding hours. The final journey was on foot or on an open cart, accompanied by a small procession: at the head of the party was a religious, holding a crucifix, followed by a line of penitents dressed in a black or white habit with their faces covered. Two of their number flanked the condemned person, speaking to them, reciting prayers, and singing psalms, accompanied by the others. One of them held a small board painting *(tavoletta)* with images of Christian martyrs, scenes from Christ's Passion, or Madonnas. This was held up in front of the condemned person's eyes and served to block the crowd from their vision, with all the feelings of hatred or love that faces might evoke, distracting them from contemplation of the divine tribunal awaiting them. The litanies and psalms sung by the *confratelli* conferred a sense of the religious ritual and acted as a restraining influence on the crowd. Along the route acts of devotion in front of churches and sacred images broke up the acts of punitive torture envisaged by the sentence. When the condemned person arrived at the gallows, the executioner stepped forward and tied his hands. But before this happened there was a brief exchange between the two. The executioner asked forgiveness for what he was about to do, and the prisoner replied. This was a crucial moment, signaling the success or otherwise of the comforters' fundamental mission, to convert vengeance into reconciliation. It was also a risky moment, due to the contact with the figure most closely associated with the negative values of the whole culture of the age. The executioner was the instrument of vengeance. The sword of Justice, the noble peplos-clad female image, was wielded by a person with brutal and irredeemably negative attributes, bordering on the demonic world of the accursed dead. The crowd hated him and reacted violently if the condemned suffered too much due to any lack of skill on his part. For the comforters, the danger to avoid was that the executioner might rob them of their trade and, influenced by the atmosphere of devotion and forgiveness, might take on a role that was not his. Once again, in short, any overlapping of functions had to be avoided. *Confratelli* sometimes felt constrained to complain to the authorities after an execution because the executioner had tried to put them out of a job by assuming a devout role that did not pertain to him. One instance can be found in a report about an execution carried out in Bologna in January 1710: the executioner, "though prohibited from speaking at excessive length in requesting forgiveness on the gallows insisted on doing so anyway";[10] a few years later, it was again considered necessary to point out that "the executioner went way beyond the time he had to take away his [the condemned's] strength, as he wanted to act as a consoler, persuading him to die willingly."[11]

The ritual then continued with the reciting of prayers by the condemned, often accompanied by the crowd. Prisoners sometimes made a public request for forgiveness for the bad example they had set. The service was considered a complete success when there was a reciprocal exchange between the prisoner on the gallows and the crowd in the square, consisting of requests and promises of prayers and of blessing, those addressed to the condemned for their soul and those of the person about to become a soul in the sky, who undertook to thank his benefactors from on high. There was still time then for a low-voiced exchange between the priest and the condemned: a sign of blessing marked absolution for the final sins. The condemned kissed the crucifix, and climbed up to the gallows murmuring prayers. Moved, the crowd followed the unfolding ritual, conscious that they were participating in a sacred event, and that the eternal fate of a soul was being decided. To this end they offered up their prayers, conscious too that in so doing they would acquire an important spiritual benefit—the indulgence that reduced the sufferings of purgatory and brought them closer to entering into heaven. The singing of psalms and *laude* accompanied a human being's journey toward death—a robber or a murderer, a political or a religious rebel. The condemned had been transformed by religious intercession from their real condition as a common criminal or political adversary into the figure of a penitent sinner, if not a martyr.

Then came the execution proper. If it was for a crime of blood or if the offender was of noble stock, the punishment was beheading, whereas robbers, brigands, and other base criminals were hanged. Heretics, sodomites, Jews, and Muslims went to the stake; if they had repented or converted, they were hung first. Sometimes the punishment was supplemented by special torments or by the amputation of limbs. The picture of suffering found in the sentences handed down by the courts are couched in the terms of blacksmiths and butchers—to pincer, to hammer, to slaughter, to quarter. All this was entrusted to the executioner, with whom the comforters had to relate as they had done from the start in their dealings with the mechanisms of the tribunal, maintaining their distance and avoiding any risk of appearing to the condemned as if they were instruments of the power to kill. At the final moment, then, the comforter's movements had to be coordinated with those of the executioner, without helping or being helped by him in any way. It was absolutely forbidden to interfere with the work of the executioner, either by helping him or by speeding things up. If the condemned was hauled up the steps to the level of the noose, the comforter had to clamber up behind them, so the victim could see and kiss the crucifix, all the time reciting the prayer formulas which the prisoner had been assured were effective. If execution was by beheading, the comforter knelt down to be at the same level as the head resting on the block, continuing to pray and to display the crucifix right to the end, heedless of the proximity of the axe. Indeed, precisely in that final instant the victim's eyes, which continued to see, and the mind in which all activity had not yet ceased might lose faith in an instant, undoing all the confraternity's hard work. If the behavior of the condemned in this very last moment of their life offered some demonstration of conversion, the body would be gathered up in the evening by the devout and taken in procession for burial in the church of the confraternity, unless special provision had been made for it to be used for anatomical purposes, in exchange for alms and commemorative masses. If the "certain sign of remorse" attested in the records was missing, though this was very rare, no ecclesiastical burial took place.[12]

This was the model, the basic procedure for consoling the "afflicted," that was practiced, with local variants, by the confraternities operating in Italian cities in the modern age. The central protagonist of the ritual was the condemned, a figure who was obviously different each time, but whose diversity was smoothed down and forced into the stereotype of the penitent sinner set on the path to an exemplary and devout death. It was a "theater of devotion" in which the lead actor always changed but the script remained the same. The play was directed by the *conforteria*. The noisy, ferocious spectacle had given way to an orderly and solemn religious ritual, at the core of which was still the confession of the condemned we encountered in the scene described by Dante Alighieri. But a complex ritual had been built around the sacrament of purging sin. It was a change that resulted from an overall reorganization of the confraternities that took place under pressure from threatened powers, those of states and those of the Church.

15

Political Crimes

THE CITY CHRONICLES of the mid and late fifteenth century abound with stories of betrayal, conspiracy, and murder, often ending in quick and harsh death penalties. In Venice the general of the Republic Francesco Carmagnola was sentenced to death for treason in 1432;[1] a plot hatched by the Accademia Romana of Pomponius Laetus against Pope Paul II was discovered in Rome in 1468, the first in a series of similar episodes.[2] The Pazzi conspiracy in 1478 attempted to eliminate Lorenzo de' Medici and his brother Giuliano in Florence Cathedral. The Bolognese chronicle of Gaspare Nadi recounts that the whole family of the signore, Giovanni Bentivoglio, was to have been killed at three o'clock in the morning of November 27, 1488. The plot was discovered though, and during the night of December 3 eleven conspirators were hung from the battlements of the Palazzo del Podestà.[3] These are just some of many episodes that show how the new political setup of Italian cities and states was gaining ground against a backdrop of betrayals and conspiracies. The administration of justice was significantly affected as a result, in terms of both doctrine and praxis. One category of crime in particular began to be drawn on in penal practice, quickly becoming commonplace even though it remained cloaked in mystery: the crime of lèse-majesté. Originating in pagan Rome, it gained fresh vigor and new and unpredictable possibilities of application in the new context of papal Rome. The ancient historian Tacitus recounted how the emperor Tiberius used it to punish those who had dishonored his wife Julia, and observed that until then it had been used to protect the *maiestas* of the Roman people against those who betrayed its security or governed it badly. From then on the attribute of *maiestas* had migrated into the deified figure of the emperor.[4] This legacy had been taken on board by medieval Christianity, first with the punishment of people who offended divine majesty by blaspheming and then by applying the same category of crime to any offense against the supreme powers, insofar as they were representatives of God and thus, literally, bearers of "God's person," of the *imago divinae maiestatis,* with *maiestas* remaining divine by definition.[5] The crime of lèse-majesté would be abolished together with the death penalty in Peter Leopold's reform of Tuscany's penal legislation in 1786, being deemed a product of the "despotism of the Roman Empire." The definition of its characteristics over this long time span was possible only by way of *exempla* for penologists as well, as Mario Sbriccoli observes.[6] This is because the crime was invariably recognized and punished when someone disobeyed or betrayed a power that was suspicious and insecure and hence liable to see traitors everywhere. In its configuration Sbriccoli sees "certain aspects of the same attitude taken by the Christian churches (apostasy, excommunication, or Saint Cyprian of Carthage's principle 'salus extra ecclesiam non est' [there is no salvation outside the Church]."[7] We can go further: the Church played a decisive role in the reappearance of the Roman penal category of lèse-majesté in legal culture and in the work of the medieval courts.[8] The charge of "divine lèse-majesté" was used against the crimes of heresy and apostasy; indeed, it was placed at the top of the scale of seriousness of crimes, followed immediately by that of "human lèse-majesté" (conspiracy, rebellion against the legitimate political power). On a par with, or indeed worse than, lèse-majesté, as Tiberio Deciani sustained, heresy was a crime to which the normal rules did not apply.[9] It was the supreme crime, so serious as to justify the suspension of the limitations placed on the use of torture by the generally strict regulations: the one requiring the existence of at least two prosecution witnesses was fundamental. Instead, a person suspected of lèse-majesté could be tortured without limit—and suspicion alone sufficed. What is more, it was enough to get the suspect to admit their intention, that they had simply had the thought. The crime of opinion, that of the negation of *fides,* lent itself to being used against the enemy even before thoughts were turned into words and deeds. Between the thirteenth and fourteenth centuries, the papal bulls against *haeretica pravitas* (malignant heresy) laid the foundations for the inquisitorial procedure designed to root out heresy and apostasy. In defining the rules for the punishment of the heretic, the papal authority established once and for all the boundary between mercy and vengeance: the former had the maternal countenance of the Church, the latter the ruthless face of the temporal power. The repentant heretic could be forgiven, but this did not stop the "relapsed" heretic from being sent to their death by the "secular arm." That the possibility of obtaining a reprieve for those who repented and abjured was becoming ever more remote is shown by the long history of interpretations of the bull *Ad abolendam* issued by Pope Lucius III, who had left that possibility open. True, the Church did not shut its doors to anyone wishing to return to the maternal womb, as Pope Alexander IV wrote in the decretal *Super eo*. But this just meant that it maternally offered the sacraments to those who repented, leaving it to the secular judge to pass the death sentence.[10] The Church provided the fundamental model in the interpretation of lèse-majesté. It was immediately apparent that this category of crime was well suited to becoming the most effective instrument of any sovereign power to impose its norms and will—not just that of the emperor but also of the ruling houses. It is no accident that Emperor Frederick II's Constitutions of Melfi rivaled in harshness those that were being drawn up by the Roman popes in their battle against heretics. Boniface VIII was himself denounced for heresy by Guillaume de Nogaret in 1303, in the course of the pope's conflict with King Philip IV of France. And charges of heresy and apostasy were used soon after in the monstrous trial of members of the Order of Templars, which saw Philip IV, but also the new pope, Clement V, in action.[11] There is a further element, pointed out by Mario Sbriccoli, that takes us into the religious sphere: to ascertain the existence of *crimen lesae maiestatis,* it was crucial to obtain a confession, an act based on collaboration, indeed connivance, between the adversary to power and the power trying that adversary. It was the accused who, by confessing, would themselves provide the evidence against them: "qui delinquit amat poenam," says Bartolus of Saxoferrato.[12]

It was the suspicion dwelling in the corridors of power that generated a fear of hidden perils and stimulated the search for guilty parties, giving rise to a type of crime that is actually very hard to define. The penologist Girolamo Giganti made an attempt in the sixteenth century with a long description. Centuries later Frederic W. Maitland got by with an eloquent image, representing it as a vague circumference with more than one center.[13] The center could be approached by descending from the plane of abstract definition to the concrete one of judicial practice. In effect, the rebirth of the Roman criminal category of lèse-majesté from the inexhaustible repertoire of Roman law offered political and religious powers an instrument to strike against any form of disobedience and insubordination: divine lèse-majesté was the crime of the heretic, human lèse-majesté that of the person who attacked the sovereign. Crucial in both cases was the affirmation of the canon law category of the "mystic body" to denote the personifications of collective bodies and the special relationship between them and their head, whether pope or prince. By virtue of this metaphor, which became fairly commonplace around 1300,[14] any refusal to obey orthodox doctrines (in the case of the Church) or the laws of the prince (in that of the State) could be depicted as lèse-majesté. And as the absence of loyalty might be concealed in the shadows of plots and conspiracies but also in the darkness of the human heart, special methods were established to seek out ("inquisitio") the truth. One of them was torture. Legally, as we have seen, it was only permitted when an accusation was backed by more than one piece of probative testimony. But lèse-majesté was considered a "crimen exceptum," a special and particularly heinous crime, the discovery and punishment of which justified the setting aside of any limitations on the use of torture. Both the "mystical body" of the Church and the "moral and political body" of the State had to be kept safe from attack. One was modeled on the other: the Church brought to it the concept of the mental nature of the betrayal of faith, which triggered *latae sententiae* excommunication, with all the consequences thereof coming into play at the very moment in which the heresy was embraced. Fragile powers drew inspiration from this, trying and torturing on the grounds of suspicion alone, and sending people to their deaths on the simple charge of having entertained thoughts of rebellion. Now for the Church, the repentant sinner's confession of hidden sins was covered by the seal of secrecy. With the decree of the Fourth Lateran Council, which separated individual and secret sacramental confession from the public confession before the judge, a divarication took place which had important consequences. On the one hand, as we saw, the French judges refused to allow the condemned to receive sacramental confession and imposed that of the public court instead; on the other hand, northern and central Italy saw the spread of sacramental confession. But a special problem was posed here: Just how inviolable was the seal of confession? Might it be broken in certain circumstances or not? Constantly denied on the theoretical plane, such a possibility did emerge in practice both through the development of models of examining the conscience whereby the inner space of the conscience was built and furnished by the ecclesiastical body, and through the automatic transfer of certain hidden sins revealed in confession from the sacramental field to that of the public court. For example, the sinner might be admonished by the confessor so that they themselves revealed before witnesses what had been said under the sacramental seal—a method that made its appearance in the fight against heresy, from the campaign against the Albigenses in the thirteenth century to the one against readers of prohibited books in the sixteenth century.[15]

From the religious sphere there was a shift to the political sphere; from the non-obedience to the ecclesiastical authorities implicit in heresy to the supposed or suspected lack of loyalty to the sovereign. Suspicion alone was enough to arrest and torture without any legal limitation. The secret nature of the crime then became associated with the public character of the punishment: the enemy was to appear as hidden and dangerous as the act of justice was theatrical and sensational. A special role was carved out in this tangled web by the men—hooded and preceded by a crucifix—who figured increasingly frequently as the real directors of the spectacle. They were permitted access to the condemned in the hours before the execution, and their chaplain was charged with gaining access to the conscience and final revelations of the person about to die. The special aura that was being created around their rituals had a lot to do with the need felt by the personal powers that were establishing themselves in the small Italian states to bolster their sometimes dubious legitimacy. Calculations based on a substantial sample of chronicles and execution lists have shown that the crime of lèse-majesté was resorted to with increasing frequency in Italy precisely around the middle of the fifteenth century.[16] Insecure and suspicious powers seized on it in their struggle to control and transform the communal political arrangements from within. As Leon Battista Alberti acutely observed in the dialogue *Momus,* it was with the spread of the charge of lèse-majesté that the new shape of power pushed forward behind the appearance of the communal institutions.[17] Humanistic culture fanned the renewal of interest in heroic memories of ancient Rome and the fight against tyrants in the context of the rebirth of ancient paganism. Executions became an opportunity for victors to settle scores with the defeated, and the city square was the setting where the *popolo* turned from being an actor to being a spectator. Conspiracies, either real or feared, unleashed the violent arm of the power: the bodies of the hanged dangling from the windows of the Palazzo Pubblico, or the gory public rituals performed in the city square, served to educate the people to be obedient. The pedagogy of power fed off a special mixture of secrecy and clamor: the secrecy of real or presumed conspiracies and of the repressive measures enacted by the powerful, the clamor and publicizing of the repression. In these cases there was no tolling bell of the Palazzo Pubblico, a signal used throughout Europe to communicate the sentence to the populace and invite them to the public spectacle of the imminent execution.[18] Instead, people would wake up in the morning to discover bodies hanging from the iron bars of the Palazzo Pubblico. "Eighty or more men were hanged for the Pazzi conspiracy and died without the Company," according to the record of the Florentine Compagnia dei Neri. Among those whose bodies Florentines saw dangling from the windows of the Palazzo Vecchio was the archbishop of Pisa, Francesco Salviati; and on December 28, 1479, the people saw that Giuliano de Medici's killer, Bernardo di Giovanni Bandini Baroncelli, had met a similar fate. He had fled to Constantinople after the assassination but was sent back to Florence in chains and in "Turkish dress, and was hung in it."[19] This was when the crime of lèse-majesté first appeared in Florence, in the midst of wild scenes of vengeance identical to the ancient ones of factional strife: Iacopo dei Pazzi, captured on the road to Rome, was brought back to be killed in Florence, where so many people had been put to death that "the streets were filled with the parts of men."[20] His body, first buried in the family tomb, was then removed and reburied with the excommunicated along the walls. Finally, it was dug up once again and "dragged, naked, all through the city" with the noose around the neck.[21] This was the vengeance of the winning side: death without forgiveness, without the devout offices of the Company. Nocturnal executions without religious comforts, bodies displayed in the morning, attached to the windows of public palaces, abandoned to the fury of the people. How and why the sentence had been reached was something that required no explanation. We are not yet at the formulaic phrase "State secret," with the dark and solemn overtones of mystery that this carries.[22] But we can catch a first glimpse of it here in the midst of the tumultuous factional violence in the medieval communes. In 1478 Florence was, formally at least, a free commune and not a monarchy: and Lorenzo de' Medici was just a private citizen. It took the conspiracy and the ensuing violent repression for the reality to find a way to be expressed. This was when the meaning of the word "state" changed: for Lorenzo, who had just escaped the conspirators' daggers and taken refuge in the palace, the word "state" slid off his pen spontaneously in the frantic dispatch he sent to his Milanese ally, Ludovico il Moro. What was in danger was his "state," that condition of family and personal preeminence in the city, which had turned the commune's institutions into an empty shell and was becoming a form of sovereignty. But how could the summary execution of those implicated in a conspiracy without having taken part in the crime be justified? Those people "could not die 'de iure,'" the ambassador of the duke of Ferrara wrote to his lord at the time. So it was necessary to resort to the charge of lèse-majesté, thereby revealing the true position held at that time by Lorenzo as the *signore* of the Florentine State.[23] It was no accident that the critical observation was made by a diplomat from Ferrara, where the sovereignty of the house of Este was ancient and well-rooted. It was here that the juridical category of Roman origin that was beginning to attract the definitions of criminalists first made its official appearance at the head of the list of cases dealt with by the confraternity which assisted the condemned. And it was no accident that Peter Leopold's abolition of the death penalty for all crimes in the Grand Duchy of Tuscany in 1784 carried with it the elimination of the crime of lèse-majesté. That same year the governor of the Duchy of Milan, with a decree dated August 24, disbanded the Confraternita di San Giovanni Decollato alle Case Rotte. The document was recorded in the codex that included the list of executed prisoners assisted by the confraternity since 1552. The first name on the list was that of one "Giorgio, Sienese," who was quartered alive on June 8, 1552, for having plotted on behalf of the French.[24] The knot that had held together the political crime, the death penalty, and the political and social function of the confraternity of justice was thus untied.

Three Exemplary Cases between the Renaissance and the Reformation: Andrea Viarani, Pietro Paolo Boscoli, and Pietro Fatinelli

The records of the Ferrarese confraternity list many cases of lèse-majesté where special emphasis is placed on the harsh punishments inflicted by the duke. Not that there needed to be a genuine conspiracy against the ruling prince: every theft or murder represented a rebellion against power, an attack on the role he had in ensuring peace and obedience. The sovereign's presence looms large in the mind of the chronicler tasked with keeping a record of executions. The heading of each side of the document bears first of all the name of the holder of power. The prominence given to reporting the sentences of conspirators and political enemies formed part of the pedagogy of terror, as did the images the reader came across. The function of the confraternity, with its rituals and symbols, effectively became more and more that of legitimating the sentence of the earthly sovereign in the name of God's will. Several examples will help to illustrate this.

On August 12, 1469, the register of the Ferrarese company recorded the beheading of two men: "the magnificent Zohane Ludovico di Pi(i) from Carpi and one Andrea da Vairana, his chancellor." Their execution was organized in a particularly solemn setting accessible to the public: the square situated between the ducal palace and the Palazzo della Ragione: "A tribunal was constructed right in front of the court, so the people had a good view." It was an exceptional choice, given that executions generally took place "on the other side of the Po." The reason lay in their crime: lèse-majesté: "They wanted to betray our Most Illustrious S[ignor] Meser Borso, duke of Ferrara."[25] The Pio family, the lords of Carpi, had planned to depose and perhaps to kill Borso d'Este, the marchese of Ferrara since 1450, to pave the way for his brother Ercole d'Este to take his place. The conspiracy involved a complex set of agreements with the duke of Milan, Galeazzo Maria Sforza, and with Cosimo de' Medici and his son Lorenzo. But Ercole, who had initially gone along with the plan, then told his brother everything. So when Giovanni Ludovico Pio and Andrea Viarani, the secretary of the Pio family, traveled to Modena to finalize the plot, they were arrested in July 1469, imprisoned in the Torre dei Leoni in Ferrara, and sentenced to death. The other Pio brothers also ended up in jail, with the sole exception of Giovanni Niccolò. One of them, Giovanni Marco, was beheaded on September 22 inside Castel Vecchio. It was a sensational case, and required the services of the Ferrarese confraternity. A trace of the work they did has been preserved in an exceptional document: three poetic compositions—one long sirvente and two sonnets—written in prison by Andrea Viarani. Long preserved by the manuscript tradition, they were finally published in the nineteenth century. But in the meantime they were immediately incorporated into the meditative and instructional text that, from the late fifteenth century onward, guided the work of the Bolognese School of Comforters and the whole Po Valley area influenced by it. Viarani's voice can be immediately discerned amid a series of compositions of varying origin, asking for God's forgiveness and the mercy and intercession of the Virgin Mary and of the saints. What the texts have in common is that they are "meditatio mortis," invoking "the help of God, of Christ, and of the Virgin in the supreme hour: what prevails in all of them is a consciousness of sin, anguish for the imminent torment, and a terror of death."[26] Viarani's compositions stand out not just for the author's refined Petrarchan culture and his sense of form: what enables us to identify his voice is the modernity of his inner dialogue, dominated by the urgent call to lift the mind up toward God, to search for the deep feeling that touches the "hard heart." Hardness of heart was the chief obstacle that stood before him as he tried to enter into contact with the divine figure before whom he was preparing to appear. We do not know exactly when in his detention these texts were written, though certainly not in the night before the execution. But Viarani did not need to wait for the sentence to imagine what his fate would be. And in this "contemplation, or devout and moral meditation," and turning his back on the "blind traitor [the] fallacious world," he focuses on the figure on the crucifix. He describes Christ as a man, a "poor fellow" subjected to endless abuse but always there, with open arms, ready to forgive those who turned to him with a contrite heart. Hardness of heart had to yield to the tears of the repentant sinner—and with an hour's crying the stain of sin could be washed away completely. The medicine of tears was what had saved Mary Magdalene and the Apostle Peter. And for the good robber it had sufficed to commend himself to Christ with faith to be forgiven: that was the perfect model of inspiration for those who, like Viarani, could see death approaching. The robber, by commending himself to Christ, "deserved forgiveness in just that moment."

While Viarani's thoughts on the eve of his execution have been preserved, nothing is known about those of many others who shared his fate. In Ferrara the vicissitudes of a dynasty that was threatened, not only by other Italian powers (Venice, the Church), but first and foremost by the ambitions and fratricidal struggles of its own members, led to continual arrests and trials on charges of lèse-majesté. Even just a cursory perusal of Ugo Caleffini's chronicle of the city shows this quite clearly: lèse-majesté appears alongside notes about snow and the dearth of rain, about famine and the price of grain, saints' feast days and the city *palio* dedicated to Saint George. It was in this way that in the late fifteenth century lèse-majesté and the rituals of justice, with sudden arrests and equally sudden executions or pardons, became a feature of everyday life. Even a woman, Francesca, the wife of a wine carrier named Girardino, was "seized and taken to Castel Vecchio" on June 6, 1474, charged with lèse-majesté. On the next day, Tuesday, June 7, she was joined by three others accused of the same crime. One was sentenced "to have his head cut off immediately in the square of Ferrara," but was then reprieved and imprisoned instead, while the others were banished on pain of death.[27] Among the death sentences handed out for political reasons, there was one that must be mentioned here because it was so sensational that it is remembered not only in words but also in images. In September 1506 the statistics of the Battuti Neri of Ferrara recorded, under the number of the year from Christ's birth and under the name of the ruling duke, Ercole, an event so important that the author felt the need to describe it in a miniature (Plate 11). The scene depicts an execution carried out in the central space of civic life, between the cathedral and the Palazzo della Ragione. In it can be seen the main figures associated with justice: the notary reading out the sentence, a judge, guards armed with pikes, the platform of the gallows surrounded at the base by severed heads and other body parts. A condemned man climbs on to the platform and advances toward the executioner, while a cleric presents him with a large crucifix. Three men dressed in black habits are kneeling behind him, praying and holding up a processional cross. Other hooded *confratelli* look on from the bottom of the steps leading to the platform. This is the story: On September 12, 1506, Count Albertino Boschetti da San Cesario; his son-in-law, Gherardo di Niccolò Ariberti, or Roberti; and one Franceschino da Rubiera, the attendant of Don Ferrante d'Este—the conspirators who had plotted to assassinate the duke of Ferrara—went to the gallows. They had "talked again and again among themselves, and with deliberate intention, about killing our Most Illustrious lord Duke of Ferrara," but the conspiracy had been discovered by "divine providence," as the sentence read. And it was "shocking to hear [the details of] that plot read and made public." The text of the register relates the particulars of the execution, first the fate of the offenders' bodies and then of their souls. In compliance with the wishes of the sovereign, the condemned were first "stunned" and "then their heads were cut off with an axe before being cut into four quarters on a tribune in the square of Ferrara." The quarters were displayed at the three gates of the "Terranova" of the city, and the heads at the top of the Arengo tower, impaled on three spears to instill "terror in every wrongdoer." The victims' innards received different treatment, following a pattern inspired by the funeral practices of the Este dynasty:[28] "the innards were buried honorably in the church of Santo Romano." This was the sign that the violence of the punishment for the crime of lèse-majesté could go hand in hand with respect for the social status of the offenders, who had displayed remorse for their deeds: the condemned had faced death "with a good spirit and attitude toward God, and [were] very regretful for their sins."[29] And if, on the one hand, this example offered to the spectators marked the success of the comforters' endeavors, on the other it ensured that the laceration within the social and political order could knit together and heal, reinforcing the authority of the Este family.

The history of those condemned for political crimes also features the case of the rebel Pietro Paolo Boscoli, whose last thoughts were remembered by a friend and put down in writing. The text lay undiscovered and unpublished for hundreds of years, before being found by Luigi Filippo Polidori in the middle of the nineteenth century, when the struggle for Italian freedom was in full swing. An exile from the Marche who had taken refuge in Tuscany, Polidori had it published in print form. The text is the account of the dialogue that took place in the Bargello prison in Florence in 1513 between Luca della Robbia and Pietro Paolo Boscoli. One of the first to read the document was the Swiss historian Jacob Burckhardt, who saw in it a first glimpse of a modern sense of individuality, by now detached from the Christian religious tradition and nurtured by the models of republican freedom that the rebirth of ancient paganism had made topical again. But the fact that the document exists at all is because in this case it was not the Blacks but Luca della Robbia who "diligently" took note of "all his words, both questions and replies," remembering and then writing them down afterward. He called on "God, and the Confraternity of the Blacks," besides all the other bystanders, to bear witness to the faithfulness of his account. The Blacks effectively remained in the background on this occasion, and indeed were asked by Boscoli to keep quiet so he could concentrate on what awaited him. This is an exceptional case: we normally know very little about the thoughts and words of the condemned. Collective prayers and ritual exhortations usually drowned out their voice and feelings. The whole legacy of thoughts and memories of the person about to be executed was considered a dangerous distraction from the duty to concentrate on penitence and the salvation of the soul. For that same reason, efforts were made to keep friends and relatives away. It is precisely in the contrast between the thoughts and questions of Pietro Paolo Boscoli and the comfort that the Blacks were accustomed to providing that we can see the emergence of a new reality. Boscoli had been condemned for his part in an anti-Medici conspiracy inspired by ideals of republican liberty and the struggle against tyranny. Those ideals were embodied for him in Marcus Junius Brutus—the same Brutus immortalized by another Florentine, a young Michelangelo, in a bust offering a proud, heroic image of Julius Caesar's assassin in line with the sculptor's republican political sentiments. In the conversation between Boscoli and Della Robbia, who spoke to him about the soul and the need to prepare for death, a conflict emerges between the ancient ideal of giving one's life for the freedom of the republic and the Christian idea of the salvation of the individual soul. It is a dramatic, but brief, conflict. As soon as he recognizes the imminence of death, Boscoli yields and succumbs, imploring his friend: "Ah, Luca, pull Brutus from my head, so that I make this passage entirely as a Christian."[30] He wants to die as a Christian, but his thoughts are still pervaded by Brutus and by those ancient Romans. He is not a heretic: "My intellect believes the faith," he says to his friend. But the obstacle lies in the heart. "I seem to have a hard heart." Just like Andrea Viarani, for Pietro Paolo Boscoli the impediment is the hardness of the heart, not that of the mind. His prayer is that his heart might soften: "Ah, if only I could cry a little at the passion of my Lord! Turn to liquid, hard heart of mine. Do you not know that I die willingly? Come with me sweetly."[31]

This exchange between the two men took place in a place crowded with curious onlookers and officers of justice. It was what happened normally: noise, shouts, a desire to see the condemned, curiosity to know how they were facing up to their fate and what they had to say about their affairs, their enemies, their story. Death was like this in the everyday normality of the home as well: at birth and at death there was always a crowd of people moving around the woman about to give birth as there was around the person about to die. The images illustrating the art of dying well show notaries, confessors, friends, and relatives gathered around the sickbed. There were lots of people around Pietro Paolo as well. But this time there was an outburst of anger, a rebuff: "Turning to those standing around, he said: 'Ah! Be still! Don't bother me!'—because they came up to him one after another. 'Luca here is enough for me; he knows my nature. If I want anything, I'll tell him. You others pray to God for me.'"[32]

This need to feel in his heart the assurance of a direct relationship with God shows that something had changed in the moral economy, to the point of undermining the very rituals of the preparation for death, even in material details. Boscoli had been offered a hearty dinner, as was the norm. Laying on the dinner was one of the most important cost items in the organization of the spectacle, and was met by the confraternities. In the German tradition what was called the executioner's dinner involved consuming an immoderate amount of food and alcohol.[33] And we have seen how in the case of the company of Padua the idea behind the preparation of this meal was that the body needed to be comforted in order to be able to tend to the soul. Instead, Boscoli complained repeatedly about the difficulty posed by all that food: "They gave me too much to eat. How can I turn my spirit towards God?"[34] There is a moment in the dialogue in which Boscoli accepts his friend's suggestion and offers his heart up to God. One of the bystanders sees in Boscoli's words a sign of conversion and immediately urges the hooded *confratello* from the Company of Blacks: "Let him see the *tavoluccia*." But on this occasion the prisoner reacts in a new and unexpected way: "No need for the *tavoluccia*. I'll be in a bad way, if I don't recognize him without the *tavoluccia*."[35] The image of Christ he was looking for was something that had to take shape within himself: a human and welcoming image, different from that of the wounded, suffering body depicted on the *tavoluccia*: "I wish," he says to Luca, "that the humanity of Christ would offer itself to me and I want to understand it as if he were to come out of the woods and run into me."[36]

The refusal of the *tavoluccia* was the sign of a sensibility that was new and different from the one that had prevailed until then, which had been inspired by Franciscan preaching and by the practice, also Franciscan, of visualized meditation. The representation of Calvary and of Christ's journey to the Cross had been the theme of meditation offered to pilgrims visiting the "sacred mountains." In these images, the cruelty of the guards, depicted with caricatural Jewish features, and the twisted anatomy of the two thieves, Gestas and Dismas, on each side of the Cross, presented a theater of suffering and death. Boscoli was searching for something else. He needed to picture his meeting with Christ as that of one man running into another. Only in this way could he imagine being able to entrust himself to him with an immediacy of feeling that completely did away with the mediation of the Church. This can be seen more clearly when, as he repeated the words suggested to him by his confessor, he had to be continually corrected.

> And for the first, he spoke thus:
> "I must believe what Christ commands."
> "Yes, and what the church commands," Fra Cipriano added.
> "What God commands."
> "And the church, which is the same thing."
> "Ok. I do."[37]

With the same docility Boscoli declared his readiness to become "all spiritual": a word that would have great resonance during that century, coming to define a religious trend viewed with suspicion by the Roman Inquisition. Talk of becoming spiritual described a religious conversion that no longer translated into the choice of taking the habit and obligations of a regular order. It was an entirely inner choice—indifferent, if not actually hostile, to ecclesiastic institutions and the obligations of ceremonial observances. Just when theological conflicts were beginning to rage between the Roman Church and the Protestant Reformation, the decision to describe oneself as "spiritual" meant setting ecclesiastical mediation to one side and trusting in a view of faith as sentiment and inspiration. Revealed here is the basic feature that would make the doctrine of justification by faith the most dangerous heresy for every type of power. As E. P. Thompson wrote, "It displaced the authority of institutions and of received worldly wisdom with that of the individual's inner light."[38] The organ called upon was the heart, not the mind, even though the care taken by Fra Cipriano to correct and modify the wording used by Boscoli offers a glimpse of the intervention of the ecclesiastical authorities charged with controlling orthodoxy and bringing back onto the straight and narrow those who ventured dangerously along the path of a religion of the spirit. In the night of comforting of Pietro Paolo Boscoli these things were already present in an embryonic form. But it was clear then that the confraternities' traditional forms of Christian brotherhood risked appearing inadequate, and even liable to provoke rejection. The devout image of the *tavoluccia* and the choral singing of litanies and penitential psalms were no longer enough in the search for a personal relationship with God, which required concentration and silence. When the Blacks began to sing penitential psalms, Boscoli's reaction was immediate: "Then Pietro Paolo spoke up energetically, 'Fathers and brothers, I don't need this noise in my ears, it bothers me a lot. I have little time, please be quiet so that I can confess. This singing of yours doesn't please me. If you want quietly, by yourselves, to pray to God for me, I beg that of you, and will be indebted to you.'"[39]

That same sound of chanting voices in the night disturbed another prisoner as well, under inquisition on the same charge and locked in a nearby cell: his name was Niccolò Machiavelli. After getting out of prison alive, Machiavelli evoked that night in a composition dedicated to Giuliano di Lorenzo de' Medici. He recalled the sound of chains and locks, the weight of shackles, and the pain of being subjected six times to the *corda* torture— having his hands tied behind his back with a rope and then being suspended from it. And he added:

> Quel che mi fe' più guerra
> Fu che dormendo presso a la aurora
> Cantando sentii dire: "per voi s'òra."
> Or vadano in malora . . .

(What gave me most torment was that, sleeping near dawn, I heard them chanting the words: "We are praying for you.")[40]

The historian and politician who not long after, from his exile on the estate of Albergaccio, would devote himself to an analysis of politics as violence and astuteness ("lion" and "fox"), was also the person who reflected on ancient Roman religion as a political tie capable of binding the citizen to the fight for the defense and greatness of the state; on the other hand, the dominant thought of Christianity, the salvation of the individual soul, seemed to him to move in an entirely different direction.

The crisis in the communal system and the advance of territorial states stained the scaffolds with blood. What had happened in Florence with the Medici's return to power would be repeated in Siena in the middle of the century with the protracted resistance to Florentine conquest. The records of the Sienese Compagnia della Morte for 1553 featured long lists of names of people condemned for treason.[41] This trend in Italian politics became intermeshed with the wider crisis in European religious unity. We have already said that the conversion of Pietro Paolo Boscoli was for him about becoming "all spiritual." And it must also be added that he was comforted before his death by Luca della Robbia and by a Florentine Dominican monk: two witnesses of the Savonarolan tradition, both convinced that political rebellion against a tyrant was legitimate from a religious point of view as well. Tyrannicide could therefore be sustained not just on the basis of the rebirth of pagan models but also on that of the Thomistic tradition as renewed in the work and testimony of Fra Girolamo Savonarola. The web of ancient pagan and Christian sources and of modern conflicts can be found in the developments in the reality of life in sixteenth-century Italy, where, as mentioned, a special thread connoted tendencies defined as spiritual: some understood them as a form of adherence to the ideas of the Protestant Reformation, and there were those who embraced them with a view to achieving a nonsubversive renewal of the structure of the Catholic Church.

The interweaving of political struggle and new religious tendencies in the public life of Italy's cities translated in effect into new cases of capital punishment that sorely tested the function of the traditional *misericordie* and confraternities. A particularly significant episode was the condemnation and execution of the nobleman Pietro Fatinelli (1512–1543), found guilty of having organized a conspiracy against the ruling oligarchy in Lucca. Arrested and sentenced to death, the details of his final hours were recounted by a witness whose identity is concealed behind the initials F. C., in a text included around 1572 in one of the manuscripts of Matteo Civitali's chronicle of Lucca. It is a further example, alongside that of the heretical friar Michele da Calci and of the political conspirator Pietro Paolo Boscoli, of a secretly transmitted narrative of a death considered to be memorable and exemplary. And here too the, as it were, officially appointed comforters seemed inadequate, and remained on the fringes of the scene. In Lucca, a Compagnia della Croce had been active since the end of the fourteenth century. The regulations for assisting the condemned had been clearly established in statutes drawn up in 1492: two of their members were to spend "the night before the said execution is to be carried out" with the condemned, in order to procure "the comfort of the said [person] designated for execution." In the morning thirteen *confratelli* had to accompany the prisoner to the scaffold, carrying the "small Crucifix" in front of them.[42]

In F. C.'s account, mention is made of the presence, alongside Pietro Fatinelli, of three laypeople, a canon from San Frediano, and a friar.[43] This is what
they saw when they entered Fatinelli's cell on the evening of October 28,
1543: the prisoner was sitting at a table writing some thoughts on prayer. It
was a topical theme, having been recently treated in a book by a Genoese
nobleman turned man of the Church, Cardinal Federico Fregoso, testi-
fying to how much influence Luther's ideas had had in his circles. No trace
has remained of similar readings in Fatinelli's life up until his long imprisonment: but the ones picked up by the account of what he said in those
final hours were clearly Lutheran. When his visitors arrived, Fatinelli interrupted his writing, greeted them happily, and thanked them for the "good
news" they bore. Great sinner that he was, he expressed his gratitude to
God for the salvation brought to him, not by works—because "insofar as
I am human I cannot do any good thing"—but "by faith, by His goodness
and mercy alone."[44] He spent the night reading the Gospel: and it was Fatinelli
who offered "interpretations so fine that he amazed everyone who heard
him." He declared that he had learned the truth by "true faith" and had requested and obtained eternal salvation after having been for his whole life
an "enemy of God and of Christ's truth." The Passion of Christ had been
"sufficient to cancel everything," making him sure of election: just three
days earlier he almost did not believe "there was either God or Christ," whom
he called to mind only when blaspheming against them. But now God's
mercy had "elected" him, and "the faith of Jesus Christ" had saved him.
Fatinelli's language is revelatory of a new faith, where the idea of God's immense mercy is expressed in the words of the doctrine of the Protestant
Reformation: a predestination to salvation earned by faith alone, and a rejection of any possible idea of good works. And when they removed his
shackles the following morning and took him through the rooms of the
palace toward the square, Fatinelli grasped the opportunity that presented
itself, when he encountered the city's notables, to vehemently abjure his
earlier political convictions and the pagan shadows that had accompanied
them: "Behold the man," he says, "behold Magnificent Lords, that [Gaius]
Marius, that Sulla who had thought to bloody his hands in civil blood, not
out of enmity but for his own ambition." The *Ecce homo* of the Passion
(John 19:5) sweeps away pagan ethics and politics, the ambitions of the
struggle for and conquest of absolute power. Fatinelli appealed to the citizens

of Lucca gathered in the square "in a very great number" in similar terms: "Behold the man! Behold here, my people, the greatest sinner ever to have been in the world, he who, during his life, has done all the evil things a rational creature can do. Nonetheless, God's mercy has not looked at his sins and has forgiven him." His case should be held up as an example for everyone, "so that no sinner should despair, because all those who have faith in Jesus Christ, as I have at present, will be forgiven their sins. And I have come to this death by the will of God thanks to my deeds, to testify to everyone his truth, which is that which I have said."[45]

As in Boscoli's case, the truth that Fatinelli claims to have learned also found its way into a textual account that remained undiscovered for a long time. The two documents share a family resemblance that has prompted one scholar to suggest the existence not just of an abstractly textual link but one involving the material transmission of ideas inherited from the thinking and writings of Fra Girolamo Savonarola.[46] What is clear as a matter of fact is that a doctrine of salvation by faith was gaining ground during the crisis troubling the city-states in the years of the Italian wars and of the Reformation, a doctrine based on the idea of an immense divine mercy that offered corrupt and undeserving humanity the way to salvation through the death of Christ. As in Florence when Michele da Calci had been sent to his death, among the crowd watching Pietro Fatinelli's execution in Lucca there were members of a dissident religious minority: an embryonic "Ecclesia Lucensis" that would become involved in a lively standoff with Rome and would end with an emigration toward Geneva of collective proportions. In the meantime, word spread that Pier Paolo Vergerio was preparing a short treatise about consoling "the infirm and the condemned" from a Lutheran point of view.[47]

The way was opening up for comforting that appealed to an interpretation of divine mercy and of the precept of forgiveness as a salvific formula without the need for the contribution of the sinner's works: an idea that had strong roots in the Italian religious tradition but that, against the backdrop of the conflict of the Reformation, acquired connotations subversive of ecclesiastical mediation and dangerous for the entire structure of the Church. In Italian cities, meanwhile, the holders of political power were demanding forms of symbolic legitimation that would bend the functioning of the devout lay associations in their favor.

The reaction came, with Faenza being an emblematic case in point. A vigorous reforming movement in the city was opposed and wiped out by a violent campaign conducted by the new Roman Inquisition, which literally decapitated its followers and modified the city's institutional setup. An echo of this can be found in the statutes of 1567 (the most dramatic year of the repression) of the local Compagnia di San Giovanni Decollato, in which the importance of works was placed very much to the fore: "In these works of charity, then, lies everything."[48] The art of comforting was incorporating and replacing the "art of dying well." What had long been a work of mercy carried out by laypeople for their devotion was being transformed into a function of increasing importance for secular and ecclesiastical powers: to begin with, it was possible to legitimate the sovereign's power to kill in the name of God's will insofar as the condemned could be transformed into the guarantor of the justness and of the providential nature of the sentence. It was an important and delicate task, arousing jealousy and suspicion in both ecclesiastical and political quarters—not solely because of the knowledge that might be gleaned during the nighttime conversations with the more important prisoners, but also due to the delicacy and theological riskiness of the arguments used to provide comfort and assurances of eternal salvation. The most important of these was the ideal of divine mercy itself, so deeply felt by those who, by joining those confraternities, had pinned all their hopes of salvation on the reciprocal pact between human works of mercy and divine forgiveness. The comforters held out eternal salvation and access to the kingdom of heaven as a gift to those who accepted capital punishment as the occasion offered by divine providence to convert and repent of one's sins. This, as we shall see, was the idea sustained in a *Libro devotissimo della Misericordia di Dio* published in Bologna in 1521: and onto this dramatic idea, which resolved all fears, there was grafted the new morality nourished by the Lutheran theology of the Cross. One could be saved by faith alone, not by way of human works: faith in the benefit earned by Jesus Christ on the Cross. In the middle of the sixteenth century there was convergence on this point from various quarters—from those directly touched by the preaching of Reformation ideas to those seeking religious renewal of traditional forms of piety. Shortly before the execution of Pietro Fatinelli in Lucca, in Verona the Rieti-born cleric Tullio Crispoldi had anonymously published his meditation on *Alcune ragione del perdonare,* in which the law of the reciprocity of forgiveness had been extended from the relationship between humans and God to that between all members of a society:

> It is certain that they [soldiers and lords] and every rank and condi-
> tion of person and every republic and reign is worthy of perpetual war
> and to never have peace, where there are many who hate forgiveness. . . .
> When we ask what the cause of this blessed law of forgiveness is, we
> must answer that it is so because God fulfils the promises he made to
> forgive everyone, Gentiles and Jews, and to give his blessing to all, and
> it is to save everyone that he wishes everyone to be forgiven.[49]

The idea of a divine mercy capable of embracing everyone without distinguishing between religious affiliations had to come to terms with the outbreak of a war of religion within Christianity. The harshness of the ultimate
punishment for those who strayed from the "truth" protected by the Church
was called for and supported, not just at a theoretical level, by a chorus of
voices: that it was right to put heretics to death was reaffirmed with fanatic
rigor by the Spanish Franciscan Alfonso de Castro, an exponent of the
column formation of an alliance of power between religion and the State.[50]
Events led rapidly to the obligation to choose between two opposing camps:
and Tullio Crispoldi, despite having shared with Marcantonio Flaminio the
reforming ideas circulating in Veronese circles, chose the anti-heretical in-
transigence of the Church of Rome, and argued in one of his theological
manuals that heretics should be punished with severity.[51] But the evolution
of his thinking reflects the persistence of the motif of forgiveness in new
forms. Having moved close to the circle of the Oratorio di San Filippo Neri
and of the Capuchin Order, he began publishing treatises of devout meditation and consolation for the dying. He was responsible for the instructions
for comforting the dying that circulated in the libraries of the companies of
justice. In the new climate of religious war forgiveness became an extreme
resource for the dying: they could be forgiven and save their souls on condition that they penitently gathered together under the protection of the
Church's sacraments. The person who gave poetic voice to this idea of forgiveness was Torquato Tasso, in the episode of the death of Clorinda. Vanquished and fatally wounded, Clorinda dies—but as she dies, she forgives her

killer and asks him for the sacrament that will give her eternal life. It is a memorable scene, the leitmotif of which is the word "forgiveness":

> "Friend, you have won. I pardon you. Do you
> Pardon me also—not my body, no—
> It fears naught—but my soul, yes."[52]

It is a celebrated episode, which not by chance became immediately popular. The solution to the conflict consisted of killing the body and at the same time saving the soul. One's best enemy is a dead enemy: but in order to kill that enemy definitively, it is necessary to remove the possibility of them dying as an enemy. The soul will be saved, and the ferocious armed adversary will then reveal the hidden identity of a tender, forgiving female figure. Embroiled in the wars of religion, Europe at the end of the sixteenth century was losing sight of the ideals of tolerance and peace of faiths, and nurturing dreams of death and conversion. Torquato Tasso's poetry recorded the change: while Ariosto missed the "noble chivalry of knights of yore," when a Muslim and Christian, "two rivals, of opposed belief," could still ride the same horse,[53] Tasso came up with a very different outcome for the encounter between the Christian knight Tancredi and the Muslim virgin Clorinda.

Tasso was obsessed by the fear of heresy, and witnessed executions of heretics. He had smelt burnt human flesh in Mantua, and was to experience it again in Ferrara at the execution of members of the heretical sect of Giorgio Siculo, carefully listed in the books of the city's company of justice. In those books there are very few cases where the condemned died unrepentant. The chronicler almost always noted down signs that boded well for the eternal fate of the executed. In the case of Clorinda, Tasso took the model of forgiving death to the extreme, as the occasion for gaining access to the kingdom of the blessed.

That the enemy should be vanquished by forgiveness was an ancient and profound Christian aspiration; that war should be replaced by peace and swords transformed into plowshares had been forcefully affirmed by the prophet Isaiah. But the prophesy had been belied by reality, and onto the hope of the Jewish Messiah there descended the construction of the Christian Church, the ally of the greatest empire in the ancient world. The collapse of the Roman empire had prompted Augustine of Hippo to call for the fate of the earthly city to be separated from that of the heavenly Jerusalem.

Speculation about the soul had replaced reflection on the world. The walls of the city, which fell before the invasion of the Germanic barbarians, had been substituted by an intangible boundary: baptism. And from then on war—which had not disappeared—had been legitimated by the new religion as the conquest of holy places or of souls. Against the background of a profound crisis in the Western Church, the rebirth of antiquity had taken with Machiavelli the form of a reflection on the force of religion as the foundation for a sense of belonging to the State. In the context of the political and religious crisis of Europe, the death to be inflicted on enemies and those who were different found potent legitimation in their final extreme conversion and acceptance of the justness and providence of the sentence.

The relationship between the administration of earthly justice and the religious tribunal of the sacrament of penance had found a point of intersection in the overlap and inextricable tangle of sins and crimes. Emphasis has been placed on "the continual intertwining between the plane of sin, the plane of canon law, contentious and criminal, and the plane of secular law, civil and criminal" that took place in papal Rome, the seat of a vast and complex system for administering justice.[54] So it is no accident that at the opportune moment the network of confraternities of justice found their capital in Rome.

16

Rome, a Capital

THE REVIVAL OF THE PAPACY in the late fifteenth and early sixteenth centuries, following the years of the schism and the conciliar crisis, turned Rome into an essential focus for communities of merchants and financiers, artists and literati. From the Florentine community came the decisive impulse to launch a religious initiative providing comfort to the condemned. After the changes that had taken place in the Italian cities of the Po plain, this was a decisive step. The fact that the initiative came from laymen engaged in trade and banking shows that saving the souls of criminals and the wretched poor was viewed as a profitable investment in the treasures of the sky.

The Roman community of Florentine merchants and bankers gave rise to what would prove to be the most important confraternal institution in Catholicism: the Compagnia di San Giovanni Decollato, known as the company of the Florentines. In Rome, the city where the splendor of a papacy that had defeated the threat of conciliarism attracted people from all over Europe, the important Florentine community created a *misericordia* company named after the patron saint of Florence, Saint John the Baptist, which began, in April 1488, to "accompany those who went to be executed."[1] They received official approval in the shape of a bull issued by Pope Innocent VIII on February 25, 1490. Drawing on the words used in the entreaty presented by the *confratelli,* the bull recognized that there was a need to assist many people ("quamplurimi") who were sentenced to death in the city and had no one to remind them of what they needed to do to save their souls. The bull also granted permission for the bodies of the assisted to be buried at the foot of the Capitoline Hill, in Santa Maria della Fossa, where the confraternity church dedicated to Saint John the Baptist was subsequently built.

On August 5, 1497, the Roman company of San Giovanni Decollato responded to the last wishes of a condemned man named Organtino di Persona, from Rome. "Of sound mind and intellect, and due to die in the evening," he declared that he wanted to make a will "for the health of his soul."[2] Thus began the series of records of the new confraternity, which was to acquire a dominant position in the general panorama of such institutions, marching in step with the Roman papacy's ascent to hegemony over the Italian peninsula. The whole history of papal power, temporal and spiritual, left its mark in the long trail of physical death and of the salvation of souls remembered by the company. One scholar who tried to quantify the death sentences carried out in Rome from the sixteenth to the nineteenth century did not find any particular differences compared to what happened in other European cities, but he did have to acknowledge the intention, with the work of the company, to propose a special moral model in Rome.[3] In the testaments and declarations of those who died in the papal state, we find the knot which, through the work of the company of justice, linked death with the hope of eternal life, crime with remorse, ruthless legal violence with religious piety. This continued for many years, until the end of the temporal power of the popes, with the brief interruptions of the Napoleonic empire and Mazzini's Republic of 1848.

The work of the Roman confraternity was not limited to the papal state. Founded with little fanfare, its fortunes were determined by the development of the papacy in the years of the sixteenth-century religious crisis. It was not a peaceable initiative. The body of clerics grouped together in the "Romana fraternitas" claimed a monopoly on burials, a monopoly guaranteed by a bull issued by Pope Gregory IX in 1237. The clergy's lucrative privilege regarding burials could be eluded only by members of the confraternities, who had their own chaplains and places of burial. This was the situation in times of normality; but if there were plague epidemics, things changed, and charitable lay initiatives to help the sick and bury the dead were permitted. During the pestilence of 1448, for instance, the members of the Florentine community grouped together in the association of the Pietà and carried out these tasks. The Confraternita di San Giovanni Battista della Nazione Fiorentina, founded in 1456, introduced to Rome the devotion to the saint of the Florentine "nation," and with it that special form of mercy consisting of accompanying the condemned to the scaffold. According to one chronicler, the *confratelli* of this association, "considering that poor offenders sentenced to death by the judicial authorities did not have the spiritual and temporal assistance to convert them with charity and indeed to better set them on the all important path of eternal well-being ... resolved (heedless, therefore, of human concerns) to assist them right to the very end, dressing in black sackcloth tied with a cord belt and with the [emblem of the] head of Saint John the Baptist in the basin on the front."[4] The Roman confraternity was thus the fruit of a plant whose roots lay elsewhere, in the model provided by the Florentine Compagnia dei Battuti known as Santa Maria della Croce al Tempio: the transplant occurred as a result of the growing political clout of Medici Florence and its special ties with papal Rome. It is a perfect example of the process whereby these associations were transplanted and spread elsewhere.

In those years Rome was open to people from many other cities, and the initiative of the Florentine community was just one of many. Another community of merchants and investors with a very visible presence in Rome were the Genoese, especially in the years of Pope Julius II, born in Albisola (Republic of Genoa) as Giuliano della Rovere. From this direction came another proposal that arose similarly from the experience of a confraternity of justice and was developed by the Genoese notary Ettore Vernazza. His name is little known. Fond of secrecy by choice and character, he left few and uncertain traces of his religious activities, which, however, were many. He had grown up in the oligarchic Republic of Genoa, where a multi-branched web of lay associations *(casacce)* performed primary social functions and offered networks of assistance in a territory united much more by maritime and financial trade than by a state structure. He was the promoter of initiatives to provide assistance to the poor, sick, and condemned, and some of the most important charitable institutions in early sixteenth-century Italy can be traced back to him. One theme dominates in particular in these initiatives: divine love. A charismatic inspirer of this had been Caterina Fieschi Adorno, the woman who revived the model of Saint Catherine of Siena in fifteenth-century Genoa. The group of devotees that had formed around her in the Compagnia del Mandiletto was supported by Vernazza. What Caterina's teaching consisted of can be seen in the *Libro de la vita mirabile et dottrina Santa de la Beata Caterinetta da Genova,* published posthumously in Genoa in 1551. A central core of the book dealt with the theme of purgatory—viewed as a place, not of affliction, but of divine love, where the soul can be purged of wrongdoing in order to attain blessed life with God.[5] The question of purgatory had become central to the doctrinal controversy that raged in the age of Luther and the Reformation, and it is possible that the reworking of Caterina's ideas by her disciples was influenced by this. However, there can be no doubt about the basic inspiration that Caterina's followers drew from her teaching: the God whose children they felt themselves to be was a loving god, who asked his children to plant the bond of charity in their hearts—the same charity exalted in a celebrated passage from Saint Paul's Letter to the Corinthians. The spirit of charity had to be channeled into work to save souls—those in purgatory, the prison beyond this world, and those suffering in the hospitals and prisons of this one. As we saw earlier, Caterina had prayed to God and his divine power to enter into human hearts so that the soul of a condemned prisoner might be saved. Her example determined the goal of Vernazza's secret confraternity. Secrecy, so familiar to the Genoese trading and financial world, was the rule for practicing a charity that was to be only the reflection of divine love in human hearts. Among the companies of Divine Love that sprang from Vernazza's work was one that had particular importance, due both to where it was established (papal Rome) and who its members were—men of the Roman Curia, forming part of cardinals' courts and the pontiff's secretariat, laypeople and clergy, who, against the backdrop of Leo X's lavish court, devoted themselves to works of charity and practiced a rigorous asceticism. The Lutheran historian Leopold von Ranke was struck by the discovery that experiences of this kind were cultivated in the heart of a Rome censured by Luther's preaching, and saw in them some analogies with the Protestant Reformation. In actual fact, the path of spiritual perfection and charitable works went in a direction completely different from the one taken by those who pinned their hopes for the salvation of a humanity imprisoned by sin on faith in the efficacy of the free gift offered to humankind by Christ's death on the Cross. But only with time would the irreconcilable difference between the two paths—of charity and of faith—become fully clear. They related to two different divine figures, that of the benevolent father ready to forgive every misdeed and that of a terrifying and remote God who predestines humanity to damnation.

The confraternities established or revived by Vernazza helped prisoners and the sick, renewing the tradition of merciful works amid the dramatic problems created by an illness of epidemic proportions, which was deemed "incurable" and considered to be particularly shameful and disgusting:

syphilis. Among the causes of what seemed to be a particularly serious emergency were the movements of French troops during the Italian wars, the masses of Jews expelled from the Iberian Peninsula, and the pauperism resulting from the revolution in prices, and it inspired devotees of charity to practice what lay at the heart of their commitment by helping those in need of care and assistance. But once again hospital assistance—the cornerstone of merciful works—gave rise to or revived the work of comforting the condemned. Ettore Vernazza's name is associated with the establishment of the Confraternita Santa Maria Succurre Miseria, also known as the Compagnia dei Bianchi della Giustizia—the name of the association that did this work in Naples, the largest city in Italy and the capital of the kingdom whose possession had sparked the Italian wars. Here there was no sort of assistance for the condemned at all. The report of an earlier fifteenth-century initiative associated with the presence in Naples of the celebrated Franciscan preacher Fra Giacomo della Marca probably falls under the rubric of the invention of tradition.[6] The origin of the company dates to 1519, when Vernazza visited Naples together with the Augustinian canon regular Callisto Fornari from Piacenza. The first known chapters were drawn up in 1525.[7] As Ettore's daughter, Battistina Vernazza, later recalled, the Genoese notary was struck by how the condemned were abandoned and despised. Accustomed to the intense social life of his own native city, where bank stock counted for much more than being of noble stock, Ettore was appalled by the haughtiness of the Neapolitan aristocrats, who considered being associated in any way with the infliction of the death penalty on thieves and murderers to be "the vilest" and most dishonorable thing in the world.[8] In actual fact, the company was an immediate success with the Neapolitan social and cultural elite, and attracted members from very different backgrounds, such as the circle of Juan de Valdés and the Theatines of Gian Pietro Carafa. Soon destined to go their separate ways and indeed to become ferocious enemies, in the 1530s these groups shared a desire to practice a renewed personal faith. This was the start of one of the most active and important institutions operating on the boundary between political power and religion: from then on, the stories of the executed, an extremely representative fragment of the reality of a great city, would pass through the filter of the institutional network created by the Compagnia dei Bianchi della Giustizia. The company's chapel, situated in the heart of the city near the ancient Ospedale degli Incurabili, opened to the public in July 2017. It is now finally possible to fully appreciate the imposing nature of the place and its sumptuous pictorial decoration, which is a monument to the art and religiosity of the age: Neapolitan culture, characterized by a special and obsessive sense of death and of the relationship with the dead, created there what is perhaps the most significant expression of its interpretation of Counter-Reformation religiosity. The chapel was used as a meeting place by confraternity members, who, in compliance with their statutes, were engaged not just in "procuring the well-being of the soul of those condemned to death," but also in "visiting imprisoned wretches and hospitals for the sick, especially those infirm with incurable illnesses."[9]

Naples was by far the largest European city of the age, and the weight of this great capital in the system of Spanish power in Italy was decisive, adding to the hereditary dominion of the House of Aragon over Sicily. The influx of Italian models of religious life led to the establishment of a company of justice on the island as well. The Franciscan preacher Pietro Paolo Caporella provided the stimulus for the foundation of the Compagnia del Santissimo Crocifisso, known also as the "Bianchi," in 1541. Its first act was performed on May 2 of the same year, with the comforting of two condemned prisoners. This was a big success, according to the chapters of 1572, because "never did such docile lambs as they go to their deaths disposed to the Lord."[10] In a very short space of time, the company effectively became the main confraternity and was granted the privilege of leading solemn processions.

But the capital of the companies of justice was not established in Naples or Palermo, but in Rome. It was the Roman confraternity of San Giovanni Decollato that was to exercise a crucial influence on subsequent developments of scaffold devotion, becoming the central institution. Decisive to its development was the context of the political and religious conflicts that broke out in the late fifteenth and the early sixteenth centuries. The papacy was constrained to attribute renewed value to the more strictly religious component of Roman power. While Leo X limited himself to reinforcing the "national" character of the confraternity by restricting membership to those belonging to the "Florentine nation," the fundamental step from being Florentine to being Roman was the work of Pope Paul III, born Alessandro Farnese. He injected fresh impulse into the association by making it an arch-confraternity and granting it a very special privilege—the power to free someone who had been condemned to death, solemnly restoring their full liberty on the feast day of the patron saint.[11]

The Power to Pardon

From then on, in addition to the special indulgences rewarding their work, the members of the confraternity could boast a genuine power to pardon: it was the seal that the companies of justice had previously lacked to accede to the highest levels of social prestige. The power of pardon was the area in which the supremely arbitrary nature of sovereign authority was expressed more than anywhere else. The papacy, which in vying with the monarchy rediscovered the valuable asset of spiritual power, had nothing to learn in this area. As the holder of temporal power, the papacy exercised it with all necessary severity through the different tribunals it had in place, sustained by legal doctrines based on the model of Roman law and by theologians who judged the use of the death penalty to be entirely legitimate and grounded in the holy Scriptures. As for pardon, it was the divine variety that was dispensed by the Church through the channels of the sacraments: there was baptism, which washed away original sin and all other wrongs, leaving the soul pure white and immaculate (as comforters were at pains to remind condemned prisoners who were not baptized); for the baptized who had fallen into sin, the function of forgiving and reconciling the sinner lay with the court of sacramental confession. But as far as earthly life was concerned, it was the supreme pontiff, as absolute sovereign of the Church State, who had the power of pardon: and he now delegated it to an association dedicated to comforting the condemned. Added together here were the two aspects of the power of the person who was sovereign in both the spiritual and the temporal domains—for the sins of remorseful and converted criminal-sinners were forgiven and their lives pardoned. That it was communicated by the association of devout *confratelli* who had interceded for them did not cancel what remained the "extreme manifestation of a 'total' power, over bodies and over minds."[12] The possibility of saving a human life thus reflected a special light on the salvation of souls and brought a glimmer of hope to the dreams of all those condemned to death. The interweaving of the temporal and the spiritual percolated all the way down to the roots of the administration of justice, as would be seen when the task of managing the organization of jails was given to the Confraternita della "Pietà dei carcerati."[13]

Like all papal acts and concessions, the privilege of pardon, though defined as *perpetuo,* was subject to reconfirmation when there was a change of pope. But the fact remains that the most important and prestigious sign of sovereign power—the right of life and death—in the Papal State had been entrusted to the mediation of a devout company and to the protection of a saint. The privilege was not exclusive to the Compagnia di San Giovanni Decollato dei Fiorentini. In the scramble to win signs of favor, the homonymous confraternity of the Genoese community managed to obtain the same privilege as well, under Pope Gregory XIII, as did other devout associations, including the Archiconfraternita della Santissima Madonna della Consolazione, also from Gregory XIII, and the Santissima Madonna del Suffragio, from Clement VIII.[14] Giving the power of entreaty to the devout proved to be the model best suited to a soft management of the punishment system, such as to achieve harmony between the temporal and spiritual sides of papal sovereignty. But what counted was the establishment of a strategy that would characterize the papacy in the Tridentine age. By conferring the power to pardon on a confraternity, albeit with rules that excluded certain categories of crimes and guaranteed that he had the final word, the pope pointed out the way that would be taken by his successors, in the period that saw the reaffirmation and reinforcement of the papacy as a spiritual power.

The pattern of delegating the running of judicial affairs to the confraternities quickly caught on. By linking themselves to the Roman confraternity that had become an archconfraternity, other similar associations requested and generally obtained the same privileges and indulgences. The most violent function of justice was thus cloaked by paternal solicitude and Christian charity: the divine love for the souls to be saved and the offer of a papal pardon for the candidates selected annually by the *confratelli* abounded in devotion and gave extraordinary emphasis to the ritual of the eponymous saint's annual feast day.

The ritual subsequently drawn up and published together with the company's other prayers and liturgical formulas included the special prayer that the pardoned prisoner, dressed in white and accompanied to the altar by two *confratelli,* had to recite immediately after the choral singing of the Te Deum and the psalms:

Oh most glorious Saint John the Baptist, I acknowledge that I have been liberated from death, and brought here to new life by the mercy of the Lord God by virtue of your merits. I confess my utter gratitude to you, and to render infinite thanks, illuminate me, I pray, and keep me always as your devout servant, to lead a new and better life in observance of the saints and holy commandments and of the saintly virtues of Our Lord Jesus Christ, with whose grace and help I here propose and promise. Amen.[15]

It is a model that we find being widely reproduced by the confraternities of justice. From then on, among the multitude of the condemned there was also a minority of people who were pardoned thanks to the privileges granted by the pope and ratified by local political powers. The procedure for periodically selecting a candidate and the rituals of the solemn concluding celebration were a very important moment in the life of these associations, and were the concrete manifestation of a possibility of forgiveness that was not limited to the soul, but really did restore life and liberty to someone facing the imminent prospect of death. It was the exception that confirmed the rule—or at least it masked the bloody violence, reflecting a paternally merciful light on power.

The faculty of pardon was used immediately in the cities of the Papal State. In Perugia, after a rebellion over the introduction of a salt tax led to harsh repression and the city being stripped of its communal freedom, the Confraternita dei Santi Andrea e Bernardino inserted itself into a tradition of pardons that the papal legates were accustomed to granting on Christmas Day and Good Friday. In the confraternity's records, the list of pardoned prisoners begins on Christmas Day 1548, with acts drawn up by the notary Ser Giovanni Maffani. He was also the author of the first printed instructions about how to comfort the condemned.[16] Evidence of the spread of the recourse to the privilege of pardon can also be found in the papal bulls that the confraternities associated with the Roman archconfraternity conserved jealously in their archives. Let us consider one random example. Like all the other privileges, the one granted by Pope Paul V in 1619 to the Compagnia di Stroncone in the diocese of Narni listed the excluded crimes: heresy, lèse-majesté, forgery of coins and papal bulls, murder, sacrilege, sodomy. It also specified, as a preliminary condition, that peace was to be made with the wronged.[17] The document offers a significant indication of how the Roman model had been able to spread due to the privileges granted by the papacy. In a small commune of the Papal State, the existent Compagnia della Misericordia sprouted a Compagnia di San Giovanni Decollato, and requested association with the Roman archconfraternity in order to enjoy the same privileges. These were numerous, and besides the power of intercession and pardon, they dispensed many spiritual indulgences. The revival of the traditional works of charity was thus linked to the affirmation of papal power over the souls of the living and the dead that Luther had so vigorously contested. While Christian Europe split on this point, the papacy reinforced and multiplied the forms of diffusion of what were popularly known as *perdonanze.* Everyone who performed charitable works was rewarded. With the transmission of these powers and spiritual benefits, the associative network, which brought together and rewarded the devout lay-people who were engaged in the same works of charity, acquired a pyramid structure with a Roman vertex and a special tie with papal Rome. That those privileges were greatly sought after can be seen from the number of entreaties made to Rome, a significant number of which have been preserved in the archconfraternity's archives. This enhanced not only the importance of the Roman company of San Giovanni Decollato, but also the effectiveness of its action to convert the condemned, to whom it could offer not just the spiritual benefits resulting from the aggregation—that is, the indulgences useful in the life to come and a religious burial—but also the hope of a pardon that might arrive at the last moment. So the individual situations of those facing the scaffold were impacted by the reverberating effects of a European-wide religious battle. Rome offered the Catholic world the spectacle of a most violent function of justice cloaked with paternal solicitude and Christian charity: the divine love for the souls to be saved, and the offer of a pardon for one condemned prisoner each year, abounded in devotion for the eponymous saint of the confraternity and gave extraordinary emphasis to the ritual of the annual feast.

This basic model of the functioning of the confraternities of justice was widespread. Apart from the uncertainties that arose when the privilege was up for renewal, and when limitations and exclusions were introduced for certain crimes, its concession was each time a sign of the sovereign's favor. The Confraternita di Santa Maria della Morte in Bologna received it in 1576 from the Bolognese pope Gregory XIII, and it was solemnly reconfirmed by the other Bolognese pope, Benedict XIV, a former *confratello* of the School of Comforters.[18] In Faenza, a minor city in the Papal State, the rituals devised by the Compagnia di San Giovanni Decollato (known as the Compagnia della Morte) around the annual pardon made it into a very atmospheric and long-lived event in the city's life, while placing the confraternity at the center of social and political dynamics that guaranteed its prestige. The ritual of the "liberation from death" normally took place there on August 29, the feast of Saint John the Baptist, and followed the exact same path, but with a reverse outcome, as the journey to the gallows, symbolizing the restoration to life of someone who had entered into the shadow of death. The condemned was received at the prison gate and accompanied to the church, where, freed from shackles and dressed in a white habit, the lucky person listened to Mass and was then taken to the confraternity building before being allowed to put on their normal clothing and go free.[19] Among the surviving documents of the confraternity of Ravenna there is a record of the pardon granted in 1683 to an infanticide, Maria Morigi, and the solemn rite that was celebrated when the woman was taken to church accompanied by the singing of psalms. In this case the ceremony took place on the Feast of Assumption: it was to the Virgin Mary that the pardoned woman wished to devote herself.[20]

But it was not just in the Papal State that the right to pardon was placed in the hands of a devout brotherhood. Around this privilege, which in social terms completed and crowned the spiritual indulgences granted to the *confratelli*, an intense dynamic of relations evolved between the Roman confraternity and all the other ones that had been established or were coming into being. The goal of obtaining such a prestigious and evocative power prompted companies of justice old and new to forge epistolary relations and, if necessary, to send representatives to Rome from peripheral towns in the Papal State and from other Italian cities. The sixteenth-century letter book of the archconfraternity in Rome offers a substantial repertoire of how a system of hierarchical relations was being built up between the center and the periphery, for the greater glory of the Holy See. The Compagnia della Misericordia of Foligno declared itself to be "devoted" to the Roman archconfraternity because it had obtained the privilege of "pardoning a bandit facing the death sentence" and had proceeded accordingly on the feast day of the saint in August 1567; however, the news that Pius IV had revoked the privilege in a *motu proprio* had caused great consternation.[21] Revocation of the privilege was cause for alarm among the members of the Compagnia del Crocifisso in Cingoli as well, as it was for those of the Compagnia del Gesù in Parma.[22] The bull with which Pius V reconfirmed all the privileges, including the faculty to free a condemned person, came as a special reward and confirmation of the public role that the companies of justice were taking on everywhere. But above all it marked the supremacy of the Roman company as the one with which it paid to be associated, in order to enjoy the same spiritual and temporal privileges. A flurry of applications ensued from dozens of confraternities in big and small cities alike, all determined to reach an associative agreement that would enable them to share in the fruits of an intangible yet incalculably valuable treasure. It was also a means by which the papacy was achieving one of its general and lucidly pursued objectives in the early modern age: to make Rome the holy city of Christianity, attracting worshippers from the whole Catholic world and binding them with indulgences and privileges. The company in Rome thus became the archconfraternity, the top of the pyramid, in line with a tendency toward verticalization and hierarchical obedience to the papacy that was typical of the period. In Bolsena the members of the Compagnia della Misericordia handed to the Capuchin preacher who had founded the company an entreaty declaring their wish to be entirely dependent on the archconfraternity in Rome, which they considered the "leading and principal" one in "all of Christendom." And they included a sentence that was revelatory of their desires: "We understand that the Company of Rome has a great many privileges, indults, and exemptions."[23] It was a general movement that stimulated the setting up of new companies of justice and transformed the traditional relations between devout associations, which had been proud of their own specificity, into a tendency toward subordination and imitation. The Misericordia di San Rocco in Pavia, for instance, having learned that the Confraternita di San Giacomo Minore in Piacenza enjoyed the same privileges as the Roman company, decided to write to the latter to see if they could have them as well.[24] Even if the place where they were operating was too small and unimportant for there to be occasions to comfort condemned prisoners or free bandits, this did not mean that associations were not set up anyway, determined to imitate the Roman model, if for no other reason than to acquire the spiritual privileges and indulgences. This was the case of the Compagnia della Misericordia of Montefalco, on whose behalf the priors of the community sent a letter to Rome attesting to the merits of the pious works carried out by its members: visiting prisoners in jail, dispensing alms, and assisting them in their dealings with the judicial authorities, and also visiting the infirm and seeing to the burial of the dead. Until then, however, there had been no executions, and so the confraternity had not had occasion to "comfort and accompany condemned prisoners to their deaths." But the priors guaranteed that "when such a case arises, they will not fail to engage in works of piety to comfort and accompany them." They therefore considered it right that privileges and indulgences should be granted to them as well.[25] It was through networks of relations like these that the fate of criminals who lived in hope of a pardon was played out. This was the case of a certain Giovanni della Cucipella, a young man from Montefiascone, who the local *misericordia* company brought to the attention of the Roman *confratelli* so that they might undertake to get the go-ahead from the pontiff. Giovanni had killed a man in a brawl five years earlier. Attacked by a rival while he went "to sing at night, as the young do," he had snatched his assailant's sword and killed him, and was now going "into exile . . . poor, indeed a beggar."[26] But there were also those who wrote in with negative information about the candidates for a pardon. For instance, a certain Piero Bonaccorsi sent a letter from Cisterna voicing his opposition to the liberation of Vincenzo Calabrese da Sermoneta, who, in his view, was a "killer, thief, and liar," a spy responsible for the killing of nine or ten men in a war between factions.[27]

Episodes like these show how a whole web of recommendations, exchanges, and clashes was quick to develop in local contexts, bringing the confraternities into the dynamics of the balance of forces in a given place and into the general micropolitical model of a State whose ruler guaranteed an exchange of benefits and pardons between earth and sky.[28] But in the meantime the power to pardon, though limited by regulations and liable to unexpected modifications by one pope or another, was something that broke the boundary between the sphere of the soul and that of the body. It demanded an at least embryonic specialization and articulation of competences from people endowed with a legal culture besides the theological grounding provided by the spiritual fathers and by preachers. Sucked into the sphere of power, the confraternities changed in nature—becoming increasingly an instrument of the authority that handed down death sentences. They were asked to provide religious legitimation for legal killing, in exchange for the privilege of proposing a pardon in certain specific cases.

Justice and mercy met and embraced, as can be read in one of the Bible passages most familiar to the Christian culture and imagination of the ancien régime. But how that encounter happened in the reality of the Italian States was completely different from what had taken root in monarchies elsewhere in Europe. The power to pardon had played a central role when the French monarchy developed a dimension of sacrality: the intention behind granting a pardon to those guilty of the most serious crimes was precisely to emphasize the sacrality of the sovereign, and that he necessarily belonged to the religious sphere.[29] The Easter privilege of freeing a condemned person was the rite of a power that presented itself as the instrument of God in exercising the divine work par excellence. But the widespread reality of the Italian confraternities appears to have differed from other European realities in how the rite was interpreted. If there is a divine dimension to power, it is concentrated in its capacity to donate life. This was clearly perceived in a religious tradition relating to the biblical God, the one to whom vengeance and retribution belonged (Deut. 32:35; Rom. 12:19), but founded also, and indeed above all, on the Christian promise of forgiveness. Exercising the power to pardon was the means favored by the ruling European dynasties to acquire the aura of being representatives of God. The ritual of the royal pardon celebrated on the Iberian Peninsula on Good Friday reflected divine glory upon the Christian sovereign. The importance of this aspect of the exercising of power emerges above all in the history of the French monarchy, which demonstrated a keen awareness of it. The constant flow of pleas presented to the sovereign's attention from the early fourteenth century onward was encouraged and increased by the liberal dispensing of "letters of remission"—full-blown forms of total amnesty with no strings attached—which were often used to extinguish all punishment and responsibility for the most serious crimes. In the direct relationship created between the supplicants requesting remission for their wrongs and the king granting it, an image was being built of the sovereign as someone above the law, the sole and absolute holder of the power to condemn and forgive. By exercising the power to pardon, the king affirmed his superiority over the ordinary administration of justice and the dense network of signorial jurisdictions and local powers that held sway over subjects. The principle was affirmed that the sovereign was the absolute master of the law and could pardon crimes, however serious, before the judges had even considered the case.

All this is well known and widely studied, but it is mentioned here to provide a comparison between two models of exercising the power to pardon. What in France was a fundamental instrument for affirming sovereign power was, in the Italian model, a privilege recognized as being of religion in general and of the companies of justice in particular. The fortunate cases in which the condemned placed their final hopes of receiving a pardon were all dominated by the power of religion and of the clergy. There was the—extremely rare—possibility of taking refuge in a church and asking for the right of exile. Or one might have the good fortune to run into a priest as he was taking the sacraments to an ill or dying person—which was enough to secure the gift of life. It was even better if one met a cardinal. This special prerogative of the princes of the Church was known to jurists: a cardinal who approached an execution procession and placed his skullcap on the prisoner's head had the power to cancel all guilt.[30] It was something that did actually happen from time to time. In Naples, for example, in 1606, the procession taking the twenty-three-year-old Tommaso Pandone to the execution site was noted by a cardinal who happened to be passing in a carriage together with the viceroy. The cardinal inquired "what gathering of people was that"— sufficient for the viceroy to send a man on horseback to tell Tommaso that his life had been spared, "which the afflicted learned as he was confessing."[31] We can imagine the anxious looks of the condemned peeking out over the comforters' *tavolette* on some of these occasions. But the institutional route to a pardon was the one that went by way of the privilege of the local confraternities, who stood as mediators between the criminal about to be executed and the authorities. Comparison between the pardons granted by the king of France and those given by members of a company of justice reveals the great difference in conceptions of sovereignty. In the first case the light of divine omnipotence reflects onto the sovereign: the plea, which would include an extensive and detailed narrative of the crime, was addressed to him, and it was up to his inscrutable judgment to make the gesture of giving life and a pardon to someone deserving death. As a result, the sovereign was exalted as a lofty point of reference for the whole of French society and as a final hope for those facing the gallows. The power to pardon was the necessary attribute of a sovereignty lying above the law, a perpetual exception, and it was also thanks to this that the State religion which characterized French life in the thirteenth and fourteenth centuries became delineated.[32] The medieval papacy also claimed total sovereignty, and not just within the bounds of one State. But in its capacity as the temporal sovereign of a State, it left to the courts the administering of punishments, including that of the death penalty, and entrusted the privilege of graciously freeing the condemned to the intercession of a devout lay confraternity. This gave rise to a mechanism of weblike propagation of the privilege by way of communication to all the other confraternities associated with the Roman one. As far as the reality of Italian life was concerned, the primacy of Rome was reinforced. The earlier setup, disseminated locally and generated from the bottom up by the devout initiatives of the *confratelli,* was giving way to a pyramidal structure dominated by papal Rome. And the base of the pyramid broadened through the aggregation of confraternities from other Italian cities that sought the privileges of the Roman archconfraternity. It was up to the power-holders of the minor Italian states to decide whether to make that privilege executive in their own territories—in effect, they hardly ever failed to do so. One case that stood out for being different was the Republic of Venice, which was jealous of its powers. When the local company of justice aggregated with the Roman one in 1613, the *confratelli* were given only the indulgences granted by the pope.[33] On the other hand, in Modena, which the Este had made the capital of their duchy with the devolution of Ferrara to the Holy See, the Compagnia della Morte obtained, among other signs of their enhanced prestige (such as the transfer of their headquarters to the ducal palace), the concession of the power to pardon. As usual, the very serious crimes of heresy, lèse-majesté, sodomy (an "unspeakable sin"), and brigandage were excluded.[34] The first ritual of pardon was solemnly celebrated in 1602 with a procession that took an infanticide "through the city, torch in hand and crowned with flowers."[35]

Anyone interested in studying the formation of the modern State in Italy will need to consider this aspect in order to understand how and by what paths a multiform entity federated under the papal government gradually took shape. In its effective transposition into local realities, the Roman comforting model acquired different forms. The function of justice was too important and prestigious for it not to become tangled up with the ambitions of the baronial and aristocratic families and for the central powers not to try to exert influence. One particularly significant example comes from Sicily. Here the Compagnia del Santissimo Crocifisso in Palermo, known as "the Whites"—set up, as we have seen, in 1541 and consisting of forty members—had strongly aristocratic social connotations (the original chapters talk of "gentlemen and honored persons"[36]). The company had obtained the privilege to save a condemned prisoner from death in 1580, thanks to the intervention of the viceroy Marcantonio Colonna. It was the most important and sought-after sign of the prestige enjoyed by the company. Exercised somewhat intermittently (for example, it was never used between 1710 and 1720), whether due to the distraction of the noble *confratelli* or because of suspensions imposed by the sovereigns, it represented the gift of life for many Sicilian men and women. The list opens with the name of Giovanni Pietro Sanguigno from Naro, a "country robber" pardoned in 1580, and closes in 1820 with that of Francesco Carollo from Comiso.[37] How the noble *confratelli* managed their power to pardon is not clear. But it is worth noting that the king suspended the privilege in 1790 after hearing that they were taking it in turns to use it to save men loyal to them, and who had been condemned by the feudal courts, from the gallows—the inevitable outcome of the company's rigidly aristocratic composition. King Ferdinand IV decreed that from then on the company would only have the power to propose a pardon: the sovereign would then choose the name from a short list of three after having gathered appropriate information about them.

The Sicilian ritual was very elaborate. The proposal of the person to pardon was to be made on Passion Sunday, whereas the solemn ritual of the pardon itself was celebrated on Good Friday, in memory of the liberation from sins made possible by the death and resurrection of Christ. The condemned person who had been preparing to die during the three days following the communication of the sentence, and had received the Eucharist and absolution "in articulo mortis," might then suddenly be informed by the governor that the viceroy—a member of the company by right—had issued a "pardon card." When the prisoner saw the prison gates opening, the emotion must have been overwhelming. This was envisaged by the *confratelli*, who had prepared "cordial conserves with icy water." After the shackles had been removed, the prisoner took part in a collective dinner. Then the *confratelli* washed the pardoned person's feet, dressed them with a smock, canvas pants, and "white silk stockings," and in a rite of conferring the pardon, handed over the keys of the prison and a crucifix, and warned them to "lead a devout life" to thank God for having freed them from an "opprobrious death." An image of the crucified Jesus was placed around their neck, and they were given a lit torch as a symbol of the fire of divine love. Then the pardoned person was taken in a public procession to the execution site, where a homily elaborated on the moral significance of the pardon that had canceled the "terrible point of having to end one's life hanging from that wooden beam." And finally, after returning to the oratory and receiving a sacramental blessing, the pardoned person was collected and taken home by their relatives.[38] This was the ceremonial procedure as described by a company register. An idea of how the populace saw it can be gleaned from the words of a German traveler who arrived in Palermo on April 13, 1786. On that day a certain Don Giuseppe Stoc from Palermo had been pardoned, and the traveler—Johann Wolfgang von Goethe—was sitting at a table eating, describing in his diary the beauty of the island, and the delights of the food and drink to be had there. But then a shouting crowd attracted his attention:

> But let's leave the table now and go to the window to look down into the street. As always happens at this season, a criminal has been reprieved in honour of Holy Week, and is being accompanied by a religious brotherhood to a mock gallows. There he says his prayers, kisses the ladder and is led away again. He is a good-looking, well-kempt man of the middle class, dressed completely in white, white tail coat, white hat. He carries his hat in his hand. Pin some coloured ribbons on him here and there, and he could attend any fancy-dress ball as a shepherd.[39]

In love with the island, Goethe writes that "to have seen Italy without having seen Sicily is not to have seen Italy at all, for Sicily is the clue to everything."[40] And yet it must be remembered that the clue to deciphering the scene described in his diary was not Sicilian but Roman.

The fresh impetus given to the centrality of papal Rome as the capital of the Catholic world had created the conditions for the systematic spread of the model of the Roman confraternity to the Italian states in that age. This emerges from just a cursory examination of the *Libro grande* of the head of the Roman company of San Giovanni Decollato dei Fiorentini. The year 1575—the year of the jubilee that marked the new religious and political protagonism of a papacy boosted by the outcome of the Council of Trent— began with a knock on the door from the procurator of the Compagnia della Misericordia di Castelnuovo, in the diocese of Tortona. He wanted to present a request for aggregation in order to "ask for our indulgences."[41] The indulgences that had provoked Luther's religious protests now bound together the most remote towns in the peninsula to the Roman capital of the Catholic Church. The political and religious ties with the restored Savoy dynasty in Turin and with the Medici grand duchy of Tuscany were reflected in the establishment of what might be described as the branches of the Roman company of San Giovanni Decollato. The Confraternita della Misericordia was founded in Turin on March 5, 1578, and would have a long history as an efficient presence in the rituals of criminal justice. Looked on favorably by King Emanuele Filiberto and his successors, it obtained the privilege to free a condemned person once a year.[42] It had been preceded by the confraternities of Alessandria, Casale, Vercelli, and Cuneo, and was followed by those of Savigliano, Bra, Carmagnola, and Cavallermaggiore. Before its foundation the task of accompanying the condemned to the gallows had been carried out by the confraternity of Grugliasco.[43] The year after, it was the turn of the confraternity of Chieri, with the approval document being signed by Monsignor Della Rovere on May 7 and by Emanuele Filiberto on May 20.[44]

It is worth looking quickly through the list of the places of origin of the requests sent to the Roman confraternity, in order to gain an idea of the network that was forming.[45] The map has a certain eloquence, dotted as it is with places of all sizes from around Italy, some so small that it is not easy to find them in the list of placenames that still exist today. There are names like Bisignano, Garlasco, Matelica, Norcia, Voghera, Demonte, Monte San Savino, Sondrio, Fossano, Foligno, Tortona, Todi, Trevi, Stroncone, Civitavecchia, Castiglion Fiorentino, Velletri, Grosseto, Fucecchio, Vetralla, Saluzzo. Mixed in with these Italian names are a few confraternities from other countries: two in France (Avignon, Chambery) and two in Hispanic territory (Santiago de Compostela and Mexico City). The time span is from the

seventeenth to the nineteenth century, and often what is involved are letters requesting the confirmation and reactivation of preexisting ties. It is a
geography of devotion that is principally Italian, with a few other branches
elsewhere in the Catholic world. The expressions of fervid desire and the descriptions of the duties habitually performed by these associations present
readers with a mixture of mangled bodies and devotion for souls that made
up the holy routine of the *confratelli*'s experiences, uniting them above and
beyond time and space. The tasks were relatively uniform, centering above
all on the burial of bodies. The account given by members of the Confraternita della Beata Vergine del Suffragio in Sondrio, in the request presented
in 1772, offers a typical sample. Their "particular mission" was "to gather up
the corpses of the executed, and take them for burial in their church, in
which, besides a specific burial place for the said corpses, they have also . . .
erected a chapel dedicated to Saint John the Baptist, where . . . anniversaries
are celebrated during the year, together with a large number of masses for
those souls." The *confratelli* of Bisignano attached to their request a letter
from the archbishop of Pavia, Bartolomeo Olivati (dated October 3, 1782),
which specified that the Confraternita di San Giovanni Battista e Santo
Spirito was engaged in comforting those inmates of the public prisons who
had been condemned to death, and that they assisted them until the sentence
was carried out, taking part then in the burial of the bodies. The *misericordia* company of Mexico City, in requesting aggregation with an entreaty
dated August 17, 1717, described its duties as follows: The *confratelli* took
the bodies down from the gallows and carried them to their church. In cases
where the sentence envisaged quartering and the display of the body parts in
the places where the crimes had been committed, it was necessary to wait
for some religious festivity or other to gain permission from the authorities
to gather them up and hold the funeral in the church of San Francesco. The
chief focus of their attention was on the organization of the funeral. A procession "with a very large number of candles" followed by "a large number of
people" carried the coffin into the church and placed it in "a magnificent tomb."
A mass and homily followed. The question of the burial of quartered bodies
also engaged the attention of the confraternity of Nuestro Padre Jesús Naz-
areno y la Santísima Virgen de los Dolores in Santiago de Compostela,
which, however, also provided spiritual assistance for the condemned. This
emerges from the description of a concrete, recent case that accompanied

the Spanish confraternity's request for association with the Roman arch-confraternity. The case in question was the hanging of a man named Emanuele García Sexto, carried out on April 27, 1819. The *alcalde* had handed over the prisoner to the brethren, who assisted him right up to when he was hanged; the body had then been quartered. The confraternity had asked for the return of the remains excluded from the sentence, so they could be buried.

From this correspondence we can discern a world of relationships between remote provinces of the Catholic world, united by the intangible bond of voluntary devotion to assisting the condemned: a complex task, which saw the brethren working alongside the executioner and in conjunction with the political and judicial authorities. But of all that work, what stands out from the succinct descriptions with which the various devout associations asked to be affiliated with the Roman archconfraternity is the function of burying the bodies, or what remained of them, after executions had taken place.

The picture that emerges from these papers is one of repetitive duties and rituals grounded in ancient tradition, of conflicts with parish priests over responsibility, of heated disputes with competing confraternities, and not always smooth relations with the civil authorities. The provision of assistance to the condemned seems here to have been reduced to arranging funerals and devout practices of intercession. But it had not always been like that. Originally, there had been a much more ambitious design.

⅛ 17 ⅜

Reasoning on Death Row: The Birth and Development of the Arts of Comforting

FROM THE SECOND HALF of the fifteenth century, an increasingly dense network of confraternities began to cover the peninsula, and branched out beyond the political and geographic borders of the Italian states. If we were to count the number of *stretta* companies established within preexisting *misericordie* associations, the figure would be considerable. But the importance of the task they performed cannot be measured in quantitative terms. Their members were male laypeople who belonged at least in part to the world of the intellectual professions. They were attracted by the prospect of a special kind of conquest, that of souls, and to achieve it they had to be willing to risk failure before a crowd of spectators and the public authorities. The horizons of charitable work had been changing. At the beginning, in the fourteenth century, it revolved around being present at the execution ritual, providing religious comfort to the condemned, and ensuring that their bodies were buried afterward. There was a marked distinction at that time, bordering on contestation, between the office of Christian piety and the power to condemn. But a century later a new political and social role began to emerge in the confraternities of justice— that of preserving the social peace and supporting the political power. This change in direction led to a shake-up in the internal composition of the associations, and to an increase in their public prestige and power. In the middle of the fifteenth century there were more and more signs of the new prestige surrounding the comforter's role. Guardian of the passage from earth to heaven, with the delicate and difficult task of rapidly transforming an enemy of law and order into a reconciled and protective spirit, the comforter was entrusted with an undertaking as honorable as it was taxing. It was no longer just a matter of performing straightforward acts of lay charity, such as singing *laude* and psalms. The figure of the comforter brought together the vengeance of an inexorable wordly power and the forgiveness of a God willing to compensate all suffering. He had to deal with people from very different walks of life, dispel doubts, and reconstruct, in a few short hours, a horizon of Christian beliefs and practices that had almost been erased. Men like Andrea Viarani and Pietro Paolo Boscoli demanded interlocutors able to engage on equal terms with their culture and sensibility. But so too did the river Po boatsman Piero da Codigoro, sentenced to death in Ferrara in August 1495: after initially pretending to "have passed out" so as not to have to listen to the comforters, he firmly rejected the invitation to confess, saying: "What do you want me to say, I have not sinned" (he had been condemned for murder and theft). "He ate very well," and after dinner, to avoid listening to the comforters, "he pretended to be asleep." He was hung from the window of the Palazzo Comunale, and "his body was thrown into the Po as animal bait, just as he deserved."[1] He represented a failure for the *confratelli,* though their religious sanction in declaring him possessed by the devil was important for the city. When there was no sanction, its absence was felt. Not for nothing did a city chronicler point out the exceptional nature of a summary execution that was ordered by Ercole I d'Este in 1488 without involving the confraternity.[2] The Christian regulation of the justice ritual was particularly important for a power like the Este, which in taking on the guise of a state sought sacred legitimacy, to the point of inventing the cult of a "living saint" and its stigmata. More generally, in the Italy of the small states, the ritual of death by execution became an eagerly awaited event with a key role to play in educating citizens to become "faithful" subjects and Christians. Hence the need for preparation. This took place in periodic meetings, during which the company's chapters were read out aloud, a traditional exercise of spiritual improvement. Those chosen by lot for the "service" would have an encounter with the person called "the patient" or even "the afflicted": they knew nothing about the condemned beforehand, except for their name, age, sex, and the crime they had committed. It was hard to foresee how the prisoner might react, and the night spent in their company would be long. How to comfort them? And how to answer their questions while trying to convince them that they could expect a better life than the one about to be taken away from them? To respond to these challenges they engaged in intense and concentrated reflection that found its way into the company's in-house instructions but also gave rise, thanks in part to printing, to a new literary genre spawned by experience.

The brief recommendations in the chapters of the confraternities were revised and elaborated upon with more precise instructions. But the "service" always threw up different cases and unpredictable questions. Chanting litanies and singing songs was no longer enough. It was a problem of intellectual refinement and divulgation similar to the one that had presented itself in the field of confession, the sacrament that played such a fundamental role in scaffold rituals. The answer there had been the science of cases: the organizing of scholastic moral theology into casuistic epitomes in Latin provided sufficient instruction for friars, who were by now universal specialists in that sacrament, while brief vernacular handbooks on confession helped laypeople learn what they had to say and how to practice the "medicine of the soul" (as the archbishop of Florence, the Dominican Antonino Pierozzi, put it in a text composed for simple priests unversed in Latin). The confessor, according to Innocent III, was the judge of wrongdoings and the physician of the soul's wounds. Medicating souls was the task taken on by the specialists in this field, those who had to teach how to provide reassurance and guidance to the dying in hospital or in their beds: that was the moment to sow hope and faith in the efficacy of repentance and forgiveness. The "art of dying well," like the confession handbooks that provided assistance in quickly meeting the obligation of the Easter precept, had to make the cancellation of sins appear readily achievable and facilitate in every way possible the payment of the penalties: the practice of indulgences was spreading rapidly, and not long after would prompt the theological rebellion of a young German Augustinian monk. It was not just a question of money. Admittedly, alms and donations for devout causes did play a large part in the dynamics of ecclesiastical pardons. But the rapidly evolving society of the rich trading cities, exposed to the risks of foreign voyages and adventures of all kinds, was demanding full-blown bills of exchange to cash in upon arrival in the kingdom of heaven: the letters of indulgence and the concessions providing absolution from all sins if one was in danger of death were the response to an insecurity that manifested itself in the proliferation of magic remedies— amulets, *abitelli,* charms—and had clients thronging the cells of women and men reputed to be holy.

The condition the condemned found themselves in encapsulated the extreme forms of danger most distressing to normal humanity—that of dying suddenly, and without having time to settle the accounts of the soul. Because the issue was this: confession and the absolution of sins opened up the path of penance and making amends for misdeeds with good works, the return of ill-gotten gains, and the sweeping away of all traces of hatred and enmity from human relations. It was necessary to speak about this with people who were burdened by the weight of their crimes but no longer had time to make amends for their wrongdoings. What is more, in this case the condemned prisoner had already been up before a judge. What they needed was a doctor able to console them and treat their wounds, preparing them to face the second judgment, that of God.

It was an extreme case, but it combined and concentrated the problems of every Christian—hence its fascination, not just for theologians and expert canonists, but for simple lay folk as well. A new literary genre sprang up, into which flowed the formats of consolation literature and the *Ars moriendi*. And at the very start of this strand of writing we find the groundbreaking work, the unsurpassed model, the text that, while taking on board the medieval tradition of the impersonal and collective work of mercy, gave voice to the new need for psychological penetration, personal dialogue, and the ability to move and to persuade. The work in question is a manual composed in Bologna sometime in the second half of the fifteenth century to assist the work of the School of Comforters, the new association that had quickly risen to a position of primacy in the city's religious rituality. This manual conceived of and created the task of showing how to talk to someone who had been condemned to death and to direct their thoughts along the path of a detachment from life, of forgiveness, and of a fraternal adhesion to the inscrutable will of God. The anonymity of devotion has left in the shadows the identity of the author—or rather, the authors, as the two texts forming the first and second parts of the work differ in style, and there is a discernible presence of a second author explicitly determined to differentiate his position.[3] The confidence with which the first part of the work—the *Libro de la vita beata*—deals with theological problems that attracted much discussion at the time, such as the dependence of human cases on the conjunctions of the stars, has led to the suggestion that it was written by a friar, perhaps the spiritual father of the Bolognese confraternity for which the text was composed. A clue in support of this is offered by the Ferrara copy: an attestation of the copyist Niccolò Mascarin, dated 1478, attributes the *Libro de la vita beata* to the Augustinian Cristoforo da Bologna (ca. 1380–1450), who seemingly also translated it into the vernacular.[4] The second part is more practical, instructing comforters what to do step by step in the hours between the announcement of the sentence and the execution. Its author may have been one of the School's lay members.[5] Rounding off the work is a collection of *laude* and spiritual poems of various origin (including those of Andrea Viarani). And so the union of theology, practical norms, and liturgy made up the complete design for a special art of dying well that was offered to the School of Comforters for study purposes.

The Principles of Spiritual Comfort

Though the authors of this indisputably fine work remain shrouded in anonymity, readers will note an objective difference between the first and the second text. And what can be described as the spiritual instruction proper is certainly not the work of a jobbing writer. The author displays a skillful use of the vernacular and an ability to infuse his prose with an effective mix of persuasive force and gentleness. The resulting text rightfully belongs to the best tradition of fifteenth-century vernacular religious literature. It was an immediate success with readers, becoming a manual for everyday use: it was adopted by many charitable confraternities, and numerous copies were made for the benefit of comforting companies in central and northern Italian cities such as Bologna, Ravenna, Ferrara, Padua, and Genoa. All memory has been lost of the Bolognese original. The one "for the use" of the *confratelli* in Genoa was copied from the original in the second half of the fifteenth century, and opens with an elaborate initial letter that shows two comforters at the bars of a prison in front of a condemned man.[6]

It was, as the Bolognese version of the manual states in its title, "the procedure and the way to prepare and make ready those who must go to comfort and console the people who are condemned to death" (Plate 7).[7] Indeed, the text that so effectively expressed the feelings of those who undertook this work of mercy remained closely bound up with the function for which its author had written it: to shape and guide how comforters needed to think in order to perform their task effectively. The author was not seeking literary glory, and indeed he did not receive it. This first and noblest example of an incipient literary genre circulated in manuscript form alone, and only within the circuit of the confraternities of justice. This is quite singular, considering that confession handbook literature, a competing body of work partially incorporated within the literary genre under discussion, moved from manuscript to print as soon as the new technology became available. Yet this text, which bordered on it, remained in manuscript form for centuries, and only appeared in print in historical studies of our own age, when, with the dying out of the confraternities and the dispersal of manuscript collections, traces of it were being lost. The work stands as testimony to the duration and efficacy of the general rule of preserving the secrets of the trade within the corporative associations, and of the special regulation that members were reminded of in their confraternity statutes. The diffusion of manuscript copies in the second half of the fifteenth century attests to a keen and widespread interest, and also to the care taken by the Bologna School for what was considered a glorious product and a fundamental instrument. The singularity of this fact deserves explanation.

That channels of manuscript circulation continued to survive in the print age is well known. During the Reformation and Counter-Reformation, for example, religious propaganda was distributed in manuscripts as a way to elude prohibitions and hostile control. In general, in the print age, communication by manuscript was used for special circuits of power and confidential knowledge. In the case of the Bolognese manual, a survey of the copies reveals the pattern of diffusion of the work.

The fifteen surviving manuscript copies were made in the late fifteenth and early sixteenth centuries, not for personal use but for the benefit of other companies of justice: their diffusion draws a map of confraternal relations in central-northern Italy, radiating out from Bologna in various directions.[8] In the religious economy governing the networks of lay associations, the concession of this book for copying purposes and for use by other aggregations had a precise significance: to multiply the production of the special merchandise that consisted of souls to be saved. Copied and transmitted from one confraternity to another, for centuries the manual acted as a locus for members of confraternities based in various northern Italian cities. The associative phenomenon and the importance of the function are reflected in the exceptional fortunes of a work that traversed the whole age of the print revolution without leaving a trace.

What prevented its divulgation outside of the confraternities was the secrecy surrounding the work of the *confratelli*, in compliance with the Gospel precept not to parade one's own good works. But the ancient argument was soon re-elaborated and complicated by considerations regarding the reality of the power and knowledge acquired by the companies of justice in the civic world—a reality that gave their members a prominent place in the eyes of society. For this reason the first warning found in the manual cautioned against doing the work for "any aspect of glory or mundane pomp, or to be held in high esteem by the people of this world, or to avoid disrespect of your fellow man, or for any worldy gain, or to be on everyone's lips, or to be praised, or to be able to learn the secrets or the deeds of those people, or out of revenge or out of ill will, or for faction, or for reward."[9] The list of "vain reasons" paints a picture of the change that had taken place in the companies of justice. The humble and despised task of participating in executions had been transformed into an office of great importance, for which one was "praised" and where one might learn "the secrets or deeds of those people." In the exchanges with people who had just a few hours left to live, confidences were received and circumstances revealed, turning the *confratello* dressed in the attire of the confraternity into a kind of lay confessor.

But amid the changing social considerations and the growth in prestige, the voice of the anonymous author bears the legacy of the loftiest tradition of the spirit of charity toward the condemned. And the series of warnings about how members of the School should prepare themselves for their task was inspired by this. Charity was the most fundamental thing, in the dual sense of love for God and love for one's fellow human being. The goal was to win over the soul that risked being lost. The image that springs to mind is worthy of a mercantile city and culture: "Remember that by doing this act you become a merchant of heaven, that is, you gain for God, always by his grace, new merchandise—that is, the soul of your brother." It was a very special kind of merchandise, rendering the comforter worthy of "joining together with the angels of God." The comforter had to prepare for this through prayer, confession, and Communion, and by being sober in food and drink. Then the meeting would take place with the condemned, who needed to be reminded that what was happening formed part of God's mysterious design, because it is He who "allows and lets [people] go in different ways, on different paths, and on different roads and routes under the banner of various and different deaths."[10] It was important for those about to face death to consider "how great and unknown God's judgment is." Life is in the hands of "the predestination, the providence, and the firm sentence of God." Consider "how many generations, peoples, nations, and individuals there are and have been and will be" whom God has made run under the banner of death. What was happening to the Christian brother awaiting death could be encountered by anyone: "by great lords, great masters, great princes, great barons, counts, chevaliers, doctors, merchants, and by different generations of people, the great, the small, the young, the old, the healthy, the sick, the rich, the poor, the wise and the not-so-wise, the gentleman, the courtiers, the artisans, the foreigners, and the locals." It is a rich vision of the world, of history, and society, expressed in a soaring and impassioned style, with a solemn and deeply felt eloquence where the discourse tends to assume the rhythmic and iterative course of a litany. The world is full of adversity and persecution. The condemned person should consider the Passion of Christ, the "pure lamb," who nonetheless "let himself be so mistreated, taken and tied, beaten and flogged, his bones broken, spit at, mocked and tormented, his face covered and muddied, his hair pulled and crowned, dressed in white torn rags, shouted at and cursed in his face, put on the cross and nailed, and above all else, despised."[11] Later on the author would offer up, as an example to imitate, the saints and martyrs awaiting the condemned person's soul in heaven, and recalled their sufferings, torments, and ignominious deaths. Enduring the punishments and doing as the martyrs did—that was the way to attain the well-being of the soul. The soul is like a candle inside the lantern of the body: if the soul is saved, the body will also shine once again like the lantern with a lit candle. This link between soul and body runs throughout the text, a focus on the unity of the person where we find a strongly realistic sense of the individual, something that would be lost in the subsequent development of the literary genre. It is also found in the way in which the central issue of the treatise is presented: forgiveness is "the first and holy rule," the duty to forgive every person for every wrong received and for those that will be received in the future. The word of Christ as set out in the Gospel (Matt. 18:35) is quite clear: "the forgiveness of sins is a commandment." Nor is it enough to forgive those wrongs: one must pray to God for those who have and will cause offense.[12] "You are well aware that he who does not forgive is not well in order nor tranquil nor relaxed." Not forgiving "weighs down" the soul and is "not useful for the body in any way," making it impossible to rise to heaven, "which is a temple of peace and tranquility." This is the fundamental rule governing the reciprocal relationship between creature and creator, that "if you don't forgive all of your enemies, then God will not forgive you." God will forgive if the sinner turns to him and says: "My dear Lord, do not look at the multitude of my sins, which are more than the sands of the sea and the stars of the sky and the drops of the rain; rather, look at your mercy and your immense pity, at your sweetness and your abundant benevolence."[13] Then come the rules for making a good confession and for receiving the Eucharistic sacrament, where we learn that it was customary to grant Communion to the condemned. But the sacraments are not presented in monkish terms, nor is there any concern to conform with canonic rules. What counts is the way in which the sacraments are received. There is no need to prepare the stomach, says the anonymous author, indirectly citing Augustine: to explain how to approach the sacrament, he evokes the redemption of Christ and stirs the emotions with images of intense mysticism. From the peak of emotion experienced with the sacrament it will be possible to face the test and "the shame of public execution." The condemned must remember what Christ suffered, in order not to bother about "worldly shame" when hearing the tolling of the bell and facing the crowd. The devil will try to encourage the condemned to say something in their defense, but they must not. To do so would be to fall into temptation but it would also be pointless, because if a "protest be sufficient, very many would go free." And so even if the condemned were in the right and was being put to death unjustly, they should keep their reasons to themselves—it will be of great worth in eternal life. Starting with this piece of advice about how the prisoner should behave on their final journey to the scaffold, the author concentrates his reader's attention on the description of the other world, the one that would provide the title for the Ferrara version—the *Libro de la vita beata*. There is a description of the vision of the Trinity, of the Virgin Mary, of the angelic hierarchies, of the patriarchs and prophets, and of Saint John the Baptist, who was "beheaded and his blood spilled . . . not, to speak truly, for his fault."[14] Martyrs, doctors, confessors, and virgins are listed to introduce the description of life in heaven: the "desire without need," the songs and

the sweet, continual sounds, not like here, where "today we sing and tomorrow we cry them, today we dance and tomorrow we fight to them."
This is what awaits those who die with the right disposition: because it is
the will of divine justice that the "soul shall live eternally and remain with
the intention and the disposition it had upon leaving the world."[15]

In this doctrine lies the final form of the whole argument deployed by
the author, whose aim is this, and who for good measure adds a meticulous
and insistent confutation of astral determinism—which was, in his view, an
"error that many stumble on," a very widespread heretical doctrine. There
can be no doubt that it was commonplace: the rebirth of ancient paganism
had brought with it the spread of astrology, the study of the zodiac, the practice of generations and of horoscopes; the Italian courts and the universities had opened their doors to people who occupied themselves with these
things, despite the hostile reaction of theologians and the condemnation of
the Church. And the issue was of unquestionable importance for those who
had to convince prisoners awaiting execution of the providence of a paternal
and benevolent God. Not that there was any shortage of reasons. The thesis
that the circumstances of one's death were determined by the "planet they
are born under" must have had a certain popularity in the prisons and around
the scaffolds: a final refuge in the face of the irreparable, the Egyptian science of the stars offered a way out for the desperation of the condemned.
The theologian countered the passiveness of astral determinism with a doctrine of free human will such as to limit the very omnipotence of the Christian God, who became more of a notary than a supreme judge. God's sole
task was to record a single point of all the life and of all the works and
thoughts of a life: the intention and disposition of the soul "upon leaving
the world."

If this doctrine was preached by an Augustinian hermit, as the traditional
attribution of the text to a certain Cristoforo da Bologna would have it, we
would be in the presence of a fairly singular case. The Augustine of the anti-
Pelagianistic controversy had been of an entirely different view. The long tradition of the Christian idea and practice of "conversion" had hinged on the
combination of divine grace and free human will, mixed in varying degrees.
Behind the model of Saint Dismas, the "good thief" of the Gospel story, many
stories of end-of-life repentance had been advanced.[16] Domenico Cavalca
had included in his *Leggendario dei santi* the edifying tale of the brigand who

had repented and been immediately admitted into heaven, and of the hermit who had at the last moment lost a patrimony of good works and penance. And Jacobus de Voragine had related how, for Saint Dismas, the shame of the cross had suddenly been transformed into glory: "Yet shameful as it then was, the cross is now a sign of unbounded glory."[17] All these precedents are like many streams flowing into the riverbed of the doctrine of forgiveness, which had become the foundation of scaffold comforting practices in Italian cities. Just as the prices of goods and the exchange rates for coins were fixed in market squares, so too at the public execution site the "merchant of heaven" bought the condemned person's final conversion and request for forgiveness, paying with a letter of exchange that was valid—so it was claimed—in the kingdom of heaven.

Advice and Casuistry

Earning "new merchandise" was also the aim of the second book in the Bolognese comforting manual. It resumes the plan to teach the method and form of comforting, but departs immediately and explicitly from the elaborate and extensive proposal of the author of the first part. Practical and concrete, the second book stresses the conditions and behavior required to make comforting effective. A precise goal had to be reached, and to do so it was necessary to foresee all the possible obstacles and avoid them. The condemned prisoner was to be continually presented with a crucial choice regarding the fate of their soul, which was to be done above all at the end of the final journey, before the scaffold. At this moment the person had to be told: "Let me remind you that the disposition with which the soul leaves the body is the one that will remain with you eternally."[18] The "disposition" of the soul when it leaves the body must be one of acceptance of the sentence and of forgiveness both requested and offered: it must be forged from the very beginning and protected through to the very end, when the comforter would kneel down at the level of the execution block or climb up the steps leading to the gallows. But for the comforter's advice to be accepted, it was necessary to create the conditions for being heard, in the very difficult circumstances in which the dialogue would take place. The author addresses his "companions," inviting them to adopt a simple style in their conversation with the condemned, "without creating any reputation of arrogance or vainglory."

These two characteristics were risks associated with the particular social status of the city comforters. While in much of Europe the scaffold was considered to be an inherently denigrating context, in Italy shame and dishonor were entirely absent from the viewpoint of those who donned the penitent's habit and joined the execution procession. On the contrary, the walk-on actors in the ritual had to take care not to flaunt the pride they took in what they were doing. These premises having been stated, the author offers appropriate advice for every stage of the course to death, from the moment of the sentence through to that of the execution: any signs of shame and suffering were to be transfigured in every instant into a perspective of glory and eternal pleasure.

It is worth looking at the different steps in the process as they are articulated in the manual. Upon entering the prison, some space had to be created straightaway in order to be able to speak with the condemned person. Other prisoners would tend to gather around to talk to and console the condemned person. Relatives—parents, wives, children—would also be arriving. To gain the prisoner's attention, curious onlookers and fellow inmates had to be sent away, and communication with the family kept to a minimum. All this was to be done kindly, enlisting the others, if possible, as assistants and, as required, stepping in between them. It will be necessary, says the author, "to be daring and keep speaking," so that "the weakness of the flesh" does not erase the arguments of the spirit. Once the condemned has been isolated from other people, the comforter can begin talking to them. But to say what? Certainly not to utter the solemn entreaties proposed by the author of the first part of the work. Comforters needed to bear in mind their interlocutor's abilities, language, and social and cultural background, and gain an idea of the person's character and desires. For those inclined to listen, there were stories at hand, about miracles and wrongdoers and converted Jews, of the kind used by preachers to rouse their distracted audiences. Those inclined to read were to be given devotional books, such as the Life of Christ (for example, the widely available one by Ludolph of Saxony) or Jacobus de Voragine's *Golden Legend*. If the condemned person preferred to talk, one could begin by inviting him to recite a prayer together. But experience had shown that the irremediable imminence of death tended to produce a psychological detachment or absence, a kind of mental apocalypse: the end of the world, the disappearance of any prospect of a future led to a greatly reduced capacity to listen, a state of dazed stupor. The condemned had to be shaken out of this torpor, if needs be roughly. At the same time, it was important not to exaggerate, because there was the risk of antagonizing someone who was already ill-disposed. One should use kindness and gentle words, then, taking care not to break the thread of the relationship, not least because there might always be the opportunity to secure a bequest for the Hospital of Death. The hours passed talking in this way, and the comforter had to be ready to console those who complained because they did not want to leave their wealth behind or because they were too young to die. The leitmotif was always the same: ask for forgiveness and forgive—this was the only way to save one's soul. But if at this point the "patient" wanted to know what the soul was exactly, a prudent approach was required: best not to delve into matters that are too deep, better to be like the simple, who are blessed by Christ, and to follow the rule of leaving the "secret mysteries of our Lord God Almighty" alone. Nonetheless, one could express a willingness to say something about the matter, and with all the talk the condemned person might in any case drop off to sleep for a while. And so, eventually, the first light of dawn will filter into the cell. At this point the prisoner must be gently awakened and prepared for an event that would shortly be announced by the ringing of a bell. The priest then arrives, bearing the consecrated Host, and administers the sacraments: first confession, then Communion. The comforter must "make him [the condemned] ask all those present for forgiveness."[19] At this point the tolling of a very different bell will be heard, that of the Podestà's palace. When this happens, experience shows that "most of them become completely overwhelmed and that many grow faint." The prisoner must therefore be comforted, and helped to face the three enemies battling against him: the devil, the world, the flesh. There is the thought of the public shame announced by the bell, when everyone will see him "tied and led before the people," and of the personal enemies who will be happy. The remedy is to warn the condemned about what will happen and remind him that the crowd has been summoned to pray for him, and that even his enemies know "that the soul does not leave the body in any way more secure than this."[20] The "cavalier" then arrives, ties the prisoner's hands, and leads him outside. The condemned must ask all the other prisoners and the "multitude of people" gathered in the square in front of the Podestà's palace for "forgiveness"; and he must forgive everyone in turn, from the "cavalier" to the executioner. During every phase the comforter must remain to the prisoner's right, while a companion stands to his left: "As for you, always keep beside him holding the *tavoletta* high so that he has that to see and nothing else."[21] The painted image, depicting the torments of Christ's Passion or those of the martyrs, must give an idea of the model into which the condemned person's own experience is being transfigured.

The procedure as described by the manual involved the condemned, flanked by the two comforters, being led to the *ringhiera* (orator's stand) of the Podestà's palace, where he listened to the reading of the sentence. He needed to be distracted at this point, so he did not hear the list of his crimes—he might discover it included some that he had not committed. In the meantime, the bell signaling the raising of the Host in the basilica of Saint Petronio might sound, in which case special prayers would be said. Then the prisoner left the palace and the execution procession set off (at that time it headed toward the church of San Giovanni Decollato in the market field, on the northern boundary of the city walls). There the prisoner knelt on the threshold of the church and prayed. Finally, he arrived at the execution site. And here he had to be reminded "forcefully" that if he had kept some sin or other to himself, then this was the last chance to confess it. He was to be told: "And know that you have no more time for penance and that your salvation rests in four or five words that you still have to say."[22] The end was close: the condemned placed his head on the block, and the executioner secured around his neck a yoke-like brace fitted with a blade in a slot, which the executioner would strike with a mallet to decapitate him; or, if the prisoner was to die by hanging, he would ascend the ladder to the gallows. Here the comforter had to be very careful to follow the prisoner's every movement, to keep his sight occupied by the *tavoletta* and his hearing with the words of prayer. Right up to the final instant: any movement of the *tavoletta* not synchronized with those of the executioner would put at risk not only the concentration of the "patient" but also the smooth course of the, as it were, technical side of the execution.

Of the entire tradition left to us by the medieval confraternities, what we have here is the most serious meditation on the human condition of those sentenced to death. The figure of the condemned is the focus of attention of the spiritual teacher of the Bolognese confraternity and of one of its members, who consider the prisoner's state of mind, get inside his thoughts, and try to find the best way to show their own human compassion and to offer the help that could be decisive in saving the prisoner's soul. The sentence passed down by the authorities is not called into question, and it is openly requested that all forms of collaboration with jailors and executioners should be avoided. What is brought to the attention of the condemned is the boundlessness of divine mercy. The bond between God and the world is found in the idea of the providence and benevolence of God: only by starting from here is it possible to find a positive meaning in the sentence, because it is thanks to this that the sinner will have the opportunity to consciously face up to their death and say those few words that will decide their eternal fate: "Salvation rests in four or five words," writes the Bolognese comforter. Even fewer than that, according to Dante: it is "for a tear" that the angel vanquishes the devil in the struggle to win over the soul of Buonconte (*Purgatorio,* V, 106–108). The pictorial tradition of the dispute between the white angel and the black angel now sees the appearance of a new and decisive protagonist, the confessor. An extreme case is Boccaccio's tale about Ser Ciappelletto, the notary Cepperello da Prato, who, besides leading a wicked and unreligious life, adds the final mockery of a totally fake confession, thus becoming, in death, a saint in the eyes of the people—a false saint. But we should note that Boccaccio did not stop here, with this worldly scene that, with the laughter of disenchantment, records the triumph of a usurer's astuteness and simulation over popular credulity. Inscribed within the author's Christian background and life experiences was a final possibility: that the false saint, with a last leap of remorse, became a real saint. Perhaps there was—there could have been—a final act of contrition such that "God had mercy on him and received him into his kingdom."[23] Which means that in the heaven of Ser Ciappelletto there was space for everyone. Boccaccio's God was still the God of Dante that "willingly forgives," who "takes those that turn to Him." This was the mercy, or *misericordia,* after which the confraternal associations were named, and it was in order to have a share of the beatitude promised to the merciful that would-be brothers preferred to join, if possible, the one dealing with people found guilty of serious crimes and who faced imminent death with no possibility of making amends for their wrongs. As has been observed, "the experience of the person condemned to death, or at any rate of someone who knows they are to die, is not comparable to any other, and involves an exceptional degree of tension (perhaps also religious). But symptomatically the experience became, in this period, the subject of many devotional writings."[24] Words and images from the Bolognese manuscript appear not coincidentally in Fra Francesco da Mozzanica's *Ricordo di fare il transito felice de la morte,* printed in Milan in 1510: "No one should despair of God's mercy, even if he has committed more robberies, thefts, and murders, and other very great and repulsive sins, than there are drops of water in the sea or grains of sand, even if he has never performed penance in his life, nor confessed, not even if, when dying, he was unable to confess." And the anonymous author of a *Trattato devotissimo della misericordia de Dio,* printed in Bologna in 1521 and very probably linked to the School of Comforters, even promised a Christ so merciful as to forgive any sin, including one committed against the Holy Spirit—and not just once but "the thousands of millions of sins against the Holy Spirit."[25] If it was possible that concentrated in one person there were

> the sins of all the infernal devils and, again, of all the men who in this world have ever been and ever will be heretics, schismatics, Moors, Saracens, Turks, and Jews, and also of all perverse Christians tainted and sullied by all the wicked acts and vices that can possibly be said and thought [and this person] wanted to return to God and convert and be fully contrite, God is so good and so charitable, so merciful and clement, that He will graciously receive him and confer his mercy upon him.[26]

The example is again the Gospel story relating to Saint Dismas: "the thief deserved to be in heaven for a single moment of penitence in the hour of his final confession . . . as he was suffering, he repented, and by virtue of a single word of confession he deserved to have heaven as his abode. . . . Do not delay, then, oh soul burdened by sins, to convert to God while you have time, because as you have seen, conversion is never too late."[27] The general argument was reaffirmed in the conclusion of the book: "By his mercy and compassion God frees every sinner that converts to him with true contrition from all the pestiferous effects of sin and receives him among the chosen ones to enjoy the glory of heaven in perpetuity *in secula seculorum.* Amen."[28] The only condition was the "tear," the sign and expression of true contrition. It was in the tear that remorse was summed up and concentrated, and where conversion took place. This entailed a setting aside of the whole complicated structure of moral cases developed for the use of confessors, in which different types of sins were distinguished and special powers requested to remit the more serious ones. A confession made in the imminence of death ("in articulo mortis") was a special one: the person who was to die had the right to have all their sins canceled, without distinction and by any priest. It was an extraordinary privilege, which those embarking on long and dangerous journeys consequently tried to obtain. The papal bulls granting them were highly prized documents, preserved with care and held ready for any necessity. Now the situation of the condemned officially met the conditions for the granting of this privilege, a prospect that could hold a certain dark appeal to consciences burdened by the weight of shameful, unconfessable sins. It would be seen in operation in certain extreme cases when the decision to go to the gallows was taken deliberately in order to benefit from the privilege of being absolved by special sentence from the torment of intolerable sins or from the fear of being predestined to hell: this is how the would-be regicide Jean Chastel explained his decision to assassinate Henry IV in 1598.[29] Such was also the case (to which we will return) of those who chose the path described as "indirect suicide"—killing innocent children (destined for heaven) in order to be certain of being put to death but also of having time to express remorse.[30] These constituted extremes in the use of the sacramental powers of the remission of sins. Effectively, it was around this time that the case of those condemned to death became the most advanced field of experimentation for an issue that divided consciences and set the whole of Europe on fire. What we have here are the premises of the Lutheran revolt against the sale of indulgences, when the Saxon monk overturned the logic of a penance fragmented and dramatized in exceptional, discontinuous acts and gestures, and in its place proposed the idea that the Gospel invitation to convert meant something quite different: that the penance required of the Christian should affect the whole of one's life. The fact remains that on the eve of the Lutheran Reformation the bulls of indulgence, like the letters of confession to use when one's life was endangered, were very precious to the institutions and people who managed to obtain them. This was the case, for example, with the plenary indulgence granted by the Spanish pope Alexander VI in 1496 to visitors to the Portuguese hospital of Santa Maria del Popolo at the request of Queen Eleonora of Portugal.[31] Concessions like these encouraged an influx of devotees and almsgiving. The sanctuary or hospital that possessed such an indulgence guaranteed pilgrims, the devout, and the people who went there a much appreciated opportunity. This gave the condemned person's confession a special attraction.

To understand why the question of conversion *in extremis* found its most powerfully dramatic locus in the scaffold, we need to take account of the fact that God's boundless mercy was being emphasized against the backdrop of increasing violence being done by the earthly courts: the machinery of execution worked without pause in the fifteenth and sixteenth centuries. The forms of legal violence illustrated in images accompanying the first European penal codes, and in paintings, speak volumes, just as the partial statistics currently known to us document the growing cruelty of political and religious powers. The language of mercy and the real scenarios of suffering and death inflicted in the name of justice went, as it were, hand in hand in city squares. They were bound together by an institutional tie to the power that punished and the one that forgave: the division between spiritual and temporal guaranteed their autonomy and regulated the alliance. In the ritual procession to the scaffold the comforter walked alongside the executioner, but he did so to obtain the sign of conversion. This is what the confession and the granting of the sacraments were for, this was the aim of the words of contrition requested of the condemned and offered as a possibility right to the very last moment of life. An interpretation of mercy as the boundless dispensing of God's forgiveness, capable of breaking up all juridical rigidity and formalism, threw up other possibilities as well. In the sixteenth century, the extent of God's mercy was the picklock that opened the door to extreme heretical outcomes involving a rejection of institutional membership in any church whatsoever. It also provided the comforter confraternities with grounds for exalting the importance of sacramental confession and consequently the powers of the Church as the sole holder of the right of access of the body to burial and of the soul to eternal salvation. This contradiction marked the experience of the comforting companies in the century that saw them spreading in a capillary fashion throughout Italy and expanding beyond the boundaries of the peninsula and even of the European world.

The history of the rules and recommendations for members of the companies of justice seems repetitive and unchanged, but this was only apparently the case. The course of the procedures and rhetoric of persuasion remained that of a timeless devout murmuring, but there were changes not only in the social and political framework of the confraternity but also in the theological inflection that the authors drew from the various religious orders to which they belonged, which were the prevalent and almost exclusive origin of such literature. After the early fifteenth-century production of anonymous devout vernacular texts, the sixteenth century began with an extensive literature of manuals preparing readers for death. Many of these were the work of preachers belonging to religious orders that, following the model of Girolamo Savonarola, printed reflections, advice, or formulas which, they assured, would be efficacious in the event of grave and imminent danger. But the question of how to face up to death and the judgment of God was too important for it not to also inspire a culture of simple laypeople, often engaged directly and personally in comforting. Once the flames of controversy surrounding the movement of Martin Luther had taken hold, the issue of how to set at rest consciences disturbed by the threat of death and the burden of sins gave rise to contrasting and increasingly divergent choices. The autonomous voice of the companies of justice remained confined within manuals and regulations for internal use, but it also made headway as a general message of exaltation of God's mercy. From the second half of the sixteenth century onward, a specialized literature sprang up in this regard, produced almost exclusively by members of religious orders, with one or two rare offerings by the spiritual directors of the confraternities. It was too delicate a matter to risk opinions not backed by collective bodies able to vouch for and conclusively demonstrate the author's orthodoxy. This literature dealt with the preparation for death of a special category, which, however, became an experimental sample for the condition of all humanity.

The Rules: Instructions and Manuals

As we have seen, the art of comforting had begun during the late fifteenth century as an autonomous section of the literary genre of the *Ars moriendi*. Its rules had been fixed in the statutes of the *stretta* companies established within the Battuti confraternities. The collections of *laude* and prayers in the popular "books of companionship," illustrated with devout images and circulated by publishers from the very early days of movable-type printing, sufficed for members of the *larga* companies. The rhythm and rhymes of these compositions facilitated mnemonic learning and stirred the emotions, moving people to contrition and forgiveness. The prayer to recite "in the cemetery for dead Christian worshippers" was combined with the exhortation to draw from the death of others the stimulus to ask God's forgiveness for one's own sins:

> Leva su non dormire
> se troppo indusii per tua negligentia
> udirai la sententia:
> vanne all'inferno ingrato peccatore.
> O Iesu salvatore
> Mia [*sic*] miserere mei
> Di fallimenti mei
> Dico mia colpa con el contrito core.[32]

> (Rouse yourself! Don't sleep!
> If you tarry too long in your negligence
> You will hear the sentence:
> Get to hell, ungrateful sinner.
> Oh Savior Jesus,
> Have mercy upon me,
> Upon my failings.
> I confess my sin with contrite heart.)

God's answer provided the reassurance of the most extensive forgiveness:

> Io sono el dolce Idio anima ingrata
> I son Iesu che ti feci sí bella
> I son lo sposo tuo che t'ho sposata
> I son facto fratel di te sorella
> . . . .
> I son perdonator di colpe e pene
> Perché non torni a me anima mia?

> (Ungrateful soul, I am the sweet Lord
> I am Jesus, who made you so beautiful.
> I am your groom, who married you.
> Became brother to you, sister
> . . . .

I am he who remits sins and punishments
Why don't you return to me, my soul?)

And the soul that confessed itself worthy of hell was addressed by the spiritual father of the company, who recalled "the ineffably bitter passion that our Lord steadfastly bore when crucified upon the cross . . . for which, most human brothers, we do not wish to be ungrateful for such immense goodness."

In becoming involved with matters of justice and execution, the Christian charity of the lay companies had ended up creating a professional specialization with the establishment of the socially and culturally selective *stretta* companies operating in conjunction with those who had the power over life and death. What had been conceived as an extension of the charitable work of assisting the dying and burying the dead in holy ground had been transformed into a function of increasing importance for the secular and ecclesiastical powers. Fragile and threatened, the uncertain powers of the Italian cities had particular need for religious legitimation in the crucial area of the administration of justice. Here there was no unction of the sacred ampulla of the French kings or the sacred aura of the empire to guarantee divine sanction in an age in which it was possible to legitimate the power to kill the sovereign only in the name of God's will. The proof of the redemptive function of power had to be sought out from the bottom up: if the wrongdoer was transformed into a penitent sinner, into a model of Christian death, the whole scene of power was redeemed.

It was an important and delicate task, and it stirred up jealousies and suspicions in both the ecclesiastic and the political camps—not just for the knowledge that might be gleaned during the nighttime conversations with the more important condemned prisoners, but also because of the theological sensitivity and riskiness of the arguments used to comfort and guarantee eternal salvation. Among these, the original one had been the ideal of divine mercy itself, so deeply felt by those who, by joining the confraternities, had pinned all their hopes of salvation on the reciprocal pact between human works of mercy and divine forgiveness. The comforters promised eternal salvation and immediate access to the kingdom of heaven for those who accepted capital punishment as an opportunity offered by divine providence to convert and repent of one's sins. This was the idea sustained by the *Libro devotissimo della misericordia:* and it was onto this extreme conviction, resolving every fear, that the new morality fueled by the Lutheran theology of the Cross was grafted. One could be saved by faith alone, not by human works: faith in the benefit earned by Jesus Christ on the Cross. In the middle of the sixteenth century there was convergence on this point from various circles: from those influenced directly by the preaching of Reformation ideas to those that tried to give expression to traditional themes and forms of religious piety. Although in Lucca in 1543 the final words of the conspirator Pietro Fatinelli to his fellow citizens before dying on the scaffold had a distinctly Reformist ring, the theme of "general forgiveness" and of the general predestination to salvation ensured the extraordinary success of a small book that has been described as the best seller of the Italian Reformation—the *Trattato utilissimo del beneficio di Cristo.* The theme of the immense breadth of the heavenly kingdom, able to receive everyone, would become the core of the extreme message of Italian heresy with Celio Secondo Curione.

In this case too the literary genre grew out of a tradition rooted in experience. The members of the *conforterie* were generally cultured laypeople, led by churchmen who acted as spiritual leaders but also as active members of the confraternities, or as experts in legal and theological issues. The problems manifested themselves more and more in the transition from providing the condemned with a comforting human presence to the duty to bend their will to the requirements of the political and religious powers. Members were attracted by the prospect of performing the feat that, more than any other, was extolled and celebrated by the culture and religious propaganda of the age: to save souls. What the missionaries did by embarking on dangerous journeys and visiting unknown lands could be achieved on the comforters' own doorstep. The condemned was the closest and at the same time the most remote figure imaginable: already torn from their habitual social setting by their crime, they were about to take the definitive step from life to death. Through contact with the condemned, comforters could test their own fear of death while at the same time earning merit in God's eyes. But there was the risk of failing before the watching crowd and the public authorities, hence the need for preparation. This was done in periodic meetings during which the chapters of the company were read—a traditional exercise of spiritual perfecting common to all the confraternities. But what awaited those who would be drawn by lot for the "service" was an encounter fraught with uncertainties: the "patient," or "afflicted," was not known to them, and the person's behavior from the moment they were notified of the sentence would have been entirely unpredictable. A long night together awaited them, during which it was not a question of comforting with fraternal company, with food and drink. Indeed, the instructions on this were clear: material comforts were to be kept to a bare minimum, as overly abundant wine and food would dull their minds. A total "conversion" needed to be obtained from the condemned, from this life to the promised one in the afterlife, from the court that had condemned them on earth to that of God. How could their thoughts and emotions be governed? They were people rendered impotent by shackles and by being entirely in the grip of power: it was necessary to transform that weakness into collaboration, to turn criminals brutalized by prison into obedient protagonists of a sacred representation, human beings terrorized by death into fearless martyrs, and to convince those about to die that their executioner was doing it for their own good. At the end the condemned was to be the one who thanked the judges and the executioner, and offered the crowd the example of a willingly accepted death. There was very little time for all this, so how could such a difficult challenge be met? The comforters would need to be able to answer the prisoners' questions, of which there would be many. Efforts would be made to convince them that another life awaited them, better than the present one. This was what prompted the long text on the *vita beata* for the use of the *confratelli,* and the text instructing them how to proceed depending on the personality of the "patient." These first preparation writings remained in manuscript form, the invaluable patrimony of a very particular craft, the trade secrets of a corporation that could be copied for companies in other cities as a gesture of spiritual fraternity but that remained the jealously guarded property of the confraternity. The copies that have survived, embellished with carefully illuminated scenes, bear witness to the presence of the work in the life and in the periodic meetings of the confraternity. More than a century later, the author of another substantial manual of instructions, Pompeo Serni, would explained very clearly the

212 · CRIME AND FORGIVENESS

pride the Roman confraternity took in its craft and why it was resistant to rendering public its wealth of accumulated experience and knowledge. Setting such things down in writing was already viewed with suspicion: the members of the confraternity were not "happy for our customs and ways of practicing this work of piety to be propagated in writing": there were competitors ready to undertake the work if given half a chance. It was therefore necessary to keep the secrets of the art to themselves and to try to "be able to do it better than any one else with complete exactness." All the more so as mistakes and the presumption of knowing how to do it without having learned first might "endanger the soul of some of the executed," for which "serious account would have to be rendered to God."[33]

But with the age of printing and the religious upheavals in European Christianity, the secrets for winning over souls on the scaffold had become invaluable for the rulers of society. Mention has already been made of the need that political powers had for religious sanction to discipline society. For their own part, the ecclesiastical hierarchies of the Catholic Church were anxious to demonstrate—in the face of the challenge posed by the Reformation—that their work was precious and that the spiritual power of the clergy was needed to ensure social peace. It was thanks to the Church, according to Giovanni Botero, that subjects could be led to bind "not only their bodies and faculties but also their souls and consciences" to princes, putting up with "everything in order not to disturb the peace."[34] This was the answer to the question that troubled political thinking at the time: How and why was the power of a single person endured and obeyed by entire peoples? The people were like a wild beast to be tamed. The outcome of the prime spectacle of power—the behavior of the condemned on the scaffold—had to encapsulate the substance of the lesson of obedience. The people were inclined to conform, provided that the peace was not disturbed and everyone could continue to lead their normal lives. And they would do so even more willingly after witnessing the triumph of a power that acted against the disobedient and against dangerous rebels who flouted the law, a power thanked and legitimated by the very people who were being put to death. This was true also because the public did not feel passive but were involved emotionally in the religious ritual of judicial killing: they contributed to its successful outcome with prayers and alms, granted and asked for forgiveness, and displayed abhorrence for the crime while preparing to invoke the protection of the criminal who had become a saintly soul in heaven.

Irrespective of its political and social significance, the feat of transforming or converting the condemned was viewed by those who took part in it as being of fundamental importance. This is borne out by a body of documentary and narrative sources that, judging by what has remained, must once have been extraordinarily large. A significant place in this tradition was held by the treatises and manuals that aimed to put the rules of comforting down in writing. Having become institutional entities, the lay *misericordia* confraternities had to deal with the competition of the religious orders, especially with regard to the most sought-after and difficult task: comforting those who had been sentenced to death. The organization of the *stretta* company had been the decisive choice. The creation of a specialized group professionally devoted to providing spiritual assistance to the condemned and to orchestrating the public phase of the execution ritual was the winning card in vying with the religious orders. The *stretta* was made up of an elite group representative of the hegemonic classes in society, associated by culture and social status with the circles of power. The statute rules normally envisaged periodic meetings given over to preparation and in-depth study of the methods of spiritual comforting. This was done by reading the statutes themselves, but also through meditation and discussion, which was where the activity of the authors of instructions and manuals was particularly intense: it was the members of the religious orders above all who placed their experience and theological learning at the service of the laypeople operating in prisons and at execution sites. However, simple lay folk also addressed the task. This gave rise to a new literary genre that flourished remarkably in the sixteenth and seventeenth centuries. The catalogue of titles in the library of the Bologna confraternity, published in 1729 by Carlo Antonio Macchiavelli, the prior of the Bologna School of Comforters and a jealous preserver of its memories, consists of around a hundred works.[35] Another similarly rich list was drawn up in the same period by Girolamo Baruffaldi, the archpriest of Cento, who did a survey of the volumes owned by the Ferrara confraternity of Santa Maria Annunziata.[36] The sense of belonging to their respective confraternities and the quest for literary glory spurred on the two erudite men to special efforts in gathering together sources, drawing up documents, and composing detailed accounts. These literary and erudite aspirations

chart the evolution of the ancient confraternities into full-blown academies. The abbot Carlo Antonio Macchiavelli, unable to resist the desire to
ennoble himself and his lineage, even invented an ancestor, Luigi di Lion-
ardo Macchiavelli, and attributed to him the masterpiece of comforting literature, the fifteenth-century *Modo e forma,* falsifying the name of the author on the copies he managed to get his hands on. He wanted to insert
himself and a whole string of forebears into the history of a powerful and
respected institution, "composed," as can be read in the catalogue's dedication, "of subjects distinguished for their offices, nobility, and virtue."[37] He
was not held back by the obligation to perform his office "only out of love
for God and for the charity and health of one's fellow citizens," as stated in
the first lines of the treatise. In his age, and that of his colleague and imitator Girolamo Baruffaldi, the authorial ambitions of moralists, theologians,
and jurists had invaded the literature of instructions regarding assistance for
the condemned. Hanging over their ordering of memories, organizing of archives, and writing of regulations was something of the spirit of Ludovico
Antonio Muratori. But their ordering enables us to see how much the production of writing about comforting the condemned had grown in the space
of two centuries.

This literature—apparently timeless, given its generalizing nature and the
common core of theological teachings, legal norms, and religious readings—
sprang from local contexts and attempted to work through real experiences
in order to draw suggestions and precepts from them. When, in the sixteenth
century, printing became a major player in what was a revived and very top-
ically pertinent literary genre, the contribution of laypeople began to fade
increasingly. The subject was too delicate for it to be left to confraternity
members to shape and elaborate. And yet there were instances of lay members printing rules and advice designed to facilitate the effective course of
their shared endeavor—where, that is, their presence was not undermined
by the advance of the religious orders. Unfortunately, the first book of printed
instructions about regulating one of these confraternities cannot currently
be traced: it was written by the Perugian notary Ser Giovanni Maffani for
the company of justice of his native city, which had been recently reformed
with the merging of the confraternities of Sant'Andrea and San Bernardino.[38]
But in the meantime the new vernacular literature and the printing press

intersected with some of the outcomes of the impassioned religious discussions of the early sixteenth century. We have already come across a *Libro devotissimo della misericordia de Dio* in Bologna, which may have been written in circles close to the School of Comforters. For the Roman confraternities, on the other hand, a treatise was printed under the names of the Florentine Dominican Fra Zanobio and the cleric and scholar Tullio Crispoldi from Rieti, published—as Pompeo Serni would attest a century later—"with the common intent and approval" of the confraternity.[39] From trust in the universal law of forgiveness, extolled in his pamphlet of 1537, Crispoldi had moved toward an increasingly pious rigidity that had led him to raise the bar for eternal salvation. Perhaps in part due to his experience of collaborating with the Roman confraternity, he had come to realize that many of the condemned "who desperately were for living and for dying" had converted "because of the example of this thief [Saint Dismas]"; and for this reason judged it best to warn of the risk of falling into the "license of sinning for this example, drawing hope of saving oneself at the end with just a few words."[40]

But in the field of comforting the condemned, the work that left the most profound and lasting trace sprang from the fledgling Society of Jesus. It was written by the historian, organizer, and author Juan Alonso de Polanco (1516–1576), the most outstanding mind among the companions of Ignatius of Loyola. Already the author of a brief instruction to "help" confessors, printed in Rome in 1554 and then published and translated numerous times, Polanco wrote a manual of instructions that laid down the principles of a special method to help the dying (*Methodus ad eos adiuvandos qui moriuntur*).[41] The method was based on a simple but effective idea, that of considering those who were about to die as a category that included all the living. Just like the physician, for whom all human beings fall sick and require treatment, the Jesuit confessor saw before him a humanity made up of people who were to die: reminding everyone that they are only temporarily alive was the first step in meditating on how to prepare for death. In itself this was not an original thought. Earthly life as illusionary reality in contrast with the eternal life that awaits everyone after death had been the key theme of the medieval monastic asceticism that spread throughout society with the epidemics and wars of the fourteenth and fifteenth centuries. But now, in a changed scenario, the theme of the precariousness of earthly existence was presented together with the offer of sacramental help as a stable bond of the lay community with the ecclesiastical body. The image of the dying in the engravings of the fifteenth century had been that of a man lying on his bed, dictating his will to a notary and confessing to a priest, while an angel and the devil contended for the outcome of his soul. Around him was a stable, well-ordered society. But that context had now disappeared: death loomed large for everyone, and was liable to be sudden, hence the need to be ready to offer the necessary spiritual help to convince the dying person to confess and thus to save their soul. The exemplary case in this regard was those condemned to death, burdened by the weight of their misdeeds and needing to undergo, in the very brief span of time left to them, a profound conversion, from their culpable ties with the world to a total trust in divine mercy. The Jesuit offered the help of the confessor as a mediator of divine forgiveness, armed with the twin arguments of God's mercy and the easiness of salvation.

Polanco's recipe was universal. Death invaded the whole of life because it could occur at any moment, and it affected all human beings. So the invitation to see themselves in the condition of the condemned was directed at everyone. The Jesuit confessor had to be ready to seize any opportunity to win souls. The contest was played out in precarious conditions and over a short period of time. This explains why Polanco's text was like a handy reference book. One point that must be mentioned about this work relates to the dominant role that the Jesuits would soon also acquire in the prisons and by the scaffold. Polanco was the first Jesuit to formulate norms and suggestions about "tricks" *(industriae)*—the art of "adapting" to different contexts and individuals, exploiting the possibilities offered by concrete reality, and resorting to astuteness and dissimulation in the practice of religious conquest.[42] His *Methodus* applied that general principle to the situation of the relationship between the confessor and the person who was to die: reminding the latter that their condition was the general one of all living beings was the first step toward getting them to make their confession.

The success of the Jesuits' proposal could be measured by their ability to carve out space for themselves in the comforting of the condemned. The reports that came back from their initial outposts spoke increasingly of confessions secured from condemned people. In Florence, where they presented themselves armed with words of caution and advice from Polanco himself, they were, already in 1585, "busy confessing the infirm in the hospitals and the prisoners in jail, especially when these were to be executed." And they were able to report that they had won the contest against other competitors in the art of consoling, of which there was no shortage in the city ("many virtuous and religious men"). They had demonstrated it by saving from despair a condemned man "who did not want to listen in any way to talk about matters of God."[43] A success story in the hometown of the ancient and well-established Compagnia dei Neri was no mean achievement, especially as it took place in a context marked by other successes of the same kind. In the meantime, Polanco's *Methodus* had a significant reception in Italian cultural circles as well. It was in the milieu of Tasso and the Italian literary world that the work was translated into the vernacular. This was important for two reasons. First, for the person who figured as the author, even though he was not: Ercole Tasso, a man of letters from Bergamo now much less well-known than his renowned cousin but who at the time was a prominent and active presence among Italian literati and publishers, as shown by the collection of dedicatory letters that the publisher Comino Ventura linked to his name in 1601.[44]

In his free translation of Polanco's work, Ercole Tasso, while not concealing the identity of the original author, claimed the merit for it with readers: as he wrote in the dedication, what he had contributed was not only the language but also the actual practice of what was indicated in the title, which was *Il confortatore,* the comforter.[45] Tasso was one of four administrators of the Misericordia Maggiore of Bergamo, the city's centuries-old charitable institution, and as can be deduced from his words, he was active as a comforter. In the dedication to "his loving fellow men," Ercole addressed the *confratelli* with whom he shared comforting duties. He asked those special companions to prepare him for death at the opportune moment. He did not ask his wife and children, "because the natural tenderness toward one's dying [loved ones] breaks almost everyone's heart." Tasso confessed that he was weak in the face of the biggest tests, of which death was the biggest of them all, so great that all the defenses of philosophy did not suffice to face it. But in reading Polanco's writing he had found the medicine he had been looking for. This was the "only and certain antidote"—the true and universal remedy for curing the fear of death. And just like an antidote, the medicine needed to be applied to the dying person by experts. The confession of weakness and need that prompted his request was, at that time and on the part of an author with his name, a declaration of surrender to religion by the Italian literary and philosophical culture of the age. In the Tasso family's circles the scruple of orthodoxy and the fear of heresy constrained the literary work to defer to the school of Jesuits and to fear the danger of heresy above all else. Dominating here was the religious poetry of the Benedictine Angelo Grillo, who, having survived the season of the heretical sect of Giorgio Siculo, directed his entire output toward a gloomy meditation on death.[46]

The advice offered by Ercole Tasso to lay comforters consisted of the by now canonic suggestions: it was necessary to persuade the "languishing" that the desperation over eternal salvation was a diabolic temptation and that the only judge who could condemn human beings was Christ: "who does not sentence before death, having given us until the very last breath of life the faculty to deserve"; and if the despair stemmed from the burden of sins committed, the person about to die should be reminded that they could always present, as amends for their faults, what they were now suffering and had suffered throughout their life.[47] It was a version, and one that would be very successful, of the doctrine of the value of works that the Roman Church had set out in opposition to the Lutheran thesis of justification by faith alone. The God it portrayed was not the judge of the Apocalypse, who opens the book where everything a human being has done is written down and will be used to judge them. Nor was he the merciful father from the Gospels. This God is a tax collector, who waits at the passage of death, carefully checking the means of payment possessed by the arriving soul. We are a long way here from the mysticism of God's immense mercy, and likewise from the Lutheran theology of the Cross or the Calvinist doctrine of predestination. A specific line of reasoning was used to explain to the condemned the middle way to take: it was necessary to avoid extremes, that of placing too much trust in the value of one's works and the opposite one of attributing "everything to the mercy of God."[48] Everyone in danger of death had to keep this in mind: but the principle applied especially to those "condemned to death by earthly justice." The third and final part of the work was devoted to them.[49] And here the religion of works was transformed into a religion of intentions, adapting to the circumstances of the person who had no more time to work in the world: was one not condemned by divine justice to the eternal flames for homicidal intentions or desire for another man's woman, just as one was for homicide and adultery? Following the same criteria, it would be enough to offer God the desire to give alms and to fast if there was no time to actually do these things. As for making amends for wrongs committed, the good example of steadfastly enduring the punishment would be enough to make up for the scandal caused by the crime. The condemned person who thinks it is no longer possible to compensate for their misdeeds with a Christian life is to be told that the torments of the executioner and death on the scaffold are good works that can represent the right weight on the scales of justice, if only they are faced with the intention to offer them as atonement for their sins. In this way, the judge passing sentence for a crime becomes a vehicle of providence: the punishment he inflicts on the criminal is transformed—so the skilled comforter argues—into the penance of the confessor.[50] Judge and confessor exchange roles, crime and sin lose all distinction.

The work ends with a series of brief formulas and prayers whose function was to earn, for the person about to die, the remission of all punishment in the life to come. Not that this was guaranteed, but reliance was placed on the final thoughts of a person who, by repeating the formulas of prayer a given number of times, imagines they will be able to ascend to the blessed life of the saints immediately after death. In this way, Ercole Tasso, a lay man of letters and an important member of a city *misericordia,* by making Polanco's text his own and offering it with full honors to the literary society of his time, adhered to the new Tridentine morality of intentions and works, and proposed an alliance of secular literary culture with the Society of Jesus on the decisive terrain of the conversion of the dying and those condemned to death.

From other texts there emerged a different and more practical, concrete kind of advice born out of experience rooted in individual confraternities. The sensibilities of the authors varied, and there were local variables in terms of rituals, but the compactness of the model, by now formalized in the literary comforting genre, appears clear. Not for nothing was the manual written by the churchman Domenico Caparozzi for the Compagnia di San Giovanni Decollato in Viterbo, presented in the author's dedication to the *confratelli* as "drawn wholly from the holy Scriptures, from many doctors and theologians of the Holy Church, and from other approved authors, who have written extensively on this subject."[51] Divided into three parts, the work first describes the ritual as it was to be observed by members of the confraternity. It starts with the *confratelli* coming outside "dressed in their garments, with crowns in hand, with our customary crucifix, hooded, in pairs and in silence." This is followed by the public procession, the execution, and then the final steps: "remove the dead [body] from the gallows, and place it in the coffin, cover it with our usual cloth, all of this with love and in silence." The lay brothers charged with the task "were not to be disgusted" by it. They should think of the example of Nicodemus, who buried Christ. They also buried the criminal's body in the company's church, or elsewhere if so ordered. The noose would be removed from the hanged person's neck and replaced "in the customary box with the others, with all faith and good care."[52] The brothers also had to remember to keep silent about everything that had been said or done by the condemned person, and they were to write to the dead person's family and try to console them with the news that their relative had died in a Christian manner. Among the suggestions and things for the company to remember, there was the obligation to maintain a rigorous distinction of roles between priests and laypeople: the former were to avoid any risk of irregularity by giving material assistance. Their task was to administer the sacraments: confession, Communion, and perhaps reconciliation. A priest would say Mass, and, depending on the view of the confessor, would consecrate a particle, which the condemned would then receive "by way of comfort":[53] it was just necessary to ensure that this took place at least three hours before the execution, in the opinion of the renowned doctor Navarro, Martín de Azpilcueta.[54]

The *confratelli* in Viterbo sometimes came across prisoners who, fearful of being tortured, accused themselves, and others, of concocted crimes: here provision needed to be made for a special form of reparation, to be effected with a formal deed drawn up and signed by two witnesses, "or at the site of execution, out aloud and in a clear voice, publicly."[55] Details of the reparations and the bequests made by the condemned would be noted by the company archivist, who would keep an orderly record of many things:

> Name, surname, place of origin, and age of the criminal; under whose authority he had been condemned, the reason why, the day, month, and year; likewise, if he exculpates anyone, either in the chapel or at

the place of execution, in the presence of whom, again noting the names, surnames, and places of origin of witnesses with the notary, if any are present; where and in what place the execution was carried out; if he died as a good Christian, if he had a wife, and finally, where he was buried.

A second and more substantial part of the treatise deals with the things imagined as being said to the condemned in order to convince them to accept the sentence. The principle remained the same: "human justice is the minister of divine providence . . . This sentence derives from God."[56] They could, then, be "certain and sure that the sentences and determinations of our temporal superiors are decrees of God."[57] And they should be consoled by the knowledge "that heaven is fuller with those who have died this violent death at the hands of the judges than with others."[58] The same concept would be expressed centuries later in a satirical sonnet written in Roman dialect by Giuseppe Gioacchino Belli.

Along the course of the route taken, in full sight of the assembled crowd, the comforters had to be constantly engaged. There were words to say and prayers to recite, and the *tavoletta* had to be kissed constantly while the priest sprinkled holy water over the condemned. And then the arrival of the procession at the scaffold (transfigured into Mount Calvary in the image suggested to the person who was to die), the kneeling in front of the gallows, further sprinkling of holy water, and the climb up the ladder, followed by the *confratello,* who would cover the victim's face well with the *tavoletta.*[59] The raised position of the scaffold could be seen by the condemned person as offering the occasion to publicly "absolve" those who may have wrongly accused them. But from the comforters' perspective this was risky and to be avoided. Finally, there was the final act of faith, in response to the question: "Do you believe everything that the Holy Roman Catholic Church holds and confesses, and confirm that you wish to die in it?"[60] After the crucifix had been kissed and the name of Jesus uttered, it was time for the executioner to do his work, bringing the spectacle to a close. At this point the *confratelli* "left, rosaries in hand and hooded, silently and in procession," returning to the oratory, where they recited the customary prayers.

Of course, everything did not always go smoothly, as prisoners were sometimes recalcitrant. The third part of the work suggests some strategies for dealing with those who resisted, if needs be by resorting to threats. For instance, they might be told: "Your body will be buried together with animals, and your soul will immediately become prey for devils, tormented for all eternity in hell. All men will condemn you for your dishonor."[61] The comforters might cry, implore, curse, and even pretend to leave and abandon the prisoner, but they would not desist right until the end, And if, climbing the ladder to the scaffold, the condemned finally decided to repent, an adequate suspension could be obtained from the officials of justice so the person could confess.

Among the works written by ecclesiastics, it is worth mentioning that of the canon Francesco Isella, the spiritual father of the Compagnia della Misericordia di Santa Maria del Sole in Lodi, who printed his *Istruttione* in 1586.[62] He had been inspired by the work of Polanco, referred to right from the very first pages. And he was driven by the conviction that the task undertaken by his company was the "office of Apostles, of Angels, or rather, of God."[63] To make the work more effective, he made suggestions to his fellow *confratelli* but also offered them in ideal terms to anyone engaged in the same enterprise. His text dealt with the practical procedures required of the *confratelli*. Experience prompted him to suggest that it was useful to maintain a regular presence in the prisons, so that the appearance of the *confratelli* there was not automatically associated with executions, potentially creating panic. It was also a way of learning more about the prisoners. Knowing their origins *(patria)*, habits, job, and relatives could help the *confratelli* to be better prepared for the moment when they might have to intervene to comfort someone if news arrived of an imminent sentence. In any case, Isella suggested not being the first people to present themselves to the prisoner after notification of the execution order, waiting instead "in a separate place from the others."[64] The condemned would be prompted to make a general confession, according to the Jesuit model that seemed by now to be in common use. As for preparing for the suffering that lay ahead, the work contains a long repertoire of martyred saints, with appropriate examples for the most disparate categories of person. It is what all these writings tried to do. But Isella did something more: he extended the list to include women, offering examples of female saints. We do in fact know that the *tavolette* used by the confraternities also bore images of martyred female saints.[65] And this is a demonstration of the adherence of Isella's work to the actual practice of comforting. His main concern was to overcome the resistance of those who he described as stubborn. Among the arguments used, he suggests recalling the names of those who, though innocent, patiently accepted death, including recent Catholic martyrs "such as Thomas More, the leading man and grand chancellor of Henry VIII," and "the most reverend cardinal Roffense" (John Fisher). But if the prisoner's resistance was hard to break down, then one could switch to a harsh and threatening tone, addressing the stubborn prisoner with words like this: "Pitiful and unhappy, how have you dared to contradict the Creator, given that you are a most base creature, engendered from base and stinking material, a pot of garbage and food for worms?"[66] The tactic to win the battle described by Isella might involve verbal aggression and the threat of abandoning the prisoner. But if this did not work either, then the comforter had to be prepared to change tack and once again open the treasury of divine mercy and the inexhaustible strongbox of indulgences. The Gospels of the Passion were to be read to the afflicted, but it was also important to respond concretely to the condemned man's fears, promising to see to the "care and protection of his relatives, like his father, mother, children, brothers; and they would think in particular of the honor of the wife and sisters, and assist them in their need as far as is possible."[67] The company should also bear in mind the duty of the condemned to make amends for their misdeeds. The confessor would remind the prisoner of the obligation to restore the good name of those who had been wronged. Often, "in order not to feel pain" under torture, the defendants accused themselves and others of crimes they had not committed. The restitution had to happen "either by public act, or in the presence of witnesses, or on the point of execution, in the presence of the public, with a loud and clear voice."[68] In any case, the comforters had to keep a record of their words "in their annals, so that if they were not noted by others, they might be of benefit to the innocent."

Following execution, it was up to the *confratelli* to attend to the burial, a "most welcome act, and pleasing to the divine Majesty": four of their number would be charged to carry the coffin containing the body on their shoulders to the burial place, "in accordance with the obligation of the Company, and good manners, and Christian piety. And those who perform this office with love should know," Isella observes, "that they will receive great merit from God."[69] The liturgy of suffrage for the dead person's soul would follow with masses according to the alms that had been collected, and would in any case be guaranteed for everyone.

A whole life was to be observed and judged by its end point, and that end point had to be the focus of attention—not in the sense of informing every moment in life with a strict morality, thinking of God's final judgment, but in the sense that the vital game was played out entirely and exclusively in that final moment. This entailed a devaluation of the whole of a person's previous existence until then. As an erudite Neapolitan professor wrote, "Living is nothing other than continual dying, and dying is a perpetual living. Therefore he who wants to live a long time should die early. In the end a bad death casts into doubt a good past life, and a good death excuses a bad life."[70] Only those who played their final card well won the game. It was a view coherent with the emphasis placed by the comforters on the model of the "good thief," but was at odds with the convictions of the author of the work prefaced by the professor. Father Bartolomeo d'Angelo was a Dominican, a firm believer in the Thomist doctrine of the value of good works. And from the very beginning of his *Ricordo di ben morire* he admonished readers that "the first thing for dying well is living well, and doing good while you are alive."[71] This was the lesson of his theological school: one had to act well as long as one could and not wait till the last moment. However, he decided to add to the work a final concluding section devoted to the "method and form of comforting and consoling those condemned to death at the hands of justice."[72] He drew the content for it "from the book of the devout company of certain gentlemen who take pleasure in similar works of piety" (the Neapolitan Bianchi, or Whites).

The procedures followed by the Whites were formally similar to those of other companies of justice, but took place over three days, as did those of the Sicilian companies. This would account for the particularly long and detailed description of the obligations and advice that filled the lengthy treatise of Diego de Córdoba, published half a century later.[73] In the work of Bartolomeo d'Angelo those three days form the backdrop for suggestions about what the comforter should say and do in relation to the condemned: find out about the state and condition of the condemned person, whether he was "literate or not, if he had children," what he was accused of, what additional punishments he would receive, in order to present model martyr saints suited to the circumstances. There then conveniently follows a list of saints who had been "suffocated and hung," condemned to "death on the Cross," or had been "beheaded," "burned," "pincered," "dragged," and "quartered," without forgetting the "martyred women." But the monk's advice was not to linger on this point; fears and anxieties needed to be allayed by playing down the suffering on the scaffold and the quartering and ill treatment of the body after death. Above all, it was necessary to silence those who believed they were victims of injustice and had only confessed on pain of torture: "to whom it will be answered that it is true, but that God wishes it to be so, to give him purgatory in this life for some of his other sins, and that Christ and many martyrs also died innocently, among whom he will find a place."[74] There is then a relationship of contiguity and exchange between the scaffold on earth and the purgatory that loomed so large in the devotions and collective imagination of the age, especially in Naples.[75] The Dominican monk imagines that the comforter's persuasion will lead the condemned person to want to make confession, which will then happen. Nothing is said about Communion, a sign that some theological perplexity still surrounded this issue. But at this point, when the trust of the "afflicted" has been earned, D'Angelo asks that the dangers to faith should be addressed. The devil lays snares for the salvation of the soul, with doubts over faith and through the grave threat of despair. A careful examination of all the articles of faith must therefore be carried out. And at the end there is a dire warning for the "wretch": "That if he does not remain firm, and goes back on what is held by the holy mother and guide, the Roman and Catholic Church, he will undoubtedly be lost."[76] Having said this, the prisoner should go "to death with good heart and good will," taking the cross given to him by the judge, he should remember that Christ went "cheerfully" to die for him, and should not be worried by the list of his crimes, which, at the sound of the trumpet, are proclaimed in the square by the "injurious voice" of the city crier. He should remind himself that this is the occasion to "make amends for his previous sins."[77]

If, on the other hand, we open the *Guida spirituale de gli afflitti* written by the Jesuit Giovan Pietro Castello for the company of Santa Maria della Pietà in Messina (known as the company "dell'Azori"), we find just one point in common with D'Angelo's work: concern over the danger of despair. But this is just the "eighth discourse," and it concludes with the thesis that "Christ, through his suffering, gave sinners great confidence to convert" and that the offer of the sacraments, the medicine of salvation, suffices to demonstrate God's salvific will.[78] The work sets out to sum up and present what was practiced and had been learned from the experience of the company. Castello begins immediately by citing examples of conversions of misbelievers and "infidels": of a Neapolitan knight who did not want to confess, and of a Muslim (a non-Christian "Moor"). Divine illumination had resulted in the conversion of both, after much talk in the chapel, including a "comparison of the Holy Faith of Christ, based on the truth, with that of Mohammad, [based] on the force and freedom of living [in sin]."[79] To obtain such results had required, according to the Jesuit, great commitment on the part of the *confratelli* in examining themselves and performing acts of contrition. So he encouraged them to read "spiritual books" and suggested acts and phrases for every moment of the comforting process. The main "industry" (the word pertained to the language of the Jesuits and implied not only effort and commitment but also shrewdness, "prudence," and therefore astuteness) consisted, according to the author, in "making the afflicted resolve to die willingly." This could be achieved by suiting the means to the end. If the prisoner was disheartened by the weight of his sins, "it will be necessary to animate him with the readiness of God's mercy." Conversely, if the condemned is stubborn or desperate, it will be necessary "to terrify him with the eternal punishments of hell."[80] He is to be instructed in the Christian faith, because the condemned, for the most part "coarse poorly educated persons from the countryside or woods, are usually very ignorant of matters of faith." A brief and essential catechesis was required, after which the prisoner was to be prepared for confession with mnemonic techniques typical of a missionary order: the afflicted had to examine himself by running through the Ten Commandments of God, the five precepts of the Church, the seven mortal sins, the five senses, recalling "places, companions, activities, and works."[81] There was no need to list particular circumstances of the sin—the category sufficed. If there was time, the general confession beloved of the Jesuits could be done, if not, then just the unconfessed sins should be heard. When dealing with reserved sins it was to be borne in mind that the confession was "in articulo mortis." And it was important that the "afflicted" should make amends, where possible, for the consequences of his crime and the damage done to others, restoring the good name and possessions to those to whom they were due. Communion was to be given as laid down in the agreement between Philip II and Pius V; and no account was to be taken of the one-day gap between Communion and execution, as this was a "pious custom" rather than a norm. It was also necessary to combat the human passions—above all, the fear of dying. Here the example of Socrates could be cited; though he was a "blind man of our faith," he believed in the immortality of the soul and for this reason he drank the fatal poison without fear.[82] But it is when it came to convincing the "afflicted" to accept the sentence that we find a fixed point of all this literature, repeated without distinction by authors from different religious orders: what the legitimate authorities decided was the will of God. "All that is decreed and carried out by the superiors, and earthly governors, is directly inspired by God."[83] They are like doctors who prescribe bitter medicine: the sick must not ask to know any more, but should be content to accept the remedy for their own health. "We must, then, be ready to accept what is imposed on us by human justice, the minister of God's providence, even death."[84] This applied even if the sentence was unjust and the judge had believed false testimony, because "that sentence derived from God." The condemned should be thankful for the privilege of knowing the time and day of their death. And if they were threatened by despair, they should be aware that "an act of bad or perverse interior will" in just one moment would be enough to be damned. Similarly, "in a blink of the eye," there could be sufficient pain to convert, as the good thief did.[85] Other pieces of advice concerned the final journey to the scaffold, during which appropriate meditations were to be offered. The "ministers" who bound the prisoner would do so "with kind words, and gentle actions." Even the crowd was different from the one that insulted Christ, who had been "tied like a murderer." They felt pity for the condemned person's misdeeds and desired his liberty, and in any case he was a sinner, not Christ.[86] The confessor was to remind the prisoner to confess any forgotten sins, give him all possible indulgences, and sprinkle him with holy water. The *confratelli* accompanying the afflicted "were always to maintain the customary silence," assisting with inner oration or by reciting psalms. The final prayer was to be said by the brother who climbed the ladder to the scaffold. Here the author praises the company's custom of saying a prayer in the first person, as if by the condemned person, and getting him to repeat it. This was to ensure that, right up to the end, the mind did not remain unguarded and susceptible to the devil's temptations. In the suggested prayers, the request for forgiveness dominates: the last prayer is addressed to "My Lord Jesus Christ, your natural disposition is to forgive."[87]

The *Sicuro viaggio de giustitiandi* by the Milanese Dominican monk Girolamo Gattico is also chiefly directed at condemned prisoners, though it is generally pertinent for anyone close to death.[88] The long subtitle guarantees that the work provides "all the help necessary to announce death to those who are to be executed," and also "all the diligent measures for any other dying person." And it does so "in a much more copious, orderly, and fruitful way than has been expressed to this day by others." This indicates that competition was tough in this special niche of the publishing market. To make things easier for readers, they were offered an "instruction for using the book," in which the author warns that some special parts are marked with a symbol (a "small hand"), which would serve to reassure the person who was to die that they would certainly go to heaven. Leafing through the work, as perhaps the Milanese comforters would have done when they had to deal with the despair of condemned prisoners, we can see some of these key points. For instance, there is a "very important declaration" *(protesta)* the prisoner had to make (or have done for him if he was unable to read) immediately after receiving Communion. From this he will gain the "final security for his health."[89] The *protesta* was a text that the companies of justice had ready for the "patient" to read and ratify at the appropriate moment, and which had the bureaucratic ring of a notary deed. The following, for example, is the first part of the one used by the Florentine company of the Blacks:

> In nomine Patris, et Filli et Spiritus Sancti Amen. I [name], wretched sinner, declare in the presence of the divine Majesty, the Most Blessed Virgin Mary, all the angels and saints in heaven, and all of you that are here present, that I desire and wish to die believing, and confessing everything that the Holy Roman Catholic Church believes, holds, and confesses. So I expressly declare that I believe everything that is in the Holy Scriptures, as is taught by the Holy Roman Church. I believe in the most holy sacraments of the Church, in the most holy sacrifice of the Mass, I believe in the glory of the blessed, the eternal punishments of hell, purgatory, indulgences, the resurrection of the dead, the last and specific judgment of each person, to be carried out by my Lord

Jesus Christ. I am sorry for all the wrongs I have done in any way to his Divine Majesty and to my fellow men from the day I received the holy baptism to the present hour . . . For the sins which, through neglect, I forgot to confess and which I did not explain well and with due detail, declaring that I would willingly confess them if I could remember them; and I ask forgiveness of all those whom I have wronged in any way, and pardon all those who have wronged me in any way. I now likewise declare, while I am of sound mind, that if, for the anxiety of death, the temptation of the devil, or for any other reason, from which may God preserve me, I should fall into despair, or into blasphemy, or into complaint against God, or in any other condition that might impede my salvation, I now hereby renounce, annul, and revoke it, declaring that I accept this death as remission for my sins, as being fitting for my ill deeds, acknowledging that I am deserving of this and further torment, and that I do not desire to live even one short moment more than is pleasing to his Divine Majesty, in whose infinite mercy I trust to save my soul.[90]

In a society where the written word held particular fascination for the unlettered and illiterate masses—consider the numerous pacts with the devil signed in blood that ended up in the hands of confessors and inquisitors—a *protesta* like this one, signed or in any case ratified before witnesses immediately before going to the scaffold, would doubtless have been effective in consolidating the "positive" determination of those about to die.

The Milanese Dominican's *protesta* was a particularly elaborate version. It was a legalistic declaration running to twenty-seven paragraphs, presumably made by the condemned "now instead of then," valid before a judging court consisting of angels and saints in heaven and presided over by the Virgin Mary and by Jesus. In it the subject accuses himself of his wrongs, declares ("protesta") that he is ready to confess everything that God will bring to his mind, contests every claim that might be advanced by the "enemy of his health," refuses to acknowledge doubts and temptations that might stem from the work of the devil, asks to be forgiven, and affirms that he harbors no memories of offenses received. Finally, he declares that he wishes to die in God's grace, undertakes to believe as long as he lives "what the holy faith holds and the Holy Roman Catholic and Apostolic Church teaches and commands," abjures and detests everything that he might have done or believed against it, declares that he expects his soul, "after leaving, as it will, his body, will belong not to demons but to God," promises to abstain from sinning forever in the event of being allowed to relive his life from the age of reason and henceforth for thousands of years. And finally, he brings the devil before the tribunal of God in order to win the case against him on the basis of this formal act that the condemned must recite and make his own.

Making a formal declaration before witnesses in order to prevent the angel of shadows from emerging victorious over the person about to die was an ancient tradition, and is also attested in the Jewish one.[91] The uncertainties over what approaching death might produce in human minds and behavior had long since assumed the shape of an external aggression on the part of malign spirits. A formal declaration before witnesses by the condemned person while he was still in command of his faculties was the way to strip any evidence that might be used by the devil of all judicial value and to assure a favorable divine sentence. Girolamo Gattico drew on this tradition to guarantee the salvation of those who were to die and to dispel all their apprehensions. True to the juridical and theological culture of his order, but also to his preferred devotions—he cited a series of twelve miracles of souls that had been saved thanks to devotions made to the Our Lady of the Rosary—he seized the opportunity to praise the "famous convent of San Domenico in Bologna," with its many learned monks distinguished by the goodness of their lives.[92] He was particularly concerned about the orthodoxy of the condemned, and so he proposed that they should not receive Communion without having first answered a long list of "most useful and very important questions"—all of which were, of course, doctrinal. The only permitted answer was "yes." Antiheretical conscientiousness, the theology of good works, attention to legal formalities—these were the defining traits of Gattico's culture. He had one point in common with all the other authors producing this kind of literature: his insistence that the condemned person had to accept the judge's sentence, for the fundamental reason that "human justice [is] subordinate to the divine" one.[93]

One religious order that felt professionally called upon to comfort the condemned was the body founded by Saint Camillus de Lellis, which assumed the name and office of "ministers of the infirm." From providing religious assistance to the infirm in hospitals, regulated by the strict norm to care for the soul through confession before caring for the body, to attending to the condemned was but a brief step. For this reason the instructions and manuals drawn up to prepare the sick for death were soon expanded to include the case of those who were to be executed. But in the work of Marcello Mansi, the general consultor of the order, the relationship ended up being reversed. His "documents for comforting" were devoted primarily to the condemned, even though the title pointed to the general utility of the advice it contained.[94] A muddled piece of writing, it covers the themes common to all this literature, in order to convince the condemned that what was about to happen to them was the will of God, and that rebelling against it would not only be wrong but would lead to serious consequences: "too much damage, in the end, for you yourself, confusion for your family, outrage for your fellow men, besides the pain of your eternal ill that you would leave to those desiring your health, not to mention the joy it would give the enemies of our souls."[95] But by this time the path of devotion was awash with instructions and prayers, including the now-customary juridical declaration before the tribunal of Christ of the wish to die in his grace.[96] The comforter even undertook to explain the symbolic significance of the vestments worn by the priest celebrating the Mass and administering the sacraments. Nor did he neglect to refer to the holy oil of the infirm, which he imagined the condemned would also want. He explained, however, that they were barred from receiving it for various reasons—they were not infirm; even if they were they could not and should not be healed from it; and it was not right to anoint feet that would soon walk to the scaffold.[97]

A contribution to this literature also inevitably came from the Capuchins, the religious order which, in the age of the Counter-Reformation, renewed the ardor of the Franciscans' appeal to poverty, personal witness, and conversion, combining it with a fierce antiheretical and anti-Muslim stance. An example of this can be found in a treatise published by the Capuchin monk Carlo Verri from Cremona.[98] But the original spirit of Franciscan poverty and humility seems very much in abeyance in the special attention he devotes to the social categories of the condemned. The comforter, he writes, must learn the prisoner's standing before entering his cell. There were two possibilities, nobles or commoners, and the rules changed accordingly. If the person was a noble, the comforter was to excuse himself, saying "that he comes to that office more to fulfill his office and satisfy his conscience than for need," because he is sure that as a "well-born person, Christian and able to understand, he will comply with his will to that of God." The comforter would tell stories about prominent figures who faced death with courage, giving a fine example of entrusting themselves to God's will. With commoners, on the other hand, the approach was to be quite different. "When the condemned person is common, with little under-standing, the good and prudent comforter should leave aside any sort of fine talk and artfulness, and using just a few words, will announce to the criminal that he is to die."[99] This comes at the beginning of the indications about what to say, things which we have already come across: that death by execution was a "precious thing," a privilege, a gift of God; that worldly jus-tice was an expression of divine will, "ordered by God to this end"; and the (usual) guaranteed reward for those who accepted the chance to save them-selves, as the good thief did. But Verri's thoughts on the good thief were as-tutely calculating: Saint Dismas was someone who quickly decided what it was in his best interest to do in the presence of the figure alongside him on the Cross, and who decided to commend himself to Christ because he sensed that he was "a great king, very different from other kings."[100] Packed with a cultural mishmash of episodes and names, flitting between Socrates, Job, and the queen of Scotland, the text has a harsh and violent tone that surfaces continually in the pages dealing with how to crush the resistance of Satan's stubborn slaves. Miracles and visions feature in abundance, as do promises of heaven and scenes of the sufferings of hell.

Verri's work offers a glimpse of the terrifying inventions produced by the hallucinated imagination of devout figures prepared to do anything in order to save a soul. By contrast, a very different culture can be sensed in the trea-tise of an anonymous writer from Turin, who warns: "It is not good, gener-ally speaking, to make loud noises, or hidden sounds, or fake shouts to frighten the offender, as if demons had come from hell to take him away"; they are "inventions" that make no impression on the prisoner and provide occasion for those present "to make fun of comforters."[101] Public mockers were representatives of a restive and irreverent public opinion that needed to be taken into account. The author believed in the devil—indeed, he did not rule out that he and his fellow brothers might see the devil appearing before them while comforting—but those mockers should be given no cause to laugh at religion or criticize Church tribunals. Prudence and dissimulation were needed to defend the Church. Among the hypothetical cases presented by the author is that of a "patient" condemned by the Inquisition for heresy, but who, the confessor realizes, is entirely without blame. What should be done? The answer was clear. The person should be comforted discreetly, but "with such prudence that in assisting him no indication is given that he is dying a Catholic, out of consideration for the Holy Tribunal of the Inquisition, by which he has been recognized as a heretic, and as such condemned by public knowledge."[102] On the other hand, great attention was paid to the rules of "civility," the forms of good manners to observe in the prisons, with the executioner, and with the condemned—everything from avoiding the "tu" form when dealing with the prisoner, even if he was "of extremely low condition," to the clean clothes and the white handkerchief to have ready at hand to present him in public and blindfold his eyes. Nor did it make any sense to oblige the prisoner to read and sign those "declarations printed in various books, certainly devout but very long."[103] Better to opt for some brief acts of contrition. One also had to be prepared to cope with the failure of all their efforts, when the criminal obstinately refused to convert: "Remember, the offender is endowed with liberty."[104] The dedication to Saint John the Baptist extols the testimony of those who died for the truth and for justice. Even more than the extremely detailed series of practical warnings (the ones relating to the body of the prisoner and the behavior of the executioner are particularly noteworthy), Verri's vocabulary indicates that the baroque feast of justice was being transformed into an austere ritual of power and religion.

An entirely different style prevailed at the other end of Italy, in Sicily, which was part of the Spanish State but maintained an Italian language and culture. The penal regime long practiced by the Spanish authorities on the island was violent and merciless. The impact of the new Spanish Inquisition had been immediate, with the brunt of this being borne by the Jewish minority, and with surveillance taking the harsh forms typical of the political-religious nature of the institution. For this reason too the assistance given to those condemned for inquisitorial crimes was not left up to the Whites. Established immediately after them was the Confraternita dell'Assunta (Our Lady of the Assumption), under the control of the Dominicans, who were granted all the privileges enjoyed by the Whites, including the faculty of pardon. It was this new company that organized the *autos-da-fé* (acts of faith) and provided spiritual assistance to those condemned by the tribunal of the Inquisition.

In Sicily, where the administration of royal justice had to reckon with the powers of the communities and the feudal ones of the big baronial families, the composition of the Whites was distinguished from the outset by the preeminence of the nobility and high clergy. A first difference from the model operating in the rest of Italy was the duration of the comforting. With his penal constitution of 1532, Charles V had established an obligatory three days between the sentence and the execution, and set out the general terms for the exercising of spiritual assistance. The novelty introduced by his son Philip was the admission of repentant condemned prisoners to the sacrament of Communion. The protracted resistance that had blocked this concession in the kingdoms of the large European dynasties was overcome thanks to the close political and religious ties established between the monarchy and the Counter-Reformation papacy. A *motu proprio* by Pius V dated January 25, 1569, accepted and ratified by a "royal pragmatic" of March 27 regulated the matter: the condemned could, if they had repented and confessed, receive the Eucharist. These normative and social differences as a whole characterized the functioning of the Whites. A special manual quickly prepared for their use by Don Baldassare, a member of the noble Beccadelli di Bologna family from Palermo, was printed in 1583.[105] An unbending aristocratic and feudal ideology informed all his recommendations, starting with the obligation, repeated several times, to immediately ascertain whether the "afflicted" was of noble birth or of "base lineage and with little or no understanding." In this latter case, the matter was to be attended to with "few words, and without other excessive talk," putting an immediate stop to any attempt to dispute the sentence, "because one must not allow such people to become equals in disputes."[106] On the other hand, "if the person who must die is noble and of understanding, it will be enough for our brother to briefly mention the examples." This is because it was assumed that a "person of repute and understanding, and a Christian, knows all those things without others saying anything to him."[107] This did not stop the noble and learned *confratello* turning out hundreds of pages of advice of every kind, not just theological and juridical but practical as well. The three-day time lapse meant that the comforting was extended over a much longer period than was the case in the other Italian confraternities, which also lent a distinctive feature to the measure of pardon. The comforters moved into the oratory and spent the nights there, though their direct contact with the condemned prisoner was limited to ritual exhortations to express contrition in the morning and evening. The rest of the night they spent sleeping in comfortable beds near the prisoner's cell. On the morning of the third day they accompanied the condemned to the execution site in Piazza della Marina, in a procession punctuated by acts of torture and additional punishments, forms of suffering ironically referred to as the *succàro* ("sugar")—being tied to a horse tail and dragged, pincering with hot irons, having a hand amputated or fire applied to their feet. Baldassare di Bologna's instructions recommended paying attention to the wrist ties, which had to be tight when the executioner cut off the condemned person's hands. A freshly gutted hen needed to be kept ready, and the prisoner told to put the stump "into that."[108] The procession might also be animated by burlesque and carnivalesque displays. Upon arrival in the square, the procession split up. The condemned, together with members of the *conforteria,* the executioner, and his assistant entered an enclosure closed off to everyone else. The prisoner knelt before the gallows. He was then asked if he wished to die as a Christian, and if he replied in the affirmative, he received absolution from the company priest. Then he climbed the ladder to where the noose was positioned. Right up to that moment a pardon could still arrive, and we can imagine with what anxiety the condemned tried to detect in the shouts of the crowd some signal that the magistrate had arrived in the square bearing the note sparing his life. Just occasionally the scene of liberation and of a return to life described by Goethe broke the monotony of the gloomy baroque theatricality of the execution ritual.

In all this literature, arising out of the needs of many different local communities, there are quite a few common features, demonstrating that the culture of the confraternities was becoming unified. One of these is particularly striking in a literary genre characterized in ideal terms by the aim of envisaging the questions, desires, and fears of people suddenly faced by the prospect of their own imminent death: the silence of the condemned. The weighty body of argumentation is hardly ever scratched by the recollections,

faces, and words of real people encountered by the authors in their experience. There is nothing casual about this silence. The literature we have sam-
pled and dipped into here and there, stemming as it did from the need to
predict in advance the protests and complaints of those who had just learned
of their fate, had rapidly evolved into systematic argumentation that reflected
a situation from which there was no way out: the condemned were regarded
as recipients to fill up rather than as human beings to listen to. They just
needed to be convinced that the horizon was one and one alone, and to decide whether to accept it or not. It was the comforter's task to lead the condemned person onto the path of acceptance with his words. This was the
core of the matter. Everything else—the crafty ploys, threats, prayers, tales
of miracles and of martyrs' deaths—revolved around that choice. As for the
things that were actually said, it was not the task of the authors to recount
them. The rule in the comforting chapels was for witnesses to remain silent
about what they heard there. The late statutes of the Modenese company of
San Giovanni Battista della Morte explain it with the rough concreteness
of a mercantile culture: "As secrecy is the soul of business, the *confratelli* shall
take care not to talk around the city about the matters dealt with in the gath-
erings." Members who could not resist talking about them in public risked
expulsion.[109] Surrounded by the curiosity of those who imagined they were
privy to secrets about the crimes of the condemned and their behavior in
the *conforteria,* they were duty-bound not to ask for details about the condemned as a person and to say nothing about what they heard. Of course,
tactical considerations dictated that they should find out about all these
things on the quiet, to avoid mistakes when deciding how to speak to the
prisoner and what to say. But it was otherwise necessary to steer away from
questions about "who he is, or where from, or from what family, relatives,
etc." The condemned themselves requested it: "they are ashamed of disclosing
what family they are from, and where their origins lie."[110] The constraint of
secrecy naturally had to be respected regarding the content of declarations
made in the repeated confessions during the night. But the condemned were
animated by the desire to talk, and to do so in public. They wanted to excul-
pate themselves, send messages to friends and enemies alike, safeguard the
memory others had of them. They viewed the scaffold as the final pulpit from
which to address the public. However, the instructions were very clear on
this: everything possible had to be done to prevent it happening. The con-

demned who emerged from the cell or chapel in the morning on the way to their execution had to move as if they were already dead. The comforter's job was to shut the prisoner's eyes, ears, and mouth. This is explained particularly well in the treatise written by Pompeo Serni in the seventeenth century for the Roman archconfraternity of San Giovanni Decollato. The text circulated in manuscript form within the confraternities associated with the Roman one. Like the first treatise of the genre prepared for the Bologna *conforteria,* Pompeo Serni's was also a devotional work that scrupulously eschewed the quest for literary glory.

The text is particularly rich in minute observations about every moment of the service. Here we will just mention the rules concerning the prisoner's senses in the public phase of the ritual. First the eyes:

> In the street he [the condemned] must stay with them all the time, his mind and eyes concentrating on the *tavoletta* held before him; nor should his eyes wander, but must remain fixed on the crucified Christ, because to do otherwise would only distract the mind.[111]

The ears and the tongue:

> Two comforters, with the condemned between them, remain behind and with him, without anyone else, on the cart or walking through the street holding the *tavoletta* up in front of his eyes, keeping him occupied all the time with vocal prayers, such as getting him to devoutly say the *Pater Noster* and the *Ave Maria* to each wound of the cross, kissing the wounds in the image of the *tavoletta* and thanking him at each wound with specific words about the grace—bestowed on the world, and on him in particular—of the most holy sacraments arising from, and whose efficacy lies in, the blood of those same wounds.[112]

But if he wanted to say something? In this case he was invited

> to communicate with the comforters, if he is of a mind to say something to the people on the scaffold or on the street. And effectively he should remain in agreement about the words he must utter because, either out of passion or ignorance, he might be tempted to say things that represented a charge of injustice or such like, burdening his conscience with sin, regarding which, at that final point, it would be difficult to be able to confess and retract. But to avoid that danger and to

stymy the opportunity for the devil to tempt him and make him let slip some aggravating words, which could easily happen while blinded by the passion and distress of death, he might not have time to measure everything and all his words, it will be best to remain silent and say nothing if not for the benefit of his soul. Let him say a *Pater* and *Ave Maria,* persuading him to leave off saying anything else, which in any case will not be understood due to the tumult of the people, or will serve no good effect.[113]

See nothing, hear nothing, say nothing. The condemned was a dead man walking.

❧ 18 ❧

A Charity of Nobles and the Powerful: The New Social Composition of the Companies

BUT FOR WHOM were these manuals and books of instructions written? What changes occurred in the intended readers of these recommendations and teachings? To answer these questions, we need to reconstruct at least the main lines of the changes that took place in the composition of the companies of justice during the long time span of their maximum development in Italy—that is, from the fifteenth to the eighteenth century. The general framework is well known: there were increasing signs of a general crisis in production and trade in Italian society during this period, combined with the establishment of aristocratic models. Landed property dominated, and persons who aspired to climb the social ladder pinned their hopes on an ecclesiastical or military career, or on financial activities. All this was reflected in the makeup of the companies of justice. The first sign of their special nature was the disappearance of women. The mysticism of redemption had inspired female figures such as Saint Catherine of Siena, and from the outset women had engaged in the charitable works of the confraternities. But their presence faded as comforting became a specialist activity and the *stretta* companies separated from the general bodies of the original confraternities. Women passed from being subjects active in charitable endeavors to being objects.[1] In the case of the companies of justice, their disappearance was the inevitable outcome of the special functions entrusted to those associations: justice was a matter for men. Only in exceptional circumstances, such as when female condemned prisoners required some form of material assistance, were women called in to help, as they alone were permitted to have access to the bodies of women. While the image of the accepting, motherly Virgin Mary dominated in the general iconography of the *misericordie,* in the companies of justice it was generally the bearded head of the decapitated saint, John the Baptist, that stood out. Besides women, artisans and members of the lower orders also disappeared or faded into the background. Into their place stepped men of law and gentlemen. For the most part it was men from the ruling elites, clad in habit and hood, who comforted the condemned and acted as their intermediaries with the outside world. The prisoner passed from their hands directly into those of the executioner. It is worth taking a look at their identity, concealed by their hoods and habits but well known to contemporaries and carefully recorded in confraternity proceedings. Over the long term the composition of the confraternities reflected and accentuated the pattern of changes in the ruling groups of Italian society: an analysis of membership of the Bolognese *conforteria* reveals that the artisans, merchants, and "rag-traders without knowledge" still present in the fifteenth century were giving way in the second half of the sixteenth century to solemn, authoritative figures such as notaries, university professors, and members of the city elites, with a special component consisting of members of the religious orders (especially Capuchins and Jesuits, who dealt with those convicted for heresy).[2] During the eighteenth century a special register even began to be kept of "executed nobility."[3] This was the inevitable outcome of a social system mirrored in penal norms: "Fitting regard must be accorded to their noble or civil condition," states the Este criminal code in the chapter "On punishments," "keeping them immune from demeaning punishments, to be commuted into others that do not bring disgrace but are appropriate for the crime."[4] This regulation corresponded to the transformation of the social composition of the companies of justice operating both in Ferrara and in the nearby legations of the Papal State. In Ferrara the arrival of the papal government in 1598 had also marked a further turning point: as Girolamo Baruffaldi recounts in the historic information prefacing the company's *Direttorio,* the comforters' office had been entrusted at that time to members of the secular and regular clergy. The laity were left with the task of joining the execution ritual and burying the bodies of the condemned.[5] When the company was refounded in 1679, a comforters' school similar to the one in Bologna was set up and placed in the hands of a body of noblemen. The governor then was Count Pinamonte Bonacossi, and the first meeting, held on May 11, was organized by the Marchese Ippolito Bentivoglio d'Aragona. Marchesi, counts, and cardinals from then on constituted the twelve Masters of the *conforteria.* This was the local version of a general phenomenon. In Venice the list of "clerics, noblemen, and brothers of the school" was dominated in the eighteenth century by the names of the republic's leading aristocratic families.[6] In Milan the confraternity regulations drawn up in 1564 distinguished clearly between noble members, co-opted in variable and practically unlimited numbers, and the fixed thirty-member group of the so-called *funerari,* who were responsible for the demeaning tasks—gathering up and rearranging body parts and taking them off for burial.[7]

Control of the secrets disclosed in *conforteria* confessions, and the power to interfere with the ordinary procedures of the courts through the privilege of pardon, were too important to leave in the hands of base and inexpert members of the lower orders. A process of ennoblement and clericalization also effectively occurred in many other companies of the same type. The result was that in the prisons and chapels, the condemned were increasingly likely to encounter individuals belonging to the governing elite of the State and Church. These elite lent themselves to a work of charity that brought them in contact with the dregs of society because this is what the ethics of the Counter-Reformation asked of them. Similarly, in the penitential processions held during the course of the liturgical year, the nobles and magnates were urged to be at the back, as an example to others. In the symbolic overturning of the social order that put itself on display in public rituals, the iniquity in the distribution of power and wealth was covered over and legitimated by a rhetorical Christianity of appearances. But appearances had their own weight. The fact that the powerful went so far as to humiliatingly present themselves as the Christian brothers of thieves and killers in places of suffering and death had its own importance in the strategy of "conversion." We can imagine the effect it must have had on the condemned to find themselves before those grave, austere figures who had stepped down from their raised chairs and left their palaces. One such case can be found in the memories of Marco Gambarucci, the sacristan of the Roman company of San Giovanni Decollato. It concerned a notary of the Capitoline Hill, Girolamo Ceccani della Sabina, put to death on July 14, 1662, for having committed no fewer than twenty-two homicides in his hometown. He wanted at all costs to be confessed and assisted by a Capuchin whom he trusted, and when the comforters pressed him to use the confessor they were offering, he showed great reluctance. He asked them "if among the brothers present who were assisting him there was some titled person." After the comforters, the *provveditore,* and the chaplain had briefly conferred, it was decided to reveal the identity of all the *confratelli,* and they gathered around the prisoner. Gambarucci then asked him if he really wanted to know who they were. When he said "yes," the sacristan was able to triumphantly reel off names and titles:

> This is the lord abbot Francesco Maruscelli, our *provveditore;* this is Monsignor Carlo De Ricci, consistorial lawyer; this is Monsignor Onofrio Ippoliti, canon of Saint Peter's; this is the reverend abbot Giulio Ricci, canon of Saint Peter's, this is the lord abbot Castiglioni; this is the lord abbot Palagi; this is signor Matteo Baldosii; this is the signor cavalier Bellarmini; and this is the signor prince of Palestrina D. Maffeo Barberini, nephew of the sacred memory of Pope Urban VIII, blessed vicar of Christ.

At the mention of Barberini's name, shrewdly left to the end, "the poor patient threw himself off his seat, kneeling to kiss the feet of the lord prince, and broke into great wailing, saying: 'My Lord Jesus Christ, what grace is this that you do me, that at the death of an unworthy sinner such as me, you have assisting a nephew of your vicar, with many other eminent lords.'"[8] The humiliation of the powerful exalted the faith of the humble, all the more so if that powerful person was so close to the one who held the keys of heaven.

In the lists of the *confratelli* we can see the progressive emergence of university professors and members of religious orders, the high clergy, and the nobility. The power elites appropriated the forms and symbols of civic religion in order to exercise their social hegemony.[9] This was also because, in the meantime, the communal-style political setups had been replaced by regimes of a very different kind. In Modena, which in 1599 became the capital of the Este state, the Confraternita di San Giovanni Battista underwent a process of ennoblement and clericalization that was evident in the care devoted to details of clothing in the *Capitoli per la conforteria* presented to the duke for approval in 1719. There were strict rules regarding the obligation to wear "white gloves" when touching the condemned person—which gloves, immediately after use, were to be thrown into the prisoner's grave in the church of San Domenico. Contact with the crowd was also unwelcome: a squad of the duke's police guarded the *conforteria* and kept people away.[10] In the "catalogue of living *confratelli*" printed in the 1782 edition of the chapters, we find, alongside the bishop and the cathedral canons, all the leading figures in Modenese society. Standing out in the string of nobles and prelates are the names of the Marchese Giovanni Battista Cortese, of Count Benedetto Manzoli, of the count and provost Francesco Fontana, and the count and marchese Massimiliano Montecuccoli.[11]

The variegated world of artisans' workshops and Renaissance courts was yielding to an austere procession of monsignors and gentlemen. In the general pattern of change in society the confraternities of justice were immediately marked by the new forms of social and political dominion, as required by the delicate functions of administering the punishment system in the Counter-Reformation states, where political power and religious power were closely intertwined and demanded loyalty and obedience. The concern for orthodoxy made itself felt with the exclusion of suspected heretics or restless men of letters. In the first half of the sixteenth century, the membership of the Compagnia dei Bianchi della Giustizia in Naples included churchmen and literati variously representative of the current ideas on Church reform. There were names like Gaetano da Thiene, the cofounder, together with Gian Pietro Carafa, of the Congregation of Clerics Regular (or Theatines); Antonio Minturno, man of letters and then bishop; and many others. Between 1536 and 1540, various followers of Juan de Valdés held important posts, from Mario Galeota to Pietrantonio da Capua and Ferrante Brancaccio. But when the congregation of cardinals of the Roman Inquisition began its work, there was a shakeup in the company. The Valdesian group ended up on trial, while the Theatine order became involved in systematic policing. The revival following the crisis showed that the lesson had been learned: the *confratelli* requested and obtained indulgences and privileges by becoming associated with the Roman confraternity. It was a declaration of deference to the papal power contested by the Lutherans. The bishop of Sessa at that time, Galeazzo Florimonte, to whom they had turned as a mediator, urged them in vain to trust in Jesus Christ, the "first and principal granter of all grace." In this way the Neapolitan company gained the concession of the fundamental privilege of pardon, which was then redistributed to the other confraternities of the kingdom, like the one in Lecce. In the meantime ecclesiastics began to be an increasing presence in the social composition of the Whites. The Neapolitan aristocracy continued to be in a majority and to retain powers of control. But in the end, after a complicated period of divergences between Rome and

Madrid, Philip II, suspicious of possible political plotting by the Neapolitan nobility under cover of confraternal secrecy, ordered the replacement of all lay members with churchmen in April 1583.[12]

The Milanese confraternity of San Giovanni alle Case Rotte also underwent a marked process of Counter-Reformation disciplining and aristocratization. The reorganization of the ecclesiastical government of the archdiocese, carried out by Cardinal Charles Borromeo, resulted in substantial change. During his time in Rome, when he had been the cardinal-nephew of Pius V, Borromeo had come to know and admire the work of the Roman confraternity. So when he returned to Lombardy as archbishop, he decided to revitalize and reorganize the one in Milan, so that those "condemned by the world may, by virtue of divine mercy, be redeemed by the Lord." In doing so, he gave the confraternity a character different from the traditional popular one. The rigidly hierarchical view of governing society typical of Borromeo was reflected in the archbishop's direct interventions and in the social composition of the confraternity, whose members came prevalently from the city's nobility. The resulting body was a company of gentlemen. Highly critical of the bottom-up associative tradition of the confraternal world and determined to impose a Christian discipline on the ruling class of the duchy of Milan, Borromeo involved a large number of Milanese noblemen, thereby putting his stamp on the association. It was necessary, his biographer Carlo Morigia wrote, for gentlemen to become involved "as much to benefit themselves, so that by teaching others to die they might learn to live, as to help the wretched condemned."[13] The subsequent modifications introduced by the Spanish governor maintained and reinforced this composition: it was no accident that thereafter it was referred to as the "company of nobles of the consolation of Saint John," or as the "most noble School of Saint John the Baptist." The new statutes followed the Roman model in establishing the forms of ritual to adopt, but they specified, in response to the pious concerns of Philip II, that no one could be put to death on the day in which they received the sacraments. The confraternity, which enjoyed numerous privileges for collecting and administering alms and bequests, in addition to special rights regarding the person and assets of the condemned and the power to pardon two condemned prisoners each year, experienced in that period what has been described as its "golden age."[14]

Some idea of the confraternity's prestige can be gauged from the names of the dedicatees chosen by the authors of the instructions for comforters. The *Sicuro viaggio de giustitiandi* by the Dominican Girolamo Gattico was dedicated by the printer Giovanni Battista Bidelli to the "most illustrious lords of the Company of Saint John the Baptist of Milan," and to the Marchese Ambrogio Spinola, governor and captain general of the State of Milan, who held the title of "protector" of the confraternity.

Some forty years later another book of *ricordi* for companies of justice, by the Cremonese Capuchin monk Carlo Verri, carried a dedication to the "Most noble congregation of Saint John the Baptist."[15] There then followed a list of the *confratelli,* which shows how justified the emphasis on the word "nobility" was. The office of protector was held permanently by the governor of the State of Milan. The members were divided into three categories: fully entitled members, "funeral brothers," and supernumeraries. In the first category we find princes, counts, viscounts, and marchesi, together with knights, abbots, ambassadors of Spain, generals, tournament masters, and militia captains. The names were a kind of who's who of Milanese society: Visconti, Borromeo, Trivulzio, and so on. Carlo Verri explains in the first pages of his text that although helping the condemned to die a Christian death was a duty for all Christians, "nevertheless it is with particular entitlement and reason the concern of the lords of this most illustrious and noble confraternity."[16] The attribute of "Confraternitas nobilissima Divi Ioannis Baptistae Decollati" then featured in all the company's proceedings. It appeared at the top of the elegant printed invitations sent by the prefect of the company to notify members of their duty to take part in comforting practices and executions.[17] The list of prefects during the course of the eighteenth century includes, among others, the names of the marchese of Cislago, Marchese Don Luigi Cagnola, Count Giovanni Luca Pallavicini, Count Don Gaspare Bigli, Count Don Carlo Annone, Marchese Ludovico Trotti, Marchese Don Alberto Visconti, Count Francesco Antonio Visconti Pirovano, and Count Giovanni Antonio Visconti Borromeo. The judges were highborn, the comforters even more so: in their noble hands the sword of justice killed the body and saved the soul. And not infrequently the hooded figure who comforted the person about to be executed was the very same person who shortly before had passed judgment on them. The ancient confraternity of women, artisans, and merchants had been transformed into a company of noblemen devoted to the practice of saving souls in the spare intervals between their many earthly and governmental concerns.

Something similar also took place in the oldest and most celebrated *conforteria* of them all, the one in Bologna: whereas in Milan the political hierarchy dominated, here the profile of the School was defined by those at the top of the ecclesiastical and university orders. An analysis of the social composition of the Bologna *conforteria* reveals that a clear shift took place around the middle of the sixteenth century.[18] From then on, instead of artisans and merchants, we find almost exclusively the names of university professors and members of the local senate. The new statutes approved in 1556 were drawn up by the notary Cristoforo Pensabene, a member of the city's governing elite. Though initially caught up in an inquisition trial, he nonetheless became a member of the Bolognese tribunal of faith and the vicar of Archbishop Gabriele Paleotti in the years that saw the harshest repression of heresy in the city. The tendency to turn the School into a strictly controlled and culturally elevated academy can be seen by the introduction of the new figure of the censor, a post derived from the model of the societies of men of letters that were developing rapidly at the time. Loyalty to the papacy was sealed by the request to aggregate with the Roman confraternity, submitted in 1571, though it took great powers of persuasion to overcome the resistance of the Bolognese in the face of what appeared to them to be a humiliating form of subordination. From that time on, the entanglement between university professors and members of the lay and ecclesiastical governing elite was a constant. Symbolizing the mechanisms of integration of the city's leading authorities in the *conforteria* is the fact that the most famous name we come across there in the eighteenth century was that of Archbishop Prospero Lambertini, later Pope Benedict XIV—who, mindful of his own earlier participation in the confraternity's work, solemnly renewed all its privileges and indulgences.

Heavy clericalization and the customary mix of nobles and prelates was the dominant feature of the companies of justice operating in the Papal State. Cardinals, nephews of popes, and members of the most important congregations and magistracies figured in the lists of the Confraternita di San Giovanni Decollato dei Fiorentini. And looking through the seventeenth-century registers of the confraternity of the Ferrara legation we find that it was by no means exceptional for thieves, highwaymen, and very poor common folk from the Comacchio valleys to find themselves face to face with the most illustrious members of Ferrara's nobility. The minutes of the meeting held on May 13, 1674, to solemnly celebrate the resumption by the lay brothers of the work of "comforting patients and accompanying them to the scaffold," after a long interlude in which they had been replaced by clerics, indicate that the governor was Marchese Roberto degli Obizzi, while other titled Ferrarese noblemen were among the members.[19]

These examples give an idea of the overall process whereby the companies of justice became places of aggregation for members of the dominant orders. Mention can be made of the geographically marginal but important case of the confraternity of Turin; its list for 1717 indicates that it was made up of "a goodly number of members of the nobility and bourgeoisie, comprising lawyers and some doctors."[20]

At the other end of the Italian peninsula from the Piedmont of the House of Savoy lay Spanish Sicily. Here the evolution of the social composition of the companies of justice followed a rather particular course. The members of the Company of Whites in Palermo were prevalently "gentlemen and honored people" from the outset, though in the early days there was some provision for poor members, who were exempt "by the love of God" from paying membership fees (which were used to fund dowries and other benefits for the children of needy *confratelli*). Over time, however, hereditary membership of the nobility became obligatory. The chapters of 1766 spelled this out definitively by requiring, as a prerequisite for membership, "one hundred and fifty years of true nobility of the family of one's own surname."[21] The Sicilian nobles were so jealous of their privileges that they reserved for themselves the exclusive right to enter the fenced-off area where sentences were carried out. In 1669, the mere fact that the standard-bearer entered the enclosure with the banner of justice was enough to spark a bitter controversy between the company and the president of the court. In protest against the entrance of a "base minister on horseback" into the area reserved for the *confratelli*, the nobles decided on and implemented a very singular form of retaliation: for years the company desisted from helping the condemned. This "comforting strike" went on until 1676, and it required the intervention of the king of Spain to bring it to an end.[22]

The shift in the social standing of members toward the higher levels of society was thus a general feature of the long evolution of these associations, which ultimately became select bodies endowed with prestige and power. As a consequence, the "high" responsibility of providing spiritual comfort and being a public presence at the ritual was separated from the "low" tasks relating to the dead body and the paraphernalia of execution. Suffice it to say that taking down the bodies, whole or quartered, from the scaffold or the display pikes in order to recompose and bury them was normally delegated to specially recruited porters. But the change in the social composition of the confraternities is only part of the story of the different perspective on comforting taken over the course of time.

Historic sources relating to the work of the *confratelli* show a progressive change in the figure of the condemned, both in terms of their soul and the treatment of their body. As far as the soul is concerned, all that was requested, as we have seen, was the confession of sins. But few things were discussed more heatedly than confession in the period between the Fourth Lateran Council and the dispute between Catholics and Protestants in the age of the Counter-Reformation. The confession of the condemned had a rather special character: coming as it did right at the very end of their earthly lives, it excluded any possibility of performing adequate penance for their misdeeds. Only a powerful mysticism of Redemption had enabled Catherine of Siena to comfort Niccolò di Toldo and allow him to experience his death sentence as an identification with Christ's sacrifice on the Cross. From here too came the argument, oft repeated in *conforterie,* of the example of the good thief: if faith and prayer had turned a thief into one of the blessed in heaven, why was a similar metamorphosis not possible for thieves and murderers in the final moments of their lives? The theme of God's immense mercy cropped up continually in the nocturnal conversations with those destined for the scaffold. But during the early sixteenth century it was felt that there was an advancing danger of heresy in this area—and the echo of the Protestant doctrines that denied value to human works and entrusted everything to justification by faith reverberated around the squares of Italian cities precisely when followers of the Reformation were executed. We have already seen this in the case of Pietro Fatinelli, sent to his death in Lucca in 1543: turning to the assembled crowd, he declared remorse for his political ambitions, and said he had been converted by heroic models of republican Romanity to a religion of justification by faith that gave him the certainty of divine predestination.[23] This was the shift away from a collective religion of rites to a religion of faith as choice and personal responsibility.[24] The crisis of traditional religion that had driven Pietro Paolo Boscoli to reject the ritual comforting methods of the Blacks seemed to be ending with a move toward Calvinism. But then came the vigorous revival of the Church of Rome and the reaffirmation of the value of ecclesiastic mediation, together with good works, in winning eternal salvation The definition of penance approved by the Council of Trent in 1551 specified its parts (contrition, confession to the priest, satisfaction) and confirmed that those who confessed when death was imminent could be absolved from every sin and by any confessor. The bitter conflict with the Protestant Reformation led to a mistrust of any insistence on the penitent sinner's placing their faith in the mercy of God, emphasizing instead the judicial nature of the tribunal of confession, such as to render divine pardon effective even in the absence of profound sorrow for the sin committed (contrition), considered until then to have been an essential condition. What remained unchanged was the request that the confession of the penitent sinner be followed by "satisfaction"—that is, by adequate amends for the wrong committed, which would in any case be punished with the torments of purgatory. The medieval construction of the ultramundane place for expiating sins became the point of discrimination between orthodoxy and heresy, and lay at the center of terror-inducing preaching about sufferings in the afterlife, which was immediately echoed in the exercises of persuading the condemned. In the meantime, the start of the work of the Roman Inquisition offered the occasion for returning to and stiffening the traditional rules regarding the confession and forgiveness of repentant heretics—they could be forgiven and could save their souls if they confessed, but that did not mean they would be allowed to live. In the notes of the Roman jurisconsult Pietro Belo, who was appointed consultor of the Roman Inquisition in the middle of the sixteenth century, we find an annotated response to the case of a stubborn heretic in Parma, who, having been brought to the pyre to be burned, declared his repentance. The question was: after sacramental confession, could he be forgiven or should he be handed back to the secular court for execution? Belo answered that the maternal womb of the Church was always open to the repentant son, but forgiveness only concerned the penitential court and the fate of the soul. Relapsed heretics and fake converts should not be spared the punishment of death.[25]

From then on there was effectively a growing climate of caution and mistrust about last-minute conversions at the foot of the scaffold. In the comforters' texts we no longer find Saint Catherine of Siena's certainty regarding the immediate ascent of Niccolò di Toldo's soul to the celestial wedding, but only cautious annotations about the hopes that could be entertained, in the best of cases, about the eternal fate of the executed person. The spectacle of death at the hands of justice took on increasingly gloomy and disturbing overtones. The horror of the crimes and the cruelty of the punishments had to instill into readers and spectators a healthy fear of sin and of disobeying the legitimate authorities. The suffering and fears of those who converted only when execution was imminent and who died fearing that they would not be saved for all eternity were underlined for harsh pedagogical purposes. The most popular figure in the comforting tradition, the good thief of the Gospel story, paid the price for this new climate. Saint Dismas—as the devotion of Christians had called him—had offered the most solid foundation for the arguments of consolers trying to dispel the pall of despair hanging over the condemned: Christ himself had assured him that he would be welcomed into heaven on the very day of his death on the Cross. The condition of the person condemned to death and awaiting execution reflected the general condition of humanity as a whole and of individual human beings. There had been a change in the economy of the relationship between Christians and their God, which was increasingly and unilaterally regulated by the will of a God that did not take human merits and wrongdoings into account at all, but castigated and saved in an inscrutable fashion. This was the outcome stemming from the popular diffusion, through grassroots preaching, of the dominant theology in the Franciscan order, which proposed an idea of divine power that was not subject to any rule, whereas the Dominicans tried to guarantee the rationality of the relationship between the natural and the supernatural. That is why the model of the good thief Saint Dismas, whisked from a disgraceful death on earth to the glory of heaven on the basis solely of a last-second invocation, came to inspire the work of the companies of justice in the cities of Italy, and then spread from there. From that same foundation, the sense that it was totally impossible for a human plant with corrupt roots to work well would lead the Augustinianism of Luther to overturn the complex structure of the system of ecclesiastical pardons that had grown up like a climbing evergreen on the hard trunk of the gallows tree.

But in his *De arte bene moriendi*—a best seller of that particular genre— Robert Bellarmine established the general principle that was dominant not only in Catholic religious culture: in order to die well, it was necessary to have lived well. Those who lived badly therefore died badly. Only a life rigorously inspired by good principles could ensure a good death. And if the good thief had been saved and beatified on the cross, it was surely because he had lived a saintly life.[26] And as for the mode of confession, Bellarmine called for caution and the use of stricter methods to ensure the efficacy of the sacrament.[27] Ideas of this kind obviously could not circulate in the places where thieves were persuaded to confess. But grave doubts about the chances of the condemned being saved in the afterlife circulated in the closed confines of convents among monks responsible for confessions.[28] Such doubts became palpable in both erudite and popular literature. The deaths of sinners were awful, and it was a terrible error not to make penance immediately after committing a sin: those who put everything off to the end of their lives should harbor no illusions about the goodness of God, warned Paolo Aringhi, the priest of the Roman oratory in an imposing work of encyclopedic doctrine.[29]

The representation of the delinquent in the popular literature that flourished around the scaffold was no less harsh and negative.[30] In rhyming verse or in prose, the many pamphlets printed in the sixteenth to eighteenth centuries presented a dark and terrifying image of the delinquent that underpinned the extolling of justice for having done away with the criminal. The start of the ballad that opens "the wicked life of Arrigo Gabertinga, highway murderer," is a case in point:

> Signori se mi serve la memoria
> e insieme col giuditio l'intelletto
> voglio cantarvi una crudel historia
> d'un perfido villano maladetto.[31]

(If memory serves me well
and together with judgment, intellect,
I want to sing for you a cruel story
of a wicked, cursed villain.)

Thieves and murderers were the chief protagonists of these stories, which were spawned and sold in city squares; they are mainly peopled by men, though there are also women who poison their husbands, such as the Signora Prudenza from Ancona.[32] There also is space here for ungrateful sons who find in the final punishment the occasion for tardy remorse.[33] The height of the pleasure of narrating such tales came when there was the opportunity to sing about the execution of a particularly hated figure—the executioner.[34] The moralizing intent veils the pleasure in the dreadful and the monstrous, the abomination of those who leave the domain of a normal life. The notorious Neapolitan bandit chief, Benedetto Mangone, condemned to death for rebellion against the king, was the leading character of a poem in *ottava rima* offering the reader a specific description of the theater of punishments in all its horror.[35] Here the path taken by the bandit on the executioner's cart is a grotesque inversion of the triumphal entries of sovereigns: he has a fake gold crown on his head, is tortured with red-hot pincers, and is subjected to the final, terrible torment of the wheel, while his "strong and stubborn . . . errors" are recalled by "the angelic *confratelli*" of the company of justice.[36] Here too their presence and their admonitions—the invitation to think of Christ's Passion and the promise of final salvation—do not alter the nature of a representation of justice as the liberation of humanity from a diabolic presence. The large city of Naples was the setting for some particularly elaborate rituals: and the popular life of the city produced some very effective poetic literature, full-blown versified chronicles such as the one written by Marchese Giovan Battista Del Tufo about the procession of justice in his late sixteenth-century "portrait" of the city. Here the protagonist is:

> quel dolente [che] vien fuor di carcere tra pur troppa gente
> scalzo e avvinto il meschin col capo ignudo,
> portando ne la man legate a gionte
> quel che spirò sovra il Calvario monte.[37]

(that pitiful wretch [who] came out of prison amid so many people
barefoot and bound, with bare head,

carrying in his tied, joined hands
[an image of] he who died on Mount Calvary.)

Also featuring in these stories were members of the higher orders, who, when it came to wrongdoing, appeared endowed with a superior and even monstrous wickedness—for example, the "most eminent gentleman" of Milan, executed in 1609 for having committed "120 homicides, buried a priest alive, slaughtered a young child, and other things of unprecedented ferocity." In his case too, this Italian gallows literature differed from a genre that was very widespread at the time in other European countries in the attention it devoted to the presence of comforters. The gentleman prompted the mobilization of "ten Capuchins, and three priests," in addition to the *confratelli* of San Giovanni alle Case Rotte, "who comforted him continually," making him kneel before all the sacred images and recite prayers and inviting the people to "shout mercy." But that his soul was truly saved is cast into doubt by the final detail, when the nobleman came to a halt in front of the black-draped platform. Turning pale and with his legs buckling under him, he said to the monks that he did "not know if he was sorry for his sins, or only sorry that he felt no contrition."[38]

"Who lives well, dies well": Bellarmine's principle returns by way of conclusion in one of the many "execution reports" which, in the eighteenth century, contributed moral teachings and journalistic information to the great current of gallows literature. The account of the execution of three condemned prisoners in Livorno on September 12, 1745, stressed the "great cruelties" they had committed and included the text of the speech purportedly uttered on the scaffold by one of the three, the Florentine Giacomo Lenzi.[39] The "example of these wretches" was necessary so that sinners might correct their ways—this is how it was put by another pamphlet of the same ilk and by the same publisher, dealing with the "wicked" death of an unrepentant murderer, Angiolo Secchiarolo known as Bigaratta, from Ripe in the diocese of Senigallia. He died on the gallows in Ancona in June 1729, entirely unmoved by all exhortations to show a sign of contrition.[40] And he had had lots of comforters of noble stock as well. One of them was the future pontiff, Prospero Lambertini, recently appointed the archbishop of Ancona. The man had even been subjected to the test of fire, to give him an idea of what the flames of hell might be like: they had held his hand over a lit candle, making his "flesh burn for nearly a quarter of an hour." To no avail. He died invoking the devil, and his body was carried outside the city and buried in the place reserved for animal carcasses, "as a universal, terrible example."

A tradition of stories of facts and characters associated with the gallows was thus developing—an important source for the image of crime and criminals, to which we shall return. But the question that arises at this point is whether the condemned left any final messages, and what they were. In the mass of documentation collected by the comforters about the final hours of the "afflicted," was there any space for their final words—for the "vividness of words" that attracted Michel Foucault in the lives of "infamous men"?[41] For now, if there was a "vividness," a splendor, surrounding the protagonists of Italian scaffold stories, it was that of the triumphs of baroque altars.

19

The Voices of the Condemned

IN THIS HISTORY there is an evident imbalance between the very many words of the comforters, and their masters and spiritual guides, and the very few we have of the condemned themselves. This imbalance is not casual, and it would be strange if it were not so. In it we find, multiplied a hundredfold, the gap so familiar to historians between those who hold power and those subjected to it. The wealth of literature stemming from the need to anticipate the protests, complaints, and questions of those who had just learned what fate awaited them, had rapidly evolved into systematic argumentation that reflected a situation from which there was no way out: this was the prospect facing the condemned, and it was up to them to decide whether to accept it or rail against it. The comforter's task was to guide them onto the path of acceptance. This was the inescapable crux of the matter, and everything else—stratagems, threats, prayers, tales about the miracles and deaths of martyrs—revolved around this choice. As for the things that were actually said, these were shrouded in secrecy when they were not formalized in the schemes envisaged by the comforting procedures. The manuals of instruction were very clear about the obligation to attend to every detail of the contact with "patients," from how they should be addressed to suggestions about the best way to overcome their resistance. But what was learned about their crimes had to remain covered by silence. The raison d'être of the secrecy rule, habitually present in confraternity statutes as in all those governing the functioning of corporative associations, lay in the rule of forgiveness. Nothing that came to light during the hours of comforting should leak out. The forgiveness promised to the condemned was to cancel out forever all memory of their wrongdoings—in this world and in the next.[1] The constraint of silence had to be respected regarding the content of declarations made during the repeated confessions that took place during the night. But sacramental confession was not the only occasion to hear what the condemned had to say. One night is a short period of time, but to those for whom it was their last it seemed very long indeed. What was said in those hours? Very little filters out from confraternity papers. And yet the reticence about the nighttime conversations is still minimal compared to the silence of the condemned during the daytime ritual. The goal of the *confratelli* was to exhibit a human being going to their death contrite and silent. As Pompeo Serni clearly explained in the instructions we cited earlier, it was necessary that the condemned should walk among the comforters without communicating with the world, keeping their eyes and minds focused on the *tavoletta,* listening to and repeating prayers and litanies, avoiding at all cost what was considered the greatest danger—the impulse to talk to the crowd. Everything was to be directed toward a rituality of devotion, and silence to cover what had happened. Though this was not always achieved, in the vast majority of cases things worked out in exactly that way. There were a number of justifications, not just religious but also political and social: the salvation of the soul was linked to acceptance of the sentence as an expression of God's will. To contest it, accusing the ruling authorities of injustice, put the whole strategy of the companies at risk. But perhaps there was something more, and different, besides the choice of pure political and social opportunism that emerges at first sight from the activities of a body linked to the power that had the passed sentence. In order to try to answer this, let us look at the ritual of justice as it was experienced in Italian cities, and what its outcome was in the eyes of contemporaries.

In the orchestration of capital punishment as public spectacle, the comforters were instructed to prevent the condemned from speaking, unless it was to recite prayers. But before the final act, there was a dialogue with those about to die, and this is how their stories and voices found some space in the papers of the confraternities. Whether the person was saved or damned, the companies of justice wanted to keep a record of them in their accounts. In the rich but dispersed patrimony of the companies' records, the one that figures most often is precisely the *libro dei condannati,* the book of the condemned. Anyone leafing through the surviving lists will find a long procession of names of those who went to the scaffold: men and women, laypeople and clergy, nobles and commoners—for the most part baptized and Christian, but Jews and Muslims as well. United only by their common fate, they came into contact for a generally brief period of time (a few hours or days) with the companies of justice active in Italian cities. Traces of that short phase have survived in the documents of the companies: a name, a date, occasionally some information about the crime and the form of death, more often a judgment about their religious behavior and what could be deduced about the eternal fate of their soul.

Regarding a man named Camillo, beheaded in Siena on June 7, 1521, the register of the local company of death made only this brief and rather doubtful comment about his fate in the life to come: "Average expectations for the soul. That God may have had mercy on him." The case of Pietro, hung for murder in 1572, was treated more fully. He had killed a woman and her granddaughter, and buried the bodies in a field. But a peasant who had seen the grass growing vigorously on the burial spot had discovered the crime and Pietro had been captured. He appeared hard and stubborn to the comforters, who noted: "His wickedness was so great that he would willingly have died if he had been able with his own hand to take vengeance on his accuser. And when it was pointed out to him that this was a great mistake, in the end he simply said that Christ would take vengeance for him." Hence the negative conclusion: "So may the merciful Lord not have looked at his obstinacy."[2]

With a few variants, this is the normal pattern of the profiles of the condemned outlined in the companies' books of records: a name, a date, sometimes an indication of the kind of crime, a brief account of the way in which the comforting had been carried out, and often a final comment about the chances of the person's soul being saved or not. For Camillo the hopes were "average"; for his fellow citizen Pietro they were almost nil, and it was necessary to entrust him to the inscrutable mercy of God. In others—the majority—the *confratelli* could record a complete success.

Prisoners who resisted the comforters' entreaties received only scornful notes of disappointment and rejection. We gain some idea of this from the annotation about Piero da Codigoro, the Po boatman condemned for murder and theft in Ferrara in 1495. He "did not want to confess," and so, after his death, he was thrown into the river "as animal bait, just as he deserved."[3]

Failures like this were a small minority of cases: common people who refused through silence, pretending to sleep, or by declaring they wanted to be left in peace while they ate an abundant dinner to which they were not accustomed. Or people unwilling to renounce a religious or intellectual choice for which they were prepared to give up their life.

The question of what these sources can tell us about the condemned must therefore come to terms with the very nature of the sources. As we have seen, in the model of comforted death everything was mediated by the companies of justice. Once the prisoner had been transferred from the prison to the chapel, the relationship between the "patient" and outside reality was filtered by the comforters. While the person was in prison, some messages might still have been exchanged between inside and outside, but what happened on the eve of execution is known to us only through what was noted down by the comforters.

The condemned who walked to the scaffold on their own two feet—or arrived in a cart, or were tied to a horse's tail and dragged there—their faces covered by the *tavoletta,* could not see, could not hear, and could not speak. Or rather, they saw what they had to see, heard what they had to hear, and said what they had to say. Like the martyr saints on the painted *tavolette,* they were considered, and had to think of themselves, as already being outside this world, composed in an edifying fixity or in a frightful inhumanity. They could pray, forgive, and ask for forgiveness—or die vilified and damned in body and spirit. A whole category of human beings, the condemned, seems to be composed of people without their own voice. In effect, the notes recorded in the lists of the confraternities consisted initially only of a summary description of the crime and the punishment. A few examples of criminals assisted by the Company of Blacks in Florence will suffice to illustrate this: in 1423, Dolfo di Antonio was "beheaded for treacherous homicide and other crimes"; in 1426, Piero di Cavalcante di Piero from Città di Castello was "pincered on the cart, hung, and burned on the Podestà's orders because he killed a notary in his house to rob him, and cut him into pieces, throwing part [of the remains] in the Arno, and part in the latrine."[4] Likewise in Bologna, where, on July 6, 1440, "Tomaso Canetoli and Battista Bernabò, rag dealer, were beheaded for trying to let the army of Francesco da Cotignuola in through the Porta di San Felice to drive out the Bentivoglios";[5] and in Ferrara, where in 1541, "on the fourteenth day of January . . . Zohane de Zaneto da Vicenza, thief, was hung at the gallows on the other side of the Po."[6] Names and misdeeds succeed one another like this. A little more information is forthcoming when the executed person did not have time to confess, or refused to do so, or if something else unusual happened during the course of the execution: for example, if the body of the murder victim shed blood as the killer went by, as occurred in Milan on March 10, 1554.[7]

The records of the activity of the Milanese confraternity are generally quite spare. A list detailing executions carried out in the 292-year period between 1471 and 1763 contains 3,124 names.[8] Many things changed over this long arc of time, commencing with the place of execution—Piazza del Duomo; the *broletto* (the palace where justice was administered and the city council met); the Castello Sforzesco; outside Porta Ticinese; and Piazza Vetra. Initially the annotations give barely the name and type of punishment: the list begins with a woman named Lucia Fontana, beheaded on January 26, 1471, in Vigentino, a village on the southern edge of Milan, and "buried in said place," and an Antonio and a Friano da Padova, hung in Piazza del Duomo and buried in the cemetery of San Giovanni. The numbers increased and their punishments fleshed out with details in the age of the Borromeo family. The year 1566 alone saw the deaths of a Fermo Castoldi and a Paolo di Farino known as "il Calcagno," "pincered and hung" on May 9; a Battista da Boixo, street murderer, who was quartered on May 15; a Giacomo da Prato and a Battista da Ronchi, common murderers, who received the punishment of the wheel on May 27; as many as four men were executed on June 27— one, a sixteen-year-old, was hung, three were "dragged through Milan by horsetail," two were given the wheel ("inrodati vivi"). There then follow other cases of prisoners being "pincered" and "dragged" through the streets tied to a horsetail. The exercising of ecclesiastical justice by the House of Borromeo saw the appearance of burned heretics—a priest, a monk, a Lutheran spinner. The episode that caused the greatest stir was the execution of four would-be assassins of Cardinal Charles Borromeo in August 1570. Sentences for heresy, sodomy, infanticide, and witchcraft became more frequent over the century. With the plague of 1630, the political use of justice led to a series of sentences that, thanks to Alessandro Manzoni, have gone down in history as being particularly unjust and infamous—those against *untori*, or plague spreaders. The victims of horrendous tortures, and forced to confess to crimes they had not committed, Guglielmo Piazza and Gian Giacomo Mora were condemned to death "as authors of the iniquities of plague spreading," "hauled onto a cart and pincered, and then, after their right hand was cut off, they were put on the wheel alive in the usual place, and kept alive two hours, and burned to death, and their ashes scattered." In the meantime, Gian Giacomo Mora's house was razed, and two city criers on horseback distributed notices and, to the blare of a trumpet, announced on every street corner the death of those responsible for the fate of five thousand plague victims.[9]

These lists were, however, just one kind of document charting the work of the comforters: besides the series of names and dates of a concise annals writing, the archives of the confraternities were accumulating many other traces of their dealings with the condemned and of what was said and done in those circumstances. But there was a more powerful reason for the bureaucratic regularity of the annotations and writings of chancellors and notaries than celebrating the comforters' devout work, or the need to leave a memory of unusual events and individuals. It was of course important for confraternities to preserve information about the work they did to save imperiled souls: these were glorious memories for generations of individuals who joined charitable associations and then learned how to proceed along that path. But when the work of comforting started to be recognized and encouraged by ecclesiastical and state powers, the records took on the shape of a diligent and alacritous bureaucracy. The confraternities of death were effectively responsible before the State and the Church for the successful outcome of the scaffold ritual. Having become at once a heavenly and an earthly bureaucracy, intent on reconciling the justice of God and that of the prince (or pope), and presenting them jointly to the condemned, they had a difficult path to tread—they were literally on a knife edge. It was necessary to overcome deep resistance, to silence desperate protests, organize solemn public rituals, and operate in the narrow space between the condemned, the power that condemned and killed, and the public summoned to watch. The primary reason for keeping accurate records of their activities was therefore to measure the efficacy of their work. The initially embryonic and then more extensive accounts of the scaffold ritual, with the recording of the condemned person's last wishes and the expression of their feelings, developed from this. And it is to these accounts and these pieces of testimony that we must turn if we want to try to hear the voices of people who were facing the most dramatic moment in their lives. So let us look now at some randomly chosen cases drawn from the surviving papers of a number of these confraternities.

Conversion and Repentance

We can begin in Rome, with some records from the mid and late sixteenth century. Book 11 of the "Libro Grande del Proveditore" and the corresponding "Giornale" of the Roman company of San Giovanni Decollato contain the minutes of the brothers' Sunday meetings and the reports of executions carried out in the period from 1581 to 1584. A note on the inside front cover page proposes a count of 256 executed prisoners. However, the reader's curiosity will be immediately drawn to the report of one man who was "reprieved when he was about to go to the scaffold."[10] On Friday February 18, 1583, the company was called on to deal with four men who, as a result of a sentence passed by the Roman Inquisition, had been excommunicated as heretics and entrusted to the secular arm—the court of the governor of Rome—for execution. In its pious hypocrisy, the holy tribunal did not speak of killing, and indeed asked that the sentence should be carried out without bloodshed. But effectively what it required was that the men should be put to death. Their names were Domenico Danzerello da Piperno; Prospero d'Imperatore of "Barbary Africa"; Gabriel Enriquez, a Portuguese Jew; and a Dominican monk who is well known to historians: Giacomo Paleologo.[11] This was the man who, from his native Chio, had begun an adventurous life that saw him play a leading part in the attempt to establish a church in Transylvania based on the religious ideas of Michael Servetus, the Spanish Erasmian who denied the Trinity. He, like the other three men, was put through the exercise of comforting by the *confratelli* of San Giovanni, who were determined to persuade them to repent of their heresies and to confess. With two of them, their efforts were quickly rewarded: Domenico Danzerello and Prospero d'Imperatore repented of their sins and declared their wish to die as good Christians. The sentence in the report for one of them reads as follows:

> Having confessed and repented of his sins he said that he wished to die as a good Christian, and thanked God for dying as a son of the Holy Church, and prayed the Lord that he might forgive him his sins, and he, out of his own love, forgave all those who had offended him, and

prayed that those who he had offended might forgive him, and he declared his wish to die with the holy confession of the Catholic truth.[12]

His words? Hardly. Instead, they are the formulaic wordings of the bureaucracy of the soul. We find similar expressions, sometimes textually identical, attributed to other condemned prisoners who accepted the comforters' invitations to repent and confess—that is, almost the entirety of cases. This, for example, is how the final wishes of a certain Gianmaria Ferrari, from Genoa, were recorded on January 7, 1565:

> Confessed and sorrowful and repentant of his sins, he asked God for forgiveness, commending his soul to Him with great humility of heart, praying to the glorious Virgin and the whole heavenly court that they might see fit to intercede for him in the hour of his death: he forgave all the offenses done to him and begged forgiveness of all those whom he had wronged, declaring that he wished to die as a good and faithful Christian.[13]

And with very similar words three centuries later, a condemned man declared that he wished "to die as a good Christian, and, submitting to the will of God, to accept death as atonement for sins, begging forgiveness of his fellow men for every wrong and forgiving them every wrong, as he hopes God will forgive him."[14]

The man in question was Gaetano Tognetti, executed in Rome on November 24, 1868, together with his companion Giuseppe Monti for political conspiracy against the papal regime. Quite irrespective of his story, to which we shall return presently, the point to stress here is the repetition of basically identical expressions centuries later. We can regard them as a preconstructed mold impressed onto the thoughts of the condemned, at least those who declared contrition.

On the other hand, the thoughts of the unrepentant have not been saved. In that group of executions in 1581, not one but two condemned men refused to bow in the face of the comforters. It is no accident that they were followers of two faiths incompatible with Roman Catholicism. The Portuguese Jew Gabriel Enriquez, who, after baptism was imposed on him, went back "wickedly to Judaizing and to observing the rites and superstitions of the Jews," proved unbending and staunchly faithful to his religion. The efforts of the confraternity members and of some theological experts to convert him were to no avail, and so, "persevering in his error and obstinacy, he was wretchedly burned alive." In the case of Giacomo Paleologo, they were dealing with a radical heretic who in his writings had espoused the anti-Trinitarian ideas of Michael Servetus. Paleologo was a long-pursued enemy who had escaped the clutches of the Inquisition several times. He was also an adversary well equipped to rebut the arguments of the brothers—and in fact he too, like Enriquez, proved impervious to the persuasions of a whole gaggle of comforters. All the best efforts of the "many theological monks and Jesuits" who hurried to assist the Compagnia di San Giovanni Decollato were in vain. The following morning they dressed him in the heretic's garb, a canvas "habit" decorated with the flames of hell, and led him out into the city square. But along the route to the scaffold, he began to display signs of wanting to convert. We do not know why, though it is not hard to imagine. With death imminent, the long experience of a world where pretense and dissimulation were part and parcel of life, as his protector, Bishop Andreas Dudith, had taught him, must have pushed him to a last-resort fake conversion. The register of the comforters states that Paleologo acknowledged the error of his ways, declaring himself subject to the Holy Catholic and Apostolic Mother Church; and as proof of this, he openly venerated the crucifix that the brothers placed before him. A miracle: a pious later narrative attributed the merit for this to Saint Philip Neri, who approached him when "the fire stake was now close, now close to burning Paleologo." Philip purportedly "said to the Court . . . that they should stop and to the ministers that they should not carry out [the execution], otherwise castigation [awaited], and as Philip had, in that brief space of time, softened the heart of that wretch, he also induced him, in the same place and having got him to climb onto a bench, to publicly renounce his error, to the admiration of all the people present there to see the outcome."[15] The story of this miracle was also propagated by a devout popular image representing the scene as a sudden event, the chief protagonist and mover of which was Saint Philip Neri, who was not mentioned by the comforters at all (Plate 17). But at any rate that sudden conversion was the desired turn of events, albeit rather late in the day. What was to be done? The procession had already nearly reached the Campo de' Fiori, where the crowd was waiting. While the first sentences were carried out, and fires lit for two of the condemned, the *provveditore* and the chaplain hurried off to speak to Cardinal Savelli, the vicar of Rome. He promptly referred them to the governor, because the heretic had been handed over to the secular court and no longer came under his jurisdiction. The governor sent an urgent message to the pope and in the meantime asked the *bargello* (police chief) to suspend the execution. Giacomo Paleologo was taken into a nearby workshop while they waited for an answer, which eventually arrived. It had been decided that the conversion of this particularly dangerous heretic should be held up as an example. Pope Gregory XIII ordered that Paleologo was to express contrition for everything he had done and said against the Church: a declaration was drawn up in writing and authenticated by the chief notary of the criminal court, who read it to the people from on top of a bench in the middle of the square. That was not all: Paleologo also had to read out the letter in public, confirming everything said in it on oath and prostrating himself in adoration before the crucifix. At this point the choir of *confratelli* sung the Te Deum and the procession took the penitent heretic back to prison.[16] But it was only a temporary and partial reprieve. Paleologo remained in jail for a long time, where it seems that Philip Neri really did visit him and tried to negotiate conditions for the prisoner's life and liberty. These were not accepted, and four years later he was put to death on the orders of the fearsome Pope Sixtus V.

Pope Sixtus kept the executioner in regular employment during his reign and, before Paleologo, proved implacable with many others: a notable example of his style was the condemnation of the most powerful member of the Bolognese feudal aristocracy, Giovanni Pepoli. He was put to death with very little forewarning in 1585 for having allowed bandits to stay in his feudal domains. The principle adopted on this occasion was that, as Traiano Boccalini wrote, "an example made of a great [man] suffices to make everyone observe it."[17] The suspension of Paleologo's sentence had also been justified by the utility of the public example of a repentant arch heretic. The tally of that day in 1583 had been one impenitent burned alive and three repentant prisoners, two of whom had been hung and then burned, and one sent back to jail. The report documents the brothers' great commitment in performing their task of saving souls, which in the case of Giacomo Paleologo achieved the maximum desired success with a public conversion *in extremis*—an example for all, a triumph of faith rewarded with the reprieving of a life. And it reinforced the image of the Church as a benign mother interceding for children who return to the house of the Father.

In the registers of the Roman company the long series of penitent condemned prisoners was interrupted every now and then by unyielding Jews and the occasional stubborn heretic. In the sixteenth century the violent religious conflict and the spread of doctrinal dissent led to the execution, in Italy's city squares, especially in Rome, of a considerable number of people who had been condemned by the tribunal of the Inquisition. And as that tribunal, though nominally invested with universal power, exercised its jurisdiction especially over Italy, many presumed heretics from various parts of the peninsula ended up in Roman jails and went to the scaffold in the city of the pope. Traces of them have not always survived. The purpose of the Inquisition was to curb the threat of heresy, regarded as a plague of the soul and therefore as something even more dangerous than the kind that killed the body. For this reason efforts were made to erase all memory of them, and of names and ideas. When dealing with heretics, the confraternities of justice tried to obtain at least an abjuration from them before execution, and they had something important to offer in exchange—the possibility of not being burned alive: that is, of being hung before they were burned. People died for the crime of heresy in other Italian cities as well. The proceedings of the School of Comforters in Bologna record ten executions for heresy in 1567 in which the ashes of the dead were buried, a sign that they had abjured. They were burned alive "as most obstinate Lutherans," and were all painters.[18] Another painter also went to the stake the following year in Conegliano, in the territories of the Venetian Republic: his name was Riccardo Perucolo, put to death on an unspecified day in February or March of that year, to the great satisfaction of the papal nuncio in Venice and of the Roman authorities: he had "relapsed" back into heresy, and so the fact that he had succumbed to the exhortations of a Franciscan monk and a priest, who visited and comforted him in prison, did him no good. His whole story, and all but a few fragments of his work, were then carefully erased, and it took the painstaking research of an enthusiastic historian to piece together his story.[19] The only thing public about the case was his being "burned publicly in Conegliano." This encouraged the nuncio's hope to see many more of the same kind, as a terrifying "example for others," thereby modifying the customary Venetian practice of drowning heretics in the lagoon in the silence and darkness of the night.

We are indebted to the records of the companies of justice for having at least preserved written memory of the names of the condemned, with a little more information if there had been conversion and repentance. When the statistical annotations extend into narrative accounts, we read stories of dogged resistance—above all, though not exclusively, on the part of those who had abandoned the Church of Rome for other religious confessions. Religious barriers went up in the face of the invitation to abjure. But while Jews generally refused to be baptized, for the most part followers of the Protestant Reformation or of radical heresies eventually yielded and proved to be "well disposed"—that is, they repented and agreed to confess. The call of the old Church might have stirred profound echoes, all the more so as in their case the execution arrived after long and trying periods of imprisonment, during which they were subject to the assiduous and insidious work of persuaders chosen in particular from among the ranks of the Jesuits and Capuchins, who were determined at any cost to offer public proof of the triumph of faith over heresy. This was the experience, among others, of the Erasmian humanist Aonio Paleario, arrested and tried by the Roman Inquisition and rightly considered a martyr of the Italian religious reform movement. After lengthy imprisonment he was taken off for execution on July 4, 1570, and gave the watching crowd the spectacle of a repentant heretic. According to the register of the Roman confraternity he had been persuaded of his errors: "confessed and contrite, he begged forgiveness of God and his glorious mother the Virgin Mary, and of the whole heavenly court, and said that he wished to die as a good Christian and believed everything that the Holy Roman Church believes."[20] What actually happened we do not know. In his long spell in the Inquisition jail, he had been subjected to the care of the wily Jesuit Giacomo Ledesma, who probably managed to undermine some of his convictions, or perhaps produced a distorted version of the decisions taken by Aonio Paleario. In fact, he did not formally abjure his beliefs, and if he was condemned to death by the tribunal, it was due to a flash of humanistic dignity—the refusal to wear the habit of the repentant heretic. He died accompanied by the execration of those who, like the Florentine correspondent of Piero Usimbardi, the secretary of the duke of Florence, maintained that he had shown himself to "care very little for God in this end" and was amazed that "they did not burn him alive."[21] But the organization of the spectacle by the Roman confraternity was more effective than the rigor of the tribunal of faith, and it was thanks to the former that the Roman people were presented with the image of a lost lamb brought back into the

Catholic flock. On the other hand, the "terrible obstinacy" of Luca da Faenza was unyielding. Hung and burned in front of the bridge of Castel Sant' Angelo on February 28, 1569, he had refused to confess despite the insistent pressure of two Capuchin monks who had been called in to help by the brothers of the company. The monks had "fought" with him all night, "even kneeling at his feet and praying for the visitation of Jesus Christ." But all their efforts proved useless, and in the end "the Company left with very great regret at having seen so much obstinacy."[22] Devout *confratelli* had similar disappointments in other cities as well. In Modena, the unrepentant death of the heretic Magnavacca in 1567 caused a wave of shock: "He died in his bad opinion, even though he had been warned and comforted by many Catholics of the need to do otherwise," as the *podestà* reported to his ruling duke. For this reason it was decided to kill him in the night and burn his body straightaway "outside the city."[23]

These stories of a minority of individuals recalcitrant to the forgiving embrace of the Roman Church stand out for their solitariness against the background of a plebiscitary rush into the arms of penitence and conversion. One "impenitent burned heretic" was a certain brother Celestino, otherwise known as Giovanni Antonio da Verona, who died at dawn on September 25, 1599, stripped naked and burned at the stake in Campo de' Fiori. Not only had the lay brothers endeavored to convert him, so too had a succession of monks: two Capuchins, two Jesuits, and two Oratorians had deployed "very efficacious reasons" right up to the end, but at the final moment Celestino "arrived without showing any sign of repentance."[24] Just a few months later (Thursday, February 17, 1600), Campo de' Fiori would also be the setting for another famous "execution of an impenitent heretic," the burning at the stake of Giordano Bruno, whose tongue was nailed to stop him from talking to the crowd.[25] From then on the flow of unrepentant heretics dried up. But as Luigi Firpo has observed, in the absence of heretics the Roman Inquisition found ways of exercising its power in other directions, striking against anyone who offended the figure of the pope in any way. Between 1605 and 1636, five heads rolled "for harsh judgments about the pope."[26]

After the sixteenth century the choice of impenitence at the expense even of one's life was a rare phenomenon in the experience of the Compagnia di San Giovanni Decollato. When it did happen, it involved not so much dissident Christians or followers of other confessions but rather Jews who, at the moment of death, rediscovered the force of their old faith. One emblematic instance was the case of Abramo Caivani and Angeluccio Della Riccia, two young Jews from the ghetto of Rome who were found guilty of theft and hung on the morning of November 24, 1736, at Ponte Sant' Angelo. They were poor men, with little or no religious instruction. However, the imminence of death rekindled their Jewish faith, and they resisted all attempts to press the Christian sacraments on them: "These wretches never wanted to convert," noted the abbot Placido Ghezzi. Their bodies were buried by night in the Ortaccio, a kind of ghetto for prostitutes.[27] It was only thanks to the testimony of an anonymous fellow Jew, in much the same way as in the story of Michele da Calci, that a memory of their heroic resistance has survived.[28]

Such cases were very rare, emphasized each time in confraternity records and vilified in the black tales of scaffold literature. Less rare were those in which the condemned person held out at length and refused almost up to the end to repent and confess. Quite apparent here is a widespread awareness of the fact that the comforters' need to secure a declaration of repentance provided an opportunity to haggle for concessions. Among other episodes, the sacristan Marco Gambarucci dwelt on the case of a bag-maker named Giovan Tommaso Cornovaglia, who was to be hung at the Ponte di Castel Sant' Angelo on July 14, 1662, but who proved a tough nut to crack: among various other "diabolic" things he said, he declared "not to know Jesus Christ nor the Holy Virgin his mother and the saints in heaven," and not to understand "what those comforters were saying."[29] The night envisaged for his conversion went by without any results. At dawn, with everything ready for the execution, things went from bad to worse and the comforters feared they would fail. But then finally Giovan Tommaso gave in: he revealed that he had not confessed for years and had made a blood pact with the devil, proving it by pointing to a mark on his arm. The comforters convinced him that "repentance alone, and detestation for such a shameful contract was enough, while he was still alive, to obtain forgiveness from the Lord Almighty." Giovan Tommaso then made a general confession that took two hours. The pact with the devil was declared null and void with a formal declaration, and he died "with excellent hope for his well-being."

A contributing factor in the multiplication of episodes like these was the prestige of the company, the fame of its powers, the social rank of its members: protracted resistance to conversion was one of the means employed by those who sought right up to the end to obtain, if not a pardon, then at least the possibility of a delay to their execution, or a less infamous or less painful death. Naturally, the condemned clung on to a flicker of hope that they might benefit from the privilege of pardon enjoyed by the confraternity. But many of those who considered themselves innocent or who, betrayed by an accomplice who had then been rewarded with a pardon, protested at the unfairness of their treatment, wished to obtain justice. In all these cases the *confratelli* found themselves being urged to pass on complaints and perhaps even evidence to the authorities. This opened up a path fraught with risk, partly because of the danger of failure but also because anyone awaiting a potential revision of their sentence would not be inclined to cross the boundary of repentance and preparation for death toward which the confraternity was pushing them.

In almost all cases, though, the end result was penitence and a devout death. The examples recorded by the companies of justice demonstrate this quite clearly; and those that the Roman archconfraternity could hold up and display to the city's population are a significant sample. The starring role in these edifying representations was played by a succession of common criminals—especially thieves—but also by prominent members of the Roman nobility. One celebrated case was that of Beatrice Cenci, put to death in September 1599 together with her mother, Lucrezia, for having killed her father. The ritual formula of her final declarations underwent a rhetoric amplification, in which we catch a glimpse of the deference and compunction of a company led by male members of the nobility:

> Exhorted by comforters to forbear and to resign herself to the will of God, she prepared herself with great contrition and, having made her confession to our chaplain, said she wished to die as a good Christian and in the bosom of the holy Mother Church, asked God for forgiveness for her sins, and also asked forgiveness to those she had offended in any way whatsoever, as she also forgave those who had offended her, and said that she did all this with all her heart.[30]

The body of Beatrice's mother, Lucrezia, was buried, not in the company's cemetery, but in a chapel in San Pietro in Montorio. It was not in the power of the condemned to decide where their body should go. But in a society where privilege outweighed rights, members of the higher orders quite frequently indicated their preferred burial place. However, the story of Beatrice Cenci was exceptional not only because of her social rank but also because she was a woman. There was a difference between how women and men went to the scaffold. But of what kind?

Female Death

There was a gender difference at least in the words in use to denote death. It is well known that the neo-Latin languages have generally opted for the feminine (*la morte* in Italian), whereas the Germanic languages use a masculine noun (*der Tod* in German) or a genderless noun (*death* in English). But if we look at the figurative tradition, the answer in medieval Europe is clear: in fourteenth-century iconography the living person is followed and taken by the hand by a skeleton that is a specular image of themselves, their truth—a skeleton with scraps of putrid flesh. In this macabre dance the living king gives his hand to the dead king; the fat, richly dressed ecclesiastic is pursued by his skeleton; and the young, proudly beautiful woman has a double in her temporal projection beyond death. The dead extends their hand to the living and annuls the illusions of worldly life. But it is *il morto*—Italian uses the masculine gender for "the dead." For there to be a shift toward the feminine *morte,* an alliance was required between humanistic culture and Christian sensibility. Situated here is the process of abstraction and mythicization that presided over the *trionfo della Morte* (triumph of death) as a divinity superior to individuals and at the same time a mediator of inner processes involving a detachment from the earthly world and a move toward the heavenly one. Nothing expresses this alliance better than Masaccio's famous fresco in the church of Santa Maria Novella in Florence. Here, in the sober classicizing architecture of one of the side chapels, two praying figures look at the crucified Christ above whom God the Father looms. Their gaze is directed upward; but below them, opening beneath their feet, the viewer sees a tomb from which a skeleton says to those watching: "Io fu[i] già quel che voi sete: e quel ch'i son voi ancor sarete" (What you are, I once was; what I am, you will become). The dead figure is no longer the skeleton with putrescent flesh dancing on the same plane as the living one. The bones of Adam occupy a temporal low section which is the past of all humanity: his threat *(quel ch'i son voi ancor sarete)* is averted by the mediation of Christ above him. The horizontal relationship between the living and the dead, one the negation of the other, is replaced by the vertical relationship between a death lying in the past of the human species—Adam, a skeleton without individual identity, stripped of any trace of life—and a divine and vital identity in the future.

Death *(la morte),* the classical female entity ready to join forces with the world of Christian representations, did, however, evoke paths of ideal preparation from which pagan culture had tried to eliminate every feminine weakness: the masculine / feminine dualism had found a locus of strong characterization in the Stoic tradition and in the Roman elaboration of the military virtue of dying for the fatherland. This tradition, linked in various ways to medieval Christian morality, connoted a particular type of death and specific ways of dying as "manly," which made the end of life something freely accepted and assumed as a positive value. Solitude, meditation, and the shunning of the false values of life were the Stoic ingredients taken on board by Christianity and adapted to the idea of death as a passage to a higher eternal life.

The context of impending capital punishment offered a kind of synthesis of all this, concentrated into a measured and limited time span. The condemned went out into the square to face a painful and infamous death decided by others. No terrestrial glory awaited them on the scaffold. And yet it was not rare for the comforters to note the courage and "great spirit" displayed by both men and women. The declaration that they were dying "willingly" is the one that recurs most frequently in confraternity sources, and sometimes the spectators also had cause to be amazed by the cheerfulness of the victims. Catherine of Siena recounts that Niccolò di Toldo smiled when he saw her arrive. And when Pietro Fatinelli went to the scaffold, the anonymous chronicler claimed to have heard "some who said: Oh how cheerfully he goes!"[31] Similar expressions of wonder were heard in squares all across Europe on the special occasion of heresy sentences: in the age of the European religious revolutions, the deaths of new martyrs—followers of the Reformation in Catholic territories, Catholic missionaries in Anglican England—amazed a hostile public locked into the narrow horizons of an intolerant orthodoxy. The return of martyrdom as a form of religious testimony gave rise to bitter polemic and subtle theological distinctions, which did not curb their use for propaganda purposes in controversies between the Christian confessions.[32]

The stereotype of a gender difference between dying like a man and dying like a woman found no place in the literature and work of comforting. However, one thing is certain: what was appreciated and sought from those rightly described as "patients" was the remissive and devout attitude of the repentant sinner typical of the female stereotype, while any attitude of rebellion and of manly, disdainful refusal of comforting in preparing for death was considered an indicator of future damnation. The courage that the comforters tried to instill in the "afflicted" no longer had anything to do with the masculine virtues of pagan death. It seems, wrote Machiavelli, "that the world has become effeminate and Heaven disarmed."[33]

The virtues of charity, the protective figure of the Virgin, the model of Magdalene the penitent sinner were all female, as were the attitudes of passivity and obedience recommended to those about to die. Moving on from stereotypes to real flesh-and-blood people, we find instead that it was fairly rare for women to be sent to the scaffold. When Isabella Signorini was hung in Modena on July 3, 1623, the compiler of the register of the executed recorded the exceptional nature of the episode: "She is the first woman in memory to have been hung as a thief."[34] In fact, most of the names on the list are male. Nor does the instruction literature have much to say about specific problems regarding women facing the death penalty. Having disappeared from the life of the confraternities as active members, women sometimes reappeared among the "afflicted." But women were a distinct minority of the total number of executed prisoners. Men were the almost exclusive protagonists of crime and religious dissidence. That said, there were some sensational episodes involving the execution of women, and a special female criminality associated with poisons, the magical arts, and witchcraft. Stories of love and death in which women played the leading roles inspired poetic compositions and historic laments printed for a popular market. With cases of witchcraft on the decline following the bursts of inquisitorial zeal in various parts of the peninsula in the fifteenth and sixteenth centuries, what came to prominence was the figure of the woman who poisoned and killed for love or out of hatred. The "magic-women-poison trinomial," Giovanna Fiume observes, "recurs with such frequency in the history of modern Sicily and in such a close relationship as to have left persistent linguistic traces as well."[35] It should be said that the figure of the poisoning woman also crops up beyond Sicily. One example is Adriana di Mariotto Massetti, who was beheaded in her home city of Siena in 1570 for having tried to murder her husband and another woman by poison. The description of her in the written record is fulsome in its praise: Adriana showed herself to be "of admirable constancy, ready and confident in her words, and gave such a good account of herself that all our brothers who were present testified that never in their time had there been either man or woman with a constancy like it. That the blessed Lord may have given her peace in eternal life.[36] Girolama Spanna, on the other hand, was from Palermo in Sicily. Sentenced to death in Rome in July 1659 together with four other accomplices for being "producers of [poisonous] water," she put up a quite different display of character. Marco Gambarucci, sacristan of the Roman company, recounts in his diary what happened on the night of July 5, 1659. While the five women were being comforted, Girolama Spanna asked insistently for her handcuffs to be removed so she could satisfy "some needs." This was granted a first time, but not again, whereupon Girolama exclaimed "that our Saint had especially assisted us at that point, because she had decided that if she found herself again without handcuffs she would have made them see some grave spectacle." After her pockets were searched and a two-bladed knife found, the woman confessed: "With this pocket knife I wanted first to slit the throat of Giovanna de Grandis"—one of the other women, known as Tintora—"and then wound anyone who came close to me, and slit my own throat as well."[37] It was known to be dangerous to leave condemned prisoners unchained during comforting; but it is also noteworthy that Girolama's intrepid homicidal and suicidal wish came to the Roman sacristan's mind. Female condemned prisoners, then, despite being less numerous than their male counterparts, also included figures endowed with manly courage and ferocity. And among them there were also those who avoided the whole spectacle by committing suicide: on September 2, 1673, the Bolognese Lucia Marzocchi "was found dead in prison, having throttled herself with a [makeshift] noose."[38]

If we consider the charges for which they were sent to the scaffold, it appears evident that the majority of women were found guilty of crimes of a "private" nature, played out within the four walls of the home and in the intrigues of illicit love affairs and of the hatreds and violence of the domestic environment. Prevalent over all others was infanticide, a crime and sin that ever since the Tridentine age carried the punishment of death, especially if the newborn had not been baptized. In 1701, in the Florence of the bigot Grand Duke Cosimo III, two Catherines ended up on the gallows in July alone. Immediately afterward a memorandum from the grand duke instructed judges to introduce the figure of the "guarantor of birth" to prevent abortions and infanticides.[39] Other crimes punishable by death were having plotted to eliminate a husband or father by means of poison or with the help of assassins. With these stories of love and hate, sex and transgression, women began to occupy the stage of the scaffold. But they were incomparably fewer than the number of men executed. Women's social status in ancien régime culture generally excluded them from the spheres of conflict and violence for power and riches. However, there was a price to pay for this relatively protected condition: the rarity of occasions to see women executed aroused a special curiosity, which in turn posed special problems for the companies of justice. How was a woman to be put to death? There was a female dimension to death on the scaffold that was different to the male one. While the priority with men was to prevail over and shape their thoughts, the key issue with women was the body. Caring for the body was a female specialty, and in this case also the only solution was to resort to the help of another woman, who undertook to assist the condemned with their natural needs. As for the public part of the ritual, the fundamental problem was how to prevent the display of the female body from turning the execution spectacle into an occasion for "scandal," for sin. It was well known that there was a big turnout when women were involved. The crowd was stirred by a special curiosity that focused precisely on the body. The death of saintly women and the torments of female flesh filled Catholic churches with erotic images: what stood out was the suffering and the impotent abandonment to the violence of a male power. And the scene at the scaffold promised a real-life reproduction of those images. The crucial concern, therefore, was to hide the body of the condemned woman throughout the journey to the scaffold. The sacristan Marco Gambarucci issued specific warnings about this. The *provveditore* was to be responsible for the woman's clothing, checking that she had *sottocalzoni*—a pair of drawers—beneath her gown. "And if by any chance she does not, he must immediately give orders to the sacristans, or the steward, that they be procured at the expense of the

Company."[40] Once this had been done, someone had to make sure they were put on—and who had access to the body of the condemned woman? The answer: "To make her put them on, tell the captain of the jail to find some woman, and this so that no scandal is given to the people during the act of execution."

Hanging a woman also meant that spectators would see her body from below. Even while climbing the ladder to the level of the noose, the woman would necessarily be subject to the indiscreet gaze of onlookers. But there was a remedy for this too. It was enough "to remind the execution master to have her dress tied around her feet when climbing the ladder." And indeed this is what was done in such cases.

> Women did not as a rule have the right to an independent public life; and in crimes they rarely acted alone. Even in this abnormal dimension of women's existence, they moved for the most part in the shadow of a man, the one with whom or for whom they had committed the crime. And they went to the scaffold with him too. But at this point it was necessary to break the tie: "And in the event that a woman and a man are executed together, between whom some transaction had occurred, or even if they were wife and husband, in these cases the Company is accustomed to keep them apart so they cannot see each other, in order to better persuade them."[41]

Such measures were not necessary if the crime had involved two women. This happened especially in cases of infanticide, which tended to be committed in the secrecy of the home with the aid of another woman, such as a mother or midwife. Mothers and daughters led separate lives with respect to the male members of the family. While the males went to school or the workshop, or at any rate participated in social life under paternal supervision, the mother of the household was responsible for bringing up the daughters and protecting their "honesty." It was up to mothers to ensure that the girls were virgins when given in marriage or entrusted to the convent. Sometimes even the condemnation of one or the other for some crime did not release them from this close bond. Maddalena da Linara and her mother, Livia, ended up on the scaffold together in Ravenna on November 29, 1608; the priest assisting Maddalena, Don Bernardino Sacchi, described in a long report how they had prepared for death.[42]

It is not known with certainty what crime the two women had committed together. Don Bernardino says only that they had been "worshippers of the world and the flesh." Maddalena had given birth fifteen days earlier, so perhaps she was guilty of attempted infanticide. (The child was still alive at the time of execution.) But whatever the reason for the sentence, their behavior during the night of comforting appeared so exceptional to their confessor Don Bernardino Sacchi that he felt compelled to write an account of it. He was thinking of a readership attracted by stories of extraordinary deaths, and was sure that anyone reading his narrative would feel their "soul filling with wonder, compassion, desire, and fear all together." His account remained in manuscript form, as had Luca della Robbia's report about Boscoli. And the Boscoli case comes to mind here as the most appropriate model for comparison: on one hand, a young Florentine living in the age of Machiavelli, attracted by the heroism of ancient tyrannicides; on the other, two women who had been raised in the religious thought and devotion of the Counter-Reformation. It is hard to imagine two more different periods and stories, and yet, as we shall see, they did share something in common.

Don Bernardino arrived at the prison on Friday evening, together with other brothers from the Company of Death. He consulted with them and prepared himself for the task awaiting them—the conversion of the "afflicted sisters." They entered the *segreta,* the isolation cell positioned away from where other prisoners were kept, and found Livia sitting on the bed reciting the Hail Mary, and her daughter Maddalena, beads in hand, saying the Rosary. Don Bernardino stepped forward, showing them the *tavoletta* with the image of Christ on the Cross, and greeted them, invoking the Virgin, the angels, and the saints to protect them. With a smile ("almost laughing"), Maddalena replied: "So be it." From that moment on an extraordinary harmony of intent was established between the priest, who invited her to think devout thoughts, and the woman, who showed herself more than willing to accept his invitation. With obedient docility, Maddalena not only displayed profound contrition but also helped the comforter to rouse her more silent mother with sentences such as: "My mother, get dressed, for the Lord is calling us to death, and to heaven." Don Bernardino began by listing the deaths of apostles and martyrs, and reminded them that "Saint Peter, so grateful to God, was crucified upside down, that Saint Paul had his head cut off, that Saint Bartholomew was flayed alive, that Saint Thomas was first made to walk on red-hot sheets of iron and then thrown into a burning oven." Maddalena, the "resolute young woman," replied immediately: "I am willingly content, here is my soul and this life together, do of them what the Lord pleases. I am very ready to suffer and to endure any torment and death if that appeases my Lord." The priest reassured her: "This willing deliberation of yours was enough to satisfy the supreme goodness of God." Appeasing the Lord, paying for one's misdeeds: Maddalena's religion was that of a sinner who had to make amends for her wrongs with suffering and penance before presenting herself for God's judgment. She left the prison exchanging words of reciprocal forgiveness with the prison warden's wife. This was just the start of a series of declarations of forgiveness. The gaze of many spectators at the windows and loggias of the palace followed Maddalena as she descended the stairs and walked toward the execution site. What they saw was a self-confident combatant, or, as Don Bernardino put it—mindful of ancient martyrologies and perhaps a reader of Tasso's poem—an "indomitable warrior of Jesus Christ."

In the chapel, in front of an altar illuminated by lit candles, the priest had her say a prayer to the crucified Christ structured around the evocation of the senses: sight (thorns, blood, tears, spits); hearing ("ears surrounded by insults, abuse, incivility"); taste ("the mouth and tongue revived with vinegar and bile"); and touch ("the holy hands pierced with sharp nails, the flank opened with the spear iron"). Maddalena listened, and repeated the prayer. But she went further, saying one on her own initiative: addressed to the Virgin, it was "impassioned." They then moved from the chapel to the *conforteria*. Here Don Bernardino exhorted her to comply with what God had decreed for her "before the world was created"—namely, that she had to die a "violent death" and in this way obtain the possibility of going to heaven. Maddalena was not frightened by the thought, and indeed offered warm thanks to God. In the meantime a messenger arrived to say that her mother Livia was crying in the chapel. The priest imagined she was crying at the thought of the death that awaited her and the things of the world she had to leave behind. But he was mistaken, as the woman showed no fear either: "Sir," Livia said, "I am not bothered at dying in this manner, because, deserving it for my sins, I hope the Lord will forgive me in his infinite goodness." This interplay between the comforter and the two women carried on throughout the proceedings. Mother and daughter proved ever more fervent and ready to spontaneously tread the path indicated to them. Don Bernardino spoke of the "atrocious punishment of purgatory, and of hell as well," illustrating them with revelations and visions, and reminding them that hell was eternal punishment. Contrite at the thought of her sins, Maddalena went to make her confession. Afterward she emerged from the chapel "so cheerful, serene, and beautiful in the face that one could truly say that, having received the remission of her sins, the inner part corresponded to the countenance." Her mother looked at her and, overcome with emotion, began to cry. At this point Maddalena herself comforted and reassured her, saying that she was truly happy to die and that she was certain that God would forgive their sins and they would meet again in heaven. They hugged each other, crying, and her mother blessed her: "Remain cheerful, my daughter, as these shadows, this night, and torments will soon pass together." Whereupon Maddalena said: "We wish to die as Christians. We wish to die in the grace of the Lord. We wish to die willingly together."[43] Then she focused her gaze on the *tavoletta:* she looked at the image of the Virgin with the dead Christ in her lap, "kissing one then the other many times." The priest got them to recite a long invocation to the Virgin Mary. Maddalena said she felt so "devout, and stirred by, and enamored" of the Virgin that it was as if "[I] have her in my soul and that here she is in my company."[44]

At this point the priest decided the moment had come to get Livia and Maddalena to say the *protesta,* the usual testamentary declaration, uttered while they were still lucid and in control of themselves, that they wished to die in the Catholic faith of the Roman Church, avoiding the opposing dangers of desperation and presumption. In signing it the condemned protected themselves from themselves, from that self which the torments of death might render different and uncontrollable. After the declaration had been made, the comforter realized that Maddalena, who had been kneeling at his feet from the beginning, had freezing hands, so much so that it was like touching "a cold iron." He asked for a brazier to be brought to warm up the room, but Maddalena refused with an irrefutable argument: "There is no need, she said, to further warm the hands, as soon they must be completely cold."[45] More than by a fire, she was comforted by a brief rest—she fell asleep, her head slumped forward. Then she roused herself and decided to make a will. She asked that her marriage settlement and that of her mother be given "to her dear little son delivered fifteen days ago," and the priest promised that he would see to it.[46] Now was the moment to celebrate Mass, and the two women received Communion.[47] There were then kisses and embraces, amid the general emotion of those present. The end was near, and Don Bernardino totted up the balance of his accounting: "This night was truly long and cold, as it was wintertime: but lengthy and frequent were also the sighs, the prayers, and the tears, all applied in satisfaction of the due punishments."[48] It was now time to talk about heaven. The women listened to the priest's description of it as the place where the eternal sun of supreme good shines, where "you will always live, and where you will no longer need fear death or any suffering, but will enjoy supreme joyousness, glorious happiness, and everlasting beatitude."[49] The night was now coming to an end, and preparations were made for the final phase. Don Bernardino invited Maddalena to thank the "gentlemen" present—and here we learn that all the proceedings had taken place in the presence of nobles and other eminent members of the company. Among others there was also the chamberlain of cardinal legate Caetani. Maddalena thanked them and said she was not afraid. She was thinking of Christ led to his death "with a rope round his neck" (this may have been how it was depicted in Stations of the Cross after it had been painted in this way by Mantegna), and recognized that "it is a rightful duty, that in the same way, with this rope, I should also pay for the many wrongs done to you Lord."[50]

They went out of the palace door into the street, amid the crowd. And here a minor incident occurred: Maddalena was about to lose a shoe and feared she might offer an inappropriate spectacle to those watching. So she removed the other shoe as well, and left them both in the street. She walked cheerfully, reached the execution site, knelt down, recited the Creed and the Confiteor, invoked the name of Jesus three times, received the final blessing from the confessor, and climbed the ladder to the gallows. The end was close. The minister of justice beckoned to her, and Don Bernardino writes: "'Generous Maddalena,' I said, 'Glory to the living Jesus': and she, looking at me with a serene and happy face, and then immediately at the *tavoletta* before her, replied: 'Glory to the living Jesus.'"[51] Livia, in the meantime, was still in the chapel: the priest went to tell her that "Maddalena had already gone to heaven" and that her constancy and devotion and hope and faith had "amazed everyone."[52] Her mother cut no less of a figure, and she too ended her "wretched and mortal life, making amends for her wrongs."

The conclusion is worthy of note: the two women had deserved eternal salvation because they had paid for their wrongs in an adequate measure. Here the deep current of the mysticism of immense divine mercy and of the salvation earned by Christ meets that of the Tridentine theology of meritorious works, a bulwark against the doctrines that devalued good works and ecclesiastical mediation. But it was enough to flow into the conclusion sought by the comforter: "From the success achieved," Don Bernardino affirms, "we could draw great example, and together devoutly believe that both have been gathered into eternal glory by compassionate God, therein to praise and magnify the greatness of his infinite mercy forever."

This female way of dying on the scaffold was the one that the comforters liked: different from how men died, not just for what is absent from the comparison, but also and above all for what is present. Surfacing here is a life of domestic interiors, of loves and errors: there are no adventures of violence and of crimes committed in streets and workshops, no scandal of doctrinal dissent, religious and political rebellion. But even if the age of the Pietro Paolo Boscoli case was remote, we find here the exact same openness and docility toward the invitations of the comforter, the same immediate and unreserved acceptance of the offers of a sentimental religion rooted in the heart. What is new and different is the sum of debit and credit between penances as meritorious works and eternal salvation, so far removed from the idea of the immense mercy of a God who saves the thief for free in return for a word of faith. There is also the fact that the two women were already steeped and expert in the devotions suggested to them: the priest's offers fell on terrain already plowed by Catholic devotionalism. The fervent prayers of Maddalena da Linara and her spontaneous assent to what the priest urged her to do reveal a predisposition to obey the churchman, a readiness to immediately embrace the suggestion to have hope in a reality different from "wretched and mortal life" on earth. This was also because the sacraments, rites, and offerings of a sentimental and emotive devotion thronging with heavenly mediators and protectors, as preached by popular missions and cultivated by the Tridentine clergy, had found a particularly receptive audience in women. Protagonists for a day on the world stage, some of these women seem to have emerged from the closed confines of family life to fit, without resistance, into the part of Saint Magdalene, the prototype of the redeemed sinner.

It would not be until the French Revolution and the Sanfedist reaction to the Jacobins that another type of woman would come onto the public stage of the scaffold. The hanging of Eleonora Pimentel Fonseca in 1799, a victim of the defeat of the Neapolitan Republic, gave a measure of the success of a protracted religious disciplining that did not tolerate the idea of women being given political and intellectual functions. A street ballad of the time went like this:

> A signora donna Lionora
> Che cantava 'ncopp'o triato
> Mo abballa mmiezo o Mercato.
> Viva viva u papa santo
> C'ha mannato i cannuncini
> Pe scaccià I giacubini!
> Viva a forca e masto Donato
> Sant'Antonio sia priato![53]

This translates roughly as:

> To the lady Eleonora,
> who once sang on the theater stage,
> but now dances in the marketplace.
> Long live the holy pope
> who sent the cannons
> to drive out the Jacobins!
> Long live the gallows and Master Donato[54]
> and praise to Sant' Antonio.

Wills, Letters, *Proteste,* and the Unburdening of the Conscience

The mediation of the *confratelli* gave everyone who repented, without distinction, the possibility to indicate their final wishes. This was another of the privileges granted to the *conforterie,* and which they offered to those who died penitent, thereby effectively annulling the regulation that, with the passing of the death sentence, the condemned forfeited the right to make a will regarding their possessions and funeral arrangements. Wills were drawn up by the confessors as a matter of course: they were the traditional means for compensating those who had been wronged and for leaving warnings and instructions intended to assist the future well-being of the family.

The wills of those about to be executed were looked after with particular care by confraternity archivists, also because the destiny of assets left to the confraternity depended on them. In Rome, among the documents still preserved in what was once a very extensive archive, the series of wills opens with the name of Organtino in 1497 and ends with a certain Agapito Bellomo, "a countryman from Palestrina," who, on July 9, 1870, shortly before the capture of Rome by Italian troops, was preparing to die on the scaffold, commending "his poor elderly mother to the charity of the Archconfraternity, to support her when it could."[55] Throughout the previous centuries, the brothers of the Roman company, besides comforting the condemned, had recorded their final wishes. The same thing had taken place in other Italian cities.

In these declarations the preliminary and fundamental part was the one that, in a normal will, concerned the commendation of the soul and the instructions for burial. The condemned were only required to declare that they intended to die as good Christians. Anyone reading the successive formulaic wordings in the registers will be struck by the continual repetition of such attestations over the centuries. In 1568 Lorenzo da Mugnano, sentenced to death by the Inquisition, declared that he intended "to die willingly and in the bosom of the Holy Roman Church."[56] Centuries later, Cesare Berretta, sentenced and executed on January 9, 1856, "in a very brief space of time," just had time to declared his wish "to die as a good Christian, to forgive any wrongs he might have received as he hopes to obtain forgiveness for his own sins through the mercy of God, for the love of whom he affirms that he rejoices at the death he means and declares to receive in the bosom of the Holy Church."[57] The formulaic expressions suggested by the brothers were inscribed in tradition. It should be said, though, that when the condemned wished to dictate a personal text, the company notary respected its content. On January 26, 1565, Benedetto Accolti, who had been sentenced to death for conspiring against the pope, was still suffering from the pain of the torture inflicted on him, and had yet to face the terrible torments envisaged by the sentence, declared that he wished "to die as a good Christian," as the norm dictated. However, in the record of his wishes there is a glimpse of a Calvinistic faith in divine predestination.[58]

Sometimes the final wishes took the form of a letter to family members. Directly addressing their loved ones, the condemned left testimony and advice about how to live the good life that they themselves had not led. A type of document was created that would become rooted in custom well beyond the life span of the traditional *conforterie:* the condemned prisoner's final letter. The age of religious conflicts left its mark on this literary genre. The martyrologies of the Protestant Reformation, starting with Jean Crespin's celebrated *Livres des martyrs,* published letters and testaments of those condemned to death by the Roman Inquisition, whereas the archives of the confraternities collected letters imbued with a strong Catholic piety and professions of obedience to the Church. In one case that we have already come across, that of Aonio Paleario (Antonio della Paglia), the two traditions overlapped: he died repentant and confessed, according to the company—and as a martyr of truth, according to the Protestant tradition. The fact remains that he was killed at the orders of the Inquisition. Beneath the date July 3, 1570, on the eve of the execution, the Company's register bears the transcription of two letters written by Paleario himself.[59]

The first was for his wife Marietta:

My dear wife, I would not wish you to receive grief from my pleasure, and ill from my good. The hour has come for me to pass from this life to my Lord and Father, and God. I go there as joyously as to the wedding of the son of the great king, for which I have always prayed to my lord that, in his infinite goodness and generosity, he might grant to me and my beloved wife [sic]. Take comfort in the will of God and in my contentedness, and attend to the dismayed family that it will remain to you to bring up and protect with the fear of God, and to be a mother and father to them. I was already 70 years old and of no use. With virtue and sweat, the children must strive to live honorably. May God the Father, and our Lord Jesus Christ, and the communion of the Holy Spirit be with your spirit. From Rome on the 3rd day of July 1570.

Your husband Aonio Paleario[60]

The letter to his children begins: "Lampridio and Fedro, most beloved sons, these most courteous gentlemen have not withheld their courtesy from me at the end, and permit me to write to you" and ends with these words: "My hour approaches, may the spirit of God console and gladden me with his grace. Rome, the 3rd day of July, 1570. Your father Aonio Paleario." The report, signed by the chaplain, a Dominican friar, and five brothers, ends: "Then he was taken to the Ponte [di Castel Sant'Angelo], where he was hung and then burned."

Many other letters of this kind are preserved among the papers of the Roman company and of other confraternities. They form part of a genre of writing that grew out of a devout context where the spiritual warning left by the condemned consisted of reminding wives and children of the obligation to be faithful to religion and moral discipline. Collected and often materially written by confraternity confessors and notaries, they contained messages of subjection to the religious and political authorities. The presence of these particular mediators inevitably colored the language and imagery. A different religious perspective would only be established after the work of the confraternities died out, when the final letters of the condemned stopped being private testimony restricted to the family and became public mediums for a new morality, though not without links with the original religious tradition. We need only mention the celebrated book of the archpriest Luigi Martini, who gathered the testimony of the "martyrs of Belfiore," the patriots sent to their deaths between 1851 and 1855.[61] Another new, and more recent, kind are the final letters of condemned Second World War Resistance fighters, which, with their staunchly ethical and civil-minded message, form a compendium of the moral and political rebirth of Italy in the twentieth century.

But in the Italy of the ancien régime the letters of the condemned to their families were relatively isolated and exceptional documents. Much more ordinary were their *proteste,* declarations that were kept in special registers. Perusing the seventeenth-century ones of several confraternities (Ferrara, Bologna, and Naples) that contain the "*proteste* and wills of the condemned," we enter into a landscape different from that of Rome in the previous century. The resistance of religious dissidents is nowhere to be found: the *proteste* only in exceptional cases took the form of a genuine and resolute contestation of the sentence. There were some, however. In Bologna in 1693, a "robust young man" named Gilio Sandonati poured scorn on a sentence that was sending him to his death without him knowing the reason: "Whence," he added, "he knew full well that justice was not done if not in the eyes of simpletons, and he would never believe that God had let him die despite his innocence." But his comforters rebuked him harshly: "It was immediately replied that human justice was directed by divine [justice]."[62] Innocence was an empty word. All that counted was obedience to power. As the Jesuit Juan de Polanco had written, one had to die without hatred for the person who put him to death, accepting the sentence as an expression of the "pure will of the Lord, *even if he really was innocent.*"[63]

In general, though, the definition of *protesta* was used to denote its exact opposite—that is, the testamentary act whereby the condemned declared that they accepted their fate and professed themselves to be devout and obedient children of the Church. We have already seen how the legalistic practice of getting the condemned to ratify *proteste,* which were a kind of contract valid for the future that guarded against any potential error or shortcoming, was a habitual part of the work of the *conforterie.* As happened elsewhere as well, in the chapel of the Ferrara confraternity declarations of this kind were an obligatory part of the ritual. And here too people were seen and heard who had no desire other than to manifest their submission to the will of God and their convictions as true Catholics. It is worth looking at some examples of the language of the sources. On April 21, 1679, three condemned men entered the chapel. The first, Michele Collorato, dictated his will "after having edified everyone with his ready submission to divine will and having made holy confession." It was a repetitive formula: the same words recur for Andrea Romanelli, also invited to make his will "after having edified everyone with very ready submission to divine will and having made holy confession." The third man, Francesco Schiavoni, "initially became downhearted," but then recovered and showed himself to have "true Catholic sentiments."[64] The three men were thieves, with no property to leave, and had an obligation to recompense their victims that they could not meet. Michele said he had stolen "firewood, fish, and such like for his needs," but that he did not have the means to pay those damaged by his actions. It was not a serious offense. The condition of the indigent who procured the means for survival was contemplated by the moral tradition. And in any case there was a means of payment. Michele "offers his life in penance for his sins," the report says, and then continues:

> Finally, the aforementioned Michele Collorato declares that he was born, lived, and was brought up Christian, and that he wishes to live and die in the bosom and faith of the Holy Roman Catholic and Apostolic Church. He likewise declares that as he, with all his heart, begs forgiveness for his sins to God and his fellow men, so too does he, with all his heart, [forgive] anyone who might have offended him.

We frequently come across similar such *proteste* and affirmations of "true Catholic sentiments." And sometimes we also catch a glimpse of the mediators and prompters of conversion. The case of Angelo Padovano known as Antonio Sotto, from Nogara, comforted on June 9, 1679, was dealt with by the provost of the Theatines, Angelo Geverati, and various priests from the *conforteria*. But special praise was accorded to the "most illustrious and excellent" Marchese Ippolito Bentivogli. He was the one, in the view of the obsequious writer of the record, who demonstrated "incomparable eloquence," as the complex syntax of the declarations attributed to the "patient" shows: "As he asks forgiveness of God for his sins, and of his fellow men for all offenses . . . so, in order to merit the forgiveness promised by God to those who forgive others, he forgives generally, and with all his heart, anyone by whom he has in any way been wronged, even in the trial of the case for which he has been condemned."[65]

Perhaps closer to Angelo's real words is the message he wanted his family to receive. He asked them to celebrate masses for his soul and promised "that if God, in his mercy, as he hopes and trusts, grants him the glory of heaven, he too will pray for them, and he will not be ungrateful."

In the papers of the confraternity we can see what feelings and convictions underpinned the order of this strongly hierarchical society, placed under the legatine authority of a cardinal representing the pope. Here, as an example, is the *protesta* of Lucrezia Pasquali da Comacchio, who on October 13, 1679, was preparing for execution for the crime of infanticide:

> As, by the grace of God, I was born and brought up in the bosom of the Holy Roman Catholic and Apostolic mother Church, I thus wish

to die in the holy and true faith that it professes and teaches; and if any temptation or doubt to the contrary should ever come to me, I hereby declare I will never acquiesce to them, and so too for any other temptation, especially distrust in divine mercy, while I know and believe that this exceeds and is greater than all my iniquities . . . I so declare before the image of this crucified Christ which I hold here in front of me.[66]

To be born and to die in the same mother Church, welcoming and ready to guide them in death—this is a line of thought recorded for many men and women. Caterina Quaresima made it her own on May 7, 1710, the day of her death: "By the grace of God I was born and brought up in the bosom of the Holy Roman Catholic and Apostolic mother Church. I thus wish to die in the holy and true faith that it professes and teaches." And she added: "If I have become worthy of praying, I promise [to pray] for all those who are assisting me with such charity, so they too can see me in that blessed room."[67]

These are all examples of the testament of the "patient," the concluding document detailing the outcome of the nocturnal comforting. After this had been drawn up, it was time for the public spectacle, which would fix forever the image of the condemned person in people's minds. But the confraternities kept for themselves the detailed accounts of what went on during the long hours of the night, the uncertainties and difficulties of the initial meeting, and the successive steps toward the new character who went on display at the execution site. Those secret reports were material for study, to gauge where they may have gone wrong and how to overcome the resistance of "patients." The *conforteria* taken as a model was that of Bologna, which of all the similar institutions operating in Italy was the one most evidently characterized by intellectual activity, as it was a meeting place for doctors of theology and jurists from the university. We will see later how much and what kind of testimony has been preserved in the Bolognese archive. The Company of Death in Ferrara followed the Bologna model during its late seventeenth-century revival, carefully recording the whole course of their dealings with the condemned, from when the prisoner was handed over to them through to the final act of execution. The following is a report of the procedures adopted in a specific case, that of Gasparo Giorgi, condemned to death on October 9, 1683, for having been an accomplice in a murder.[68]

The proceedings began when the brothers were alerted to news that workmen had received urgent instructions to erect a scaffold in the square. Confirmation arrived late in the evening—a capital sentence had been passed by the criminal congregation. Marchese Bentivogli, the director of the *conforteria,* appointed the two comforters (a priest and a lay brother) to assist the "patient." But the rector, Marchese Francesco Sacrati, did not wait for the prisoner to be handed over, and sent two brothers to the prison straightaway. This was a mistake. Gasparo Giorgi, "not knowing he was to die, was sleeping peacefully in prison." Awakened suddenly, and "seeing the two brothers presenting him with the crucifix, he was dumbstruck and beside himself." The first words he managed to say were: "Oh God, with such innocence?" And then: "Oh, what a great spectacle." He continued to complain during the journey from the prison to the chapel, protesting at the sentence and despairing of the fate of his brother, who was also in prison. The comforters finally managed to interrupt the flow of complaints and went on the attack. They frightened Gasparo by saying that his rash comments about the judges were mortal sins and there was the risk that his soul would end up in hell as a consequence. And at this point they deployed the chief argument in their arsenal: "The death to which he had been condemned would not have come about without the will of God, perhaps in order to save his soul, which, by dying in another way would have been damned." This thought "persuaded him to confess that what he was being told was true and to accept God's will and die as a good Christian." But patience was required: it would take hours for the man's initial agitation to subside, and so "the prudent comforters did not hurry at all to send him before the confessor." Taking a sacrament in the wrong frame of mind might have turned into a sacrilege, with the risk of the day of judgment becoming the day of anger. The report-writer's account reveals that at this point a squabble broke out among the brothers: some, driven by "excessive ardor," could not understand why it was taking so long. But the men in charge of the comforting, who were shrewder, did not change their minds. They waited, preparing Gasparo and instructing him carefully "about all that was expected in order to make a valid confession and examine the conscience." As a result, everything went smoothly: the "patient" made his confession, performed his penance and then, fully consoled, returned to the table and "had brother Piccinardi, the notary and secretary of the School, draw up his will and the usual *protesta.*" At this point it was a question of perfecting their work: Gasparo, whose initial agitation had given way to the serenity of a man at peace with his conscience, was now led bit by bit toward a state of mystic exaltation. The comforters' "insinuations" helped him to perform "acts of virtue" with associated eternal rewards: and he became so enthused that "one time he himself spent more than a quarter of an hour kissing the crucifix, now saying the ejaculatory prayer: 'Jesus and Mary are my heart and soul.'" But the night was long, and the prisoner's state of mind fluctuated abruptly. He remembered further unconfessed sins, and it was necessary to "reconcile him." But the confessor had left, so another religious had to be called. Then Gasparo had difficulty getting to sleep; he was "tired and tormented," but managed to calm down by reciting the Rosary. At dawn they woke him, brought him close to the fire and prepared him to receive the viaticum. This he did at a first mass, then he heard another, and another again, accumulating merits in the process. It was then time to go out into the square, and Gasparo steeled himself, receiving the special indulgences that the Company was empowered to distribute. By now, though, he was exhausted: they had tried to fortify him with biscuits and wine, but he needed to be supported and almost carried across the square. He received the commendation of the soul, got through the preliminary face to face with the executioner, and accompanied "with a weak voice" the words of prayer suggested to him by the comforter, and finally died while repeating the names of Jesus and Mary. There was good reason, then, to believe "that that soul flew to the place of salvation." In summing up and reviewing the proceedings, it was evident that there had been a breakdown in the discipline of the confraternity, because someone had acted without waiting for the orders of their superiors. Moreover, the agitated "patient" should not have been made to mechanically recite Our Fathers; the best course of action would have been to sit him down and calm his anxieties by reasoning with him and presenting solid arguments. Another lesson was that no dissent was to emerge among the comforters: if someone was in disagreement, they could at most whisper their doubts in their colleague's ear. Another mistake had been made by the comforter who had been in a hurry to get Gasparo to do his confession. As for the confessor, he always had to be present, in the eventuality that additional sins might be remembered.

What emerges from documents like these is that the Ferrarese confraternity was distinguished by the same characteristics as the period's literary academies—places where the elite met and engaged in secret intellectual exchanges, read and discussed texts, and tackled theoretical issues. The style and the social composition of the membership was the same, as the companies of justice brought together the elite of local society. And the lugubrious Arcadia, which was replacing sixteenth-century classicism in the literary academies, found genuine nourishment in the weekly "congregations" of the confraternities, where reports like that of Gasparo Giorgi offered material for discussion and theological, juridical, and moral elaboration, all the more so as the voices of the condemned raised issues touching upon the original heart of the relationship between sacramental confession and judicial confession. This was the issue of what was described by the terms *scolpatione* or *scarico di coscienza*—the unburdening of the conscience. It was under this heading that the voice of the condemned was prompted and channeled into legally defined forms habitually practiced from one end of Italy to the other. The Ferrara register offers a number of examples.

On October 6, 1683, Ambrogio Bartolomeo, from Villa Bartolomea in the territory of Verona, who had been sentenced to death for murder, signed with three shaky signs of the cross a deposition authenticated by three comforters. In it, he declared that he had unjustly accused several people of complicity in his crime: "a certain Caporalino, from Mantua, Domenico Castellano, a certain Lorenzo, and others." It was all false: he had only accused them because the judge had questioned him about those names, and it had been the only way of making the torture stop, or, as he put it, "to release me from the pain of the torments." It is true that he had then ratified his confession, as the rules of criminal procedure required. But he had done so for one reason alone: "out of fear of being tortured again, which I dreaded more than death." Ambrogio Bartolomeo had made his confession, and was now preparing to account for his whole life before "the fearsome tribunal of God, the just judge to whom all the secrets of hearts are known." He had been warned not to "aggravate" his soul by lying, and also knew he was "obliged in conscience to restore the reputation, and relieve as much as I am able others from charges unjustly made against them, with the declaration to speak the truth before God, and before men, before rendering the spirit to my Jesus, to the will of whom I totally submit."[69] The words used in the text were probably not part of Bartolomeo's usual vocabulary. Nor was his case an isolated one. In the records of the confraternities the question of the "restitutions" was not regulated just with bequests to pay off debts and to compensate material damage: what emerged as a key matter to resolve in some way was the reparation of damage done with denunciations and false admissions made for purposes of vendetta, self-preservation, or simply as a consequence of torture. This gave rise to the registers of *scarichi di coscienza* or *escolpazioni.* The ones that have survived show that this was a particularly delicate part of the comforters' work. The keeper of the register of *escolpazioni* at the Bologna confraternity declared that they were "true and just," in which one must have unquestioning faith—all the more so as each of these documents bore notarial authentication.[70] This practice was followed elsewhere as well, for example in nearby Ravenna, as attested by the only register known to date for that city.[71] Much more substantial documentation can be found for more important cities such as Rome, Naples, and Palermo.

The unburdening of the conscience was an integral and necessary part of conversion, offering proof of the authenticity of the repentance. In the procedures of religious comforting a special form of reparation for wrongs done, to oneself and others, thus appeared. Behind it lay the ancient principle of "restitution," which thus emerged in the shadow of the scaffold. The *escolpazione,* that is to say, an attestation of the untruths said by the condemned in the course of the trial torture, was the method employed by the Italian model of confession to fulfill in its own way the desire of judges to hear from the mouth of the person about to be executed the complete truth about accomplices and crimes. It was an old problem for court prosecutors, and corresponding to it was the crucial need of those on the wrong end of a cruel and unjust sentence to be heard when they protested their innocence or when they did not want to wrongly accuse someone else. Thanks to Alessandro Manzoni this dramatic phenomenon was embodied for Italian history in the figure of Gian Giacomo Mora and in that of Guglielmo Piazza, his companion in misfortune and accuser during the Milanese trial of the plague-spreaders in 1630. The declarations of innocence they made before the interrogating judges and to their confessors before execution were to no avail. We have seen how the comforters were accustomed to disregarding anything the condemned might have to say about their innocence. But *escolpazioni* for unjust accusations leveled at others were of great importance in the history of the confraternities, and contributed to cementing their social and institutional position in the middle ground they occupied between the Church and the State, operating between earthly judges and God's tribunal.

Recompensing the injured party, making amends for wrongs done, is an old need that has always been a constituent part of the very idea of justice: in European cultures the colors and words of Christian morality have long run alongside reality and sought a compromise with the hard substance of advancing state power. In the proximity of the scaffold, where thieves, infanticides, murderers, heretics, and rebels died amid atrocious suffering, the words we have seen being constantly repeated were remission, reconciliation, forgiveness. The obligatory step to restore the social bond broken by the crime had been found in the Christian sacrament of penance. But as Ivo of Chartres had written in the eleventh century, without the restitution of what had wrongly been taken away, penance was regarded as a fiction; and Gratian's *Decretum* contained Saint Augustine's severe words, which had become a juridical norm, declaring the remission of sins to be null and void if there was no restitution.[72] Such restitutions were mentioned habitually in the wills of the condemned, involving full-blown notarial acts when it was a question of paying off material debts. The *escolpatione* was a special form of restitution, the natural offspring of the inquisitorial process and of judicial torture. It referred to the act whereby a person expressed their wish to make formal amends and cancel the damage done to oneself or to others through the attribution of inexistent misdeeds in the course of the trial. It was a matter of restoring a reputation damaged by false or unfounded charges and confessions of guilt. The ancient rule of repairing the reputation thus found a place among the mediating duties of the comforters, taking on a dramatic urgency. The violence of judicial torture, but above all the threat of capital punishment, had distorted the value and substance of what had been an act of reparation of economic or moral damage—money to pay back, blots to remove from the reputation and good name of others. It was a question of redressing the injury caused to a person's name by the leveling of false charges, which might lead to innocent people ending up on the scaffold: the final truth needed to be told about one's own crimes and those of others. It is a well-established fact, and one that was well-known at the time too, that torture, or simply the fear of it, drove people to confess to anything: they would own up to crimes they had never committed, and reel off name after name of supposed accomplices. It was part of everyday reality in trials for all kinds of crimes, and familiar to jurists, who reassured themselves and their clients by listing the many prerequisites that had to be met before resorting to torture.[73] But those with eyes to see the reality of the situation in the courts were fully aware that the fear of torture alone was enough to induce confessions of wrongs that had never been committed: as the jurist Giovanni Nevizzano da Asti observed, even if an accused person was taken somewhere other than the torture chamber in order to ratify their confession, he was still filled with fear. Serious miscarriages of justice therefore occurred on a regular basis.[74] But that did not stop the depositions being relied on by investigators, who had no qualms about resorting to torture. Indeed, they did so "with a calm, just, and Christian spirit," to use the words of the Venetian treatise writer Lorenzo Priori, according to whom the suffering commenced when "the culprit was frightened by the judge threatening to torture him." This was the first degree, where "one understands the terror he [the accused] feels as he is led to the *corda,* stripped, and tied." Next came a "second degree," when the accused was hauled up and suspended from the ropes, and a third degree, "when he is tortured and shaken."[75] The fear aroused even prior to the "first degree" drove the victim to lie at their own and others' expense—accusing themselves of crimes they had not committed, accusing others who were innocent—and it happened habitually, to save oneself or at least to put an end to the torture. Some effort was made, at least in principle, to remedy what was a recognized problem, but the multiplication of precautionary measures did little to prevent the continual use of torture, especially when the crime allowed for exceptions to the rules, such as heresy and lèse-majesté. The devastating nature of the witchcraft trials, for example, stemmed from the fact that the judges, starting from the preconception of the existence of a demoniacal sect, forced the accused to list a whole string of accomplices, who, when they in turn were tortured, added to the pool of suspects to be arrested and tried.

Only when the definitive death sentence was passed were the condemned offered a final opportunity to voice their truth. In other judicial systems—like those in France and England—that truth could be learned from the actual voices of the condemned in the *amende honorable* or the last speech uttered in front of or on the scaffold. By contrast, in Italian cities the condemned unburdened their consciences in the secrecy of the nighttime sessions, pouring the weight of what they had on their minds into the comforters' report. The resulting documents were called *escolpazioni,* or also *disgravi* and *discarichi di coscienza.* The confessions made by the condemned just prior to their death were saved in written declarations used to correct other confessions made under torture to the chancellors of the court. If, during their trial, they had accused other innocent people in order to escape torture, they now had an opportunity to retract. Yet again the different strands of confession multiplied and became interwoven: that of the external court, signed in front of the investigator and recorded by the tribunal; the one of the court of conscience, whispered into the confessor's ear; and this third version, which lay somewhere between the two. It had a double seal of truth, that of the sacramental confession made to the priest on the point of death and that of the written declaration handed over to the confraternity, to be then reported to the judge who was deciding the fate of other accused. The tradition of public confession beneath the scaffold, used from the thirteenth century onward by French judges, here took on a guise that lay halfway between sacramental mediation with the afterlife and bureaucratic mediation with earthly life. The abjuration of the heretic and the conversion of the criminal thus took the conclusive form of an unburdening of the conscience: spontaneous confessions somewhere between the religious sacrament and the revelations of a *pentito* useful for policing purposes.

The Neapolitan register of *escolpazioni* begins with the confession of a Spanish soldier, Pedro Cabello, who on November 2, 1587, put it on record that he had unjustly accused a fellow soldier while he was being tortured ("su la cuerda").[76] Those that followed invariably referred to the *corda* torture to explain how and why they had leveled accusations against innocent people. It was not just at the brothers' suggestion or in order to save their soul that they wanted to tell the truth: they also had a clear idea of the social infamy they had heaped on others with their charges. For this reason, Antonio Coppola, sent to the scaffold in February 1606, made a special request for his retraction to be communicated in public: he had falsely accused his mother-in-law, Maria Russo, of having urged him to kill his wife, Cecilia, and his father-in-law "so we could then marry each other." He wished this retraction to be made public in Capodimonte, so he wrote, "where I have defamed her, there will her reputation be restored."[77]

The members of the companies of justice were keenly aware of the delicacy and importance of these final reparations. For this reason the Bolognese comforters asked that the *escolpazioni* recorded in their books be given the credence they deserved, "because truly they can be taken to be true and just things."[78] What happened to them is revealed by the rich sources of the Neapolitan Company of the Whites. Careful research by Giovanni Romeo has found that they were already recorded as a matter of course in the middle of the sixteenth century.[79] But it was in Naples that the abnormal development of the interwoven connections between the criminal court and the Inquisition, the almost incredibly tangled nature of which has been clearly reconstructed by Romeo, ended up posing the question of how to keep the declarations in view of the use that some innocent party might make of them to defend themselves from unfounded charges. And so, from 1587 onward, the *escolpazioni* were kept away from the public eye and entrusted to the filter of the Company.[80] A special register of *escolpazioni* was kept inside the chapel in the Vicaria prison. One example is the document dictated and signed by the condemned prisoner Giovanni Velasco in Naples on July 13, 1630, the same year as the plague-spreading trial in Milan. The document begins like this: "I Giovanni Velasco say in this last [moment] of my life, to unburden my conscience, that the charge I made against Marco Antonio d'Ascioli when I was imprisoned in Longonne . . . was not true at all." And it ends as follows: "And to unburden my soul I have prepared this document in the hand of my confessor, signed with my hand on this 13th day of July 1630."[81] Passing before the eyes of the reader in the series of exculpations are the justifications of those who reveal the truth at the last moment: "I said it believing I would escape with my life, and for fear of torture," Onofrio Schiavariello declared on October 5, 1649, having been arrested and tried in relation to the revolt of Masaniello: he had named some innocent people as accomplices in a conspiracy "to make Naples rise up again."[82] Likewise, Francesco Giannella retracted his accusation that the prince of Montesarchio wished "to put the palace to blood and fire": he had said it "out of fear of torture."[83] And Orazio Capuano: "I said it thinking by this that I would be able to escape with my life."[84]

The eleventh-hour disclosure of the truth took concrete form in a document recorded by the confessor within the four walls of the prison chapel. This was one of the many consequences of the transformation of a crime into a sin. And the truth about the crime and about accomplices, if it differed from what had been confessed to the judge, found a space in the comforting procedure, with recorded declarations left in the hands of the confraternities. They were not always prompt in communicating them to the judging authorities. But the people who gathered around the prison, anxious about the fate of their unjustly condemned relatives, knew about such revelations and did everything they could to obtain certified documents to produce in their favor. And here we can see the casual and unpredictable paths of decisions made by the political authorities, faced with the alternative of annulling sentences that had already been handed down or exploiting the terror of execution to keep the populace in check during times of unrest and revolt.

Reparation, from being a fundamental part of sacramental penance, thus became juxtaposed with the trial phase of ascertaining the truth, correcting it and setting in train a dynamic that interfered with state justice. For instance, on October 5, 1649, Onofrio Schiavariello retracted the accusation he had made against Domenico Fabbricatore. Three days later, on October 8, Fabbricatore presented a formal plea to the Company of Whites: he had learned of the *disgravio di coscienza* concerning him and was requesting an authentic attestation of that unburdening to use in his trial, promptly issued the following day.[85] It is one of the many clues as to how the heavenly bureaucracy of the mediators of the salvation of the soul had become firmly established in the intermediate space between the individual conscience and the apparatuses of Church and State. This was assured on the basis of the social consensus that had been earned through works of mercy. Not for nothing was the company dedicated to "Sancta Maria succurre miseris." The money raised from alms and bequests was spent on masses for the souls of the executed, but also to help their family and relatives. Regular announcements were made to publicize the acts of charity performed by the company, including the payment of prisoners' debts and the freeing of slaves.[86]

Charity occupied the interstices of a cruel justice. It was out of charity that the brothers sometimes tried to correct sentences when it transpired from a sacramental confession that an innocent person was going to be put to death. But here the distracted, anonymous, and mean face of bureaucracy in a society of privilege also emerged. One example is the case of a young Neapolitan called Nicola Fanfano, condemned in 1696 for the crime of sodomy together with Giuseppe Lopez: in his *escolpazione* of October 23 Giuseppe declared that he had denounced Nicola "out of fear of torture."

Sancta MARIA Succurre Miseris.

I fà noto, e fono avifati li Parenti poveri di quelli Condennati à Morte dal Regio Tribunale di Campagna, li quali fono ftati giuftiziati dal Mefe di Aprile dell'Anno 1715. fin oggi, e per l'avvenire ; e che fono ftati affiftiti alla Morte dalla Venerabile Congregazione delli Bianchi della Torre del greco ; che volendo le Mogli, Figlie femine, e Sorelle carnali, povere, e non maritate delli detti Giuftiziati, effere partecipi dell'aumento di loro dote lafciato dal quond.Signor D. Domenico Caracciolo della Torella all' Illuftre Compagnia de' Bianchi della Giuftizia della Fedeliffima Città di Napoli ; prima di contraere il Matrimonio portino la Fede della Morte del giuftiziato, e di effere ftato affiftito dalla fopradetta Venerabile Congregazione delli Bianchi della Torre del greco ; la Fede del Paroco del Matrimonio col giuftiziato, fe è Vidua di effo ; ò pure del Battefimo, & Attestato, fe è figlia, ò forella del giuftiziato ; e fimilmente Fede del Reverendo Paroco, e dell'Univerfità dove habita la Donna, dell'Onestà, e Povertà vera di effa congionta come di fopra del giuftiziato, la quale domanda il Suffidio, & aumento fodetto di dote : e le accennate Fedi autentiche, e fuggellate, con il Memoriale diretto al P.Governatore della detta Illuftre Compagnia le prefentino al Rev. P. Confeffore, e Cappellano della medefima Illuftre Compagnia di Napoli dentro il Cortile dell'Ofpedale dell'Incurabili di Napoli, il quale le confegnerà al detto P. Governatore, che le farà fpicciare prefto ; e verificati li fopradetti Requifiti dal Fratello Procurator Generale di detta Illuftre Compagnia, fe li prometteranno docati Diece ; doppo della quale promeffa, e non prima, contraeranno il Matrimonio avanti il proprio Paroco ; ricordandofi li Spofi di Confeffarfi facramentalmente prima di contraere : e portata la Fede del Matrimonio al medefimo P. Cappellano in Napoli, fe li fpedirà la polifa dal Fratello Procurator Generale delli fudetti docati diece per ciafcheduna di quante vi capiranno ; & il tutto fenza interpofizione di mezzo, nè raccomandazione alcuna, & affatto gratis, anche per li ademplimenti, & obbligo dello Spofo, dal Magn. Notare di detta Illuftre Compagnia : e preghe-ranno il Signore IDDIO per il fopradetto pio Teftatore : la di cui volontà acciò fia puntualmente efeguita, & offervata, e le povere fopradette facilmente fovvenute, la medefima Illuftre Compagnia di Napoli le fà avifate col prefen-te affiffo in tutte le Terre, e Paefi, e Città convicine.

FIGURE 19.1. Printed notice, "Sancta Maria succurre miseris," Naples, 1725.
NAPLES: ARCHIVIO STORICO DIOCESANO.

The confessor passed on this information in writing to the governor of the company, who initially thought of consulting with the other members, but then, prompted by the need to act quickly to prevent the death of an innocent person, had the attestation delivered to one of the judges of the criminal court. From him the document passed into the hands of the viceroy, the duke of Medinaceli, who entrusted it to the Collateral Council with the recommendation "that it should act in conscience."

The conscience of the viceroy was governed by one of the numerous "councils" that assisted those exercising sovereign power in Europe at the time. The decisions made there formed jurisprudence. And in a collection of the decisions of the "Council of Conscience" of the other Spanish viceroy, the one who ruled Sicily, we find a good example of how *escolpazioni* were taken in account. The case in question dates to October 1607: a man condemned to death for murder denounced a series of accomplices while being subjected to torture, but when he passed into the hands of the comforters, he retracted all his accusations in a formal unburdening of the conscience. He reiterated this right to the end, on the scaffold and the moment before his death. The matter was discussed by the Council of Conscience, the opinions of Baldus de Ubaldis and Bartolus of Saxoferrato were cited, and it was determined that the confession made in the *conforteria* and reaffirmed on the scaffold before the man's decapitation had the juridical value of sworn testimony. The council thus upheld what Prospero Farinacci sustained— namely, that an exculpation of this kind totally canceled the charge. This conclusion was reported to the viceroy, and everyone who had been unjustly accused was freed without torture.[87]

This was the correct and exemplary course of action. However, the reality of criminal practice did not always obey the principles of this special kind of jurisprudence. Returning to the case of Nicola Fanfano and Giuseppe Lopez in Naples, the final decision lay in the hands of a deputy of the Collateral Council, the last person in the chain of command, who distractedly replied "that the sentence should be left to be carried out." On the morning of October 25, Giuseppe and Nicola found themselves together in the market square in front of the scaffold: Nicola had just received the sacrament of confirmation. There was time only for a final farewell: "Giuseppe said to Nicola: forgive me friend for what I have done to you, see you in heaven."[88]

Adding to the chorus the voices recorded in the formal acts of exculpation preserved by the Company of Whites in Palermo would perhaps compound the monotony of a bleak story that invariably unfolded in the same way.[89] But behind the repetitiveness of words and situations, those who parade before us through the residual papers of a large archive are people who lost their lives not because of the harshness of the law but due to the casual superficiality of judges who based their sentences on confessions extracted under torture.

"What I said was a lie, and I said it because I was not able to endure the torture of the *corda*." This is what we read in the unburdening of the conscience dictated by Tommaso Cuté (or Cuti) in Palermo on March 13, 1680.[90] In compliance with the company's rules, this declaration was recorded in the book set aside specifically for that purpose, which was immediately put in a cupboard with three different keys, kept respectively by the governor, one of the secretaries, and a brother. The following morning, after the sentence had been carried out, a copy of the declaration was sent by the chaplain to the court. The confidentiality of its contents was guaranteed by a rigorous oath: if a member of the Company revealed something, they were to be expelled immediately.[91] The outcome of this and other cases like it is unknown. In the interweaving of the secrecy and slowness of the bureaucracy, the lives of innocently condemned people were at stake.

20

Compassionate Cruelty:
Michel de Montaigne and Catena

BUT WHAT DID SPECTATORS make of the ritual of justice? This can be asked of the many travelers who visited Italy as an essential part of their journey of formation and who recorded in their diaries the scenes of everyday life and the customs that struck them most. Among these, the spectacle of capital punishment was obviously the one most liable to stir feelings and stimulate richly colorful descriptions. We are often indebted to these travelers for detailed accounts of the whole mechanism of criminal justice, from torture through to final execution.[1] One exceptional witness was Michel de Montaigne. The travel notes in his *Journal* allow us to view with the eyes of a curious traveler a scene that took place habitually in Rome and in other Italian cities, that of a public execution. Montaigne stopped to watch one such spectacle.[2] The condemned prisoner was a bandit named "il Catena," notorious for the number of people he was reputed to have killed—no fewer than fifty-four, according to the "Rome announcements" printed several days later. The scene that morning and the spectacle that followed are described in detail in the *Journal* kept by Montaigne's secretary on his behalf. Of course, France had its own executions in that period, but there were differences, and it was precisely these that were recorded in the annotations: compared to French customs, what struck Montaigne about the Roman ritual were the devotional trappings. At the head of the procession was a large crucifix covered with a black cloth, and the prisoner was surrounded and followed by a large number of men dressed in habits, their eyes covered by hoods made from the same material. It was said of them that they were gentlemen and people of distinction, members of a confraternity who took it upon themselves to accompany criminals on their journey to the scaffold and to bury their bodies afterward. Two of them stayed next to Catena on the cart carrying him to the execution site. The others followed on foot. A swarthy man of around thirty, Catena was a known bandit and gang leader famous throughout Italy for the enormity of his crimes: among other things, there was a story that he had murdered two Capuchin monks after forcing them to repudiate God.[3] His face could not be seen from the street because the two members of the confraternity hid it behind an image of Christ that they held up in front of his eyes all the time, right up until the moment when the executioner cast him off the gallows and hung him. His death seemed unremarkable to the French onlookers, because the condemned man made no movement and said nothing. Immediately afterward his body was taken down and cut into four parts. As soon as the sentence had been carried out, one or two Jesuits or other members of religious orders stood up on makeshift pulpits and began preaching to the crowd, inviting everyone to reflect on the example of religious death they had witnessed.

The Romans, Montaigne's secretary noted, had made the condemned die a "simple" death—that is, without any special forms of torture. The observation grasped a peculiar feature of the prevalent punishment system in Italian cities, where the additional punishments customary in France were resorted to in a much more limited way. The examination of sources relating to the criminal court in Bologna shows that, of 316 death sentences carried out between 1613 and 1673, extra punishments in the form of torture and corporal afflictions were meted out in just 64 cases—a fifth of the total.[4] It is very likely that the mediation of the confraternities played an important part in the limited resort to such methods. In Rome, where the pincering of living flesh and other tortures were sometimes carried out, the *confratelli* of San Giovanni Decollato had their work cut out to help the condemned overcome their terror of these excruciating forms of suffering—and in standing beside them on the cart or on the route by foot to the scaffold they witnessed those tortures from close up. So it can be no accident that at one of the company's meetings a formal proposal was made by one of their number to "go to the pope and request the favor that the executed not be pincered." A long and impassioned discussion ensued, with numerous contributions ("there was much talk"). But there was no dissent: the proposal was approved unanimously and "representatives were chosen to go to the pope."[5]

The impressions of Montaigne and his secretary did then grasp a real aspect of execution practices in Rome. And the agonies inflicted on Catena must have appeared insignificant in comparison to the French reality of the time. In Rome the violence of the executioner was unleashed on the body of the condemned after death. Montaigne noted with amazement that the spectators, having watched the hanging in silence, reacted with wails and cries to each blow of the axe delivered to the corpse. The scene remained impressed on his mind, and he included a recollection of the episode in his reworked version of the short but dense chapter (book 2, chapter 11) on cruelty that appeared in the 1582 edition of the *Essays*.[6] From it he drew some particularly noteworthy conclusions, to which we shall return shortly.

In the meantime it is worth noting the observation about the "simple" nature of the death on the gallows of someone who had been a terrible bandit, and who here was silent, faceless, and wordless, entirely absorbed in devout murmuring with his two comforters. What was seen in French justice rituals was entirely different: as Montaigne well knew, the sacraments were not permitted in France, and the confession of the condemned was the *amende honorable,* a declaration made out loud and in public before the stone cross that marked the execution site. In Rome, on the other hand, the public part of the execution ritual did not involve criminals being presented with the burden of their misdeeds and being forced to look the crowd in the face and publicly account for their crimes. The scene centered on a faceless person, a completely absorbed penitent waiting for the judgment of God in the hope that their soul might be saved.

Montaigne, like all the other spectators, knew nothing about the secret part of the "service." If he had been able to read the company's report he would have found this brief account:

> On Tuesday January 10, two hours into the night before Wednesday, our Company was informed that there would be an execution the following morning. For this reason, the comforters were summoned to Sant'Orsola and at the ninth hour they went to Torre di Nona, where Bartolomeo Vallante [corrected elsewhere to Valente] known as "il Catena" was handed over to us, as he was to die at the hands of justice.
>
> Confessed and contrite, he said he wanted to die a good Christian in remission of his sins, asking for the mercy of our Lord and forgiving everyone who had wronged him and requesting forgiveness of all those who had been wronged by him, confessing that he was dying justly. Nothing else he said needs to be recorded. Present were Messer Ulisse,

our chaplain, Messer Vincentio Cenciolini, Messer Alessandro Vecchiani, Messer Averardo Serristori, Messer Francesco Scarfantone Girolamo Romoli, comforters, Carlo Strozzi, *provveditore,* sacristan, and steward.

In the morning at dawn the Holy Mass was said, and he took Communion with great devotion. Then at the 16th hour he was taken through Rome on a cart and pincered in various places, and then led to Ponte, where he was hung and quartered.[7]

At dawn on January 11, just before leaving the chapel, Catena had dictated his last wishes to the comforters. These were that he

> wanted to die a good Christian in remission of his sins, asking for the mercy of our Lord and forgiving everyone who had wronged him and requesting forgiveness of all those who had been wronged by him, confessing that he was dying justly. Nothing else he said needs to be recorded.[8]

That was all. And not just for Catena: the whole register that opens with his name is filled with many other cases. Each was different, but for each the words that recur in the reports are the same: confession, contrition, acceptance of the punishment "in remission of sins" (not crimes, note, but sins), the request for and granting of forgiveness. Murderers, highwaymen, and heretics entered the *conforteria* with their burden of crimes. By the time they left they had to have been transformed into repentant sinners prepared to consider death on the scaffold as a gift of divine providence to earn a place in heaven. Not everyone toed the line: some, albeit not many, resisted. Looking through the register, we find hundreds of names from very varied social backgrounds, guilty of a range of different crimes—from theft, always the primary cause of death on the scaffold, to murder, heresy, and apostasy. But the personal identities are lost and their life stories vanish behind a wording that is almost always the same, in which the condemned person accepts the punishment, recognizes the justice of his death, asks for forgiveness and forgives, and declares that he wishes to die a "good Christian." The words of devotion and forgiveness attributed to them are almost invariably the same. We find them in the declarations of Alfonso Ceccarello, a doctor from Bevagna, and in those of Giovan Battista and Gabriele Venessi, two Piedmontese brothers who were wine merchants in Naples.

Catena's execution had also been a straightforward affair, and one, furthermore, brimming with devotion. But, Montaigne observed in another section of the *Essays* that it would not be arbitrary to link to the Roman case, this display of devotion—requested of and inculcated in the person about to die and in the crowd—formed part of a strategy of diversion, a way of distracting the condemned from the thought of their imminent death and preventing them from really facing up to the trial awaiting them. In those condemned prisoners who fixed their eyes on the image of Christ, raised their hands to the sky, used their voice for prayer and their ears to follow the comforter's instructions, Montaigne saw people who were fleeing from the struggle, distracting themselves from their approaching death. He recalled the case of an acquaintance who got into a fight and was stabbed repeatedly; in imminent danger of dying, he heard everyone around him telling him to think of his conscience, but he reacted and killed his assailant. Instead, all that devotion was a mechanism of diversion, which reminded him of another scene, when a surgeon had to use a lancet on a child to cut a fistula, and as he stepped up to perform his task everyone present tried to occupy the young boy by amusing him and playing games with him.[9] The religious devotion surrounding the execution, then, made adults into children, preventing them from really addressing the reality of their punishment.

The key reflection into which Montaigne inserted his recollection of the Roman execution scene dealt with the theme of cruelty (book 2, chapter 11). He begins by praising moral virtues, in particular the firmness and constancy shown by great men in the ancient world, from Socrates to Cato, in the face of death. He mentions the virtues of Epicurus and Stoic morality, talks about death, suffering, and tears, and compares the cannibalism of the American savages with the agonies of execution rituals. Here Montaigne comes to the core of his thinking, and the subject dealt with in the chapter "On Coaches," where his comparison of the anthropophagy of Brazilian savages and the violence of the religious conflicts in France ends with the celebrated relativization of the concept of "barbarities," which is very probably indebted to Sebastiano Castellione's notion of heresy.[10] What he saw in Europe was ritualized death transformed into spectacle. It is not the cannibal who roasts and eats the bodies of the dead that offends his senses and moves him to tears, but the cruelty exercised on the living in Christian Europe. This time the comparison between different cultures takes place within European history,

1. Giotto, *Desperatio,* fresco, 1306. PADUA: CAPPELLA DEGLI SCROVEGNI.

2. Filippo Dolciati, attributed to *Storia di Antonio di Giuseppe Rinaldeschi,*
tempera on wood, 1502. FLORENCE: MUSEO STIBBERT.

3. Cristoforo di Jacopo da Bologna, *Flagellation, Crucifixion, Martyrdom of Saints Lorenzo and Biagio, tavoletta,* ca. 1360. STUTTGART: STAATSGALERIE.

4. Giovanni di Paolo, circle of, *Decapitation of Saint John the Baptist, tavoletta* no. 105, fifteenth century. SIENA: ARCHIVIO DI STATO, ARCHIVIO DELLA COMPAGNIA DI SAN GIOVANNI BATTISTA DELLA MORTE.

5. Cristoforo de Predis, scene of torture and condemnation in a medieval city, miniature, 1470. MODENA: BIBLIOTECA ESTENSE, *DE SPHAERA D'ESTE*, FOL. 6*V*.

6. Niccolò dell'Arca, *Lament for the Dead Christ,* terracotta, 1463. BOLOGNA: CHIESA DI SANTA MARIA DELLA VITA.

7. "This is the procedure and the way to prepare and make ready those who must go to comfort and console the people who are condemned to death." Preamble to book I of *Il Manuale quattrocentesco della Conforteria di Bologna,* miniature, Bologna, second half of the fifteenth century. NEW YORK: PIERPONT MORGAN LIBRARY, MS. M. 188 F. 5R.

8. Piero della Francesca, *Polyptych of Mercy,* tempera on wood, ca. 1445, central tableau. SANSEPOLCRO: PINACOTECA COMUNALE.

9. Three condemned men and three offering comfort, against the background of a city, ex voto, sixteenth century. NAPLES: MUSEO DEGLI EX VOTO, SANTUARIO MADONNA DELL'ARCO IN SANT'ANASTASIA.

10. Torture scene, ex voto for grace received by Giovanna Zaya, 1599. NAPLES: MUSEO DEGLI EX VOTO, SANTUARIO MADONNA DELL'ARCO IN SANT' ANASTASIA.

11. Execution scene in Ferrara, miniature, 1506. FERRARA: BIBLIOTECA
ARIOSTEA, MS CL. I, 404, CC. 16V–17R.

12. Prayer of the condemned man, from *Oration to recite to assist the condemned to die,* eighteenth century. BOLOGNA: ARCHIVIO ARCIVESCOVILE.

13. Jacopino del Conte, *The Preaching of Saint John the Baptist,* mural painting, 1538. ROME: ORATORY DELL'ARCICONFRATERNITA DI SAN GIOVANNI DECOLLATO.

Sacræ Conſolatorum Scholæ
Bononiæ Patronus.

14. Emblem of the Conforteria of Bologna: oval with images of the executioner who chops off the head of the condemned and the text, "Sacrae Consolatorum Scholae Bononiae Patronus (c.s.)," eighteenth century. BOLOGNA:
BIBLIOTECA ARCIVESCOVILE.

SACRÆ CONSOLATORUM SCHOLÆ
BONON: PATRONUS.

15. *Decapitation of Saint John the Baptist,* engraving of Silvestro Neri, drawing of Domenico Fratta, Bologna, 1733. PRIVATE COLLECTION.

16. Madonna of the Conforteria of Bologna, miniature, 1562. BOLOGNA:
BIBLIOTECA COMUNALE DELL'ARCHIGINNASIO, MS FONDO OSPEDALI
DELL'ARCHIGINNASIO.

DETESTA IL NOVATOR LO SPARSO ERRORE
CHE A LE FIAMME IL DANNÒ.FILIPPO SPETRA
DE L'UOM SUPERBO L'OSTINATO CUORE (a)
QUALI GRAZIE DAL CIEL FILIPPO IMPETRA!

(a) Il Paleologo Eresiarca condannato ad esser abbruciato vivo, mentre erasi per eseguir la sentenza,
alle parole di S.Filippo, ritratta pubblicamente le sue Eresie, e salva la vita).

Nº 53.

17. Innocente Alessandri, *The Converted Heretic: Giacomo Paleologo on the Scaffold, Converted by Philip Neri,* engraving, Venice, 1792. PRIVATE COLLECTION.

18. Bonfire of Sister Geltruda and of Ignazio Barberi, in Antonino Mongitore, *The public act of faith solemnly celebrated in the city of Palermo on 6 April 1724 by the tribunal of the Holy Office in Sicily,* Palermo, Epiro, 1724. TURIN: BIBLIO-TECA NAZIONALE UNIVERSITARIA, DEPOSITED AT THE FONDAZIONE FIRPO, FONDO ANTICO, COLL. FIRPO 1684.

at the highest level: it is a comparison between the practice of death on the scaffold in Christian Rome and pagan cultures. Montaigne compares the cruelty of the present times with the practices of the ancient world; he suggests imitating the Egyptians and Persians, for example by directing punishments not at the living body but at the clothing and headwear of the individuals to punish.

Everything about capital punishment that went beyond the straightforward putting to death appears to him to be pure cruelty. This is especially the case for Christians, observes Montaigne, as they should be concerned to ensure that souls made the transition from life to death in a good state, not sending them on their way in a condition of total despair and anguish caused by unbearable torments. So Montaigne does not, at least in appearance, either explicitly condemn or approve of the death penalty; the focus of his concern seems instead to be the excess of additional agonies with which it was administered. Montaigne points out that those torments were so unbearable that the very idea of them drove some people to try to kill themselves. He tells the story of a soldier imprisoned in a tower who, seeing carpenters at work and imagining that they were making preparations for his execution, tried to commit suicide with a rusty nail. He did not die though, and lived to hear the reading of his sentence, which condemned him to be beheaded. He was so immensely relieved ("infiniment resjoui") that he thanked the judges for the unexpected gentleness of the punishment.

Montaigne's observation grasps a well-known reality. Terror of the agonies that sometimes preceded the execution proper dominated minds in Italy as well, and could turn into obsession. Montaigne could not have known about it, but not long before there had been a case in Florence that bore out his view. It was that of Giovambattista di Bindaccio Ricasoli Baroni, who fell into a deep depression (the word used in those days was "melancholy") that took the form of terror at the idea of being condemned to death. Galileo Galilei was a friend of his, and did what he could to help until Giovambattista died. A long deposition on this affair has been preserved among the papers of a Florentine court. It was unquestionably a case of madness, of "bizarre mental infirmity." But there was method in that madness, with the ingredients of a culture where Christian religion and pagan models were fighting it out. Galileo told the judges that Giovambattista was obsessed by the thought of how he should behave in prison. For instance, he asked himself "if it would be better, when he was taken to prison, to deny and withstand the torments, or confess everything, or else deny a part. And in this period Giovambattista expected to read examples of men strong in the face of death, and spent a large part of his evenings in orations to God, and would have liked law books to study cases." He had "many times thought of killing himself, either by throwing himself off some high place, or killing himself with a blade; but, he added, that was rejected by the Christian religion."[11] Here, then, was the same mix of ancient models and Christian precepts that Montaigne was attempting to analyze.

In the essay on cruelty the memory of the Roman crowd's behavior during the execution of Catena resurfaces and prompts a thought: could cruelty not be directed at the dead bodies of criminals? Seeing them deprived of burial, boiled, and quartered would have had just as much impact on the onlookers as the suffering inflicted on the living. In this way, the rigor necessary to keep a brake on the people would be displayed, without any need to make living beings suffer. This brings us back to the central point, the question of whether putting someone to death was an act of justice. Montaigne does not tackle the issue directly. It was not easy to do so. Rejecting the right to kill on the basis of the Gospels would have meant taking sides with the Anabaptists whose evangelical radicalism had cost them their lives. Even the humanistic tradition inspired by Erasmus which had touched on the matter had found it prudent to take refuge in complaints about the hardness of the times, in moral exhortations, and in the praising of mildness. Or it had taken shelter behind models offered by other societies in distant antiquity, or in the even more remote area of utopia. The example for this had been offered by a work which became immediately famous when it was first published in 1516—Thomas More's *Utopia*. Here "supreme justice" is described as "supreme injustice," applying the Ciceronian motto "summum ius, summa iniuria." God's commandment was at odds with the practice of the age and with the terrible readiness with which thieves were put to death: "God has said, 'Thou shalt not kill'; shall we kill so readily for the theft of a bit of small change?"[12] How could the evidence of God's prohibition on killing be eluded? Simple: in the justice system the person who materially killed the victims was the executioner, the only person exempted by human convention from the divine prohibition—an exception that confirmed the rule. But once divine law had been suspended on this point, the path was open to introduce so many other exceptions that every trace of God's commandments was canceled from human society.

The success of *Utopia* among sixteenth-century readers offers a useful pointer for grasping the doubts and reservations that jurists also had about the violence of criminal law. As mentioned in Chapter 2, the name of Thomas More crops up on several occasions in the very popular and oft-reprinted *Sylva nuptialis* by Giovanni Nevizzano da Asti, together with negative judgments about the cruelty and pointlessness of torture.[13] A renowned and attentive reader of Erasmus, the canonist Martín de Azpilcueta otherwise known as Doctor Navarrus, seriously posed the question of whether it was right to excommunicate for mortal sin (consequently taking their life) someone who just stole a needle from a tailor, a sewing awl from a shoemaker, or a dozen eggs from a peasant. And in the face of the handing down of death penalties for those guilty of such minor thefts, he observed: "It seems that Christian mildness is repugnant to the law, which takes away a person's life for something that is not, nor presumes to be, mortal sin."[14] The prevailing position among criminologists was different: they supported the harshness of the death penalty on the grounds of the need to keep a brake on human beings and guarantee the safety of goods and life in society. In the years in which Montaigne was traveling in Italy, one of the most celebrated of these, the criminologist and magistrate Giulio Claro, reiterated in his famous "liber quintus" the necessity of capital punishment to govern a human species which, unlike other animal species, appeared to him to be ever ready to cruelly spill the blood of their fellow human beings for the most insignificant reasons.[15] Human beings seemed cruel to Montaigne as well, but for him the height of cruelty was precisely the resort to the death penalty. He said this from behind the protective shield of a quote from Seneca—"That man should kill man not in anger or in fear but merely for the spectacle"[16]—but that this was his opinion could not have been clearer. Montaigne then moved on to other even more radical considerations. For example, if a people as devout as the ancient Egyptians ("si devotieux") offered painted pigs to the gods as a way of satisfying divine justice, what should be said of the present age, in which human bodies were dismembered with axe blows, and unusual tortures and new forms of killing were invented not out of personal hatred or for reasons of gain, but simply in order to enjoy the spectacle of the screams and agony of the dying? Further and bolder passages extended the notion of pity for the living to beyond the human species, taking in animals as well. Why kill animals, who lodge in the same worldly palace as we do and who were put there by the only Master? Historic experience is summoned to the aid of theology: ultimately, Montaigne observes, the ancient Romans became accustomed to producing a spectacle of death in the circus by moving on from killing animals to killing human beings. The considerations of the essay on cruelty, in recalling the cousinship ("cousinage") between men and animals, suggested a general feeling of respect for nature, including trees and plants. And the example of ancient peoples was once again invoked to suggest that dogs, horses, birds, and other beasts had a right to a respectful burial, in recognition of the services they rendered to adults as working animals and as play companions for children.

This part of the *Essays* did not pass unobserved by the Roman authorities, and Montaigne was called to explain himself before the supreme ecclesiastical authority responsible for the censorship of books, the Master of the Sacred Apostolic Palace, Sisto Fabbri.[17] The latter was a Dominican friar, Montaigne relates, who did not know French but had received a report from a French friar signaling various points of concern. There is no doubt that on certain key issues the text did appear at first sight to clash with the suspicious orthodoxy of the Counter-Reformation. But the ones mentioned by the friar concerned hardly any of the themes that might have been expected to jar on Tridentine ears. Montaigne recounts that what was contested of him was precisely the phrase that defined cruelty as anything that, in capital punishment, went beyond "simple" death.[18] The Roman censor's sensibility was decidedly singular: he had found nothing to object about in the praise of Epicurus, the observations on metempsychosis, and the burial of animals, but his suspicions had been aroused by the criticism of the current practices of tortures and torments added to the death penalty.

❦ 21 ❦

The Fate of the Body

> In the evening, at the 22nd hour, the quartered body was removed and taken by our Company for burial in our church, and the head of the above-mentioned, at the order of the Governor of Rome, was handed over to the master of justice.[1]

Let us now return to the account of Catena's death and look more closely at the final part of the penal ritual. As the final lines of the company's report indicate, the working day of the *confratelli* did not end with the execution. Now they had to deal with the body of the executed man, after the executioner had cut him to pieces. In Rome, the parts were gathered up before nightfall and taken to their final destination in a ritual procession comprising thirty deputies. The rule generally stipulated in the statutes of the companies of justice was for the corpses of those who died penitent and reconciled to be taken down from the scaffold, or from where they had been put on display, after which they were recomposed and buried in holy ground, either that of the confraternity or that of other churches if the dead person or their family had the privilege of burial there. Like all the others, the Florentine company of the Blacks had the task of gathering up the body:

> As the head will have been severed from the bust, the comforter who had the *tavoletta* will take it [the head] in both hands by the cheeks, face upward, and will place it in the prepared coffin. At the same time four other brothers chosen to carry the said coffin will take the corpse, two by the arms and two by the feet, and will place it in said coffin.[2]

Criminals lost ownership of their body at the moment in which they were sentenced to death. For this reason it might be used for vivisection, or to test the efficacy of poisons and antidotes to poisons, as Duke Cosimo I dei Medici did.[3] It was the property of the authorities and, generally speaking, was left to the confraternity. But there was no one single rule governing this area. The reality was that certain categories of people—the clergy, nobles—enjoyed privileges that guaranteed them special treatment in death, while the bodies of others remained available for other possible practices after execution. The body of Beatrice Cenci, for instance, was "carried in procession with great honor to San Pietro Montorio, where it was buried."[4] Catena's head, on the other hand, ended up with the executioner. Irrespective of the requests made by the condemned and the promises made during comforting, their bodies no longer belonged to their owners, who had lost all rights over them when sentenced. Nor, basically, did it belong to their heirs either, though the corpse might be granted as a benign gift where an important family was involved. All the personal effects of the dead person went to the confraternity that had assisted them—on this matter the privileges granted by the popes were explicit.[5] The dead person's soul was assured of remembrance masses: the fate of their body had to be sorted out between the powers who had taken part in the killing operation, from the sovereign to the comforters to the executioner. Elsewhere in Europe the Reformation Churches retreated in the face of death: as they could not influence divine judgment in any way they forewent all forms of remembrance and left the rites of memory to family and friends. In Calvinist Europe the principle of the private nature of funeral rites and burial would become established, given that the Church recognized that it could do nothing more for the dead: in London, following execution the body was left to anyone who wanted to take it away. By contrast, in the Italian tradition burial in holy ground was guaranteed as a work of mercy to those who died in the communion of the Church: the abhorrence of nonpenitents and suicides was marked by their bodies being dumped outside the city walls. In Modena, for example, they were thrown into a space next to the city walls,[6] in Rome near the pyramid of Cestius or along the Muro Torto.[7] But if the condemned died penitent and confessed their body was to be interred in holy ground as confirmation of a Christian death. Meanwhile, the comforters had to make sure that the crowd did not enter into possession of any part of the dead person's body, and none of the paraphernalia used to carry out the execution. If the hand of a thief or murderer had been cut off along the execution route, it had to be gathered up for later burial, and the same applied for all other organic remains. As for the body, it had to be removed from the stage or from the gallows as soon as possible: the same evening, according to the confraternity's regulations and in accordance with any additional punishments or ritual humiliations decreed by the sentence. In Modena, for example, the principle established by the statutes was the following: "As the soul will have departed, all the brothers must carry the body off for burial and honor it according to its condition."[8] The body, reunited with its head, or recomposed if it had been quartered and the four sections gruesomely displayed in public places, had to be accompanied to the place of burial ("according to its condition," that is, to the family chapel or the church chosen by the condemned if they were of noble birth, otherwise to the confraternity's graveyard) and with the alms that had been collected masses were to be said for their soul. Furthermore, special care had to be taken to recover and burn the halter and ropes used in the hanging, to prevent them ending up on the secret market of necromantic practices and popular medicine. This was an operation that all the companies of justice performed with great attention. The *confratelli* of San Giovanni Battista in Modena were especially meticulous in meeting this obligation. At the end of every execution, in the presence of the brothers, the executioner, and sometimes "many people" from the crowd, the hanging ropes and every other object used to cause suffering to and kill the condemned were set on fire in the church sacristy: in 1706 witnesses attested that what went into the flames in the sacristy were "the halters and the nails of the hands" used in the execution, and that "the two large halters and the two small ones," and "also the two nails of the hands" were burned in their presence.[9] There was nothing symbolic about this ritual: it was necessary to be absolutely sure that the ropes to be burned really were the ones used for the hanging and that they had not been cunningly substituted with other ones. The rope-maker had to examine them and reply on oath when asked if they were the ones he had supplied to the executioner on the morning of the execution.[10] This concern must have been very widespread in confraternity circles: traces of similar rituals in other cities indicate how important it was considered to prevent those materials from falling into other hands.[11] New companies wrote to the archconfraternity in Rome for information about "the form of ceremonies they used in burning the nooses of the executed on the feast day of the beheading of Saint John the Baptist."[12] They were objects that occupied a special place in people's minds, something that was noted by an English traveler at the end of the sixteenth century: in Italy, when the priest turned to the congregation during Mass, urging them to lift up their hearts with the words "sursum corda," the assembled faithful made the sign of the cross on their throat "because in the Italian language the noose is called 'corda.'"[13]

But why did the remnants of the bodies and the materials used on the scaffold receive such attention? What we find here is confirmation of the profound reasons that from the very start had motivated those who volunteered to bury the executed. The life that had been ended with violence continued to linger in the remains of the dead person, and imbued the instruments of execution with mysterious powers. This raised the curtain on the effective protagonist, albeit concealed, of the whole ritual of saving the soul of the condemned: their body. It should not be forgotten that the need to give it a Christian burial had been the reason for the widespread beginning of these works of mercy, which then became specialized in the city *conforterie*. The devotion of such care to the body was grounded in a world of deep-rooted cultural beliefs and practices, both official and folkloristic. The human body was, by common conviction, one of the most powerful concentrations of natural secrets, indispensable for a long life and good health. And for the person condemned to death this was so in a special way. A forcibly interrupted life left its sources—blood, breath, flesh—suspended and still available in the limbs of an organism that was no longer attended by its owner or by others. If there is something that always leaves one stunned and incredulous in the face of the death of a human being it is the disappearance of life: something that was there until a moment ago has gone, has disappeared, and is irremediably lost. Lost or hidden, invisible but still present. Death on the scaffold was the supreme example of the sudden and immediate interruption of a still-full and vigorous life. The sentence had expropriated the body, forcing the inhabitant to resign themselves to death with the promise that their soul would be saved and their body buried in holy ground. This is what somehow curbed the protests, the complaints, the sense of shame at that infamous public display, in a word all the expressions of the jealous sense of self awoken by the idea of the scorn that others were preparing to heap on the abandoned body parts.

But irrespective of every promise, what remained on the scaffold once the execution had been carried out was commonly considered to be a precious repository of secrets and powers. And everyone, without exception, tried to take advantage. Here more than elsewhere, the crossover between

high and low culture was intense, between folkloristic traditions and erudite learning. Blood was the substance of life, sought after and drunk avidly
even on the platform of the scaffold itself, and often distributed to epileptics as it gushed from the bust severed by the executioner's axe. This was an
ancient practice, found far beyond Italy's borders, prompting one scholar
who found it in German historical sources from the seventeenth century onward to see in it the indirect effect on folkloristic traditions of the cancellation of the cult of saints and relics by Protestant reformers.[14] In reality, as
was well known to the German antiquarian and medical tradition of the seventeenth century, it was already customary in ancient Rome to resort to the
powers concentrated in the bodies of the hanged. Pliny the Elder's scientific
encyclopedia offers testimony that the Romans habitually drank the blood
of gladiators to cure epilepsy. The most obvious explanation was given for
this—namely, that it was a case of exploiting the curative power of the blood
of human beings who were still young and vigorous, a liquid even believed
capable of reacting to the presence of the person who had killed its owner.[15]
A treatise (by Heinrich Kornmann) about the miraculous operations of
human bodies affirmed that executioners had the habit of drinking human
blood and listed the therapeutic properties of the executioner's noose and
even the brain of the hanged person, as places where vital spirits found a final
refuge.[16] In the view of this learned Protestant reader of Paracelsus, this was
the origin of the Catholic habit of venerating relics and of baptizing with
new names the bones dug up in Roman catacombs. Effectively, there is no
doubt that the idea of the human body as a repository of natural secrets, and
especially of blood as a vital force, a life-bearing vehicle in the generation
and preservation of bodies, exercised an extraordinary attraction. It was the
spiritual substance that transmitted from father to son the legacy of life and
of the soul, including the sin of the first father, Adam. The life of the body
depended on its heat. Those who tried to grasp its secrets as a way of prolonging existence were attracted by the investigation of the mysteries of blood
and by the original substance that gave the human being not just the power
to grow and remain in life, but also to return in possession of one's body
at the moment of resurrection. It was spoken of as a "radical dampness,"
distinct from other natural juices like milk for its being innate to the
living being.[17] It was described as living silver or as gold. Popes wishing to
prolong their lives were advised to drink liquid gold.[18] Meanwhile, in "low"

practice, those who had no gold tried to procure the vital liquid par excellence—blood. That is why the fresh blood of executed criminals was collected and drunk at the scene. Epileptics used to drink it avidly and then run for a long time so the medicine would work its effect. All this could take place quite peaceably, like a normal procuring of a curative liquid: so, in Modena in 1756, a lackey of Marchese Giuseppe Montecuccoli di Modena was politely served by the executioner with two cups of blood from an Irish officer who had just been beheaded. The marchese needed it because he suffered from epilepsy, but his lackey decided to drink some of it himself and then immediately set off on the recommended run. On the other hand, in Rome in 1713, the whole crowd around the scaffold, "having seen . . . someone who had drunk the blood running, and not knowing why he was running, immediately fled."[19]

Despite the strong legal prohibitions and the rule of burial in holy ground, ways did exist to get around them. There was a trade in human flesh, bones, and skulls that was no less widespread for being banned. In this respect the thief and the murderer who died on the scaffold ended up being subjected to the same treatment reserved for the relics of martyr saints of the Church or of those rumored to be destined for sainthood: the thaumaturgic powers attributed to canonized saints and conveyed by their remains rubbed shoulders and sometimes overlapped with beliefs about the medicinal preparations that could be derived from scaffold remains. The Florentine chronicles of the age relate that a crowd threw itself upon the ashes resulting from the burning of Savonarola and his fellow brothers in 1498. The narrative told by his devotees was that they were looking for relics of saints. But around the scaffolds there was normally no shortage of people searching for human relics attributed with miraculous powers not so very different from the ones that the relics of saints were recognized as having by the official culture of the Church. The body of the executed criminal and the management of these mysterious and wonderful powers often gave rise to full-blown scenes of butchery, where the crowd of onlookers stocked up on blood and human flesh. The body abandoned by the spirit was transformed into a source of precious ingredients, there for the taking, without anyone being concerned to ensure respect for the dead person's corpse.

In Forlì in 1488 one such scene was recorded and described by the barber turned chronicler Andrea Bernardi known as Novacula, who had an unblemished faith in the Ciceronian maxim of history as the teacher of life. On May 1, 1488, three men found guilty of treason, Pagliarino, Marco Scozzacaro, and Piero Albanese, were executed. Pagliarino was hung from a window in Palazzo del Podestà and then thrown into the square. The crowd set to abusing the dead enemy: his penis was cut off and stuffed into his mouth, then "the viscera and all the innards" were removed and his fat collected by hand and tooth "because he was a young man" (around twenty-eight years old). Marco Scozzocaro received even worse treatment: he was "slit in half and the viscera removed and taken away . . . the fat was taken off as well." He was of small stature, "white and with good complexion," well nourished and plump, never having fasted on the days when this was commanded. Piero Albanese also had "a fine manly body, white and of good complexion." As a result there was plenty of "fat to collect."[20] The Confraternita dei Battuti, whose job it was to assist the condemned, was notably absent from this scene. Similarly missing was the granting of the sacraments to the condemned men, a practice that was normally observed in Forlì.[21] And yet it was up to the confraternities of justice to gather up the innards: in Vicenza in 1527 the *confratelli* had a special "bucket for the innards."[22] Generally they were buried with the rest of the body, though there are attested cases of the executioner being given special rights of preemption, like the one permitting the Roman executioner to take Catena's head home with him. In seventeenth-century Florence the nominal wage of the "master of justice" envisaged detailed fees in addition to that for the execution proper: for example, "for the display of each bandit's head, ramming onto the spikes," "for the hanging and quartering of each person, including the ropes," especially if it was necessary "to put up the quarters outside Florence:"[23] but the actual wage packet that is not officially mentioned generally included permission to take the hanged person's fat and sell it. There was a proverb that circulated about the difference between lawyers and executioners: executioners sold flesh, lawyers sold their tongue, the difference being that executioners really did sell flesh, while the lawyer kept his tongue even if he had sold it.[24] This private trading that went on in the master of justice's home can be found in proceedings of trials for magic and necromancy, because this is where one could find body fragments useful for ensuring success at the gambling table, to win a woman's love, secure the death of an enemy, or the wealth of hidden treasure. What surfaces in such proceedings are random traces, but they shed light on deep-rooted and widespread habits and ways of thinking. We find them above all in Inquisition papers, for official reasons so to speak: the confessors' ears picked up stories of superstitions and suspect rituals that were then passed on and recorded in the documents of the inquisitors. So, for example, on April 11, 1699, Antonia Margherita, the daughter of Giovanni Battista Bedetti from the parish of Mascarella, presented herself to the inquisitor of Bologna to report her sweetheart, one Pier Giovanni Genasio da San Cesario. The young man was an inveterate gambler, fond of a card game known as *bassetta*. He believed that all he needed to do to win was to "get hold of the noose of the hanged person, the heart, and the jawbone of the same hanged person, and then say some words." He had instructed Antonia Margherita to "get hold of the hanged person's noose and he would then venture to find the rest." But the woman had refused: "I told him that they were things to go to the Holy Office about,"[25] a sign that the pedagogy of the Inquisition had made its mark. In the Protestant world too, the threat of special punishments hung over those who used the remains of the executed for magical practices, while if they appropriated them for anatomical studies they could count on leniency from the judge.[26]

The fear of being hauled before the tribunal of the Inquisition stemmed from the awareness of how close all this was to necromancy: those remains were powerful because a soul dwelt in them. The confessor who made the Tuscan sculptor Cosini bury an executed man's skin with which he had clad a small body fully understood the magic significance of the operation: Cosini attributed "some great virtues" to that skin (which he had had no difficulty in procuring because he was the member of a company of justice).[27] But there was also a more humdrum and less dangerous use of the resources controlled by the executioner, one which saw people come knocking at his door as if to a kind of pharmacy or place of cure. In 1712 a certain Agostino De Sanctis confessed to the bishop of Chieti that the year before he had gone to the executioner to ask for a "little human fat to use as grease for sciatica." There was nothing exceptional or prohibited about this: the trade in medicinal substances made from the human body was still commonplace at the time, from fat to "mummy flesh" (derived, it was said, from Egyptian mummies). What complicated matters was that the executioner now saw himself not just as a pharmacist but as a physician as well. He had decided to treat De Sanctis himself, shaving his patient's thigh with a knife used for executions. But while doing so, "he made crosses and said certain words."[28] That is why Agostino decided, probably on the advice of his confessor, to go to the bishop. The executioner had staged a rite of magic, of the kind that disturbed the guardians of orthodoxy: cross signs and incomprehensible words mimed the rite of exorcism and suggested the evocation of spirits in the afterlife, those souls whom the executioner was accustomed to separating from their bodies. As for the execution knife, it was attributed with powers of the same order as that of the hanging ropes: the ropes that had closed the passageway to the vital spirits could transfer their efficacy to those who suffered from headaches. And the knife that killed could heal. At the heart of all this there was always the special contact with the body of the condemned at the moment of death.

What emerges once again from this welter of practices and beliefs, and from comparison with other European Christian cultures, is the complexity of the functions performed by the companies of justice. What they contributed in the relationship between society and the person who died on the scaffold was the mediation of a body endowed with visible sacred attributes and political power, qualified to operate in the liminal area between death and life, and to legitimate and discipline the unleashing of the instinctive impulses of a feral world. It was under their jurisdiction that the final phase of the desecration of the condemned person's body took place: public anatomy.

22

Public Anatomy

MONTAIGNE OBSERVED THAT the commotion among spectators at executions was caused not by the killing itself but by the quartering. Their collective cries denoted an emotion that did not just stem from pity. The secrets hidden beneath the surface of the skin exercised a very strong pull on those present. Spectators did, however, have other occasions to satisfy their thrilled curiosity about the mysteries and secret forms of what the sixteenth-century Flemish anatomist Andreas Vesalius called the "fabric of the human body." The key moment when everyone could get a glimpse of human viscera being brought to light was during public anatomy. Here, as has been noted with regard to eighteenth-century London, the history of the poor met the history of science.[1] In reality, what was presented to viewers of public anatomical dissections had little to do with science. Their purpose was not to verify scientific hypotheses but to entertain the public with carnivalesque spectacles, with the opening up of the human body being the high point in terms of subverting rules. In the public squares of Italy, in a show that over time also started to be staged in other European cities (for example, Holland), the body of the condemned was subjected to the ultimate humiliation, completing the process of desecration and reification that had begun with the punishments and tortures prior to execution. When the condemned discovered that this was the fate that awaited their corpse, their reaction was one of profound anguish, the risk being that this would put paid to the strategy based on the splitting of soul and body. The mediation carried out by the companies of justice tended, on the one hand, to attenuate the sense of shame experienced by the condemned, while, on the other hand, legitimating the use of the bodies in displays of public anatomy. But the sense of shame was acute all the same, as is confirmed by the fact that the preferred choice was to use the bodies of members of the lower orders. As far as possible, efforts were also made to avoid exhibiting the bodies of fellow citizens in the public dissections, due to the dishonor that fell upon the city. The fact is that in Italy the encounter between science and the poor was not marked by disorder and angry clashes between body bearers sent by the surgeons and the relatives of the hanged. Far from it. Thanks to the mediation of the solemn, hooded *confratelli,* everything took place with official religious blessing and in a precise and carefully regulated sequence of acts. It was in accordance with an earlier choice that the body was taken down from the gibbet and given to the physicians' guild for dissection. And so, as has been observed, the link between science and criminal justice, both engaged in cutting up the same body, was constituted by the dishonor inflicted on the condemned on the basis of the deep connection between honor and physical integrity.[2]

Scaffolds and anatomy had been closely related since the dissection of bodies resumed in the universities. In Bologna the master Mondino de' Luzzi had just started the practice of anatomy when, in November 1319, another master, Alberto, went on trial for having disinterred by night the body of a recently executed prisoner who had been buried in the cemetery of the church of San Barnaba, near the bridge over the river Reno.[3] These beginnings soon led to provisions being made to ensure a systematic supply of bodies.

In all of this the companies of justice ended up interpreting very freely their primary commitment to ensuring a Christian burial for the condemned, and which had led the members of the *misericordie* to gather around the scaffold. For this reason the companies of justice often had to intercede to try to secure the attenuation or withdrawal of special decrees ordering the prolonged display of the whole or quartered bodies of scaffold victims. But soon the beginning of the practice of anatomy led to a derogation of the rule of burial immediately after execution. Not that there were any religious obstacles to this, as was long thought to be the case by a liberal historiography quick to conclude that the needs of the advancement of studies were irreconcilable with the Catholic Church. On the contrary, what was of value to the Church, and needed protecting, was the soul. The bodies were up for negotiation, saving appearances and monetizing the granting of them in spiritual benefits (lots of masses for the souls in purgatory).

The practice of the fragmentation of bodies and differentiated burials, with the soft parts being separated from the skeleton by boiling, first started for practical reasons, when the problem arose as to how to bring back home the remains of sovereigns and noblemen who had died on the Crusades. A bull of Pope Boniface VIII, the "Detestandae feritatis," had sought to curb such practices. But in the meantime the fragmentation of the bodies of saints with a view to multiplying their protective presence was being transferred to the bodies of kings as well: the sacralization of the king's body attested in the French tradition and introduced into the rites of the Italian dynasty with the closest ties with France, the house of Este, had generated the custom of burying the noble parts, such as the heart or the head, in different churches or in monuments.[4] But it was above all in the case of those condemned to death that the reuse of bodies developed in an extensive and systematic fashion. Whereas their souls were regarded as resting in the kingdom of heaven, their bodies frequently took a path other than that of burial. Anatomy, an ancient science given new life in medieval universities, involved studying parts of the body from texts read aloud by professors, but also practical "demonstrations": a surgeon would be on hand at lessons to show real examples of the limbs and organs discussed by the professor. Hospitals for the poor and scaffolds were a natural source, as it were, where the necessary bodies could be procured. It was from here that Leonardo and Michelangelo received bodies for dissection. As for the university practice of teaching anatomy, the need for bodies sometimes even led to them being disinterred from cemeteries during the night. Generally considered a nonserious crime, in the seventeenth century the theft of bodies for anatomy received light punishment, while a very different view was taken if it was committed for purposes of magic.[5] The scaffold became the simplest source of supply: in eighteenth-century London porters and relatives of the hanged used to brawl over the bodies at Tyburn. Instead, in the Catholic world the existence of confraternities set up in the main precisely in order to bury those bodies was a fundamental condition for establishing a regular and peaceful trade. Supply was guaranteed in exchange for alms and remembrance masses for souls—a trade that functioned for centuries. It was the organs of political and religious power that determined that the bodies of executed members of the lower orders should be handed over for anatomical purposes, a practice which appears to have been consolidated in the fifteenth century when public anatomy became a habitual civic ritual in the large university of Bologna. In Modena the practice of giving the bodies of the executed to physicians for teaching and demonstration purposes is attested in city chronicles from 1494; and there is a celebrated case of an instance of public anatomy carried out by Gabriele Falloppia on December 13 and 14, 1544, on the body of an executed prisoner in the Ospedale di San Giovanni della Morte.[6] In Bologna the first public dissection by Andreas Vesalius took place in January 1540. The diary of an excited German student recorded not just the content of the lessons, where the already famous anatomist demonstrated how many errors there were in Galen's writings, but also the ritual of solemnly transporting the bodies ("cum pompa") from the gallows to the Ospedale della Morte. He also noted that there was a general preference for robust, well-fleshed bodies.[7]

The first reference in the registers of the Roman Confraternita di San Giovanni Decollato to the granting of the body of an executed person for anatomical purposes is on March 22, 1512. In accordance with the university statutes of 1531, surgeons and barbers paid a tax in order to watch the show. From it they were able to obtain alms for the soul that had inhabited the body, now owned by the public power that had condemned the prisoner.[8]

But physicians were not always willing to pay, and grotesque arguments sometimes broke out as a result, like the one over the body of Pellegrino da San Cesario, a poor wretch hung for "many thefts" in Bologna in 1636: his body was granted to the popular feast of public anatomy, but the doctor who was to perform it refused to pay the customary large ducat to the priest whose job it was to celebrate the remembrance mass. In response, the prior of the confraternity "had it buried, and refused to hand it over until he had received the large ducat." The doctor "gave it to him immediately and the lord prior had it [the body] disinterred."[9]

The mechanism of supplying bodies in exchange for masses became habitual not just in the field of the executed and the confraternities: in Bologna, when a poor person died, students would forcibly take the body despite resistance from family members, who were shut up by promises of remembrance masses for the dead person's soul.[10] And the religious legitimation guaranteed by the ecclesiastical authorities helped to quell the anatomists' own feelings of guilt and instinctive resistance in the face of the violation of human bodies: alms and offerings in memory of souls was the price paid for a ritual reparation.

Dissection and social discrimination are laced together in this story: the bodies of thieves, murderers, and infanticides were the ones that ended up on the anatomy table.[11] The statutes of the medical colleges regulated the forms this might take. It was an important appointment, a spectacle attracting the same crowd that turned out for executions. In Rome, Bologna, Padua, and Pisa the anatomical dissection of human bodies was a special event during Carnival. And this was not just because bodies decomposed less quickly in the winter, as the official provisions stated. Carnival was the feast during which order was overturned. Nothing could more appropriately symbolize the extreme infraction of rules and taboos than the violation of the secrets of the human body: the authorities knew this, and took special care to preserve public order on such occasions. The supply of bodies was assured by carefully choosing the dates for executions. In Pisa, it was the rector of the Studio (university) who asked for the condemned to be sent from where they had been incarcerated: whether by river or by land, the prisoner arrived in the university city and was placed at the disposition of the rector, who was responsible for signing the act of execution on the eve of the public anatomy. And so, on January 30, 1590, a prisoner in Pietrasanta named Giovanni Antonio da Chianni, having been sentenced to be hung and quartered, was brought down the coast to Pisa and put to death by the *bargello:* his body—not quartered—was earmarked for the rector, "for the service of this Studio and as a subject for anatomy."[12] It was a "service" that required a regular supply of bodies. The Studio's statutes obliged the rector to procure two corpses of executed prisoners each winter, one male and one female, to use for anatomical purposes during Carnival. The condemned were handed over by the grand duke's police chief to the rector: after being strangled by the executioner beneath the vault of the palazzo of the grand duke's representative, they were delivered to the students, who took them off to the premises set aside for anatomy next to the Palazzo della Sapienza. This is where the dissections were conducted during the Carnival holidays.[13] If no human bodies were available, animals were dissected instead. This is what happened in February 1642, because the "strapping young man" due to end up on the dissection table was apparently pardoned as the result of an exceptional event.[14] Public anatomy was also practiced at the University of Ferrara, where, in the middle of the sixteenth century, Gabriele Falloppia, besides ordinary dissections, according to the testimony of Ludovico

Castelvetro, "yearned to publicly cut up another body." And in Mantua the statutes of the college of physicians had a record book "regarding the anatomical dissection to do each year."[15] But it was above all in Bologna, the second most important city of the Papal State, with its celebrated Studio and its ancient and prestigious comforting school, that the institutional connection between criminal justice and the religious ritual of comforting found its most spectacular form in the organization of public anatomy: a triumph of university knowledge, a theater where morbid curiosity about the secrets concealed inside bodies—especially female ones—found what it was looking for.[16] The great spectacle of public anatomy attracted people to the city square during Carnival. Here, finally, the ritual of justice became that great cruel feast that had been curbed and repressed by religious rituals on execution day. People partied, ate, and drank in the theatrical setting of public anatomy, enjoying a freedom from rules that offered plenty of work for thieves and prostitutes. And so it could come about that unbridled instincts led to new crimes, and that nine months later a young woman might find herself giving birth to, and suffocating, an infant conceived behind a building in an act of casual intercourse—the result being that she might be transformed, in the space of a year, from spectator to protagonist of the anatomical demonstration held during Carnival.[17]

23

Art and Spectacle at the Service of Justice

JUSTICE THRIVES ON symbols, myths, and images, and it thrived on them in particular in ancient societies. In mass societies, and especially in the democratic systems of the contemporary age, one can count on what H. L. A. Hart called "the *internal aspect* of rules," that which ensures the existence of commonly accepted rules of play.[1] But this automatic efficacy of rules is the result of a social discipline and a habit of obedience that required lengthy processes and great investment in persuasion and violence by power. The arc of time considered in this study lies in a preliminary phase of the process, and was characterized by the need to translate forms of social control, especially those culminating in the execution of offenders and enemies, into myths and rituals. It will be clear from this premise why the full gamut of the arts was drawn on in the scaffold ritual to express emotions and communicate values. A key work by Gherardo Ortalli demonstrates just how widespread was the medieval custom of painting images of wrongdoers on the walls of public buildings for purposes of defamation.[2] The repertoire of practices employed to express abhorrence of crimes and their perpetrators was not limited to images. The sentences that were handed down envisaged other harsher and more radical forms of social condemnation: the exiling of offenders' children, the pulling down of their houses, the erection of columns bearing written memory of the reasons for the sentences (the *colonna infame*). The violent face of the sentence as vendetta found expression in painting: here too a survey of the most significant outputs of figurative art has highlighted the extraordinary wealth of images of legalized violence pertaining to the highest European tradition.[3]

This vast field also encompasses the creativity of the companies of justice, produced both for internal use—to animate the religious spirit and the sense of their own work—and to communicate to the condemned and the society in which they were operating the meanings and values of what was practiced on the scaffold. This dual requirement gave rise, from the very start of their activities, to a series of original inventions that addressed three different audiences at the same time: the *confratelli,* the condemned, and the general public.

The women and men who, in compliance with the Gospel teachings and the preaching of the clergy, devoted themselves to the merciful office of assisting those about to die, in hospitals or on the scaffold, made their presence felt amid the crowd of onlookers by singing *laude* and psalms, and chanting prayers. Besides the liturgical tradition of psalms and litanies, *laude* were also produced by authors from the Franciscan tradition and by improvised poets as well, such as the condemned prisoner Andrea Viarani, who while in prison composed texts that then found their way into the shared heritage of the confraternities. As we have seen, it was in the Bologna comforting school that the first structured collection of *laude* was compiled, attached in a separate section to the instructions given to members.

The justice ritual required an intense stimulation of the senses and of feelings in order to produce a mental conversion from immediate reality to that of the afterlife, on which the condemned person's thoughts and the collective feelings of the spectators had to focus. Consequently, besides singing *laude* and psalms, special resort was made to images. The first and most fundamental of all these was naturally that of the crucified Christ, often flanked by the two thieves. The crucifixion of Christ and the Passion scenes were the subjects of a supranational culture of the penal ritual that found expression in painting and sculpture. Mention was made earlier of the stone cross that Pierre de Craon had erected before the scaffold in Paris: it was the first of the monuments of what has been described as the microarchitecture of capital punishment, a genre that also features constructions of a certain size, such as the Spinnerin am Kreuz (Spinner at the Cross) erected in Vienna in the mid-fifteenth century, together with the Zderad Column in Brno and other similar structures that sprang up from then on in various European cities. The cross and the symbols of the Passion were for both the condemned and for spectators to see. It was in these years that crucifixion images with contorted, lacerated, blood-drenched bodies became commonplace in the German-speaking world, where the pain- and torture-deformed bodies of the two thieves also made an appearance in the works of artists like Lucas Cranach the Elder. In depictions of the robbers, more than in that of Christ, artists could give free rein to representing the execution torture practices of their own age.[4] The climate of the incipient Protestant Reformation is discernible in these works: suffering humanity, a prisoner of sin and death, would find expression in Luther's "theology of the Cross."

The images spoke to very different gazes—those of the public and those of the condemned. Between the two extremes were the mediators, who used the images to give religious sense to legal killing. As for the condemned, the effect that those images exercised on them by prompting an identification with the suffering of Christ has been described as a kind of "visual anesthetic."[5]

If it was anesthetic, it must be said that very high doses were administered in Italian rituals. The corpus of images produced as a result of commissions from the confraternities was particularly rich. Here too the image of Christ on the Cross or the Lamentation over the Dead Christ were central. In the place of the judging Christ of the Romanesque cathedrals before whom justice was administered, the new religious culture of the fourteenth-century cities found expression in the devotion of the suffering and wounded Christ, the man of pain evoked and propounded by Franciscan preaching. Then there was a symbolic image that occupied a crucial place in the world of the *misericordie*—that of the Virgin. The masterpiece painted by Piero della Francesca for the Misericordia di Sansepolcro was the finest version of an iconography that was widespread in painting and low reliefs in the churches and chapels of the confraternities (Plate 8). In prisons and on scaffold platforms comforters presented themselves by speaking in the name of a maternal figure represented in images with a broad open cloak that embraced their group, dressed in a black or white habit and in an entreating attitude of prayer. It was on the basis of a special relationship with her that the members of the *conforterie* addressed their "patients" as mediators. The stories of saints and miracles narrated in *The Golden Legend* of Jacobus de Voragine offered material for a pedagogy transmitted by way of paintings in churches and on the streets. In the specific case of the confraternities of justice, account must be taken of the way in which the suggestions offered to the *confratelli* by the paintings in their own premises and those presented to the condemned during the "service" were combined. The iconography of the interiors followed the evolution of pictorial culture dealing with religious themes. If the fourteenth-century frescos in the small church of the Tuscan confraternity of Cascina, near Pisa, present the theme of divine judgment as a subject for meditation, the sixteenth-century paintings in the Oratorio dell'Annunziata in Ferrara are about the story of the "Invention of the Cross," while the ones in the Roman confraternity of San Giovanni Decollato (painted by Giorgio Vasari) feature the eponymous saint as the protagonist of a large-scale apparatus of images.

These works would also have been seen by condemned prisoners, during the hours of comforting in the chapel. But as has already been said, there was a kind of artistic production especially for them—the *tavolette.* The execution ritual required the devising of a special form of itinerant painting offering models of faith and martyrdom to the condemned (and to spectators too), and which stimulated repentance and forgiveness in everyone. Once again the crucifix occupied a fundamental place. Normally it was held by the prior at the head of the public procession to the scaffold, and the comforter following him would show it to and make the condemned person kiss it. The identification between Christ and the condemned was taken so far that Mantegna's *Ecce Homo* was actually depicted with a hangman's rope around his neck. But the devout image had to engage the prisoner's gaze all the way to the scaffold, which is why the *tavoletta* was invented (known as *tavoluccia* in Florence and *tolella* in Venice): a small board painting equipped with a handle, which could be held before the eyes of the condemned, who would then be urged to kiss it devoutly and continually, especially in the moments before the execution. Manuals of instruction and statutes set out how they were to be employed, and they formed part of a tradition dating back to the years when the companies of justice were founded. They must have been commonly used and present as a matter of course in all confraternities. The loss of their original function over time meant that, when the handles were removed, they became mixed up with the whole mass of paintings on board that has come down to us from those centuries. It took a scholar's acute intuition to discover the connections between pictorial *maniera* and *mannaia* (the guillotine-like device used for beheadings), and to enable these singular icons of justice to emerge from the indistinct background of museum collections.[6]

Florentine Quattrocento painting was the first area to be explored, but the horizons of subsequent research broadened and the contribution of the Po Valley region became apparent—the first known *tavolette* from there date to the years around 1360 (Plate 3). They were images of pain and hope: the pain of Christ's Passion or of tortured martyrs, hope in the embracing gesture of the Virgin in glory between two condemned prisoners. The works were two-sided, sometimes showing the Crucifixion on one side, and the Virgin and tormented souls on the other; in other cases they depicted scenes of martyred saints.[7] In one case, that of the company of justice of Ascoli Piceno, the *tavoletta* had the form of a miniature, three-panel altarpiece (Figures 23.1 and 23.2): the central image was for the condemned's devotion and kisses, which in one case almost entirely wore it away; the two side panels were hinged, making it possible to completely block the prisoner's lateral vision. As Massimo Ferretti has observed, "just one gaze was to rest on them, thereby separating it from all the others."[8] The one painted by Titian for the Venetian company of San Fantin depicted "Saint Jerome in penitence, which was highly praised by other artisans."[9] From then on the use of the *tavoletta* became generalized and habitual, receiving mention in execution reports and in statutes. It featured images that clearly illustrated the comforter's persuasive aims: to remind condemned prisoners of divine mercy, to present the sufferings of the martyrs as models with which to identify, to silence any protests about an unjust sentence by showing them, in the Crucifix, the supreme injustice. At the same time, the painting offered the crowd an image of martyrdom and devotion that substituted and hid the real face of the condemned. Words found in the image the persuasive and emotive force to convince.

The pictures of tortured and executed saints found in confraternity buildings and literature were primarily for the common devotion of the *confratelli* but also helped to support the meditations suggested to the condemned by the comforters. One fine example is the "martyrology of the Battuti Neri of Ferrara," a parchment manuscript comprising 32 illuminations realized in the course of the fifteenth century, in a context where painters were very much at home.[10] It is an extraordinarily revealing document of how images were used in the comforting phase proper. This is shown first of all by the juxtaposition of the illuminations with commentary texts: the comforter would read the text and point out the image to the patient. The sequence of images has a precise thematic organization: it begins with the Passion scenes, from the Last Supper to the Crucifixion, the Resurrection and the Descent into Limbo (where Christ is shown taking Adam and Eve by the hand, and is followed by the good thief with the cross on his shoulder). Then come various martyrs designed to offer models of meritorious suffering to those steeling themselves for torture and death on the scaffold: here there are a number of cases ordered according to a roughly historical and ideal criterion, beginning with Saint Stephen and ending with Saint James the Mutilated, and also includes several martyred female saints to show to condemned women. The images illustrate various types of torture and execution, from stoning to beheading and flaying. It is an important document of the devout meditation of the Battuti Neri, but also a source which, by itself, gives an idea of the cultural sophistication and social prestige that the Ferrara company enjoyed in the fifteenth century.

Later developments in the pictorial tradition attested by the patronage of the confraternities were linked to the evolution of religious sensibility and to that of the juridical and social forms of criminal justice. The Byzantine modules of the early images were soon dropped, and the figure of Christ as seen in Quattrocento painting was that of a young man with a harmonious, perfect body, even when depicted in death. Contemplation of the body of the dead Christ was a very widespread form of devotion: his day was Good Friday. At the time, visiting the Holy Sepulcher engaged all Christians in rituals of contemplation and lamentation before images and groups of statues displayed in the churches. The intention was to prompt Christians to meditate upon their sins, which had been the cause of the Son of God's incarnation and death. Mourning Jesus was a very deep-rooted form of devotion, also because, much more than the subsequent feast of Corpus Domini, it permitted a ritualization of the reflection on death, sin, and forgiveness before the image of the dead Christ. If the feast of Christmas celebrated the revival of nature in the depths of winter, represented in Nativity scenes with scenarios of everyday life, that of the visit to the Holy Sepulcher was linked to the season of flowers and fertility, with the guarantee of making peace with God. It was also the day in which the annual confession was to take place, with the forgiveness of sins by divine justice. All this was translated into words and images: it was necessary to recount Christ's death reflected in the pain of the apostles and of the devout women, re-creating the scene of

FIGURES 23.1 AND 23.2. Anonymous, Two *tavolette* with three moments from the Passion, ca. 1590–1610. ASCOLI PICENO: PINACOTECA CIVICA.

funerary mourning as an everyday reality with which everyone could iden-tify and thus move emotionally closer to the Christian mystery of faith. The devotional contribution of the Franciscan tradition was not limited to sermons, but also took the form of *laude* and of the theater of sacred repre-sentation *(sacra rappresentazione),* reaching extraordinary heights of expres-

siveness with Jacopone da Todi. But the scene needed to be visualized, offering the support of figures to the rite commemorating Christ's death. This is what was undertaken through the artisanal production of terracotta images, the medium best suited to telling stories by way of figures, as the success of Christmas Nativity scenes had already demonstrated. The figures populating the churches of northern and central Italy were the product of artisan workshops that specialized in representations of the Lamentation over the Dead Christ in response to commissions from devout confraternities and wealthy private citizens. At least two examples are worth mentioning here, both of which are interwoven with the historic experience of the companies of justice. One is the diligent activity and high-quality work of Guido Mazzoni and his workshop, whose output and reputation spread far and wide, reaching beyond the borders of Lombardy and Italy, into France and south to Naples. His natural sphere of activity was between Modena, Ferrara, and Reggio. He produced a beautiful *Lamentation over the Dead Christ* in Modena to a commission from the Confraternita di San Giovanni (known as the Buona Morte), set up in the company's church between 1477 and 1479.[11] Of extremely fine workmanship, and infused with pathos and feeling, it tapped into the devotion and self-identity of the *confratelli* engaged in assisting the condemned, transforming the chapel where they met into a special oratory. The diffusion of statuary groups like this, a sacred theater of feelings captured and frozen in terracotta, delineates the map of an area, that of Emilia Romagna, which stands out with its own characteristics amid the general tendency to create theatrical representations of the Passion scenes. An instance of this can be found in Brisighella, a small town on the slopes of the Tuscan-Emilian Apennines: here, around the middle of the fifteenth century, a group of eight polychrome terracotta statues produced by an anonymous artist were placed in the oratory of the Confraternita di Santa Croce, devoted to assisting the dying and the condemned.

But the absolute highlight of this new art of Lamentation was the masterpiece created by Niccolò dell'Arca for the church of Santa Maria della Vita in Bologna, where it is still housed today (Plate 6). As an indulgence granted to the confraternity's hospital in 1464 states, it is a "commemoratio Sepulchri Dominici cum figuris et imaginibus pulcherrimis."[12] These were the years when the comforter's school was just getting established, focusing on the connection between sin, condemnation, and salvation. A stone's throw from the company's church was the Palazzo del Podestà, from the loggia *(ringhiera)* of which sentences were announced and executions orchestrated: statues of Fortitude and Justice had been placed on the two sides of the *ringhiera* in 1464.[13] The stage set of the urban spectacle of capital punishment thus had a compact design: the comforters went from the church to assist the condemned in the prison of the nearby Palazzo; the procession of justice then moved out from here in the morning for a representation of contrition and forgiveness that served as a lesson for the onlookers. The Lamentation over the Dead Christ was the scene to contemplate for those preparing to die or to see a death: it was a reminder of what underpinned the hope in eternal life. For this reason the statuary group created by Niccolò dell'Arca was set up in the oratory where the members of the Bolognese *conforteria* met, and where the condemned spent the night before execution. In places like this the ritual Good Friday visit to the Holy Sepulcher attained the peak of religious emotion: people who were really about to die mirrored themselves in the image of the dead Christ, while their comforters drew on it for their arguments.

In the beauty of a sleeping body shaped into forms of classical composure viewers contemplated a death reconciled by sacrifice and forgiveness, the premise for the reawakening of the resurrection. We will look in vain for the spasm of death that deformed the figures of the suffering Christ and of the two thieves in the Franciscan-inspired iconography circulating at the time in the German-speaking world. In the rooms where the comforting school's periodic meetings were held (currently well preserved and restored), there is another imposing sculptural group that shares with Niccolò dell'Arca's work the same aura of classicizing composure, but also contains a specific Christian anti-Judaic message. Commissioned by the School, the sculptor depicted a dramatic moment of religious conversion, that of the Jew who is miraculously stopped while trying to turn over the dead Virgin's body and throw it to the ground. It shows the sorrow of the angels and of the group of apostles around the Virgin's lifeless body, dominated in the foreground by the desecrating gesture of the Jew, miraculously halted by a divine intervention that prompts him to convert.[14] The work was executed by the Ferrarese sculptor Alfonso Lombardi between 1519 and 1522, and earned him "fame and a glorious name," according to Giorgio Vasari.[15] The violent campaign of anti-Jewish writing and preaching conducted by Franciscan and Augustinian friars had left indelible marks in the pictorial furnishings of the confraternities, as we noted with regard to Paolo Uccello's predella about the miracle of the Host—and now the mood and the echoes of the expulsion of the "Jews" from the Iberian Peninsula reached Italy as well.

Sometimes the ancient inventories of the artworks contained in churches and oratories enable a reconstruction of the figurative apparatus of confraternity buildings. One of these has revealed how many and which paintings were housed in the headquarters of the "most ancient and most noble Archconfraternity, hospital, and church of Death" in Bologna.[16] But it is difficult to piece together, even partially, the jungle of devout images that thronged the symbolic universe of scaffold piety: here, even more than the crucifix, what conjured up the merciful intercession to which the fate of the soul in the life to come was to be entrusted were the name and images of the Virgin Mary. Anonymous groups of confraternity members took their place beneath her cloak in the gonfalons and in the carved or painted images of the group. As for the host of saints and martyrs depicted in images or remembered in comforting documents, their arrangement was governed by the miracles ascribed to them in the tradition consecrated by Jacobus de Voragine in *The Golden Legend*. But standing above all the others was the eponymous saint of the companies of justice, Saint John the Baptist, the nature of whose death was recalled by the addition of the title "Decollato" (beheaded). The bearded head sitting on the platter or handed over by the executioner to female hands was the eloquent symbol of the special work of mercy carried out by the devout association: in the form of sculpture, engraving, or painting, it spread in a capillary fashion both within and outside the confraternity. This population of celestial patrons remained the habitual population of the Italian urban world, present in churches, oratories, and tabernacles, and circulating through prints and other channels of devotion. The divergence from the religious imagination of the other European countries became profound when the iconoclastic wave of the Reformation swept away this type of representation from their churches—one in which the condemned figured in some way, collectively represented among the souls engulfed in the flames of purgatory or depicted as grateful protectors of those who had arranged masses in suffrage for them.

But the key, regularly employed image was that of Christ on the Cross, or in the throes of the Passion. During the comforting phase, when seeking to overcome the resistance of the condemned and direct their thoughts toward repentance and the confession of sins, exhibiting the image of the tormented Christ was regarded as a strategic gambit: the instructions of the Florentine company of the Blacks recommended, when the "afflicted" were particularly stubborn, that they should be reminded that the alternative was to repent or be damned:

> And after some time, some holy image of Jesus's Passion will be suddenly placed before his eyes, and with great devotion they will persuade him to respond to the call of God, by threatening him that the blood flowing from those wounds for his health will soon serve to light the fire of his damnation even more. They will also let him suddenly see some skulls, to suggest how he would be in a few hours' time.[17]

When the public execution procession began, the condemned was given a crucifix to hold in their hand or to kiss. And their eyes and thoughts had to be occupied by the *tavoletta,* a functional, indispensable item to be used with great care so that the condemned person's eyes never strayed from it, not even at the very end. In the event of decapitation, the instructions of the Company of Blacks warned:

> When the executioner has blindfolded the afflicted, the brothers who will have been around the scaffold will go to their places, and the comforters, having put the afflicted in their midst, will follow him to the scaffold, holding the *tavoletta* in front of his face. After arriving there, they will kneel down with him and, pulling the said *tavoletta* back from his face, will carry on comforting him, and then the executioner will get the afflicted to place his head beneath the *mannaia.*[18]

Quite different from these working instruments were the forms of artistic expression elaborated for the internal use of the confraternities as their social and political importance grew in the cities. While the sixteenth- and seventeenth-century patrimony of images housed in the premises of the Roman archconfraternity is perfectly conserved, and offers an idea of the rapid ascent of the institution, in other cases it would be necessary to reconstruct at least in approximate terms the history of commissioned art works from what remains of the administrative papers. The assiduous care devoted to conserving, restoring, and updating the collection of images in their meeting rooms emerges from the administrative records of the confraternities, even when time or the ravages of war have destroyed the works that had gradually been accumulated in their premises. In some fortunate cases, restoration and historic study have proceeded hand in hand. This is what happened with regard to the oratory of the company of the Annunziata in Ferrara, which has been carefully restored after suffering heavy bomb damage during the Second World War. On the large wall of the oratory is a fifteenth-century fresco of the Resurrection of Christ, a theme we also find in one of the illuminations of the martyrology of the Battuti Neri; and the realization of the sixteenth-century story in images devoted to the legend of the True Cross (from the Garden of Eden to Constantine), which involved, among others the Ferrara-born artist Sebastiano Filippi known as Bastianino.[19]

Besides painting there was music. The musical culture cultivated at the court of Este in Ferrara had an outcome in the activities of the confraternity of justice as well: the recourse to singers and to the accompaniment of the organ of the duke's chapel for the liturgies of the Compagnia della Morte during the feast of the Holy Cross gradually became more and more important. In a pilgrimage of the *confratelli* to Reggio Emilia in 1596 we find a twenty-one-strong "musical body" that included a very young Girolamo Frescobaldi. The seventeenth century saw the emergence of an independent association of musicians known as the "Accademia della Morte."[20]

The music and singing of sacred oratorios brings us to theater and melodrama. The center of the triumph of melodrama was in the city of Bologna, thanks to the compositions produced by the *conforteria* to celebrate Good Friday in a fitting manner. The day commemorating the death of Jesus Christ had for centuries been the focus of the holy events and liturgies of the Christian world. It was, as we have seen, the day favored for the various forms taken by the precept of forgiveness: from the confession of sins to the pardons and amnesties of sovereign powers. Divine justice and human justice went hand in hand on that day, presenting a united front to the crowd of subjects-worshippers. No means coincidentally, papal justice under Boniface VIII had chosen that day to solemnly promulgate from the Loggia delle Benedizioni the bull entitled *In coena Domini*. Naturally, the date was also important in the liturgies of the confraternities of justice. Their confraternity feast was the one dedicated to their patron saint, Saint John the Baptist, on his feast day of August 29. This was often chosen as the date for the most significant and poignant ritual: the freeing of a condemned prisoner. But it was on Good Friday that the sacred representations of oratorios were performed in Bologna between the seventeenth and eighteenth centuries.[21]

The history of the "special functions" within the Bologna confraternity began in 1533, when, as the eighteenth-century archivist noted, the "miraculous image of the Madonna of Saint Luke" was carried into the oratory.[22] Among the special events that began to grow in number from that date on we find the funeral rites of illustrious civic figures to which the company was invited, solemn meetings with members of other confraternities, pilgrimages to Loreto and Rome, and special sung masses with leading musicians. But it was in the eighteenth century that musical oratorios became regular annual events. Their almost exclusive focus was the Crucifixion, as a list of titles indicates: *Gesù al sepolcro,* a poetic text by Giacomo Antonio Bergamori, with music by Giacomo Antonio Perti, performed on the Good Friday of 1718; *Morte di Cristo,* poetry by Giovanni Battista Taroni, set to the music of Count Pirro Capacelli Albergati. From then on there was a constant flow of oratorios, the librettos of which, carefully ordered and jealously preserved, plunge the reader into a parallel universe with respect to the drama played out on the scaffold of criminal justice.[23] A few citations will help to give an idea of the musical messages offered to audiences.

L'angelica costanza dell'umanità ne' suoi dolori, an oratorio for four voices, consists of a dialogue between Divinity, Divine Love, Sorrow, and Humanity. The following is a duet between Humanity and Divine Love:

> *Umanità:*
> Dopo lungo penar s'accosta infine
> Quella, che tanto bramo, amata morte
> . . . .
> Morir mi sento,
> Non ho più vita,
> Già vengo meno:
> Cieli pietà.
> Lo spirto lento,
> Per qual ferita
> Parta dal seno
> Trovar non sa.
>
> *Amor divino:*
> Degli eterni voleri
> Essecutor fedele ecco il Dolore.

Tutti I tormenti tuoi cangia in piaceri.
Così penare,
Che soave, che dolce piacer!
Son troppo care
Tutte le pene,
Se promettono eterno goder.

(*Humanity:* After long suffering the cherished death which I yearn for so greatly finally draws close . . . I feel myself dying, I have no more life. Already I am slipping away: heaven have mercy. The spirit, faint from the wound which starts from the breast, is lost. *Divine Love:* The faithful executor of God's will is Sorrow. All your torments are transformed into pleasures, and thus suffering—what gentle, sweet pleasure! All punishments are so dear if they promise eternal joy.)

Good Friday of 1725 saw the performance of the oratorio *I conforti di Maria Vergine addolorata per la morte del suo divin figliuolo,* a poetic text by Carlo Innocenzo Frugoni with the music of Giacomo Antonio Perti. The voices of four protagonists are interwoven here: Divine Love, Divine Justice, Divine Wisdom, and the Virgin Mary. This is Divine Justice comforting the Virgin:

Maria, pensa qual fui
Quando, immutabil, sorda
Ai prieghi, ed ai sospir tendea dal cielo
L'inevitabil arco, e a' cenni miei
L'Abisso apria l'ampia vorage ingorda;
e pensa or qual mi sono
doppo che la grand'ostia
Fu prezzo di salute e di perdono.

(Mary, think how I was when, unswerving and deaf to prayers and sighs, from the sky I drew taut the inevitable bow, and at my sign the abyss opened its wide, voracious chasm; and think of how I am now, after the great Host was the price of health and forgiveness.)

This was a youthful effort by Frugoni, a poet who had found success in Bologna and employed his talents to satisfy the tastes of the polite society that packed "the theaters, the academies, the salons, and public conversation," combining "luxury, ease, amusements, banquets and beautiful ladies."[24]

In the background of these dramas one can constantly perceive the presence of the Jews, "the wicked Judea" that wanted the death of Christ. And there was also the occasion to oppose the blood sacrifices of the Jewish religion with the divine victim immolated on the altar of the Mass:

> Non più (lassa!) vedrai le tue tiare
> del sangue tinte d'olocausto e intorno
> del tabernacol tuo stendersi il manto.
> Nuova vittima or chiede, e nuovo altare
> Quel Dio, ch'or fa tra noi lieto soggiorno
> Tra noi popolo suo felice e santo.[25]

(No longer shall you sorrowfully see your tiaras stained with the blood of burned offerings, and the cloak spread around your tabernacle. That God which now dwells joyously among us, his happy and holy people, now asks for a new victim, and a new altar.)

The image of blood bathing the altar perhaps emerged from the repressed background of the sacrifice legitimated by religion that was habitually celebrated on the scaffold. But it was with the delicacy of melodrama that its presence was perceived among the upper classes in the city, while the lower orders gathered into crowds for the public anatomy sessions of Carnival.

24

Capital Punishment as a Rite of Passage

THE SPECTACLE WITNESSED by Montaigne in Rome in 1581 represented the loftiest model, the one that inspired organized scaffold rituals at a local level throughout the Italian peninsula. It can be viewed as an embryonic form of national unity that encompassed all Italians, because the most powerfully symbolic moment of justice—the administration of the death sentence—appeared to all Italians in similar forms, adapted as required to suit the characteristics and traditions of different places.

Common to the various local realities was the mechanism whereby, in the short period of time between the sentence and the execution, murderers, thieves, and heretics were transformed into penitent, devout individuals, obedient to the Church and ready to declare that their punishment was just. This path of conversion matured rapidly and concluded with a death on the scaffold, which the preachers who witnessed it greeted as the salvation of a soul. Rituals of this kind took place regularly in Italian cities over the course of the centuries. The ones held in Rome were the most solemn and long-lived. The Roman company of San Giovanni Decollato was active from the year of its foundation until 1870, when the troops of the Kingdom of Italy breached the city walls near Porta Pia and put an end to the temporal power of the popes. For hundreds of years an extraordinarily efficient structure provided religious comfort to the condemned, recorded their behavior, and executed their wills. Unfortunately, the mass of documentation gathered together in the company's archive over time has reached us in a partially impoverished state. Nonetheless, we can draw on numerous collateral sources, such as a partial list of executed prisoners drawn up by Abbot Placido Eustachio Ghezzi, a member of the Confraternita degli Agonizzanti (one of the many devout associations that collaborated with the Arciconfraternita di San Giovanni), in which considerable attention is given to the behavior of the crowd and the individual profiles of the condemned.[1] Moreover, the organization of the comforting procedures and the advice for the *con-fratelli* fill pages and pages of Pompeo Serni's manual of instruction, which was circulated systematically among the most important companies of justice operating in Italy. Lists of the condemned, manuals of instruction, detailed reports, and discussions of events occurring elsewhere at a local level emerge from various archives and libraries. We have seen, for instance, how a wealth of sources sheds light on the history and culture of the *conforteria* in Bologna. From sources like these it is possible to gain an idea not only of what the "ritual city" was in this age,[2] but also a great deal of knowledge about the methods, powers, and successes of the work of providing religious comfort to the condemned. Even though the Roman model generally served as inspiration for confraternities of the same type, conferring a unitary stamp on the bloody ritual of justice, there was no lack of local variants determined by specific features of political power and different types of social relations. But there can be no doubt at all that capital punishment was experienced as an act of supreme mercy and Christian fraternity: the theme that dominated it was expressed in a single word—forgiveness. The condemned forgave his executioner and asked for forgiveness for his wrong-doings; the executioner also forgave and asked for forgiveness. This formula, taken from the Lord's Prayer, offered assurance to the person who was to die that God would forgive and receive them into heaven. But it was also the key word enabling the curious crowd to transform a bandit, murderer, or thief from a vilified, cursed being into a protecting and benevolent soul. If in medieval folklore the shadow of the hanged person was a member of the Furious Host, an evil, vindictive spirit, those conversions and those public rituals elevated him to be a candidate for heaven: from the bloody brigand, killer, or heretic he had once been, he became a devout and simplified stereotype of a saintly soul.

A great deal has already emerged about these fundamental characteristics of capital punishment in Italy in various studies of the history of the administration of justice in the Italian states of the ancien régime. But representations and interpretations have continued to be strongly influenced by the paradigm proposed by Michel Foucault:[3] an execution scene consisting of bodies tortured with extreme, refined cruelty, a death sentence as the outcome of the war between power and subjects, the key moment of a deaf conflict always liable to explode. Encapsulated in those bodies, in the "spectacle of the scaffold"—to use Foucault's celebrated phrase, which crops up repeatedly in historiographic literature—was the sovereign power's message to the people, that they might see his vengeance at work and, trembling, bow in obedience. If in the eyes of power any infraction of the law contained an implicit wish to rebel and therefore a crime of lèse-majesté, for the people who crowded around the scaffold the condemned person embodied rebellion. "Public execution," writes Foucault, "allowed the luxury of these momentary saturnalia, when nothing remained to prohibit or to punish. Under the protection of imminent death, the criminal could say everything and the crowd cheered." Here Foucault refers to the view expressed by Antoine-Gaspard Boucher d'Argis, a collaborator on Diderot and d'Alembert's *Encyclopédie,* according to whom if the final words of the condemned were reported correctly, one would discover "that no one who had died on the wheel did not accuse heaven for the misery that brought him to the crime, reproach his judges for their barbarity, curse the minister of the altars who accompanies them and blaspheme against the God whose organ he is."[4] But very few features of this representation can be found in the execution rites performed for centuries in Italian city squares. Admittedly, here too the bodies of the condemned were subjected to violence and torture: in Montaigne's diary his secretary noted that he had seen what was meted out on January 14 to the bodies of two brothers condemned for having murdered the secretary of the pope's son, Jacopo Boncompagni. But even at that time everything followed the same pattern dominated by devout, reverent ritual. In the Roman tradition, and in the Italian one in general, the key feature of capital punishment stably remained that of proposing models of religious conversion. For the most part there were none of the signs of the carnivalesque subversion of a popular culture in which, following the suggestion of Mikhail Bakhtin, Foucault wrote that "rules were inverted, authority mocked and criminals transformed into heroes"; nor was there that exaltation of the courage of the person about to die which Foucault found in English historical sources.[5] The crowd watched the scene of a devout death in silence, and only became excited if a rope broke or a delay to the procession raised hopes of a pardon. "Pardon! Pardon!" was the cry that went up in Piazza Grande in Modena on November 12, 1598, where the expectancy surrounding the execution of "four sorry wretches" attracted so many people "that one could stay there only with difficulty," according to the chronicler.[6]

But the judge was simply late, while the company of death had set off early, and the four prisoners, who had begun to harbor hopes that they might be freed, ended up on the gallows as planned. In Italian cities the crowd watched the drama of a soul that needed to be saved, was moved by the plea for forgiveness, prayed for the condemned person's soul, and urged him to repent: "Convert, convert!" shouted the crowd, where there was always someone performing "the office of the comforter."[7] What was of concern was the fate of the soul, and in fact only very rarely was the expectation of repentance disappointed. The comforters were the first to acknowledge the singularity of their almost invariable success, and their proceedings contain many traces of a need to be believed: it was necessary to have "complete and unquestioned faith" in what was stated in their records, as we read in a register of the wills of the condemned. There were two reasons to justify this: on the one hand because they were appointed to that office only "for the well-being of the souls of those poor patients," and so their hearts contained nothing but "truth and candidness"; on the other, because "it is likely that . . . the patients, who are about to be put to death and know that they will die, will not want to damn their soul to humor the world, unless, that is, they are animals."[8] These, then, were the intentions and the conditions of both the "patients" and the comforters. Indeed, even if we were to hypothesize for a moment that the compilers of the confraternity books set out to systematically falsify the true state of affairs, there still remains the reliable testimony of Michel de Montaigne. It is no coincidence that he stressed that there was something "outre la forme de France" in the devout compunction of behavior demonstrated by Catena, who had a "mort commune, sans mouvemant et sans parole," and by the crowd, which was filled with compassion at the sight of the man's limbs being severed. The episode forms part of a more general Italian history, where the differences between it and the French and English models were profound and persistent, to the point of suggesting the need to revise the paradigm of the "spectacle of the scaffold" and the "theatre of horror" proposed by Foucault.[9]

What struck Montaigne about the scene he witnessed in Rome was the religious discipline of the spectacle—an aspect which, in the centuries of the modern age, was not limited to Italy, as we shall see. Also in seventeenth- and eighteenth-century Germany, the administration of the death penalty was marked by a solemn religious rituality. What was organized with great care in the German cities were the rites of a retributive justice, where death was the end point of a journey charged with moral and religious meanings. Here, the condemned figured as a poor sinner ("arme Sünder"), assisted by a Catholic priest or a Lutheran pastor for the whole period between the communication of the sentence and the execution. It is no accident, in fact, that the chief work of reference on this aspect of German history stresses, right from the title, the term "rituals."[10]

The fundamental feature of the model of ritual which, for convenience, we shall call the Italian one was the attempt, generally successful, to take over the thoughts of the condemned person, isolating him from the surrounding context and presenting him to the attention of the public as a soul journeying toward another world. This is what crowds saw when they gathered around the *conforteria* on the eve of execution and then at the procession on the day itself. The hubbub of the onlookers who assembled outside the prison or chapel cropped up frequently in the complaints of the comforters. Their goal, both theoretically and practically, was always to categorically exclude any contact between the condemned and their relatives and friends. It was a singular ban: the cases of Niccolò di Toldo and Pietro Paolo Boscoli are just the visible tip of the deep and very human need for a final contact with one's loved ones, something of which the confraternity members were certainly fully aware. But it was precisely against the tug of earthly bonds that the whole strategy of the companies of justice was directed. In this way, the person who learned of their imminent execution and instinctively sought the comfort of a friendly face discovered that they would not have it. In vain would they ask to say a final goodbye to their wife, children, or family members. In their place arrived men dressed in habit and hood, messengers of impending death. With the exception of the executioners, they would be the sole intermediaries of the condemned person with outside reality right up to the end. The liminal condition of the prisoner was thus apparent to everyone: he was suspended from this moment on between earth and sky, attached for a little while longer to the earth but now irreversibly embarked on the journey to the other world. An uncertain journey, filled with risk. The fundamental phase took place during the night, the period of time normally granted to the condemned. Following this nocturnal isolation, the prisoner was brought out for execution, usually in the morning and in public, though sometimes—in Venice and Naples, for instance—in the afternoon.

Regimes that fear the reaction of the people execute their enemies by night, in the secrecy of their palaces, a practice that distinguished the oligarchic Republic of Venice in particular. The condemned were strangled in prison or drowned by night in the Orfano canal, especially when heretics were involved. During the tensions of the war waged by the League of Cambrai against Venice in 1509, the public execution of some Paduans guilty of having sided with Emperor Maximilian I prompted harsh criticism: many said, according to Marino Sanudo, that "they should have been put to death in 'secret,' and that it was not the moment for such commotion."[11] Even in the event of nighttime executions in prison, the body was sometimes put out on display the morning after, hung from the prison bars or in some other public place. This happened to Pietro Paolo Boscoli, who was beheaded in the courtyard of the Palazzo del Bargello in Florence. Secrecy was a sign of power and of a wish to avoid the judgment of the people. A sudden uproar among the populace could jeopardize the execution proceedings, snatch the condemned from the jaws of death, and degenerate into revolt. When the execution was public—that is, in the majority of cases—it was signaled by a tolling bell, whereupon the population gathered along the execution route and in the place where the scaffold had been erected. Here, as with many other details of the system of civic justice, the overall design was complicated by and adapted to local circumstances and traditions. The central square, the locus of the seats and symbols of power, was generally chosen in order to give greater public visibility to the act. In Venice it was reached by water, on a barge along the Grand Canal. In the cities of the Po Valley—Ferrara, Modena, Bologna—it involved a short route from the prison inside the *palazzo pubblico* to the main square. The journey might be longer when the scaffold was set up outside the city walls and it was necessary to go through the city, as happened in the early phase of this history and as continued to be the norm in Florence. The expulsion of evil from the sacred space within the city walls was one of the traits of the communal tradition, which was maintained even when the city became the capital of an important territorial state. There were due exceptions, however. Piazza della Signoria was chosen as the site for the execution of Fra Girolamo Savonarola and his three companions, as this was the outcome of a bitter political conflict and the authorities wished to emphasize it as much as possible. In general, efforts were made to avoid a lengthy route to the scaffold, as it was the final opportunity for the condemned to find some barely hoped-for salvation. The prisoner might make an improvised escape attempt, taking refuge in a providentially open church and daring the guards to violate ecclesiastical immunity. That same immunity was triggered by embracing a priest on his way back from administering Communion to a sick person; and if one happened to encounter a cardinal, a pardon was almost certain.[12] Then there was always the residual, inerasable hope placed in exchanges with and in the reaction of the crowd, who might put the result at risk by interrupting or altering the state of separateness between the person condemned to die and those who continued to belong to the living. But this was precisely the goal of the model pursued by the companies of justice: the lack of communication between one and the other.

Everything that the condemned saw, heard, and said referred to the reality of another world. Their face was covered by the *tavoletta,* an essential piece of equipment in the whole tradition of the *conforterie.* Their eyes could not be allowed to search among those present for the faces of children, wives, friends: they had to see only the devout images of saints, martyrs, and Virgin Marys. Their ears did not hear the voices of the crowd but only the exhortations and prayers murmured by the comforter and the litanies recited by the *confratelli.* No words of dialogue with others emerged from their mouths, just prayers, repetitive and ritualized formulas of a dialogue with God and with the saints in heaven. The instructions they received were very clear: no contact with those they were about to leave behind in this world, no public declaration about people or events. Anything they might want to say was considered dangerous because it brought them back to the present life, of which they should no longer feel a part. The sole thing they were to do was to pray, ask for forgiveness, and forgive. Projected toward the other world, they had to sever all contact with the one surrounding them. The definition coined for the short journey of the condemned prisoner along the corridor of death row in American prisons applied here: dead man walking. Of course, society in the ancien régime was not as impermeable to human contact as the high-security jails of a great world power of our times. In Venice, on the afternoon of September 22, 1513, five condemned prisoners were sent to their deaths, but as they crossed the square in the midst of the comforters they still found a way to embrace and kiss people they knew and to beg for their prayers.[13] Whereas in modern conceptions the passage from life to death lasts an instant, in the society of the ancien régime there persisted the notion of a longer period of time, part of a deep-rooted tradition of which ritual had to take account. The death of the condemned person was regulated by norms similar to those of other human beings. For him too, death was not a clear-cut and definitive change, but a transition from the world of the living to that of the dead—a passage, not a brusque change. Only that in his case the whole process was altered by virtue of the nature of the death, deliberated by other human beings and a result of his own wrongdoings. It began at the moment when the sentence determined his expulsion from the society of the living. From then on the Christian sensibility of the *confratelli* saw in him only a soul facing a transition from this to another world: a peculiar condition, similar to the one illustrated by a brilliant, young French scholar of primitive cultures in a ground-breaking study written at the beginning of the twentieth century. In that transition, Robert Hertz wrote, the soul "lives, as it were, marginally in the two worlds: if it ventures into the after-world, it is treated there like an intruder; here on earth it is an importunate guest whose proximity is dreaded."[14] Sacred symbols and the work of the comforters alongside the condemned protected the society of the living from contact with a threatening and tainting presence during the phase of transition into the world of the dead. Those condemned to die, situated as they were in a pitiful yet dangerous condition, stirred contradictory feelings of fear and compassion in the living. They were thought to harbor a spirit of vendetta, as the dead were, because it was already as if they were dead; what is more, compared to the ordinary dead, they had a special and very powerful reason to detest and hurt those who had taken away their lives ahead of time. Furthermore, if for others the duration lasted from the moment of natural death to that of final burial, for the condemned that time was concentrated by the judge's decision to between the moment of the sentence and the imminent elimination and transformation of their body, which replaced natural processes and accelerated the period of time. For now, the condition of the condemned was that of a dead person who still resided among the living, and who, among them, was the embodiment of evil. It was a combined evil of crime and sin: in the shared consciousness of the age and in the rules governing justice there was no clear-cut distinction between the two fields. People died on the scaffold for wrongdoings ranging without interruption from violence against other human beings and things to rebellion against the Church and the infringing of the laws of morality and religion: from theft and murder to sacrilege, blasphemy, and heresy. The Christian endeavors of the *confratelli* dealt with those wrongs from within the dimension of religious sin, and it was for this reason that repentance and expiation were demanded. And it was here that the mediation of the comforters intervened. Everything was concentrated in the insistence on confession and forgiveness: that between the condemned and society was linked to the other forgiveness, the one requested of God. The condemned was offered the possibility of confession and forgiveness. To deny them this possibility would have meant keeping their souls in the condition of accursed spirits, without a final, reconciled abode and driven by hatred and the desire for revenge on the living.

The person who was engaged and comforted thus found himself in a prematurely dead state: the death awaiting him was already reality. A relationship was formed with him during the long night. The voyage of the soul was also nocturnal, according to a widespread representation expressed in the literature of mystical and penitential meditation. Hence the particular features of that nighttime dialogue: the person with whom the comforters spoke was a soul setting out along a passage full of perils; someone who ran the risk of getting lost, who was torn between the bonds that kept him clinging to the body and to the earth, and the invitation to enter the world of reconciled and forgiven spirits. The relationship of the condemned person's soul with their body took to the extreme the danger posed by the link with the body, because before execution the living, vigorous body was still dominant. What unfolded in the dialogue between comforter and assisted was the drama of the attempt to dissolve that tie: all the comforters' arguments were directed to this purpose. But here the analogies between the representation of death in primitive cultures and what was at play in the ritual of comforting the condemned end, and the differences begin. The imagined tie between the soul of the dead person and his body led primitive cultures to develop the rite of double burial, with a period of mourning that began with the first, provisional interment and ended with the definitive giving up to the earth of the dead person's bones. In the rituals of the death penalty, the link was broken with violence. The body was tormented before and after execution: cut to pieces, quartered, displayed in public, used for shady forms of trade. The transition period was thus accelerated, demanding concentrated sacred interventions, with the multiplication of sacraments, blessings, and devout protections to see off the danger, which in the end was condensed in the quartered body and in the instruments used for the execution. Here too the confraternities, through the burning of the hanging ropes, anatomical dissection, and burial of the collected body parts in their cemeteries, sought to end the period of danger for the community as soon as possible. This evident symbology is borne out by the ritual of sparing the life of a condemned person. On such occasions the prisoner awaiting execution was taken in procession to church; then, freed from shackles and dressed in a white habit with a crown of laurel on his head, he was presented as a soul who had returned to earthly life, which he would be free to reenter at the end of the Mass and Communion—transparent repetitions of the sacrament of birth, baptism.

25

The Arrival of the Jesuits:
Confession and the Science of Cases

IN THE LARGE FRESCO *Preaching of Saint John the Baptist* that greets the eye when stepping into the entrance room of the oratory of the Roman archconfraternity (Plate 13), one male profile stands out amid the crowd of listeners—a young man with curly dark-brown hair and a short beard framing his lips and chin. It appears evident that the painter's intention was to represent a specific person known to him, something that Michelangelo Buonarroti, the unparalleled master who dominated his horizons and that of the age, did habitually. Given that Michelangelo was a member of the Roman company in whose oratory Jacopino was working, one might reasonably expect the figure to be a tribute to the great artist by someone who followed his "manner." This seems all the more likely as the fresco is entirely Michelangelesque in the anatomy and movements of the bodies of the men and women listening to Saint John the Baptist preaching. But actually the serious, attentive face of the soberly dressed young man, who, in his position to the right of John, seems to present himself as a follower and reviver of the saint's preaching of the Messiah, is not that of Michelangelo. Instead, it has been proposed that it is a portrait of Ignatius of Loyola.[1] The fresco dates to around 1538, in the period of the mid-1530s to the mid-1550s, when the oratory was being built and decorated at the initiative and expense of the wealthy Florentine bankers and merchants who were members. Ignatius had not been in Rome for long—he arrived in 1537—but had already begun preaching and was starting to attract curiosity but also accusations and suspicion. The work of the confraternity must have stirred his interest straightaway. While Michelangelo Buonarotti was quite a distracted and absent *confratello* (from 1514),[2] preferring the sermons of Bernardino Ochino and the conversation of the group of Cardinal Pole and the poetess Vittoria Colonna,

Ignatius was different. He was not drawn to the exclusive circles and initiatory settings where his fellow Spaniard and mystic rival Juan de Valdés was speaking about faith, but was much more interested in the idea of transforming the world through good works, the Christian's path to salvation.

The Italian model of the companies of justice would provide special impulse to the work of the Jesuits. Here, as we have seen, the simple popular piety of the early lay confraternities was followed, in the fifteenth and sixteenth centuries, by a second phase dominated by more selective groups comprising members of the upper orders of society. This is what was demanded by suspicious powers intent on employing the spectacle of capital punishment to educate the people to obedience. A typical feature of the Italian scaffold ritual at the time was the use of religious devotion to instill subjection to political power in the hearts and consciences of which the Church held the keys, as Giovanni Botero underlined. This explains why members of the regular clergy became an increasingly widespread presence alongside and sometimes in place of laypeople. In Naples a decree issued by Philip II led to the complete substitution of laypeople with members of the clergy, but elsewhere the presence of churchmen was increasingly requested by the confraternities. In Rome, Capuchins and Jesuits were called in as a matter of course to deal with heretics and particularly recalcitrant prisoners. And the Jesuit and Capuchin orders were again the ones from which the Compagnia di San Giovanni Battista in Modena prevalently chose "the subjects best qualified and best known and reputed to be best suited to the case," as Monsignor Sabbatini observed. As we have seen, comforting literature developed remarkably during the sixteenth century, coming to rival the two dominant literary genres appealing to the religious piety of laypeople: confession handbooks and *Ars moriendi*. But in dealing with matters of conscience this literature also inevitably moved toward casuistry—and it was here that the Company of Jesus made its entrance.[3]

The Jesuits' arrival on the execution scene came about through the firsthand practice of comforting, but also and above all through the elaboration of a science of cases that adapted the general precepts of Christian morality to the most disparate situations. Specialists in moral theology, they invested all their resources in the task of religious conquest. In the vocabulary of the founder of the order, as evinced from his letters and from sources relating to his rule, the word "help" occupies a special place. For him, helping was the duty of the Christian who believed in the positive value of good works and therefore rejected the Protestant Reformation's doctrine of predestination. This is one of the reasons why Ignatius exempted the scholastics of his company from the obligation to recite the Breviary. The Jesuits' time was to be occupied by works to the greater glory of God, and the society drew up many different human categories in need of help: young men to be steered clear of the perils of university life; girls in need of a husband; the sick and dying to be prepared for death; heretics, unbelievers, and pagans to be converted. Spiritual help was provided by way of material support and activities directed at resolving conflicts and removing factional enmity. In the age of the wars of religion, the problem of pacification—the central issue of the moral tradition of societies—put the resources of the European Christian Churches to the test, and led to the emergence of unexpected protagonists in the new and combative elites which had sprung up in the course of the century, from the Puritans to the Jesuits.[4] The contribution of the Jesuits was the idea of mission and the emphasis on confession as means of constructing a lasting relationship with the penitent. Instead of the fearsome God who made himself known in Luther's Augustinian theology through the abjection of the Cross—the opposite of glory—the God of the Jesuits reached out to sinners and saw his glory magnified with every soul saved and every triumph of the true faith.

Introducing themselves into the dense fabric of the confraternities and of charitable works, the Jesuits quickly carved out a prominent role for themselves. It is not clear when exactly they perceived the importance of comforting the condemned. Only the traditional works of mercy figured in the "Formula of the Institute" of 1540, including assistance for prisoners and the hospital sick, to be exercised "for the glory of God and for the universal good." In Rome, Ignatius, Diego Laínez, and Nicolás Bobadilla gained experience in the hospital of Santo Spirito in Sassia, and it was Ignatius himself who intervened to reestablish compliance with the disposition of the Fourth Lateran Council obliging patients to confess, with failure to do so resulting in the suspension of treatment. For the Jesuits, confession was the decisive step in obtaining the conversion of sinners, setting them on the path of religious improvement. Active between Rome and the Spanish world, the Jesuits could not ignore the importance of comforting the condemned, a particularly dramatic moment in which confession was the key to saving souls.

Their presence in the prisons and at the foot of the scaffold began to be felt very soon. In Rome the confraternity of San Giovanni Decollato often had to draw on their services to win over the most stubborn condemned prisoners. The same was true in Naples, with the company of the Bianchi della Giustizia. Jesuits dispatched to the city sent back reports to the General Curia in Rome in which they talked a great deal about their work with prisoners and galley slaves. Down by the docks they met long lines of men condemned to serve in galleys, in shackles and chained to each other. The Jesuits reported that they had given them essential aid: something to drink and eat, clothes, but also offers of legal representation for those who could not afford it.[5] The prisons were a world of indigence and shadows ("tenebras pauperum," wrote the Modenese prelate Gian Battista Scanaroli in his great work of instructions about the practice of prison visiting).[6] And incarceration was employed more and more indiscriminately as a means of seizing the poor and making them serve the various needs of the powerful. Jails were also the antechamber to the scaffold, and besides prisons the Jesuits began turning up at execution sites to offer the condemned their services as confessors. They very quickly became a presence in various parts of Italy and the Spanish Empire, engaged in works of mercy either alongside existing confraternities or independently. When they arrived in Palermo, they found the Compagnia del Santissimo Crocifisso, known as the Whites, which had been founded in 1541 at the initiative of the Franciscan preacher Pietro Paolo Caporella. The Jesuits talked about it in the first reports they dispatched from Sicily—as usual stressing the success of their work to overcome the resistance of the Sicilians and to make scaffold devotion more effective and widespread. The biggest obstacle was, in their view, the fear that the souls of the hanged would then harass those who had accompanied them to the scaffold.[7] In fact, from the middle of the sixteenth century the Jesuits showed that they had grasped the importance of this particular kind of merciful endeavor, and from then on would become the most convinced and active supporters of it. Once again, the key word was "help." If there was a human condition in which help was necessary and urgent it was that of those about to die. Preachers of penitence had traditionally been unsparing in their efforts to instill terror of the moment of death—fear of God's judgment and fear of human fragility in the final moment had encouraged the practice of drawing up wills while one was still in good health. The preambles to these documents chart the boundless diffusion of a need for protection which, in anticipation of that final moment and the risks it carried, was entrusted to the saints and the Virgin.[8] This was when it was necessary to persuade the person about to die to confess. And that last moment had been the focus of the tradition of the *Ars moriendi* (The Art of Dying)—a best seller, the success of which was eclipsed around the decade 1530–1540 by the new Erasmian morality.[9] But it was the Jesuits who left a decisive imprint on the new orientations assumed by the art of dying well in a Europe riven by the problem of the justification of the sinner before God. With the Catholic revival of the Tridentine age, a Jesuit literature became established, the archetype of which was Juan de Polanco's *Methodus ad eos adiuvandos qui moriuntur.* This text offers an example of how the Company of Jesus interpreted the function of help for the condemned and adapted the work of the confessor / comforter: a man invested with the decisive holy power of administering on earth the divine forgiveness of all sins and of suggesting the means of avoiding punishment in the life to come. The sacrament sufficed to dispense forgiveness. And the intention of the penitent was enough to transform the torments of the scaffold into the equivalent of the punishments to pay in the afterlife.

The current embodied by the Jesuits in the broader Catholic response to the Protestant Reformation led to a special way of understanding the meaning and potential of confession. Whereas the Counter-Reformation version of the confessor as a severe judge invested by God with the task of investigating and discovering the number, nature, and seriousness of sins gained more and more ground, the members of the Society trained themselves to exercise the skills of the physician in healing sores and assuaging suffering. The path described in the "Spiritual Exercises" elaborated by its founder was grounded in frequent confession together with Communion. This interpretation of the Catholic sacrament was the one best suited to making it the instrument for consoling the condemned, driving away memories of their crimes and misdeeds, and leaving in the shadows the question of how to do penance and make amends for their wrongdoings. Reappearing here was the mysticism of Redemption that we saw at work in the episode of Saint Catherine of Siena and Niccolò di Toldo. It was a sentiment that now tended to take the form of adherence to the doctrine of justification by faith, as seen in the case of Pietro Fatinelli in Lucca. So, even though the Jesuits were safe from such charges, confession was changing. The definition of the sacrament of penance approved by the Council of Trent imposed very specific rules, insisting above all on the judicial aspect of the sacrament—which did not prevent the Jesuits from making it the instrument for a non-terrifying relationship with penitents, set onto a path of conversion and regeneration through the general confession of a lifetime of sins. However, suspicions soon began to abound that what was confessed to their ears was then revealed to judges and authorities—a malevolent but not entirely unfounded accusation given that collaboration between confessors and judges was not unusual. The resulting controversy prompted a scholarly disquisition from the Jesuit Juan de Mariana.[10]

The consequences on the ground of the practice of comforting would be felt not so much in general principles but in a climate of caution and suspicion surrounding the presumed confessions beneath the scaffold. The essential features of this new atmosphere can be found in the interpretation given by the Jesuit Cardinal Robert Bellarmine to the Gospel story of the good thief—or Saint Dismas, as he was called by Christian devotion—the most popular figure associated with the scaffold throughout the Middle Ages. The promise of immediate ascent into heaven on the very same day as his death on the cross offered an assurance of forgiveness and salvation for the many thieves and killers who died at the hands of justice. His name, and the sentence addressed to him by Jesus, crossed the lips of comforters innumerable times. In the martyrology of the Battuti Neri of Ferrara, Saint Dismas figures behind Christ in the descent into Limbo, and the image must have suggested hopeful thoughts of future life to the condemned when they were shown it by the Ferrarese comforters. It was the decisive example, able to dissipate the cloud of despair hanging over the condemned. But things had been changing as the task of opening the doors to heaven gradually passed from the divine judge to the confessor-judges of the Church. Conscious of their own power and of the duty to govern the world in the name of God, these churchmen no longer intended to guarantee criminals and heretics an easy way out from earthly life toward the delights of heaven. They lived in a society threatened by violence and rebellion, and the necessary measure for dealing with it was a strict disciplining of mores, a pedagogy based on severity rather than gentleness. This point of view was not exclusive to Catholicism, the religion of works. Throughout Christian Europe courts were lashing out without distinguishing between crimes and sins, infractions of the sovereign's laws and of religion.[11] But the solution adopted by Jesuit culture, in this greatest expression of Catholicism, was that of a scission of theoretical convictions and practical strategies. Bellarmine's interpretation of the story of the good thief is as follows: right at the beginning of his treatise *De arte bene moriendi,* the work that established itself as the new model in the evolution of the genre, he addressed the traditional interpretation of the episode. According to Bellarmine, as we have seen, only a morally strict life could guarantee a good death: anyone wanting to die well had to live well.[12] Dismas must therefore have deserved the immediate ascent into heaven promised to him on the cross by having led a saintly life. Aside from this forcing of the Gospel text, it must be said that such a mentality was very widespread in Europe at the time. Around the scaffold in England, onlookers listened to sermons proclaiming that crimes were only the final product of small sins: the condemned person's last speech was an exhortation to the young to avoid drunkenness, profanation of the Sabbath, and the company of women of ill repute, the start of a slippery path to crime.[13] The new climate is also discernible in Bellarmine's recommendations about the necessity to make the conduct of confessors more rigid and intransigent.[14] The cardinal was aware that the social practice of confession was moving in the opposite direction. Edwin Sandys, an English traveler in Italy struck by the analogies between the Anglican and Catholic Church, wrote his own report about the state of religion in Italy in those years, commenting harshly on the readiness with which those guilty of serious crimes were absolved in the confessional and allowed to return to their wicked habits with the sole penance of a few prayers.[15]

Yet ideas like Bellarmine's struggled to find their way into practice. This was also because, in the effort to counter the attack on the power of the clergy, the defense of the efficacy of the sacraments led to the sustaining of the argument that the remission of sins occurred even if the sinner was not truly contrite but confessed only out of fear of eternal punishment. And in any case it was hard to show a stern face when trying to convince killers and thieves to confess beneath the scaffold. Anyone who thought that the hung thief, even if he was repentant, could not be saved kept it to himself and said it elsewhere.

As for the Jesuits, their intellectual contribution was certainly not limited to Polanco's text and the short treatise by Bellarmine. The question of

justice and law ("de iustitia et iure") was at the center of the imposing theoretical constructs of leading Jesuit thinkers, who reworked the thinking of
Thomas of Aquinas to give life to "second scholasticism." But the most
important ground for the exercise of confession was that of the science of
cases, or casuistry. It was here that their work left its biggest mark and influence on the activities of the companies of justice, supplementing the instructions contained in their chapters and in printed manuals. To the framework of rules it was necessary to add solutions for the concrete cases that
they might encounter in real life: this was the intellectual training that the
elite body of professional comforters felt they needed.

This, then, was the start of casuistry, a moral science that developed to an
extraordinary degree in the early modern age, linked as it was with the wars
of religion and the moral perplexities of a world that had suddenly become
bigger and more complicated. This depended in large part on the centrality
acquired by confession in the government of religious life. And confession
was the main point of comfort for those who were in jail, preparing for their
final journey to the scaffold. Widespread in the whole of European religious
culture, casuistry initially emerged above all (though not exclusively) in the
Catholic world.[16] It has been calculated that approximately 1,300 casuistic
works were produced by Catholic authors between 1550 and 1799.[17] Casuistry was cultivated especially by the Jesuits, acknowledged masters of the
science, who made it the key subject on the curriculum at their colleges in
the *Ratio studiorum* (1586). In administering the sacrament of confession,
confirmed at the Council of Trent as the central moment of pastoral government, the clergy caring for souls turned to the collections of cases prepared by Jesuit writers. It is no surprise, then, that the Jesuit tradition yielded
the large manual of casuistry specifically intended for comforters, a work we
have already come across and which has the suggestive title of *Notti malinconiche*. Composed by the Jesuit Giacinto Manara, and published in Bologna
in 1658,[18] it contains an immense range of answers to possible questions
and doubts, based on an analysis of real or hypothetical cases and a vast
canon and criminal law literature, besides information drawn from other
cultures—ancient and modern, European and non-European. Manara had
an author to draw on in Juan de Polanco, and a model of reference in the

weekly sessions of theoretical discussion at the School of Comforters in Bologna. This institution had become an academy dominated by scholars from the university and churchmen, who debated theoretical comforting themes and untangled problems arising from practice. Manara had grasped the spirit of the Bolognese model and channeled the invaluable experience he gained there into his book, designed for comforters who were not adequately prepared for the task. There were plenty of potential users, given that, as Manara wrote, "no one is ever put to death by the executioner in Catholic cities without many people being involved: the condemned man's confessor, the comforters, and the executioner who carries out the sentence, the police or wardens who accompany [the prisoner] to the scaffold."[19] Often they lacked experience, especially in towns where capital sentences were rare. The work therefore set out to offer answers to possible doubts. The deliberately jumbled organization of the subject matter was the kind of order for which the Jesuit said he had a preference—and it was not casual, for that was not only the literary taste of the time but also the style of casuistic literature. But the muddle of the cases lay within a very precise framework. The dedication to readers offers a general notion of humanity that is a prelude to the first, decisive *interrogatione,* whether "it is truly licit to put wrongdoers to death." The final *interrogatione* concerns the crimes for which the death penalty was envisaged. In his dedication, Manara proposes, under the authority of the founder of the Company, Saint Ignatius of Loyola, a typically baroque and counter-reformist reversal of the humanistic theme of Man as the measure of things. Created by God in his own image—the "compendium of all things created, little world, delight of the Lord of heaven, beauty of the universe, mirror of divine greatness, companion of the angels, restorer of the thrones lost by rebel minds, adopted son of God"—this man suddenly appears transformed into a pitiful being, consumed by fevers, illnesses, poverty, and hunger, the prey of enemies, who has finally become a miserable delinquent destined to be "hung from the gallows, beheaded, shot with bolts, flayed, broken on the wheel." Appearing behind the image of man as the microcosm of Renaissance culture are the worms and putridity of a body "that in the end is reduced to seven ounces of dust," as Manara succinctly writes at the end of his treatise.[20] From this the author derives the thesis that the power of God is manifested in the making of the beautiful creature but also in reserving "the power and authority to unmake it." God has delegated part of that power to the princes "who rule the people," while retaining for himself the decision about whether or not to destroy the "more important and superior part, which is the soul."[21]

The doubts about the rightness of capital punishment were dealt with not only with written arguments but, even prior to them, in the etching preceding the frontispiece to the first edition. In it three robust woodsmen are cutting through the roots of the leafless, fruitless tree of the wicked. The branches of the tree carry the names of the damned who must be uprooted from the earth, ranging from heretics to those guilty of lèse-majesté, and from murderers, thieves, counterfeiters, and pimps through to sodomites, adulterers, blasphemers, and those guilty of abortion and incest. The image leaves no doubt as to the author's view on the lawfulness of the death penalty. Manara knew that there were contrasting opinions. In Chapter 2 we saw how he reported the sense of perturbation and the feelings of basic humanity aroused in comforters by the scenes they witnessed. He responded to the doubtful by referring to Roman law and the commentary of Baldus de Ubaldis: judges must be ready to punish because the preservation of public order required it. But the question of whether one could do so by killing remained open: after all, was it not forbidden by the fifth commandment? And what about the parable of the sower (Matt. 13:18–23)? And did the Bible not say that God wanted the sinner, not to die, but to convert and live? Manara also recalled that Duns Scotus had noted the absence of thieves and adulterers from the list of crimes to be punished with death in Exodus 22, and had emphasized the Gospel episode of the adulteress saved from stoning by Jesus himself. Manara shrugged off all these objections, declaring them to be "dangerous"—that is, at risk of heresy. It was necessary to adhere to Saint Thomas, and also to another Thomas, the illustrious Master of the Order of Preachers, Thomas Cajetan, also known as Gaetanus, and in general to the authors of second scholasticism, who had all justified the death penalty. Was it not lawful to defend oneself from a murderer by killing him? And if one amputates a diseased limb from a person's body, the diseased limb of the "moral body of citizens" must also be cut off to prevent the healthy organism from sickening. And so, "to say that putting wrongdoers to death is unlawful, because it goes against God's teaching, is a sin against the Catholic faith."[22] The evildoer is an accident to be eliminated, against whom there stands a pyramid with God and the prince—his voice on earth—at the top, and the moral body of citizens as the base.

The mass of cases presented and solved by Manara do not just relate to themes touched on by the manuals. With imagination and readings, they also probe a welter of dark, shadowy hypotheses. His analysis of the ways and forms of granting sacraments supports the rightness of doing so without uncertainty, recounting the story of how Pius V intervened with Philip II to obtain assent to give Communion to the condemned.[23] But immediately afterward he ventures into a forest of imaginary cases, such as, for example, whether one could give a poisoned Host to a condemned prisoner, and whether the latter could vomit it, and how the resulting vomit should be devoutly gathered up, and finally what sin the priest would be committing in consecrating such a Host.[24] Respect for existing laws and obedience to sovereigns are the political framework within which the Jesuit's moral discourse places the fate of the individual soul and interprets the value of the intentions of the single person. If the prince's will is law, even when he condemns unjustly, the condemned have the right to save their lives, even if doing so requires killing those present, comforters included. A shiver of retrospective fear can be found at just one point, where Manara describes a night spent alongside a prisoner who, instead of resting, "frequently lifted his head and looked at the door of the *conforteria*." The Jesuit saw those furtive glances and movements in the darkness and asked him "why he was doing that, and so frequently: he answered sincerely: 'I was looking to see if I could escape.'"[25] This is one of the rare glimpses of those "melancholic nights" of which Manara claims to have seen so many in his life. The man pretending to rest but who, "lying on a mattress," raised his head in the dark to see if the door was open conjures up a scene worthy of Alessandro Magnasco. But the reason Manara described it is that here too his science had something to say, something destined to astound those devout comforters who, Manara writes with evident derision, are "accustomed to fingering their crown a hundred times a day." They will think that the prisoner's desperate desire to flee is a diabolic temptation, but it is not so. Even those who have been justly condemned have the right to try to save their lives. If to do this it were necessary to kill the judge, guards, and comforters, the offender would not be committing a sin. It would certainly be a crime, but not a sin. The solid foundations of the doctrine of Saint Thomas and the elaborations of second scholasticism that confirm the power to kill for the good of society also underpin the right of the single person to do anything to protect themselves.

But in this moral system supported by the principle of the lesser evil and governed by casuists, another power was gradually emerging, not that of the prince but of the ecclesiastical tribunal of the Inquisition. And when the ecclesiastical Inquisition came on the scene the rules were rewritten. The heretic, the unbeliever, and the Jew are characters who appear regularly in the theater of justice. Now it was a possibility that the rules of the sacramental court of penance and those of the external court of the Inquisition might enter into conflict, for example in the imaginary case of a person condemned to death for heresy revealing in the confessional that they had been unjustly punished. Which truth would win over—the one discovered in the depths of the conscience or that of a mistaken inquisitorial sentence? The answer was simple: the confessor was to secretly absolve the offender, but the comforters would not accompany the prisoner to the scaffold. One must have respect for the Inquisition.[26]

The *boia*—executioner—also merited respect, because he was a man who performed "an office very necessary and useful for the public. That he may somehow enjoy peace."[27] The word *boia* had a special place in the semiotics of the scaffold: together with its synonyms—*manigoldo, ribaldo, barattiere*—it denoted a piece of human trash, an infamous being by definition, an indispensable mediator with the accursed kingdom of death and the butchery of bodies, the object of all the disdain and rejection of a society that imposed that role on him as an everlasting condemnation.[28] Here, instead, he exercised a worthy "office," like other state functionaries: his civil and religious merit was to be respected and recompensed, on earth and in heaven. And as we shall see, the vigilant piety of the Counter-Reformation had already acted to give the "executors of justice" a protector saint as well, like every other order of social life. For Manara, the executioner could be a fine Christian. In any case he had his rights, which, among others, included the right to remove the fat from the executed person's body. Though that might prompt protests and calls for it to be stopped by those unable to bear the thought of their body being opened up by anatomists or exploited as a source of sellable medicines by the executioner, there was nothing to be done: if the prince had given the necessary permission, those things would be done. This did not mean that the use of human fat did not disgust the Jesuit as well ("This seems to have something very barbarous about it").[29]

Manara's firm conviction was that the death penalty was required for a pacified and well-ordered world. It amounted to the sacrifice of necessary victims, and was pleasing to God. Indeed, "one cannot sacrifice victim[s] more acceptable to God than by removing troublemakers from the world."[30] God did, though, permit those troublemakers to save their souls. Of course, there were those who had serious doubts about this. While talking in the *conforteria,* Manara had heard it said by a "wise person" that not only was there no certainty regarding the eternal salvation of those souls but even that "the majority of these wretches are damned."[31] But this was wrong, according to Manara: the grounds of those convictions had not been understood well, and in any case it was necessary to think differently, also in terms of miraculous testimony. But it was not a particularly important point for the Jesuit, who was anxious above all to confirm the utility of the punishment and the central role of comforting as a school of thought and an office of Christian good manners. The cases offered by the age formed a kind of landscape to be explored with the curiosity of a detached observer capable of appreciating the courage shown by Charles I of England in facing his death—though there was no doubt that as soon as his head was severed from his royal bust the English sovereign would "be tormented eternally in hell."[32] Manara had witnessed the execution of two brothers in Imola, and was thus able to give a firsthand description of the moment in which the executioner knocked them unconscious with a mallet blow to the temple before they were flayed. And he had gathered information about some very cruel executions, like that of the regicide François Ravaillac. He had also read the proceedings of a trial describing how "a barber known as 'il Morra,' who made unguents to infect people with the plague so that they died and he made greater profit, was removed from the world in Milan in the year 1630." Manara was in no doubt that "he [Gian Giacomo Mora] and his accomplices deservedly had their bones shattered, and, twisted on the spokes of the wheel, remained alive for six hours; he had plenty of time to perform acts of contrition for past wrongs and to earn merit by enduring such dire torment, and enabled the religious men who were assisting to merit greatly."[33] It is no accident that the brief accounts provided by Manara contained a repeated allusion to the question of merits. The length of Mora's torments provided him with an opportunity to earn merits before appearing in the presence of God. But it was the people who religiously assisted him that merited "greatly." There were no gray areas in the justice system: torment and death settled accounts with wrongs done and provided merits to avoid or reduce (eternal) punishment for the condemned and to earn a place in heaven for the comforters—the only ones who made a net profit. The bill of exchange signed on earth would be paid in heaven. In the meantime the delinquents were to be "removed from the world."

The name of Gian Giacomo Mora, the victim of an atrocious judicial case that was celebrated at the time and would become so again in the reflections of later centuries, is one of the very few instances in which a real person appeared in the burgeoning literature of the comforters. It took a Jesuit expert in casuistry to include the unfortunate barber among the remote figures of saints and famous historical characters. But the names and real features of the condemned were covered by an almost complete veil of silence. The concrete human profile of the prisoner receiving the death sentence remains a timeless silhouette. The condemned person's only task was to choose between acceptance of their fate (including the offering of thanks to those who had put them in that situation) and stubborn refusal, which was destined to be punished on earth and in heaven. The proposed dialogues were unilateral: like in a bureaucratic handbook, the comforter imagined doubts and hypothetical situations, and indicated solutions. What the condemned said, and their actual situation, seemed not to concern him much. His mental gymnastics was performed on the most extreme hypotheses, and consisted of rendering rational the most absurd countenance that the real was capable of assuming.

26

Laboratories of Uniformity:
Theoretical Cases and Real People

GIACINTO MANARA'S "MELANCHOLIC NIGHTS" evolved in the context of the work performed by Bologna's Sacra Scuola di Conforteria—a name which very soon lost its original sense of a confraternity and took on that of a place of study, which is what it effectively ended up becoming. The surviving archive material contains significant traces of intense, serious, and continuous intellectual endeavor and teaching activity. It was directed by one of the members, who held the office of censor. A figure typical of the literary academies that flourished in Italy from the mid sixteenth century onward, the censor's role was to guide the collective work, correcting the intellectual output where necessary and ensuring that it remained on the narrow path marked by the internal rules of rhetoric and language, and the external ones of the Church and of the political authorities. The rules drawn up around the middle of the seventeenth century to regulate the ordinary meetings of the Bolognese School (one every Sunday) stipulated that the censor was to plan and oversee each session according to an unvarying pattern: twelve "masters" were to "reason about and address those things which shall seem useful, opportune, and necessary for the instruction, doctrine, and training of novices and disciples." It was the censor's job to organize the meetings, "proposing the issues or cases, both theoretical and practical," and to inform the brothers of them in advance so they could prepare and perhaps put down "in writing the main foundations of the reasoning of that day, so they might be preserved for the benefit of the School."[1] Outlines of the cases for discussion were normally printed, and copies of many of these have been preserved in the School's archive. We can imagine that the meetings were very strict and regimented. They were presided over by the masters, most of whom were professors at the city's Studio (university) or canons from the basilica of San Petronio. In the middle of the seventeenth century, when the debating activity got under way regularly, the censor was Ovidio Montalbani, a university professor of philosophy and mathematics. Many of the cases he proposed were printed. One of the masters at that time was Giovanni Battista Gargiaria, a jurist, university professor, and the author of *Conforto de gli afflitti condannati a morte,* published in 1650 and reprinted several times.[2] If we add Giacinto Manara's volume, and the other printed texts, we have a significant corpus of the products that came out of the meetings. But did they come out or go in? The members of the Bolognese Studio were bookish men of science. One only needs to leaf through the lists of the books in their libraries, recorded by the notary who worked for the School of Comforters, to gain an idea of the vast and curious erudition that lay between them and the practice of comforting,[3] acting as a filter for the experience of those "hideous and frightful functions of torments and deaths," where, as Gargiaria writes, "it is customary to see dumbstruck onlookers, like blockheads, with pallid, bloodless faces; some faint, some cry, some shout, some sigh."[4]

As this subject matter accumulated in the structures of the casuistry of conscience, it lost the concrete connotations of the people who had received comforting and died amid the torments of the scaffold: from flesh and blood reality it became abstract potential and repetitiveness, providing the stimulus for an intellectual game that was a habitual feature of such circles. Casuistry was at the peak of its development in that period, studied as a form of moral theology in European universities well beyond the borders of the Catholic world, and providing the basis for the training of priests and pastors. The practice of printing, on loose sheets, cases for discussion taken from the experience of the confessional had been introduced among ecclesiastics caring for people's souls back in the late sixteenth century thanks to Bishop Gabriele Paleotti, who had entrusted the Jesuits with the task. But there was a fundamental difference in the casuistry practiced in the School of Comforters: the cases discussed here often arose out of the experience of providing assistance to the condemned during "melancholic nights." What we are faced with here is an intellectual exercise where scholarly pens were, as it were, dipped in human blood. This is suggested by the elegant, intertwined motif of a sword and a pen placed on the frontispiece of Carlo Antonio Macchiavelli's catalogue by the Bolognese publisher Lelio dalla Volpe. And the comment in the cartouche qualified the work of study with what we might describe as a wholly Christian Enlightenment: *illuminare eos qui in umbra mortis sedent*—"bring light to the shadows of he who awaits death." This was the formula repeated most frequently in company of justice circles, expressing the sense of the undertaking in which the members of the *conforteria* were proud to participate.

The procedure used in formulating cases for discussion involved imagining possible situations or drawing them from real-life experiences. And as the functioning of justice in the important Bolognese legation provided regular opportunities to renew such experience, there was no pressing need to invent abstract cases: it sufficed to elaborate actual events, stripping them of their concrete connotations and generalizing them. Real events can, however, often be glimpsed behind the abstract formulations of the cases presented during the School's Sunday sessions. For example, in the first semester of 1641 the censor, who at the time was the "master" Giovanni Bertalotti, proposed some *Motivi per li discorsi ordinarii della Scola,* taking them from a recent case in which the *conforteria* had been involved. The censor did not name the "patient," but the events were still fresh in the city's memory and the outcry over the case had left a profound mark. Bertalotti described the protagonist as "a subject who was executed in his prime, accustomed to living according to the inclinations of the senses, an atheist at heart and who boasted some intelligence."[5] The word "atheist" tells us that this was a heresy case. In the record of prisoners executed in those years, kept up to date by the city's criminal court (known as the Torrone), we find, among a host of thieves, murderers, and others punished for various crimes (sodomy, infanticide, and so on), just two cases of heresy. In both instances the sentences had been handed down by the Holy Office of Bologna, which had then passed them on to the police of the Torrone for execution. One involved a German student named Assuero Bispiach, hung and then burned on November 4, 1618. The other, on November 28, 1622, saw the hanging and burning of Costantino Sacardino and his son Bernardino, and of Pellegrino Tedeschi and his son Girolamo. In Assuero's case the notary at the Torrone observed that the mildness of the punishment—he was strangled before being burned—was due to the fact that he had shown signs of conversion.[6] The same must be presumed for the later group, who were not Lutherans but atheists, an extremely serious charge that had been included not long before in the theological matrix of the Inquisition together with the shades of

Machiavelli, ancient epicureanism, and modern libertines.[7] Evidence of Costantino's final conversion can be found in his last wishes, dictated on Monday, November 28, 1622: in them he declared himself "desirous to render his soul to God with as much contrition as possible" and left instructions regarding his assets, "in order to spend what little life remained to him in begging forgiveness of his Divine Majesty, and bewailing his sins after having sacramentally confessed."[8] The episode had caused an outcry in the city, and the *conforteria* had needed to deploy its full energies. In the immediate aftermath, one of the masters, the canon and count Ridolfo Campeggi, wrote an account of the affair entitled *Racconto degli eretici iconomiasti,* which had been immediately reprinted.[9] The heretics were described as "iconomiasti" because the group's subversive action had targeted sacred images of the Virgin Mary around the city, which were the focus of great devotion and indeed of a full-blown cult due to the miracle-working powers attributed to them. Thorough historic research into what has been described as the "conspiracy of a buffoon" has reconstructed the culture and life path of a singularly theatrical personality and popular libertine who chose Bologna for an experiment in revolt against Counter-Reformation religion.[10] Both the German Lutheran and the Italian atheists had died penitent and converted, and so could be considered two success stories from the comforters' point of view. It was now a case of studying what one of the atheists—Bernardino, the youngest of the four—had said in the *conforteria,* so the trainees could learn how to adapt to particularly difficult situations like this one. The exercise was structured as a dialogue where the arguments of the condemned man were given and it was necessary to fill in the gaps with the comforter's half of the conversation. Each separate point marked a step in the construction of a relationship in which the comforters had to insert their voice and make themselves heard. It quickly became apparent that the task was very difficult: the prisoner did not listen and had a feverish state of mind, combining a desperate fear of death with angry protests and attempts to contest the sentence. When the news arrived that he was to die, Bernardino "burst out into many blasphemies," and immediately afterward, "agitated by a fit of rage, sought to hurt those present as much as he could, and indeed, banging his head on the walls, tried to kill himself." Gradually he tired, and it was finally possible to speak to him. However, he refused to countenance the prospect of death because he said "presumptuously that God had exempted and freed him from this death." He also revealed a vision (dream?) he had had, the truth of which he "stubbornly" sustained, and "indeed called anyone who did not believe it a heretic." But was he not an atheist? Well, this would be discussed in the eighth point of the exercise. Immediately before this he had tried to justify his political crimes, which he summed up as "having reproved the bad government of the authorities." But was it a crime to tell the truth? Because he had said the truth when he had "reproved the bad government of the authorities with placards and defamatory pamphlets." And as what he had done was right, he should not be punished, or at least not so harshly. Verbal crimes against the powerful in heaven and on earth—blasphemies and defamatory statements—could be forgiven: "if offense given to God is forgiven, one can also forgive that made against men."[11] We do not know what responses the trainees came up with to counter Bernardino's argument. But he had been excommunicated by the Inquisition not for blasphemy but for atheism. And he was being sent to his death by the civil authorities, and so Bernardino could rightly say he had been forgiven for his crimes against God. But who was God for him? This was probably the question by the comforter that we should insert into the blank space on the questionnaire immediately before the next point (number 9). Here we read that Bernardino styled himself as a "natural philosopher" who reasoned "in the ethnic way"—as the ancient pagans did: for him God was "a first cause, or first entity, whose help he intended to invoke though he did not know him." It was a pretext for talking about the Christian God, the immortality of the soul, and eternal punishments. At point ten we find Bernardino "assailed by a very grave fear of death," who reacted to the reminder that he should not fear this death but that of the soul by asking: "So if the soul must die, why so much effort to save it?" In the following point we read that it had been explained to him what the death of the soul involved: "the disgrace of God, and the punishments of hell." He had also been presented with the alternative—namely, "heavenly glory"—to which "he responded brutishly: 'So there is no purgatory.'" Bernardino had homed in on an important point, that the comforting of the condemned was based on an instrumental simplification that said nothing about purgatory. Therefore, he had retorted not "brutishly" but rationally, pointing them to one of the key points of their own faith. But what amounted to the beginnings of a doctrinal discussion was dropped. A decisive turning point came when Bernardino "began to show signs of conversion, but had no faith in the mercy of God." He repented, confessed, and received Communion, but then asked to see his father, who had been "condemned for the same crimes and [was being] comforted in another room." Should this be permitted or not? It is not hard to imagine how the trainees were expected to answer: as we have seen, all the manuals of instruction for comforters regarded such contact as "very dangerous," and the censor pointed this out in formulating the question. Then came four further themes for the scholastic exercise: how to comfort the young man who, while he spoke, heard "sounds of the nailing of planks and the moving of carts," and thinking immediately of the "harsh torments" awaiting him, "fell into a great fear, with tears and sighs," revealing all the fragility and tenderness of his character. This "delicacy" emerged again in the final point, when the young man was handed over to the executioner, who stripped him and placed the noose around his neck: thinking they were about to pincer him, he "broke down in tears." But before that he had posed a problem for the comforters, by asking for permission to speak to the people from the gallows. He had remembered that he was "obliged to restore his own reputation." The condemned were normally reminded of their duty to restore the good names of others, the expectation being that they would reveal the names of accomplices or clear people they had wrongly accused. However, Bernardino wanted to restore his own good name and, what is more, to do it from the scaffold, explaining that the crime he had committed— sullying some sacred images after his father had been incarcerated—had been done "out of love for his father," in order to create an alibi for him. A noble motive, perhaps capable of attenuating the abomination heaped on him. But here too, for those who knew the instructions, the answer to the quiz was not difficult—it had to be no.

As this example shows, casuistic exercises were designed for the intellectual training of new comforters at the School, but their publication in print form meant that they also became an important sector of the literature produced by Italian Counter-Reformation culture. They were neither manuals for confessors nor theological or canonistic texts; often they had a link with real events and problems that arose in concrete cases, but they might also explore the vast territories of an abstract moral theology. Nor did they form part of devotional literature. They drew on ingredients from all these fields, but elaborated them with a much more ambitious goal in mind. They were presented as a bridge capable of harmoniously uniting positive law and theology in order to cover every possible gap in experience. And they followed the rule of always and completely transforming crime into sin, and of legitimating the sovereign's punishment as the emanation of a divine decree. This took place not just and not so much on the theoretical plane, but by making the condemned person the actor and witness: the scaffold thus became the truth-theater where the melodrama of martyrdom was staged, the one which in the meantime the confraternity itself was also offering as a theatrical model in the *sacre rappresentazioni* organized for the city's devout entertainment.

The model developed in Bologna was echoed and imitated in other places too. A bundle of questions presented and solved by the confraternity of San Giovanni Battista in Modena is what remains of the meetings to discuss cases organized by the School of Comforters in a phase of revival following a long period in which the assistance for the condemned had been carried out by Jesuits and Capuchins.[12] In the records of these sessions kept by the canon Giuseppe Antonio Lotti from 1758 onward, we find a series of situations thought up around a table, taken from current moral-theological literature and resolved with an abundance of citations and references to treatises. A range of possible situations were imagined: condemned prisoners who pretended to be mad to avoid the sentence; or took poison so they died before having to climb onto the scaffold; or who perjured themselves during their trial and were now troubled by scruples that the comforter needed to know how to solve and for which copious and erudite explanations were provided. These documents offer revealing glimpses of the shared values of an Italian city in the ancien régime. One regarded a condemned man "of respectable standing" who declared to his confessor that he wanted to make a public declaration of innocence in order "to render his death less dishonorable."[13] He needed to be dissuaded, as this was a "blind passion for glory, vain and fallacious," but above all cause for scandal, which would mar the outcome of the spectacle. The confessor therefore had to convince him that it was a diabolical temptation to distract him from what should be the sole object of his thoughts—repentance and God's impending judgment.

These texts remained in manuscript form in the archive. In Bologna, on the other hand, efforts were made to bridge the gap between the in-house manuscript and the print circulation of the news and work documents of the *conforteria,* to which a wider intellectual value was evidently attached.

This took place with the publication, around the middle of the eighteenth century, of a handful of texts written by the abbot Carlo Antonio Macchia-velli while he held the office of censor. They consisted of answers to issues which he claimed were raised by condemned prisoners, and which were printed in italics before the response given by the "consoler," as the traditional role was now called. Unlike the casuistic exercises of Manara, here a connec-tion was made, sometimes with precision, between theoretical elaboration and real experiences of comforting. But the questions were articulated and threaded together in such a way as to delineate an ideal type of "patient," with all the negative traits the comforters came across on various occasions in reality—a person resistant to comforting, who tries to save his life with legal arguments or desperate fabrications, who moans disappointedly about the lack of satisfaction he obtains, and succumbs only after a great effort by those urging acceptance of the sentence as an inevitable outcome. It is like looking at the path taken by an animal trapped in a labyrinth with just one way out: the abattoir. The prisoner is pushed there by the inexorable "consoler." The authoritativeness of the publication was guaranteed by the name of the prior and principal of the confraternity, Marchese Costanzo Zambeccari, printed on the frontispiece, and even more so by the list of the twelve masters of 1744. This opened with the name of Benedict XIV, and also included the marchesi Niccolò Tanara and Giuseppe Nicola Spada. There were various professors from the university, for example Gaetano Tacconi, an anatomist and teacher of philosophy and medicine, and doctors of theology and civil and canon law who were also canons at the basilica of San Petronio. One of them, Giuseppe Maria Vernizzi, beside his teaching duties, was also the pro-moter fiscal of the Holy Office and advocate for the poor. Rounding off the list was the name of the parish priest of San Sigismondo, Giuseppe Gaetano Malisardi, a professor of theology.[14] The following are some examples of the issues:

(1) A condemned man refuses to be comforted because the court mes-senger has just handed him a summons to appear in court for the sentence. The man is in possession of evidence proving the falsity of the testimony against him and is counting on the opportunity to appear before the judge to present the evidence he has gathered and to ask to be cleared. But the an-swer is unequivocal: "the hope is vain." The "consoler" patiently explains that the summons the prisoner has received is pure form: it is what remains

of the ancient custom of criminals going with their consolers "to hear their sentence at the *ringhiera* in the square, where it was read out publicly." Everything has now been reduced to a written summons, done so hurriedly that in one case (on January 27, 1703) the School had even thought they might be able to get the culprit released because the summons did not specify that the sentence was a death sentence. The condemned man is thus advised not to waste time and to start preparing straightaway for what awaited him at the end of the night. As for the decisive proof he claims to have, it would be neither "heard nor admitted," because the main evidence against him is his confession: "his sentence derives from his own confession."[15]

(2) In the second issue, the "patient" claims to be in possession of "a secret of the greatest importance." He wants to disclose it exclusively to the cardinal legate, hoping to obtain a pardon in return. But also in this case the consoler must remain unmoved in the face of "our patient's pleas," while at the same time adopting "kind and amenable manners." Giving him leave to write to a superior is impossible: "just thinking of writing to him is an outrage that has no like, because it is too bold." He should disclose his secret to court notaries and fiscals, or at least to the "consoler," and should do so quickly because it is a duty of his conscience. "Here it is a matter of damage to third parties, and of a prejudice that the government may have, and if not remedied in time, as he was obliged to do, his punishment will be eternal." In short, there was no recompense for the secret: he was to reveal it or God would add to his earthly sentence that of the soul in hell. When the "consolers," with skillful and appropriate "insinuations," then come into possession of the revelation—oral, not written—they are not to rush off to tell the authorities: their task is to save the soul, without running the risk of becoming embroiled in matters dangerous for the decorum of the School.[16] Quite clearly, responses like this were anything but consoling.

(3) The third question regards a "patient" who is protesting and, "half despairing," accuses the School's methods of being "tyrannies," so much so that he regrets not having "ended up just in the hands of ecclesiastics," as they might have shown more compassion for him. This is a singular argument, before a group of "masters" the first of whom was the reigning pope, but it reveals an awareness (of the consolers? of the patients?) that the law had taken the place of the Gospels. The response is, as always, gentle in tone but clear-cut in substance: not even an ecclesiastic could consent to improper

requests, "intrinsically bad and at odds with equity." Once again the fault is "entirely of he [the condemned man] who asks for things that are against the dictates of reason." The goddess Reason appears here alongside her companion Justice: "one must request just things to obtain justice." Naturally, all this was to be said in an appropriate way, so that "the offenders are won over by their pleasantness."[17]

(4) The fourth issue is a variant of the third: this time the patient, "satisfied" by the reasons put forward, says he is ready to suffer the punishments that await him as "just castigation for his misdeeds." But he wants to be consoled by priests, as they are the best suited to speaking "of God's love, of regret, and of patience for condemned wretches." Here the prisoner seems to breach the defenses of the consoler, who admits that priests are the ones best suited to assisting those about to die: God grants them that "divine knowledge" so necessary "in the distressing hours and in the most melancholic nights of the miserable offenders." There is an implicit reference to Manara's work here, but it is also an opportunity to settle accounts with Jesuit claims. Because, it is observed, the miracle of converting a sinner could also be performed by laypeople *(secolari)*. Indeed, that was precisely what laypeople had been doing in Bologna for the last four centuries. Nonetheless, if the patient insisted, his request should be accepted and the layman would stay to keep him company only until the priests arrived.

The next topics in the sequence return to the traditional pattern of how to combat the condemned man's desperation and his fear of not being forgiven by God as he has only repented out of fear. He is to be asked to acknowledge that the sentence has been inflicted for his sins and that the punishments have been sent by God as a penalty for his errors."[18] One question concerns the use of alms collected for masses for the soul: Could they not be given to the man's wife, who has four "young children in very grave necessity"? The answer is no: those who have offered alms have done so for masses to be said in suffrage for the soul, and the wishes of others cannot be modified or altered in any way, all the more so as disillusion would spread among alms-givers if this were to come out. If anything, it would be better to personally ask those present at the execution for a "new and separate collection to help his family"; this had been done on many previous occasions, indicated here very precisely, and with excellent results, because "the wretched offenders, who were greatly troubled at leaving their wives and children beset with poverty," were rendered "peaceful and consoled."[19] The careful orchestration of the scene emerges from a question about how to calm the "patient" who despairs because he does not know the different devout "acts" he is required to utter and requests more time to learn how to say them properly. This could be granted: it would suffice to extend the comforting by a few hours, as envisaged and permitted by the closely coordinated dealings between the court and the School, which are described here:

> It is customary in our city of Bologna, before the Arringo [the bell announcing an impending execution] tolls and the sentence is carried out, for the curia to send someone to the *conforteria* to ask how the offender is carrying himself, how repentant, and what disposition he shows: and on the basis of the replies the said curia then decides the appropriate orders for performing the act of justice, in such a way as to show both humanity and charity.

In a word, the condemned must not complain, "it being more charitable toward him than he thinks."[20] Obstacles also arose from the welter of legitimate devotions: for example, it needed to be explained to the patient that though the "habit" of the Madonna del Carmine would save him from the risk of dying a bad death, this was only in the sense that it would prevent the death of his soul. In any case, he would be told that demanding a miracle from the Madonna "is tempting [the wrath] of God himself in expecting that he will perform miracles through his own most holy mother."[21] That does not mean God would not do so; there had been several in Bologna (and here some cases are cited, with specific dates). The series of topics eventually comes around to dealing with the usual problems: the infamy of the condemned man's name, the mockery of the body. The patient asks for the customary notices *(polizzotti)* not to be affixed in public places because of the infamy this would heap upon his name. Here he was to be told that by dying a good death he would leave "a good name for himself to posterity," transforming infamy into honor and leaving his family with the glory of his conversion. A more difficult task was calming down the patient who, upon leaving the Palazzo del Podestà and while walking toward the scaffold, discovers that his body will be quartered after he has died. What should one do if, in a "loud, ringing voice, he calls for the judge who passed sentence on him to be brought before the tribunal of God"? Situations of this kind were to be avoided by keeping the manner in which the sentence was to be carried out concealed from him by all means possible. If he did find out, the comforters had to ask those present to pray in unison to drown out his cries, explaining to him that the judge had condemned him justly to such punishments because he was guilty of the crimes to which he had confessed—in short, the time for consoling was over, now was the moment to get on with things. This was the harsh reality: "he should not have been guilty if he did not want to be condemned."[22]

This is just one example of how things played out in one of the confraternities of justice, probably the one which for the university city where it operated was best suited to being transformed into an academy of moral and theological exercises. The necessary premise for such an evolution had been the construction of an archive memory of treated cases, from which ideas could be taken to dissert on how to answer doubts and protests, and overcome difficulties. It was not just in Bologna that the shift of lay companies like these toward the exercising of public functions had prompted increasing attention about how to keep a rigorous memory of what they did and what happened during execution rituals. From the early sixteenth century onward the Roman company of San Giovanni Decollato kept a careful record of executions, noting down in the *Giornale del Provveditore* the various everyday occurrences, and in particular "all the final wishes of those who leave this life at the hand of justice."[23] Annotations made in the heat of the moment were then copied and put into order in the *Libro del Provveditore,* while the final wishes of the executed were recorded in the *Libro dei Testamenti.* A special series of personal files related to individual prisoners. The *scarichi di coscienza,* the declarations in which the condemned corrected trial depositions or cleared innocent people who had been falsely accused, were often kept separately.[24] The subsidiarity of religion with respect to criminal justice appears here in all its evidence: a person who, under torture, had accused innocent people of being jointly responsible for their crimes had to restore the good name of the slurred party to make amends for their sin. At the same time the secular judge could better ascertain the truth. And so the religious rule underpinning confession as a sacrament, and the duty of criminal justice to strike against all, and only genuine, culprits, came together and overlapped. How this happened, and how events often differed in reality from the ideal design of the confraternities' statutes, will become clearer by examining the documents preserved in the archives of some of the most important companies of justice, for example the Whites in Naples and the like-named company in Palermo.

But first it would be useful to complete the picture of the exercises devised to study and perfect comforting techniques, once again looking at the case of Bologna. Here, in 1674, the School of Comforters, directed by elite members of the city government—noblemen, high-ranking clergymen, university professors—decided there needed to be greater uniformity in the information they gathered about each execution. They did this by devising a preprinted module which was to be filled out straightaway by the pair of comforters on duty. The first modules in the archive series were filled out on the occasion of two executions carried out in 1674.[25] A certain Agostino Pizzola went to his death in Piazza Maggiore on September 15, while a man named Girolamo Parisini met the same fate on December 12. The comforters only filled in the first sheet of the many questions on the module. We learn that on the eve of their execution the condemned men were handed over to the prior, Count Filippo Maria Bentivogli, and to the comforters who had gone in procession to the jail: after being taken to the *conforteria* the prisoners were greeted by the master on duty and his assistant. The comforters were completely successful: in both cases, the condemned made their confession within an hour and were freed from their shackles. Later they received Communion. Agostino suffered from the "temptation" of "not detaching himself from earthly things," of leaving "his family in need and abandoned by everyone," but then "submitted everything to God." With Girolamo Parisini there was a special problem. When he had been handed over to the brothers the evening before the execution, and was walking with them through Piazza Maggiore, he had seen the platform being prepared for the execution, "above which he feared he would have to make a spectacle of his body." He had asked, "full of grief, if that scaffold was really destined for him, showing himself most saddened by that, and as a result, a great dampening in the fervor of his spirit."

From then on, the comforters diligently compiled the many parts of the module, which mirrored the successive steps leading to the execution and of the dialogue with the condemned. These were: (1) taking delivery of the "patient," initially received at the prison gates by a small procession of hooded brothers but then subsequently handed over by police officers to the prior on the threshold of the *conforteria* chapel; (2) recording the time that elapsed between the first confession, the removal of the shackles, and Communion; (3) listing the areas of resistance shown during the comforting and an account of how they had been tackled; (4) listing the patient's devotions and an indication of the way in which they had been "cultivated," meaning nourished and strengthened; (5) any last wishes conveyed to the comforters; (6) behavior of the prisoner at the *banchetta* (the moment when the condemned person met the executioner), then during the walk to the scaffold, and finally on the scaffold; (7) the comforters' evaluation of the behavior of everyone who had played an official part in proceedings, from the prior to the pupils and any "other ministers." The spaces in the module were filled in according to this sequence, though more attention was given to the phases that posed greater problems. This is illustrated by a case dating to January 27, 1703, which attracted the attention of the censor Carlo Antonio Macchiavelli. Here we find extensive annotations about the protests made by the condemned man, whose name was Domenico Grignani, or "degli Arcangeli." He railed vociferously against the injustice of the sentence, saying he had endured a long spell in prison and had been condemned because he was poor (they had asked him if he had any "stuff"). "He replied several times that the justice of God was true, but that of the world iniquitous"; he complained about the notary, the magistrate, and even the cardinal legate, and cursed "with the most violent exaggerations, declaring the wish to ask, on the scaffold, for heaven's vengeance for his supposedly unjust condemnation." He was told "that the justice of the world was the minister of that of God, and therefore from the righteousness of one came that of the other." The customary examples of Christ and of the martyrs were then produced to reaffirm "the specific necessity to forgive anyone who had played a part in his death." A sensitive issue also arose: the sentence had not been cited, and so the comforters turned to the prison lawyer to see if the punishment could be reduced in any way—whereupon it emerged that this was the style of the court. After this turbulent start to proceedings, the condemned behaved in an exemplary fashion, preparing himself "with total calm" and cooperating spontaneously every step of the way: he forgave the executioner, prayed on the scaffold for the people to forgive him for having been cause for scandal, and asked them to pray for him.

The initial violent complaint about the injustice of the sentence thus petered out without consequences, and the comforters could successfully complete their work. Also included on the module was the length of time it took: in this case, five hours elapsed between taking delivery of the man and his first confession, the sign of successful "conversion." This was an exceptionally long period of time, even longer than in the case of Gian Matteo Bertoldi, beheaded in Piazza Maggiore on Wednesday, September 3, 1710, for whom three hours were required. In turn, this was a bit longer than the average, which was about two hours, but here the reason why proceedings were rather protracted was quite different from that of Domenico Grignani. The master who assisted the prisoner explained that Bertoldi prepared for confession with such devotion that "it seemed as if he wanted to slip into scrupulousness." He intended to make a confession such as "to merit the forgiveness of his sins by his Divine Majesty." He had also insisted on making confession repeatedly, and was extremely profuse in his devotions, to the point that no more were needed. In his will he asked that the alms collected for masses for his soul be given instead to suffrages for the souls that he had harmed. And during the meeting at the *banchetta* with the "Master of Justice"—the executioner, who was making his debut in the role—he again went further than what was asked of him: not only did he accept the request for forgiveness, but he also "caressed, thanked, and kissed the executioner." It was this excess of devotion that had brought him to the scaffold in the first place: Bertoldi had been condemned by the Holy Office because, though he only had minor orders, he had publicly celebrated Mass "many, many times." As a result, he had been degraded by the Roman Inquisition and handed over to the secular arm.

Quicker and easier to deal with were the "temptations" of Giuseppe Collina from Bologna, delivered to the *conforteria* on the afternoon of March 20, 1703, though they did reveal an awareness of the ties between the company and the city's political and judicial authorities. Collina had asked to see his wife, a request that had been denied; moreover, he was convinced that one of the judges had been unduly harsh on him by punishing him with death. With an "adroit ploy by the consoler himself," which was emphasized in the report, he was told what had happened in the management of his case, and that everything possible had been done to fulfill his desire. This does effectively sound like an "adroit ploy," given what we know about the comforters' stance on allowing meetings with family members.

Thoughts of wives and children cropped up regularly: Tommaso Capra, hung with two accomplices on March 21, 1703, complained about having "to leave his wife and children abandoned." But it was easy to calm him with the reminder that he was leaving them in the hands of God's mercy, and that the only help he could give them was to do everything possible "to save his soul, and go to a place where he would be able to intercede with God"; he would help them much more in this way than by "remaining in this world and setting them a bad example." Tommaso also feared that his late contrition would not suffice to earn God's forgiveness. But this doubt was likewise quickly allayed by the consoler Gregorio Malisandi, who invited him to reflect that "the mercy of the Lord could forgive much more than he was capable of sinning." One final complication was that Tommaso was the second of the group to be hung, and a dexterous and careful use of the *tavoletta* was required to prevent him seeing the body of the first man to die.

Santo Persichini da Calcara, hung on Saturday, November 17, 1703, also worried about his family, which was one of the most frequent "temptations" of thought: "the sorrow of leaving his family, consisting of his wife and three daughters, two young and one nubile, in a needy state." His principal concern was that "the elder one should not serve in an *osteria,* as he had been told she did at present." Once again the comforter resorted to the argument of God's providence, telling him that "as regards the family, he was leaving it in the arms of the Lord, who in his infinite providence neglects no one, all the more so as he was going to a place of well-being, where he would beg for more special assistance." But reports of daughters at risk of losing their virtue sometimes triggered conditioned reflexes in the charitable system of the age. Santo Persichini was given reassurances that "due to the compassion of these gentlemen [an undertaking] had been secured to find a place for the younger daughters," which the comforter said he would see to personally.

Just one hour went by on June 17, 1695, between the arrival of Pietro della Vedova—known as "il Todesco," who was hung the next day in Piazza Maggiore in front of the basilica of San Petronio—in the *conforteria* and his making confession. Yet his "temptation" stemmed from a situation that seemed almost deliberately contrived to undermine faith in justice: although he had been imprisoned together with other accomplices, and they had all been found guilty of the same crime, he was the only one sentenced to death. Moreover, he claimed, it was the accomplices who had "seduced and led [him] to wrongdoing." Situations like this arose from within the very heart of the penal system, based on the granting of rewards and pardons to those who collaborated and reported or helped to get accomplices captured: in public notices issued by the cardinal legate, it was customary to offer immunity and other rewards, such as the freeing of a bandit from punishment, to those who handed over criminals to the police. And no one was better placed to do so than accomplices. The master and pupil comforting duo—Carlo Antonio Bedori and Pietro degli Antoni—wrote at length in their report about the arguments they used to convince "il Todesco," and it is worth reading it to grasp just how firmly aligned the *conforteria* was in support of the power to condemn:

> No one, nor he himself, was to think that either the Prince or the judges had been so thirsty for his blood that they had wanted to punish him in that way without him having deserved it, but rather he should consider the sentence most just, while those who had passed it had been guided by justice alone. He should not and could not fathom or seek the judgments of the Lord God, because of the three accomplices he had had in his misdeeds one had already died in prison, and perhaps without the assistance which God was granting to him in that moment. The other two were still in the hands of justice, and therefore it could not be known what castigation divine justice had in store for them, though he was not to desire it; but knowing that the limits of justness were not being exceeded in his case, the castigation of others could not in any way benefit either his soul or body: and therefore he was only to wish for reparation and all spiritual well-being.

This reference to the fate of the soul put the prisoner's mind to rest ("he was very satisfied"), and he added some thoughts of his own: "He said that he knew that in order to save himself it was necessary to lay down all hatred, and desire every happiness even for those who had offended him."

It was Todesco, then, and not his comforters, who recalled the Gospel precept of forgiveness, which just goes to show to what extent the *conforteria* could count on a preexisting foundation of religious convictions on which to build the legitimation of the power to condemn to death. Not only was Todesco satisfied, but he also responded by shifting the discussion to the law of forgiveness. And he experienced it at the most densely emotional encounter, the one with the executioner at the *banchetta:* here "not only did he courageously forgive the executioner, but he also immediately begged him with great tenderness to pray to God for him." He proved so docile and willing to conform to what was presented to him as "divine will" that the comforters' report concluded by observing that "each of the onlookers could do no less than to imagine a well-founded moral assurance regarding his well-being."

Nicola Raimondi known as Budella da Bologna was a thief and high-wayman. He was sentenced to death by hanging "for many crimes of armed assault, robbery, and theft, committed by him both in the city and the countryside," as could be read on the posters affixed at the corners of Piazza Maggiore on February 7, 1714. He made his confession two hours after entering the *conforteria,* but the two comforters noted in him a "tepidity, that is, a relaxing of the spirit." He expressed the desire for everything to be done quickly, "that the hour of death might arrive once and for all to remove him from the tedium and affliction in which he found himself." He displayed a spark of engagement when he asked to see two Jesuit fathers, though quite why is not known. However, he was ably dissuaded by the members of the School. His sole possessions were the clothes he was wearing, which he asked to be given in alms to the poor.

The forms compiled by the comforters reveal a kaleidoscope of faces differing in social standing, age, sex, and crime, but the rhythm of the steps during the fast-moving nighttime hours remained constant and the same. The punishments varied according to the gravity of the crime. Francesco Fantoni, who had robbed and killed his master, Don Antonio Albertini, the curate of Zola Predosa, was clubbed to death, flayed, and quartered on May 9, 1716: he manifested no "temptation," said he had no particular devotion, and showed himself to be "obedient and very accepting of God's will," kneeling without resistance when the moment came to be "clubbed." On the other hand, Giacomo d'Antonio Stegani, guilty of homicide and robbery, did have one specific "temptation," expressing a desire for tobacco, but desisted in his requests when asked "that he be patient for a little while" (until dawn on December 2, 1719). The form about him concludes by declaring that "his spirit expired with the signs and demonstrations of a true Christian, and of a true penitent." Signs and demonstrations: the words refer to what was seen, to the behaviors witnessed by the public. The "consolers" did not express personal opinions about what they thought would come of the souls of the executed. They reported the outcome of an undertaking that had to achieve the result of moving and edifying the crowd summoned to watch the great spectacle of Christian death. The success they aspired to was that of a theater director: the admiration of the public, the spectators' gratitude for those who had worked to stage the event. "The whole city remained full of admiration for such comforting" is how one pupil rounded off his report on October 10, 1722, expressing his pride about a job well done. But this case offers an opportunity to get a better view of what went on backstage. The pupil in question was Carlo Antonio Macchiavelli, who was then just starting out as a comforter. The man whose misfortune it was to play the part of sacrificial victim and lead actor was Leonardo Antonio Gaetano Capobianchi, originally from Naples but who lived in Bologna, and who had been sentenced to death by hanging for "great theft" and possession of a prohibited weapon (a dagger). In his case we do not have the usual preprinted form, but three distinct manuscript reports: one by Macchiavelli, the pupil, another by Pietro Soprani, the master, and a third unsigned one. Reading them it becomes apparent why there was a departure from the established rules in this case (the final module should have been the work of the pupil, then checked and corrected by the master). During the night of October 9–10, Leonardo Antonio had arrived in the chapel of Santa Maria della Morte, where he had been greeted by the members of the School, presided over at that time by Marchese Paris Maria Grassi. The first master-and-pupil pair had gone to work. According to Macchiavelli their exchanges with the prisoner immediately appeared to be "of great satisfaction to the patient himself, who was most obedient in all and everything demanded of him. He showed himself always to be utterly resigned to God's will, and never gave any sign of a change in the sentiments he had had right from the beginning, that is, of not wishing to seek anything other than to save his soul": as for his having been sentenced to death, Leonardo "fully recognized he was deserving not just of the death that had been prescribed by justice as punishment for his crimes," but also of the other, second death. He even displayed enthusiasm when the final moment came: he received "cheerfully, and with the admiration of all, the summons to go to his death." Along the route to the scaffold, he never took his eyes off the *tavoletta*. A successful outcome, then, and unexpected too—because when he had first been informed of the sentence he had manifested the "feelings of a desperate person."

In his report the master Pietro Soprani described those feelings. Leonardo had received the news of his sentence from the prior of the Celestines, who normally followed the ritual of execution with special devotions. In the presence of the prior and two other churchmen—a lay priest and a Jesuit—the condemned man protested loudly: he said "that he was innocent, and that it was a great injustice to make him die, he who had been led astray, and to send his companion, who had led him astray, to jail." He declared that "the following morning he wanted to make it very clear to all the people, even on the scaffold, the great injustice that was being done to him." Furious and desperate, he said that "for his own part he was willing to give his body to the executioner and his soul to the devil." When asked why he wanted to "so wickedly damn his soul," he replied: "to give remorse to his Eminence and to the judges." He did not want to listen to objections, nor was he moved by threats of hell. But how, they asked him, did he think he could endure the fires of hell when he had been unable to resist the *veglia,* the terrible torment rendered notorious by the case of Tommaso Campanella and which involved keeping the prisoner awake for forty hours in excruciating pain. An argument began at this point: Leonardo asked what hell was, and instead of meekly accepting the declaration that believing in hell was a matter of faith, he had shouted that "as the soul had to burn, he wanted the body to burn as well, and the ashes scattered in the wind." He yelled other things as well. But then, following an affectionate intervention by the lay priest, the man's mood changed: "two tears formed in the eyes of that one [the prisoner]." The priest embraced him, and Leonardo, "addressing that one [the priest], said: 'So will I, such a great sinner, be saved?'" And the priest said: "I assure you of it, and when you want it God wants it." From that moment on, things took the desired course: Leonardo made his confession to the Celestine curate and, fully contrite, then arrived in the School's chapel.

The third report, manuscript and unsigned, omitted this initial phase of desperation and was given over to a very detailed account, but without any mention of incidents or difficulties, of the path of events prior to the execution: Prior Grassi being informed of the impending execution; the summoning of the confraternity; the meeting in the company's headquarters, with the usual prayers and the handing over of the *tavoletta* to be held in front of the condemned man's eyes; the transfer to the chapel of Santa Maria del Popolo in Piazza Maggiore; the reciting of prayers before the people gathered "in very great number"; the transfer to the *conforteria;* and the arrival and handing over of Leonardo. Here we read of the affectionate greeting the condemned man received, to which he responded with many "niceties of feeling and of submission to divine will," after which the comforting began, with Leonardo's account, "in a low, subdued voice," of how he had become resigned to his fate. What emerges is the portrait of a profoundly devout man: he said that he was accustomed to going to the shrine of the Madonna di San Luca every Saturday, and listed many other similar practices; he recited the Miserere, the Prayer of Repentance, demonstrating that he knew Latin; and he "was most fond of certain verses, and these he repeated with the greatest tenderness and tears of regret." He wanted to make a general confession and accepted all the indulgences granted to him. He declared that "he was dying willingly to satisfy the will of the Supreme Omnipotent Almighty and the justice of men, regulated by that of the Lord himself." He had just one doubt: he had "heard it said many times that the father Saint Augustine says that of a hundred who die at the hands of justice barely one is saved." This was a widespread opinion in the prison world and often came up during conversations in the *conforteria.* He was told that Augustine had never written anything of the sort, and his fears were allayed by this. The details of his final walk to the gallows stress his exemplary and spontaneous behavior, through to the very last act, when Leonardo wanted to cover his eyes with a cap "in order not to be distracted by any external object," and fell from the ladder, "saying, in a voice clearly heard by onlookers, 'Glory to the living Jesus and Mary.'" And on this occasion the report-writer concluded that one must firmly believe in the salvation of the man's soul. Three reports, three different faces of one man, whose deep-rooted devotion could not in any case be doubted.

Not all the "patients" were so steeped in religious practices and so prone to devout tears. A certain Stefano Sartoni, hung on Saturday, May 16, 1722, proved to be quite withdrawn, though he was not "at all coarse and uncultured" either. The ritual was complicated in his case by the fact that the cardinal legate, disgusted by the scenes of death in Piazza Maggiore, decided that the execution should take place on the outskirts of the city, in the area occupied by the market (today's Montagnola). This meant that the comforters had to be transported on a cart pulled by two oxen and led by a peasant, who, in being visibly such ("without being dressed up"), would have appeared unsightly to the upper-class *confratelli*. Sartoni followed on foot together with the executioner, who kept him on a rope like an animal being taken off for slaughter. On this occasion too there were "innumerable people." Everything went off in an orderly fashion: in the afternoon the procession of company members arrived at the church of San Giovanni al Mercato, where the body was buried, while one of the brothers (Carlo Antonio Macchiavelli) climbed onto the scaffold to remove the noose. A hint of frustration can nonetheless be detected in the final report, and not just because the rain had soaked the brothers' hoods. There had been something of a dip in style, which had perplexed and displeased the comforter.

The execution ritual followed a repetitive routine. Everyone in the city was familiar with it, and expected events to occur with the same order and timing. This is what normally happened, and postponements were not allowed. For instance, a "patient" who begged for the opportunity to see his brother who lived some distance from the city was told that the hour of execution could not be deferred. And the sixteen-year-old boy who could not believe that he was going to die so young was not even given the time to cry for himself. Protests about injustices, high-handed behavior, and disparities in treatment were always silenced. Gianfrancesco Carbonati, executed in Piazza Maggiore on April 3, 1751, for having helped to gild some silver coins, was told that he should not complain about the gravity of the punishment and the difference between his sentence and the happier fate of others who had been more directly responsible for the counterfeiting—he had after all been involved in a crime of lèse-majesté. As for those who had gone unpunished, he was reminded to intercede for them in God's tribunal so that they too might have the good fortune to enjoy a Christian death like his.

The form of execution was not the same for everyone: those from noble stock could count on decapitation, a death that "was not ignominious even in the world," as Giuseppe Gessi, put to death on March 13, 1745, was told. Commoners, on the other hand, had to resign themselves to an infamous death on the gallows. And if anyone demonstrated reluctance—like the fisherman Pellegrino Torri, executed on May 28, 1727—it was explained to him that he had to endure the "scandal" (his word) of the gallows in the city square and of having his body left dangling there, while his desire was to "be quickly detached and taken down from the scaffold." The written reports recount how people of every age and condition went down this route. But the diversity of the individuals and the crimes committed disappeared in the fixity of the ritual—a combination of sacred liturgy and theater, a *sacra rappresentazione* in which the condemned were figurants who performed, with few variations, a part known to the spectators in advance. And everyone, or almost everyone, behaved in the preestablished and desired manner. Everyone, or almost everyone, converted, confessed, received Communion, attended the masses celebrated for them, went out into the square and died, displaying signs of devotion. Respect for the Aristotelian rule of the unity of time appears to have been absolute. In the brief interval of time between arrival in the *conforteria* in the evening and the tolling of the bell of justice in the morning, the drama behind closed doors saw the central figurant changing each time but without any possibility of altering the script. The final dénouement before the crowd in the city square was connoted by varying degrees of commotion, but virtually all the condemned did nothing other than commit themselves to God and pray. If on occasion one of them said something to the onlookers it was only to ask them to pray for him and to promise that he would then do the same for them from heaven. Now while the unity of time and its fixed rhythm shaped the final outcome, preventing any of the condemned person's wishes being granted and forcing him to start contemplating his impending and inevitable death straightaway, another condition had to be respected to achieve such a uniformity in the result. Everyone—bandit, highwayman, aristocrat, murderer, infanticide—shared with the members of the *conforteria* a series of habits instilled in them from early childhood: prayers (the Rosary, the Pater, the Ave Maria), sacraments, sacred rites, patron saints, and so on. They moved in a society where the ringing of the church bell, the outline of the campanile, and the shrine combined with images in language, habitual gestures (the sign of the cross, kissing the crucifix, kneeling in front of a niche containing a sacred image). The imminence of death and the inexorability of the sentence, filtered through the enticing offers of consolation made by solemn figures with a cross emblazoned on their attire, reactivated, in the closed confines of the *conforteria,* all that life experience and shifted their thoughts from the actions of the criminal court to the sentence of the other court, peopled with saints and martyrs, and awaiting them in the life to come. From the most illiterate person to the most cultured, everyone had certain "devotions": it is no accident that a question about devotions was near the top of the list in the comforters' module. First there was a question about the prisoner's "passions," with an unburdening of the feelings provoked by the recent discovery of their fate. Then there were the "temptations"—the mistaken thoughts toward which the mind might turn. And then came the question about what the condemned person's habitual devotions were, together with the invitation to duly "cultivate them."

The coercive force of criminal law and the persuasive one of religion would not in themselves have been enough to ensure the smooth unfolding of the scaffold ritual. Another essential element was the widespread consensus of society. This can be illustrated by the case of Pellegrino Stefani, sentenced to death for homicide in August 1778. He had already been in jail for a year and a half. When he was taken to the *conforteria* he saw the familiar face of his parish priest, together with members of the School. Also familiar to him were the patterns of devotion and beliefs proposed to him: he immediately showed himself to be "sufficiently educated, and he always paid the greatest attention to the instructions that were given to him regarding doctrine, and for the whole night it gave him great pleasure that they suggested heart-stirring thoughts and prayers to him." He was "very resigned, full of docility, and so grateful for the office of charity performed for him by the gentlemen masters and pupils that he thanked each one in the most affectionate terms, and promised that when he arrived in heaven he would be sure to remember such charity." But then came a sign of how society at large gathered around to follow the course of the ritual. There was still one thought that troubled Pellegrino: what would come of his wife and three children (a boy and two girls) after his death? At this point it seemed to the comforter that the Almighty intervened. Passing amid the many curious onlookers gathered in front of the Palazzo Pretorio was Marchese Giuseppe Giovagnoni, who inquired how things were going. The reply was reassuring: they were going well, but the patient was worried about his family. The marchese went home, and wrote a note to the censor, telling him to let the patient know that he, Marchese Giovagnoni, would give fifteen ducats a month to the widow (naturally only "as long as she lived in a state of widowhood"). One can only imagine "how this news was received" by the "patient" and how "he became even more fervent in his resignation." Stefani wanted to respond in some way to such civic charity: when the procession set out for Piazza del Mercato, surrounded by a great crowd restrained with difficulty by the Swiss guard, he went beyond what was expected of him. The comforter asked him to repeat in a low voice the suggested prayers and invocations, but he was determined to repeat them in a loud voice, "saying he wished in this way to give a good example to the people."[26]

Was it possible to remain unaffected by the influence of shared cultural and religious horizons, to elude the blackmail of divine justice as the inspirer of human justice? The "atheist" of 1622 had not managed it. Nor did the various people condemned by the Holy Office, among whom we will search in vain for someone capable of defending a different conception of the world and of God. Not the Lutheran, far less the fake priest desirous to practice such an important, venerated, and socially protected profession. The rituals of the Holy Office's sentence were perfectly welded together and overlapped with those of the *conforteria*. An idea of how this came to be so can be gleaned from the printed report on the treatment handed out to a man from Modena named Giovanni Menghi, known as "la bella Gioanna," who stole the pyx and the monstrance, together with the consecrated Hosts they contained, from the church of Castelguelfo.[27] Chased "a furor di popolo" to the sound of alarm bells, he took refuge in Faenza but it did him little good. Imprisoned for a year in San Domenico di Bologna, on June 19, 1744, the inquisitor of Bologna proclaimed the sentence of excommunication from a "lugubrious platform," accompanied by a solemn speech. Giovanni Menghi, immediately handed over to the secular arm, was assisted during the night by the company of justice before being hung and then quartered the following morning. His behavior left all the people, who had already been "softened and made contrite" by the Inquisitor's speech, edified and immersed in devout thoughts.

Sometimes difficulties arose due to the overly scrupulous behavior of the condemned, who took the call to repent too seriously. For example, there was a murderer who worried that he had caused the eternal damnation of those he had killed: this was the case of Francesco Borghi, executed on December 10, 1777. In order to ease his fears, it was necessary to evoke the boundless mercy of God, who would have "forgiven Judah as well, and his crucifiers, if they had repented." It proved more difficult to placate a young man from the Veneto, Giacomo Naldi, on November 14, 1784, who was "of acute and great ingenuity" and had a keen interest in theological issues. He was convinced "that the path to heaven was narrow" and therefore reserved only for the just. Well versed in the Holy Scriptures, he had Jansenistic leanings, and the controversies of the age about the wide and the narrow path to heaven had made an impression on him. His only devotion was "a lengthy meditation on the life and passion of the Lord," which is how in his case the public part of the ritual set a fine religious example.

We have to wait until the end of the eighteenth century to find an instance of anomalous behavior: Luigi Tamburini, a young Bolognese, was brought to the *conforteria* on March 13, 1790. When he arrived, he was "hostile, with the obstinate declaration that he did not want to convert and that he wanted to be damned." He had already shown his strength of mind in prison, with an attitude of "stubborn impenitence," and he reacted to his death sentence "with mocking contempt." He stuck to this position for several hours, with "affected nonchalance." The comforters even resorted to the old ploy used with heretics and Jews in the previous century: making him feel the heat of a lit candle to instill terror at the thought of the sufferings of hell. Everything seemed to be of no avail, until the parish priest of Santa Caterina di Saragozza, who had admitted Tamburini to his first Communion, came to visit him. This affectionate contact and the recollection of his adolescence was all it took for him to break down in tears, paving the way for a devout end. The impulse provided by the man's memory of his first Communion led him back to an ingrained religion he had moved away from but never forgotten. There is something in this that recalls the case of Pietro Paolo Boscoli. And, what is more, signs that times had changed can also be seen in the final cases of the dossier. "Very ignorant" and in need of being instructed in the "rudiments of Christian doctrine" was, for example, the description given of Vincenzo Cottignola, known as "la creatura" ("the creature"), executed on the Montagnola on February 26, 1791.

These were the unsettled times of the French Revolution, and notions of liberty were spreading through Italy as well. And it was on the Montagnola in Bologna—to where the execution site had been moved when the sensibilities of the ruling orders had begun to find the scenes of human butchery in the city center unbearable—that the execution of Giovan Battista De Rolandis took place on April 23, 1796. A young Piedmontese student, little more than twenty years old, he had been involved in a plot to foment a popular uprising in the name of liberty. He arrived at the scaffold almost in a swoon. During the previous night he had appeared to the School's comforters to be "too oppressed by passion," unable to engage in "long conversations," tormented by the thought of the pain he was about to give his mother—voiced by the intermittent lament "My poor mother." He had remained in bed virtually all the time, and the cakes and wine offered to him by the comforters had not revived him either. He had been physically brought to the place where the executioner had dispensed the blow to his temple to stun him. Then, having been placed on a chair, he had been taken to the Montagnola, where, "with Catholic sentiments, his soul passed away."[28] Before him, on August 17, 1795, his friend Luigi Zamboni had committed suicide in prison, leaving on the walls of his cell a final farewell to the woman he loved, an epigraph in French expressing his ideals of liberty and equality, together with his signature ("Luigi Zamboni, Bolognese democrat") beneath a denunciation of Antonio Socci, the traitor who had obtained impunity as a reward for revealing the conspiracy. Zamboni's body was buried in a place called "'il Malcantone,' where unbelievers are usually buried."

The attempt to get the city to embrace the cause of liberty ended like this: leaflets handed out by the conspirators by night spoke the new language of freedom and of rights—those of citizens, to set against the abuses of the ruling orders. But the people had not reacted, and the liberty dreamed of by Luigi Zamboni was brought to Bologna by the troops of Napoleon Bonaparte. With the cardinal legate, who was ignominiously expelled from the city, went the forms of religious ritual of the death penalty. A proclamation to the people issued by the Jacobin club of Bologna promised the advent of real justice. But the fracture between old and new would prove less radical and more fraught with compromise than what was promised, as was promptly demonstrated by the brief return of the old regime with the interlude created by the Austrian-Russian army. One example of this was the career of the man of letters and publisher Angelo Sassoli, who had been part of Zamboni's conspiracy but had then secretly reported it to the papal authorities. He devoted his life after that to the search for literary glory, but the betrayals continued, no longer of people but of texts. His cobbling together of Ugo Foscoli's *Ultime lettere di Jacopo Ortis (The Last Letters of Jacopo Ortis)* in the first Bolognese edition was inspired by an attempt to adapt the texts to suit the rapidly changing times.

27

Devotions for Executed Souls: Precepts and Folklore

ONCE IT HAD BEEN brought into the heart of the city, the great spectacle of capital punishment also conquered the heart of every strand of civic culture, from the erudition of the universities and academies to popular devotions. The basic ingredients were curiosity about the secrets of the human body and the fate of souls in the world to come. It is hard to deal, even roughly, with the many forms this took in the local traditions of the Catholic world. If we were to name the causes in order of importance, we would have to list them under the key dimensions of the Catholic revival in the age of the Counter-Reformation: the revitalization of ecclesiastic mediation between the living and the dead linked to devotion for souls in purgatory, and the centrality of the sacraments of confession and Communion as efficacious channels of divine grace. The Christ of the Good Friday rituals, wounded and crowned with thorns; the Forty Hours' Devotion of the Blessed Sacrament; and the vast spread of the practice of general confession and of spiritual direction gave expression to the idea that humanity was burdened by sin, threatened by the prospect of looming death, and in search of heavenly protectors. The plight of the prisoner facing execution thus came to symbolize a general human condition. The figure of Saint Joseph, who until then had been a shadowy presence in the history of devotion, became extraordinarily popular. Traditionally represented as a very elderly person, more a grandfather than a husband for the Virgin Mary, given the need to banish any suspicion of sexual relations between them, he was afforded a special patronage over those nearing the end of their lives. The image of the death of Saint Joseph as a model of Christian death thus assumed an important place in devout iconography and religious patronage.[1] In this way he ended up in competition with Saint John the Baptist as the protector of those destined for the scaffold, taking his place among the patron saints of the companies of justice. The attribution of patrons to the many devout associations that sprang up to form a dense undergrowth around the large, ancient trees of the companies of justice brought particular popularity. Of these, the Congregazione degli Agonizzanti—the Congregation of the Dying—was especially successful. Set up with the blessing of Pope Paul V to ensure that those who were about to die had a religious end, it specialized in a range of devout strategies, including prayers and masses. The congregation in Palermo was dedicated to the Virgin, whereas the one in Bologna chose Michael the Archangel, the saint positioned at the gates of heaven with a flaming sword. The Sicilian congregation of the Agonizzanti was founded in 1614 after comforters met with failure in one of their cases: "a poor wretch who had been sentenced to the gallows, though the brothers of the noble Company of the Whites endeavored with all their ability to lead the unhappy stubborn heart to a timely conversion, . . . rendered vain their most pious labors; their efforts were to no avail, and he ended life leaving everyone uncertain, afflicted with doubt, and critical of his end."[2] The social composition of the Agonizzanti was similar to the Company of the Whites, as membership was reserved for "either knights, or doctors of law, or lay priests."[3] The statutes of the Bolognese company, founded in 1627, drew instead on the vocabulary of merchant trading. The members were described as "merchants of souls," because "they labor with the divine merchant Christ for the health of those [souls], with the capital of the merits of Christ himself, obtaining for Christ the profit of glory, and merit and reward for themselves." But behind the traditional language of trade, a military language was emerging as well: the Agonizzanti could in fact be defined as a military company in the service of captain Christ, because it fought "on behalf of the dying in the perilous conflict of the death throes."[4] The company's heraldic device was not the image of the crucified Christ but that of a Christ who was "dying, half-alive, and breathing his last."[5] Naturally, the members of these congregations played a role in the rituals of justice, organizing special "exercises of piety" and collectively reciting short prayers and litanies on the days when executions took place to "beg for the well-being of the soul of the condemned."[6] They were not the only ones. Other bodies sprang up as well, whose members would line the route taken by the ritual procession of justice. Later, in the cosmopolitan climate of the eighteenth century, Pope Benedict had the idea of promoting a "Pious Union to bring comfort to the souls of executed wretches in the whole Catholic world."[7] The Italian context provided fertile ground for initiatives like these, as over the previous century a great many associations and religious orders had been engaged in devout exercises to transform capital punishment into a great holy ritual. This movement was facilitated by a reduction in the number of executions and in the violence of aggravated punishments, welcomed by an Enlightenment culture which was reflecting on the legacy of an uncomfortable past. The erudite abbots active in the *conforterie* also voiced their satisfaction about the change in atmosphere: "Today's comforters," wrote Abbot Girolamo Baruffaldi, "should be consoled [by the fact] that the slaughters once ordered by the courts to torment condemned wretches are no longer in use. Besides the noose and beheading, few other punishments continue to be exercised in Italy, and these are hammering, pincering, and cutting off of the hand; and it must be said that the crime of the condemned person must have been atrocious to arrive at such a horrible resolution."[8] In actual fact, Baruffaldi's view that the sufferings inflicted by the courts in eighteenth-century Europe had eased off was decidedly optimistic. In comparison with the criminal procedures outside Italy, the impression is that the court practices of other European countries were much harsher. To cite just one example, which made a big impact on public opinion in western Europe at the time, it is hard to remain unmoved when reading Voltaire's description of the execution of Johann Reinhold Patkul, a nobleman from Livonia, carried out at the behest of King Charles XII of Sweden on October 10, 1707. As Voltaire related in his *Histoire de Charles XII,* Patkul bravely endured terrible, protracted torture on the wheel, which broke his limbs one by one without killing him. Eventually he was hanged, and after his heart and entrails had been removed, the body was cut into four and the head impaled on a pike, while the executioner took the fat that was due to him.[9]

The blessed sacrament was displayed on altars and boxes were circulated in the neighborhood to collect alms to pay for the many masses said in remembrance of the dead, a significant ledger-book item for a clergy that was continually growing in number. If the church of a convent or religious body was situated on the route taken by the procession of justice, the door was left open as an invitation to the condemned person to make a final stop. This was a custom associated with devotion for souls in purgatory, which had put down solid roots in religion and folklore, making it possible to bind together family remembrance and that of society as a whole. As Natalie Zemon Davis once suggested, Protestantism, by doing away with purgatory, channeled the tie with ancestors into private feelings of family and stock.[10] In Catholic society, on the other hand, the relationship with the dead continued to find a collective outcome in the generalized exchange of protection and spiritual help between the living and the dead. This is where the idea came from that the plight of the executed—the most wretched imaginable—would render their souls particularly grateful to those who remembered them in their prayers. But there was more to it than that, because those were the souls which, to recompense the living who had expressed devotion for them, should be the most ready to save those in danger of losing their lives. Learned theologians, always fearful of the devil's presence in stories of spirits, resisted this notion. But even the most doubtful, though pointing out that such apparitions might be the work of demons "pretending to be the souls of purgatory," added reassuringly: "The common and truest opinion of the doctors is that sometimes the souls of purgatory, by divine permission, come to help us."[11] The Jesuit preacher Paolo Segneri tapped into popular opinion very forthrightly in his sermons, with stories like this one:

> In the year 1620, near Rome, there was a man who, despite his various dissolute ways, professed a special affection for the souls of purgatory, whom he succored with frequent suffrages. Now it so happened that, having become caught up in some very bad blood and in order not to lose his life, he went off alone one night on horseback toward the city of Tivoli, fleeing from the might of his enemies. But the wretch did not realize that though he was fleeing their might he was heading toward their deception, because his adversaries had learned of his journey and four armed men were already waiting for him along the road, hidden behind a bush. He was already close to falling into the ambush, when, coming upon an oak from which there hung the quarters of a notorious killer who had not long before been executed nearby, he halted for a while to say a few prayers for the soul of the dead man. It was then that he saw something of the utmost wonder. He saw those parts joining together again under their head to form a man, who, leaping upright, approached our friend and, grabbing his horse by the bridle, said: "Be pleased to dismount and wait for me here without

leaving, I'll be back in a moment." Be in no doubt that he was very quick to obey the order he had received to stand still. He was so frozen with fear that he could not even loosen his tongue to reply, nor his legs to flee. He stood motionless, and the other man mounted and continued along the path on horseback, until, after just a few steps he ran into the ambush set by the four armed men, who, in the dimness of the night, believing him to be their enemy, fired at him with all their harquebuses; and, seeing him fall to the ground, they promptly ran off, as it were, before people rushed [to the scene]. The man feigning death got back to his feet and led the horse back to where he had stopped its owner, to whom he revealed the singular good he had done him, saying that the ambush had been organized for him, in which he would undoubtedly have died, in body and soul, if he, in the name of purgatory, which he knew well and which rewards its benefactors, had not hurried to his aid. . . . Having said that, and returning to being a corpse like before, dividing into four parts in the original place under the oak, he left the man so changed in his heart that a few days later he donned the habit of a very strict religious order, finishing there in a saintly fashion the life that had been in danger of ending so unfortunately.[12]

Stories like this one originated in folklore, where the miracle of the hanged man was an old tradition: but now, instead of the Virgin or a saint intervening to miraculously save a devout condemned criminal, it was the dead hanged man who became the protector and savior of the person who prayed for him. This change also owes something to the prolonged efforts of the companies of justice in plugging the legitimacy and religious utility of capital punishment. Confirmation of the elevation of the hanged person to the role of celestial protector can be found in a painted image in the oratory of Taggia in Liguria: an anonymous painter of ex-votos depicted an episode similar to the one narrated by Segneri. It shows a bodyguard of skeletons brandishing weapons and sticks, and rushing to save a wayfarer being attacked right in front of the oratory. The inscription in the cartouche reads: "Don't touch our friends and benefactors."[13]

The conviction that succor needed to be offered to souls in purgatory was spread by terrifying representations of their sufferings: in that place, a Jesuit wrote, "every torment . . . is greater than any torment in the present life." And so, he asked, "will being buried in flame, in comparison to which our flames are cold ash, not be the most terrible constriction?"[14] Help could come from those who, in the grace of God, dedicated to souls in purgatory the merits they earned through fasts, alms-giving, and prayers. But "such work is neither meritorious nor satisfactory" when offered by those "in the disfavor of God," unless, that is, it "has virtue *ex opere operato,* like the Mass," in which case "it will benefit them, even if the priest is a villain."[15] That the sacraments were efficacious irrespective of the moral defects of the officiant was a well-established tenet of ancient Church doctrine, having taken root in the struggle with the Patarine reform movement in the Middle Ages. In this context though, it had the effect of channeling all the resources in a single direction, and indeed the alms collected when there was an execution primarily went on masses.

However, the devotion for souls in purgatory, when applied to the souls of the condemned, yielded an outcome which the masters of orthodox devotion had not envisaged: people who died at the hands of justice were attributed with mysterious powers, and their souls were invoked in rites of magic. Between the sixteenth and seventeenth century the inquisitors of the Holy Office found themselves dealing with the spread of short prayers addressed to executed souls, like the one below:

> Anime giustitiate,
> per tutto il mondo andate,
> foste levate, accompagnate, foste impiccate,
> foste squartate, toccaste la fune,
> tutte quante in piedi vi rizzarete,
> al cuore del popolo voi andrete,
> se qui me lo merrete,
> tanto bene da me harete.[16]

> (Souls of the executed,
> Go throughout the world,
> You were dragged and accompanied, you were hung,
> You were quartered, your lot was the rope,
> All of you will rise to your feet,
> To the heart of the people you will go,
> If you serve me here,
> Much good you will have from me.)

This short invocation was reported to the inquisitor of Tuscany in 1639 by a Florentine prostitute, Margherita Cucchi. Its purpose, she said, was to induce unfaithful lovers to return. A set number of prayers had to be said before reciting it (nine Our Fathers and nine Hail Marys), and precise rituals were to be observed while doing so: "the hands had to be kept behind [your back], holding the crown, and while saying and doing these things you had to walk around the house." There is an evident mimesis of the hanging scene here: the hands tied behind the back, the crown, the walking around the house. They were scenes with which Margherita must have been very familiar. She lived, according to the trial reports, in a street near the Tempio, the place where the executed were buried. This is no coincidence: the same mechanism of social rejection generally forced prostitutes to occupy the same area as cemeteries of this kind. However, it was not an individual action, intended to re-elaborate autobiographic experiences. What Margherita did had been taught to her as part of an oral transmission of knowledge that accompanies the culture of writing like an underground river. Practices such as the one described by Margherita seem timeless, part of a patrimony transmitted without any trace of the circumstances of the first occurrence or of the author's name. The date of the record certainly does not tell us even approximately when the practice started. If anything, it might help us to understand why texts which had long been circulating in social practices surfaced in writing and in the circles of power. It is a fact that between the end of the sixteenth and the beginning of the seventeenth century the judicial and policing machine of the ecclesiastic Inquisition devoted itself to uprooting a series of practices and beliefs—rituals and myths—deemed to be magical, superstitious, or heretical. Among these a separate space was occupied by the use of particular "prayers" that were recited with specific rules of execution and which were generically classified as *ad amorem*. Jealous lovers, abandoned women, and vengeful partners turned to the relevant specialists for remedies designed to make the loved one return or at any rate to prevent them from finding comfort with anyone else. Specialists of this kind were found in the world of paid love—prostitutes. They could be asked to recite the prayers *ad amorem,* or to teach customers how to say them at home. This is how the courts responsible for controlling faith ended up accusing many prostitutes from the sixteenth century onward. These were not just ecclesiastic courts, nor were prostitutes the only ones involved: in Lucca, for example, in 1571, the "office for religion" put a woman on trial for witchcraft, and she also confessed to having used the incantation of the executed.[17] The machinery of the Catholic inquisitions swung into action, then, against this field of incantations and prayers: between the end of the sixteenth and the beginning of the seventeenth century, from Catholic Italy to the most far-flung Spanish colonies, the inquisitorial tribunals systematically recorded, among other rites and myths, those based on the invocation of the executed.

When these orally transmitted texts started to be used is not known with certainty. They appear timeless, the fruit of ancient lore. For those attempting to interpret them, though, the question of their meaning is posited in historical terms: the appeal to the "souls of the executed" relates in fact to two quite distinct social practices of great importance in the history of preindustrial culture and religion: capital punishment and relations with the dead.

Those who died at the hands of the executioner resisted, by the very nature of their death, the order imposed on the dead as an age group with the creation of a special space—purgatory. The violence that truncated their lives prevented them being peaceably slotted into the ordinary category. These forcibly interrupted lives still found expression in the vengeful wandering of souls who, according to a common representation, roamed the places of earthly life. That restless moving about the house, which Margherita described to the inquisitor, evoked the wanderings of the wild army upon whom death had been forced, and whose power people invoked.

Inquisition documents reveal other traces of the diffusion of this ritual and myth. In Venice, in 1587, two women, Valeria Brugnalesco and her daughter Splandiana Mariani, after being denounced by a certain Lucrezio Cilla, were brought before the Holy Office on charges of performing divinatory practices of a magical nature. One of these practices is described as follows: "They go disheveled at all hours of the night, and beseech the clouds with diabolic incantations for five hanged men, for five quartered men, for five damned men, for five who died in irons, for the five greatest demons in hell, who must rise up and go and torment the heart of the one she wanted."[18] One particular prayer was addressed to a named suicide, known as "the one of the golden apple who hung himself from its tree." The incantation is reported indirectly, but recognizable in it is the one related firsthand by Margherita Cucchi a century later: "Going to the balcony at night, beseeching the clouds for the five hanged, for the five quartered, for the five damned, for the five who died in irons, for the five greatest demons in hell, who had to rise up and go into the heart of the one she wanted brought back home."[19] The mechanism of the analogy was obvious: "She said that she did that because, as that soul . . . had torment, so too the one for whom she said these Our Fathers might have torment."[20] This testimony shows the limits of the success of the companies in gaining acceptance for the notion of the eternal salvation of those condemned to death: the hanged person, like the suicide and in general those who died a violent death, was imagined to be a soul afflicted by the punishments of hell. A Venetian variant of the incantation went like this: "I beseech you on behalf of that Great Devil who has people quartered, has people burned, has people hanged."[21]

Torment and punishment are the leitmotifs of an incantation found widely in a popular culture that combined various local expressions of devotion. The protagonists were once again those who died on the scaffold, and they vary in number between five and three. In Venice there are five, in Sicily three:

> San Giuvanni decullatu | tri brizzi, tri mpisi e tri nnigati | tutti novi v' aviti a uniri | Avanti a Diu nn'aviti a ghiri | E tantu lu priati e lu strinciti | Ca a mmia di sti peni mi livati.[22]
>
> (Saint John the Beheaded | three murdered, three hanged and three drowned | you must all nine unite | before God you must present yourselves | and pray to him and enjoin him | until you release me from these torments.)

The release from torments—a problem of the living reflected in the dead as an age group. For victims of the scaffold the torments of the afterlife must have been particularly onerous due to the crimes that weighed upon their souls. But there was more: though they were defined as "saintly souls," they could be asked for help concerning the torments of love with greater frankness and freedom than with others who dwelt in the heavenly world. So this was how a distant husband or disaffected lover could be brought back:

> San Giuvanni decullatu | tri brizzi, tri impisi e tri nnigati | tutti novi v' aviti a uniri | Avanti a Diu vi 'naviti a gghiri | E tantu lu priati e lu strinciti | Ca a mmia di sti peni mi livati | Porta battiri | Campani sunari

| Friscu friscari | Cani abbairi | Tantu mi partu di Vui Signuri |
Quandu sentu battituri.[23]

(Saint John the Beheaded | three murdered, three hanged, and
three drowned | you must all nine unite | before God you must present
yourselves | and pray to him and enjoin him | until you release me
from these torments | Doors that slam | Bells that ring | Whistles that
whistle | Dogs that bark | I will take my leave of you Lord | When I
hear knocking.)

Another version of the prayer, which still seems to have been widespread
in Sicily, is the one recited "to get a distant husband or disaffected lover to
return home":

Armuzzi santi decullati | Tri accisi, tri mpisi e tri anniati | Tutti novi vi
iunciti | Avanzi all'eternu patri vinni iti | Ci cuntati li me nicissitati |
Animi santi nun m'abbandunati | E a . . . [name] intra mmannati.[24]

(Dear beheaded saintly souls, | three murdered, three hung, and
three drowned, | you must all nine unite | before God you must present
yourselves | tell him of my needs, | saintly souls, do not abandon me,
and send [name] back home.)

The Sicilian strand of this special form of devotion seems to have developed at different times and later with respect to other areas of Italy. While
a company of justice did not begin operating in Palermo, the capital of the
viceroyalty, until 1541, the delay was offset by the blossoming of devotions
in the baroque age and the great popularity associated with tangible signs
of the brothers' activities. The impetus provided by the clergy to devotion
for souls in purgatory certainly contributed to this. The authoritative ecclesiastic endorsement for devotion regarding those who had died on the scaffold was most notably manifested by the church of the Madonna in Palermo:
situated near the Ponte dell'Ammiraglio, where, in 1785, a special cemetery
was consecrated for the bodies of the executed, it became a point of reference and a model for similar devotions in other towns and cities on the
island. The church had to be enlarged in 1857–1865 because of the growing
popularity of the cult. Many ex-votos were hung there by combatants in
the Risorgimento. And the devotion continued to live on in Sicily, where
Giuseppe Pitrè, a celebrated scholar of folkloristic tradition, found living

testimony of devotion for executed souls. The interweaving between clerical encouragement and popular reception had fueled a special devotion for the emarginated category of humankind comprising thieves and brigands who had ended up on the scaffold. They had attracted a kind of projection of identity, which was not limited to Sicily but spread throughout the peninsula, leaving traces in the folklore of various Italian regions.[25]

One scholar of Italian folklore wondered what it was that transformed the way in which Catholic Italy viewed the souls of executed criminals between the sixteenth and seventeenth century.[26] He pointed to "popular creativity" as the category that provided an answer to this question. Indeed, thanks to the cultural investment of the companies of justice in the overall Catholic framework of devout emphasis on the theme of purgatory, popular creativity had developed a special relationship with that particular category of souls, because it was possible to ask them things that were not permitted in prayers to saints and the Virgin.

In the old, deep-rooted fear of the dead, the devout investment in purgatory and the work of mediation carried out by the companies and, more generally, by the Catholic Church, had changed something. To understand what had happened we need to take account of a point emphasized by Aron Gurevič—namely, that people's perception of the world at that time stemmed from a "complex and contradictory interaction of the reservoir of traditional folklore and Christianity."[27] From this came a familiarity with the presence of the dead similar to the one identified by Robert Hertz in primitive societies: present as an age group, they watched over the society of the living in a way that could be vengeful but also protective. From the world of the afterlife the shadows of the dead carried powers of second sight and magic: as Marc Bloch has shown, the evocation of the shadow of Solomon narrated in the Jewish Bible resonated for a long time in medieval culture.[28] Despite efforts by theologians and clerical authorities to impose some kind of discipline on the dead by dividing them into different containers—hell, purgatory, heaven—in folkloristic culture the souls of the dead retained an unassailable freedom to interfere with the living. In the end, due to the effect of the arrangement imposed by erudite culture, exchanges, though still possible, were legitimated and encouraged only within certain limits: one could offer prayers and suffrages to the inhabitants of purgatory, and receive from them an intercession with the heavenly world. It was not permitted to invoke those in hell, the world of demons: the barrier imposed by the Inquisition in combating necromancy and pacts with Satan prohibited any attempt to make contact with the diabolic world of the damned. It was imagined that the souls of unrepentant criminals went there, and this was used as a threat to overcome the resistance of the condemned—and if they did not yield it was deduced that they were destined for certain damnation.

Preaching and folkloristic culture had very early on found in the figure of the impenitent condemned a protagonist of terrifying tales.[29] There was reason to fear that executed criminals would return after their deaths to inflict harm not on the living in general—this was feared from all the dead—but specifically on those who had accompanied them to the scaffold. The ritual of mutual forgiveness at the foot of the scaffold, the alms, and the remembrance masses were the currency of exchange designed to achieve a peaceful agreement. But fear of the envy of the dead remained, and the strong emphasis given to the theme of purgatory in the struggle with the Protestant Reformation exploited it extensively and systematically. With the devotion for souls in purgatory the precarious armistice in the battle between living and dead took on the appearance of a contract for the reciprocal supply of services. On the part of the living, remembrance masses provided the guarantee that memory of the dead remained undimmed; the latter were asked in exchange to transform a vengeful attitude into a protective one. From this came the appeal to the souls of the executed, which inevitably turned into devotion. While the devotion for souls in purgatory resulted in a proliferation of altars dedicated to them, at the initiative of the clergy, in the parallel world of practices of popular medicine and magic there took root the variant of devotion for the souls of the executed, who were called on to release the living from their torments in the name of those which they themselves had experienced. Suffering united the living and the dead: and when it came to matters of earthly hatred and love the souls of the condemned were the ones best suited to help.

In the first years of the nineteenth century a detailed investigation of popular rituals concerning birth, marriage, and death in the Napoleonic Kingdom of Italy uncovered many traces of a nonpacified relationship with the dead, who were feared and regarded as vengeful. Even the dying were considered dangerous: "in the event of death, if the dying person calls someone, it is said that this is the one who must follow him first."[30] But what were avoided and feared above all else were occasions of contact with those who died a violent death. There is recorded evidence of an identical custom being practiced in various parts of Italy: along roads where a cross marked and remembered a case of violent death, it was customary for passers-by to throw a stone at the foot of the cross. The classical culture that provided a common parameter to government officials of the age suggested to many the Latin formula for greeting the dead: *Sit tibi terra levis*—"May the earth rest lightly on you."[31] One attentive observer has noted the incongruence between the well-wishing greeting and the stone, which "indicates the opposite," as it is anything but light earth.[32] In actual fact, it takes little to understand the significance of the gesture: the wish to confine a threatening and potentially aggressive presence beneath the "heavy weight" of the stones.

The nineteenth-century investigation also touches on the theme of devotion for "executed souls." An informer in the Valtellina signaled "a marked bias in favor of the souls of the executed," and attempted to explain the phenomenon as follows: "Whether the bloody spectacle that the afflicted offer of themselves instills, together with fear, a feeling of compassion and affection; or whether the common people believe that no one dies more contrite and mollified than one who leaves his head on the stage, the fact is that these souls are invoked in many places with the formula *Dear executed souls*."[33]

From the Valtellina to Sicily the devotion for executed souls seemed at this time to be a component of Italian religion, drawing together the beliefs of folkloristic traditions and suggestions from preachers and missionaries. The meeting of these two threads resulted in a plethora of initiatives that brought into church spaces many confraternities from different denominations, all dedicated to offering devotions for souls in purgatory. While bodies and scaffold materials were traded outside the churches, confraternities of Prayer and Death, of Remembrance and of purgatory, sprang up inside, invariably in areas occupied by the remains of the dead. Churches dedicated to the "Anime del Purgatorio" (souls in purgatory) filled up with images of tormented souls, of skeletons and bones.[34] Instead of the "Bibliothèque bleu" (blue library) in France, which divulged literature dealing with lives of saints and marvelous tales, creating a special popular category of readers, peasant Italy had its "biblioteca nera"—black library—of short books of prayers. Good examples of such works were the black funeral booklets of

Saint Alfonso Maria de' Liguori's "eternal maxims," and other publications distributed during the popular missions—meditations and prayers printed in large red characters, for centuries the only books that circulated in a world of widespread and devout illiteracy. The exchange of forms of benefit and protection was multiplied by the mechanism of aggregations, whereby a patrimony of indulgences was built up that yielded substantial rewards for the members of the more remote and tiny confraternities. It was in this context that the "Pious Union" for devotions offered to the souls of the executed throughout the Catholic world was planned and set up.

This was the result of a major ecclesiastical investment in the relations of exchange and mutual assistance between the living and the dead, designed to weld Christian society into a bond of solidarity, exalting the function of reciprocal help and projecting it beyond the barriers of death. However, this flourishing form of devoutness began to be met by the resistance and re-forming aspirations of an enlightened Catholicism, which led to a first abrupt change in direction. It was in the sphere of devotion for executed souls that the history of Italy experienced one of its many fractures between north and south. In Austrian-ruled Lombardy, Emperor Joseph II put a stop to the work of the Milanese confraternity of San Giovanni alle Case Rotte, precisely in order to discourage the spread of the cult of executed souls, which was judged to be superstitious. This resulted in a parting of the ways for a special kind of devotion, the fruit of the impetus given by the post-Tridentine Church to the theme of purgatory and to the religious legitimation of the power to put people to death.

❧ 28 ❧

Dying without Trembling: The Carlo Sala Case and the End of the Milanese Confraternity

CHANGE WAS IN the offing, and this could be sensed in the experience of the confraternities as well, with a proliferation of cases where condemned prisoners showed that they no longer shared the metaphysical foundations of what the comforters proposed to them.

One such instance was the episode regarding Carlo Sala, recorded in the proceedings of the Scuola di San Giovanni alle Case Rotte when he entered the *conforteria* on September 23, 1775. Guilty of around thirty crimes of sacrilegious theft and of trading in and reading prohibited books, he tenaciously resisted all attempts to get him to abandon "perverse maxims" concerning religion in general and Christianity in particular. He was visited in jail by the "count regent Verri" (Gabriele), by whom he was "stimulated and enjoined to lay down his perverse maxims and retreat from his terrible condition of disbelief."[1] The sight of Count Verri in the guise of a Christian apologist is a rather unusual one for those who know about his son Pietro's battles in favor of the Enlightenment. In any case his comforting work "was all in vain." Carlo Sala spent the night before execution conversing with important visitors and with the company's comforters. He did not just engage in amiable chat, but gave further demonstration of exceptional self-control: "he ate well, always talking cheerfully and responding frankly to the kindness of the above-mentioned." In his replies he discussed religion, revealing himself to be a deist with a highly critical attitude toward Christianity, which he defined as a "very likely religion, divided, however, into various sects, some stricter, others gentler." He had embraced these convictions, wrote the *confratelli,* "under the dictation of Mons. Volterre [Voltaire]." Their horror over this miscreant prompted them to express themselves in terms worthy of the most superstitious medieval chronicler when describing what happened to his body following execution:

> The executioner went to Piazza Vetra with his helper and some foot soldiers, removed the corpse of the said impenitent—which had become as hideous as a monster—from the gallows and dragged it to one of the bastions of Porta Tosa, where, a deep trench having been made, he was buried, then carefully and thickly covered with earth, above which a headstone could be placed with the following inscription: "Iacet hic Carolus Sala turpiter suspensus in furcis. Vita, moribus et religione Satan."

These were not the details reported by Pietro Verri in a letter to his brother Alessandro, who was living in Rome at the time. What had struck him was Sala's behavior during the execution of the sentence and in the face of death: while the executioner cut off his hand "he remained as still as a marble." Verri, who held government office and was attentive to the public mood, reacted with dismay and concern: Sala's display of religious indifference bordering on derision had been cause for a "notorious scandal." And in his view the *confratelli* of San Giovanni Decollato had contributed to it by recounting details of Sala's behavior and "repeating the dialogues [they had had] with him." It would have been better to say nothing, as the result demonstrated: "One hears talk of insidious blasphemies that no one spoke about before."[2]

Pietro Verri and the Milanese social and cultural elite, well represented in the confraternity, were worried by a new climate of religious indifference and impiety. In his letter of reply, Alessandro said that the episode had provoked considerable comment in the city of the pope as well. But far from sharing his brother's concerns, he felt human admiration for Sala's courageous behavior: "It grieves me that such a soul is damned and such a man hanged."[3] What reemerges in their correspondence is the theme of the manner of dying on the scaffold, which had already arisen previously in the context of the fairly begrudging attention given to the international success of Cesare Beccaria's writings. During a trip Alessandro made to London, the brothers had exchanged news and impressions of the difference between the "English" and the "Italian" way of dying. Alessandro had described in abundant detail the execution of four condemned men from different social backgrounds (a sailor, a peasant, a lawyer, and a captain). The behavior of all four had been distinguished by "great sangfroid": one of them had even helped the executioner put the noose around his neck, as if putting on a piece of clothing. When they all had nooses on, they had begun praying and preaching to the audience. For an hour the men had sung psalms together with the friars, then they had been hung. Their lack of concern was not just due to the climate, in Alessandro's view, but also to the spread of irreligiousness: "Fears of a life to come are not very deep here."[4] A few days earlier Pietro had recounted to his brother that a killer named Mantegazza had been hung in Milan. The sentence had been just, in his view, but Pietro had been struck by the behavior of the condemned man, who had spontaneously thrown himself off the ladder "with the intrepidness of a man who clearly cares not a jot about the other life." This had caused consternation in the people, "who have no idea that it is possible to die without trembling."[5]

Pietro Verri's reaction to the Carlo Sala execution and his sensitivity toward the attitudes of the people give an idea of the contradictions nestling in the heart and mind of a Lombard aristocrat—not just any old nobleman, but a man with Verri's culture and past. Irrespective of his own personal case these contradictions help us to understand how and why the religious scaffold ritual had become so firmly rooted in Italian society, enjoying the support and collaboration of the dominant classes. The man who shared the enthusiasm for Beccaria's views to the extent of boasting of having been their author, and who fought Enlightenment causes like the one regarding judicial torture, had been dismayed by Sala's behavior and disapproved of the effects, fearing the collapse in people's minds of religious beliefs that had acted as a brake on crime and revolt. This was the limit of a class that was unwilling and unable to let go of the function performed by religion of conserving the social order.

Elsewhere too, prominent members of the companies of justice noted with concern in the behavior of "patients" the signs of a crisis in traditional religion. The School of Comforters in Bologna, where members of the city's nobility took turns to serve as the censor, reported signs of the scarce efficacy of religious arguments in dealing with the condemned. The report about Vincenzo Cottignola, who was among those executed in 1791 (see Chapter 26), states that "he died with sangfroid, and may it be that the Lord has wished to save his soul."[6] And in relation to Girolamo Ridolfi, condemned to death in February 1791 for theft at Monte di San Petronio, we read that "he certainly proved to be more [of a] philosopher than [a] Christian": according to the comforter Gian Battista Morandi, Ridolfi had been "animated in faith with the fervent sayings of Saint Augustine, and never with Italian sentiments," and with those sayings "he presumed to demonstrate his talent and nobility."[7]

The philosophy that was undermining the traditional "Italian sentiments" of attachment to the Catholic faith, and which required a refined theological doctrine to combat it, was especially at home in Verri and Beccaria's home region of Lombardy. The latter was well aware of what went on close by in the oratory of San Giovanni alle Case Rotte, where the "Nobilissima Confraternita" of San Giovanni Decollato used to meet. It was certainly no accident that in the controversy unleashed by the publication of his work he resorted, on the frontispiece of the third edition published in 1765, to an image of Justice—designed by Giovanni Lapi to his instructions—averting her gaze in horror from the sight of the severed head presented by the executioner, and indicating instead the tools of forced labor with which the condemned would serve their punishment.[8] More effective than words, the image polemically overturned the representations of the martyrdom of Saint John the Baptist that adorned the printed summons sent to the *confratelli* on the occasion of every execution.[9] By refusing to countenance the display of John the Baptist's severed head, the goddess Justice of Cesare Beccaria rejected the foundations of a form of devotion that had sprung up and prospered at the foot of the scaffold.

But it was precisely in Milan—and not for merit of Pietro Verri—that the history of Italy experienced one of the instances of differentiated development between the cultures of the different regional areas that characterized it, and which political vicissitudes had contributed to widen. Here, as we have seen, Emperor Joseph II put an end to the work of the Milanese confraternity of San Giovanni alle Case Rotte. He did so in steps, first by requiring the presentation of detailed accounts and of information about its composition and administration, in line with a procedure applied to all of Lombardy's religious institutions but that dealt a severe blow to the confraternity's finances. Subsequent checks on its administration and deposit funds, and above all the ban on sending out representatives to collect alms, plunged the finances of the already shaky structure of the Nobilissima Compagnia into crisis. Admittedly, the company was permitted to make collections, but on the condition that this was done by the titled brothers and not by the *bussolanti*—people who gathered alms in the streets, rattling tin cups to encourage passers-by to give coins—at their service. This jarred with the haughtiness of the nobility and the now limited and distracted participation of the *confratelli* in traditional activities. The storm of the suppressions, which had not spared the Inquisition either, finally hit the confraternity as well. Forewarning of the next and definitive sanction came in the shape of a government dispatch in 1780, stating that "the corpses of executed wrongdoers must no longer be buried in churches and oratories, nor must almsboxes remain on display for donations in suffrage for them." This order stemmed from Joseph II's wish to "rectify the abuse of those superstitious practices that arise from the recourse made by worshippers to the souls of purgatory, especially of those punished by justice with death."[10]

This marked the end for the Confraternita di San Giovanni Decollato alle Case Rotte. In its end was its beginning: the emperor's decree prohibited the church burial of the bodies of the executed, which is what the original practice of the *misericordia* had been as conceived by the devout women, merchants, and artisans who, centuries earlier, had first started the confraternity. The ordinance of suppression was signed on August 24, 1784, and communicated to the prefect of San Giovanni alle Case Rotte on August 29. The choice of date—the day dedicated to Saint John the Baptist—was certainly not casual. The comforting ritual thus passed away just as Beccaria's work was moving toward its crowning fulfillment with the abolition of the death penalty, which happened for the first time in that very same year in the Lorraine grand duchy of Tuscany. It is a suggestive coincidence—disappearing with that penalty was the ritual that had constituted the religious legitimation of human butchery. But its roots were robust: Pietro Verri's concern that the people might lose their fear of the other world had shown how much resistance there was to abandoning the anchor provided to society by religion. The bond between religion and capital punishment performed many functions, and had concerned all the European cultures. It is to them that we must now direct our attention, at least in general terms, before following subsequent developments in the Italian Catholic world.

29

Comforting of the Condemned in Catholic Europe

IN FRANCE, as we have seen, the condemned used to be denied sacramental confession, which led to Jean Gerson's protest and eventually to the edict of February 1397. Before this was introduced, the scaffold ritual in Paris envisaged that the condemned could make two stops along the route, one at the Hôpital Sainte-Catherine, where food and drink was available, and the other in the courtyard of the Filles-Dieu (daughters of God), where, in front of a wooden crucifix, the nuns' confessor said some prayers, blessed the condemned with holy water, proffered a cross to kiss, and made them eat bread and drink wine—a symbolic form of Communion. Subsequently, even where the custom of attending executions to pray for the souls of the condemned spread through France, granting of the sacraments was limited and uncertain. Even as late as the end of the seventeenth century, a French theologian criticized it for being sacrilegious on two counts: first of all because, with the Eucharist, the body of Christ entered a human body destined immediately afterward to meet a violent and infamous end; but also because the condemned were liable to conceal their crimes from the confessor out of fear that the latter would report them to the judge—something that does in fact appear to have been fairly commonplace.[1] However, that same theologian, returning to and amplifying Gerson's recognition of how things were done in Lombardy in his age, observed that sacraments had long been granted as a matter of course in Italy—an area where France, proud of its Christian primogeniture, was outdone by Italy. But even after Gerson's authoritative appeal, capital punishment in France did not cease to characteristically entail a harsh and ignominious exclusion of the condemned from the social body. The public confession made by the condemned was described as the *amende honorable,* but in reality it had all the hallmarks of a shaming ritual because those about to die publicly declared the crimes which had made them deserving of their end. As for the most important concession obtained as a result of Gerson's protest, the possibility of confessing to a priest, powerful limitations were imposed in practice on those who wanted to avail themselves of it. In Paris, for example, even though there were hundreds of confraternities providing mutual assistance and interceding for the souls of the dead, the job of comforting the condemned was the exclusive task of two professors from the Sorbonne, for the very simple reason that they could be relied on to collaborate with the judges in the search for accomplices. The testimony of a lawyer in the early eighteenth century indicates a widespread awareness that absolution was habitually denied to anyone who did not reveal the names of accomplices—names that were then passed on to the judges. And it was well known that on this point the method adopted by the Sorbonne confessors differed from the one used by the Capuchin monks, who were excluded from comforting duties for precisely this reason.[2] The weight of the king's power in these areas did not guarantee respect for the secrecy of sacramental confession. During the trial of François Ravaillac, Henry IV's assassin, the accused stated that he trusted in God's mercy because Christ's Passion was greater than the act which he had committed. But how, his questioners objected, could he hope for divine mercy if he did not confess his regicidal design? Why, for example, had he not told any confessor what he was planning? Ravaillac replied that if he had, he would have been thrown in jail straightaway, because when matters of state were involved, priests had an obligation to reveal what they heard in the confessional.[3] In France, then, the confessor was more of an intermediary between the condemned person and the king than he was between the condemned person and God: and in fact it was to the king that the final act of contrition was offered as a return to obedience.[4] Other fundamental differences between the French ritual and that of the Italian cities derived from this: in France, the condemned were not just denied the Eucharist but also burial in holy ground. These were evident signs of an exclusion from the Christian body, an exclusion that weighed more heavily than any thoughts of their imminent suffering on the scaffold, judging by the pleas and attempts to obtain by gracious dispensation what was denied by the law. But if the privilege of burial was readily granted to those from noble stock, that of Communion was just as readily denied. In the sentence passed on the count of

Luxembourg, Louis de Saint-Pol, executed in 1475 for the crime of lèse-majesté, we read that his body should have been quartered and the parts displayed in public spaces, but that the court granted permission for him to be buried in holy ground. But when the count asked if he could receive the Eucharist, his request was turned down. As a special privilege he was allowed to be comforted by four theologians, and to hear a mass celebrated in his presence, after which he was offered some blessed bread. He received this with great devotion and after having eaten it, he did not touch any other food or drink.[5] The bodies of commoners, on the other hand, were subjected to unlimited exposition, and an idea of how much the thought of that dismayed them can be seen in François Villon's *Ballade des pendus*. As a threat, it was even more effective than capital punishment at educating subjects to obey the law, as Jean Muret observed in his survey of the funeral ceremonies of all peoples.[6] But the absence, in the French ritual, of a visible form of reconciliation and divine forgiveness had the effect of exalting the values of political loyalty and individual courage, completely eclipsing the issue of the salvation of the soul. The model of the "death spectacle" had an important function in forging a social discipline of obedience to the state. The confessions made by the condemned to unburden their consciences remained a public matter of criminal justice, and did not have much in common with the secret examining of sins carried out under the guidance of a priest that characterized the Italian tradition. The occasional granting of burial in consecrated ground has prompted some scholars to speak of an attempt to rehabilitate the condemned socially within a religious ritual tending toward the restoration of a collective communion.[7] To others the design to impose sovereign authority as something legitimated by God, similar to what happened at that time in England and the Protestant nations, appeared preeminent.[8] In actual fact, as we shall see, aside from a shared function of the moralization of everyday life that distinguished the various different forms of Christianity in modern Europe, the differences were fairly deep. According to a Florentine Augustinian theologian, the ancient ban was still effectively in force in eighteenth-century France.[9]

However, the impulse that reached papal Rome from Florence and gave rise to the Confraternita di San Giovanni Decollato ("dei Fiorentini") put down some roots in France as well. A company of Black Penitents of Saint John the Baptist—of the *florentins*—was founded in Avignon at roughly the same time as the one in Rome, though it did not work with the condemned. Only in 1586 was a Misericordia founded, perhaps due to a scission, which, judging by the statutes approved in 1596 by archbishop Francesco Maria Tarugi, appears to have been devoted to assisting those in jail, including condemned prisoners: aggregated to the Roman archconfraternity from 1609, it enjoyed the privilege of freeing one prisoner each year. In Marseilles, two distinct confraternities, also aggregated to the one in Rome, dealt, from the end of the sixteenth century, with the burial of the executed—one was for the nobility, the other for those of common stock.[10] Through aggregation it was possible for devout Catholics from every country to earn a treasure trove of indulgences deriving from the opportunity to meditate upon death and sin through the experience had *in corpore vili*—that of the condemned. And the work of the religious orders most closely linked to the Catholic rebirth of the Tridentine age played an important part in encouraging the foundation of associations similar to the Roman one.

Tridentine Catholic patterns of devotion flourished particularly in seventeenth-century France. An example of this can be found in Lyon, where, more than any other city, there was traditionally a marked presence of Italians, as merchants, printers, and exiles. Home to important charitable institutions providing assistance to the poor and sick, Lyon had no devout association tending to the needs of the imprisoned and condemned. This lack was noted by a silk merchant of Milanese origin, Cesare Lauro. In an entreaty to the pope, he described how condemned prisoners were effectively abandoned to their fate. Before going to the scaffold they could only count on the possibility of making confession. After execution they were buried directly on the spot, and sometimes were dug up and eaten by dogs,[11] hence the idea of building a chapel where the bodies could be buried and of founding an association to help them and pray for the salvation of their souls. Lauro had the chapel built at his own expense in 1625–1627, and the confraternity was canonically established by the archbishop of Lyon on March 2, 1636. On August 26 of the same year consent was obtained from the civil authorities, the Senechaussée of Lyon, for the brothers, dressed in sackcloth, to enter the prison two at a time on the day of execution, to accompany the condemned criminal to the scaffold. But that was as far as the political powers were willing to go in admitting religious models into the functioning of justice: the request for the privilege of freeing a condemned prisoner was granted by Rome but not ratified by the crown. Instead, the work of helping those in jail for debt met with greater success: thanks to the collection of voluntary offerings, the release of many debtors was secured. As for the condemned, the rules laid down in the statutes of 1639 stipulated that two-man teams of lay members were to take turns in keeping the condemned company so they were never alone from the moment they received notification of the sentence to when it was carried out. The burial rites were particularly solemn: the body was to be removed from the scaffold the same evening, wrapped in a shroud and placed in a coffin, and then carried on the shoulders of four *confratelli* to the chapel, publicly accompanied in procession by all the members. Burial was to take place the following day, with a mass and prayers of suffrage. This ritual was suspended in the many cases in which the body was handed over to trainee surgeons for exercises in anatomy. In the requests made by physicians to the Criminal Lieutenant of Lyon assurances were given that, in exchange for the body, they would undertake to bury it afterward and have prayers said for the salvation of the dead person's soul. All this is unmistakably reminiscent of the *conforterie* on the Italian peninsula: the Italian style of the Societas Misericordiae can be detected in the instructions for the brothers and in their choice of symbol, the head of Saint John the Baptist. But for France it was a novelty. Cesare Lauro was conscious of this, and stressed it in an entreaty to the pope requesting the title of Archconfraternity of France for the institution he had founded. As observed in a draft version of the letter of entreaty to the pope, there were still no confraternities of this kind in France, and the example of Lyon might encourage the establishment of others.[12] The dominant line in French Catholicism was the one connoted by the Compagnie du Saint Sacrement, which, from 1629, had given rise to a vast campaign of devout, anti-Protestant propaganda and of the moralization of every area of French society. Supporters of this project set out to combat the spread of works dangerous to faith and to promote devotion to the Eucharist, besides taking part in many social initiatives.[13] Cesare Lauro's project also lay within this Counter-Reformation Catholic revival in the years after the wars of religion and the reign of Henry IV. But once again it was the Jesuits who promoted the devout themes of comforting. And it was to the magistrates in Lyon that a scholarly treatise by the French Jesuit Joseph Filère, dealing with the spiritual consolation of prisoners and the condemned, was dedicated. The work expounds principles that were present as a matter of course in Italian comforting literature by that time: the harmony between human and divine justice, the superimposition of sins and crimes, the obligation to accept the death sentence as the fulfillment of God's design to offer the condemned an opportunity to show remorse and to use the torments of the scaffold as currency to pay necessary penance for their sins. The Jesuit's own reflections were in line with the somber tones of baroque religion: how could one doubt divine providence, he asked, given that earthly life is nothing other than a prison where every human being awaits the sentence of condemnation or salvation?[14] Nor should the power that sent people to the scaffold be criticized: the sword wielded by the king was nothing other than the instrument of the "justice de Dieu pour la terreur des méchans."[15]

But of greater practical usefulness to the *confratelli* in Lyon seems to have been a short instruction, anonymous and undated, written in Italian and preserved in the confraternity's archive. The rule regarding their behavior sums up clearly and simply what was to be found in Italian literature on the topic in that period. The incipit of the text gives an idea of the spirit that animated the founder:

> The brother of our Company, who, either having been picked by lot, or, as it is customary to say, having been chosen by a show of hands, that is, by election, has accepted the office of comforter, considering himself called by God to a truly angelic ministry, just as the Eternal Father sent an angel to comfort his only Son in the Garden of Gethsemane before the Passion, will immediately have to apply his mind to this great work by preparing his soul so that, pure and free from all sin, it remains so empty and free that divine grace might dwell in it.[16]

The first thing to do was to prepare the soul, but there was also plenty of very concrete and detailed practical advice. In his four-month period in office, the *confratello* had to be sober in his diet, so he would be able to remain awake during the night if any comforting needed to be done. So as to be ready to answer the nighttime call, he was to sleep on the side of the house giving on to the street, so that the person who came to call him would not have to knock for too long, which would wake up the neighbors. In all things he was to use "that silence by which devotion is always accustomed to be accompanied." He had to carry the company's sackcloth with him, to put on as required, making sure that no hose of a "very bright" color was visible. It was also recommended that he carry "some small pieces of perfume" with him, as the prison was a foul-smelling place; and that he had something to chew on to keep his stomach down in "case he had to assist someone who had his hand or head cut off." He was also to find out "about the qualities of the condemned, that is, whether they are noble or mean, rich or poor, civil or plebeian, literate or ignorant, whether they have fanciful or peaceable minds." There were three kinds: "Either they are low and doltish people, and consequently ignorant, such as peasants, sailors, vagabonds, and so forth. Or they are noble and civil, persons of learning, such as ecclesiastics, doctors, courtiers. Or they are mediocre people, such as artisans, merchants, servants, who, having associated with civil men, have some small degree of manners and some understanding of spiritual things." And their predispositions are likewise of three kinds: "some are obstinate, angry, inadequate, unreasonable, and half despairing. Some others are all saintly, all devout, all contrite, humble, and obedient. Others have some good inclination but, being greatly assailed by honor, fear, pain, and temptations, are unsteady, volatile, timid, and fearful."

It was important to learn about the differences in social standing, but without mechanically adopting different approaches. Each individual case required an appropriate form of behavior: for example, one way of treating mean and generally despised people was to pretend to esteem them "as if they were kings and monarchs," trying in this way to lead them on the path to confession, which, if time permitted, was to be a general one. After confession, and having done the requested penance, the condemned could go to the table of the company's *provveditore,* who would help them to write letters, wills, and documents restoring the good name of others who may have been falsely accused. Finally there was a mass, during which the condemned could receive a simple Communion with blessed bread rather than with the consecrated Host. They would recite "the declarations for the point of death according to the formula of Saint Charles [Borromeo]." When the condemned went to the scaffold, they would be accompanied, agreement having first been reached about what prayers to recite and what to say. If prisoners wished to speak to the crowd, they should be advised against it. Having taken their final steps, they would be absolved again with some catch-all phrase and instructed to say: "Jesus, Mary" at the moment of execution.

No memory has survived of the people assisted by the confraternity. On the other hand, the members' names are known. The changes in the social make-up of the company from when it was established through to its abolition in 1792 echo familiar patterns: an initial phase in which artisans were recruited gave way, in the eighteenth century, to the presence of nobles and the clergy, culminating with the explicit exclusion, in the statutes of 1728, of those belonging to the "mechanical" arts. The French Revolution then shut down the Lyon confraternity. A final attempt to revive it in 1797 stemmed from the recognition that the prisons were in a disastrous state and the government was unable to do much about it, prompting a call for a return to the old form of confraternal charity. But nothing came of it.

This marked the conclusion of efforts to establish the Italian model of comforting in France. Shortly before that, the final word had been pronounced on the ancient controversy between the papacy and France regarding the granting or otherwise of the Eucharist. As archbishop of Bologna, Prospero Lambertini had initially sustained that it was right and in compliance with Christian piety to grant Communion to condemned prisoners, even those guilty of serious crimes, provided they asked for and were willing to receive it.[17] After being elected pontiff as Pope Benedict XIV, and having further studied the issue, he returned to it in the second edition of the treatise *De Synodo dioecesana*. Having read Pius V's letter to Philip II on the subject, he was of the view that a different approach was necessary: the bishops were to be given the task of introducing into their dioceses the practice of granting the Eucharist to the condemned, and also to insert it into their synods.[18] In this way the confrontation with the French State was circumvented. As he wrote in the treatise *De Missae sacrificio,* it was up to the bishops to follow local practice. The pope had no intention of judging the direction of state policies.[19]

Iberian Cultures of Mercy

The rituals of capital punishment in Portugal and Spain had a religious dimension similar in some ways to that of the Italian states. There was, though, one important difference: both imperial states had a strong central power to whose will the administration of justice, and its evolution from medieval forms toward the use of the spectacle of the death sentence as a means of social disciplining, was subjected.[20] It was at the wishes and under the auspices of the queen mother Eleanor and of King Manuel I that the Confraternity of Mercy was established in Lisbon Cathedral in August 1498. This marked a turning point with respect to an earlier tradition governed by the principle of the "eschatological exclusion" of the condemned: a death without sacraments and without burial of the body.[21] During this period the city was experiencing immigration pressure as a result of the expulsion of Jews from Castile and Aragon. The precedent set by the expulsion of the Jewish and Muslim minorities offered a model to the Portuguese dynasty. But in the meantime the monarchy moved into the field of assistance and charity with a plan to concentrate resources and aid. In many respects this anticipated forms of social control that would later distinguish all the modern European states. The question of the poor and of charitable institutions became more and more interwoven with an increasingly hegemonic model of justice, giving rise to new ties between violence and charity under the paternal influence of central powers and of ever more pervasive forms of control. The initiative to set up a confraternity under the protection of the Virgin was an important sign of how the Portuguese monarchy intended to use within the country the religious legitimation that had paved the way for its non-European conquests. The papacy in Rome was quick to offer spiritual incentives to ensure a flow of visitors and benefactors to Portuguese charitable institutions. An idea of this can be gained from the bulls of Alexander VI, in particular the one dated May 24, 1496, which granted a plenary indulgence "in articulo mortis" to anyone who, dying duly penitent and confessed in Lisbon hospital, left some of their possessions to the hospital itself.[22] The newly established *misericordia* effectively presented itself as an agency responsible for a vast range of tasks, and destined to concentrate in its hands the financial means to tackle them. The language of the document draws on themes from the traditional religious repertoire and from the great tradition of the medieval Portuguese confraternities: but the scattered and variegated world of lay associations gave way here before a design of concentration and centralized control. Not for nothing did the sovereign precede it with a systematic inventory of existing institutions in order to rationalize the use of resources.[23] This was a widely felt concern in European society. The Portuguese monarchy's systematic intent is reflected in the regulation of the new association set up in Lisbon: there was an overall scheme for the two series of charitable works that it intended to carry out—seven corporal and seven spiritual. Norms were drawn up to govern the charitable structure, and the situations listed in which it would intervene to help the poor, the imprisoned, and the dying, assist the living and bury the dead. The scope of intervention was strictly limited to those who were baptized: the religious division running through Portuguese society between Christians, Jews, and Muslims was confirmed and consolidated. Works of charity could only be done within the circle of those belonging to the Church. There were instructions about how to administer bequests, alms (to be collected in certain places in the city), and sums charged to those who were assisted or collected for masses. Besides the traditional categories of the poor, sick, and dying, in the overall scheme of charitable works there was space too for the condemned.[24] This was the first time. Until then the ritual had involved a procession through the city from the prison to the execution site, with a stop in front of the cathedral on the way, where the condemned could attend the celebration of the Mass and adore the Eucharist.[25] The corpses were left hanging on the gallows or in quarters on spikes, and were devoured by dogs. But in the regulations ("Comprimisso") of the Lisbon Misericordia special attention was now given to the pious work of spiritually attending to the condemned and burying their remains. A long, detailed chapter dealt with what the confraternity should do with those who suffered at the hands of justice ("que padecem per justiça"). Specific norms indicated how the thirteen brothers of the Misericordia had to line up in procession. To begin with, they had to conceal their identity with their habit and hood in order to defend themselves from the sin of vainglory ("cubertos da vam Gloria destem undo"), a clear indicator of just how socially prestigious the office was. Thus attired they would head the procession of the condemned, holding up the gonfalon with the image of the Virgin together with the large processional cross, inviting everyone to congregate by sounding a bell. In candlelight, the procession would chant litanies while the Misericordia's chaplain walked to the right of the condemned person, consoling and preparing him to die in the holy Catholic faith. In addition to providing spiritual comfort, one of their number would also walk on the prisoner's left to provide the "padescente"—the patient—with succor as required. On top of this there were repeated aspersions of holy water, which another company member held ready for use. Other penitents could also join the procession to display their contrition and to encourage the condemned by their example to do likewise: the protagonist of the drama would wear an identical habit of white linen, in which he would then be buried; sewn to this was a hat that would cover his face following execution. At the moment of execution the chaplains would sing the Gregorian chant of the responsory of the dead. The invocation begging God to forget human sins when he comes to judge the world in the apocalypse of fire would accompany the moment of greatest suffering and the death of the condemned, who were to be sprinkled with holy water. Alms were to be gathered for their souls, if they were poor, while if they were rich their burial expenses would be paid for with their assets. If they were quartered and put on display at the city gates, the officials of the Misericordia were instructed to remove the parts with great devotion on the third day.

There was no rush to bury the body parts in the confraternity's cemetery. This emerges from interventions made by King Manuel and from detailed indications in the Misericordia statutes, where further specifications and rules regarding the fate of the bodies of the executed were laid down.[26] The burial function was ritualized with the solemn "procession of the bones": once a year, on All Saints Day, a procession made its way to the scaffold site and collected what could be found there—bones, the flesh-stripped, unburied remains of the executed. A selection was made between what was to be taken off to the confraternity's cemetery and what was to be buried beneath the gallows. The significance of this was to make a distinction between those whose souls they thought could still be saved through the brothers' prayers and those whose souls were left to die. The ritual first began in Lisbon in November 1498, but was not limited to the capital. The network of *misericordia* organizations gradually grew until it covered the whole of Portugal and extended into the colonies as well. In 1500 the confraternity in Beja marked the start of its work with a solemn procession of this kind.

The ritual of taking part in the execution proceedings was intended to bring comfort not only to the condemned but to the whole crowd watching the penitential procession and taking part in the penitential drama—a drama culminating in the death of a person who had been transformed before everyone's eyes from a delinquent into a contrite sinner, the lost sheep returning to the fold. In the charged atmosphere of devotion, and under the direction of the *confratelli* clad in their ritual vestments, the suffering and death inflicted for crimes committed were put on the condemned person's account to offset accrued sins. What we have here is the construction of a theatrical machine that culminated with the execution, and then dissolved into the devout contrition of a crowd absorbed in a meditation upon death and divine justice, having experienced a collective rite of pacification: the violence of the crimes and that of the punishment gave way to thoughts of forgiveness given and received on the scene of the scaffold. "That all may live in love, concord, and peace" are the closing words of the short final chapter following the instructions about executions. The confraternity leaders were asked to gather information about wrongs, quarrels, enmities, questions of inheritance, and vendettas. They were also required, at least once a year, during Lent, to arrange a rite of reciprocal forgiveness in order to completely settle conflicts. A record was to be kept of these acts of forgiveness, indicating the names of the people who had forgiven. The purpose of all this activity, and the raison d'être of the confraternity itself, was summed up in a single sentence: everyone should live "em paz e em amor com o proximo e irmãos em Christo nosso Salvador" ("in peace and love with one's neighbors and brothers in Christ our Savior").[27]

The idea of civic peace as a positive value to be protected with the spontaneous contribution of people gathered together in an association is something we have already come across in the Italian companies of justice. But this project to give an association set up at the wishes of the sovereign the task of settling conflicts and divisions was the Portuguese form of an organic and carefully controlled view of Christian society. Instead of a penitential and prophetic movement, such as the one created by Venturino of Bergamo with his crusade of criminals, eliminating violence and hatred from social relations was to be achieved here through constant surveillance by a powerful and well-resourced corporation. But from where and how had the simple and suggestive idea of using death as an instrument for social pacification, with the inclusion of attendance at executions among the exercises of mercy, arrived in Portugal? We can only advance some hypotheses about this. But one thing is certain: no precedent for this type of pious work has been found in the many confraternities which, for centuries, had provided occasions for solidarity and devotion to the inhabitants of a small country clinging to the southern edges of the continent, facing Muslim Africa. One suggestion is that here too the mediators were Florentine merchants active in Lisbon in the fifteenth century, and it has been pointed out that the Portuguese sovereigns had dealings with Italian cities. What is more, in his will King Don John II cited the Florentine hospital of Ognissanti as a model.[28] But there is a substantive difference between the host of civic confraternities in Italy, which sprang up spontaneously as a result of initiatives by groups of citizens proud of their own specific identity, and the monolithic structure of the Portuguese *misericordia* organizations. A generic resemblance stems from the body of beliefs and sentiments shared by Christianity in that age: mercy as a currency of exchange between merits and sins, the guarantee of recognition at the moment of God's judgment, a way of reducing or canceling out the punishments of purgatory, liberating souls from the prison of fire that tormented them in the afterlife. These tendencies were nurtured by the great Dominican and Franciscan religious orders; their members moved freely in a domain extending across borders, upholding, in their sermons, a theology of sin and salvation based on the Passion of Christ. And the model of the transformation of capital execution into a religious ritual probably came from Rome. What is certain is that the project of mercy received the assent of a papacy that had forged a special relationship with the Portuguese sovereigns during the second half of the fifteenth century. As is known, the start of ocean navigation and the establishment of colonies in Africa and the Indies had taken place with the blessing and crucial aid of a papacy that was emerging from the conciliar crisis by building relations directly with the ruling houses. Nicholas V's bulls of 1455 had granted Portuguese navigators and conquistadors the right to enslave non-Christian peoples and to take possession of their territories. This was the decisive premise for the development of early European colonialism. The religious legitimation of the right of conquest would provide the ideological foundations for the two great empires of the early modern period, the Portuguese one and the Spanish one. We could say that Portugal's most important discovery was not the route to the Indies but the route to Rome. And it is quite likely that in the dense network of relations built up in the late fifteenth century between Lisbon and Rome the idea of copying the Roman model of comforting the condemned also gained ground. Portugal's *misericordia* system was based on the image of royal power as the interpreter and holder of the divine power to forgive and to protect. This is borne out by the way in which the ideology of merciful regality accompanied the new organization of social control. It will suffice to mention the example of how an early sixteenth-century *sacra rappresentazione* presented the theme of the contrast between Mercy and Justice. It recounted how in the end Mercy overcame Justice: God had been convinced by her to send his Son down to earth to cancel the curse of Adam's sin and free all humanity from original sin.[29] It was hoped that the confraternity of mercy would therefore succeed in redeeming the guilty from crimes and perhaps eradicate violence from social relations. Indeed, the humanist Cataldo Siculo declared at the time, in an epistle in Latin praising one of the founders of the newly established confraternity, that it had immediately been so successful that its mere presence had been enough to eliminate the recourse to the death penalty almost entirely.[30]

The reality of events subsequently belied this. The design of a Christian monarchy that dominated a society cleansed of all impurity and all religious difference was charged with a violence that was not slow to manifest itself in many ways. The outcome was one of a full-scale triumph of death at the hands of justice. Portugal and neighboring Spain were the countries where death elevated to spectacle, and the executions where heretics and "Judaizers" died in large numbers, went by the name of *auto-da-fé*—"theater of faith."

In this, Portugal copied the model of the neighboring kingdoms of Castile and Aragon. The religious legitimation of the power to punish had played a fundamental role in the growth of the Portuguese and Spanish monarchies. This also gave rise to the widespread use of images and rites intended to reflect the light of a special divine protection and a faithful observance of Gospel teachings onto the acts of sovereigns. Those of justice had been among the most significant, and the theme of Gospel forgiveness had remained dominant. In the Siete Partidas (1348), or "Seven-part Code," of King Alfonso X of Castile, known as "the Wise," we read that on Good Friday the king "generally pardons all the men that he has prisoner," to the extent that the day was called "the day of Indulgence."[31] The choice of day derived from the fact that it was "on such a day, Good Friday of the Cross, that Our Lord Jesus Christ received death and passion to save the human race and forgave his death." The sovereign forgave so God might forgive the sins of his forebears and of himself in the other world. The practice of the Good Friday pardon continued in the later tradition of the Spanish sovereigns. In the Cortes of Saragozza of 1447, Don Juan de Aragón asked for the whole year's pardons to be concentrated on that one day: his confessor was to receive the list and prepare a detailed report. This measure was intended to reduce the number of pardons granted and to rationalize procedures. But we should bear in mind the wording used by the king on Good Friday: "I pardon you so God might pardon me."[32]

Of a quite different ilk were the forms taken by the dominant religion in the administration of justice by Ferdinand of Aragon and his successors. The political unification of Castile, Aragon, and the other smaller Iberian territories, which were different in their language, culture, and traditions, took place as the continuation of the Reconquista, in the name of a bellicose mission by the Spanish people to establish a spotless religion at home and abroad. The sovereign became the interpreter of that mission, and the close bond he formed with his people thanks to religion enabled him to sweep away the autonomy and privileges underpinning the local elites. This idea of the historic vocation of the Spanish people had been embodied in the expulsion of the religious minorities—Jews, Muslims—and in the structure of the tribunal of the Inquisition, an instrument controlled by the sovereign but invested by the pope with the power of excommunication, which made it superior to any other. While the *misericordia* model was established in Portugal and its colonial dependencies, in the Iberian kingdoms of Ferdinand and Isabella the new reality was that of the tribunals of the Inquisition, holders of a power superior to any judicial right or privilege held by local autonomies. In both cases, ecclesiastical powers were ceded to the monarchy: the tribunal of the Inquisition was the instrument for the affirmation of central power. The unity of Spain came about in that period of the fifteenth century amid political and religious violence: the creation of the new Inquisition of Castile, subsequently generalized, the conquest of the Moorish kingdom of Grenada, and the expulsion of unbaptized Jews in 1492 paved the way for a season in which the violence of burnings and the spectacle of the executions of "Judaizers" made intolerance and suspicion the new glue holding the country together. In Portugal, the elimination of Jewish difference was achieved by resorting to the artifice of forced conversion, thereby avoiding expulsion. The enforced baptism, "standing up," imposed upon the Portuguese Jews officially eradicated the non-Christian minority from the country, but laid the foundations for an obsessive suspicion that would find an outlet in collective violence before eventually being channeled into the work of the Portuguese Inquisition. As early as 1506 the pogrom sparked in Lisbon by the incendiary preaching of two Dominicans ended with the friars being burned at the stake and dozens of hangings.[33] Meanwhile, in the kingdoms of Castile and Aragon, the "Suprema," the central tribunal of the Inquisition, had already rendered fully operational the machinery for trying, torturing, and condemning Judaizers. Even though in Portugal the action against forcibly baptized Jews was suspended temporarily due to an awareness of the violent nature of the imposed conversion, that did not make ordinary criminal justice less violent. Extant sources testify to a "harsh and exemplary use of the death penalty."[34]

The model in Portugal came down from the center and spread throughout society. Created at the wishes of the monarchy, the *misericordia* structures proliferated rapidly not only in Portugal itself—there were sixty-four when King Manuel died in 1521—but also in the archipelagos of the Azores and Madeira, and in the main cities of the overseas empire. These institutions were used for many different purposes. Like the Spanish ones, they devoted particular attention to organizing the public Easter week rituals, such as the traditional visit to devoutly revere an image of the dead Christ on display in churches, and the great Good Friday procession: bleak rituals that nurtured hatred for the Jews, destined to become a collective obsession after the violent erasure of the Jewish presence.

One thing is certain: whatever suggestions were made by the preachers and whatever was known about the Italian models, we are faced here not by a lay movement inspired by preachers or religious leaders, but a top-down monarchic design intended to concentrate resources and tackle the question of poverty and societal control: this small state, with a monarchy of enhanced power and wealth, achieved a secularization of charity that was removed from Church control with an act of rule unlike anything to be found in the complicated procedures of Tridentine Italy.[35] Quite evident in that design was the intention to establish a centralized setup for the whole complex world of lay charity. The social composition of the *misericordia* associations effectively marked the preservation of the structure of power by accepting members from the dominant classes. But where the difference is most clear-cut is in the sphere of assistance for the condemned. First of all, the burial of the bodies that had initially stimulated the spontaneous setting up of the

Italian *misericordie* was here the subject of a norm dictated by the sovereign; and as we have seen, instead of gathering up the bodies as soon as possible in order to solemnly bury them in the confraternity cemetery, in Portugal we find the so-called procession of bones. This practice was ostensibly meant to put limits on the cruelty of displaying the corpses and the ghastly sight of what stray dogs did to the bodies. But in reality it provided a final religious legitimation for the horror-inducing function of the memory of the crime and of the punishment, as all that remained to be gathered up of those bodies were the bones, a cause of impurity and social unworthiness.

Anyone viewing the landscape in Spain would not have found a very different situation. Here the spectacle of death at the hands of justice was an elaborate construction, the outcome of a significant investment of resources. The supreme model of this tradition was the "act of faith," the execution of sentences against heretics. But here too the vilification of the condemned exposed travelers to the spectacle of corpses hanging by the dozen from gallows in the woods: Miguel de Cervantes describes the feet and legs ("pies y piernas") dangling from the trees as a typical sight in a Barcelona where bandits and robbers were hung "twenty by twenty and thirty by thirty."[36]

Another complicated issue, widely debated in Spain as well, was whether the condemned should be allowed to receive Communion. The experience of ecclesiastical trials for matters of faith weighed on this discussion: in Portugal the mechanisms of exclusion from the unitary body of the Christian kingdom had been reinforced with the start of the procedures of the tribunal of the Inquisition, approved in 1547 and given its first set of regulations *(regimento)* in 1552. To grant admission to the Eucharistic Communion amounted to readmitting to the community those who had undermined its foundations. Even just managing the final confession could throw up complex problems: the Inquisition wanted to know what was said. And the seductive arts of the Jesuit confessors, who played an important role in the functioning of the Inquisition in Portugal, were ill tolerated by the Dominicans. In fact, in Spain too there was a very strong tendency to bar the condemned from receiving the sacraments. It took intervention from Pope Pius V to obtain from Philip II the suspension of the ban on allowing the condemned access to the sacraments: the papal *motu proprio* of January 25, 1568, called for by Bishop Pedro Guerrero, was ratified by the sovereign with the *pragmatica real* of March 27, 1569.[37] But the devoutly Catholic Spanish king laid down some precise conditions: Communion was to be granted the day before the execution during a mass to be celebrated in prison. Furthermore, in no circumstances whatsoever was the execution to be deferred. The rigorous image of royal justice evidently could not tolerate the delays and complications that might arise from the intervention of magistracies of the soul—and what went on in the Spanish viceroyalty of Naples at the time show that the king's concerns were not ungrounded: the imagination and astuteness of the condemned would make Neapolitan judicial rituals an endless source of surprising outcomes and twists and turns in events.[38]

The advent of the Habsburg monarchy and the union with Spain made the *pragmatica* of 1569 obligatory for Portugal as well, and it was included in the compilation of norms known as the *Nueva recopilación*.[39] These were taken into account after Portugal came under the crown of Spain with the agreement of the Cortes of Tomar (1581). Having become king of Portugal, Philip of Habsburg decided to become a *confratello* of the Lisbon Misericordia, consolidating the role of the confraternity as a close ally of sovereign power.[40] Subsequently, the laws that had been passed by the Portuguese king (the Manueline Ordinations of 1514, the definitive edition of which was emanated in 1521), and which gave to the *misericordie* the central role that we have seen, were absorbed with few changes into the Ordinations of Philip III (the Ordinazioni Filippine of 1603), in line with a policy of avoiding, where possible, the introduction of substantial modifications to earlier tradition. In the ordinations it was established that notification of a death sentence was to take place in the evening, so the condemned person had time to confess and ask God's forgiveness for their sins. From that moment on, some "religious persons"—in other words, not laypeople—were to undertake comforting duties. On the morning of the second day, the prisoner was to be allowed to receive the Eucharist. The sentence was then to be carried out on the morning of the third day, If there was a local *misericordia* confraternity, it was to be alerted so its members could take part in the ritual and console the condemned person.[41] A different emphasis, though, was placed on the role of the clergy with respect to that of the *misericordia* laypeople: the latter had an essentially ceremonial role, while the comforting and spiritual assistance lay in the hands of the clergy. This also had repercussions in the Italian part of the Spanish Empire; here, as we have seen, the Confraternita dei Bianchi della Giustizia in Naples, which played a key role in the comforting ritual, had to disband as a lay association and be reestablished as a body consisting exclusively of members of religious orders. The Spanish rulers were anxious to ensure that a prestigious and powerful body of lay-people did not oversee the final hours of condemned prisoners, who might reveal important secrets. From the monarchy's point of view it was much better for everything to be bound by the secrecy of the confessional. Similar logics of power also emerged in the way in which the question of whether or not to grant the Eucharist to those who were to die on the scaffold was addressed. This was the same old problem that had arisen in the fourteenth century with the clash between the papacy and the French monarchy: the complete readmission of the condemned to the Christian communion amounted to a cancellation of their sins, while the king's justice intended to make an appalling use of punishment. The discussion became further complicated, touching on issues of a theological nature: it was pointed out that having received, with the Eucharist, the flesh and blood of Christ, the body of the condemned person could not be subjected to vilification and suffering, because to do so would be to commit sacrilege.

On the other hand, even though the agreement between Philip II and Pius V formally opened the door to granting the Eucharist to the condemned, it is hard to gauge just how much the official rule was obeyed. Indeed, the question still appeared to be unresolved and controversial in the seventeenth century, not just to the Portuguese Jesuit Manuel de Sá, in a work that would condense the official doctrine on confession in brief aphorisms, but also to the German Paracelsian Heinrich Kornmann.[42] As for the intervention of confraternities or friars for the burial of the executed dead, envisaged by the Ordinations, it seems that friars did sometimes ask the authorities for permission to gather up and give a Christian burial to executed individuals on display near their convent; and at the beginning of the eighteenth century there was a confraternity called Our Lady of Charity that used to bury the quartered parts of the executed, provided they had permission from the authorities and an assurance that they had not died impenitent.[43] A confraternity of this name, active in Cáceres in Estremadura, has left traces of its work in the period between 1792 and 1909: surviving documents indicate that the length of time between sentence and execution oscillated between two and three days.[44] Essentially though, in neither Spain nor Portugal do we find the same level of concern to bury the executed dead that had inspired the work of the Italian confraternities.

The official rules were unable to bring order to the welter of problems that arose constantly in concrete practice, especially when it came to managing cases involving forcibly baptized Jews, so-called New Christians, who returned to their former religion. It was here that the legitimation given by religion to the death sentence was fixed in the public execution ritual with the *auto-da-fé,* or act of public penance, a triumph of faith designed to reinforce in the collective mentality the conviction that the state religion was spotlessly pure. As Giuseppe Marcocci has written, the celebration of the *auto-da-fé* "contributed to establishing, in a majestic public ritual, the official image of a Catholic crown that purified the community of subjects from the threat of heresy."[45] As regards common crimes, on the other hand, there appears to have been a gradual drop in capital punishments. However, this seems to have been the effect of a broader process that did not just affect the Iberian region, and which indicated that society no longer relied on the terror of the scaffold to achieve discipline and order.[46] Before this there had been time for legal experts and moralists to focus on the spectacle of death by justice and on the comforting of the condemned, and we will turn our attention to some examples of this.

The Death Penalty in the Mid-Sixteenth Century: Testimony and Discussion

In the eyes of a sixteenth-century Portuguese witness, the jurist Antonio da Gama, the work carried out by the *misericordia* associations in his country appeared to be the most just kind, combining as it did justice and Christian piety.[47] He could hardly have expressed himself any differently in a work whose frontispiece bore a dedication printed entirely in capital letters to Henry, infante and cardinal of the realm. But behind the show of patriotism is a glimpse of a propensity for other ways of treating the condemned. Antonio da Gama had seen with his own eyes what went on in Catalonia, in France, and in Italy, and his account offers an interesting taste of comparative anthropology regarding the rituals of justice. It is worth looking at what he has to say: in France and Spain bodies were left on display in public by order of the judges, so their presence would terrorize the population and keep alive a sense of horror and repugnance for the atrocious deeds of which the executed had been guilty. Sometimes animals were ritually sentenced and executed for the same reason, when they had been instrumental in a crime or had caused the death of human beings. Along roads in Catalonia, Antonio da Gama had seen corpses hanging from trees, and bones tied to trunks to serve as a permanent warning; and on the public street in Montpellier he had come across the bodies of two brigands, who had been hung for robbing and murdering a Spanish nobleman.

The testimony of the Portuguese jurist confirms what the great European literature had related about the scenes of horror that presented themselves to travelers. In France, the condition of the hung already had its poet in François Villon:

> Vous nous voiez cy attachez cinq, six
>
> . . . .
>
> La pluye nous a debuez et lavez,
> Et le soleil dessechiez e noircis;
> Pies, corbeaulx, nous ont les yeuz cavez,
> Et arrachié le barbe et les sourcis.

> (We five or six strung up to view
>
> . . . .
>
> Showered and rinsed with rain, we dead
> the sun has dried out black and blue.
> Magpie and crow gouge out each head
> for eyes and pluck the hairs.)

Those five or six bodies all hanging together, washed out by the rain and blackened and dried by the sun, the eyes picked from their sockets by crows, imploring mercy from the living and absolution from God, conjure up an unforgettable scene. Here divine forgiveness and the appeasement of the consciences of the living are not guaranteed by the ritual of comforting. The interminable exposition of the hung was the sign of an implacable vendetta. Yet this extreme model of the harshness of justice as vendetta gave rise, with Villon's poetry, to the supreme and most authentic example of the plea for Christian forgiveness as a rule of exchange between human beings and as a condition of the relationship between humankind and God:

> Frères humains qui après nous vivez
> N'ayez les cuers contre nous endurcis,
> Car, se pitié de nous povres avez,
> Dieu en aura plus tost de vous mercis.

(Brothers that live when we are dead,
don't set yourselves against us too.
If you could pity us instead,
then God may sooner pity you.)[48]

The executions recorded in his *Journal* by Nicolas Versoris, lawyer at the Parlement of Paris, in the first decades of the sixteenth century paint a picture in which the space devoted to the religious comforting of the condemned was very limited: there continued to be a place for confession, even though not everyone used it and at least one person refused it on the grounds of his convictions.[49] There were those who showed their devotion in the face of death by reciting many prayers, and there was also the chance of a royal pardon at the last minute. Another hope nurtured to the end was that of a direct intervention by the Virgin or saints: it was said of one person who had been hung, but was found to be still alive, that the Virgin had wished to give him time to finish a prayer addressed to her. The crowd pulled him down from the scaffold and handed him over to the nearby Carmelite church.[50]

In the course of his travels Antonio da Gama did not fail to note how different the rituals were in Italy. He had studied at the Royal Spanish College in Bologna, and recollected having seen executions in other cities. In Siena he had witnessed the punishment of a man guilty of homicide, who, before being led off to be beheaded in the square, was first taken to in front of his victim's house, where the executioner cut off the hand which had committed the deed. But Da Gama was struck above all by the ritual of burying the bodies, describing in particular how things were done in Bologna. Executions took place early in the morning, and already as evening fell the body was cut down from the gallows and taken off for burial. He offered this to his readers as a positive example, noting that the rules of canon law were followed here and the prescriptions of the Bible obeyed.[51] In Portugal, Spain, and France, on the other hand, things worked differently. The jurist's suggestion to the ruling dynasty was to pay greater attention in exercising the authority God had given to sovereigns over the administration of justice and the fate of the bodies of the executed. In particular he believed it important to remedy the many abuses that had been introduced into universities with the granting of bodies for anatomical studies; the death sentence only permitted the execution of the condemned, and perhaps for their bodies to be quartered. That they were then handed over to anatomists was an additional affront, not envisaged by the law. The problem could, however, be resolved: all the sovereign had to do was to grant a special license. This example shows just how rooted in the jurist's mind—a man of vast culture and experience—was the conviction that the king wielded total power not just over the lives of his subjects but over their bodies as well.

It was not matters such as these, though, that prompted him to write his erudite treatise. What he primarily wanted to do was to address a plea to the sovereign on an old issue concerning the salvation of the souls of the condemned. He was convinced that the firm authority of the monarch's power over the administration of justice could resolve the ancient problem regarding the granting of the sacraments to the condemned, in particular the Eucharist. The old question, a genuine leitmotif in the history of the death penalty in the Christian West, cropped up once again in a context marked by the lacerating theological question of the justification of sinners before God, and the new equilibria being established between spiritual power and temporal power, ecclesiastical bodies and national monarchs. Antonio da Gama did not touch on the substance of the crisis opened up by currents of reform in the Church and the religious conflicts that had ensued. His cultural horizons were those of a Portuguese jurist. And what seemed to him to be the fundamental opinion on the matter was that of an eminent Spanish canonist, who also taught at the university of Coimbra, Martín de Azpilcueta, known as Doctor Navarrus. According to Navarrus, the secular authorities did not commit a sin by withholding the Eucharist because Clement V's decretal, arising out of the dispute with the French judges, condemned the denial of the sacraments to the condemned as an abuse, but was only meant to refer to penitence.[52] For Antonio da Gama, on the other hand, the text also held good for the Eucharist, and in any case the Portuguese judges had the duty to obey the ecclesiastic canons and pursue the path of augmenting the Catholic faith and the tribute paid to the Roman see. For this reason it was important to ensure that the condemned were not denied the Eucharist. Only in this way could the condemned be certain of attaining the glory of heaven: confession alone was not enough, because the penitent might not be contrite enough to deserve the remission of the punishment. Instead, the Eucharist offered the perfect contrition that had opened the gates of heaven to the good thief: it alone removed hardness from the heart and guaranteed the cancellation of the punishment due for sins.[53] Da Gama therefore vigorously sustained the thesis that the Eucharist needed to be given to all the contrite condemned, despite being aware that the king and his cardinal brother were hostile to the idea. But to have any chance of success he had to take great pains to head off any possibility that the notion of sacraments as vehicles of spiritual life might entail consequences for earthly life. Consequently, he examined the sacraments separately one by one, demonstrating that granting baptism to non-Christians, just like giving the Eucharist to the baptized, was no cause for fear that the sentence might be canceled. Admittedly, there was the tradition that had it that encountering a priest while he was carrying the Host was due cause for granting a pardon to the condemned. But Antonio da Gama methodically examined all the reasons in favor of granting the individual sacraments to those who asked for them, from baptism to confirmation to the Eucharist. Each time he concluded that the salvation of the soul had nothing to do with the salvation of earthly life. In any case, the sentence had to follow its due course. In his view, the Eucharist should also be given to relapsed heretics and even to apostates—that is, to Jews converted to Christianity who had then returned to their old faith—a widespread condition in Portugal, to the extent that a tribunal of the Inquisition had been set up there along the lines of the Spanish one. For Antonio da Gama, the condition of the apostates was the most serious one: and yet the sacraments could not be denied even to them, if they were penitent. Once again, the argument for forgiveness and the restoration of communion with the Church could only be sustained by severing any link with the right to life on earth.

Alliances and distinctions between the two powers were made in a context where new ideas were gaining ground and the crisis of traditional religion was becoming manifest. The Lutheran Church had entrusted itself to the power of the territorial princes and Luther, having preached his theology of the Cross, had guaranteed that the exercising of earthly power would receive divine approval and promised a place in heaven to those who took the sword to peasants in revolt. But not everyone was willing to follow Luther down this path. One indirect but very clear expression of dissent can be found in the *Praeparatio ad mortem* that Erasmus wrote for Thomas Boleyn.

According to Erasmus, an abyss separated divine justice from the temporal variety, and no one had the right to deduce the eternal fate of the soul from the form of death: a situation might arise, in his view, that "a man whose body is quartered because he has incited sedition may pass into the company of the angels."[54] On the other hand, Erasmus also took issue with the Catholic obsession about the need for the dying to receive the sacraments, and tried to curb the anxieties of those who were deprived of confession and Communion. Anyone disturbed by the fear of not being given the sacraments on the point of death was invited to seek peace by trusting in God, abandoning a way of thinking based on human appearances. Hell might await even those who died having received the Holy Unction; and, moreover, ardent faith could save anyone. The examples cited by Erasmus are pertinent to our case: "Let examples . . . be persons who have died through shipwreck or by execution or, for instance, through a sudden illness or accident."[55] Views like this spread throughout Europe: the discredit into which ecclesiastical mediation fell was the other side of the need to achieve what one very widely read text described as "the tranquility of the soul." How could one assure the serenity of a conscience which, though conscious of sins and their inevitable alliance with human nature, sought a solid foothold, a reassuring certainty of the possible salvation of the soul? This is what was offered by the doctrine of justification by faith, or, as it was called in Italy, the "benefit of Christ for Christians," a message that found an audience beyond the sphere occupied by ferocious doctrinal controversies among theologians. It was a simple and clear alternative to the insecurity that drove people to procure indulgences and blessed amulets, to endlessly recite the prayers of the Rosary, to trust in the short Latin formulas put about by popular preachers. And what about the search for letters of confession that guaranteed absolution from any sin by any confessor in the event of being in danger of death? These were the insurance policies devised at the time for the needs and fears of those who set out on long and dangerous journeys. But the multiplication of remedies did not resolve the problem, rather it increased the uncertainty. The medieval tradition of the "art of dying well," an invitation to detach oneself from the fallacious world and to meditate upon death, had experienced a turning point with the Black Plague of 1348 and the wars that ravaged late medieval Europe. Ecclesiastical culture had responded to the sense of insecurity and the perception of the fleetingness of life with writings that offered a guide to confession as the tie to be established between the laity and ecclesiastical power, the only authority able to identify and cure the illnesses of sin. One had to live with the expectancy of death as the instant that would decide one's eternal fate, and be ready to make confession and, thanks to ecclesiastic mediation, be presented before God's tribunal free from sin. The fear of sin and of hell was a feeling experienced in dramatic fashion by the young Luther: and one of his first writings as a reformer was in fact a *Sermon on Preparing to Die,* which ran to no fewer than twenty-two editions between 1519 and 1525. His proposal was to free oneself from the anxiety multiplied by the mechanism of indulgences and the danger of scruples and to trust in the certainty of the justification obtained by the Passion and death of Jesus Christ; the new proposal quickly led to manuals on comforting and preparing for death that entered circulation alongside Luther's catechism and the instructions for pastors. Caspar Huberinus and Urbanus Rhegius were the first to produce texts that enjoyed rapid success, also because they were illustrated and enriched by the engravings of Hans Holbein. In Catholic Italy, the work by Urbanus Rhegius, the humanist reformer of Augsburg, circulated anonymously under a title which, translating the original exactly, sounded identical to the one used by the Dominican archbishop of Florence, Saint Antonio Pierozzi, for his highly popular instruction treatise on how to confess: *Medicina dell'anima.*[56] It was a medicine with a simple prescription: let go of the obsession with scruples and the quest for meritorious works and trust in faith; for sins "there is no other satisfaction than the death of Christ."[57] The alternative solution was the one that enjoyed the favor of the Church as a corporation of clergy, who went into battle to defend the power to remit sins.

So in places where the ecclesiastical structure remained strong and widespread, opinions like those expressed in the *Medicina dell'anima* appeared dangerous. A growing number of people stepped onto the stage of the scaffold, not just thieves and murderers but many who were tried and sentenced for their religious ideas. They were judged by state and ecclesiastical powers that considered doctrinal dissidence a crime of human and divine lèsemajesté—a rebellion against God and his representatives on earth. The division ran between the Iberian monarchies, where an ecclesiastical tribunal of the Inquisition subject to the king's power was operating, and the French and English ones, where the power of the sovereign lashed out at dissidents considered guilty of treason. The theoretically universal authority of the cardinals' congregation of the Roman Inquisition was actually recognized almost only in the Italian states. One feature common to the different institutions of justice was the idea of the divine origins of the power to punish: the condemned thus had to accept their fate as something willed by God. The differences emerged in the answers to the problem of whether and how to grant them access to the sacraments. We have already seen how the question of the confession of the condemned had been an area of conflict between the papacy and the king of France since the end of the fourteenth century. From then on the rite of confession before the scaffold had become generalized, and the *Constitutio Criminalis Carolina* promulgated for the empire on the authority of Charles V in 1532 had established the rule. But the forms of that confession diverged according to the confessional divisions. In Lutheran Germany the Catholic doctrine of the power of the clergy to absolve sins was not valid: humanity was so radically corrupt that the only possibility was to entrust oneself to the justification of sinners obtained by Christ with his death on the Cross. So the rule was to send a pastor to talk to the condemned, inviting them to repent and to consider their punishment as the manifestation of God's wrath for their sins, as we read in the diary of the Nuremberg pastor Veit Dietrich.[58]

The rules laid out in the *Carolina* were articulated with precision in the practical instructions published under the name of the Flemish judge Joost Damhouder, a text to which Antonio da Gama also made reference. Damhouder's work amplified, adapted, and published in various languages a short practical instruction by another writer. It circulated widely in the territories of the empire, providing judges with a shared culture and a repertoire of images that simplified and unified judicial procedure. In it, the confession of the condemned was described in words and images.[59] But the question that now troubled jurists, canonists, and the political and religious authorities was whether the condemned should or should not be able to receive Communion. The widespread practice—"generalis consuetudo"—that Antonio da Gama saw around him was to withhold it. This is what happened in France, Spain, and Portugal.

But the overall panorama had in the meantime changed profoundly. While western Europe was being torn by religious divisions and conflicts, the world had expanded. Advance groups of conquistadors had begun venturing out to conquer new lands and peoples. Material conquest was accompanied by the design to achieve religious conquest as well. Here, too, we find the Jesuits very much at the fore. And among the proposals they made to peoples and sovereigns, we find the Italian model for comforting the condemned.

". . . y piddiendo a Dios misericordia lo matan":
The Jesuits and the Export of Comforting
around the World

IN 1600 a Jesuit priest from Navarre, Jerome Xavier, the great-nephew of Francis Xavier (who had played a leading role in the early contact with cultures in the Far East), dedicated to the Moghul emperor Akbar the Great an apologetics book that presented the fundamental principles of Christianity and compared them with the Muslim religion. One of the arguments intended to convince Akbar of the superiority of the law of Christians concerned the victorious expansion in America. In the New World, wrote Father Xavier, there is not "a single Moor who follows Mohammed," and because all Europe was Christian, he concluded that the followers of Christ were more numerous than the Moors.[1] Among the aspects of European Christian culture as presented by Father Xavier we also find the comforted death of the condemned. The key phases in this ritual are described with care. The sentence is pronounced, with the execution due to take place shortly afterward. The job of making the announcement is given to a friar (a "father"), so the prisoner might be persuaded to accept the punishment in the best way possible, with courage and patience, preparing himself in good time through confession to entrust his soul to God. A procession forms, led by a choir of innocent orphans, who will pray to the saints in heaven that they might intercede with God. Then comes the condemned, who will have at least two friars by his side, intent on persuading him to accept his death as penance for his sins, casting aside all hatred, forgiving his accusers, and asking forgiveness for his wrongs. He will be killed at the precise moment in which he is invoking the holy name of Jesus and asking for God's mercy ("y invocando el santo nombre de Jesus y piddiendo a Dios misericordia lo matan"). At this point the "father" will preach a sermon to the onlookers, taking advantage of the general commotion caused by the execution to talk to them about God, about sin, about death which is certain, and the hour of death which is not. He will ask them to pray for the dead person's soul and offer alms in suffrage. After this, everyone will return to their homes, moved by events and consoled by the help they have given to the poor "patient." No such help was to be found among Moors and pagans, because they treated the condemned without compassion, as if butchering an animal for its meat. The Christian ritual, on the other hand, is dominated by the "father," who takes the patient's confession, instructs him in what he must believe and do, and helps him to die. He does all this because he is well prepared to perform his task: he knows medicine and philosophy, and has studied in a college where he has learned to perform the role of the spiritual father. In short, he is a Jesuit.

By the time Father Xavier wrote his book, the Jesuits had accumulated a vast experience in this specific field. The world that Ignatius had seen as a battlefield dominated by the clash between two opposing armies flying the flags of God and the Devil was divided and torn by religious conflicts in Europe, but it was also united in a network of information and experiences by the letters of Jesuits operating in far-flung corners of the globe. The West Indies, with its naked, welcoming populations, was a world that gave missionaries the powerful emotion of a protective and salvific paternity together with the shiver of the risk of ending up being eaten by cannibals. In the meantime, news trickled in of sophisticated diatribes between their advance scouts in the Far East and Confucian men of letters. In Europe the conquest of souls was now a vast field, with martyrdom being promised to those who operated in England, and plenty of occasions for doctrinal comparison and dispute in that part of Europe conquered by the Reformation. Taking confessions and comforting were duties to perform in the most varied conditions, for instance alongside *confratelli* sent to the scaffold as traitors by the courts of Elizabethan England, or among the Waldensian peoples of Calabria and Piedmont, or the Muslim minorities of Spain.

Father Xavier's description reveals the sense of pride that the Catholic way of putting someone to death stimulated in a missionary. The baroque spectacle of death exalted churchmen and made them experience the emotion of a return to the apostolic age and the triumphs of the martyrs. This is exemplified by the testimony of Cardinal Federico Borromeo, who, moved by the spectacle "of intense penitence" on the scaffold, observed: "And now I understand the reason why the martyrs thanked those who condemned them, and incited the wild animals against them in the amphitheater."[2] The work of the Jesuits, experts in the art of comforting and conversion, was full of instances of intense penitence. In prisons and hospitals, as in the preparation of those condemned to the scaffold, their presence was sought after, appreciated, and considered crucial. They were called to Inquisition jails to try to win over the most stubborn heretics, and they figured as members in the companies of justice of the Spanish viceroyalties in Italy. And they tended to transplant that model wherever possible. As we have seen, it was due to their influence that the themes and the forms of spiritual assistance given to the condemned spread in seventeenth-century France. They were actively engaged in the places where it was deemed necessary to extirpate forms of religion viewed as pagan, idolatrous, or simply heretical; from the Waldensians of Calabria, Lucania, and the alpine valleys of Piedmont to the Moriscos of Andalusia and the "infidels" and "pagans" of the East and West Indies. They made a particularly precocious appearance on the scene in Goa. Here the first decades of Portuguese dominion had seen a harsh and violent justice at work; even as late as 1546 an Indian woman who had murdered her husband was put to death, together with her lover, in accordance with a horrific ancient Roman ritual—she was thrown into the water inside a barrel together with various animals and without any religious comforting. But already in 1549 a letter from Goa informed the members of the Society that one of their brothers who had been ordained into the priesthood by Francis Xavier "used to visit the condemned when they were taken to the gallows."[3] From then on there was a proliferation of reports by Jesuit missionaries about their successes as confessors and comforters. Executions offered them a final chance to convert and baptize Hindus and Muslims, and to obtain the abjuration of "New Christians" who had returned to Judaism. The relations between the Society and the Inquisition on the one hand and the *misericordia* associations on the other became ever closer. This gave rise to forms of collaboration but also to tensions: the Jesuit tendency to allow the condemned confession and Communion irked those who rejected and were suspicious of the use made by the Jesuits of their privilege to grant absolution from heresy in confession. This is not the place to chart, even briefly, the way in which the vast experience that filled Father Xavier with such pride in his apologetics book was built up. But it was in particular thanks to the work of the Jesuits that religious comforting and the elaboration of rituals of justice dominated by the theme of forgiveness and penitence spread outside of Europe and into the Iberian colonial empires.

What distinguished the Jesuits was their use of confession to persuade and to comfort. We can gain an idea of this from testimony left by members of the Society who worked in jails and below scaffolds in the Iberian Peninsula during the sixteenth century. Here the theme of comforting featured regularly in Jesuit literary and theological exercises. One of the Society's most famous and controversial authors, Juan Bautista Poza (1588–1659), composed a *Prática de ayudar a bien morir,* which, after the first edition of 1619, had no fewer than twelve reprints and translations.[4] But the richest and most important work by a Jesuit was the one composed by Pedro de León (1545–1632), which remained unpublished. Working as a missionary in Andalusia, where the violence of the powerful and the abject poverty of the people was bound up with religious and cultural conflicts between Christians and Muslims, he presented the results of his experience in a *Compendio.* Instead of dispensing theoretical advice and a generic morality, he took on the role of the attentive and curious historian, chronicling the work performed by the Jesuits between Granada and Seville from the beginning of their presence in Andalusia—that is, from 1550.[5] The realism of the work, designed as a manual of instruction for the brothers, is probably the reason why it was never published. Moreover, the expulsion of the Moriscos in 1608 had put an end to the missionary's hopes of convincing the authorities to employ nonviolent methods. Pedro de León had witnessed the execution of many Moriscos, and in his accounts revealed the injustices that were committed. More in general, what he related in his book was too rich in detail, too true: his passion as a historian and his curiosity about concrete events and the description of men and things made the work unpalatable and dangerous in the eyes of the censors, all the more so as it was written in Castilian and therefore not even obfuscated by the use of ecclesiastical Latin. The stories of the confessions that were heard probably sufficed to lay the Jesuits open to the charge that the secrecy of the sacrament had been broken. Over the course of thirty-eight years of missionary work in the most varied places in Andalusia, the author found himself for long periods acting as confessor to the imprisoned and condemned, and had carefully noted down the circumstances of the executions and the modes of comforting. When he turned historian at a late age and gathered together a lifetime's material to extract some advice for his readers, he prepared an appendix with an annotated and chronological list of all the cases.

It is a document that offers extraordinary testimony of the commitment invested by members of the Society whenever there was the possibility of winning over souls for the Catholic heaven. But Pedro de León's notes also show how, besides their practical endeavor, the Jesuits never neglected the intellectual one of study and written communication. He also drew inspiration from Polanco's work, which he referred to in the *Compendio*.[6] But in his writing he transformed brief instructions into a work worthy of the very best season of Spanish "Golden Age" literature: the *Compendio* offers impassioned and extraordinarily rich testimony of what the Jesuit had learned while comforting the imprisoned and the condemned, and of his own personal experience of the work he had undertaken. The advice and recommendations in the first part are drawn from personal experience, to which the text makes continual reference. In the appendix to the second part of the treatise we find a whole gallery of names—307 in all—of executed prisoners, together with systematic descriptions of how they met their end; these were ordered by year, starting from 1578 and running through to 1616.[7] Quite uniquely in the history of comforting literature, Pedro de León combined into a single work, dominated by the need to give an account of his activity as a missionary and confessor, the different literary and documentary genres that until then had proceeded along parallel and noncommunicating lines: the list of the condemned, the description of behavior, the theoretical and practical advice for comforters. To all of this he also added his own feelings and emotions as the narrator, for example the superstitious fear he experienced in his first post, when he was terrified that the spirits of the executed might return in search of vengeance.[8] No one, not even the Jesuits, ever admitted such a fear so frankly. But that this was the reason why people avoided any contact with the condemned was not in doubt. Around the 1550s, in a century in which the Jesuits had begun operating almost simultaneously in the prisons of the Spanish Empire, from Andalusia to Sicily, one of Pedro de León's fellow brothers active in Sicily related that the people there were convinced that the souls of the executed came back to "molest those by whom they had been accompanied to their death."⁹ As for Pedro de León, his fear had been so acute that initially he had tried to get out of doing the task. But then he had obeyed, and gradually immersed himself totally in the world of Seville's jails. Attending to the spiritual needs of the prisoners brought him into contact with a society apart, with its own special culture and characters. Living and moving around in large communal cells, the variegated population of thieves, murderers, heretics, prostitutes, pedophiles, and sodomites had developed their own special language (Pedro de León included a few words in his text) and what we might call an alternative morality. The Jesuit had come to realize, for example, that a kind of reverse image of justice and death on the scaffold circulated in prison: these marginal figures had, as it were, an everyday, habitual relationship with death by execution. They were like moths attracted to a flame: even if they escaped the gallows a first time that was where they ended up sooner or later. What is more, a kind of intense underground life existed in the prisons, with a culture of trial and punishment that was like a reverse image of the higher world. The inmates mimed trials and sentences, and improvised theater scenes worthy of the Castilian culture of Lope de Vega, with one prisoner playing the part of the executioner and another that of the condemned person. The obsessive, looming threat of death was exorcised with a transposition into the world of the imagination. And the prisoners faced up to the fear of dying by elaborating a heroic image of the victim, thus preparing for their role in the theatrical act where real death awaited them.

Pedro de León was the first observer of that hellish world to describe these aspects of the play of mirrors between the rituals of criminal justice and prison culture. Like an anthropologist among the people of a distant land he was concerned to decode their practices and mental categories, and understand their language. Comprehension of unknown languages was the first step toward entering in contact with societies to Christianize. The Jesuits were very clear about this, which is why they took particular care in translating confession manuals for non-Christian peoples. But what the condemned said in confession also had to be carefully deciphered, as this occasion represented the last chance for prisoners to try to affirm their innocence and obtain, if nothing else, a suspension of the sentence. Conscious of the extreme nature of what the condemned were facing, Pedro de León advised great prudence and the recourse to some astute stratagems. His first, crucial recommendation was to read the trial proceedings of the individuals to confess. This amounted to a reversal of the relationship between sacramental confession and judicial confession, which the Italian comforters interpreted as two separate and conflicting realities, with the sacrament being, in their view, the supreme one. Instead, the Spanish Jesuit suggested carefully finding out about the details of the judicial confession so as to better conduct the sacramental one. He claims to have always done this, right from his very first case in 1578, involving a young eighteen-year-old originally from Cagliari, Pedro de Multes, who had been found guilty of murder. The Jesuit was perfectly aware that lying was part and parcel of the desperate efforts made by the condemned to clear themselves, and even extended into what was said in the secrecy of confession. Denying the charges against them right to the end, even in confession, was one of the ways in which the condemned, hoping for intervention by the friars, tried to get their trial reopened. On one occasion, Pedro de León related, as he was climbing down the scaffold ladder after receiving the nod from the executioner, he was called back by the condemned person, who said to him: "Father, I accuse myself of having made up everything I have said to you."[10] It was therefore necessary to give him a hasty, rough-and-ready absolution, so as not to displease the spectators and delay the function. Experiences like these had taught him how desperate the stakes were with regard to the sacrament of confession. At the same time, one had to be mentally braced to hear terrible things, in some cases so horrific as to leave the confessor speechless or induce him to make comments that might ruin the whole effect of the sacrament. Without knowing the kinds of experiences that the guests in the prisons of Seville and Granada had lived through there was a concrete risk that all efforts to comfort them would fail. This is what had befallen one of Pedro de León's fellow brothers, who had filled in for him in Seville while he himself was away on a mission. His substitute, a young, shy Jesuit, was rejected as a comforter by a captain (probably an Englishman) who had been sentenced to death for treason and rebellion. The captain knelt and began his confession, recounting how he and his gang had killed eight Catholics in an ambush. Frightened, the Jesuit exclaimed: "Sweet Jesus, and did they all die?" Whereupon the captain sprang to his feet and burst out: "What are you so surprised about? Are you frightened about just eight deaths? I am not the right man for Your Reverence, nor is Your Reverence the right man for me. You know only the area around your own house and you presume to confess a man who has traveled all over the world."[11]

Stories like this shed a glimmer of light on a reality that the devout bureaucracy of the *confratelli* preferred to ignore. Not for nothing did this text remain unpublished. In the "melancholic nights" of comforting in Andalusia—but undoubtedly elsewhere as well—one heard many tales of larger than life lives, full of adventure, passion, and violence. The condemned—men, women, boys—wanted to talk about their life, which was about to end. They had lots to say and little time to do so, and the confessor was the only possible listener. It was difficult not to be swept along by the prisoners' urgent need to tell their stories in their final hours. There were stories of love and death, like that of Maria Anna de Sotomayor and her slave Jerónimo, both executed in 1588, he for having involuntarily caused the death of his master during a robbery and she for having been his lover;[12] or that of Miguel Jerónimo de Salazar, a schoolmaster from Seville, condemned by the Inquisition to death by burning for being a sodomite. He died with a display of great devotion and profound contrition, but also made it clear to the Jesuit that his vice was unbeatable—anyone who experienced it could never free himself from it.[13] Faced with all these stories, the first rule Pedro de León had set himself was that of the ancient stoics: "Nihil admirari," let nothing astonish you. Just listen, and simply say: "Go on" ("Adelante"). Having said that, it was also necessary to understand where the truth ended and deception borne of desperation began. But these episodes suffice to give an idea of what those prisons in Seville were like in the years of the war with England and the tragedy of the Moriscos following the Granada revolt of 1568 and before their general expulsion in 1609. The confessor had available the three days as stipulated by Philip II: one for confession, another for Communion, and the third one for the scaffold. It was important not to go beyond three days, according to Pedro de León, because there was the danger that their feelings might cool and the tension ease off, leading to negative effects.[14] But it was also necessary to avoid becoming caught up by the problems arising from the overcrowding and racket of spaces where several prisoners might be being prepared for death at the same time. Hence the comic and grotesque nature of many episodes related by Pedro de León. He describes a prison scene where the air is filled with noise and shouting, with men condemned to death moving around in a confined space as if in thrall

to a strange euphoria. They exchange odd recipes for escaping death (for instance, marrying a prostitute), worry about and hope they will be buried in
their hometown (because a religious burial would ensure relatives did not
remain tarred with the brush of infamy), boast of their bravery in enduring
terrible acts of torture, and speak without anxiety about death by hanging or
beheading. They talk about those who allow a hand or arm to be burned, and
get fired up when someone says: "Cheer up mate, tonight you'll be having
dinner with Jesus Christ!" And in the meantime they mechanically recite all
the prayers and devout formulas suggested by the comforters. De León tries
to restrain them, to get them to reason, inviting them to think with sorrow
about the sins they have committed. He suggests they should not recite
prayers that they do not understand, but say something personal, because an
"acto proprio" arising from one's own feelings is worth more than a hundred
suggested by us—says the Jesuit—and repeated parrot fashion. And they begin
to say: "Señor Nuestro Jesucristo, actos proprios."[15] Pedro de León is reminded
here of what he had once been told by another Jesuit, Juan de la Plaza, former
assistant to Archbishop Pedro Guerrero. During the years of the repression
of the revolt of the Moriscos in Granada, when many rebels were sent to
their deaths and many comforters were busy assisting them, Father Juan de la
Plaza urged them to think of their own prayers to say and kept repeating the
words "actos propios." That is how the expression took on and became a special exclamation, repeated with great faith by the prisoners.[16]

Another Jesuit also deserves to be mentioned here. In 1605, shortly
before Pedro de León wrote his *Compendio,* the Catalan Father Pere Gil
(1551–1622) published *Modo de aiudar a bien morir.*[17] His was an exceptional case in Spanish literature about the art of dying well: of the twenty
texts belonging to this literary genre published in Spain between 1510 and
1604, his was the only one that dealt with the category of the condemned,
with the exception of the Castilian edition of the treatise by Juan de Polanco.[18] In his work, Pere Gil, following Polanco's model, set out to instruct
those who had to assist people dying from sickness or about to be put to
death as the result of a court sentence. He had been prompted to this task
by the bishop of Barcelona, Dimas Loris, who was concerned by the igno-
rance of the parish clergy. Pere Gil wrote his work in Catalan, intending it
for a vast territorial and linguistic area of the kingdom of Spain, including
the Balearic Islands and Sardinia—an area beset by social unrest and re-

bellion, and by an epidemic of anti-witchcraft obsession. The mediator of an art that came from Italy and Rome (Pere Gil recalled with admiration what he had seen in Rome, Naples, and Sicily[19]), he also tried to ensure that the viceroy of Catalonia received the new rules drawn up by the Holy Office in Rome to put an end to the devastating practice of considering confessions made under torture by those charged with witchcraft to be proof.[20] The conditions in which the Jesuit comforters worked here were extremely difficult. Father Gil describes noisy, crowded cells where it was difficult to build up a personal relationship with the condemned. It was difficult even to be heard: sometimes the cries and blasphemies of the hapless prisoners were so loud that it was necessary to resort to the *badall,* an instrument used to force an animal's jaws open. It was not unheard of for someone to break the cell's water jug in an effort to commit suicide; in such cases it was necessary to explain that suicide was more dishonorable than the scaffold. Above all, it was difficult to combat the "most terrible" temptation of those who were innocent but had been sentenced to death and could not believe that this was the will of God. Such cases were far from infrequent, but here too the Jesuit had come up with an answer. If the condemned man was guilty, his cross was that of the good thief in the Gospel; if on the other hand he was suffering blamelessly, the cross he bore was that of Christ himself.[21]

From these Jesuit testimonies it appears that the condemned were ready to convert and present themselves to the crowd with the attitude of the penitent sinner. Yet we should not forget Giacinto Manaro's description of the anonymous prisoner in the Bologna jail, who, "lying on a mattress," lifts his head in the darkness of the night and furtively tries to see if the door to the *conforteria* is open. It is a clue reminding us of the reality lurking behind the unctuously devout descriptions of the comforters.

Historical documents sometimes offer a glimpse of the violence to which prisoners were subjected, bending them to behave as penitent sinners. The wealth of extant documentation about the administration of criminal justice on the island of Malta provides many examples of this kind. Here too Jesuits were actively engaged in "comforting," for instance Pier Francesco Rosignoli (1690–1775), well known as a writer of pious legends and apologetic texts. But the reality of Maltese courts and prisons was not best suited to devout meditations. On the island, where the powerful Knights Hospitaller had their headquarters, was a social hierarchy in which the lowest level was occupied by slaves captured in raids against Muslim pirate ships; just one rung above were those who had been condemned to the galleys by court sentences; and finally there were the volunteer sailors, known as *buonavoglia*—three categories of men with absolutely no rights and subject to the harsh laws of a Christian outpost in the middle of a Muslim Mediterranean. The dominant force on the island were the Knights Hospitaller, made up of the heirs to noble families: violent and overbearing, they dealt in piracy and slavery. The order had great powers and privileges, together with a propensity to abuse them, and their privileges were guaranteed by the papacy. But to control what happened on the island, which saw the arrival of both Muslim slaves and heretics fleeing from the Church, the papacy sent an inquisitor to judge crimes against the Catholic faith. So it was that the violence of the law and of men acquired particular characteristics in Malta, as demonstrated by the numerous suicide attempts among the incarcerated. And in the mid-eighteenth century, slaves were in such desperation that they even attempted a revolt aimed at overthrowing the existing order. The ensuing punishments were extremely harsh.

The history of the administration of justice in Malta is documented by an extraordinary abundance of sources, held in archives on the island but elsewhere as well. The copious correspondence of the inquisitors with Rome forms an important part of these sources. The letters of the inquisitor Girolamo Casanate, for example, are in the Biblioteca Casanatense in Rome, the library which is named after him and contains his very rich book collection. A recent and solid study by a Maltese historian tackles these aspects of criminal justice on the island.[22] It is a history steeped in blood and suffering: countless individual tragedies, concealed from the public gaze with the liturgies displayed by the condemned, tortured and sent to die as penitent sinners willing to face the torments of their final hours as the price to pay for an eternity of joy in heaven. Anyone who did not accept could expect even greater suffering. Not all did accept: many Muslims remained true to their faith, despite the cost. Those who gave in were forced to display their subjection to the spectators and perform the special ritual of kissing the gallows.

No one was deceived. When, in August 1761, the unbending judge Giulio Cumbo died immediately after having signed his last two capital sentences, the Maltese crowd greeted the procession taking him for burial with a barrage of insults and stones, and loud cries of "Hurrah."

31

The German World, the Reformation, and the New Image of the Executioner

JEAN GERSON'S PROTEST in France calling for the sacraments to be granted to the condemned also found an audience in neighboring Germany during the early beginnings of the religious reform movement. Thanks to the diffusion of the chancellor of the Sorbonne's work others took up the proposal to give the Christian sacraments to condemned offenders as a form of forgiveness and reconciliation. In Strasburg the popular preacher Johann Geiler von Kaiserberg (1445–1510) requested a modification to the city statutes to enable the condemned to partake of sacramental confession; together with the humanist Jacob Wimpfeling, he had published Gerson's works, whose efforts to reform the Church he shared. He had been inspired by these endeavors to propose, in 1482, in the cathedral chapter and before the diocesan synod, an amendment to the rules, which in his view ran contrary to the Holy Scriptures. The members of the chapter were all men of very high standing, prompting Erasmus to observe that if Jesus Christ himself had applied to be a canon he would have had little chance of being accepted. It is not hard to imagine, then, how little they would have been concerned about those condemned to the scaffold. But despite the resistance, for years Geiler von Kaiserberg kept up the pressure, addressing entreaties to the city authorities and also turning to the University of Heidelberg for an opinion. Finally, in 1485, the city council approved a reform of customary practice: condemned prisoners were now to be allowed a confessor immediately after being notified of their sentence, and if the confessor deemed them worthy they could be granted Communion as well. In this case, the execution was put off two days. There was, however, to be no talk of burying the body in holy ground.[1]

In the city and diocese of Constance too there was uncertainty for a long time about whether or not those who had been put to death should receive a Christian burial. In 1387, in response to a formal request, the authorities gave their assent on the condition that the condemned displayed signs of remorse at the moment of death. The granting of the sacraments is only attested from 1434 onward.[2] (Of course, the heretic Jerome of Prague did not receive them: condemned by the Council, he faced his death with the gladness of one who expected from God the reward for his faith, attracting the admiration of the humanist Poggio Bracciolini.) This is borne out by what is known more generally about judicial practices in the empire. Ritual burial was considered a kind of softening of the death penalty, and was allowed from time to time depending on requests and also on the behavior of the condemned in their final moments. One characteristic of the administration of justice in the German world was the existence of long-established common-law practices that had given rise to various different rituals of capital punishment and forms of burial, and of any eventual comforting. The German system of punishments has long been thought to have been marked by an ancient and deep-rooted ruthlessness. The records and descriptions of the tortures inflicted on the condemned, and the irreverent treatment of their corpses, have encouraged the idea that capital punishment was particularly ferocious in the German-speaking world, as attested very early on by Tacitus in his *Germania*. To this can be added the argument, proposed in the twentieth century, that capital punishment was used in ancient Germanic law as a kind of religious sacrifice and as a way of preserving racial purity.[3] Recently, a rather more careful examination of the issue has prompted historians to look not just at what the statutes stated but also at the ancient chronicles and trial proceedings still held in German city archives. As a consequence, the perceived image of German cruelty has been revised considerably, or at any rate its statistical significance greatly reduced.[4] From the end of the fifteenth century, the myriad of common-law practices gradually began to be supplanted by the framework of the Roman law model, employed as an instrument of centralization in relation to the territorial states and the empire. Despite an initially spirited reaction in defense of tradition, the new rules spread rapidly thanks to the drawing up of full-blown written criminal codes by advisors to the kings. Written in German, they were also extensively illustrated to more effectively clarify the different phases of the trial and punishment.[5] This illustrated literature started with the criminal code of Bamberg (1507) and the *Layenspiegel* (1508), a very popular book of law by Ulrich Tengler, and continued with a whole tradition of illustrated criminal codes throughout the sixteenth century.

One important part of this was the promulgation by Emperor Charles V, in 1532, of the famous criminal constitution that bore his name, the *Constitutio criminalis Carolina*. All these sources contain images specifically depicting the forms of comforting used to try to get punished criminals to convert and to behave humbly and contritely on the scaffold. Of the many etchings that illustrate the criminal codes of the various territorial states and

FIGURE 31.1. How the friar must show the crucifix to the condemned, in *Constitutio penalis Bambergensis* (Mainz, 1507). MUNICH: BAYERISCHE STAASBIBLIOTHEK.

free cities of Germany from the end of the fifteenth century onward, the most frequently recurrent one shows the condemned offender kneeling, hands tied, in front of a friar who is holding out a crucifix.[6] In some cases there is also the scene of the prisoner being confessed just prior to execution, while the scaffold is being erected in the background. The person doing the comforting is always a friar: even the devout lay movement of the "Alexian Brothers," also known as the Cellites, active between Cologne and Antwerp in the early fifteenth century in assisting the sick and dying, had then been transformed into a religious order in 1472. It was in this capacity that, in 1556, the Cellites were given permanent responsibility for assisting those condemned to death,[7] one of the signs that the norms established by Charles V were gradually being implemented. In them, besides provisions regarding how various different crimes should be punished, magistrates were also invited not to obstruct the granting of sacramental confession to the condemned.[8] In the three days between the sentence and its execution, the condemned was to be prepared for confession, which had to be, and appear to be, free and unconditional. The norm had enduring efficacy even after the Peace of Augsburg, in a Germany divided between different religious confessions. Spiritual assistance was provided by churchmen, who had the task of convincing the condemned to publicly beg for forgiveness and declare themselves contrite and convinced of the justness of their punishment. The power of the emperor could not override the criminal constitutions of individual states and free cities, but the norms proposed by Charles V functioned as a reference model and over the long term provided the foundations of a common criminal code for the judges of the German Empire. They were even taken into account in the regulatory arrangements of the new evangelical churches that arose out of the Protestant Reformation, with provision being made for providing religious assistance to the condemned, and possibly the sacraments as well. One such example can be found in the statutes of the church ordinance of Lübeck drawn up by the reformer Johannes Bugenhagen and promulgated in 1531. One chapter is specifically devoted to the charitable work of going to visit malefactors: besides accompanying the condemned to the scaffold, the pastor could also see them beforehand, in order to try to impart some understanding of the Gospels. This was indicated as the evangelical work of charity that would lead Christ, in the Final Judgment, to acknowledge his servants. If, observed Bugenhagen, the condemned then confessed the true faith and asked to receive the sacrament, it was not to be denied, but granted one or two days before execution—even though, in reality, from what can be read in the statute, such a concession was by no means habitual and indeed in many places was refused.[9] However, the progressive application of the *Carolina* would make it customary to provide assistance to the condemned, and not just the spiritual variety: the care taken in preparing a final supper—often a veritable banquet—for those about to be executed had nothing comparable in the Mediterranean world.[10] Older traditions would also gradually be subsumed within the forms of the new rules. The regulations of the Alexian Brothers approved in 1556 stated that when a death sentence was passed one of their number would go to the prison the evening before execution to comfort the condemned person, and would accompany him to the scaffold the next day, exhorting him to accept his fate. The brother's chief task was to hold out a crucifix so the prisoner could kiss it, and to do so immediately before the final moment, just as the executioner was raising his axe.[11] As for the function of the churchman, this was considered so important as to envisage the deferment of the execution by a few days if the offender did not display an adequate propensity to repent.[12] Of course, it was not always possible to guarantee the presence of a priest for Catholics and a pastor for Lutherans, and this gave rise to heated theological disputes and attempts to convert condemned prisoners to one or other confession, depending on individual cases.

As the new Churches were being built, the foundations laid by the reformers adapted according to relations with the secular power. As regards the spiritual one, the Lutheran cancellation of the "three walls" swept away indulgences, intercessions, and meritorious acts of suffrage for souls. In the theses on indulgences, Luther had affirmed (thesis 36): "Any truly remorseful Christian has a right to full remission of guilt and penalty, even without indulgence letters."[13] The doctrine of justification by faith made its entrance with the reassurance that humanity is forgiven thanks to the Passion of Christ. But the consequence of this was that temporal power remained the undisputed master of the field: with Luther, as Karl Marx wrote, bondage out of devotion was replaced with bondage out of conviction. In his work *On Secular Authority* the key passage from the Scriptures on which Luther based his argument was once again the history-laden one of Romans 13:1. The use of force was represented in the simplest and most everyday manner for the Christian masses by the sword of God; and as "power is the hand-maiden of God, its use must be allowed not only to pagans but to all man-kind."[14] So was it right to kill? In the context of the renewed topicality and urgency of the evangelical and biblical texts, the question was a very perti-nent one. Luther's response, which would soon be disputed by the former Benedictine monk Michael Sattler at the Anabaptist synod of Schleitheim, was very clear-cut: the principle of nonviolence held for relations between Christians, but did not apply to a world that was not Christian. Here the sword was needed for the benefit of "your neighbour and the whole world." Therefore, Luther urged, "if you see that there is a lack of hangmen, court officials, judges, lords or princes, and you find that you have the necessary skills, then you should offer your services and seek office, so that authority, which is so greatly needed, will never come to be held in contempt, become powerless, or perish. The world cannot get by without it."[15]

The change in the European landscape during the age of Reformation and the establishment of the hegemonic power of sovereigns in the territo-rial states was reflected in the new definition of the role of a key player in the scene acted out on the scaffold: the executioner. He was the one who, alone or with his helpers, had to carry out the sentence. It was important that he did it well, as he would bear full responsibility in the event of failure. If the rope broke, the crowd would promptly hail it as a miracle, but it was his job to prepare it correctly. Everything also had to be timed to perfection, so that at the exact moment in which the victim began to drop he, the exe-cutioner, had to jump on his shoulders, while a helper, known as a "feet puller" (*tirapiedi* in Italy), hung off the victim's feet for greater efficacy. The crowd's feelings of devout commotion and pity for the fate of the executed person's soul could always turn in an instant into the vengeful fury of a popular revolt—not against the governing power but against the executioner whose incompetence had caused undue suffering to the victim and put the salvation of their soul at risk. Generally, the executioner was a former con-demned prisoner whose life had been spared or sentence commuted on the condition that he took on a public office refused and feared by all. Such was the case of a certain Perone da Novara, who was sentenced to death in Siena in 1415 and given the job of being the *manigoldo*. He did this for two years, until he found another condemned prisoner, the Slavonian Simone da Zagabria, to take his place. Perone's request was accepted partly because

Simone shrewdly asked for the commutation of his sentence with the argument that his soul, which risked damnation, might be saved and received "among the other just souls" if he was allowed to "do executions."[16] But the job was fraught with risk. When, on March 11, 1665, Iacopo di Ippolito Cancelli da Pelago was hung in Florence by order of the Inquisition (he had celebrated Mass without being a priest), an inexpert "master of justice" got the final shove wrong and the man ended up with his feet and hands entangled in the ladder: "such disorder," the Florentine *confratelli* observed, "caused an uproar among the people," besides, naturally, "great suffering to the afflicted."[17] The contradiction between the sentiment of imaginary forgiveness and the reality of human butchery found an outlet in hatred for the executioner. The comforters were not to have any contact with him: the confraternity instructions were very strict on this. Not only were they not permitted to actively help him, they were not to exchange any words with him either: there was the danger that "patients," whose thoughts were supposed to be directed toward God and the life to come, might be nonplussed if it seemed that the very same people who talked about the soul were actually working in cahoots with the executioner to put the condemned person to death. And yet, due to the transformation of the brutal ritual of legal assassination into a theater of forgiveness and penitence, the executioner had ended up having a small part as well, though he lost none of his despicable features. It is hard to say from when exactly, but in the cruelest phase of executions, between the fifteenth and sixteenth centuries, there was an attested custom for the executioner and the victim to forgive each other. At the culminating and final moment of the ritual, when the malefactor entered his domain, the executioner stepped forward and begged forgiveness for what he was about to do. It was a necessary step in what we might call the Christianization of the executioner. Tommaso Garzoni described the horror aroused by this "lord of the scaffold and king of the gallows" when the latter appeared in the square to perform "one of the most shameful and abominable triumphs the world has."[18] Doctor Giovanni Battista Gargiaria, a member of the Bologna School of Comforters, was very familiar with the reactions that the executioner provoked: in his book of instructions for the brothers, to demonstrate how much caution was needed when dealing with the executioner, he related that even peasant women—who were right at the bottom of the social ladder—selling their produce in the market square

would shout to the executioner: "Stay away from me, get away, go to hell."
Gargiara also recalled witnessing an incident involving a peasant woman
who had been condemned to death. In the *conforteria* she "declared herself an enemy of the executioner; she did not wish to be reduced to
having to see him, nor to be touched or put to death by him."[19] But however despicable his trade was considered, and however much people
scorned and feared any contact with him in everyday life, he had a role to
play in the religious orchestration of the scene of justice, altering his profile
considerably.

The change was significant in a number of respects, and the outcome of
both political and religious factors. As we have seen, for the Jesuit Giacinto
Manara the executioner held "an office very necessary and useful for the
public." In this he was in agreement with Luther, the first to advance and
sustain the thesis of the separation of private morals and public norms, the
values cultivated in their inner self by the Christian, who forgives and turns
the other cheek, and the ethics of the obedient functionary who ensures
order is maintained in the public sphere, acting as an impersonal and implacable instrument of power. We can see here the start of something that
would mark modern European history and culture. But rather than separation it was in reality subordination, because prevailing over everything was
the hard task of disciplining society: in his *Whether Soldiers, Too, Can be
Saved* (1526), Luther defined the role of the executioner as a "divine office,"
like that of the soldier. The primary source of his teaching, taken from Romans 13, was cited repeatedly in the regulatory texts of the new sixteenth-
century evangelical Churches. They recognized secular power as the sole
valid expression of divine will, because the sword used by the Christian authorities to punish was in the service of God.[20] Crime was the consequence
of sin, and sinning humanity had to be kept under control by political power,
according to the traditional interpretation of legitimate violence in medieval political thought.[21] The offender had to be led along the path to contrition by the pastor, whose office it was to visit and prepare them for death.

When Luther was asked whether or not the executioner should request
forgiveness from the condemned, the answer was a very clear no. His job was
to punish the wicked. It would be as if a father, before beating his son to educate him, were to ask for forgiveness in advance. The executioner must kill
and the father must beat because that is what God wants—words that left

their mark, as is shown by the emphasis they received at the end of the seventeenth century in the erudite and voluminous "theater of punishments" (*Theatrum poenarum*) by the German jurist Jacob Döpler.[22] This vast repertoire of ancient and modern judicial punishments epitomized a whole epoch of German legal culture, with a wide-ranging erudition informed by an antiquarian taste and held together by an elementary conception of the punishment system: according to Döpler, it was thanks to the work of Meister Hans, the executioner, that the bond between citizens remained intact.[23]

The extent to which the social standing of the executioner had effectively changed can be gauged by considering Frantz Schmidt, the celebrated executioner of Nuremberg. Born in 1554, at the age of nineteen he began his apprenticeship in his father's occupation. He had then taken over from his father, as happened in every artisanal workshop, and plied his trade with great commitment and professionalism. But he did so by swearing an oath and receiving a regular salary, just like any other state functionary. Admittedly, a dark aura of superstitious dread continued to hang over his profession, but he exercised it with dedication and a serious awareness of his obligations. This emerges clearly in the diary he kept from 1575, where he noted down all the punishments he was called upon to exact in his long and highly esteemed career. Seriousness and application in performing his duty in the best possible way combined in him with a wish to make the death of the "poor sinners" less painful, and to help the pastor in getting them to show remorse. His Lutheran faith did not contemplate the Catholic notion of meritorious works, and considered the death penalty for serious crimes to be the correct use of the sword to curb the evil impulses of humankind. The word "mercy" nonetheless crops up frequently in his diary, as do annotations regarding the conversion of condemned Catholic prisoners to Lutheranism. He arranged for a parlor to be set up in the jail, where the prison chaplain, the pastor Hagendorn, met the condemned and made a note of the behavior of the "poor sinners" in his register.[24] With Frantz Schmidt the role of the executioner shifted from being that of a beastly figure occasionally employed for a task so odious and degrading as to make the person doing it a social pariah, to the disciplined and strict servant of the state aware of the importance of his position in the world: he was called by God to exercise his trade, his mission *(Beruf)*. For this reason, Schmidt, employed with a written contract and a fixed salary, kept a check on what he himself did, scrupulously noting down all the cases in which he was involved. His precise, elegant writing indicates a solid scholastic background and perhaps some knowledge of Latin. His professional conscientiousness earned him general respect in the cities of Bamberg and Nuremberg, where he was active during his long career. His case shows the profound change that had taken place in Germany over the century due to the new state ethics of the Reformation and the new judicial arrangements that had developed in the German states from the end of the fifteenth century.

Of course, it was not easy to eliminate the social prohibitions and taboos that surrounded the profession. Not for nothing did Frantz Schmidt, at the end of his working life, request and obtain exemption for his son from the obligation to succeed him.

At any rate, in the instructions drawn up in the Lutheran world regarding the correct way to perform this office there are various sentences that recall ones written for Catholic comforters: the invitation to repent and set a good example for spectators was followed by the assurance that while the body remained hanging from the gallows the soul would be led away with great honor by the angels toward the kingdom of God.[25] Here we find an unexpected convergence with the original tradition of the *misericordia* associations. The proposal made by John Calvin, the Geneva reformer, on the other hand, was very different. His doctrine of predestination did not free believers from the fear of God's judgment. Quite the opposite: "The foul grunting of these swine [those who abandon themselves to their instincts without concern] is duly silenced by Paul," who, Calvin says, "teaches that we have been chosen to this end: that we may lead a holy and blameless life."[26] All his work is suffused with an ethic of obedience to authority, and it is no accident that his *Institutes of the Christian Religion* ends with a heartfelt invitation to obey the law and submit to the will of public power that is once again based on the customary verse from chapter 13 of Paul's Letter to the Romans: "With hearts inclined to reverence their rulers, the subjects should prove their obedience toward them, whether by obeying their proclamations, or by paying taxes, or by undertaking public offices and burdens which pertain to the common defense, or by executing any other commands of theirs."[27] The execution of Michael Servetus along the lines of the ecclesiastical Inquisition offered a model of the violence that would be deployed by the sword-bearing arm of the law in the most strictly Calvinistic cultures. Two traditions thus emerged, which were not just alternative to the Catholic one but also profoundly different from each other.

In the vision of the afterlife proposed by the different voices of the Protestant Reformation, the absence of purgatory simplified matters; and the function of punishment administered by the Christian prince in the name of God cast the central figure in this process—the executioner—in a different light. Though it was not enough to sweep away the social prohibitions and taboos that surrounded him, separated as he was from others by the barriers of infamy that made even simple contact a source of dishonor, the executioner was nonetheless acknowledged as having the role of performing God's will, and was able to receive the sacraments.[28]

The Catholic Church attempted something more than this, moving in a different direction toward a religious legitimation of the scaffold and of capital punishment, viewed as a privileged and protected route to the eternal salvation of the soul. In the early modern age the Church did not just repress the magical practices that used to go on in relation to the powers and the pharmacopeia of the executioner. It tackled the central figure—the man with an infamous trade—head on. It was not enough just to attract the condemned toward the light of heaven—the same needed to be done with the person performing the sentence. A proposal to resolve this definitively was advanced by Giovanni Fontana, a highly educated ecclesiastic who was a pupil of Saint Charles Borromeo and worked tirelessly in his role as the bishop of Ferrara. Occupying the final and humblest position of his universal catalogue of saints, intended to ensure that every trade had its own patron saint, is a Saint Cyriacus the Executioner. He also took the opportunity to spell out to executioners how they should conduct their trade if they too wished to aspire to sainthood: they had to do everything that was requested of them, but gently, without gratuitous displays of violence: "In tying them up, in placing irons on their feet, irons on their hands, in attaching them to the rope, in readying them for the harshness of torments and tortures, proceed with Christian love."[29]

In the Catholic system the executioner became a good Christian. Giovanni Battista Bugatti, commonly referred to in Rome as "Mastro Titta," and renowned for his length of service (from 1796 to 1861), regularly made confession and received Communion. This was despite the fact that he remained in the category of *infamia,* was obliged to reside outside the city, and could only cross the bridge over the Tiber when his services were required.[30]

҈

As the figure of the executioner changed, so too did the theater of punishment. Forgiveness played a central role in the ritual of comforting the condemned. It was a key condition for God's forgiveness of sinners: and, together with confession, it transformed the crime into sin at the very moment in which that sin was erased. Furthermore, it restored the social harmony that had been disturbed by the crime, healing the wound inflicted on the body of the community. What happened on the scaffold offered the most suggestive and dramatic model for the reconciliation of conflicts. The ritual of forgiveness reciprocally requested and granted in the relationship between executioner and condemned referred to the moral economy of conflicts and the way of resolving offenses, quarrels, and violence in society. Vendettas arising from disputes between neighbors, rival families, and between and within kinship groups could only be halted when the offender or the offender's heirs asked for forgiveness from the injured party.[31] Luther, on the other hand, condemned the ritual as mistaken, as we have seen: for him the executioner was not just any old Christian brother preparing to do harm. He was invested by the Christian prince with the public office of punishing wrongdoers in order to ensure the security of all good subjects. A substantive change thus manifested itself in the pattern of relations between justice and religion set in motion by the religious Reformation of the sixteenth century. Forgiveness, justice, and justification were the most widely used and debated terms in the language of the age. The theological discussion about works and faith in the process of justification of the Christian had an immediate echo in the more narrowly criminal sphere in the sixteenth century. If Christians could not appear just in the eyes of God for their good works, and if they deserved every punishment, their salvation lay exclusively in their faith: the world was a mass of damned people. Salvation before God's tribunal could be obtained through faith alone.

If there was an area of society destined to immediately feel the consequences of the fracture in the unity of the European Church it was undoubtedly that of justice. The change in the executioner's role in the Lutheran conception of the relationship between power and society was just one aspect. This is not the place to examine, even briefly, the developments in the administration of justice that stemmed from it. Suffice it to recall that the fire Luther lit in Wittenberg in 1520 to burn the bull of excommunication also consumed the *Corpus iuris canonici* and the widely circulating *Summa de Casibus Conscientiae* for confessors by the Franciscan monk Angelo from Chivasso, known for this reason as the *Summa Angelica*. The great juridical wall protecting the members of the ecclesiastical body collapsed, and with it there fell into disuse rules and advice that had been developed for the individual confession made obligatory by Innocent III with the canon approved by the Fourth Lateran Council. It was thanks to this obligation that an extremely elaborate science of cases, or casuistry, had been developed: and as the specialist in confession was an ecclesiastic—generally a friar—who at the same time performed the roles of physician and judge, his power over simple laypeople had expanded greatly. Luther's choice deprived that power of its foundations. The efforts to provide guidance to pastors in their work were initially limited to putting together collections of pastoral advice and consolatory meditations drawn from Luther's letters and "table talk." It was not until the seventeenth century that a casuistry of conscience emerged in the Lutheran world, the aim being to prepare theology students to tackle the problems that arose when administering the sacraments, in particular confession; and here there were borrowings and links with Catholic casuistry.[32]

The conflict that began at that time between the different religious confessions inevitably impacted on the administration of justice and the system of punishments. Though the forms differed, there was a similar process of sovereign powers establishing their authority over state territory, in a difficult context marked by the devastating force of religious conflicts that threatened to shatter every other bond. One consequence was the addition of heresy to the list of traditional crimes, this being understood as any choice that departed from the religious confession of the sovereign power. While in much of the area loyal to Rome the ecclesiastic courts continued to have jurisdiction over heresy cases, in France and England—where one remained Catholic and the other rejected papal authority—cases of heresy, now considered to be treason, were judged by royal courts. In the turbulent reality of the states forming the German Empire, the religious wars repeatedly modified the political and confessional setup of the relationship between the hereditary empire of the Austrian Hapsburgs and the territorial states. However, the individual political entities within the composite system of the empire remained firmly oriented toward autonomy. The territorial princes had started drawing up criminal codes before Luther began his preaching, and common-law norms administered by village magistrates gave way to a framework of rules from the Roman legal tradition and a body of university-trained legal experts. This elaboration of criminal regulations and of forms of judicial administration went hand in hand with the Hapsburg Empire's attempt, under Maximilian I and Charles V, to introduce centralized regulations and institutions. There took root an idea of justice guaranteed by a Christian prince, who exercised harsh punishment with a mandate from God, to keep in check a humanity that Lutheran anthropology would depict as being radically corrupted by original sin. The criminal constitutions of individual states and cities, from Bamberg (1507) to Worms (1532), together with the constitutions promulgated by Charles V, imposed a model of justice in which the sentence was passed by a central power, while the inquisitorial ritual was based exclusively on the interrogation of the accused and the search for their confession. This resulted in a greater use of the death penalty and of aggravated forms of execution.[33] In the texts laying down the new regime of punishments the state-appointed judges found a catalogue of crimes and an analytic description of methods for inflicting as much suffering as possible on malefactors. The secrecy of the trial and sentence remained in the shadows behind the spectacle of public execution, as had already happened in the Italian cities. Naturally, those criminal constitutions did not neglect the question of religious assistance for those condemned to death. Engravings accompanying the texts offer a detailed illustration of the different moments in the procedure, including the one where the confessor listens to the condemned person's final words before the latter climbs up to the scaffold, dominated by the symbols of Christ's Passion and by the cross.

Generally speaking, the punishment system became harsher. An idea of this can be readily gained by looking through the *Carolina,* which was presented as a unifying model for the whole empire and which remained in force until the middle of the eighteenth century. Available statistics indicate that the number of executions was growing.[34] The process of constructing the different and conflicting European states, in competition with the birth of new Churches due to the disintegration of the single Roman Church, generally entailed the imposition of a harsh discipline and the widespread resort to sword and scaffold to bring entire peoples to heel. This tendency was reinforced by the prevailing of religious views of human life that were colored by a dark pessimism. However, Luther's rigid Augustinism, which considered humanity to have been corrupted by original sin, also had a profoundly liberating aspect: entrusting one's eternal salvation to faith did away with a whole tangle of devout practices devised over previous centuries to accumulate indulgences and reduce the time spent in the flames of purgatory. The relationship of exchange between the living and the dead also disappeared: the remembrance of the dead, fixed in the Catholic countries with periodic masses (for which ecclesiastic benefices were founded), melted away entirely. The inscriptions on graves in the Protestant countries speak of future resurrection as the occasion for meeting family members once again. Calvinism was even more radical, in its belief that death erased all ties with the dead person and in its elimination of any form of Church intervention on behalf of the soul preparing to face its Maker. With the interruption of the relationship of mutual protection between earth and heaven, and the disappearance of the ritual of saying masses for the departed, the need to remember the dead in an earthly world where they were now completely unreachable was satisfied by focusing on acts in their lives, remembered with narratives, speeches, and monuments. The depth of the abyss that now opened up between the living and the dead is shown by the fact that the cemetery no longer occupied a central place in the life of the community: the imperial ordinances of the late sixteenth century complained about their state of abandon.[35]

Comforting the sick and dying did not fade away. Nor were the condemned abandoned: for them, Charles V's criminal constitution offered the common model—a three-day interval between sentence and execution, comforting by churchmen, and the sacraments. But the judicial chronicles in modern Europe were characterized above all by the frequency of executions and the harshness of the suffering inflicted on the condemned: the public ritual took on the dominant feature of terror as a means of cowing peoples and terrorizing would-be offenders. City chronicles describe increasing numbers of public scenes of cruelty before an audience that often played an active role in a theater of horror.[36] The "theater of death" was a widespread cultural theme in the baroque age: and in surveying and illustrating the various forms of death in his *Theatrum mortis humanae,* the baron of Carniola, Johann Weichard Valvasor, devoted the most horrific etchings to death on the scaffold.[37] The analysis of political power deemed fear to be the only sentiment that could forcibly shape a human mass into a state. The dominant religious anthropology considered human beings to be carriers of evil and therefore destined to be harshly repressed by the Christian sovereign. This was the prevalent tone not just of the doctrine of triumphant predestination in Calvinism but also of Catholic theology: condemnation of the Erasmian tradition of leniency and tolerance was shared by the different European Christian confessions, and the ideas about freedom of conscience that lived on in currents of radical Erasmianism faced a general hostility on the part of both old and new Churches. In this context, the bond between the temporal justice of the sovereign and the divine justice of the life to come became even tighter than before, though its orientation and significance changed. The exaltation of divine mercy had long gone hand in hand with forms of royal forgiveness on the occasion of festivities during the liturgical year. On the other hand, the idea took root in this period that both courts— on earth and in the sky—were harsh and ruthless, and that the divine judge was no different from the human ones. As the French Oratorian Jean-François Senault wrote in the middle of the seventeenth century, "one would say that divine justice behaves toward sinners as human justice does toward the worst criminals": while human justice vented its rage not just on those who were guilty but also on their children and goods, destroying their houses and castles and persecuting their families, divine justice, not content with having castigated Adam, condemned his children and heirs to hell.[38]

Senault grasped a genuine change of atmosphere. The severe God that imposed strict rules and threatened dire punishment in the purgatory of the Catholics and the hell of the Reformed Churches was the projection in heaven of a temporal power that demanded obedience and asked those who it put to death to set an example for everyone else. What united the temporal courts was the need to appropriate a religious legitimacy that was crucial for consecrating powers determined to present themselves as a direct emanation of God. With the Protestant Reformation and the emergence of the modern state, the doctrine of the supreme spiritual and temporal authority of the Roman pontiff had to reckon with secular sovereigns unwilling to acknowledge any superior power, and who demanded total obedience from their subjects. This was the fundamental aim of the scaffold scene in which a friar holding a crucifix asked the person about to be executed to accept the death sentence imposed on them by the sovereign as the will of God. For this reason the private confession of sins remained as confirmation of the acceptance of the punishment and a necessary premise of remissive and obedient public behavior. In some parts of Europe greater emphasis was placed on a public declaration, which in France and the Low Countries went by the name of *amende honorable*—a formal, public act asking for forgiveness, which the condemned person uttered at a specific moment in the ritual pathway to the scaffold, either kneeling before the victim of the crime or before the judge in the courtroom. Here, however, the change brought by the Protestant Reformation had the effect of transforming the execution of the heretic into a "theater of martyrdom": the *amende* was restricted to those who retracted. The punishment of burning was reserved for the others. Protestant martyrologies recorded hundreds of such cases.[39] But thanks to printing it was just such literature that turned accounts of executions into a pro-Reformation propaganda weapon: the masterpiece of this genre was the *Histoire des Martyrs* by Jean Crespin.[40] The spectacle of the condemned person stepping into the fire, displaying, through a joyful willingness to die, their faith in the promise of eternal salvation, marked a turning point with respect to the traditional *ars moriendi* and the dark fear of the torments of purgatory.[41] After an initial phase dominated by the punishment of burning for the heretic, a gradual secularization of the ritual led to a different execution regime. The figure of the heretic was replaced by that of the political rebel. In the Low Countries at war with Spain the simplification of the ritual tended to result in the *amende honorable* dying out. In Amsterdam, for example, it was discontinued after 1600.[42] But the burning of heretics returned to prominence once again in England around the same time due to the bitter conflict between the English monarchy and the papacy. This was played out at various levels—the "high" one of the public debate between the English sovereign on the one hand and the pope and Cardinal Bellarmine on the other; and that of the English Catholics, faced with the choice of obeying the pope to the point of martyrdom, as was requested of them by Rome, and obedience to the crown, which claimed that its sovereign power was of divine origin. The great English literature of the

day, from William Shakespeare to John Donne, contains traces of the conflict.[43] The threat of excommunication, and the pope and Bellarmine's invitation to English Catholics to rebel and demonstrate their loyalty to Rome
through martyrdom led to a showdown, the most dramatic moment of
which was the famous Gunpowder Plot of 1605. The ritual burning of an
effigy of Guy Fawkes on November 5 in many English cities is a tangible
trace in popular culture of a drama that assailed the consciences of English
Catholics and that ended with the nation rallying around the sovereign. It
was at this time that acceptance of the Oath of Allegiance and the declaration of loyalty to the king became the nucleus of the last declaration made
by the condemned. The testimony offered by the Catholic priest Henry
Garnet is a fine example: arrested for involvement in the Gunpowder Plot,
and taken to the scaffold on May 3, 1606, Garnet publicly declared that
he deserved his punishment for having offended the king, whose forgiveness he sought. He also urged all Catholics not to embark on the path of
treason and rebellion.[44] The rite of penitence thus began to be transformed
into a declaration of loyalty to the crown, which from then on became the
English way of using the scaffold ritual for political ends. The Roman party
in the struggle, and the writings of the brothers in the companies of justice,
instead of being able to exalt a whole English Catholic population of martyrs, could only praise the Catholic martyrs of Anglican power, Thomas
More and John Fisher—tribute was constantly paid to their memory in
comforting literature.

Yet aside from the bitter and protracted conflict between Rome and the
Anglican monarchy, the scaffold ritual practiced by the Catholic companies
of justice in Italy was not as different as it might seem from those of the European societies that had severed their ties of obedience to Rome. The function of the ritual of justice in the great spectacle of execution was of decisive
importance in instilling obedience to the law in the entire social body. The
religious foundation of the right to kill was reaffirmed and particularly emphasized in the Protestant world, where the criminal legislations established
the Ten Commandments and the rules laid out in Leviticus as the foundation for the system of crimes and punishments. This is how it was demonstrated that the justice of the sovereign was simply the enactment of God's
will. In this the arguments used by the Catholic comforters were on a par
with the harshness of the sentences passed down by the courts of the states

that had emancipated themselves from obedience to the pope. Of fundamental importance on both sides of the confessional barriers was the insistence on the fact that no one who had been condemned to death could protest against the sentence, even if it was unjust. And if anyone did so, the answer was to hand—all one had to do was refer to Saint Paul.

༄ 32 ༄

Printing and Scaffold Stories:
Models Compared

THE SPREAD OF PRINTING marked the beginning of an "unacknowledged revolution" in communication, and on this terrain we can conduct an appraisal of the analogies and differences between the rituals of the Italian companies of justice and those in use in other European cultures. Up until now we have almost exclusively been exploring the nocturnal world where the comforting of the condemned took place. Their names and stories have emerged from the instruction manual literature produced for confraternity members. We must not forget, however, that those names and stories were a source of extremely lively curiosity in the world outside. The crowds that pressed around the chapel entrance to catch a glimpse of the arrival of the "patient," and then vied for a good viewing position the following morning in the square where the scaffold had been erected were hungry for details about the condemned, their crimes, and how they had passed their final hours. The political and religious authorities welcomed and encouraged that curiosity, and hoped that publicizing the punishment would help to instill an effective discipline consisting of terror and piety. But alongside the summons and incentives to get people to flock to the square, there were also a shower of bans and threats to prevent the secrecy of the condemned prisoners' final nights being violated. The extent of the phenomenon can be seen simply by looking at a sample of the *gride* emanated about this by the papal government in Bologna. The scene they describe is invariably the same, that of the "abuse of allowing people into the *conforteria* and other places where the poor wretches who have been condemned to death for their demerits are to be comforted."[1]

The threats of severe punishment contained in the proclamation issued by the vice-legate Anselmo Dandino on February 17, 1588, reiterated in similar terms by the cardinal legate Giulio Cesare Sacchetti on March 10, 1638, were evidently to no avail given that a solemn proclamation by the cardinal legate Pierluigi Carafa on April 16, 1652, was still warning that no one, "of whatever rank, station, or condition," should be allowed to enter the rooms of the *conforteria* "to listen to and see the condemned being comforted." The prohibition was repeated almost word for word by the next cardinal legate, Girolamo Lomellino, on April 22, 1653. The "great presence of people gathering together inside the chapel and rooms in which the said condemned are comforted" was a phenomenon that caused "prejudice to the condemned wretches," according to the umpteenth—but not last—proclamation issued on September 18, 1665. As a consequence, it threatened to punish transgressors with a fine of a hundred gold *scudi* and three lashes of the rope, or some other punishment at the cardinal legate's discretion.

These prohibitions, and those of the confraternity chapters imposing secrecy on their members, attest to how strong and widespread was the curiosity surrounding scaffold cases. This created a promising market for printed information, seen also as a vehicle for amplifying and prolonging the momentary, limited effect of the public ritual of death on the scaffold. One result was the emergence of the genre of "laments of the condemned" in the tradition of popular printed works. In the case of a Signora Prudenza in Tuscany we encounter the Florentine company of the "Blacks," with the narrating voice of the condemned woman expressing acceptance of the sentence in words that reveal a conflation of sin and crime, punishment and penance:

> Ero tra tutte l'altre una Fenice:
> Hor sono un animal posto al macello,
> Per quel peccato mio che dir non lice.

> (Among all the others I was a phoenix:
> Now I am an animal sent to slaughter,
> For that sin of mine that cannot be said.)

And then, addressing the court of justice:

> Ecco il mio corpo pronto e preparato
> A sopportar la vera penitenza,
> Secondo l'error mio e 'l mio peccato.[2]

> (Here is my body, ready and prepared
> To endure the true penance,
> In accordance with my error and my sin.)

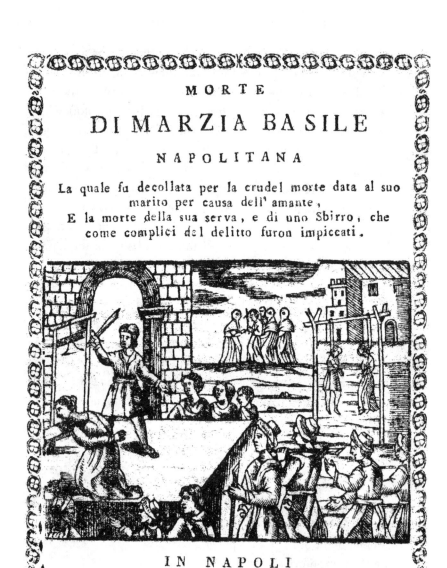

MORTE

DI MARZIA BASILE

NAPOLITANA

La quale fu decollata per la crudel morte data al suo
marito per causa dell' amante,
E la morte della sua serva, e di uno Sbirro, che
come complici del delitto furon impiccati.

IN NAPOLI

FIGURE 32.1. Giovanni della Carriola, frontispiece of the booklet *Morte di Marzia Basile* (Naples, 1603). NAPLES: FONDAZIONE BIBLIOTECA BENEDETTO CROCE, 95 C 22 BIS.

Forming part of the flood of poetic laments recounting tragic and incredible stories of crimes and punishments was a composition by the Neapolitan Giovanni della Carriola. Entitled the *Morte di Marzia Basile* (Death of Marzia Basile), it was printed in Naples in the days around the execution of the protagonist in May 1603, and subsequently reprinted several times.[3] It was a story of love and death dominated by the character of Marzia, a twenty-year-old woman of extraordinary beauty who organized the murder of her husband, Domizio, whom she had betrayed, in agreement with her lover, Narciso. The case was judged by the Vicaria criminal court and the Holy Office. While under torture, the woman accused several innocent people, for which she then made a final *escolpazione*.[4] She walked in procession to the scaffold along a route crowded with onlookers, and the whole execution ritual stretched from late afternoon into the night, lit by torches and punctuated by the tears of the woman and the crowd alike. In telling the story, the poet emphasizes the part played by the Whites in her final hours, describing their entry into her cell with verses that indicate how, for prisoners, the appearance of the brothers effectively announced that they were about to die:

> Vide un giorno poi entrar li Bianchi,
> Ohimè, diss'ella, e cadde sbalordita
> Gli spiriti vital vennero manchi,
> Fuor di se stessa attonita, smarrita.
> Lettor mio saggio, certamente credi,
> Cade trema, suda, e non si regge in piedi.

> (Then, one day, she saw the Whites entering,
> Alas, she said, and collapsed in a daze,
> Her vital spirits fading away,
> Beside herself, bewildered and lost.
> Believe without doubt, my wise reader,
> She fell, shook, sweated, and could not stand.)

The arguments used by the comforters are described like this:

> Dissero i confrati: O figlia mia,
> sta' allegramente, e non ti sbigottire.
> A Gesú Cristo figlio di Maria,

Umilmente ti voglio inchinare,
Renditi in colpa d'ogni pena ria,
pregalo che ti voglia perdonare,
Se morte pigli per li tuoi peccati,
A godere andrai con li beati.[5]

(The brothers said: My daughter,
Be cheerful, and do not be dismayed.
To Jesus Christ, son of Mary,
I want you to humbly bow,
Accept blame for every punishment given,
Pray that He may wish to forgive you.
If death you receive for your sins,
You shall go to enjoy the company of the blessed.)

Numerous examples of such literature—an adequate survey of which has yet to be attempted[6]—were produced in Bologna at the beginning of the seventeenth century. Here there had been at least one occasion in which, as we have seen, a member of the renowned School of Comforters had written an entire book, packed with details, about the case of the "iconoclastic" heretics responsible for desecrating the sacred images that then populated the city's streets and porticoes. The execution had just taken place, on November 28, 1623, when the canon and count Ridolfo Campeggi, a member of the confraternity, composed and published his book on the episode: he wrote it in Italian, obviously intending it for those who knew how to read. It was a way of sowing feelings of abomination for what the heretics had done. But it was also a response to a widespread curiosity that a journalistic form of publishing was trying to encourage and exploit. The printing of pamphlets and broadsheets was commonplace in Bologna at the time. One work destined to make a profound impact there was by an author-publisher of great and lasting popularity, Giulio Cesare Croce. Almost at the same time as Campeggi's work, and probably just before it, he produced a pamphlet with a "screaming" title promising sensational information about the "marvelous and horrible case."[7] Throughout are words expressing abhorrence for the heretics' practices and doctrines: among the aberrations they confessed to during the trial, Croce emphasizes their conviction "that the world was made by chance, that man was born from corruption, like worms from the earth." To the author the sentence was just punishment for their monstrous crimes. The presence of the comforters is just a detail of the overall scene: "The company of death, after having recited the *De Profundis* for their souls, started singing the *Te Deum laudamus,* while the bodies stripped bare by the executioner were thrown into the fire."

The pamphlet bore the joint imprimatur of the archbishop and of the inquisitor of Bologna: it was the first case of a publication about a heresy case, and the caution must have been commensurate with the strong reservations entertained by the age of the Counter-Reformation toward printed works in the vernacular. Subsequently as well, published reports about the execution of sentences against those condemned by the court of the Inquisition had their own distinct features and were checked or even written by members of the tribunal of faith, as we shall see. The ecclesiastical authorities were always very attentive in censoring printed works destined for widespread popular consumption. The formal authorization on the frontispieces of the pamphlets, if not printed, was written by hand with the formula "publicetur" and signed by the inquisitor or by his notary.[8] Even outside the Papal States printed works regularly indicated the license of the superiors.

The printing industry had devised a new strand of culture, consisting of larger than life stories and out-of-the-ordinary characters, great love affairs and great tragedies. Hack writers starting out in the trade tried their hand at them, seizing on stories of crimes and criminals that readers loved so much. This is how printing gave rise to what would become popular culture, discernible even in the typographic characters and narrative modules.[9] The demand for lurid stories coming from the squares where executions were carried out was met with a literature of ballads and fliers, sold and performed by itinerant street singers. In these stories real events and fictional elements combined and overlapped, the covers shouting for attention with promises of sensational, horrific, miraculous, and cruel episodes. The graces of the Virgin always included the miracle of some condemned prisoner being saved, as in the story of a young unnamed man who escaped with his life when the rope broke while he was being hanged.[10] The narratives that enjoyed uninterrupted publishing success between the seventeenth and eighteenth centuries were often entirely made up, and they found a permanent place in oral memory through until the late nineteenth century. This was the case, for example, of the documented success of a pamphlet about the "diabolic resolution" of the "ill-fated Isabella," an imaginary Maltese girl who, the story goes, committed the horrible crime of murdering her parents and received "just and severe castigation."[11] But what happened to the rule of confidentiality that barred the *confratelli* from divulging the secrets of their office and precluded their access to popular literature? The real cases that passed through the *conforterie* certainly attracted great curiosity, and the members of the confraternities were the ones who in a professional capacity heard confidences and details about offenses committed by criminals and the ways in which they prepared themselves for death. Yet after Campeggi, very few names of brothers appeared as authors of this literature. There was some degree of external circulation of material primarily intended for use in the *conforteria,* such as the *Notti malinconiche,* the casuistic treatise by the Jesuit Giacinto Manara, or the writings of the abbot Carlo Antonio Macchiavelli about doubts that arose while comforting.[12] But the abbot's attention toward the world of publishing can also be seen in the disparate range of texts with which he enriched the library of the *conforteria,* containing one of the largest known collections of printed reports about sentences and executions. The most frequently recurring title in this body of works is in fact *relazione,* or report, and in at least one case there is a date and a collective signature: "From our oratory of Santa Maria della Misericordia e San Rocco in Pavia, March 21, 1741."[13] The text is written in the form of a letter of convocation addressed to the brothers, and refers to the death sentence due to be carried out in Pavia on March 23. The difference between the dates indicates that this was a case where someone in the confraternity prepared and printed information about an execution that had not yet taken place. The pamphlet offered readers a gruesome account of the crimes and an even more gruesome description of the punishments: the criminals were to be "dragged by a horse's tail and taken to the place of execution, and there broken on the wheel and flayed; and then, the bones of their legs and arms also having been broken, remain exposed on the raised wheels, their corpses entangled in them, for the whole day, and then, after the heads had been cut off, these were to be taken and put on display in the public street, closer to the site of the crime committed."

This, then, is an instance where the veil of secrecy surrounding the *conforterie* is suddenly torn: the fictional artifice of a letter of convocation disguised the reality of a disclosure. The text drawn up by a member of the confraternity in the form of a letter of invitation for internal use was brought out in print to be sold in the city square. It was not an isolated incident, on the contrary. One only has to read the elegant letters of convocation printed in the course of the eighteenth century by the "most noble confraternity" in Milan (Figure 32.2) to learn the details of the crimes committed by offenders to whose executions the brothers were invited: the texts were embellished with good-quality engravings, which replicated, albeit with many variants, the same scene—the beheading of the patron saint. Quite how extensive their circulation was is hard to say, though it is a fact that surviving exemplars of such works can also be found in private collections, and not just in the confraternity's archive collection.[14]

The *polizzotti* or public notices printed by the School of Comforters in Bologna were certainly for general consumption. Affixed in the city square, they contained information like this: "Antonio Varnesi, son of the late Lorenzo from the Commune d'Anzola, is to be hanged today for robbery, committed by the same under the name of Corte in the company of others on

FIGURE 32.2. The executioner deposits the head of Saint John the Baptist, engraving, Confraternity of San Giovanni Decollato of Milan, eighteenth century. PRIVATE COLLECTION.

the night of last Christmas Eve in the Commune di S. Bartolo delle Budrie in the house of Andrea Serra, and also for other substantial thefts. This on April 26, 1692."[15]

The notices and in-house documents formed part of the printed works produced by the functioning of the institution. Alongside this official material another kind of "report" literature also sprang up, where reality and imagination vied with each other in an abundance of strange news and gruesome details. In these works readers were shown a world without boundaries, both familiar and remote, where Italian place names intermingled with those of far-off countries such as Germany and Hungary, and horrific crimes were embroidered with stories of diabolic magic and amazing miracles. Blood, death, and the devil predominated. The story of a certain Pietro Nolo, who had "quartered one of his children, buried a priest alive, and committed many murders" in Abruzzo, was published a few years before the "Distinguished report of the terrible and frightening spectacle of justice carried out in Bavaria on February 11, 1732, on six wicked sorcerers who, with their deeds and spells, caused more than 600 people to die, including around 400 children, whose blood they sucked. Other killings and betrayals are also known [to have been committed]."[16]

The report of a public execution carried out in Livorno in 1745 promised to make readers tremble and recoil in horror.[17] It was also pointed out, however, just how many useful nuggets of moral pedagogy and religious education could be gleaned from a reading of the cases presented, declared in the opening to be as follows:

Wretched is he who, in doing ill, trusts that his misdeeds will always remain hidden, because when his Divine Majesty has for a long time patiently allowed sins to go by, showing mercy toward the sinner and waiting for him to come round and repent, then sends him some tribulation, by way of which he realizes his misdeeds and errors, and turns to the true God for help, begging for mercy for the sins he has committed, so that at the same time he receives corporal remedies and also the spiritual health of the soul. But if the [heart of the] sinner still remains hard, and stubborn, like another Pharaoh, he will unknowingly bring down on himself some grave scourge, which then serves as castigation and punishment for him, and as an example and warning for others, so now you know.

Also worthy of note is a malefactor's last speech that is full of praise for the religious ritual of the scaffold: he is made to say that he had witnessed many executions where he was able to listen to the salutary warnings of "many religious fathers, who tried to save our souls." Unfortunately, he had not heeded them and was now begging the spectators to learn from his fate and to respect human and divine laws. The moralizing, sermonizing intent of these texts ensured they received the necessary authorization to be printed despite the anonymity behind which the writers hid. In actual fact, this literature was only apparently freer than the official kind produced by state or religious magistracies, such as the sentences published by the Venetian government or the "distinguished reports" of the Holy Office concerning sentences passed by the Inquisition. There are many known examples of the latter, printed and put on sale complete with the permission of superiors during the eighteenth century. The growing openness of the Holy Office to the publishing world was instrumental: it wished to exploit the efficacy of the print medium to convey to readers the execrable nature of crimes against faith and the sacraments, and to present itself as a vigilant custodian keeping watch "with the eyes of Argus" against possible attacks on the Catholic faith. From the very start, even in the frontispieces, the narratives therefore promised to provide "exact information" about the crimes, the trial, and "all the ceremonies performed on that occasion," including the participation of the company of justice. This is what was guaranteed to buyers of the report on the condemnation of Paolo Antonio Galles, a young Calabrian found guilty in 1706 of stealing a ciborium containing the consecrated Host and jars of holy oils from the church of Santa Maria in Trastevere in Rome.[18] The report describes how Galles was imprisoned and tried, and excommunicated in a public ceremony in front of Saint Peter's on April 27, 1708. "Declared unworthy of any compassion" and handed over to the governor's court to be killed, albeit with the customary hypocritical invitation "to mitigate the severity of the sentence due to him." In some cases the Inquisition's reports also contain a description of the work carried out by the Roman archconfraternity of San Giovanni Decollato: one such instance deals with the story of Domenico Spallaccini, the son of a cooper from Orvieto, condemned by the Holy Office to the harsh sentence of being hung and burned. His crime was to have celebrated Mass in Rome and in Loreto (a town and pilgrimage destination in the Marche) without being a priest. Spallaccini seems to have been "dumbstruck" by the sentence because, "not recognizing the enormity of his abominable crime, he expected a lesser punishment." But according to the report, the gravity of the offense was such that the pope himself had passed sentence. The day after the execution, the brothers of the Roman arch-confraternity gathered in Campo de' Fiori, because Spallaccini had declared sorrow and contrition for what he had done. They carefully collected up the ashes and took them during the night to the burial place for the executed in the cloister of their headquarters. However, the ritual they performed showed no sign whatsoever of forgiveness and remission: they processed lugubriously in black vestments, carrying two large black torches, and effectively "instilled terror" in everyone who gathered to watch, due also to a heavy police presence. No forgiveness, then, but vengeance—and, according to the report, it was the Virgin herself, normally depicted as a compassionate mediator for sinners before God, who exacted it. On this occasion she was unable to forgive, as the Roman temple of the Virgin and the shrine of Loreto had both been profaned. For this reason, "the Most Holy Virgin herself took her just vengeance."[19]

The printing of these reports obeyed the same logic as the solemn, public rituality of the sentences, being intended to "serve as an example" and instill "terror in others." An extensive account of a case involving a group of "atheists" in Velletri near Rome was printed "so the public might, with this report, be fully informed of this fact."[20] They were found guilty of sharing and spreading ideas that amounted to a radical rejection of religion, viewed as imposture and an instrument of dominion, and had embraced the arci-heretical doctrine of the notorious and elusive "book of the three imposters"—Moses, Christ, and Mohammed—which was taking form precisely at that time, and beginning to circulate outside Italy as well.[21] Such reports have an official tone, their purpose being to make people aware of the presence of a sacred power capable of severely punishing any transgression against persons, property, or doctrines of the Church.

No other Inquisition publication achieved the heights of a magnificent print prepared by canon Antonino Mongitore from Palermo to sing the praises of the Inquisition of Sicily (Plate 18). In a large-format volume the canon gave a detailed description of the grandiose spectacle of two human beings being burned to ashes in Palermo on April 6, 1724. Sister Geltruda and fifty-eight-year-old Ignazio Barberi had been condemned for a series of convictions and expectations catalogued as "Molinist heresy." The account of the trial and the preparation of the *auto-da-fé,* which also refers to others who abjured and fell in line with the Church, culminates with a description of the public ritual in which the "reconciled" and the two condemned individuals were led to the square where a large stage had been prepared. Readers of Mongitore's work can see a wealth of detail and admire the order of the daises erected all around the enclosure reserved for the authorities and the brothers of the Assunta, who, clad in white habits and hoods, remained with the two offenders until the very end. And they can do so, Mongitore wrote, because here "the pen makes way for sculpture, which allows the eye to see, clearly delineated, the fence and everything that can be seen inside and outside of it": in fact, there is a large, detailed copper-plate image of the square and the theater of execution, prepared with great care and complete with a caption. According to the author, it was intended as a "representation at once joyful and tearful: joyful because of the admirable Triumph of the Holy Faith over its enemies the heretics; tearful because of the loss of two stubborn souls."[22]

All this Italian literature, with its own distinct characteristics, stands out amid the broad range of "tragic stories" found in European literary output at the time. The most evident feature is the special presence of confraternities and ecclesiastical courts among the institutions organizing and disseminating the texts. This was reflected in the recourse to religious legitimation and sanction and in the tendency to make no distinction between crime and sin.[23] As for the manner in which the protagonists of these execution stories were described, there was often an exchange of roles between the figure of the penitent, forgiven sinner and that of the killer and thief: on one hand "black" literature describing crimes, and, on the other, "white" literature dealing with devout deaths on the scaffold. The lurid stories of heinous crimes and terrible delinquents recounted larger than life characters, while the devout literature presented evanescent figures of "executed souls" for the pious meditation and prayers of the faithful, celebrating the mediating function of the sacraments and the Church in saving souls—the sin was forgiven, everything else remained shrouded in silence and shadow. Realism and devotion diverged, and yet they shared a common root: the reality of the crimes and the horrifying details of the sentence were divulged by writings produced on the fringes of the scaffold scene, in circles close to the

misericordia confraternities or by members themselves. How could the celebration of the saintly deaths of the condemned be reconciled with the dissemination of horrific tales of criminal lives justly brought to an end on the
scaffold? Evidently, the function of the salvation of souls had reached the
point of being in complete accord with the legitimation of the power to put
criminals to death. The readers of criminal tales and the spectators at executions were doubly reassured by the elimination of dangerous criminals and
by their transformation into inoffensive souls, for whom one might even
mutter the odd hurried prayer.

The scaffold literature circulating in other European countries at the time
offers much scope for comparison. Developing from the religious roots of
the Protestant Reformation between the seventeenth and eighteenth centuries were movements that sought to return to the original inspiration.
Within these movements particular attention began to be given to the question of the salvation of the souls of those condemned to death. In England,
the movements most critical of the High Church, such as the Puritans and
the Quakers, were especially sensitive to the matter. The theme of evangelical forgiveness made ground there in the context of the Puritan doctrine of
predestination. According to William Perkins, forgiveness was the fundamental rule for anyone wanting to be Christian, and in his view no one
should say the Lord's Prayer if they had not first forgiven their brother. But
reconciling oneself with one's neighbor was not the condition for being forgiven by God—on the contrary. It was the sign that the person had already
been forgiven and predestined for salvation.[24] Hence the resistance of the
simple faithful to utter the final phrase of the Lord's Prayer: for anyone unable to make peace with their neighbor, to say it was to announce their own
damnation.[25] The search for peace with those sent to their deaths by the law
thus became a pressing issue in the Protestant world as well.

A special place in the English ritual of capital punishment was reserved
for the last speech made by the condemned from the scaffold. At the origin
of the ritual there was still the medieval tradition of public confession, as
an alternative form to the religious sacrament of secret penitence. This ancient ritual practice had assumed a new and important function in the age
of Henry VIII, when the assertion of the sovereign's supremacy over the

Church of England had turned into harsh repression of all dissent; in this period a long succession of condemned prisoners uttered the same old verbal formulas recognizing the justness of the sentence and admitting to the treason with which they had been charged. One scholar who was studying this chapter in English history at the time when Stalin's state trials were under way found plenty to reflect upon in it.[26] And in more recent times this whole subject has been reconsidered in the light of the phenomenon of radical Muslims seeking martyrdom by blowing themselves up in the midst of their enemies.[27] A similar cultural laceration was seen when Protestant crowds mocked Catholics as they climbed up to the scaffold muttering "popish prayers," but were then ready to believe that their martyrs in Catholic lands were blessed by the apparition of the Holy Spirit in the form of a dove.[28] The conducting of trials thus saw the poisonous outcome of the tradition of *crimen lesae maiestatis* in its extreme version, the one introduced by the medieval ecclesiastical Inquisition, whereby people could be tried not just for acts and words but also for unexpressed intentions that had simply remained thoughts in the mind. And so, tried merely on the basis of suspicions, the condemned had been constrained to publicly recite formulas in which they admitted to having harbored intentions to betray the sovereign. The ritualized act of the last speech on the scaffold had thus become a crucial and spectacular moment of the execution ritual, designed to confirm the crowd's faith in justice and the correct functioning of power. The sole remaining possibility was to speculate about how those words would be pronounced, and whether the condemned would go to their deaths bravely or display signs of weakness and cowardice. It was also expected that stories would be told about the criminal deeds and the lives of various exemplars of an accursed humanity, who had deserved their infamous death because of what they had done. And so the last words of condemned offenders provided fruitful terrain for a literature engaged in cooking up stories of crimes and violence to satisfy the appetites of popular readers.

Scaffold literature flourished in particular in the eighteenth century, at the time of the movement of religious revival inspired by John Wesley, who took great pains to visit prisons and attend to the religious animation of prisoners. This was the age in which the extreme severity of the Black Act of 1723 led to the death of an extraordinary number of poor, uprooted people, subjected to the harshest of punishments for even the smallest of thefts.[29]

That law, E. P. Thompson wrote, "put unprecedented legal power in the hands of men who had not a generalized, delegated interest, such as the maintenance of order, or even the maintenance of the privileges of their own class, but a direct and personal interest in the conviction of men who were a nuisance to them."[30] One of its very many victims was an eighteen-year-old thief named John Wilkes, sent to the gallows in 1773 for having broken into a house and for having stolen a watch and a few coins from someone on the public highway. After his death, a pastor named John Fletcher published his exhortation to Wilkes to trust in the mercy of God—a God who will pardon all sins[31]—and the story of the young man's conversion and devout death. He also included a litany in verse that could be said by the condemned, which begins: "I own my punishment is just." Other stories of this kind were recounted by a pious literature that praised the extent of divine mercy: "God willeth all men to be saved" was the theme of the sermon John Wesley addressed to prisoners in Bristol jail in 1739; and Charles Wesley recounted how he had prayed together with nine condemned prisoners on the night before their execution, and sang with them a hymn to the Savior, accompanying them to the scaffold the next morning: they were serene, "full of comfort," and "assuredly persuaded that Christ had died for them and waited to receive them into paradise."[32]

In English scaffold literature stories like these were interwoven with an extraordinary proliferation of lurid fictional narratives. While devotees of the religious movement of evangelical revival recounted edifying episodes, a significant segment of print output focused on stories of violent lives and deaths. Accounts of the final hours of condemned prisoners, their last speeches, and the journey in crime that had led them to their end formed the subject matter for a rich body of popular literature.[33] The authors who worked in this new genre were as numerous as they were obscure, and only a very few emerged as genuine writers. For every Daniel Defoe who managed to rise above this squalid industry and achieve lasting literary success, there were innumerable hacks grubbing for the meager earnings of a trade in which real facts were cooked up with ingredients better suited to arousing terror and amazement. It is no accident that Defoe's Moll Flanders ended up featuring as a "real" character in the repertoire of execution stories sold around the gallows when executions were taking place. They were composed in a mad rush in the days between capture, trial, and execution of the sentence. A glimpse of this market can be seen in a plate by Hogarth depicting the execution of Tom Idle: in it the dominant figure in the middle at the bottom is a woman inviting passers-by to buy and read a pamphlet entitled *The Last Dying Speech of Tom Idle*. Of course, it was not the real "last speech" that the man was about to give to the crowd, but an account written by someone who had gathered enough information about his crimes to capture the curiosity of readers avid for tales of out-of-the-ordinary lives and crimes. And here we find something that we have already come across in the reality of the Italian confraternities: the collaboration of those responsible for providing religious assistance in the writing of the stories sold in city squares and streets. The only difference was that in England the mechanism of cooperation was quite open and systematic. What is more, it took place in a context of free-market competition between anyone with a product to sell. The struggle to exploit the market saw the ecclesiastic prelate of Newgate Prison, on the one hand, competing with a gaggle of amateurish writers and printers, on the other. The Anglican clergyman who held the post of prison chaplain supplemented his income by writing and publishing "accounts," which began to appear from 1670 onward as regular publications of the bulletin of the Newgate jail, gradually growing from an initial folio broadsheet to pamphlets many pages long. The Ordinary's role was to prepare condemned criminals to meet their death, to organize the religious ritual that took place in public in the chapel, and then to accompany the prisoners to the scaffold. The moralizing and exemplary intent of his pamphlets offered in some way a frame for the account. But in order to obtain as much information as possible about the crimes in order to then relate them in the pamphlet, it seems that the chaplains tried to convince the condemned to make a detailed Catholic-style confession, threatening them with eternal damnation if they refused; and this, one contemporary accused, "is only to extort from them an account of their lives, that they may afterwards publish the same to fill their printed papers and get a penny."[34] The works penned by the Ordinary had to vie for sales with the offerings of a crowd of other competitors. This particular niche of publishing was "cut-throat and highly volatile, so competitive that hours counted, as the public was impatient for news and willing to spend as much as their resources allowed."[35] Spectators at an execution could then compare what they read in the pamphlets with what the condemned felon said in their last speech—printed immediately after the sentence was carried out and which readers rushed to buy.[36]

In English society the context of these scaffold stories was particularly animated: the relationship between the public and the judicial machine was the restless and quarrelsome one of a society that had lived through the upheaval of the Puritan revolution and experienced the new setup of the parliamentary monarchy and the beginnings of the Industrial Revolution. Sources indicate that public execution scenes in London were filled with sound and fury, the spectators attentive and anything but passive, capable for example of violent unrest if it got about that the bodies were going to be used for anatomy, a practice viewed as anathema.[37] The market for bodies accompanied the market for stories of violent lives—both were forms of trade where for very modest sums those responsible for the salvation of souls earned a little extra to supplement their stipends. The ferment of the evangelical revival caught on in a popular world where the promise of the salvation of the soul was the sole reason for hope. It was to prostitutes, innkeepers, and thieves, to the "outcasts of men," that Wesleyan Methodism, with its visionary and sensational manifestations, held out a hand. Alongside this religion "*for* the poor," there was also a growth in the dissident leanings of religions "*of* the poor."[38] The proliferation of invitations to seek salvation found fertile ground in a dramatic social reality. Here the promises of happiness in the life to come produced various outcomes: quietism and abandonment on the one hand, and apocalyptic expectations on the other. It was not until the end of the Napoleonic Wars that the execution scene became an occasion for the condemned to begin openly rejecting the invitation to express penitence and for popular revolts against the executioners. The hanging of a sailor named Cashman in 1817 offered a measure of the change that had taken place.[39]

It has been asked what relationship there was between (divine) grace and (earthly) justice: Why, for example, did pious comforters never protest against the violence of the law and why do their names never appear among the members of the legal reform movement active in England? This is the same question posed by the entire history of the Italian comforters. The issue also arises with regard to the relationship between the companies of justice and the Enlightenment movement in eighteenth-century Italy. The question has prompted a "fundamentalist" answer, so to speak—one, that is, that refers to the very nature of Christian theology and to the training of eccle-siastics for comforting duties: this view has it that they were moved by a tendency toward idealism, an irresistible urge to look away from the vio-lence and injustice of reality on earth in order to gaze at the eternal "reali-ties" of faith.[40] Something of this kind had been observed by Montaigne with regard to the condemned: the thought of the fate of the soul helped them avoid having to deal with the intolerable thought of the fate that awaited them. Both cases bring us back to the question of the tie that had been built up over the centuries between a religion of forgiveness and the right to kill legally.

The stories about criminals in the popular literature (understood as a form of writing for an "ideal type" of popular reader) that sprang up around the scaffold enjoyed particular success. One of their basic features was the pedagogic and moralistic use of the description of criminal lives and acts to correct human habits. The Lutheran tradition of the funeral sermon over the dead body *(Leichenpredigt)* had introduced, in place of masses in remem-brance of the soul, a new form of relationship with the memory of the dead person: the fate of the soul was no longer at stake, as this was by now defini-tively entrusted to God's judgment. But by remembering the past actions of the dead person it was possible to draw precepts and moral teachings useful for Christians still exposed to the arts of the devil. Luther himself had inau-gurated this genre with his sermon in memory of Grand Duke John of Saxony in 1532. Ever since then the practice had been carefully regulated in the ordinances of the evangelical churches, and had even ended up making an appearance in the provinces of the Catholic world that lived in close con-tact with the evangelical one.[41] Naturally, the genre was intended to offer a laudatory and comforting memory of the virtues and deeds of the dead person: it was, in short, a funeral *lauditio* of important figures in society and the realms of power. But the eloquence of a university-trained clerical body began to be directed toward other moral examples, ones that could be de-rived from the misfortunes and horrors of those who fell into a life of sin. It was here that the moralization of the scaffold ritual, which came to be the characteristic feature of the death penalty in Protestant Europe, was partic-ularly evident. In police regulations and in the early versions of criminal codes, punishment was defined in relation to the goal of improving the behavior and social conformity of the population. Not just the salvation of individual souls but the security of the State itself was thought to depend on it.[42] The production of narratives of contrite criminals fit into this more general trend—a publishing market that started in the early seventeenth century with the circulation of printed pamphlets later collated into volumes. The main feature of this literature was its low-cost morality, a trait it shared with the tradition of the last speeches of condemned prisoners in England. The paths that had led to the scaffold invariably followed the same course: from small sins to crimes. The career of murderers and infanticides in the German world began with inobservance of the Lord's day or failure to obey one's parents and ended with the crime no greater and no smaller than the one recounted in the last speech of Thomas Savage in 1668 or that of John Noyse in 1686.[43] It was the Protestant version of the change taking place in European culture with the advance of the idea that offenses that until then had been met with the terrorizing justice of punishments could be prevented with an adequate disciplining of morals, to be exercised first and foremost by the family.

In Lutheran culture this tendency took different forms. We can gain an idea of this from a work that enjoyed great and lasting success right from the very first edition of 1698: the *Historie der Wiedergebohrnen* (History of the Reborn) by Johann Heinrich Reitz, a compilation of no fewer than 161 biographies, psychological profiles, and accounts of people's deaths.[44] The author, who converted from Calvinism to the mystical and visionary tendencies of Pietism, put at the center of the biographies the experience of conversion, understood as a sudden and radical change freely wrought by God: the Spirit entered and illuminated the hearts of sinners, saving them from eternal damnation. It was in the current of this tendency that literature about the conversion of condemned prisoners destined for the scaffold was grafted.

This emphasis on the penitence and salvation of the sinner characterized the Pietist version of Lutheranism in particular. In response to the institutional teaching of the Lutheran Church and its theologians, Pietism sought to bring Christianity as a practice of sanctification into the hearts of individuals and within families. Accounts of developments in this movement record conflictual relations with Lutheran orthodoxy, given the accentuation of the sentimental and mystical aspects that abounded in Pietism, which was firmly rooted in the intimacy of homes and secret meetings (the *Collegia pietatis*). The ancient strand of medieval religiosity, that of the inner devotion of the "Imitation of Christ," found new vitality in the tradition of Pietist circles: and it was above all through the daily recording of thoughts and emotions in private diaries that the description of the experience of conversion took form as an inner certification of salvation and a feeling of joy for divine election.[45] Stemming from this was the interest in stories about human beings liable to fall prey to sin but whose hearts, thanks to divine mercy, might suddenly be touched by an awareness of the gravity of their sins and joyfully accept the invitation of the Lord. The telling of conversion tales thus became a very recurrent part of Pietist culture, and it was here that the apologetic force of the stories of remorseful malefactors was discovered. This literary genre enjoyed considerable success in German culture between the seventeenth and eighteenth centuries: stories of murderers and brigands, but also, and especially, stories of women who had fallen into sin due to what was deemed to be their incurable superficiality and lack of substance, and had become murderesses, infanticides, and poisoners. The cases that emerge from reports written in the heat of the moment, circulated separately, and then collected into volumes, present the life paths of sinners who had fallen into the devil's snares, but who, thanks to the word of the Lord preached by the pastor while they awaited execution, opened their hearts to divine grace and were saved. Many cases regarded women, and as such considered more fragile and exposed to sin, though they were ready to convert and to endure an edifying death on the scaffold.[46] Thanks to Pietism, in German culture the theme of the conversion of the penitent sinner was embodied especially in the figure of the condemned woman awaiting execution and led to conversion by the work of the pastor comforting her. A fair number of motifs apparently analogous with themes from the piety and religious life of Counter-Reformation Catholicism were thus introduced into devotion and moral teaching.

The theme of care for the souls of the condemned, already present in the Reformed ecclesiastical ordinances, acquired extraordinary prominence in Pietist religiosity. From this sphere comes a collection of stories published by an important figure in German legal and political culture, Johann Jacob Moser (1701–1785). Known as the father of German constitutionalism, Moser found time during his long career to untiringly promote the moralization of social life: marriage and relations between the sexes, the upbringing of children, obedience to the law, wrongdoing and contrition were some of the themes he addressed in his many writings, which ran alongside his monumental endeavor to systematize German public law.[47] He must be credited with the publication, between 1730 and 1745, of a long series of stories of condemned criminals who had converted, or, as the title of the overall collection states, of the "final saintly hours of executed people."[48] The theme of "revival" or "rebirth"—of how the individual sinner was touched by the hand of God and converted—was at the center of the Lutheran biographic and autobiographic tradition, which took an interest in individual lives in order to draw from them models of upright behavior and Christian morality. This is what the tradition of speeches in remembrance of the dead given on the occasion of funerals—the *Leichenpredigten*—had been about. Moser's idea was to draw positive models from the stories of the very worst sinners, who, as they had to pay for the gravity of their wrongdoings with the death penalty, found the path of redemption and the testimony of faith in the final moments of their lives. This gave rise to series of stories about the final hours of life, where confessions by the condemned and testimony of their devotion became a powerful appeal for religious renewal and personal morality. One example is the story of the repentance and devout death of Christian Friedrich Ritters, subjected to the wheel in Mecklenburg on September 18, 1738.[49] The narrative tells of how Christian fell prey to the devil and became a murderer, going astray from a very early age. He had begun by neglecting his studies, denying his parents the affection that nature demanded, and abandoning the army he had enrolled in to become a thief and murderer—in short, going down the path in which he was more and more in thrall to evil. In doing so the image of God was lost in him, and Christian became a man of the devil. After ending up in prison for his crimes, he was visited every day by four preachers and two theology students, who started by reading Luther's Small Catechism to him in order to reawaken his consciousness of faith. The rest was the work of God's grace, who melted the hardness of his heart. And so the double murderer acknowledged the gravity of his wrongs and repented profoundly, with tears and lamentations, begging for help from those assisting him. Christian's hunger for the word of God was the sign that his conversion had begun. He asked to make confession, and was told that he should not do it in the manner of the papists, with a detailed list of sins; it was not necessary to confess his crimes, because he would pay the penalty for them on the scaffold according to the biblical sentence—blood for blood.

But he was permitted to make confession as an act of penitence and humiliation. He was also made to read the account of another conversion, that of Andreas Lepsch, who had died at the stake in Potsdam in 1730. Written by the pastor Heinrich Schubert, this episode attests to how such literature was used in prisons to convert condemned offenders through the example of others who had repented and preceded them to the scaffold.

The chronicle of Ritters's final days in jail describe him as someone whose faith had been reborn, who received lots of visitors, especially young people, eager to admire the example of his conversion. Also reported were his conversations with the two pastors who came to prepare him for and accompany him to the scaffold. Once there, he knelt down and said a long prayer in which he confessed the two murders he had committed and thanked God for the grace he had received; he declared that he willingly accepted the punishment that the sovereign authority had decided, and then went toward what he called the day of his wedding, conjuring up an image that would have pleased Saint Catherine of Siena. Similarly, in the case of Anna Martha Hungerladin, executed for infanticide on November 1, 1737, the narrative published by the pastor Matthias Michael Kümmelmann consisted of a short biography followed by an account of how the woman converted. The author explained that his aim was to extend beyond the execution crowd the edifying effect of the example set by the woman in what, according to him, had been a "death-sermon" *(Todespredigt)*, rendered efficacious by the example of death. The story of Anna Martha's life followed the same pattern as that of the soldier Christian Friedrich: the first sin—in this case some casual flirting at a dance—quickly led to an undesired pregnancy and infanticide. Imprisonment, the threat of her punishment, and contact with the pastor reawakened Anna Martha's soul. Then began a battle with Satan, who tempted her with the evil spirits of falsehood, despair, and shame. The pastor narrated the outcome of this struggle and the final victory of Christ over the sinner thanks to the *punctum iustificationis*—the Lutheran doctrine of justification by faith alone. In this way the path to the scaffold became the path to the place of the mystical wedding: Anna Martha walked it joyfully, comforting those accompanying her, forbidding them to be sad, and making a long devout appeal to the spectators that moved them to tears.[50]

The success of this literary genre was measured by the large number of editions and reprints, in which there was space for the sermons and edifying narratives printed in the pamphlets of pastors responsible for comforting the condemned. After Moser's collection, it was the turn of an evangelical preacher, Ernst Gottlieb Woltersdorf, to publish another one in 1753.[51] It must be said that neither Moser nor the other authors or publishers of these texts were in any doubt about the guilt of the people who went to the scaffold, and they showed no interest in the social constrictions that had driven them to theft, murder, infanticide, and so on. In their eyes, women and men were weak beings prone to sin: the Augustinian anthropology of the Reformation suggested humanity should be regarded as being made up of obdurate sinners. Sin necessarily led to crime. The law had to punish it, and had to do so with all the severity that was required to govern the people and convey the right warnings. Nothing other than the dramatic announcement that they were soon to appear in God's presence provided sinners with an adequate impulse to repent, opening their hearts to the action of divine grace. The death penalty was what produced the conversion effect and the assurance of eternal life: if, on the other hand, an ill-judged piety had resulted in them receiving a pardon, the weakness they had displayed by falling into sin and wrongdoing would prompt a fresh fall and damnation. The "reawakenings" (Erweckungen) were only fragile flowers, as Moser put it in the preface to his collection, destined almost always to wilt without bearing fruit: those reborn to the life of the spirit might well fall again, and indeed for the most part that was their fate. Death on the scaffold, on the other hand, offered a path to certain salvation, as demonstrated by all the cases narrated in his vast collection and neatly ordered by gender and crime. The section on infanticide women, all named and with an indication of the circumstances of their crime, recounts how each of them had fallen into sin. The story of their offense, which they commented on in their talks with the pastors that comforted them, always began with them committing small sins of frivolity and vanity. They then made more serious errors, and gradually moved away from the word of God and from the law. A moment's distraction in church during the sermon was all it took to slip into sin; and yielding to the sins of the flesh was all it took to end up with an illegitimate pregnancy, from whence it was a short step to killing the newborn infant to escape dishonor and public shame. Such crimes were unpardonable in the eyes of the law, and were therefore justly punished by death, but they could be forgiven by the divine court, the only price being that the offender had to finally listen once again to the word of God. The path of return to the grace of God was marked by edifying readings and commentary on passages from the Scriptures. These stories end with the arrival of the pastor, who greets the prisoner, announcing to her on God's behalf that on this, the day of execution, her soul would be received into heaven—an announcement invariably greeted with a cry of joy. Then came the walk to the scaffold, the culminating moment of an ascent into heaven performed by a penitent quivering with enthusiasm and devotion, who would die with the name of Jesus on her lips—neither more nor less in many respects than what, according to the accounts of confraternity brothers, condemned prisoners did in Italy.

Anyone studying the narratives filling Moser's large volumes will recognize that they are repetitive modules, with stock sentences sometimes lifted from the pamphlets of scaffold literature *(Bänkelsang):* a host of condemned prisoners in a period spanning over a century do nothing other than repeat the same words.[52] It is a scene very similar to the one repeated almost fixedly in the accounts found in Italian confraternity records. Admittedly, there were many differences between the two models. It is worth recalling that in going about their work the evangelical pastors and theology students could count on a fair amount of time between the trial and the execution of the sentence, during which they performed that action of persuasion and conversion for which the Italian comforters often only had a single night. Furthermore, while in Italian cities this process took place in the secrecy of a chapel or cell during the night, in the Pietist model initially private conversations and speeches were immediately transferred into a scaffold literature that recounted life stories. But it was not just for this that the condemned person's choice was considered differently: for the Italian companies of justice, there was also a political goal associated with saving the souls of condemned felons, whose resistance had to be broken down at any cost and with any kind of pressure. In the Lutheran world, on the other hand, the choice between salvation and damnation was seen as something that had to come from the sinner's conscience. If this did not happen, it was taken as a sign of God's wrath and of an irrevocable judgment sending sinners to hell. But as these stories had an almost invariably salvific outcome, the question that springs to mind is how reliable the accounts are. Did events really play out like that on the scaffold, or were they deformed by the filter of the comforters' culture, and perhaps even deliberately distorted? A further question is how to interpret the terms of contrition and conversion that crop up continually in those documents.

The answer to the first question is simple. The hypothesis of pious falsehood, the final refuge of the incredulity and disbelief of the modern reader of these sources, collapses in the face of the concordance between the narratives of the German Pietists and the Catholic comforters, not to mention the numerous other sources of differing origin and the testimony of chroniclers and travelers. Indirect proof is also given by the fact that the cases of those who resisted the invitation to convert were not hushed up in the Reformation countries, but emphasized and signaled as abhorrent. Here we find an important trace of the different interpretive key of the two religious cultures in deciphering the meanings and outcomes of individual choices: while the Catholic comforters placed their trust in the power on earth and in heaven of the keys given by Christ to Saint Peter (thanks to which anyone could obtain eternal salvation with sacramental absolution), the invitation of the Lutheran faith was to reflect unflinchingly on the cursed nature of humankind and the hell that awaited sinners who did not trust with faith in the Redemption of Christ. The contrite and the stubborn were effectively two sides of the same coin offered for the attention of spectators contemplating the differing fates of sinners. The two traditions had a common desire to derive moral teaching and a religious message from scaffold stories, which rendered both equally indifferent to the question being debated at the time in Enlightenment culture regarding the lawfulness and tolerability of capital punishment. In both cases the transformation of crime into sin was the mechanism that underpinned the system, and it is no coincidence that this was the point of attack which Cesare Beccaria identified in drawing the new paradigm to the attention of his readers.

It is, though, worth looking further at the comparison between the Catholic path to the scaffold and the Protestant one, not on the abstract plane of morphological resemblances but on that of the concrete embodiments they assumed in the historic reality of the Protestant and Catholic countries. It is hard for readers today to distinguish between the religious "revival" of the Pietists and the "conversion" spoken about by the brothers of the *misericordie*. On both sides the death penalty was viewed as an opportunity to keep sinners reined in and to save souls. An entirely different matter was the question of the significance of acts of contrition and confession in the apparently identical scaffold devotion practiced in the Lutheran and Catholic worlds. Simplifying and summarizing a complicated issue, we might say that on one hand there were those who placed their trust in the power over souls of the sacraments administered by members of a holy order, and on the other those who worked to reawaken a consciousness of sin and to present faith in salvation as a divine gift. The conversations between a pastor and the infanticides Dorothea Elisabeth Specht and Catharina Münsters (executed respectively in 1739 and 1752) show how the women lacked an awareness of the sin they had committed—in their heart was the devil. Only the grace of God could save them, and so it was that an emotive jolt like the singing of a church *lied* opened up their hearts and brought tears of penitence gushing forth.[53] Sinners could not save themselves on their own— theirs was an extreme example of salvation without human merits, a gift freely given by God. The exclusive function of the pastor was to reawaken the condemned person's moral conscience, understood as an awareness of evil and a desire for redemption. This was very different to the concern of the Italian *confratelli* to present themselves as guarantors of divine forgiveness in exchange for the "patient" placing total trust in the efficacy of the sacraments and indulgences in the name of the holy power of the ecclesiastical body and the pope's authority over souls. And if on the one hand Catholic moral casuistry tended to examine how the norm was peppered with variations and exceptions, and how the debt of sins (and crimes) could be paid with indulgences and masses, on the other hand Protestant casuistry aimed to reawaken the voice of God in the sinner's darkened heart. Clearly we are on a very different path to the official writings and narrow Catholic orthodoxy of the Italian comforters. The norms inspired by biblical dictates demanded that a killer should be repaid with the same punishment; but the Protestant interpretation of the doctrine of salvation guaranteed the cancellation of sins for those who, with profound remorse, requested God's forgiveness in the name of the justification by faith guaranteed to all Christians.

In Lutheran Europe the conviction that death on the scaffold, if the victim was accompanied and comforted by pastors, was the gateway to eternal life not only had dissimilar roots to Catholic ones. It also produced entirely different results. Examples of this can be found in the spread of cases of suicide murderers in Germany, Prussia, and Denmark from the end of the seventeenth century. The people involved essentially committed suicide by proxy, resorting to crime—generally killing their own children or those of others—in the knowledge that they would end up on the scaffold. As the German jurist Karl Ferdinand Hommel wrote in 1766, they were individuals who, "having often heard from the pulpit that no suicide can be saved, kill the innocent children of others or other adults. Then they hand themselves in to a judge ... with the ardent desire for a public execution in order to be more certain of going to heaven."[54] At the time when Hommel was writing, a debate had long been underway about how to curb the spread of this practice. Around the middle of the eighteenth century there was much discussion about the most suitable way of halting the epidemic of indirect suicides. Pastors and preachers were aware of the risks they ran by emphasizing the certainty of eternal salvation for those who died on the scaffold. Moser himself tried to ward off such dangers in the introduction to the second edition of his work, where he issued a warning to anyone blind and crazy enough to use the narrated examples inappropriately: not one of them should harbor the illusion that they could go to heaven by committing a murder in order to then be executed. But exhortations like these did not suffice to curb those who wanted to die and be accepted into heaven by virtue of justification by faith, and who chose the path of crime in order to climb the ladder to the scaffold.

The question had particular relevance in Lutheran Denmark. Here too, as in Germany, some people killed in order to die. Historic research into cases has shown that the epidemic began in 1697 and continued for a century.[55] But here the seriousness of the phenomenon prompted a growing perception that the punishment system needed to be rethought. The first step was to aggravate the death of suicide murderers on the scaffold by inflicting atrocious suffering and humiliating punishments. Soldiers, for instance, were to receive public fustigations for two weeks before execution, which involved the terrible torment of the wheel, while ordinary citizens were tormented with red-hot pincers and had their hands cut off along the route taken by the penal procession. However, this did not solve the problem either, and in the meantime the idea that the reason for this lay in the rigorously biblical roots of the punishment systems began to gain ground. In 1758 a proposal was made to secularize the criminal code, abolishing the death penalty envisaged for crimes indicated by the Bible. And yet indirect suicides did not diminish—far from it. In 1767 the case of Anne Christophersdotter, who in order to die on the scaffold had killed the infant son of a friend, was referred to King Christian VII. Observing that the aggravation of punishments had not had the desired effect, on December 18 he approved a new decree: suicide murderers were henceforth to be sentenced to a tough prison regime and humiliating labor, a long period of detention, and to be whipped in public each year on the day on which they had committed their crime. When they finally died, their bodies were to be mutilated and exposed. In April 1768 a new decree prohibited any form of public religious rituality— such as singing hymns and reciting prayers—in places of punishment: the pastor had to wait in silence at the execution site.[56] The intent was to combat what was defined as a false fantasy: the idea that eternal salvation was assured when the pastor walked alongside the sinner reciting prayers and singing devout hymns. In this way, a little over two centuries after the establishment of the Protestant Reformation in the country (1536), Denmark abandoned at least partially the religious conception of the death penalty.

It has been asked whether a contributing factor in this was the circulation of the work of Cesare Beccaria, which had been greeted in the German translation as an immortal work *(unsterbliches Werk)* by the jurist Karl Ferdinand Hommel.[57] One thing was clear: while in Protestant culture death on the scaffold continued to be viewed as the most certain way of attaining the salvation of the soul, and the practice of suicide by proxy spread, what began to engage the minds of governors was an observation made by Beccaria: the death penalty was a convenient way out, which, far from obtaining the desired terrifying effect, was a stimulus to crime for those who wanted to sort out their relationship with the world and with God in a single stroke.

The discussion that began in the late eighteenth century in Lutheran culture, especially in Germany, dealt in particular with the question of infanticide: Goethe's *Faust* is a poetic monument arising from real events and from a widespread debate about the causes and repression of this special crime. It was in the context of Pietist culture that discussion was broadening out to include themes of pedagogy and moral philosophy that revolved around the notion of "conscience"—a theme particularly dear to the Lutheran tradition that had developed in the more general context of Reformation Europe. It is well known that one voice that commanded particular attention was that of Immanuel Kant, who, though personally touched by Pietism, countered the notion of conversion as a miracle capable of suddenly transforming the individual with that of the constancy of the moral personality resulting from persistent and strict self-control. Moral law as a rule inherent to conscience eliminated at the roots not only the science of exceptions and cases, as has been observed,[58] but also the miraculous action of external agents. This is how the modern notion of "person" took shape as a moralized form of the Christian idea of the immortal soul. In German culture the popularity of scaffold conversion stories contributed in some measure to these developments, with the insistence on a religion of the heart that ignored confessional divisions and appealed to upbringing and rigor in daily choices between good and evil. What is more, the sermonizing emphasis and pedagogic desire to bend knowledge of individual passions and wrongdoings to edifying ends was such that Rousseau's *Confessions* were a source of perplexity for that tradition precisely because it was impossible to derive any moral teaching from them.[59]

It is at any rate a fact that the emergence of the conscience as a constituent element of personal identity marked a turning point with respect to the religious construction of the idea of the soul, the body's invisible double. In this way, there was a parenthesizing of the imposing construction of the Christian afterlife, as structured by the long history of the tie between the living and the dead in the medieval tradition, which consolidated especially around Catholic purgatory. "The dread of something after death," wrote Shakespeare in Hamlet's famous monologue, "the undiscovered country, from whose bourn / No traveler returns, puzzles the will, / And makes us rather bear those ills we have."

Fear of the life to come, the unexplored territory from which no traveler had ever returned—this is what caused those who would willingly have put an end to their intolerable lives to turn pale, wrote Shakespeare. And the idea of the eternal survival of the soul had long made it possible to divert the dying person's attention away from the suffering and death that awaited them, in the same way—according to the image conjured up by Montaigne—in which attempts were made to distract the child from the surgeon's instruments with fantasies and fictions. As to what the soul was in the minds of the condemned, the question not only presupposes conditions of freedom of choice that did not exist but also ignores the fact that the soul whose salvation was talked about was, for those people and for spectators, something that became existent and actual as a consequence of the death sentence. As Michel Foucault wrote, that soul was "a factor in the mastery that power exercises over the body."[60]

But no overall picture of the literature associated with the religious comforting of the condemned would, however, be complete without taking a look at a type of document that sprang from the Puritan culture of the founders of "New England"; also because it was here, in immense spaces construed as a totally new world and imagined to have been entirely gifted to Christians by Providence, that the utopians designed (and the radical sects tried to build) a "city of God" on earth. In the criminal legislation and in the death sentences carried out in Boston during the seventeenth century the principle of a very stiff biblical literalism was closely linked to the Calvinist doctrine of predestination. In the colony's first penal code, the *Body of Liberties* (1641), the ordinances regarding crimes and punishments were organized strictly along biblical lines: crimes punishable by death were listed in the order in which they are described in the Mosaic code of Leviticus. What the Pilgrim Fathers wanted to create was a "Bible Commonwealth"; and the meaning attributed to the criminal act, viewed as the revelation of the workings of evil, was that of an attack on the very foundations of the political body. And yet wrongdoers were not abandoned to the destiny of damnation that awaited them after death. Before the sentence was carried out, they were visited in jail by clergymen and simple laypeople, and invited to express contrition—on the way from this world to the next their wayward souls had to rediscover the lost path. This was the only way to heal the fracture between the human being and God, and to restore the holy nature of the pact that bound citizens to the political body and assured them divine grace. The visits intensified after the sentence. Pastors gave sermons about the felon's case before and after the execution. The ritual followed a similar pattern to the one practiced in the mother country: after arriving at the scaffold prepared and accompanied by a pastor, the condemned could deliver a last speech inviting onlookers to learn from their bad example. As in the European Reformation societies, the penitent sinner had this final occasion to remind everyone that the path to the gallows began with the very first and most minor infractions of the moral code. The print medium was used in New England as well to draw these conclusions from the biographies of the convicted prisoners. But the accounts of wrongdoers' misdeeds and their last speeches were not published, just the texts of the sermons delivered before and after execution. As the Reverend Cotton Mather stated, preached sermons were like drops of rain that touch the earth for an instant and then disappear; when printed though, they were like snow that remains for a long time on the ground.[61] Cotton Mather was the best known and most authoritative member of the Puritan clergy: his vision of a world threatened by the presence of the devil manifested itself at the time of the events surrounding the Salem witches, when an entire city experienced the horrors of an obsession that had long dominated the European world.[62] To put all members of society on their guard against the snares of evil, Mather and other pastors began to print their sermons of theological and moral commentary on individual executions. The first case took place in 1674, when Reverend Samuel Danforth published the sermon he gave when Benjamin Goad—guilty of the crime of bestiality—was put to death. This marked the beginning of a tradition of printing sermons that continued for as long as the scaffold remained active in Boston.

This literature had an extraordinary social importance: printing meant that sermons did not just reach condemned prisoners, and the crowds that flocked to see their execution, but all members of society, "from magistrate to slave."[63] According to this Puritan tradition, magistrates, insofar as they were God's representatives in governing a community founded on divine law, were obliged to carry out God's vengeance against those who transgressed against his will. This concept, sustained by Cotton Mather in a sermon delivered in 1686 on the occasion of the execution of a man named James Morgan, was based on the distinction between private vendetta, regarded as evil, and capital punishment, seen as public vendetta legitimated by God. The scriptural grounds for this came, as always, from Romans 13—the same chapter invoked more than three centuries later by the Southern Baptist Convention in 2000 to sustain the necessity and religious legitimacy of the death penalty.[64]

Apart from these stubbornly surviving pockets in the circles of particular religious groups, we can say that criminal justice retained the features of a religious event at least until the beginning of the nineteenth century, when a collective move away from the values of tradition became apparent in the indifference of the condemned. At this point the ritual was simplified and secularized. But pastors' voices continued to be heard for a long

FIGURE 32.3. Execution of John Williams, Peter Peterson, Francis Frederick, and John P. Rog, etching, Boston, 1819.

time: the final scaffold sermon was published in 1825. And irrespective of these dates, the American idea of justice retained some characteristics of the core Puritan notion of sin and punishment: punishing the delinquent became the task of a civil government viewed as an institution based on faith in God and in the death penalty as the legitimate vengeance of a holy order against the attack of evil. As the Reverend Stephen West said in his sermon of December 6, 1787, society could not host those guilty of violent crimes, because they threatened the divine foundation of the social body. It was necessary to render thanks to the Lord for having shown the world how to free itself of those intolerable presences. This warning echoed in the context of what was a very tough period: unrest, endemic robbery, and rebellion cast a dark shadow over American society in the years following the war of the colonies against England. Among those who mounted the scaffold at that time were characters such as John Blay and Charles Rose, who, after fighting in the revolution, turned to a life of robbery and crime.[65]

Having put down deep roots in American culture, the principle of a special mandate given to the nation to carry out God's vengeance would also resurface in President Obama's announcement to the country that, with the elimination of Osama bin Laden, justice had been done. In comparison, as we have seen, there emerged what had survived in the Italian and Catholic tradition of the ancient foundation embodied by the long history of the companies of justice—which had undergone a complicated and uneven process of slow extinction.

The Slow Epilogue of Comforting in Nineteenth-Century Italy

A HISTORY OF ITALY, Benedetto Croce observed, can only be talked about starting from the date of political unification. The story of the confraternities of justice demonstrates both the truth and the limits of this axiom. The different Italys that found in the companies of justice a sign of their unity in Catholicism also imprinted them with the features of different power structures and local traditions. The differences and the continuities were maintained through the whole of the century separating the work of Cesare Beccaria and the birth of the unified state. The only thing that remained constant was the ecclesiastical condemnation of his book. The Congregation of the Index had banned it on January 3, 1766, on the basis of a report by the Jesuit Pietro Lazeri, who judged the ideas of Montesquieu and Rousseau—labeled as Protestants—to be "impure" sources. It was to be condemned, according to Lazeri, on the basis of the doctrines of Bellarmine and second scholasticism regarding the divine origin of political power. Hostility to the work remained undimmed even in liberal nineteenth-century Italy, when the ecclesiastical authorities could no longer prevent the printing of the work but, at most, could denounce the new editions as the work of the "poisoners of Italy."[1]

The unification of Italy was the result of a long and complicated process. Casting an eye over the peninsula at the time of Emperor Joseph II's suppression of the Milanese company, we see different-colored islands emerging in a landscape still largely characterized by the continuing existence of ancient institutions and rituals. The Florentine company of the Blacks met the same fate as its Milanese sister company: it was suppressed in 1785 by Grand Duke Peter Leopold, in the final stage of a process of reform that saw, in rapid and coherent succession, the abolition of the death penalty and that of the court of the Inquisition. The decree of suppression contained a blanket negative judgment of all the charitable companies: their initially praise-worthy goals were accused of having been "weakened and corrupted," and instead of setting a good example in practicing fraternal charity, they had become cause for scandal and discord due to internal divisions, conflicts over money and power, and the prodigious expense of dinners and feasts that squandered money raised in alms.[2] As for the Confraternita dei Neri, once the death penalty had been abolished, there was no justification for its continued existence: the feasts it used to organize for the patron saint at the end of August, with red watermelons providing an echo of severed heads, inevitably came to be seen as anachronistic. In the dominions of the Savoy dynasty, on the other hand, on the eve of the Revolutions of 1848, the confraternity of the Misericordia di Torino continued to provide spiritual assistance to the condemned; and the historian and politician Luigi Cibrario, a faithful subject of King Charles Albert and a follower of the philosopher and jurist Gian Domenico Romagnosi, believed its work to be indispensable, at least until such time as an improvement in habits and conduct made it possible to concentrate exclusively on helping prison inmates. While waiting for that future to materialize, he wrote, "The Misericordia hopes the hour is not distant in which, the most atrocious misdeeds having become more rare, it will be possible to abolish a punishment that, considered carefully, is a social right induced by a lamentable necessity, and as such not perpetual but temporary."[3] The social right to kill legally was a deep-rooted conviction widely shared by the dominant powers. Abolitionists, among whom the lawyer and jurist Francesco Carrara was very much to the fore at that time, found it difficult to make headway in the face of the mistrustful ruling classes, who regarded capital punishment as a vital means for keeping the criminal impulses of the subaltern classes at bay. When finally abolished, it was missed for a long time—a feeling reflected in the fact that the last noose used for a hanging was displayed as a relic for veneration. It can still be seen today in the church of the Misericordia in Turin dedicated to Saint John the Baptist.

Things were very different in southern Italy. In Naples, the Company of Whites, already disbanded once in 1583 and reestablished immediately afterward as a body reserved for diocesan and regular clergy, had, in the course of the eighteenth century, enjoyed the glory of witnessing the beatification of one of its former members, Father Francesco Caracciolo, and the popular diffusion of the *Apparecchio alla morte* by one of the company's brothers, Alfonso Maria de' Liguori, who was destined to become a famous bishop saint. When the French Revolution brought to the surface the previously subterranean turmoil of new political beliefs and ideals, it fell to the religious members of the company to try and convert those who were sent to their deaths by the Sanfedist fury of the people and the reaction of the authorities: men like the Jacobin Tommaso Amato from Messina, who went to the scaffold on May 17, 1794, with a gag-bit on his mouth to prevent him from proclaiming in a loud voice his ideas as an enemy of the king and an enemy of God. In a city terrorized by the eruption of Vesuvius, the spectacle of the execution of a person believed to be possessed by the devil was ritualized with the placing of lugubrious black hangings over sacred images to prevent the damned man's blasphemies from rising up to heaven. Instead, on October 18, 1799, the three Neapolitans "guilty of divine and human lèse-majesté, known as Jacobins," demonstrated—according to the register of the Whites, who accompanied them to the scaffold—"a truly admirable remorse"; one of them, Vincenzo Vitaliani, was particularly "remorseful and contrite," and kept yelling "May the faith of Jesus Christ live on." The day went down in the annals of the Company as a sadly memorable one, because a gunshot sparked panic and terror among a large crowd on edge with fear of the Jacobins, and transformed the spectacle into a collective tragedy, with a number of deaths and injuries in the resulting crush. But Republican virtue and the ancient model of dying for the homeland "with intrepidness and male courage," as one of the three, Emanuele De Deo, wrote in a final letter to his brother, had proven in this way to be compatible with Christian religion.[4]

In Palermo, as in Naples, the Company of Whites was a point of reference for a dense network of small congregations of the same kind operating in every city and town. After the Congress of Vienna the return to power of the Bourbon Ferdinand I as King of the Two Sicilies brought change, with the exclusion of laypeople from the congregations responsible for comforting the condemned. There were a great many of these associations, as can be deduced from the royal decree of February 16, 1820, which contains a succinct list ("in Palermo, in Torre del Greco, in Somma, in Capua, in Aversa, in Gaeta, in Sessa, in Nola, in Salerno, in Aquila, in Lecce, in Lucera, in Foggia, and in all the other communes of the Royal Domains on this and the other side of the Faro.")[5]

From then on, the Company of Whites in Palermo, deprived of its chapel and of the privilege to pardon a condemned prisoner, ceased to exist. Right until the end it had continued to keep a record of death sentences and inflicted torments in its proceedings: in 1817 the members of a band of pirates found guilty of plunder and mass murder were attached to horsetails and dragged to the execution site. Once dead, their heads and hands were severed and placed in iron cages, which were then hung up in Piazza della Marina in Palermo and in various prominent places in other cities on the island.[6] It is worth citing the description of the last trace of the rite of forgiveness that took place with the execution of Melchiorre Merenda on March 9, 1818: "When the executioner went to him in the chapel a few moments before the execution in order to tie his hands, he [Merenda] requested permission, granted by the head of the chapel, to kiss his feet. Touched by this act, the executioner cried, and wanted in turn to kiss the feet of the condemned man. This moving spectacle brought tears to the eyes of everyone present."[7]

Nothing gives a better idea of how the reality of the most extreme form of punitive violence could be masked by an imaginary forgiveness than this river of tears, overwhelming and uniting the executioner, the condemned man, and the crowd of spectators in a single embrace.

Though the Sicilian company of the Whites had come to an end, the Neapolitan one lived on, as a "wholly ecclesiastical Congregation without any interference from the lay authorities."[8] In the face of great difficulties it had managed to get through the Napoleonic age, and acquired fresh vigor with the return of the Bourbons. But when this dynasty fell it lost its raison d'être, and when Garibaldi entered Naples on September 7, 1860, the Company's secretary noted the event in the register, followed by the words "tempo *pessimo*"—apparently an observation about the awful weather but also a comment on what were seen as awful times.[9]

The age of revolution and of the Napoleonic regime marked in any case an important caesura. In the majority of cases the confraternities of justice had seen their role diminish in those years. Sometimes they were suppressed and their assets confiscated.[10] But old habits survived, and reappeared in Restoration Italy. In Modena, the practice had remained in force: on the last page of the ancient company's list of the executed, under the year 1826, is an annotation stating that in one case of the application of the death penalty "the usual charitable offices" had been performed "in accordance with the rules reestablished in their full force."[11] To make the ceremony more solemn, the two condemned people, Maria Zanni and Giovanni Battista Savigni, guilty of murdering the woman's husband, had been led to the scaffold in Piazza Grande after obtaining papal absolution *in articulo mortis*: it had been given by the bishop in person from a window high up in the bishop's palace. Everything had taken place according to ancient custom, following the rules laid down in the work of Bishop Sabbatini. The comforters, a body selected by title and standing—they were led by Count Giovanni Franco Ferrari Moreni—had played their part in line with tradition, right down to the final burial of the bodies and the burning of the nooses. There was even a "tender, moving speech" after the hanging, delivered to the crowd by a canon from a stage erected between the two gallows.[12]

In the restored Italian states of the Po Valley, the return to the ancient ways did not last long. In the meantime new faces appeared among those condemned to death. Previously there had been the heretics of the sixteenth century, who then gave way to those guilty of sacrilege and a long line of thieves, murderers, and infanticides. But stepping to the fore now were political rebels, bearers of new ideas: liberty, homeland, constitution, agrarian law. One example that was destined to make a lasting impression on the memory of the national Risorgimento was the episode regarding the "martyrs of Belfiore": the account written and published by the archpriest of Mantua Cathedral, Luigi Martini, about what happened in the city's prisons in the years between 1851 and 1855 to Don Enrico Tazzoli and his associates, gave the term "comforting" a new and unexpected flavor of martyrdom at once Christian and national.[13]

It is no coincidence that the Papal State remained the last bulwark of comforting rituals. The events of the French conquest and the Napoleonic age led to suspensions and interruptions of customary practices. But during the revival of the Restoration years it had to be decided how and what to restore. The Inquisition courts resumed their work and the function of assistance for the condemned was maintained. In some cases, however, changes that had been introduced in the Napoleonic age were kept. The most important one was that the clergy were exclusively responsible for attending to the soul, leaving the State to deal with earthly life and death. This is what happened in Bologna. Here, during the Jacobin republic, the School of Comforters continued to meet for a short period, the only novelty being that members had to adapt to the appellative of "citizens." In 1797 it was the "citizen doctor Don Adeodato Grandi" who, in his capacity as censor, presented a printed list of cases to discuss regarding testaments, beginning the introduction of the revolutionary principle of equality among children.[14] This was a not insignificant change, if one considers that the censor's book had been started in 1724 when the Marchese Giovanni Niccolò Tanara was censor.[15] But with the Napoleonic age the role of assisting the condemned was handed over definitively to the clergy, thereby creating a structural relationship between the political authorities and the ordinary ecclesiastical structure inspired by the cornerstones of the new conception of state power. They were troubled times, and the scaffold was often put to use to punish those involved in revolutionary uprisings and plots. Every time an execution took place in Bologna, the police authorities officially invited parish priests to prepare to "lend the Christian forms of aid," as we read in letters sent to the parish priest of the church of Santissima Trinità in the years between 1809 and 1812.[16] This continued to happen even after the restoration of the papal government. The priests then briefly reported to the bishop about the outcome of the comforting. In the case involving the Barnabite Ugo Bassi on August 8, 1849, it fell to the parish priest of Santa Maria della Carità, Don Agostino Bini, to report the details. While doing so, he also cautiously outlined what the condemned man's final wishes had been: Ugo Bassi "would have liked to write down an even more extensive retraction, but he was not granted paper." In Don Agostino's view, it would also have been appropriate and politically useful "to make everything public as an example."[17]

In the meantime, the tradition of keeping records of the condemned was continued: the old lists were still updated with the names of those sent to their deaths in the name of King Victor Emmanuel. Priests prepared the condemned in the *conforteria,* and the chronicler gave his opinion about what they achieved. In the case of the twenty-two-year-old Angelo Giustini, beheaded on December 2, 1826, on the field of Sant'Antonio for having slit the throat of his lover to rob her, a note was made of the "shamelessness" with which he walked to the place of execution, conversing with the police commissioner on his right, and the parish priest Don Battestini, who had confessed him, on his left. "The people were scandalized by his shamelessness and dissipation."[18] By contrast, a "highly exemplary resignation" that edified the comforters was displayed by the three men shot at the Prati di Caprara outside Porta San Felice on the morning of January 14, 1861: their final messages were gathered by the priest and conveyed by letter to the curates of their parishes.[19] And it was "under the government of Victor Emmanuel" that thirty-year-old Gaetano Prosperi, known as "the spirit," was condemned to death "for attempt of attack [*sic*] on the security of the state, and for willful murder of assault" on December 15, 1863.[20] The sentence was handed down by the superior court of the new State, and the execution took place in an enclosed space between Porta Lame and Porta San Felice. The privacy of the place, the impersonality of the court, and the new form assumed by the ancient crime of lesè-majesté indicate how much things had changed. But even more telling is the rushed and ungrammatical record, which shows just how long gone were the times of the erudite and refined discussion of cases in the ancient and holy School of Comforters. It is a case that highlights how the current of the old river was being channeled into a new river bed, carrying with it the habits and sentiments of bygone times.

Meanwhile, in other cities and towns of the former Papal State that had now become part of the Italian State, confraternities hit by decrees of abolition struggled to suddenly give up devotions and practices of suffrage for the souls of the condemned, the extreme model of the unhappiness of earthly life. In the absence of actual condemned criminals, resort was sometimes made to a kind of theatrical simulation, with one of the brothers taking the part of the condemned so that the others could practice the ancient art of comforting. It was evidently difficult to suddenly interrupt a long and deep-rooted tradition.

In the decades that preceded the turning point there had been time to reorganize the structures and rework the constitutions of the traditional confraternal associations. In Perugia, the noble doctor Omero, count of Montesperello, signed the new constitution of the Confraternita di Sant'Andrea e San Bernardino della Giustizia, published complete with imprimatur in 1846. They set out the forms and ways of comforting, including the offer of "restorative food, even dainty things, and drinks."[21] In small towns the case reports conserved in local archives recount stories like that of Giovanni Luccioni and David Zenobi, bandits from Filottrano, a town in the Marche, who were captured and sentenced to death in 1854. The comforting of the pair by the local Confraternita della Buona Morte began at seven in the evening on November 9. The long surviving report shows in detail how their initial attitude of rebelliousness and rejection quickly gave way to contrition, repentance, and mystical crisis—a full-blown "transference of holiness."[22] The religious ritual of the scaffold in the morning followed the customary pattern, with moments of intense devotion, like when Giovanni Luccioni asked to "go to his death without being blindfolded, in order to see the scaffold just as Jesus Christ looked on the Cross." He then kissed the executioner, knelt down on the ground reciting three Hail Marys, and then went to his death begging the populace for forgiveness and "invoking the most holy names of Jesus and Mary."

But in the years of the Restoration it was one of the most ancient and important confraternities of justice—the Arciconfraternita della Morte e Orazione in Ferrara—which showed how the ancient practices could be fully revived. The archconfraternity pursued a lucid design to erase everything new stemming from the ideas of Beccaria and the work of Napoleon, as is clearly shown by the surviving documentary sources.

The School of Comforters in Ferrara conducted an intense theoretical study of cases, following the ancient model of casuistry elaborated in Bologna in the seventeenth and eighteenth centuries. The collection of "ideas for possible subjects to address in the *conforteria*" preserved in its archive was based on both real and hypothetical cases. The latter included the eventuality of having to deal with condemned prisoners who were deaf, dumb, mad, or unable to speak the language of the country, in addition to heretics and Jews; and there was discussion about what to do if a Jew and a Christian needed to be comforted at the same time. These were old problems, often tackled with old arguments, just as the means and methods of the work performed by the comforters were old. The "patient" was still accompanied to the scaffold with the *tavoletta,* which continued to be used to ensure "that the patient did not see the scaffold." But something had changed, as can be seen, for example, in the hypothetical case of the Jew Abraham: he was imagined as a "wealthy merchant" aged sixty, "upright" and with "sober habits," guilty of contravening the government ban on entering the city during a cholera epidemic because he was driven by anxiety for the plight of his first-born son Isaac. Condemned to death, Abraham was urged to embrace the Christian faith. His imagined response was this: "Everyone must follow their own religion, and he, having been brought up as a Jew, wanted to die as such, changing faith not being a matter of a few hours." In any case "he would find no reason to place his religion after one that ordered the spilling of innocent blood as public vengeance." He declared that he wished to repose in the bosom of Abraham, though admitting to finding "no substantial difference between the Jewish religion and the Christian one, which is nothing other that the continuation of the former adapted to the weakness of the times." He hoped for the imminent coming of the Messiah and desired three things: "to at least see his dying Isaac in order to place a paternal blessing on his head, and to close his eyes with the kiss of peace"; "to be saved from the scaffold . . . as the divine Savior does not wish the offender to perish but to convert and live"; and to receive "food not prohibited by Mosaic Law out of simple reverence for it." The section dealing with the arguments to convert him is missing, but nonetheless what emerges from this hypothetical scenario is that the wealthy Jewish merchant and his religion are viewed with a certain respect, without the violent hostility of the sermons forced upon the local Jewish community in the seventeenth century.

Here the old form of the hypothetical case is adapted to suit the context of a different age, revealing a new sensibility. An example of this lies in the documentation regarding the (real) story of a certain Giovanni Fabbri from Monestirolo, accused of having killed his brother Luigi in 1854: his case was pending on appeal, as the evidence against him was not conclusive. The confraternity prepared at any rate for the possibility that he might be sentenced to death, tasking the *conforteria* to produce an imaginary dialogue between the man likely to be condemned and his comforter.[23] Giovanni was made out to be suspicious and mistrustful: it was imagined he would protest that they wanted to use guile to get him to confess, but that he knew no one could be sent to their death without confession. "All his companions" had told him so, forewarning him that in the *conforteria* he would face "gloom, scares, threats" to force him to confess. Now he had proof of it: "What is this semi-darkness, these black robes, this monotonous praying in whispers? I knew it, these are the deceptions to lower my spirit, to drag confession from me."

The response picks up on the theme of the opposition between darkness and light, with its figurative meanings of the contrast between religious devotion and anticlerical reason. First of all, Giovanni must be reminded of his lowly extraction (his brother, of "better fortune," was a shopkeeper): "But tell me, did you ever have as much light in your smoke-filled kitchen, lit by just a few tallow candles or some dim oil lamp?" An appeal would then be made to a notion of Christian brotherhood transcending differences of class—and this, significantly, was the new word being pronounced: "Unfortunately there is a reluctance in society between the different classes, a barrier between the commoner and the noble, the layman and the ecclesiastic, the poor and the rich, which makes it difficult for the former to approach the latter, holding them back from asking for advice, concern, help." But there was a remedy, and it had been discovered *ab antiquo,* because it was to overcome this barrier—a mental state of mind ("reluctance")—that the brothers had begun from very early times to wear penitential sackcloth, which made them neither poor nor rich, commoners nor nobles, laymen nor ecclesiastics. The only purpose of the help they offered was to get him to repent of his sins.

Just what kind of idea of class there might have been in the *conforteria* emerges from the in-house regulations printed in 1852. It was a small booklet, much shorter than the one published a century earlier.[24] The mental horizons were still the same, though, even if the old rules were threatened by the new age. A negative view of modern times surfaces continually in references to the strict forms of the ancient practice of comforting. Should handcuffs and fetters be loosened? Yes, but only if they were excessively tight. In any case it was necessary to avoid the "indecent system of negotiating with conditions the assent to confession." Should the condemned person be allowed dinner and breakfast? Unfortunately, this was inevitable, given "the indifferentism that now prevails in the prisons." The comforters would find themselves dealing with "coarse and capricious requests" from the condemned, but they had to avoid "fighting them head on," limiting themselves to "deviating them from these shameful ostentations, the unfortunate offspring of false principles." Light foods such as soups and "substantial broths" were the order of the day, thereby avoiding an unseemly revelry that would stimulate the senses and distract the mind from the only thought that should occupy it. Separate mention was made of the "indeclinable request, almost demand, to smoke." The recommendation here was to pretend nothing had been said and let the request drop, granting permission to smoke only if it was impossible to do otherwise. At this point there is a general reflection on smoking as the vice of a class, one that fills the jails with the condemned: "The class of the condemned normally belongs to that of the idle, who, not wishing to adapt to earn an honest wage, the fruit of regular labor, yield to crime to feed vices and idleness. In this [category], smoking is such a habit that it has almost become part of nutrition."[25]

This was the new category of the "dangerous classes" that was appearing on the ancient stage of comforting with the first steps of the industrial revolution. In this context the confraternity showed that it had a valuable practical function as a stronghold for the alliance between the large landowners and the clergy. A reform of the chapters in 1848 explicitly debarred from membership of the confraternity those who worked as servants, grocers, carters, or casual laborers, together with anyone whose social condition was not compatible with "civil and esteemed employment."[26]

The text was signed by the governor, Marchese Girolamo Canonici, and by the director, the canon and archpriest Guido Guitti. The hand of Canonici can probably also be recognized in one of the theoretical cases proposed to the lay and ecclesiastical brothers, undated but drawn up by the person who wrote the report on the Giovanni Fabbri case and other texts in the second half of the 1850s. This theoretical case is of special interest to us here, because it deals not only with concrete forms of execution but also with the issue of the lawfulness of the death penalty.

As with class barriers, Beccaria's arguments against the death penalty could also be swept away. A long text presented in a question and answer format shows how the *confratelli* in Ferrara were well aware that times had changed. One imaginary "case" involves a discussion of what to do with a "patient" who, having been "taken to the *conforteria,* did not want to listen to anything and wanted to be left in peace." Various forms of execution—being hanged, beheaded, shot, clubbed to death, and flayed—are then examined with a view to combatting the terror they might cause. The text observes that "extravagant torments like the ones used in different ages have not been employed in this Italy of ours for a long time now, nor do we now see the wretched condemned being burned alive, wheeled, or quartered alive, or dragged by a horse's tail." True, the crimes of lèse-majesté and parricide were exceptions, for which the culprit had their hand cut off, and then had "to go to the scaffold barefoot in a red robe." But the most significant point concerned the question of the lawfulness or otherwise of the death penalty.[27] A number of opposing theses are presented:

Thesis 1: "The death penalty runs counter to natural law," in which the preservation of one's life is a right and a duty. *Answer:* Natural law upholds the right to defend oneself to the point of killing the aggressor, who, by killing, "is excommunicated from the rule of this law." Hence the legality of inflicting the death penalty on the offender.

Thesis 2: If the aggressor is not killed in the act of his crime and is captured and rendered harmless, does sending him to his death not amount to answering a crime with another crime? *Answer:* There is an obligation of preventive defense against the threat posed by the killer. To eliminate the danger of the crime being reiterated "there is nothing for it but the death of the delinquent." This is also true because the person who has killed has "overcome the horror of spilling human blood, and is therefore disposed to repeat it," which is proven by the number of recidivists.

Thesis 3: "Crimes bearing the disgrace of the application of the death penalty did not cease, and so it is a pointless atrocity based on a fallacious hope." *Answer:* The death penalty does not put a stop to crimes but it does make them diminish. And if the terror of this punishment were to save the life of even one innocent person, that would be enough to justify maintaining it: showing "mercy for the evil who clearly put the good at risk becomes wicked piety."

Thesis 4: The argument of the social contract: "In the state of society, however, governments have no other power than that which is considered entrusted to them by the individuals comprising it. How can they have delegated to others a right to dispose of their lives which they do not themselves have?" *Answer:* By joining together in society and leaving the "isolated, wild state," human beings forgo the law of nature. The duty to preserve and protect life passes in that moment into the hands of the State, which can resort to war and the death penalty to safeguard society.

Thesis 5: "Beccaria, moreover, shaken by the horror that the atrocity of this punishment aroused in him, though he did not manage to prove unshakably that governments do not have the right of life, did, however, bring evidence to prove the lack of necessity of applying it, and the possibility of substituting it with other equivalent castigations . . . And he managed to secure its replacement by various of those governments that began to open their ears to the advancing philosophy." *Answer:* Beccaria and Filangieri had obtained from governments the substitution of the death penalty with prison. But Beccaria, by having "left too much scope for the action of the heart," was unable to prove "the absence of the right to inflict the death penalty." With time, prison was shown to be an ineffective remedy. Furthermore, "it was recognized to be more barbarous to exacerbate the life of a man than to remove it, so, having abandoned the newly introduced hard-labor prisons, there was a return to the death penalty," now practiced by "almost all governments, even the most uncivilized," ranging from "placid monarchic" to "representative, and even strictly democratic" governments.

Thesis 6: Even if capital punishment could be justified on the basis of the law of nature or Rousseau's hypothesis of the social contract, there remains the fact that it is not admitted by the word of God. Divine law has laid down the commandment not to kill. "Nor did the Gospel ever authorize it, because when the adulteress was brought before him to be stoned, Jesus Christ declared that man was illegally arrogating the right to put to death because he was always in a state of sin, and therefore incapable of exercising it and unfitting for such a right." *Answer:* There is no absolute prohibition of this kind either in the Old Testament or the New. "Countless passages in the Holy Scriptures prove its previous administration to us, but the words of Jesus Christ in the Gospel also tell us that, when surprised in the garden by Herod's soldiers, he reminded Peter, who brandished a sword against them, that *qui gladio ferit, gladio perit.*" In the case of the adulteress, finally, it was taught that "the examination of one's conscience must inspire mercy for offenders" and that "the right to punish did not lie in the association of individuals but in the governments to whom the Almighty had granted and concentrated authority—*Non est potestas nisi a Deo.*"

It was the old Pauline doctrine of the divine origin of political power, then, that concluded in ideal terms the history of the long and coherent defense of the death penalty by the Italian companies of justice.

Only ideally though: Still on its feet was what had been the most important company of them all, the Roman archconfraternity of San Giovanni Decollato dei Fiorentini. Never legally abolished, it still lives on today in its original home, where, in 1988, it celebrated the five hundredth anniversary of its foundation.[28] But its continuing existence was decisively marked by the cancellation of the temporal power of the popes imposed by the Kingdom of Italy in September 1870. The union of Rome with Italy was the final step in the birth of the new State, but it acquired a much greater symbolic value in the context of what was then a battle of ideal values between Catholicism and modern civilization. That climate was created by Pius IX's condemnation of modern notions of liberty in his *Syllabus of Errors,* together with papal censure of ideas and protagonists associated with the patriotic movement of the Risorgimento. The war of polemical writings was also occasioned by a number of famous *cause célèbres* ruled on by the papal courts. One of these involved Edgardo Mortara. Born to Jewish parents, he was forcibly removed from them by the papal police in 1858, at the age of six, after the boy's Christian wetnurse, who had secretly had him baptized at birth when she feared he might die, revealed this in confession. In the eyes of the Church authorities, baptism made him a Catholic, and this was deemed sufficient grounds for taking him away from his family, as members of other faiths were forbidden to raise Christians. The episode, which took place shortly before the capture of Rome and while Italian Jews were being freed from the restrictions imposed by the Church, triggered a press campaign throughout Europe. However, the pope refused to return the child, who was brought up in a religious institution, became a priest, and took the name Pio out of devotion to the pope.[29] But particularly sensational in an Italy pulsating with the passion of the Risorgimento was the death sentence inflicted on Giuseppe Monti and Gaetano Tognetti for conspiracy against, and an attack upon, the papal regime. Executed on November 24, 1868, a trace of their final moments entered the records of the Roman company, with the familiar words of penitence and forgiveness once again being set down in the register of final wishes. Those of Gaetano Tognetti, a young twenty-five-year-old from Rome, followed the customary pattern: "Finally, he declared [his wish] to die a good Christian, to accept death as payment for sins, [and to be] resigned to the will of God, begging forgiveness of his fellow men for every offense and forgiving them every offense, as, he hoped, God would forgive him."

Giuseppe Monti, the real leader of the plot, also left a declaration in the register of the company entitled "Testamentary recommendations of Giuseppe Monti di Benigno, native of Fermo, married with offspring, condemned to receive the death penalty in Rome on November 24, 1868, in Piazza de' Cerchi at seven o'clock in the morning."

These recommendations were all for Monti's wife, left with a child who was just twenty months old, and for two brothers. Monti requested that "it be made known to them that he died as a Christian, and begged their forgiveness for everything that he might have done to offend them." He was again thinking of her and his child in his final *protesta*. Here the ritual declaration of wanting to die "as a good Catholic Christian resigned to the will of God and asking everyone for forgiveness" concluded with an appeal to the confraternity, commending to its protection "his poor and unhappy wife Lucia Casali, and his young son of 20 months named Ciro." But then someone must have asked him to add another, politically useful, declaration to this painful private ending: he said, or was made to say, that not only did he "forgive anyone who had offended him in any way," but also that he accepted death with Christian resignation, and prayed that "this act of his, if possible, be made known to the whole world, so it might serve as enlightenment for those who had either imitated him or wanted to imitate him in his errors."[30]

Together with forgiveness for those who were putting him to death, there was a warning for those who might be tempted to follow his example. This was a novelty, and stands out among the wills registered by the confraternity over the centuries. It had taken the violent tremors of history to produce the necessary oscillation in the seismograph of recordings, which until then had never been open to requests for publicity. It was the first time that recommendations had been gathered to be made known "to the world." Quite different were the traditions associated with the last speech from the scaffold, where the condemned expressed their thoughts and demonstrated with firmness of voice and clarity of thought that they had guts. Here the intent of the message for the world evidently suggested to the condemned man must have been to use the episode in the heated controversy that accompanied the papacy's actions during the final years in which it exercised temporal power (and above all to prevent others using it against the papal regime). In fact, the fate of Monti and Tognetti triggered very lively reactions. Their last days were the subject of sensationalized re-evocations and reconstructions in the press. The whole story of their trial was told in a book, which stressed how the day of execution was deliberately chosen to coincide with the date of the opening of the Italian parliament: the description of the confraternity's work and that of the moment when the executioner held up the two heads for the crowd to see resounded with abhorrence of the papal tyranny and Jesuit devotion that the two rebels had fought against.[31]

The Jesuits responded by publishing a long report in *Civiltà cattolica,* which also appeared as a separate pamphlet. In it they used the sources available to them to counter the version of patriotic martyrdom with that of Christian martyrdom. They were able to draw on confraternity records of the two men's words of contrition and acceptance of the death sentence. Their testaments had been set down by the hand of the *provveditore,* Prince Giovanni Chigi, and various expressions were reported from these in a basically faithful manner, aside from a few additional flourishes. The account was tailored to demonstrate the dire consequences of the rebels' ideologies, which had set two people of fine Christian sentiment on the path of perdition and crime: the outcome of the trial and the execution were to demonstrate the seriousness of the error, but also the maternal mercy of the Church, which had welcomed the repentant sinners back into its arms.[32]

This was the final sensational criminal justice case under the papal regime. After Monti and Tognetti, the confraternity had few further occasions to do its work: there was space in its register for a Francesco Martini, a cobbler from Rocca di Papa, and for the already mentioned Agapito Bellomo, an "unmarried countryman" from Palestrina, who was prepared for death with some rather hurried comforting a few hours before being executed in Palestrina on July 9, 1870. As a testament he left just a few instructions regarding his possessions and debts. For himself he asked only that it be said of him that he had "died as a good Christian, resigned to the will of God." When asked if he forgave "his neighbor any offense, damage, or wrong he may have received," he responded mechanically: "Yes sir."[33]

The uttering of that "yes sir" in a jail in Palestrina brought to an end the long history of the Italian companies of justice, while in a besieged Rome Pius IX became by conciliar decree the first infallible pope in the history of the Church. In the meantime, the death penalty continued to be part of the administration of justice in Italy. It would take a big battle to win over public opinion, and was not abolished until a new criminal code entered into force in 1890.[34] Every time capital sentences were carried out in the different regulatory phases in Italy during the nineteenth and twentieth centuries, religious comforting still figured, but it was entrusted exclusively to the clergy. The liberal state showed that it wished to preserve a highly selective memory of the long history of the companies of justice, focusing on the few who had rebelled against the invitation to convert. Evidence of this can be seen in a decree passed by the Crispi government requiring the Roman archconfraternity to hand over part of its archive. It was a question of clarifying definitively whether the burning of Giordano Bruno alive at the stake in Campo de' Fiori was a legend or something that had really happened. This gave rise to the category of heretics as rebels and martyrs of "free thinking."

This long and wandering journey through the documentary sources of the companies of justice leaves open the question of the causes underlying the effectiveness of their work over many centuries. For a very long period of time the response to religious comforting by people very different in age, culture, and convictions was generally positive—in the sense that the invitation to convert, confess, and pray was almost always accepted, lending a rather special character to the execution ritual. Why was it so difficult to resist, reject, and shun the arguments of the comforters? Many years ago, a similar problem was posed not in relation to thousands of cases but to just one, that of the writer François Rabelais: Was he an atheist or not? The historian Lucien Febvre said no: it was not possible to be atheist in an age when what he called "the grip of religion over life" was widespread and omnipresent like the air one breathed. It took the mental revolution brought by the Enlightenment for that hold to be released.[35]

If we apply this model to our sample of cases, we must acknowledge that the grip of religion slackened in the eighteenth century, enough to make cases like that of Carlo Sala possible. But that did not halt the great current of the ancient river, which carried on flowing. In our own age the name of Rabelais cropped up ironically in the story of a modern example of comforting. It was the name of the director of the prison in Baton Rouge, where Sister Helen Prejean comforted the inmate Elmo Patrick Sonnier and accompanied him to the electric chair on the night of April 4, 1984.[36] The ancient form of Christian comforting is now interpreted in new ways not just on death rows in America but also in hospitals, which have long been grappling with the modern dimension of the capital sentence, that of "terminal" illnesses. Here the offer made by other human beings from voluntary associations to spend time with the sick is an attempt to give sense to life day after day, even though it is not always done for religious reasons and does not demand conversion. The fear of dying, the irrepressible need to live on, and the offer of the hope of a religion born around the crucifixion of a Jewish prophet thus find old and new reasons to meet.

> Where was it that I read of how a condemned man, just before he died, said, or thought, that if he had to live on some high crag, on a ledge so small that there was no more room for his two feet, with all about him the abyss, the ocean, eternal night, eternal solitude, eternal storm, and there he must remain, on a hand's-breadth of ground, all his life, a thousand years, through all eternity—it would be better to live so, than die within the hour? Only to live, to live! No matter how—only to live!... How true! Lord, how true! How base men are!... And he is worse who decries them on that account![37]

Afterword

THE POINT OF departure for this book was a distant analogy—and it was not until I became conscious of it that I finally discovered the roots of a curiosity that has led me to examine and pore over old archive and library documents for many decades. It is an analogy between something dramatically present today and a reality that occupied vast swaths of a remote past. The constantly recurring contemporary drama is that of "terminal" illness. How often have we heard stories about, or directly experienced, the moment when it is announced? Clinical tests are done, then the doctor arrives, already knowing the results. The patient, or his or her closest family members, waits anxiously for what is habitually described as a death sentence. From this moment on, an ambiguous relationship is established between the doctor and the sick person. The doctor has the problem of how to announce the sentence, to whom, and in what way: whether with brusque and brutal sincerity, avoiding in this way the transference of desperation; or with every possible mitigation, professionally softening the blow, offering a faint glimmer of hope, trying to find some words of consolation. For the patient, that doctor is a feared judge but often a final source of comfort as well—the person who will be asked to delay the sentence as long as possible, and whose help will be sought to die. Doctors now receive an increasing amount of psychological training, and are advised to develop the art of comforting—talking, looking the patient in the eyes, listening, drawing on literature and music. This human condition of the patient and this relationship with the doctor are the modern face of an ancient reality. They reawaken distant echoes, stirring and bringing to the surface sediments from the depths of our cultures, commencing with the very words used for the two interlocutors, the person condemned to death and the one announcing the sentence: "patient" and "comforter." These figures go back a long way, and the relationship binding them together has left a deep trace in the history of European Christian cultures—especially, but not only, in that of Italy. In the history of the death penalty as it was practiced for centuries in Christian Europe we find legions of patients and swarms of comforters. Thinking about it, we discover that before recent advances in physiology, a person's date of death could be predicted only for those who had been condemned to death. It is in the prisons, courts, and churches that the doctor and the sick person had their forebears: for many centuries the condemned person, or "patient," was assisted by the special religious associations whose members—"comforters" or "consolers"—helped those in despair by deploying the fundamental arguments of the Christian faith: hope in the life to come, faith in the survival of the soul and in the final resurrection of the dead. Nor was it rare that the very people who held the power to condemn, and the executioners themselves, took part in the work of comforting. The "distressing hours," the "melancholic nights" between sentence and execution, saw the elaboration of a science of comforting, a method of consolation, that was the fruit of prolonged and assiduous reflection on experience. If all of this occupies our consciousness today, and may become the subject of historic research, it is due to a profound revolution that has placed the question of death at the center of our cultures. "Death run wild," "obscene," hidden away in hospital, concealed from the eyes of the living: this is the diagnosis of the English anthropologist Geoffrey Gorer in "The Pornography of Death" (1955), which stimulated European historians—first and foremost, Philippe Ariès—to explore the changing representations of death down the centuries. At more or less the same time, the condemned began to make their voices heard from the dismal "death rows" of American jails. One of them was Caryl Chessman, who fought a long legal battle and before ultimately losing it, managed to highlight his condition as a world scandal. It became clear that the death penalty had lost the brutal simplicity of the scaffold in the long European Middle Ages, but that the mechanisms and guarantees of American justice, which sprang from the best tradition of the European Enlightenment and the age of the eighteenth-century revolutions, had created situations marked by a new cruelty, consisting of an unlimited extension of the period between the sentence and the execution, once measured by the hours of the final night. And it is here, out of profound solidarity between the different expressions of an age and a culture, that the condition of the "terminally ill" with which we started made its appearance. The time of the condemnation recorded and communicated by health science is also a time with a duration that varies according to the type of illness, but that remains measurable and precisely controllable, like a judge's death sentence. In both cases the lethal outcome is no longer due to an unpredictable natural event but is written in a document and projected into a future that may be more or less imminent but is foreseen and measured. But that is not all: nowadays, by studying an individual's DNA it is possible to predict the date of death even of someone who at present has no discernible illness. What the Italian writer Dino Buzzati imagined in a short black-humored tale is now becoming reality: today doctors have the means to confidently gauge not just how long the terminally sick person has to live, but also the day in which death, inscribed in the organism's cells from the very beginning of life, will come knocking on the door. Everyone is terminally ill in potentiality—but we already knew that. But now we are also in a position to move definitively beyond the boundary between the world of the approximate and the universe of precision, completing the circle which, from the stars of the Ptolemaic and then the Copernican and Galilean sky, closes more and more with knowledge of ourselves—special animals, because we are aware that we will die, but shielded until now by uncertainty about when it will happen. "If death is certain, the hour of death is uncertain," runs the popular version of an ancient maxim, now on the point of being swept away (perhaps forever) by the progress of scientific knowledge. When there is no longer even any uncertainty about the final hour we will read the literature about the comforting of the condemned in preindustrial Europe with different eyes. And the image of the doctor who now tells patients or their families how many days or months are left to them, triggering desperation and fear, will form part of a common mental horizon. Is it possible to face this prospect, tearing from before our eyes the last protective veil of Maya? We do not know. But it is not hard to predict that there will be great resistance to entering this new epoch of humanity. For now, we have basically come to accept knowledge of the hereditary defects and illnesses within the human embryo, with the possibility inherent to that knowledge of selecting the unborn on the basis of it. But when the illness and death of others become one's own illness and preannounced death, the problem of how to console those who know the final date, already an unresolved problem of our age for the terminally ill, will become for everyone the problem of how to restore a horizon of everyday life that can bear the bitter fruit of such knowledge. And the question of the quality of life and of the sense of being temporarily alive will acquire a new meaning. The alternative proposed by Shakespeare in

Hamlet's monologue will tug with renewed urgency at the conscience of humanity, unable to escape knowledge—not generic, but precise and individualized—of the finiteness of life. When that happens, the patrimony of knowledge deposited in the archives of baroque *misericordie* and *conforterie* may come to be seen as the ancient black heart of the future.

NOTES

PREFACE

1   Louis Gernet, *Anthropologie de la Grèce antique,* ed. Riccardo Di Donato (Paris: Maspero, 1968), in English as *The Anthropology of Ancient Greece,* trans. John D. B. Hamilton and Blaise Nagy (Baltimore, MD: Johns Hopkins University Press, 1981), 272.

2   Louis Gernet, *Recherches sur le développement de la pensée juridique et morale en Grèce (étude sémantique)* (Paris: Ernest Leroux, 1917).

3 Eva Cantarella, *I supplizi capitali: Origine e funzioni delle pene di morte in Grecia e a Roma* (Milan: Feltrinelli, 2005), 9. Unless otherwise stated, all the translated quotations in this book are by Jeremy Carden.

INTRODUCTION

1 The opinion pieces by Jeff Jacoby in the *Boston Globe* and Father Federico Lombardi in the *Osservatore Romano* were published on May 2, 2011; Vittorio Zucconi's article, which appeared in *la Repubblica* on May 5, 2011, prompted considerable online discussion and comment.

2 Antonio Cassesse, in *Diritto internazionale,* vol. 2, ed. Paola Gaeta (Bologna: il Mulino, 2003), 109, denounced as "humanitarian imperialism" the habitual imposition of American jurisprudence, since the Second World War, over the entire world for "crimes against humanity."

3 Niccolò Machiavelli, *Discorsi sopra la prima Deca di Tito Livio,* III, 27, in English as *The Discourses,* ed. Bernard Crick (Harmondsworth, UK: Penguin, 1970), 478. This passage in Machiavelli is the point of departure for Pier Paolo Portinaro, *I conti con il passato: Vendetta, amnistia, giustizia* (Milan: Feltrinelli, 2012), 11–12.

4 This is emphasized by Leo Zaibert, *Punishment and Retribution* (Aldershot, UK: Ashgate, 2006), 105ff.

5 See Graeme Newman, *The Punishment Response* (Albany, NY: Harrow and Heston, 1985), 27–51.

6 Gregory Vlastos, "Socrates' Rejection of Retaliation," in *Socrates: Ironist and Moral Philosopher* (Ithaca, NY: Cornell University Press, 1991), 186. The essay is also mentioned in Zaibert, *Punishment and Retribution,* 73.

7 This is the thesis of Timothy Gorringe in his *God's Just Vengeance: Crime, Violence and the Rhetoric of Salvation* (Cambridge: Cambridge University Press, 1996). Gorringe adds an ironic observation about the idealism of theologians as a reflection of a condition of social privilege that leads them "to direct attention away from the messiness and injustice of ordinary life to 'eternal' realities and truths" (6). The idea of the "suffering cross" took root in the middle of the thirteenth century (François Boespflug, *Dieu et ses images: Une histoire de l'éternel dans l'art* [Montrouge: Bayard, 2008], 200).

8 Edgar Wind, "The Criminal God," *Journal of the Warburg Institute* 1, no. 3 (1938): 243–245. The passage cited by Wind is from Friedrich Nietzsche, *Zur Genealogie der Moral: Eine Streitschrift* [1887], 2.6, but see also 2.5; in English as *On the Genealogy of Morals,* trans. Walter Kaufmann (New York: Vintage, 1967), 64–67.

9 Richard J. Evans, *Rituals of Retribution: Capital Punishment in Germany, 1600–1987* (Oxford: Oxford University Press, 1996), 712.

1. THOU SHALT NOT KILL

1 This is how René Girard put it in a paper presented to the international conference organized by Pier Cesare Bori in Bologna in 1982 on behalf of Amnesty International (René Girard, "Culture 'Primitive,' Giudaismo, Cristianesimo," in *La pena di morte nel mondo* [Casale Monferrato: Marietti, 1983], 77–104, quotation at 84).

2 "C'est sans doute un ancien usage de la Justice que de mener tuer les hommes en cérémonie. On peut craindre qu'il ne change pas de sitôt" (André-François Boureau-Deslandes, *Réflexions sur les grands hommes qui sont morts en plaisantant* [Rochefort: Jacques Le Noir, 1712]); the quotation is taken from Pascal Bastien, *Une histoire de la peine de mort: Bourreaux et supplices, 1500–1800* (Paris: Seuil, 2011), 22–23.

3 James Jones, "China's Death Row TV Hit: Interviews before Execution," *BBC News Magazine,* March 12, 2012.

4 This is the customary definition used in the prison world, which was made more widely known to the world by Sister Helen Prejean's book *Dead Man Walking* (New York: Random House, 1993) and the subsequent film directed by Tim Robbins.

5 "Hominem peccatorem occidere potest esse bonum, sicut occidere bestiam: peior enim est malus homo bestia et plus nocet" (*Secunda secundae,* q. 64, art. 2).

6 See the entry "Mort, peine de" in Heinrich Joseph Wetzer, Benedikt Welte, and Johann Goschler, *Dictionnaire encyclopédique de la théologie catholique: Rédigé par les plus savants professeurs et docteurs en théologie de l'Allemagne catholique moderne,* French trans., vol. 15 (Paris: Gaume Freres et J. Duprey, 1862), 357–368.

7 *Catechism of the Catholic Church,* no. 2267, online edition, www.vatican.va/archive /ENG0015/_INDEX.HTM.

8 See Mario Pisani, "Recenti posizioni della Chiesa cattolica sulla pena di morte," *Iustitia* 65 (2012): 15–31.

9 See Adriano Prosperi, *Giustizia bendata: Percorsi storici di un'immagine* (Turin: Einaudi, 2007), 223.

10 Hans Kelsen, "The Idea of Justice in the Holy Scriptures," *Revista Jurídica de la Universidad de Puerto Rico* 22 (1952–1953): 1–63, quotation at 2.

11 *Pie et Christiane epistole di Gratiadio da Monte Santo* [Venice, 1548], cc. 73r–v.

2. A STARTING POINT

1 Cesare Beccaria, *Dei delitti e delle pene,* vol. 1 (Milan: Mediobanca, 1984). In English as *On Crimes and Punishments and Other Writings,* ed. and trans. Richard Bellamy (Cambridge: Cambridge University Press, 1995; repr. 2000).

2 According to Cesare Cantú, *Beccaria e il diritto penale* (Florence: Barbera, 1862), 319.

3 Beccaria, *On Crimes and Punishments,* 4.

4 Ibid., 5.

5 Ibid., 22–23.

6 Ibid., 99–100. For more about the changes in Beccaria's thinking and the radical revision of the text by Pietro Verri, see Gianni Francioni's careful textual restoration and observations in Beccaria, *Dei delitti e delle pene,* 1:268–274.

7 Federico Stella, *La giustizia e le ingiustizie* (Bologna: il Mulino, 2006), 222.

8 See Aldo Mazzacane's excellent entry in *Dizionario Biografico degli Italiani* (Rome: Istituto della Enciclopedia italiana, 1960–2011) 26 (1982): 141–146.

9 Thomas More, *Utopia,* ed. George M. Logan, Robert M. Adams, and Clarence H. Miller, based on the Norton edition, trans. Robert M. Adams (Cambridge: Cambridge University Press, 1995), 69–71.

10 "The first publication of *Utopia* was loosely supervised by Erasmus," notes Carlo Ginzburg in an illuminating work on the literary tradition in which More's work lay (Carlo Ginzburg, *No Island Is an Island: Four Glances at English Literature in a World Perspective* [New York: Columbia University Press, 2000], 3).

11 "Praeceptum Domini generaliter loquitur: 'Non occides' ... quinimmo dicitur aliquando maius peccatum occidere hominem malum quam bonum ... maius esse preiudicium in amissione unius anime quam mille corporum ... Late Thomas Morus in tractatu De optimo reipublicae statu" (Giovanni Nevizzano da Asti, *Sylva nuptialis* [Lyon, 1526], f. XXIV*v*). The work of Giovanni Nevizzano, which was first printed in Asti in 1518 and circulated in the reworked version of 1522, was subsequently included in the Roman Index of 1596 (see the entry on this by Simona Feci in *Dizionario Biografico degli Italiani* 78 [2013], http://www.treccani.it/enciclopedia /giovanni-nevizzano_%28Dizionario-Biografico%29/.

12 "A principio urbis conditae, pro delictis gravioribus poena mortis reis ingerebatur ... Damnatio in metallum, vel in insulam sufficere visa est: aliquis enim eorum usus erat, cum opus facere compellerentur, et tamen merita poena afficiebantur. Siquidem ut C. Caesar apud Sallustium inquit, in luctu et miseriis, mors aerumnarum requies, non cruciatus est. At hodie in poenis mera carnificina est, et per leges municipales vel strangulantur, vel decollantur, vel exuruntur, vel mutilantur rei: qui si in opus publicum damnarentur, et perpetuam poenam subirent, idcirco acriorem, et maiori caeteris exemplo essent, publiceque utilitatem aliquam afferentur: ut negari non possit, ut in plerisque aliis rebus, hac quoque in parte ab antiquis recentiores legumlatores superari" (Andrea Alciato, *Opera omnia,* 3 vols. [Lyon, 1559–1561], vol. 3, *De verborum significatione,* c. 243r–v, "Capitalis poena").

13 Giacinto Manara della Compagnia di Gesú, *Notti malinconiche nelle quali con occasione di assister a' condannati a morte, si propongono varie difficoltà spettanti a simile materia* (Bologna, 1658), in 4to; the citation is from the 1668 reprint in 12mo, 19–20.

14 Giacinto Manara della Compagnia di Gesú, *Notti malinconiche,* 24 (in the text, chapter 13 is erroneously referred to as chapter 3).

3. THE LAW OF FORGIVENESS, THE REALITY OF VENGEANCE

1 Cited in Otto Brunner, *Land and Lordship: Structures of Governance in Medieval Austria,* trans. Howard Kaminsky and James Van Horn Melton (Philadelphia: University of Pennsylvania Press, 1992), 19–20.

2 Claude Gauvard, *"De grâce especial": Crime, État et Société en France à la fin du Moyen Age,* vol. 2 (Paris: Publications de la Sorbonne, 1991), 707–709.

3 Manlio Cortelazzo and Paolo Zolli, *Dizionario etimologico della lingua italiana,* vol. 5 (Bologna: Zanichelli, 1988), 1441; Alessandro Niccoli and Giovanni Diurni, "Vendetta," in *Enciclopedia Dantesca,* vol. 5 (Rome: Istituto della Enciclopedia Italiana, 1996), 914–915.

4 This is pointed out by Andrea Zorzi in "The Judicial System in Florence in the Fourteenth and Fifteenth Centuries," in *Crime, Society and the Law in Renaissance Italy,* ed. Trevor Dean and Kate J. P. Lowe (Cambridge: Cambridge University Press, 1994), 40–58, in particular 52–53.

5 [Andrea Alciato,] *Omnium Andreae Alciati Mediolanensis iuriconsultoris clarissimi Operum in sex tomos digestorum,* vol. 3 (Basle, 1571), cols. 181–182.

6 Francisco Tomás y Valiente, *El derecho penal de la monarquía absoluta (siglos XVI, XVII y XVIII)* (Madrid: Tecnis, 1969). The citation is from the second edition (Madrid, 1992, 48).

7 The following are just a few works from a vast bibliography featuring the terms "theater" and "spectacle" in the title: Richard Van Dülmen, *Theatre of Horror: Crime and Punishment in Early Modern Germany,* trans. Elisabeth Neu (Cambridge: Polity Press, 1990); Peter Spierenburg, *The Spectacle of Suffering: Executions and the Evolution of Repression; From a Preindustrial Metropolis to the European Experience* (Cambridge: Cambridge University Press, 1984); Mitchell B. Merback, *The Thief, the Cross and the Wheel: Pain and the Spectacle of Punishment in Medieval and Renaissance Europe* (Chicago: University of Chicago Press, 1999). Huizinga's description forms the title of chapter one of *The Waning of the Middle Ages: A Study of the Forms of Life, Art and Thought in France and the Netherlands in the Fourteenth and Fifteenth Centuries,* trans. Frederik J. Hopman (Harmondsworth, UK: Penguin, 1965).

8 See, for example, the wide-ranging survey of studies on this topic in Andrea Zorzi's introduction to Jacques Chiffoleau, Claude Gauvard, and Andrea Zorzi, eds., *Pratiques sociales et politiques judiciaires dans les villes de l'Occident à la fin du Moyen Âge* (Rome: École Française de Rome, 2007), 1–29. Among these, mention must be made of those of Mario Sbriccoli, to whom the collective volume is dedicated.

9 See Adriano Prosperi, "Les commentaires du Pater Noster entre XVᵉ et XVIᶜ siècles," in *Aux origines du catéchisme paroissial et des manuels diocésains de catéchisme en France (1500–1660),* conference proceedings, ed. Pierre Colin, Élisabeth Germain, Jean Joncheray, and Marc Venard (Paris: Desclée, 1989), 87–105.

10 See the collection *L'anima e il diritto: Figure arcaiche e concezione scientifica del mondo,* trans. and ed. Agostino Carrino and Hans Kelsen (Rome: Edizioni Lavoro, 1989), 77–91.

11 See Mauro Pesce, *Da Gesù al cristianesimo* (Brescia: Morcelliana, 2011).

4. THE MURDERER'S CONFESSION

1   "Omni die nocte ac hora visitet, eis poenitentias et sacramenta concedat" (cited by Richard Baumgart, *Die Entwicklung der Schuldhaft im italienischen Recht des Mittelalters* [Berlin: W. Rothschild, 1914], 539–540).

2   See Dario Simoni, "Antiche cose pisane: Delitti e pene," *Bollettino storico pisano,* no. 1 (1937): 88–93.

3   Gotthold Bohne, *Die Freiheitsstrafe in den italienischen Statdrechten des 12–16. Jahrhunderts* (Leipzig: T. Weicher, 1922), 2:234–248.

4   See Evelina Rinaldi, "L'istituzione della Pia Casa della Misericordia in Pisa," *Studi storici* 10 (1901): 189–215 (in ASPi, *Diplomatico Pia Casa di Misericordia,* no. 30, 1305, there is the plea of Father Giovanni, rector of the church of San Leonardo). I take this information from an unpublished study by Luigi Lazzerini, "La Confraternita della Morte di Pisa (sec. XIV–XVIII)" (degree thesis at the Faculty of Letters and Philosophy, University of Pisa, academic year 1989–1890). For more on the prison and the city statutes, the monograph by G. Bohne is still useful: see Bohne, *Die Freiheitsstrafe,* 1:139–140, 2:253–255. A later period is dealt with by Elsa Luttazzi Gregori in "La 'morte confortata' nella Toscana dell'età moderna (XV–XVIII secolo)," in *Criminalità e società in età moderna,* ed. Luigi Berlinguer and Floriana Colao (Milan: Giuffre, 1991), 12:25–91.

5   ASPi, *Diplomatico Pia Casa di Misericordia,* no. 74, June 7, 1325 (see L. Lazzerini, *La Confraternita della Morte di Pisa,* 126).

6   Giuseppe Sainati, *Diario sacro pisano* (Turin: Tipografia Salesiana, 1898), 150.

7   Ranieri Sardo, *Cronaca di Pisa,* ed. Ottavio Banti (Rome: Istituto Storico Italiano per il Medio Evo, 1963), 275.

8   Ranieri Sardo, *Cronaca di Pisa,* 131. On this episode, see Trevor Dean, *Crime and Justice in Late Medieval Italy* (Cambridge: Cambridge University Press, 2007), 64–65.

9   Paolo Prodi, *Una storia della giustizia: Dal pluralismo dei fori al moderno dualismo tra coscienza e diritto* (Bologna: il Mulino, 2000), 54–57.

10 Ibid.

11 Maureen Mulholland draws attention to the density of terms denoting "trial" and "test" in the Judeo-Christian tradition; see her introduction to *Judicial Tribunals in England and Europe, 1200–1700: The Trial in History,* ed. Maureen Mulholland and Brian Pullan (Manchester, UK: Manchester University Press, 2003), 1:2.

12 The discussion on this issue began with the research of Winfried Trusen; important contributions have been made by Paolo Prodi and Jacques Chiffoleau. An account

can be found in Bruno Lemesle, "Corriger les excès: L'extension des infractions, des délits et des crimes, et les transformations de la procédure inquisitoire dans les lettres pontificales (milieu du XIIᵉ siècle—fin du pontificat d'Innocent III)," *Revue Historique* 313 / 314, no. 660 (2011): 747–779.

13 See Vincenzo Lavenia, "Eretici sentenziati e 'reincorporati,'" in *Misericordie: Conversioni sotto il patibolo tra Medioevo ed età moderna,* ed. Adriano Prosperi (Pisa: Edizioni della Normale, 2007), 153–187, esp. 156–157.

14 "Quanquam haeretici revertentes semper recipiendi sint ad poenitentiam quotiescumque relapsi fuerint, non tamen semper sunt recipiendi et restituendi ad bonorum huius vitae participationem" (*Summa Theologiae,* Secunda Secundae, q. XI, art. IV; see Lavenia, "Eretici sentenziati e 'reincorporati,'" 158–159n).

15 Lavenia, "Eretici sentenziati e 'reincorporati,'" 159–163.

5. THE EARTHLY CITY, THE RIGHT TO KILL, AND THE ECCLESIASTICAL POWER TO INTERCEDE

1 Thomas J. Heffernan, *The Passion of Perpetua and Felicity* (New York: Oxford University Press, 2012), 130.

2 *Atti e passioni dei martiri,* intro. Antonius A. R. Bastianensen (Milan: Fondazione Valla, 1987), 131.

3 As mentioned by Pierre Duparc, *Origines de la grâce dans le droit pénal romain et français du Bas-Empire à la Renaissance* (Paris: Recueil Sirey, 1942), 27. See also Giulio Vismara, "La giurisdizione dei vescovi nel mondo antico," in *La giustizia nell'Alto Medioevo (secoli V–VIII)* (Spoleto: Centro italiano di studi sull'alto Medioevo, 1995), 1:225–251.

4 Augustine of Hippo, *Ad Vincentium—epistola 93, PL* XXXIII, 321–347, in English in *Writings of Saint Augustine,* vol. 2, trans. Sister Wilfrid Parsons (New York: Fathers of the Church, 1953), 72–73. For more on the importance of this change, see the observations of Luciano Cova in "Tra 'in te ipsum redire' e 'divinae iracundiae timor': Interiorità ed esteriorità nell'itinerario agostinano a Dio," *Esercizi filosofici* 2, no. 2 (2007): 166–194.

5 Peter Brown, *Augustine of Hippo: A Biography* (London: Faber and Faber, 1967), 214. See also the new and amplified edition (Berkeley: University of California Press, 2013), 212.

6 For more on imperial legislation after 312, see *Les lois religieuses des empereurs romains de Constantin à Théodose II (312–438),* vol. 1, Latin text by Theodor Mommsen, French translation by Jean Rouge (Paris: Cerf, 2005).

7 See Antonio Padoa Schioppa, *Storia del diritto in Europa: Dal Medioevo all'età contemporanea* (Bologna: il Mulino, 2007), 28–29.

8 Peter Brown, "Religious Coercion in the Later Roman Empire: The Case of North Africa," *History* 48, no. 164 (1963): 285–305, esp. 287.

9 Ibid., 287.

10 The image is reproduced in Adriano Prosperi, *Giustizia bendata: Percorsi storici di un'immagine* (Turin: Einaudi, 2007), 50.

11 As expressed in letter 153 of Saint Augustine to the magistrates: see Giannino Piana, "La Chiesa cattolica di fronte alla pena di morte," in *Il diritto di uccidere: L'enigma della pena di morte,* ed. Pietro Costa (Milan: Feltrinelli, 2010), 127. The most threatening sentence regarding those who do not forgive is found in Augustine's major work: "nullam indulgentiam consequuntur, si ad remittendum aliis, quod in eos quisque peccaverit, inexorabiles fuerint (dimitte nobis . . . sicut et nos dimittimus)." Augustinus, *De civitate Dei,* XXI, 27 (Augustine, *The City of God against the Pagans,* ed. and trans. R. W. Dyson [Cambridge: Cambridge University Press, 1998,] 1103).

12 "Eripe eum qui ducitur ad mortem, hoc est: eripe eum intercessione, eripe gratia tu, sacerdos, aut tu, imperator, eripe subscriptione indulgentiae, et solvisti peccata tua, exuisti te a vinculis tuis" (Ambrosius, *Expositio in psalmum 118,* serm. 8, 41, 2: *PL* XV, 1311).

13 Augustine, *The City of God,* chap. 27, 1104.

6. BODIES AND SOULS

1 See Paolo Prodi, *Una storia della giustizia: Dal pluralismo dei fori al moderno dualismo tra coscienza e diritto* (Bologna: il Mulino, 2000), 41.

2 Pietro Costa, ed., *Il diritto di uccidere: L'enigma della pena di morte* (Milan: Feltrinelli, 2010), 14.

3 This was the view of Otto of Freising, who was critical of the "vitium remissionis." See Gerd Althoff, *Amicitiae und Pacta: Bündnis, Einung, Politik und Gebetsgedenken im beginnenden 10. Jahrhundert, Schriften der Monumenta Germaniae Historica* (Stuttgart: Deutsches Institut für Erforschung des Mittelalters, 1938–), vol. 37 (Hannover: Hahnsche Buchhandlung, 1992), 57. For Gregory the Great, see *Moralia in Iob,* XVI, vi (*Corpus Christianorum,* Latin series, ed. Marcus Adriaen [Turnhout: Brepols, 1979], 800–801); and the commentary on Luke 7:36–50 contrasting the harshness of the death penalty in Mosaic law with the Gospel forgiveness of the sinning woman (*Homiliae in Evangelia: Homilia XXXIII,* ed. Raymond Etaix [Turnhout: Brepols, 1999], 296–298).

4 François Bougard, *La justice dans le Royaume d'Italie de la fin du VIIIᵉ siècle au début du XIᵉ siècle* (Rome: École Francaise de Rome, 1995), 235.

5 Cesare Beccaria, *Dei delitti e delle pene,* vol. 1 (Milan: Mediobanca, 1984), in English as *On Crimes and Punishments and Other Writings,* ed. and trans. Richard Bellamy (Cambridge: Cambridge University Press, 1995; repr. 2000), "To the Reader," 3.

6 Karl von Amira, *Die germanischen Todesstrafen: Untersuchungen zur Rechts- und Religionsgeschichte* (Munich: Verlag der Bayerischen Akademie der Wissenschaften, 1922), 198–200.

7 See Karol Modzelewski, *Barbarian Europe* [2004], trans. Ewa Macura (Frankfurt: Peter Lang, 2015), 23.

8 This episode has been researched by Mayke De Jong; see her "What was 'Public' about Public Penance? 'Paenitentia publica' and Justice in the Carolingian World," in *La giustizia nell'alto Medioevo: Secoli IX–XI* (Spoleto: Centro italiano di studi sull'alto Medioevo, 1982), 863–902, esp. 888–889; De Jong, "Power and Humility in Carolingian Society: The Public Penance of Louis the Pious," *Early Medieval Europe* 1, no. 1 (1992): 29–52. The thesis of a candid "penitential" state is presented in her more recent work, *The Penitential State: Authority and Atonement in the Age of Louis the Pious* (Cambridge: Cambridge University Press, 2009).

9 See Henri De Lubac, *Corpus mysticum: L'eucharistie et l'Église au Moyen Âge* (Paris: Aubier-Montaigne, 1944).

10 "Si quis homicidium sponte commiserit, et non violentiae resistens, sed vim faciens impetu hoc fecerit, cum isto penitus non communicandum: sic tamen ut si penitentiam egerit, in exitu ei communionis viaticum non negetur" (Gian Domenico Mansi, ed., *Sacrorum conciliorum nova et amplissima collectio,* 53 vols., vol. 10 [Florence: Antonio Zatta, 1759–1798], cols. 592–594).

11 "Et cur ad mortem condemnatis renuitur? Cum eis maxime conducat ad spem et securamen certi decessus, et praesentis agonis? Nunc autem etiam denegatur silenti Ecclesia et veluti consentienti, non obstantibus iis canonibus qui vel nunquam recepti vel saltem per usum contrarium sunt abrogate" (Mansi, *Sacrorum conciliorum nova,* vol. 10, col. 598: *Statuta synodalia Ecclesiae Rhemensis per dominum Sonnatium*).

12 Augustine, *The City of God against the Pagans,* ed. and trans. R. W. Dyson (Cambridge: Cambridge University Press, 1998), bk. 13, chap. 20, 566.

13 See Gian Marco Vidor, *Biografia di un cimitero italiano: La Certosa di Bologna* (Bologna: il Mulino, 2013), 69–88.

14 Regino of Prüm, *Liber de synodalibus causis* (written at the beginning of the tenth century for the archbishop of Mainz, *PL* CXXXII). See Roger E. Reynolds, "Rites of Separation and Reconciliation," in *Segni e riti nella Chiesa altomedievale occidentale* (Spoleto: Centro italiano di studi sull'alto Medioevo, 1987), 405–433, who refers to Edmond Martène and Ursin Durand, *De antiquis ecclesiae ritibus* (Venice, 1763–1764), 2:322.

15 Jacques Chiffoleau, in "Sur la pratique et la conjoncture de l'aveu judiciaire en France du XIIIe au XVe siècle," in *L'aveu: Antiquité et Moyen Âge* (Rome: École Française de Rome, 1986), 341–380, stresses these aspects in relation to the fourteenth-century developments of trials for lèse-majesté.

16 "Quaesitum est ab aliquibus fratribus de his qui in patibulis suspenduntur pro suis sceleribus post confessionem Deo peractam, utrum cadavera illorum ad ecclesias deferenda sint, et oblationes pro eis offerendae, et missae celebrandae, an non. Quibus respondimus: si omnibus de peccatis suis puram confessionem agentibus,

et digne poenitentibus communio in fine secundum canonicum iussum danda est, cur non eis qui pro peccatis suis poenam extremam persolvunt? . . . Perdidisset latro in cruce praemium ad Christi dexteram pendens, si illum unius horae poenitentia non iuvisset" (Concilium Moguntinum I a. 847, can. XXVII, in Mansi, *Sacrorum Conciliorum nova,* vol. 14, cols. 899–912).

17 "Per presbyteros pura inquirenda est confessio, non tamen illis imponenda quantitas poenitentiae, sed innotescenda" (ibid., vol. 14, cols. 899–912).

18 Concilium Wormatiense, a. 868, can. LXXX (Mansi, *Sacrorum Conciliorum nova,* vol. 15, cols. 865ff., esp. cols. 883–884).

19 This decisive step is summed up by Alain Guerreau, "Il significato dei luoghi nell'Occidente medievale," in *Arti e storia nel Medioevo,* ed. Enrico Castelnuovo and Giuseppe Sergi, 4 vols. (Turin: Einaudi, 2002), 1:232–233.

20 An instance of this in Venice in 1584 is reported by the writer in "Morire volentieri: Condannati a morte e sacramenti," in *Misericordie: Conversioni sotto il patibolo tra Medioevo ed età moderna,* ed. Adriano Prosperi (Pisa: Edizioni della Normale, 2007), 3–54, esp. 12–14.

21 "Si patienter ferunt mortem contriti de commissis, non ratione poenae tantum vel verecundiae, sed respectu Dei offensi, etsi non percipiant coronam martyrii, tamen salvantur. Si autem tantum dolent propter supplicium, impatientes vel incontriti ad inferna descendunt" (*Summa moralis,* pars I, tit. V, cap. I, in Saint Antoninus, *Opera Omnia,* tomo I, pars I, col. 600).

7. CONFESSION AND COMMUNION FOR THE CONDEMNED

1 Harold J. Berman, *Law and Revolution: The Formation of the Western Legal Tradition* (Cambridge, MA: Harvard University Press, 1983).

2 The key work of reference on this topic is still Mario Sbriccoli, *Crimen lesae maiestatis: Il problema del reato politico alle origini della scienza penalistica moderna* (Milan: Giuffrè, 1974).

3 See Claude Gauvard, *"De grâce especial": Crime, État et Société en France à la fin du Moyen Age,* vol. 2 (Paris: Publications de la Sorbonne, 1991), 951, but also the whole of the chapter "Pardonner et punir," 895ff.

4 See Paolo Prodi, *Una storia della giustizia: Dal pluralismo dei fori al moderno dualismo tra coscienza e diritto* (Bologna: il Mulino, 2000), 70–72.

5 For a recent investigation of deformations in the US judicial system, see Massimo La Torre and Marina Lalatta Costerbosa, *Legalizzare la tortura? Ascesa e declino dello Stato di diritto* (Bologna: il Mulino, 2012).

6 Piero Bellini, *"Denunciatio evangelica" e "denunciatio judicialis privata": Un capitolo di storia disciplinare della Chiesa* (Milan: Giuffrè, 1986).

7 Jacques Chiffoleau, *La Chiesa, il segreto e l'obbedienza* (Bologna: il Mulino, 2010), 80.

8 *Le registre d'Inquisition de Jacques Fournier (1318–1325),* ed. Jean Duvernoy, 3 vols. (Toulouse: Privat, 1965), 2:82–105; the case is also mentioned by Jacques Chiffoleau in *La Chiesa, il segreto e l'obbedienza,* 82.

9   Ministère des Affaires Culturelles, *Confessions et jugements de criminels au Parlement de Paris (1319–1350)* (Paris: S.E.V.P.E.N., 1971), 43.

10 Célestin Louis Tanon, *Histoire des justices des anciennes églises et communautés monastiques de Paris, suivie des registres inédits de Saint-Maur-des-Fossés, Sainte-Geneviève, Saint-Germain-des-Prés, et du registre de Saint-Martin-des-Champs* (Paris: Laros et Forcel, 1883), 554.

11 Marion's case is documented in the *Registre criminel du Châtelet de Paris,* 2 vols. (Paris: Societé des bibliophiles françois 1861–1864), 2:437–439; it is pointed out in Jacques Chiffoleau, "Sur la pratique et la conjoncture de l'aveu judiciaire en France du XIIIe au XVe siècle," in *L'aveu: Antiquité et Moyen Âge* (Rome: École Française de Rome, 1986), 355. On execution rituals in Paris, see Esther Cohen, "'To Die a Criminal for the Public Good': The Execution Ritual in Late Medieval Paris," in *Law, Custom and the Social Fabric in Medieval Europe: Essays in Honour of Bryce Lyon,* ed. Bernard Bachrach and David Nicholas (Kalamazoo, MI: Medieval Institute Publications, 1990), 285–304.

12 Mireille Vincent-Cassy, "La confession des condamnés à mort: L'exception française du XIVe siècle," in *Vita religiosa e identità politiche: Universalità e particolarismi nell'Europa del tardo Medioevo,* ed. Sergio Gensini (San Miniato [Pisa]: Centro studi sulla civiltà del tardo Medioevo, 1998), 383–401; on the history of the administration of criminal justice in France, see also, by the same author, "Prisons et châtiments à la fin du Moyen Age," in *Les marginaux et les exclus dans l'histoire* (Paris: Union générale d'éditions, 1979), 262–274.

13 "Si tradantur suspendio, eucharistiam denegamus, quia scandalum esset si Christus, qui adhuc creditur esse in ysofago, tradetur suspendio; ergo credat et sufficit" (Alain de Lille, *Liber poenitentialis,* book 3, chapter 24; cf. Miri Rubin, *Corpus Christi: The Eucharist in Late Medieval Culture* [Cambridge: Cambridge University Press, 1991], 69).

14 "Plures iudices temporales condemnatis hoc denegabant, et ad suam excusationem allegabant consuetudinem" (Decretali Clementine, tit. IX: *De paenitentiis et remissionibus,* in *Corpus iuris canonici,* ed. Emil Friedberg, vol. 2 [Leipzig: Tauchnitz, 1879], anastatic edition [Graz: Akademische Druck- u. Verlagsanstalt, 1959], 1190).

15 See Nicolas Jorga, *Philippe de Mézières 1327–1405 et la Croisade au XIVe siècle* (Paris: Bouillon, 1896), anastatic reprint (Geneva: Slatkine, 1976), 438–439; Johan Huizinga, *The Autumn of the Middle Ages,* trans. Rodney J. Payton and Ulrich Mammitzsch (Chicago: University of Chicago Press, 1996), 21. For more on Philippe de Mézières, see also Bernard Guenée, *Entre l'Église et l'État: Quatre vies de prélats français à la fin du Moyen Age, XIIe–XVe siècle* (Paris: Gallimard, 1987).

16 Jean Gerson, *Requête pour les condamnés à mort,* in *Opera omnia,* vol. 7: *L'œuvre française: Sermons et discours,* ed. Mons. Glorieux (Paris: Desclée, 1966–1968), no. 323, 341–343.

17 "Et s'aucun dist que plusieurs meffaits se scevent par derniere confession qui aultrement ne se scauroient mie, response que ceste cause ne excuse pas qu'on puisse

pechier la loi divine ou l'empeschier: et aussi Dieu ne veult pas que tous les maulx soient punis en ce monde car aultrement il n'auriot que jugier en l'autre" (Gerson, *Requête pour les condamnés à mort,* 342).

18 Chiffoleau, "Sur la pratique," 355.

19 Huizinga, *The Autumn of the Middle Ages,* 21.

20 The account of Lucien Merlet, "Biographie de Jean de Montagu, grand maître de France (1350–1409)," in *Bibliothèque de l'École des chartes* 13, no. 13 (1852): 248–284, is confirmed by the contemporary testimony of the *Chronique du religieux de Saint-Denys contenant le règne de Charles VI de 1380 à 1422,* ed. Bernard Guenée (Paris: Editions du Comité des travaux historiques et scientifiques, 1994), chap. 14, 272ff.

8. BURIED WITH DONKEYS

1 Anton Blok, "Mestieri infami," *Richerche storiche* 26 (1996): 59–96.

2 Giacomo Todeschini, *Visibilmente crudeli: Malviventi, persone sospette e gente qualunque dal Medioevo all'età moderna* (Bologna: il Mulino, 2007), 142–143. Here the attribute of *crudeli,* "cruel," taken from a passage in Augustine, indicates criminals and the "different," exactly the opposite of how Huizinga uses it in the passage cited below.

3 Johan Huizinga, *The Autumn of the Middle Ages,* trans. Rodney J. Payton and Ulrich Mammitzsch (Chicago: University of Chicago Press, 1996), 20.

4 Trevor Dean, *Crime and Justice in Late Medieval Italy* (Cambridge: Cambridge University Press, 2007), 62–64.

5 For example, those of Venice, Siena, and Lucca: see ibid., 65.

6 Karl Meisen, *Die Sagen vom Wütenden Heer und Wilden Jäger* (Münster: Ashendorffsche Verlagsbuchhandlung, 1935).

7 This is the thesis of Bertrand Hell, *Le sang noir: Chasse et mythe du sauvage en Europe* (Paris: Flammarion, 1994).

8 James G. Frazer, *The Fear of the Dead in Primitive Religion,* 3 vols. (London: Macmillan, 1933–1936), 1:v. See also Franz Cumont, *Lux perpetua* (Paris: Librairie orientaliste Paul Geuthner, 1949), 338–342, on the particular terror stirred by the souls of suicides.

9 Frazer, *The Fear of the Dead,* 2:53–94.

10 Of those who have, mention can be made of Mitchell B. Merback, *The Thief, the Cross and the Wheel: Pain and the Spectacle of Punishment in Medieval and Renaissance Europe* (Chicago: University of Chicago Press, 1999), 136–137: "The execution of exhumed corpses, decapitation and various forms of dismemberment . . . can all be seen as efforts to prevent the post-mortem reanimation of those most likely to torment the living."

11 Cesare Lombroso, *Delitto, genio, follia,* ed. Delia Frigessi (Turin: Bollati Boringhieri), 2000, 326–327. Adriano Favole, *Resti di umanità: Vita sociale del corpo dopo la morte* (Rome: Laterza, 2003), 142, adds nothing further on this point.

12 An argument advanced by the jurist Muyart de Vouglans (see Michel Porret, *Sul luogo del delitto: Pratica penale, inchiesta e perizia giudiziaria a Ginevra nei secoli XVIII–XIX* [Bellinzona: Casagrande, 2007], 172).

13 See Michael MacDonald and Terence R. Murphy, *Sleepless Souls: Suicide in Early Modern England* (Oxford: Clarendon Press, 1990), 18–21. A broad survey of historic practices regarding this can be found in the fundamental book of Marzio Barbagli, *Congedarsi dal mondo: Il suicidio in Occidente e in Oriente* (Bologna: il Mulino, 2009), 52ff.

14 Bernardino da Siena, *Prediche volgari sul Campo di Siena 1427,* vol. 2, ed. Carlo Delcorno (Milan: Rusconi, 1989), 1314, sermon 43.

15 The account of an English traveler visiting a German city in 1615 describes the spectacle of a condemned man who was brought before the executioner drunk (Richard J. Evans, *Rituals of Retribution: Capital Punishment in Germany, 1600–1987* [Oxford: Oxford University Press, 1996], 27). On the measures taken in the fifteenth century to prevent the condemned from committing suicide, see Uwe Israel, "Hinrichtung in spätmittelalterlichen Städten: Öffentlichkeit, Ritual, Kritik," in *Pratiques sociales et politiques judiciaires dans les villes de l'Occident à la fin du Moyen Âge,* ed. Jacques Chiffoleau, Claude Gauvard, and Andrea Zorzi (Rome: École Française de Rome, 2007), 661–687.

16 See Chiara Frugoni, *L'affare migliore di Enrico: Giotto e la Cappella Scrovegni* (Turin: Einaudi, 2008), 339–340.

17 Erwin Panofsky, *Tomb Sculpture: Its Changing Aspects from Ancient Egypt to Bernini* (London: Thames and Hudson, 1964), 9.

18 Giorgio Fornoni, "Un cammino ancora lungo," *I Amnesty: Rivista trimestrale sui diritti umani di Amnesty International* 4 (2011): 4 (the article refers to the cemetery of the Polunski prison in West Livingston, Texas).

19 Existing studies of this question all make reference to the classic work of Mommsen. See Jean-Michel David, "Du Comitium à la Roche Tarpéienne: Sur certains rituels d'exécution capitale sous la République, les règnes d'Auguste et de Tibère," in *Du châtiment dans la cité: Supplices corporels et peine de mort dans le monde antique* (Rome: École Française de Rome, 1984), 131–175. But the real reference work is Eva Cantarella, *I supplizi capitali: Origine e funzioni delle pene di morte in Grecia e a Roma* (Milan: Feltrinelli, 2005).

20 This is stressed by Jean Prieur, *La mort dans l'antiquité romaine* (La Guerche-de-Bretagne: Ouest France, 1986), 40–45.

21 Letter of Tommaso Romano, June 13, 1556, in *MHSI, Epistolae mixtae ex variis Europae locis ab anno 1537 ad 1556 scriptae, nunc primum a patribus Societatis Jesu in lucem editae,* vol. 5 (1555–1556) (Madrid: Avrial, 1901), 354–355.

22 Giovanni Nevizzano da Asti, *Sylva nuptialis* (Lyon, 1526), 47.

23 The passage is cited by Jean-Claude Schmitt, *Religione, folklore e società nell'Occidente medievale* (Rome: Laterza, 1988), 198.

24 On the symbolic significance of falling from high up, see Cantarella, *I supplizi capitali*, 129–139.

25 For Islamic food prohibitions, see Hassan S. Khalilieh, *Islamic Maritime Law: An Introduction* (Leiden: Brill Academic, 1998), 170–171; and for medieval Christian ones, see Maria Giuseppina Muzzarelli, "Norme di comportamento alimentare nei libri penitenziali," *Quaderni medievali* 13 (1982): 45–80.

26 Account of the seneschal Andrea Gatari: *Diario del Concilio di Basilea di Andrea Gatari,* ed. Giulio Coggiola, in *Concilium Basiliense: Studien und Quellen zur Geschichte des Konzils von Basel,* vol. 5: *Tagebücher und Akten* (Basel: R. Reich Vormals C. Detloffs Buchhandlung, 1904), 39–40 of the extract: see Maria R. Boes, "Jews in the Criminal-Justice System of Early Modern Germany," *Journal of Interdisciplinary History* 30, no. 3 (1999): 420.

27 See Irene Fosi, *Convertire lo straniero: Forestieri e Inquisizione a Roma in età moderna* (Rome: Viella, 2011). For more about the burial of non-Catholics ("infidels," heretics, excommunicates) lumped together with suicides and prostitutes and destined for the Muro Torto cemetery, see *The Protestant Cemetery in Rome: The "Parte antica,"* ed. Antonio Menniti Ippolito and Paolo Vian (Rome: Unione Internazionale degli Istituti di Archeologia, Storia e Storia dell'Arte, 1989).

28 This emerges from the list recorded in Peter de Backer, *Apologeticus pro defunctis* (Antwerp, 1587), 298–299.

9. A SPECIAL BURIAL PLACE

1 See Caroline Walker Bynum, *Fragmentation and Redemption: Essays on Gender and the Human Body in Medieval Religion* (New York: Zone Books, 1991).

2 See Michel Lauwers, *Naissance du cimetière: Lieux sacrés et terre des morts dans l'Occident medieval* (Paris: Aubier, 2005).

3 James R. Banker, in *Death in the Community: Memorialization and Confraternities in an Italian Commune in the Late Middle Ages* (Athens: University of Georgia Press, 1988), 2–3, describes these associations as "voluntaristic corporations that socialized death."

4 See Philippe Ariès, *L'homme devant la mort* (Seuil: Paris, 1974), in English as *The Hour of Our Death,* trans. Helen Weaver (New York: Vintage Books, 1981), chap. 4, 185.

5 For more about the Sansepolcro confraternity established in 1338, see Ercole Agnoletti, *Sansepolcro nel periodo degli abati (1012–1521)* (Sansepolcro: A. C. Grafiche, 1976).

10. THE CRIMINALS' CRUSADE

1 "Et locus ille reductus est intra ambitum murorum civitatis" (Benvenuto da Imola, *Comentum super Dantis Comoediam,* ed. Giacomo Filippo Lacaita [Florence: G. Barbera, 1887], 5:66).

2 A payment order of 1358 concerns the purchase of a "cowl" so a certain Fino could process in front of a group of condemned prisoners in chains; in 1362, a Johannes

de Mersis is recorded as having been paid 2 *soldi* to walk with a cross in front of prisoners on their way to be beheaded (Roisin Cossar, *The Transformation of the Laity in Bergamo, 1265–c.1400* [Leiden: Brill, 2006], 118–119). The Misericordia had been founded to assist the poor, the infirm, and prisoners: see Bortolo Belotti, *Storia di Bergamo e dei Bergamaschi* (Bergamo: Poligrafiche Bolis, 1959), 2:143.

3 This emerges clearly from statistics about the value of pious bequests in Siena between 1205 and 1500, as shown by Samuel K. Cohn, *Death and Property in Siena, 1205–1800: Strategies for the Afterlife* (Baltimore, MD: Johns Hopkins University Press, 1988), 47.

4 For more on this, see the very important pages in Ernest H. Kantorowicz, *The King's Two Bodies: A Study in Mediaeval Political Theology* (Princeton, NJ: Princeton University Press, 1957), 193–272.

5 Matteo Al Kalak and Marta Lucchi, *Oltre il patibolo: I fratelli della Morte di Modena tra giustizia e perdono* (Rome: Bulzoni, 2009), 200–201, where there is also an evocative image of the *Battuti bianchi* (white flagellants) of Modena (Plate 5).

6 These are the words used in the introduction to the constitutions of the Compagnia dei Neri of Florence in 1423 (BNCFi, ms Magl. VIII. 1500, no. 7, cc. n. n.).

7 See Vito Fumagalli, "Il paesaggio dei morti: Luoghi d'incontro tra i morti e i vivi sulla terra nel Medioevo," *Quaderni storici* 17, no. 50 (1982): 411–425; for a systematic collection of statute regulations in an Italian region, see Maria Giuseppina Muzzarelli, ed., *La legislazione suntuaria: Secoli XIII–XVI, Emilia Romagna* (Rome: Ministero per i beni e le attività culturali, Direzione generale per gli archivi, 2002).

8 See Lester K. Little, *Libertà carità fraternità: Confraternite laiche a Bergamo nell'età del Comune* (Bergamo: P. Lubrina, 1988), 183.

9 See Alvaro Grion, "La 'Legenda' del B. Venturino da Bergamo secondo il testo inedito del codice di Cividale," *Bergomum* 50, no. 4 (1956): 11–110, esp. 46. What is said here about this crusade picks up on my treatment of the topic in Adriano Prosperi, *Dare l'anima: Storia di un infanticidio* (Turin: Einaudi, 2005), 326–329.

10 The study by Gennaro Maria Monti, *Le confraternite medievali dell'alta e media Italia* (Venice: La Nuova Italia, 1927), is now rather dated, but the following are still invaluable: Gilles-Gérard Meersseman, *"Ordo fraternitatis": Confraternite e pietà dei laici nel Medioevo*, 3 vols. (Rome: Herder, 1972), and Giancarlo Angelozzi, *Le confraternite laicali: Un'esperienza cristiana tra Medioevo e età moderna* (Brescia: Queriniana, 1978). A rapid overview of the sixteenth century can be found in Christopher F. Black, *Italian Confraternities in the Sixteenth Century* (Cambridge: Cambridge University Press, 1989), 217–223.

11 The passage in Matteo Villani, *Cronica,* I, 7, is borne out by the extensive study of the situation in Florence by John Henderson, *The Renaissance Hospital: Healing the Body and Healing the Soul* (New Haven, CT: Yale University Press, 2006), 34ff., chap. 2.

12 Tommasino de' Bianchi detto de'Lancellotti, *Cronaca modenese* (Parma: Fiaccadori, 1867), 5:81–82; see Al Kalak and Lucchi, *Oltre il patibolo,* 13–14.

13 See *Cronache di ser Luca Dominici,* vol. 2: *Cronaca della venuta dei Bianchi e della moría 1399–1400,* ed. Giovan Carlo Gigliotti (Pistoia: Pacinotti 1933), 49–94; the passage is cited in Angelozzi, *Le confraternite laicali,* 108–109.

14 See Mario Fanti, "La Confraternita di Santa Maria della Morte e la Conforteria dei condannati a morte in Bologna nei secoli XIV e XV," *Quaderni del centro di ricerca e di studio sul movimento dei Disciplinati* 20 (1978): 3–101, esp. 13–14.

15 "Ut . . . pauperes in hospitali dicte societatis mortuos subleventur et ut mortui qui dampnantur in Communi Bononie in dicta ecclesia devocius et ferventius sepelientur et ad sepulturam portentur": ibid., 38.

16 See James R. Banker, *Death in the Community: Memorialization and Confraternities in an Italian Commune in the Late Middle Ages* (Athens: University of Georgia Press, 1988), 150, which refers, for this information, to Ercole Agnoletti, *Sansepolcro nel periodo degli abati (1012–1521)* (Sansepolcro: A. C. Grafiche, 1976).

17 See c. 102r of the *Memoriale della confraternita di S. Giovanni Battista volgarmente detta de' Neri di S. Maria della Croce al Tempio,* BTMi, ms Trivulziano 207. As Elsa Luttazzi Gregori notes in "La 'morte confortata' nella Toscana dell'età moderna (XV–XVIII secolo)," in *Criminalità e società in età moderna,* vol. 12, ed. Luigi Berlinguer and Floriana Colao (Milan: Giuffre, 1991), 25–91 (esp. 28–29), this is the book of the confraternity's deliberations and records compiled as a replacement for the original one, which was damaged by flooding in 1557. This had already been pointed out by Luigi Passerini, *Storia degli stabilimenti di beneficenza e d'istruzione elementare gratuita della città di Firenze* (Florence: Le Monnier, 1853), 481. A recent study of the Florentine confraternity is that of Gennaro Ferrante, "Control of Emotions and Comforting Practices before the Scaffold in Medieval and Early Modern Italy (with Some Remarks on Lorenzetti's Fresco)," in *Encyclopaedia Mundi: Studi di letteratura italiana in onore di Giuseppe Mazzotta,* ed. Stefano U. Baldassarri and Alessandro Polcri (Florence: Le Lettere, 2013), 1–11. I thank Dr. Ferrante for having allowed me to read his manuscript prior to its publication.

18 See Giuseppina de Sandre Gasparini, "Il movimento delle confraternite nell'area veneta," in *Le mouvement confraternel au Moyen Âge: France, Italie, Suisse,* Actes de la table ronde, Lausanne 1985 (Paris: École Française de Rome, 1987), 361–394, esp. 383.

19 The reference work here is Giuseppina de Sandre Gasparini, *Statuti di confraternite religiose di Padova nel Medioevo: Testi, studio introduttivo e cenni storici* (Padua: Istituto per la Storia ecclesiastica padovana, 1974). See also Giovanni Gorini, ed., *S. Antonio, 1231–1981: Il suo tempo, il suo culto e la sua città* (Padua: Signum, 1981), 306, mentioned by Chiara Traverso, *La Scuola di San Fantin o dei "Picai": Carità e giustizia a Venezia* (Venice: Marsilio, 2000), 39.

20 From the statutes of the confraternity of "Sancta Maria Anuncia di devoti de la morte" (1366), held in the Archivio della Parrocchia di Santo Stefano protomartire di Ferrara, *Arciconfraternita della Santissima Annunziata della Parrocchia di S. Michele di Ferrara,* b. 1. The statutes are published in Adriano Franceschini, "Spig-

olature archivistiche prime: Confraternite di disciplinati a Ferrara avanti il Concilio Tridentino," in *Atti e memorie della Deputazione provinciale ferrarese di storia
patria* 19 (1975): 5–70, esp. 42–70. In Marco Antonio Guarini, *Compendio
historico...delle Chiese...di Ferrara* (Ferrara, 1621), 60, we read that the founder of
the confraternity was "a certain Nicolo dall'Oro, son of Bertolino Ziponari," and
that the date of foundation was March 25, 1366, the Feast of the Annunciation. The
register began in 1378.

21 Monsignor Giuliano de' Conti Sabbatini, *Memorie del Pio istituto della Conforteria:
Assunto già dai primi Fondatori della Venerabile Confraternita di San Giovanni Bat-
tista di Modena detta l'Ospitale della Morte* (Modena, 1755), 7–8. See Gusmano
Soli, "Gli oratorii della Confraternita di S. Giovanni della Buona Morte," in Soli,
Chiese di Modena (Modena: Aedes Muratoriana, 1974), 157–170.

22 From the prologue to the ancient statutes cited in Sabbatini, *Memorie del Pio istituto della Conforteria,* 10–13.

23 Traverso, *La Scuola di San Fantin o dei "Picai,"* 3–6.

24 BCA, *Libro di tutti li giustiziati in Bologna incominciando l'anno 1030 per sino al
1834 con i nomi e cognomi de' medemi,* ms B 3159, 55.

25 Sabbatini, *Memorie del Pio istituto della Conforteria,* 23–24. In actual fact, the oldest
extant version of the statutes is that of 1482. See the monograph on the Modenese
confraternity by Al Kalak and Lucchi, *Oltre il patibolo,* 17.

11. "I RECEIVED HIS HEAD INTO MY HANDS"

1 Santa Caterina da Siena, *Epistolario,* vol. 1, ed. Eugenio Dupré Theseider (Rome:
Tipografia del Senato, 1940), letter 273. The letter is translated into English by Su-
zanne Noffke in *The Letters of St. Catherine of Siena,* vol. 1 (Binghamton, NY:
SUNY Center for Medieval and Renaissance Studies, 1988), 107–111, where it is
listed as letter 31.

2 As in the title of a very superficial essay by Joan P. Del Pozzo, "The Apotheosis of
Niccolò Toldo: An Execution 'Love Story,'" *Modern Language Notes,* Italian Issue,
110, no. 1 (1995): 164–177.

3 The theme is the focus of a section—more intriguing than solidly argued—in David
Biale, *Blood and Belief: The Circulation of a Symbol between Jews and Christians*
(Berkeley: University of California Press, 2007). Still fundamental with regard to
the idea of the Jewish people as a people united by blood and not by land is Franz
Rosenzweig, *The Star of Redemption,* trans. William W. Hallo (London: Routledge
and Kegan Paul, 1971).

4 See Caroline Walker Bynum, *Holy Feast and Holy Fast: The Religious Significance
of Food to Medieval Women* (Berkeley: University of California Press, 1987).

5 Dominique Rigaux, "La donna, la fede, l'immagine negli ultimi secoli del Medioevo," in *Donne e fede,* ed. Lucetta Scaraffia and Gabriella Zarri (Rome–Bari:
Laterza, 1994), 171.

6 Robert Fawtier, *Sainte Catherine de Sienne: Essai de critique des sources,* 2 vols. (Paris: De Broccard, 1921–1930).

7 Antoine Dondaine, "Saint Catherine de Sienne et Niccolò di Toldo," *Archivio fratrum praedicatorum* 19 (1949): 169–207.

8 Ibid., 176: "Tempore illo plures plectendi propter eorum demerita tamen desperati sine confessione procedebant ad mortem."

9 Ibid.: "Et etiam ulterius usque ad locum iustitie et per viam eos associabat. Et genuflectentes cum ad martirium pervenissent, suis manibus delubra recipiebat gaudebatque quantdo videbat suam vestem albam illorum stillata cruore."

10 See Mario Fanti, "La Confraternita di Santa Maria della Morte e la Conforteria dei condannati a morte in Bologna nei secoli XIV e XV," *Quaderni del centro di ricerca e di studio sul movimento dei Disciplinati* 20 (1978): 30–31.

11 As in the fifteenth-century statutes of the Disciplinati di Domodossola. See Giovanna Casagrande, "Confraternite senza barriere? Un viaggio tra casi ed esempi," in *Brotherhood and Boundaries: Fraternità e barriere,* ed. Stefania Pastore, Adriano Prosperi, and Nicholas Terpstra (Pisa: Edizioni della Normale, 2011), 20.

12 Illuminata Bembo, *Specchio di illuminazione,* ed. Silvia Mostaccio (Florence: Sismel Edizioni del Galluzzo, 2001), 13–14. The episode is illustrated in an etching and a painting by Giulio Morina, reproduced and studied by Massimo Ferretti, "Pitture per condannati a morte del Trecento bolognese," in *Misericordie: Conversioni sotto il patibolo tra Medioevo ed età moderna,* ed. Adriano Prosperi (Pisa: Edizioni della Normale, 2007), 85–151, esp. 99–108.

13 See Giovanna Balbi, "La Compagnia della Misericordia di Genova nella storia della spiritualità laica," in *Momenti di storia e arte religiosa in Liguria* (Genoa: In Palatio Archiepiscopali Ianuensi, 1963), 145–190.

14 See *Libro de la Vita mirabile et dottrina santa, de la beata Caterinetta da Genoa: Nel quale si contiene una utile et catholica dimostratione et dechiaratione del purgatorio* (Genoa, 1551), 191–192; the passage is also quoted in Daniela Solfaroli Camillocci, *I devoti della Carità: Le confraternite del Divino Amore nell'Italia del primo Cinquecento* (Naples: La Città del Sole, 2002), 47.

15 *Selected Writings of Girolamo Savonarola: Religion and Politics, 1490–1498,* trans. and ed. Anne Borelli and Maria Pastore Passaro (New Haven, CT: Yale University Press, 2006), "Ruth and Micheas," sermon 28, 33–55, quotation at 45. The text of the sermon, delivered on November 1, 1496, was, in accordance with Savonarola's wishes, printed separately from the full series (for Bartolomeo de' Libri, after November 27, 1496, see Walter Arthur Copinger, *Supplement to Hain's Repertorium bibliographicum,* 3 vols. [London: H. Sotheran and Co., 1895–1902], 14391). On the influence of Savonarola's message, see Lorenzo Polizzotto, "Dell'arte del bel morire: The Piagnone Way of Death 1494–1545," *I Tatti Studies* 3 (1989): 27–87.

12. FACTIONAL CONFLICT AND MOB JUSTICE
IN THE LATE MIDDLE AGES

1 The great works by the masters of the historic school (Antonio Pertile's *Storia del diritto italiano* is still essential reading with regard to Italy) are also referred to in the vast synthesis by Antonio Padoa Schioppa, *Storia del diritto in Europa: Dal Medioevo all'età contemporanea* (Bologna: il Mulino, 2007). In particular, see Massimo Vallerani, *La giustizia pubblica medievale* (Bologna: il Mulino, 2005).

2 These words were shouted out in Cesena in 1309, according to the city chronicle by Giuliano Fantaguzzi, *Caos,* ed. Michele Andrea Pistocchi (Rome: Istituto Storico italiano per il Medio Evo, 2012), 804.

3 This is how Andrea Zorzi summarizes the results of his studies in *L'amministrazione della giustizia penale nella repubblica fiorentina: Aspetti e problemi* (Florence: Olschki, 1988), 9–17.

4 From the 1270s onward, according to Giuliano Milani, *L'esclusione dal Comune: Conflitti e bandi politici a Bologna e in altre città italiane tra XII e XIV secolo* (Rome: Istituto Storico Italiano per il Medio Evo, 2003), 180.

5 Anthony Molho and Franek Sznura, eds., *Alle bocche della piazza: Diario di anonimo fiorentino (1382–1401)* (Florence: Olschki, 1986), 17–19 (on Giorgio Scali and the Albizzi, see Machiavelli, *Florentine Histories,* trans. Laura Banfield and Harvey C. Mansfield [Princeton, NJ: Princeton University Press, 1988], bk. 3, 18–19). The information gathered by Trevor Dean (*Crime and Justice in Late Medieval Italy* [Cambridge: Cambridge University Press, 2007], 60ff.), who examines many other city chronicles, confirms the violent aspect of the involvement of the populace in executions.

6 See Vieri Mazzoni, *Accusare e proscrivere il nemico politico: Legislazione antighibellina e persecuzione giudiziaria a Firenze (1347–1378)* (Pisa: Pacini, 2010).

7 One such case is described by Dino Compagni in *Cronica,* bk. III, XXIX (I cite from Davide Cappi's edition [Rome: Carocci, 2013], 106).

8 This is how the origins of the Compagnia are recounted in the *Libro di varie notizie e memorie della venerabil compagnia di Santa Maria della Croce al Tempio* (BNCFi, ms II. I. 138, cc. n. n.).

9 See, for example, Didier Lett, *L'enfant des miracles: Enfance et société au Moyen Age, XIIe–XIIIe siècle* (Paris: Aubier, 1997). By contrast, see Ottavia Niccoli, *Il seme della violenza: Putti, fanciulli e mammoli nell'Italia tra Cinque e Seicento* (Rome: Laterza, 2007).

10 Milani, *L'esclusione dal Comune,* 421.

11 Ibid., 418–419. For more on the development of the crime of barratry, see the perceptive analysis in Gherardo Ortalli, *Barattieri: Il gioco d'azzardo fra economia ed etica, secoli XIII–XV* (Bologna: il Mulino, 2012).

12 Molho and Sznura, *Alle bocche della piazza,* 30.

13 As reported by Giovanni Villani, *Nuova Cronica,* bk. XI, 41, ed. Giovanni Porta (Parma: Guanda, 1991), 570–571.

14 Molho and Sznura, *Alle bocche della piazza,* 83.

15 Ibid., 117–119.

16 Ibid., 146–147.

17 *Libro di varie notizie e memorie della venerabil compagnia di Santa Maria della Croce al Tempio* (BNCFi, ms II. I. 138).

18 Andrea Bernardi (Novacula), *Cronache forlivesi,* vol. 1, pt. 1, ed. Giuseppe Mazzatinti (Bologna: R. Deputazione di storia patria, 1895), 159–160.

19 Ibid., 234.

20 Ibid., vol. 1, pt. 2, 99–101.

21 Ibid., 106.

22 I cite from Anonimo Fiorentino, *Storia di fra Michele minorita,* ed. Emanuele Trevi (Rome: Salerno, 1991).

23 See my entry on "Firenze" in *Dizionario storico dell'Inquisizione* (Pisa: Edizioni della Normale, 2011), 2:605–607. For Bologna, see the entry by Guido Dall'Olio, ibid., 1:211–213.

24 The emergence of the city as a subject, and of peace as something to protect, was highlighted in Mario Sbriccoli's last work, "Justice négociée, justice hégémonique," which appeared posthumously in *Pratiques sociales et politiques judiciaires dans les villes de l'Occident à la fin du Moyen Âge,* ed. Jacques Chiffoleau, Claude Gauvard, and Andrea Zorzi (Rome: École Française de Rome, 2007), 389–421. Sbriccoli's work updates the classic study by Hermann U. Kantorowicz, *Albertus Gandinus und das Strafrecht der Scholastik* (Berlin: J. Guttentag, 1907).

25 See Gherardo Ortalli, *La peinture infamante du XIIIᵉ au XVIᵉ siècle* (Paris: Gérard Monfort, 1994). Original edition: *"Pingatur in Palatio": La pittura infamante nei secoli XIII–XVI* (Rome: Jouvence, 1979).

13. "HOLY JUSTICE"

1 Edoardo Grendi, "Le confraternite urbane nell'età moderna: L'esempio genovese," in E. Grendi, *In altri termini: Etnografia e storia di una società di antico regime,* ed. Osvaldo Raggio and Angelo Torre (Milan: Feltrinelli, 2004), 45–110.

2 Bernardino da Siena, *Prediche volgari sul Campo di Siena 1427,* ed. Carlo Delcorno (Milan: Rusconi, 1989), 1:330, sermon X. But see the whole series of sermons X–XII on *parti* (factions).

3 "Dampnatos quoque ad mortem, aliquando sociabat usque ad locum consumationis eorum, predicando eis continue ac roborando ad tollerantiam in remisionem peccatorum, rememorando eis passionem Christi ac inducendo ad firmam spem misericordie Dei" (Alvaro Grion, "La 'Legenda' del B. Venturino da Bergamo secondo il testo inedito del codice di Cividale," *Bergomum* 50, no. 4 [1956]: 11–110, esp. 46). See also Mario Fanti, "La Confraternita di Santa Maria della Morte e la

Conforteria dei condannati a morte in Bologna nei secoli XIV e XV," *Quaderni del centro di ricerca e di studio sul movimento dei Disciplinati* 20 (1978): 3–101, esp. 32.

4 As noted in Fanti, "La Confraternita," 110.

5 See Nicholas Terpstra, "Theory into Practice: Executions, Comforting and Comforters in Renaissance Italy," in *The Art of Executing Well: Rituals of Execution in Renaissance Italy,* ed. Nicholas Terpstra (Kirksville, MO: Truman University Press, 2008), 118–158, esp. 121.

6 Fanti, "La Confraternita," 46–47.

7 Ibid., 41–50. Documents relating to the important Bolognese tradition have been gathered together and studied by Elena Grottanelli in *I viaggi della Madonna di San Luca* (Bologna: Tamari, 1976).

8 Fanti, "La Confraternita," 50n.

9 The Compagnia della Morte's "resolution proceedings" from 1494 to 1847, held in the Biblioteca Universitaria di Urbino, are mentioned in Luigi Moranti, ed., *La Biblioteca Universitaria di Urbino* (Florence: Olschki, 1954). It was not possible to take account of these in the present study, or of the "books of the resolutions of the Fraternita di S. Maria della Misericordia" in the *Congregazione di carità* collection.

10 The administration of the two companies was separated as well, "with no specific obligation to keep accounts"; see Mario Fanti, ed., *Gli archivi delle istituzioni di carità e assistenza attive in Bologna nel Medioevo e nell'età moderna,* Atti del IV colloquio, Bologna, 1984 (Bologna: Istituto per la storia di Bologna, 1984), 1:23. The history of the Bolognese company is referred to in Adriano Prosperi, *Dare l'anima: Storia di un infanticidio* (Turin: Einaudi, 2005), 325ff.

11 *Ordinationi* of the Oratorio di Santa Maria della Morte, in BCA, ms Gozzadini 213, cc. 122–173; cf. c. 23r. Attention is drawn to these chapters, dating to 1436 and retained in the reformed version of 1526, by Mario Fanti in *Confraternite e città a Bologna nel Medioevo e nell'età moderna* (Rome: Herder, 2001), 114–115.

12 The *Statuti, ordinationi, et provisioni della Compagnia dell'Hospitale di S. Maria della Morte novellamente corretti, et ampliati, et riformati, et con somma diligentia dagli huomini della Compagnia revisiti*—parchment manuscript held in the BABo, *Fondo Ospedali* 42 (17)—bear the name of the rector, Count Niccolò Castelli, and, among others, those of the senator Cesare Bianchetti, of Giovanni Ludovico Bovio and Niccolò dell'Armi, and of doctors and knights.

13 See Guido Dall'Olio, *Eretici e inquisitori nella Bologna del Cinquecento* (Bologna: Istituto per la Storia di Bologna, 1999), 288–295. Avoiding "any heretic, or suspected heretical view" was the first of the "twelve laws" of the "School of comforters" drawn up by Cristoforo Pensabene and approved on April 12, 1556, by Antonio del Monte, "head and principal" of the School, and by seven comforters (BABo, ms 4857, aula 2, C. VIII, 19, p. 5).

14 "This book will be for writing down all those deprived of corporeal life by Justice, both in times past and in times to come": this is the title of the "book of the exe-

cuted" held in the archive of the *conforteria* (now in AABo, *Archivio consorziale del clero urbano,* IX, D 1).

15 Archivio di Stato di Faenza, *Archivio delle corporazioni religiose soppresse,* Pergamene B 3 (1-1), Regula della Compagnia delle Grazie, 1422, chap. 16 (the document is pointed out in the extensive research done for an unpublished degree thesis by Alessandra Parisini, *La funzione del bandito: Grazia e giustizia nelle carte della Confraternita della Morte di Faenza,* Università degli Studi di Bologna, Facoltà di Magistero, a.a. 1985–1986, 1:272.

16 The statutes preserved in the Biblioteca Ambrosiana were published by Enrico Cattaneo in "Le antiche regole de 'li disciplinati di Madona S. Maria de la morte e di S. Giovane Baptista,'" *Ambrosius* 36, supplement to no. 3 (1960): 22–46, esp. 23.

17 See Adriano Ceruti, "La chiesa di S. Giovanni alle Case rotte in Milano," *Archivio storico lombardo* 1, no. 1 (1874): 148–185, esp. 161.

18 For a cursory reading of the list, see Matteo Benvenuti, "Come facevasi giustizia nello Stato di Milano dall'anno 1471 al 1763," *Archivio storico lombardo* 9 (1882): 442–482. A list from 1471 to 1760 is in the Fondo Beccaria of the Biblioteca Ambrosiana in Milan (*Becc.* B 228); another one, from 1471 to 1766, is in the Biblioteca Nazionale Braidense, *Fondo Morbio* 149, "Registro de' giustiziati assistiti dalla nobilissima scuola . . . dell'anno 1471 al 3 aprile 1766." They are referred to in Italo Mereu, *La pena di morte a Milano nel secolo di Beccaria* (Vicenza: Neri Pozza, 1988), 12–13; Mereu notes that they offer proof "of how Beccaria had a specific and historically founded knowledge of the 'cruel' way of carrying out the death sentence in his age."

19 BAMi, ms L.128.sup., *Confraternita di san Gio. Battista Decollato in Milano: Giustiziati (1552–1611).*

20 The documentation is conserved in the Archivio di Stato di Milano, *Amministrazione del fondo di religione, Confraternite.* A study by Serafino Biffi, "Confraternita di San Defendente e Confraternita della Misericordia e Carità eretta nella Chiesa di Santa Maria del Sole in Lodi," *Archivio storico per la città e comuni del circondario di Lodi* 4, no. 10 (1885): 142–144, together with other archive and bibliographic information, was kindly pointed out to me by Maria Grazia Casali, whom I wish to thank here.

21 See Marina Olivieri Baldissarri, *I "poveri prigioni": La confraternita della Santa Croce e della Pietà dei carcerati a Milano nei secoli XVI–XVIII* (Milan: NED, 1985), 81–83; and Mario Bendiscioli, "L'età della Riforma cattolica," in *Storia di Milano,* vol. 10: *L'età della Riforma cattolica* (Milan: Fondazione Treccani degli Alfieri, 1957), 400–401.

22 As can be read in the new "Mariegola," begun in 1566 and housed in the Archivio di Stato in Venice (reproduced in the appendix of Chiara Traverso, *La Scuola di San Fantin o dei "Picai": Carità e giustizia a Venezia* [Venice: Marsilio, 2000], 165–175).

23 Angelo Maria Bianchi, *Registro di tutti li nomi, cognomi, patria e delitti commessi dalli giustiziati dall'epoca MCXII V febraro fino in presente (1806),* ms 8 of the Bib-

lioteca del Senato, Rome (see Traverso, *La Scuola di San Fantin,* 88 and 177–179, where the residual manuscript documentation listed shows that the chroniclers of the Venetian company went as far back as the year 726 in gathering information about the condemned).

24 As stated in chapters reformed in 1676 and approved by the grand duke on June 21, 1678 (*Capitoli et ordini della venerabile compagnia di Santa Maria della Croce al Tempio detta la Compagnia Grande del Tempio,* ms in ASFi, *Corporazioni religiose soppresse, Capitoli 37,* 1). Here the establishment of the company is dated 1343. A review of documents regarding the origins and development of the company between the fifteenth and sixteenth centuries can be found in Konrad Eisenbichler, "Lorenzo de' Medici e la Congregazione dei Neri nella Compagnia della Croce al Tempio," *Archivio storico italiano* 150 (1992): 343–370, where a clear distinction is made between the Compagnia di Santa Maria della Croce al Tempio, with origins dating way back to the end of the thirteenth century, its fourteenth-century refounding as a company of justice, and the formation of the restricted Compagnia dei Neri group in 1423. The rule of secrecy maintained by members of the *stretta* company and the selection by rank pointed out by Filippo Fineschi in "La rappresentazione della morte sul patibolo nella liturgia fiorentina della Congregazione dei Neri," *Archivio storico italiano* 150 (1992): 805–846, esp. 810–811, confirms this evolution toward a special magistracy with a supporting role in the administration of justice.

25 *Notizie e memorie della Compagnia di Santa Maria della Croce al Tempio di Firenze,* BNCFi, ms II. I. 138.

26 BTMi, ms Trivulziano 207, c. 103v.

27 *Costituzioni della Compagnia de' Neri,* BNCFi, ms Magl. VIII. 1488, n. 7. This is a copy from the original, made after the river Arno flooded in 1557. Not always accurate information can be found in an old work by Eugenio Cappelli, *La Compagnia dei Neri* (Florence: Cappelli, 1927); for instance, on page 39 the year of foundation is given as 1424. The existing literature is also drawn on by John Henderson, *Piety and Charity in Late Medieval Florence* (Oxford: Clarendon Press, 1994), 477–480.

28 *Capitoli et ordini della venerabile compagnia di Santa Maria della Croce al Tempio,* ms in ASFi, *Corporazioni religiose soppresse, Capitoli 37,* chap. 12, 22.

29 *Capitoli et ordini,* 14–15.

30 *Notizie e memorie della Compagnia di Santa Maria della Croce al Tempio di Firenze,* BNCFi, ms II. I. 138.

31 *Capitoli della Compagnia di Santa Croce al Tempio,* parchment manuscript in ASFi, *Corporazioni religiose soppresse, Capitoli 202,* cc. 3r–v.

32 Eisenbichler, "Lorenzo de' Medici e la Congregazione dei Neri," 348–349.

33 See Luigi Passerini, *Storia degli stabilimenti di beneficenza e di istruzione elementare gratuita della città di Firenze* (Florence: Le Monnier, 1853), 484. The information is drawn from Cappelli, *La Compagnia dei Neri,* 39–40. A list of executed prisoners

assisted by the Blacks was published by Giuseppe Rondoni, "I 'giustiziati' a Firenze (dal secolo XV al secolo XVIII)," *Archivio storico italiano,* ser. 5, vol. 28 (1901): 209–256. A systematic indexing of the data in the manuscript lists held in the Biblioteca Riccardiana and the Biblioteca Nazionale Centrale di Firenze (ms Riccardiano 2057; Magliabechiano XXV, 159; Nazionale II, I, 138) was carried out by Filippo Fineschi, and forms the still-unpublished appendix to his degree thesis at the University of Florence: "Cristo e Giuda: La rappresentazione della morte nella giustizia fiorentina tra Cinque e Seicento," supervised by Prof. Sergio Bertelli, academic year 1989–1990.

34 Cappelli, *La Compagnia dei Neri,* 14–17.

35 Benedetto Varchi, *Storia fiorentina,* ed. Lelio Arbib (Florence: Societa editrice delle storie del Nardi e del Varchi, 1838–1841), 2:109.

36 The 1466 statutes are held in ASFi, *Corporazioni religiose soppresse,* Diocesi di Pisa, F VIII, n. 1 (see Luigi Lazzerini, "La Confraternita della Morte di Pisa [sec. XIV–XVIII]," unpublished degree thesis, Faculty of Letters and Philosophy, University of Pisa, academic year 1989–1990, 183–200).

37 See the commune of Prato's attestation of 1502 for the company of justice published by Father Domenico Guglielmo M. Di Agresti, *Aspetti di vita pratese del Cinquecento* (Florence: Olschki, 1976), 50–51.

38 "Ad exercendum specialiter pium opus misericordiae erga ultimo supplicio damnatos et incarceratos" (ASFi, *Nunziature* 1, Sententiae, cc. 130r–133v).

39 The statutes of 1619 are held at the Accademia degli Euteleti in San Miniato; other sources, principally bookkeeping ledgers, can be found in the town's communal archive; cf. *Enti pubblici, assistenziali, privati ed ecclesiastici,* inventoried by Marilena Lombardi, Giancarlo Nanni, Silvia Nannipieri, Arianna Orlandi, and Ivo Regoli (San Miniato, 1994), 87–90. The work done by the confraternity in offering "spiritualia auxilia" to the condemned is described in the proceedings regarding the pastoral visits of 1650 and 1687 conserved in the Archivio della Curia vescovile.

40 Enzo Donatini, *La città ideale. Fortezza della Romagna fiorentina* (Ravenna: Edizioni del Girasole, 1979), 372.

41 Bernardino da Siena, *Prediche volgari sul Campo di Siena 1427,* ed. Carlo Delcorno (Milan: Rusconi, 1989), 2:1313–1314, sermon 43.

42 Ibid., 2:1377, sermon 45.

43 Ibid., 1:512–518.

44 BCSi, ms A.II.24, *Registro dei fratelli della Compagnia della Morte 1518–1754.* In the *Registro dei confratelli che andarono a Roma nel S. Giubileo 1575–1578,* BCSi, ms A.II.26, reference is made to porters, builders, and goldworkers.

45 BCSi, ms 380 (A.IX.45), cc. 1r, 6r–v, 21r, 23v.

46 BCSi, ms 379 (A.IX.44), cc. 1r–5r.

47 BCSi, c. 5r.

48 BCSi, cc. 8v, 11r–12v.

49 See Alfredo Liberati, "Chiese, monasteri, oratori e spedali senesi," *Bullettino senese di storia patria* 46 (1939): 157–167, esp. 165–166.

50 BCSi, ms 372 (A.IX.37), cc. 52*r*–55*r*.

51 See Giuseppina De Sandre Gasparini, ed., *Statuti di confraternite religiose di Padova nel Medioevo: Testi, studio introduttivo e cenni storici* (Padua: Istituto per la Storia ecclesiastica padovana, 1974), 173–175.

52 Ibid., 186.

53 The treatise in question is *De modo bene moriendi* (Venice, 1531). The new statutes of 1502 are included in the appendix to Giuseppina De Sandre Gasparini, ed., "La Confraternita di San Giovanni Evangelista della Morte in Padova e una 'riforma' ispirata dal vescovo Barozzi (1502)," in *Miscellanea Gilles-Gérard Meerseman* (Padua: Antenore, 1970), 2:765–815. The archive documents are held in the *Corporazioni soppresse* collection of the Archivio di Stato di Padova (53 *buste* from 1328 to 1806). I wish to thank Gianni Buganza for the information he gave me.

54 De Sandre Gasparini, "La Confraternita," 193–221, esp. 195.

55 Ibid., 224, deliberation dated 1467.

56 *Statuto della compagnia della Pietà,* 1479, in *Testi viterbesi dei secoli XIV, XV e XVI,* ed. Paola Sgrilli (Viterbo: Sette Città, 2003), 153–176, esp. 171–172. I am indebted to Alfredo Stussi for drawing my attention to this edition.

57 A survey of the rich tradition of sources and studies can now be found in Matteo Al Kalak and Marta Lucchi, *Oltre il patibolo: I fratelli della Morte di Modena tra giustizia e perdono* (Rome: Bulzoni, 2009).

58 The *Vachetta per li iustitiati 1593–1826* is in ASCMo, various registers and memorials, Lucchi II 8. A modern document summary of the old cataloguing is in Al Kalak and Lucchi, *Oltre il patibolo,* 209–226. For more on the topography of the square in Modena, see Orianna Baracchi, *Modena: Piazza Grande* (Modena: Artioli, 1981), 46.

59 Giuseppe Mazzatinti, ed., *Costituzioni dei disciplinati di S. Andrea di Perugia* (Forlí: Bordandini, 1893).

60 See Giovanni Battista Vermiglioli, *Nuova riforma delle costituzioni della venerabile Compagnia dei SS. Andrea e Bernardino in Perugia detta della giustizia con la storia del medesimo pio istituto* (Perugia: Bartelli, 1846), 14–15.

61 The document is in Clara Cutini, "I condannati a morte e l'attività assistenziale della Confraternita della Giustizia di Perugia," *Bollettino della Deputazione di storia patria per l'Umbria* 82 (1985): 173–186, esp. 174–175 n. 5. The register of "Giustiziati e oblati alla croce 1525–1826" is in ASPe, *Confraternita dei ss. Andrea e Bernardino, detta della Giustizia,* no. 3.

62 See Adriano Franceschini, "Spigolature archivistiche prime," *Atti e memorie della Deputazione provinciale ferrarese di storia patria* 19 (1975): 5–70.

63 ASDFe, *Fondo Arciconfraternita della Morte e Orazione di Ferrara,* cartella II, 1 (see my "Morire volentieri: Condannati a morte e sacramenti," in *Misericordie: Conversioni sotto il patibolo tra Medioevo ed età moderna,* ed. Adriano Prosperi [Pisa: Edizioni della Normale, 2007], 3).

64 Here I draw in part on information contained in "Statistiche criminali d'antico regime," *Annali della Scuola Normale Superiore,* Classe di Lettere e Filosofia, ser. 5, no. 3/2 (2011): 497–525. Copies of the lists of the Bolognese School, in libraries and archives in Bologna, are particularly numerous. Of these, mention should be made of the *Catalogo di tutte le Giustizie seguite in Bologna dall'anno 1030 sino al 1786 estratto da varie antiche cronache sí stampate come manoscritte* by Carlo Antonio Macchiavelli (ms 61, aula 2° C.VII.3 of the BABo) and the eighteenth-century paper ms B 4187 of BCA, *Libro di tutti li giustiziati in Bologna incominciando l'anno 1030 per sino al 1834 con i nomi e cognomi de' medemi* (bk. 1, 1030–1539; bk. 2, 1540–1752). The note affirms that it is "drawn from various authentic books"; an attached manuscript note dating to the late nineteenth century and signed Tommaso Casini briefly outlines the different families of manuscripts.

65 The expression "merchant of heaven" can be found in the Bolognese comforters' manual. See the translation of the manual by Sheila Das in Terpstra, *The Art of Executing Well,* 193.

66 Laura Graziani Secchieri, ". . . *In Hospitali Batuti Nigri Ferrariae alias Mortis . . . ,*" in *L'Oratorio dell'Annunziata di Ferrara: Arte, storia, devozione e restauri,* ed. Marinella Mazzei Traina (Ferrara: Ferrariae Decus, 2002), 71–93, esp. 73. The document is in ASDFe, *Fondo Arciconfraternita della Morte e Orazione di Ferrara,* B. 1, 5, 1378, matricola 1.

67 The coeval copy is held in the Biblioteca Ariostea in Ferrara, ms cl. I, 404.

68 The citation is from the edition of the coeval manuscript copy in the appendix to Maria Serena Mazzi, *"Gente a cui si fa notte innanzi sera": Esecuzioni capitali e potere nella Ferrara estense* (Rome: Viella, 2003), 99, 139 (the case of "Todeschino"). The most recent study of the Jewish confraternity (Elliott Horowitz, "Jewish Confraternal Piety in Sixteenth-Century Ferrara: Continuity and Change," in *The Politics of Ritual Kinship: Confraternities and Social Order in Early Modern Italy,* ed. Nicholas Terpstra [Cambridge: Cambridge University Press, 2000], 149–171) ignores this aspect of its work.

14. THE SERVICE

1 *Capitoli della Compagnia* of 1574 (BCSi, *Fondo Scuola dei confortatori,* ms 378, A.IX.43, cc. 25r–26r). On the assistance given to condemned prisoners in Siena, see Mario Ascheri and Patrizia Turrini, "La storia della Misericordia e la pietà dei laici a Siena," in *La Misericordia di Siena attraverso i secoli: Dalla Domus Misericordiae all'Arciconfraternita di misericordia* (Siena: Protagon Editori Toscani, 2004), 33–34.

2 Matteo Al Kalak and Marta Lucchi, *Oltre il patibolo: I fratelli della Morte di Modena tra giustizia e perdono* (Rome: Bulzoni, 2009), 43. The text of the chapters can be found in the appendix, on 200.

3 Ibid., 225.

4 BNCFi, ms Magl. VIII. 1500, no. 7, 15–16.

5 *Instruzione Generale del modo che deve tenere ogni fratello nell'atto del confortare,* seventeenth century, attached to an *Istruzione universale per la Compagnia de' Neri* from the same period, BNCFi, ms II. I. 138, cc. 167*r*–175*r*.

6 Paolo Sabbadini dedicated an ex voto to the Madonna as a result (BCA, *Fondo Ospedali* 67 [42], c. 61*r*).

7 See Richard van Dülmen, *Theatre of Horror: Crime and Punishment in Early Modern Germany* (Cambridge: Polity Press, 1990), 59–60. A case in Bologna is reported in Guido dall'Olio, "La 'provocatio ad vallem Josaphat' tra diritto e religione," in *Riti di passaggio, storie di giustizia: Per Adriano Prosperi,* ed. Vincenzo Lavenia and Gianna Paolin (Pisa: Edizioni della Normale, 2011), 3:283–288.

8 *Pratica di aiutare a ben morire raccolta da diversi gravi autori e divisa in quattro parti che può servire di pratico apparecchio per la morte ad ognuno* (Florence, 1733), 403. An *Instruzione universale per la Compagnia de' Neri in occasione dell'esecuzione di un condannato a morte,* undated but from the eighteenth century (BNCFi, ms II. I. 138, cc. n. n., cap. 12), suggested offering the afflicted "either biscuits or Greco [wine], or vinegar, or the queen's water to help it."

9 *De sacramentis in genere ac de sacramentalibus necnon de sacramentis Baptismi, Confirmationis, atque Extremae Unctionis decisiones, auctore Joanne Clericato praeposito Patavino,* 4th ed. (Venice, 1725), 323.

10 Carlo Antonio Macchiavelli, *Origine e progressi dela Sagra Scuola di Conforteria di Bologna dall'anno 1350 a tutto il 1759,* vol. 1, 1350–1713, 207 (BABo, ms *Fondo Scuola dei confortatori;* the condemned person was the infanticide Lucia Cremonini. For more on her case, see Adriano Prosperi, *Dare l'anima: Storia di un infanticidio* [Turin: Einaudi, 2005]).

11 Macchiavelli, *Origine,* 2:190. The process of "taking away" the condemned's strength involved stunning them immediately before execution by hitting them on the temple with a wooden mallet (there is a description in *Praxis criminalis in omnibus tribunalibus Ecclesiastici Status . . . per Josephum Caietanum Scarabellum notarium publicum Ferrariensem ad proprium usum redacta anno salutis 1717,* Biblioteca Ariostea di Ferrara, ms Cl. I, 410, cc. 117*v*–118*r*). The assertion made by the bishop of Modena, Giuliano Sabbatini, that the process consisted of tying the condemned person's hand "tight with rope" is therefore incorrect (*Memorie del Pio istituto della Conforteria: assunto già dai primi Fondatori della Venerabile Confraternita di San Giovanni Battista di Modena detta l'Ospitale della Morte* [Modena, 1755], 103).

12 One case can be found in the list of the condemned in Milan reported by Matteo Benvenuti, "Come facevasi giustizia nello Stato di Milano dall'anno 1471 al 1763," *Archivio storico lombardo* 9 (1882): 442–482.

15. POLITICAL CRIMES

1 Chiara Traverso, *La Scuola di San Fantin o dei "Picai": Carità e giustizia a Venezia* (Venice: Marsilio, 2000), 93–94.

2 There were other conspiracies against the pope in 1517 and 1523. See Kate J. P. Lowe, "The Political Crime of Conspiracy in Fifteenth- and Sixteenth-Century Rome," in *Crime, Society and the Law in Renaissance Italy*, ed. Trevor Dean and Kate J. P. Lowe (Cambridge: Cambridge University Press, 1994), 184–203.

3 *Diario bolognese di Gaspare Nadi*, ed. Corrado Ricci and Alberto Bacchi Della Lega (Bologna: Commissione per i testi di lingua, 1969), 144.

4 On its remote origins, see the useful treatment by Richard A. Bauman, *Impietas in principem: A Study of Treason against the Roman Emperor with Special Reference to the First Century A.D.* (Munich: Beck, 1974). On the medieval tradition, and in particular the *lex Romana Curiensis* which, between the eighth and ninth centuries, defined the crime of blasphemy and replaced the offense against the emperor with that against the Christian God, see Floyd Seyward Lear, *Treason in Roman and Germanic Law: Collected Papers* (Austin: University of Texas Press, 1965), 164–180. An attempted definition was provided by the jurisconsult Martino Garrati da Lodi in a late fourteenth-century treatise.

5 See Jacques Chiffoleau, "Sur le crime de majesté médiéval," in *Genèse de l'État moderne en Méditerranée* (Rome: École Française de Rome, 1993), 183–313.

6 Mario Sbriccoli, *Crimen lesae maiestatis: Il problema del reato politico alle origini della scienza penalistica moderna* (Milan: Giuffrè, 1974), 183.

7 Ibid., 151.

8 Only by adopting the perspective of the modern State and ignoring the theological and legal elaboration of the medieval Church is it possible to argue that heresy, magic, and witchcraft trials are "annexes eventuelles" of the political trial, as Bercé does when introducing the collection of studies in Yves-Marie Bercé, ed., *Les procès politiques (XIVᵉ–XVIIᵉ siècle)* (Rome: École Française de Rome, 2007), 1–9, esp. 1.

9 "Haeresis . . . aequiparari crimini lesae maiestatis imo maius esse" (Tiberio Deciani, *Tractatus criminalis* [Venice, 1614], 143).

10 See also Vincenzo Lavenia, "Eretici sentenziati e 'reincorporati,'" in *Misericordie: Conversioni sotto il patibolo tra Medioevo ed età moderna*, ed. Adriano Prosperi (Pisa: Edizioni della Normale, 2007), 155–163.

11 The indictment, with the appeal to the council and the list of papal heresies, can be found in Jean Coste, ed., *Boniface VIII en procès: Articles d'accusation et dépositions des témoins (1303–1311)* (Rome: L'Erma di Bretschneider, 1995), 140–173. See also Marco Maiorino, Pier Paolo Piergentili, Barbara Frale, and Berenger Fredol, eds., *Processus contra Templarios* (Vatican City: Archivio Segreto Vaticano, 2007).

12 Sbriccoli, *Crimen lesae maiestatis*, 160.

13 Ibid., 171; Giganti's definition is on p. 181.

14 According to Ernest H. Kantorowicz, *The King's Two Bodies: A Study in Medieval Political Theology* (Princeton, NJ: Princeton University Press, 1957), 182–183.

15 See Jacques Chiffoleau, "Ecclesia de occultis non iudicat," in *La Chiesa, il segreto e l'obbedienza* (Bologna: il Mulino, 2010), 76–90; and Adriano Prosperi, *Tribunali della coscienza: Inquisitori, confessori, missionari,* new ed. (Turin: Einaudi, 2007), 219–243.

16 "L'affirmation du procès politique pour conjuration intervient sans doute dans les années 1460–1490" (Renaud Villard, "Faux complots et vrais procès: Pouvoirs princiers et répression des conjurations dans l'Italie du XVIᵉ siècle," in Bercé, *Les procès politiques,* 531).

17 As Villard notes, ibid., 530.

18 In the Germanic empire the same signal separated the decision taken by the court in secrecy and the execution as public spectacle: see Richard Van Dülmen, *Theatre of Horror: Crime and Punishment in Early Modern Germany,* trans. Elisabeth Neu (Cambridge: Polity Press, 1990; original German ed. 1985), 107–108.

19 *Nota di giustiziati in Firenze dal 1439 al 1531,* BNCFi, ms II. III. 502, fasc. 5, cc. n. n.

20 Niccolò Machiavelli, *Florentine Histories,* trans. Laura F. Banfield and Harvey C. Mansfield (Princeton, NJ: Princeton University Press, 1988), bk. VIII, 9, 326–327.

21 Ibid., 327.

22 According to Jacques Chiffoleau, "l'écart entre les mystères de l'État (le secret du procès) et la manifestation de sa force (la publicité du châtiment)" is what emerges from the chronicles of capital executions in France (Chiffoleau, "Le crime de majesté: La politique et l'extraordinaire. Note sur les collections érudites de procès de lèse-majesté du XVIIᵉ siècle français et sur leurs exemples médiévaux," in Berce, *Les procès politiques,* 649).

23 "The Signoria with the [Council of] Seventy determined that it was *crimen lesae maiestatis,* saying that they [the conspirators] wanted to take away liberty and change this State, which was governed through Lorenzo" (letter from the ambassador Antonio Montecatini to the duke of Ferrara, Ercole d'Este, cited in Villard, "Faux complots et vrais procès," 529n). For more on the emergence of the word "Stato" and its meanings, see Nicolai Rubinstein's extensive annotation to his edition of Lorenzo's letters: Lorenzo de' Medici, *Lettere,* vol. 3: *1478–1479,* ed. Nicolai Rubinstein (Florence: Giunti-Barbera, 1977), 3–6; see also Rubinstein, "Notes on the Word 'Stato' before Machiavelli," in *Florilegium Historiale: Essays Presented to Wallace K. Ferguson,* ed. John G. Rowe and William H. Stockdale (Toronto: University of Toronto Press, 1971), 313–326.

24 The decree is the final document of ms L.128.sup. in the Biblioteca Ambrosiana di Milano, which lists those executed from 1552 onward. The case of the Sienese man named Giorgio is recorded at c. 2r. See Serafino Biffi, *Sulle antiche carceri di Milano e del Ducato milanese e sui sodalizj che vi assistevano i prigionieri ed i condannati a morte* (Milan: Bernardoni, 1884), 118.

25 From the *Libro dei giustiziati* of Ferrara, published in Maria Serena Mazzi, *"Gente a cui si fa notte innanzi sera": Esecuzioni e potere nella Ferrara estense* (Rome: Viella, 2003), 108. Literature exists on this case, considered in the important work by Alfredo Troiano, "Specchio di un condannato a morte: Le rime devote di Andrea Viarani da Faenza," *Archivio italiano per la storia della pieta* 19 (2006): 127–169, touched on again in the appendix to Alfredo Troiano, ed., *Il Laudario di S. Maria della Morte di Bologna: Il ms. 1069 della Yale Beinecke Library* (Pisa: Edizioni della Normale, 2010), 295ff.

26 Troiano, *Il Laudario di S. Maria della Morte*, 13.

27 Ugo Caleffini, *Croniche, 1471–1494* (Ferrara: Deputazione provinciale ferrarese di Storia Patria, 2006), 75–77.

28 Giovanni Ricci, *Il principe e la morte: Corpo, cuore, effigie nel Rinascimento* (Bologna: il Mulino, 1998).

29 Mazzi, *"Gente a cui si fa notte innanzi sera,"* 126.

30 Luca della Robbia, "Recitazione del caso di Pietro Paolo Boscoli e di Agostino Capponi," in Adriano Prosperi, *Misericordie*, 335. The translation is that of Alison Knowles Frazier, "Luca della Robbia's Narrative on the Execution of Pietro Paolo Boscoli and Agostino Capponi," in *The Art of Executing Well: Rituals of Execution in Renaissance Italy*, ed. Nicholas Terpstra (Kirksville, MO: Truman University Press, 2008), 307.

31 Frazier, "Luca della Robbia's Narrative," 313.

32 Ibid., 306.

33 Hans von Hentig, *Vom Ursprung der Henkersmahlzeit* (Tübingen: J. C. B. Mohr, 1958), 18–30, mentions wine being ritually offered to the condemned along the path to the gallows in German cities in the Early Modern Age, and documents how the authorities undertook to provide substantial meals at public expense. One celebrated instance involved the laying on of a genuine pre-execution banquet for an infanticide in Frankfurt in 1772 (see also Van Dülmen, *Theatre of Horror*, 62–63).

34 Frazier, "Luca della Robbia's Narrative," 304.

35 Ibid., 308.

36 Ibid., 312.

37 Ibid., 317.

38 E. P. Thompson, *Witness against the Beast: William Blake and the Moral Law* (Cambridge: Cambridge University Press, 1993), 5.

39 Frazier, "Luca della Robbia's Narrative," 316.

40 Niccolò Machiavelli, *Machiavelli: The Chief Works, and Others*, vol. 2, trans. Allan H. Gilbert (Durham, NC: Duke University Press, 1989), 1013.

41 BCSi, ms 381 (A.IX.46), cc. 62r–68v.

42 Biblioteca Governativa di Lucca, *Capitoli manoscritti della Compagnia della Croce del 1492*, ms n. 505, cap. XXX (thanks to Vittorio Antonelli and Bruno Vecoli for their indications). Other traces of the company's activity are the chapters of 1595

and a *Libro dei punti per obbligati a seppellire della Compagnia dell'Alma Croce* from the early seventeenth century (ASLu, *Compagnia della Croce,* vol. 8). Fatinelli's name does not appear in any of these sources.

43 Besides the still-fundamental study of Marino Berengo, *Nobili e mercanti nella Lucca del Cinquecento* (Turin: Einaudi, 1965), 184–190, 438–440, see Luigi Lazzerini, *Nessuno è innocente: Le tre morti di Pietro Pagolo Boscoli* (Florence: Olschki, 2002).

44 Matteo Civitali, *Historie di Lucca,* ed. Mario F. Leonardi (Rome: Istituto storico per l'eta moderna e contemporanea, 1988), 554–556, esp. 554.

45 Ibid., 555–556.

46 Lazzerini, *Nessuno è innocente,* 169–170.

47 As attested by a letter from Ercole Gonzaga, bishop of Mantua, to Fra Reginaldo Nerli on October 22, 1545 (see Pio Paschini, *Pier Paolo Vergerio, il giovane e la sua apostasia: Un episodio delle lotte religiose nel Cinquecento* [Rome: Scuola tipografica Pio X, 1925], 108). In any case, Gonzaga handed over Vergerio's treatise to the inquisitor because that book about how "to console and tame one who is about to die" had been criticized by Galeazzo Florimonte "as Lutheran" (letter from Gonzaga to Florimonte, dated April 15, 1546, in BAV, Barb. Lat. 5793, c. 194). In 1560, after Vergerio fled Catholic Italy, he did in fact compose and publish the small treatise *In che modo si portino nel morire quei che ritengono l'obedientia della sedia romana* (Tübingen, 1560), in which he described the Protestant model of preparing for death. A fresh edition of the text was produced by Silvano Cavazza; see also Gianfranco Hofer, ed., *La gloria del Signore: La Riforma protestante nell'Italia nord-orientale* (Gorizia: Edizioni della Laguna, 2006), 214–222. Gonzago himself was considered to be the author of a book of instructions for the Mantuan comforters' confraternity, of which no trace remains.

48 From the statutes of 1567, cited in Guglielmo Donati, *La Congregazione di Carità di Faenza, 1515–1856* (Faenza: Lega, 1958), 338. Still useful on the Counter-Reformation in Faenza is Francesco Lanzoni, *La Controriforma nella città e diocesi di Faenza* (Faenza: Lega, 1925).

49 [Tullio Crispoldi], *Alcune ragioni del perdonare* (Venice, 1537), cc. 4v–5r. See also Carlo Ginzburg and Adriano Prosperi, *Giochi di pazienza: Un seminario sul "Beneficio di Cristo"* (Turin: Einaudi, 1975).

50 Alfonso de Castro, *De iusta hereticorum punitione* (Venice, 1549).

51 Tullio Crispoldi, *Practica aurea, communes locos nonnullos complectens* (Venice, 1566), cc. 68r–v.

52 Torquato Tasso, *The Liberation of Jerusalem (Gerusalemme liberata),* trans. Max Wickert (Oxford: Oxford University Press, 2009), Canto 12, 66, p. 230.

53 Ludovico Ariosto, *Orlando Furioso,* 2 vols., trans. Barbara Reynolds (London: Penguin Books, 1975), Canto 1, 22, p. 122.

54 Paolo Prodi, *Una storia della giustizia: Dal pluralismo dei fori al moderno dualismo tra coscienza e diritto* (Bologna: il Mulino, 2000), 130.

16. ROME, A CAPITAL

1 *Il diario romano di Gaspare Pontani, già riferito al "Notaio del Nantiporto," dal 31 gennaio 1481 al 25 luglio 1492,* vol. 3, ed. Diomede Toni (Città di Castello: Rerum Italicarum Scriptores, 1908), II, 69. See also the institutional-historical note by Michele Di Sivo, "Archivio della Confraternita di S. Giovanni Decollato, 1497–1870," *Rivista storica del Lazio* 8, no. 12 (2000): 181–225. The text is printed in the volume celebrating the fifth centenary: *Arciconfraternita di San Giovanni Decollato detta della Misericordia della Nazione Fiorentina in Roma, 1488–1988* (Rome: Palombi, 1988), 131–133.

2 ASR, *Confraternita di S. Giovanni decollato (1497–1870),* registro 26, *Giustiziati nella città di Roma dal dí 5 agosto 1497 al dí 13 luglio 1501,* c. 2r.

3 See Tomás A. Mantecón Movellán, "La Ciudad Santa y el martirio de los criminales: Justicia e identidad urbana en la Roma moderna," in *Civitas: Ciudades y ciudadanía en la Europa moderna,* ed. Roberto López Vela, Marina Torres Arce, and Susana Truchuelo García (Santander: Servicio de Publicaciones de la Universidad de Cantabria, 2013). My thanks to Tomás Mantecón for allowing me to read the essay in the proof stage.

4 *Note storiche [. . .] scritte da D. Fabi,* 1823, archive manuscript in ASGD, cred. F, b. 15. n. 6 A. See Vincenzo Paglia, *La morte confortata: Riti della paura e mentalità religiosa a Roma nell'età moderna* (Rome: Edizioni di Storia e Letteratura, 1982), 33–34.

5 See Sosio Pezzella's entry on Caterina Adorno for *DBI* 22 (1977): 343–345. See also Daniela Solfaroli Camillocci, *I devoti della Carità: Le confraternite del Divino Amore nell'Italia del primo Cinquecento* (Naples: La Città del Sole, 2002).

6 The idea that it was a revival of an earlier fifteenth-century confraternity was advanced by Father Francesco Saverio da Brusciano in "Maria Lorenza Longo e l'opera del divino amore a Napoli," *Collectanea Franciscana* 23, nos. 1–4 (1953): 166–228. See, by contrast, the clear reconstruction in Giovanni Romeo, *Aspettando il boia: Condannati a morte, confortatori e inquisitori nella Napoli della Controriforma* (Florence: Sansoni, 1993), 105–107. Romeo's whole book is a key reference work for this story.

7 The chapters are reproduced in the appendix of the brief and superficial historic profile of the confraternity written by Father Girolamo Mascia, *La Confraternita dei Bianchi della Giustizia a Napoli "S. Maria succurre miseris"* (Naples: Convento di S. Francesco al Vomero, 1972). They are also referred to by Antonio Illibato, *La Compagnia napoletana dei Bianchi della Giustizia: Note storico-critiche e inventario dell'archivio* (Naples: D'Auria, 2004).

8 Battistina Vernazza's recollections are in Alfredo Bianconi, *L'opera delle Compagnie del "Divino Amore" nella Riforma cattolica* (Città di Castello: Lapi, 1914), 66.

9 Antonella Orefice, *I giustiziati di Napoli dal 1556 al 1862, nella documentazione dei Bianchi della Giustizia* (Naples: M. D'Auria editore, 2015).

10 Antonino Cutrera, *Cronologia dei giustiziati di Palermo, 1541–1819* (Palermo: Scuola Tipografica Boccone del Povero, 1917), 6. The history of the Sicilian confraternity is given particular attention in the study by Maria Pia Di Bella, *Essai sur les supplices: L'état de victime* (Paris: Hermann, 2011).

11 The bull, dated January 20, 1540, is reproduced in *Arciconfraternita di San Giovanni Decollato detta della Misericordia della Nazione Fiorentina in Roma, 1488–1988* (Rome: Palombi, 1988), 131–133.

12 As Diego Quaglioni observes with regard to the pardon and forgiveness granted by the bishop of Trent, Johannes Hinderbach, in 1477, to the women of the Jewish community accused of co-responsibility in the presumed infanticide of the baby Simone ("Rituali della grazia a Trento nel 1477," in *Grazia e giustizia: Figure della clemenza fra tardo medioevo ed età contemporanea,* ed. Karl Härter and Cecilia Nubola [Bologna: il Mulino, 2011], 127–145, esp. 143).

13 Vincenzo Paglia, *"La pietà dei carcerati": Confraternite e società a Roma nei secoli XVI–XVII* (Rome: Edizioni di Storia e Letteratura, 1980).

14 Mirella Mombelli Castracane, *La Confraternita di S. Giovanni Battista de' Genovesi in Roma: Inventario dell'archivio* (Florence: Olschki, 1971), 46. The documents of the other two concessions were published in the appendix to the study by Alessandro Ademollo, *Le annotazioni di Mastro Titta carnefice romano: Supplizi e suppliziati; Giustizie eseguite da Gio. Batt. Bugatti e dal suo successore (1796–1870)* (Città di Castello: S. Lapi, 1886), 94–97.

15 *Psalmi et preces recitandae per confratres Archiconfraternitatis Misericordiae de Urbe, pro gratiarum actione Condemnati liberati dum e carceribus solutus ad Ecclesiam dictae Archiconfraternitatis processionaliter associantur,* undated, 8, ASGD (copy in C.b.31.4).

16 ASPe, *Confraternita dei ss. Andrea e Bernardino, detta della Giustizia, Libro delli giustitiati et oblati alla Croce della Fraternita della Giustitia di Perugia,* cc. 77r ff.

17 The bull is in the documentary appendix to Giorgio Angeletti, *L'Oratorio e la Confraternita di San Giovanni Decollato a Stroncone* (Arrone [Terni]: Edizioni Tyrus, 1994), 87–89.

18 The bull confirming the privilege bears the date August 8, 1742, while a subsequent declaration dated March 15, 1746, clarifies that the holder of the privilege was the whole Arciconfraternita della Morte. See *Privilegia a Benedicto XIV . . . ,* in AABo, *Archivio consorziale del clero urbano, Conforteria dei condannati,* IX B 3, n. 7. In ms n. 83, pezzo 4, of the Biblioteca Universitaria di Bologna there is an account of the liberation from death of Giuseppe Tassinari, in 1741. The first person to benefit from a pardon had been an infanticide in 1577 (see Alessandra Parisini, "Pratiche extragiudiziali di amministrazione della giustizia: La 'liberazione dalla morte' a Faenza tra '500 e '700," *Quaderni storici* 23, no. 67 [1988]: 147–168, esp. 150).

19 Ibid.

20 *Libro della Ven. Compagnia della Morte di Ravenna,* in ASRa, *Fondo Ospedale S. Maria delle Croci e altre opere pie,* primo deposito, vol. 54, cc. n. n.

21 Archivio dell'Arciconfraternita di San Giovanni Decollato, Rome, *Registro copialettere per la corrispondenza con le compagnie,* B.18.C, c. 51r.

22 Letter from the Compagnia del Crocifisso di Cingoli, July 16, 1568, ibid., cc. 54r–v. And from the Compagnia del Gesù di Parma, September 21, 1568, ibid., c. 55r.

23 Ibid., c. 52v (letter dated April 25, 1568).

24 Ibid., c. 73r–v (letter dated May 19, 1574).

25 Ibid., cc. 51v–52r (letter dated January 28, 1568).

26 Ibid., cc. 54v–55r.

27 Ibid., c. 50r (letter dated August 18, 1566).

28 For more about how micropolitics was a typical feature of the Papal State in this period, see Wolfgang Reinhard, *Paul V. Borghese (1605–1621): Mikropolitische Papstgeschichte* (Stuttgart: Anton Hiersemann, 2009).

29 "L'octroi de la rémission n'est pas le signe que les crimes remis sont banals . . . Au contraire, parce qu'ils sont graves, leur rémission est tributaire de la charge sacrée que détient le souverain, de sa fonction réligieuse et de la valeur du pardon qui lui sont reconnues" (Claude Gauvard, *"De grâce especial": Crime, État et Société en France à la fin du Moyen Age,* vol. 2 [Paris: Publications de la Sorbonne, 1991], 64).

30 Giovanni Nevizzano da Asti, *Sylva nuptialis* (Lyon, 1526), bk. 6, 43. See also Sebastiano Medici, *Tractatus mors omnia solvit* (Florence, 1573), 39 ("Si reus obviet cardinali").

31 ASDNa, *Archivio dei Bianchi della Giustizia,* f. 48, c. 38r.

32 See Alain Boureau, *La Religion de l'État: La construction de la République étatique dans le discours théologique de l'Occident médiéval (1250–1350)* (Paris: Les Belles Lettres, 2006).

33 See Chiara Traverso, *La Scuola di San Fantin o dei "Picai": Carità e giustizia a Venezia* (Venice: Marsilio, 2000), 75.

34 This is established in the *Capitoli per la liberatione del prigione* of 1601, held in the Archivio del Capitolo di Modena. See also Matteo Al Kalak and Marta Lucchi, *Oltre il patibolo: I fratelli della Morte di Modena tra giustizia e perdono* (Rome: Bulzoni, 2009), 72 and note.

35 Giovan Battista Spaccini, *Cronaca di Modena: Anni 1588–1602,* ed. Albano Biondi, Rolando Bussi, and Carlo Giovannini (Modena: Panini, 1993), 131 (see also Al Kalak and Lucchi, *Oltre il patibolo,* 128).

36 See Cutrera, *Cronologia dei giustiziati di Palermo,* 6.

37 Ibid., 35. A succinct but effective picture of the evolution of the administration of justice in Sicily is offered by Francesco Figlia, *Giustizia e società in Sicilia tra il Cinquecento e il Settecento: Il vescovato di Cefalú* (Palermo: Offset Studio, 2003), 1–19.

38 Cutrera, *Cronologia dei giustiziati di Palermo,* 32–34.

39 Johann Wolfgang von Goethe, *Italian Journey* [1817], trans. W. H. Auden and Elizabeth Mayer (Harmondsworth, UK: Penguin Books, 1970), 247. The name of the pardoned man is recorded in Cutrera, *Cronologia dei giustiziati di Palermo,* 43.

40 Goethe, *Italian Journey,* 246.

41 ASR, *Confraternita di S. Giovanni decollato (1497–1870),* busta 6, reg. 10, c. 1v.

42 Later increased to two: see Giacomo Brachet Contol, "La Confraternita di San Giovanni Battista Decollato o della Misericordia, cenni storici," in *Arte, pietà e morte nella Confraternita della Misericordia di Torino* (Turin: Arciconfraternita della Misericordia, 1978), 11–38. The regulations of the oratory and other material pertaining to the archconfraternity has been given in deposit to the Archivio di Stato di Torino for reordering. The archive also possesses a "Liber mortuorum" with a list, for 1701 to 1864, of condemned prisoners who received assistance, plus a further register, more schematic and in alphabetical order, of those executed between 1682 and 1852. A short reading of the crimes of which they were guilty can be found in Alberto Lupano, "'Non iscompagnar la giustizia dalla misericordia': Aspetti penalistici nei territori sabaudi e subalpine d'età moderna," in *La giustizia criminale nell'Italia moderna (XVI–XVIII sec.),* ed. Marco Cavina (Bologna: Patron, 2012), 91–127, esp. 114–116.

43 Contol, "La Confraternita," 13, who refers to Giuseppe Martini, *Storia delle confraternite italiane con special riguardo al Piemonte: Studio di storia del diritto ecclesiastico italiano* (Turin: Franchini, 1935).

44 Anna Paolino, "Istituzione e atti dei primi cento anni (1577–1678) della Confraternita della Misericordia di Chieri," *Bollettino storico-bibliografico subalpino* 79, no. 2 (1981): 623–644.

45 ASGD, busta C. a. 8, *Lettere memoriali e attestati delle compagnie aggregate,* cc. n. n.

17. REASONING ON DEATH ROW

1 From the *Libro dei giustiziati,* 1441 to 1577, published in Maria Serena Mazzi, *"Gente a cui si fa notte innanzi sera": Esecuzioni capitali e potere nella Ferrara estense* (Rome: Viella, 2003), 121–122.

2 Girolamo Ferrarini, *Istoria della città di Ferrara dal 1476 al 1489,* ms in Biblioteca Estense, Modena, ms alpha F 5 18, cc. 244r–v: noted by Bernardo Nobile, ed., *Il libro della vita beata attribuito a Cristoforo da Bologna* (Venice: Memorie dell'Istituto Veneto di Scienze, Lettere ed Arti, 1991), 16. For more about the religious policy of the Este rulers, see Gabriella Zarri, *Le sante vive* (Turin: Rosenberg and Sellier, 1990).

3 The second part of the work begins with a formal disassociation from some advice given in the first part: "When you enter the prison, you must use the words that are written at the beginning of this book. But I warn you" (see the edition by Alfredo Troiano, *Il Manuale quattrocentesco della Conforteria di Bologna,* in *Misericordie: Conversioni sotto il patibolo tra Medioevo ed età moderna,* ed. Adriano

Prosperi (Pisa: Edizioni della Normale, 2007), 367–479, esp. 438. A first edition based on the Ferrara manuscript version appears in Nobile, *Il libro della vita beata*. The English translations by Sheila Das of this and subsequent quotations from the *Bologna Comforters' Manual* can be found in Nicholas Terpstra, ed., *The Art of Executing Well: Rituals of Execution in Renaissance Italy* (Kirksville, MO: Truman University Press, 2008), 193–275, esp. 248.

4 Nobile, *Il libro della vita beata*. The attribution is accepted by Katherine Walsh in the entry for Cristoforo da Bologna in *DBI* 31 (1985): 77–80; Walsh does note, however, that none of his works can be found today "in any identifiable manuscript." There are writings by Cristoforo in the coeval inventory of the convent library of San Giacomo di Bologna (see Marie-Hyacinte Laurent, *Fabio Vigili et les bibliothèques de Bologne au début du XVIe siècle d'après le ms. Barb. Lat. 3185* [Vatican City: Biblioteca Apostolica Vaticana, 1943], 122–136).

5 This is the view of Mario Fanti, the most meticulous and authoritative scholar of the Bolognese *conforteria*. Nicholas Terpstra also believes the second book was written "by an anonymous lay comforter" ("Comforting by the Books: Editorial Notes on the Bologna 'Comforters' Manual," in Terpstra, *The Art of Executing Well*, 183–192).

6 Biblioteca Universitaria di Genova, ms G III 2. The writing added when the manuscripts of the confraternity, abolished in 1797, were assigned to the library, describes it as the "Book of 1432 used by the brothers of the Compagnia della Misericordia to assist those condemned to death. Formerly in a small secret oratory close to the Oratorio di Sant'Ambrogio negli Orti di Sant'Andrea, abolished in the year of the revolution in Genoa in 1797."

7 *Questa sie la forma e 'l modo . . . :* Troiano, *Il Manuale quattrocentesco,* 367; Das, *The Bologna Comforters' Manual,* 193.

8 A count of the manuscripts is provided by Troiano, *Il Manuale quattrocentesco,* 361. A *stemma codicum* and some observations about the linguistic style of the different versions can be found in Silvia Ferrari, *Due note sulla versione genovese del "Libro della vita beata,"* in Prosperi, *Misericordie,* 481–489, esp. 482.

9 Das, *The Bologna Comforters' Manual,* 193.

10 Ibid., 193–195.

11 Ibid., 201.

12 Ibid., 205–206.

13 Ibid., 204–206.

14 Ibid., 220–221.

15 Ibid., 229, 231.

16 See Frederic C. Tubach, *Index exemplorum: A Handbook of Medieval Religious Tales* (Helsinki: Suomalainen tiedeakatemia, 1969), 361–365, nos. 4777, 4783, 4787; and also 106, no. 1319, the miracle of the Virgin who saves a condemned man from death by burning. See also Friedrich Lotter, "Heiliger und Gehenkter," in *Ecclesia et*

regnum: Beiträge zur Geschichte von Kirche, Recht und Staat im Mittelalter; Fest-schrift für Franz-Josef Schmale zu seinem 65. Geburtstag (Munich: Winkler, 1989), 1–19.

17 Jacobus de Voragine, *The Golden Legend: Readings on the Saints* (Princeton, NJ: Princeton University Press, 1993), 203.

18 Das, *The Bologna Comforters' Manual,* 274.

19 Ibid., 266.

20 Ibid., 268.

21 Ibid., 271.

22 Ibid., 273–274.

23 *Decameron,* I,1. In the pictorial narration of the hanging of Antonio Rinaldeschi for sacrilege in Florence in 1506 (now in the Museo Stibbert, Florence), the battle for the soul is resolved by confession.

24 Carlo Ginzburg, "Folklore, magia, religione," in *Storia d'Italia,* vol. 1: *I caratteri originali* (Turin: Einaudi, 1972), 603–676, esp. 634–635. On pp. 635–636 are the original Italian passages from Francesco da Mozzanica and from the *Trattato devotissimo della misericordia de Dio* (Bologna, 1521).

25 *Trattato devotissimo,* c. 14r.

26 Ibid., c. 18r.

27 Ibid., cc. 23v–24r.

28 Ibid., c. 24v (numbering erroneous—actually it is 26v). There then follows a series of passages from the Old and New Testaments attesting to God's immense mercy, a repertoire that seems to have been intended as a handbook for comforting the dying.

29 See Henri Fouqueray, *Histoire de la Compagnie de Jésus en France des origines à la suppression (1528–1762),* vol. 2: *La Ligue et le bannissement (1575–1604)* (Paris: Librairie A. Picard et fils, 1913), 722–725.

30 Marzio Barbagli, *Congedarsi dal mondo: Il suicidio in Occidente e in Oriente* (Bologna: il Mulino, 2009), 87–90.

31 *Portugaliae Monumenta Misericordiarum,* vol. 3: *A Fundação das Misericórdias: O Reinado de D. Manuel I,* ed. Isabel dos Guimarães Sá and José Pedro Paiva (Lisbon: União das Misericórdias Portuguesas, 2004), 32–33 (the bull is dated September 3, 1496).

32 Confraternita dei Battuti, *Libro da Compagnie della Confraternita di Battudi nuouamente stampato et diligentemente corretto con molte additione a laude de Iddio et della gloriosa Virgine Maria et delli deuoti christiani: Con le sue figure alli suoi luoghi appropriate* (Venice, 1535), cc. 107r–11v. The citation is from the exemplar of the BCA, coll. 16.K.VI.19.

33 *Memorie a' fratelli della venerabile confraternita di S. Giovanni Decollato detta della Misericordia della nazione fiorentina per la solita funzione di aiutare a ben morire i condannati a morte fatte da Pompeo Serni fratello di detta compagnia,* BCAL, ms Corsiniano 285 (38 A 14), cc. 1r–2r. I wish to thank the director of the Biblioteca

Corsiniana, Marco Guardo, for his help in consulting the work and checking the citations. There are many other manuscript copies in Roman libraries: the ms 1375 and ms 3985 at the Casanatense, and the ms Vittorio Emanuele 579 at the Biblioteca Nazionale Vittorio Emanuele. Copies are held at the BAV, Vat. Lat. 8517, 13 596 and 13 558, Reg. Lat. 2084 (incomplete). The prestige of the Roman archconfraternity is also attested by the diffusion of manuscript copies of Serni's treatise. The Bologna *conforteria* had a manuscript copy entitled *Instruttione alli Confrati della Confraternita della morte per agiutare al ben morire li condannati: Opera pississima, utilissima, e di molto merito appresso il Sig.re Dio per chi bene l'essercita composta dal Sig. Pompeo Serni Fiorentino, e serve anco alli assistenti a qualunque moribondo* (AABo, *Archivio consorziale del clero urbano,* IX B 3). The historic archive of the Curia Arcivescovile di Ferrara holds in its confraternity collection a manuscript copy preceded by the following note: "This book belongs to the Comforters' School, donated by the most illustrious and excellent brother Sig. Marchese Luigi Bentivoglio, director of the School, on this day of March 18, 1691." The Biblioteca Corsiniana of the Accademia dei Lincei also houses another useful source for the history of the Roman company: the *Libro de' ricordi scritto da me Francesco q.m Girolamo Masini di Firenze con occasione che sono entrato a servire la venerabile compagnia di S. Giovanni Decollato detta della Misericordia di Roma* (ms 2576). An edition of Pompeo Serni's work is being prepared by Mons. Vincenzo Paglia for Edizioni di Storia e Letteratura. My thanks to the editor and publisher for permission to consult the transcription of the manuscript.

34   Giovanni Botero, *La ragion di stato,* ed. Chiara Continisio (Rome: Donzelli, 1997), 76.

35   Carlo Antonio Macchiavelli, *Catalogo delli autori, e delle materie spettanti alla Conforteria* (Bologna, 1729). The collection is now almost entirely housed at the Biblioteca Arcivescovile di Bologna.

36   The important work undertaken by the archpriest for the confraternity in Ferrara is not mentioned in the entry written by Raffaele Amaturo for *DBI* 7 (1970): 6–9.

37   Macchiavelli, *Catalogo delli autori,* 4.

38   Ser Giovanni Maffani, *Operetta la qual contiene l'ordine et il modo hanno a tenere quelli de la Compagnia della giustitia di Perugia quando haveranno a confortare li condannati alla morte* (Perugia, 1545) (Sander 4084; cited from here by Anne Jakobson Schutte, *Printed Italian Vernacular Religious Books, 1465–1550: A Finding List* [Geneva: Droz, 1983], 253). There are no known exemplars of the work in public collections, already described as being "of some rarity in the nineteenth century" (Giovanni Battista Vermiglioli, *Nuova riforma delle costituzioni della venerabile Compagnia dei SS. Andrea e Bernardino in Perugia detta della giustizia con la storia del medesimo pio istituto* [Perugia: Bartelli, 1846], 32), and later as "unfindable" (Olga Marcacci Marinelli, *Confraternite di Perugia,* no. 684 of the bibliography). A copy was sold by Sotheby's in Milan in 2004.

39 [Fra Zanobi de' Medici], *Trattato utilissimo in conforto de' condennati a morte per via di giustizia*, with *Alcune ragioni da confortare coloro, che per la giustizia pubblica si trovano condannati alla morte* (Rome, 1565); a copy of a reprint (Ancona, 1572) is in the Biblioteca Arcivescovile di Bologna.

40 *Considerationi, et avertimenti spirituali de M. Tullio Chrispoldo d'Ariete, sopra la Passione di nostro Signore Giesu Christo non piú vedute* (Modena, 1559), 105 (the copy held by the Biblioteca Casanatense bears a note indicating that it belonged to the Jesuit Diego de Guzman, of the Casa Professa [mother house] of Rome).

41 The first edition came out in Macerata in 1575. Roger Chartier, in "Les arts de bien mourir, 1450–1600," *Annales ESC* 31 (1976): 63, has counted no fewer than eighteeen editions between 1577 and 1650.

42 Juan Alfonso de Polanco, *Polanci Complementa, Epistolae et commentaria,* vol. 2 (Madrid: G. Lopez del Horno, 1917), 752 (*MHSI*, vol. 54).

43 ARSI, Rom. 129 b. I, c. 246*v*. See also Adriano Prosperi, *Tribunali della coscienza: Inquisitori, confessori, missionari,* new ed. (Turin: Einaudi, 2007), 663–664.

44 *Il primo libro di lettere dedicatorie di diversi* (Bergamo, per Comino Ventura, 1601). The son of Giovanni Giacomo Tasso, Bernardo's second cousin, Ercole, corresponded with Torquato Tasso. See Armando Maggi, "Una figura poco conosciuta del tardo Rinascimento: Ercole Tasso e i suoi due canzonieri," *Esperienze letterarie* 31, no. 2 (2006): 3–38; and see also Dennis E. Rhodes, "Le opere di Ercole Tasso: Studio bibliografico," in *Studi sul Rinascimento italiano in memoria di G. Aquilecchia,* ed. Angelo Romano and Paolo Procaccioli (Manziana: Vecchiarelli, 2005), 271–280.

45 Ercole Tasso, *Il confortatore* (Bergamo, 1595).

46 This has been described as "the poetics of conversion" by Francesco Ferretti, *Le Muse del Calvario: Angelo Grillo e la poesia dei benedettini cassinesi* (Bologna: il Mulino, 2012), 256.

47 Tasso, *Il confortatore,* 107.

48 Ibid., reasoning 14: "Of those who trust too much in their own works, or too much in divine grace," 109–112.

49 Ibid., 135ff.

50 Ibid., 141–143.

51 Domenico Caparozzi, *Compendio per conforto de' rei condennati alla morte con un utile discorso spirituale per quelli, che si affaticano in questa santa opera, raccolta dal Rev. D. Domenico Caparozzi chierico viterbese et fratello della Ven. Confraternita di S. Gio. Battista Decollato* (Viterbo, 1613). On pp. 3–4 is a dedication by the author to the brothers of Viterbo, dated April 24, 1613.

52 Ibid., 15–16.

53 Ibid., 10–11.

54 For more on the complex position taken by the renowned doctor Navarro, see Vincenzo Lavenia, "Eretici sentenziati e 'reincorporati,'" in Prosperi, *Misericordie,* 170–174.

55 Caparozzi, *Compendio*, 10.

56 Ibid., 56.

57 Ibid., 55–56.

58 Ibid., 57.

59 Ibid., 91.

60 Ibid., 92.

61 Ibid., 94.

62 [Francesco Isella], *Istruttione per consolar i poveri afflitti condannati a morte: Con una breve regola spirituale per quelli, che si essercitano in così S[anta] opera* (Bergamo, 1586).

63 Ibid., 9.

64 Ibid., 25.

65 See Massimo Ferretti, "Pitture per condannati a morte del Trecento bolognese," in Prosperi, *Misericordie*, 85–151.

66 Isella, *Istruttione*, 89–90.

67 Ibid., 79.

68 Ibid., 33.

69 Ibid., 22.

70 Giovanni Andrea di Mayo, dedicatory epistle to the noblewoman Eleonora Sanseverino, dated Naples, March 11, 1576, in Bartolomeo D'Angelo, *Ricordo di ben morire, et della consolatione de' penitenti, con il modo di raccommandar l'anima a gli infermi, o condannati a morte* (Venice, 1576), cc. a 4v, a 6r.

71 D'Angelo, *Ricordo di ben morire*, 2.

72 Ibid., 319ff.

73 Diego de Córdoba y Salinas, *Aiuto de' moribondi e condannati a morte dalla Giustizia* (Naples, 1648). Some chapters are in Guido Panico, *Il carnefice e la piazza: Crudeltà di Stato e violenza popolare a Napoli in età moderna* (Naples: Edizioni scientifiche italiane, 1985), 167–169.

74 D'Angelo, *Ricordo di ben morire*, 333.

75 See Pierroberto Scaramella, *Le Madonne del Purgatorio: Iconografia e religione in Campania tra Rinascimento e Controriforma* (Genoa: Marietti, 1991).

76 D'Angelo, *Ricordo di ben morire*, 346.

77 Ibid., 351.

78 *Guida spirituale de gli afflitti condannati a morte: Dove si trattano tutti gli aiuti necessarii per la salute di un'anima, di chi è vicino a morire, composta per il M. R. P. Gio. Pietro Castello sacerdote della Compagnia di Giesú ristampata ad instanza del Signor Don Tomaso Marquet, governatore della Compagnia di S. Maria della Pietà, sotto vocabulo dell'Azori, in Messina* (Messina, 1628), 163–168.

79 Ibid., 22.

80 Ibid., 45.

81 Ibid., 55.

82 Ibid., 86–87.

83 Ibid., 104–105.

84 Ibid., 108.

85 Ibid., 201.

86 Ibid., 222–223.

87 Ibid., 240–244.

88 Girolamo Gattico, *Sicuro viaggio de giustitiandi, e di qualunque altro moriente per felicemente passare da questa all'altra vita di sicuro, e di certo in gratia di Dio* (Milan, 1630).

89 Ibid., 152–177.

90 BNCFi, ms Nazionale 138, c. 220r–v.

91 The text of a declaration of this kind, taken from an ancient commentary on the Laws, can be found in Isaac Bashevis Singer, *The Family Moskat* [1950], trans. A. H. Cross (New York: Farrar, Straus and Giroux, 2007).

92 Gattico, *Sicuro viaggio,* 258.

93 Ibid., 97.

94 Marcello Mansi, *Documenti per confortare i condannati a morte [. . .] Opera utilissima ancora per tutte le persone tribolate* (Turin, 1690).

95 Ibid., 39.

96 Ibid., 378–382.

97 Ibid., 269–271.

98 Carlo Verri, *Ricordi per essercitar il caritativo officio d'aiutar a christianamente morire quei meschini che sono dalla giustitia condannati a morte, con l'aggiunta di alcuni dubbii spettanti allo stato, e salvezza di detti Giustitiati dopo la loro morte* (Milan, 1672).

99 Ibid., 10–20.

100 Ibid., 21.

101 *Istruzzioni varie concernenti la maniera di assistere a'condannati alla morte per mano della Giustitia, raccolte da persona affettionata alla Vene. Compagnia della Misericordia di Torino, e dalla medesima dedicate a S. Gio. Battista Decollato* (Turin, 1692), 80.

102 Ibid., 61.

103 Ibid., 76.

104 Ibid., 43.

105 Baldassare di Bernardino di Bologna, *Conforto de' giustiziandi per quei tre dí che stanno nella Cappella de' Bianchi di Palermo, . . . e da lui stesso riformato e ampliato* (Palermo, 1610; copy in the Biblioteca Casanatense). The author's dedication to the governor and to the counsellors and brothers of the Compagnia dei Bianchi is dated Palermo, August 6, 1583.

106 Ibid., 4–5.

107 Ibid., 10.

108 Ibid., 181–182.

109 *Capitoli della Venerabile ducale arciconfraternita di S. Giovanni Battista detta della Morte* (Modena, 1782), 11–12. The solemn and much larger manuscript version of 1718 bore a similar expression: "Secrecy in interests is their only soul" (*Capitoli della Confraternita di S. Gio. Batta detta già Hospitale di Morte . . .*, ACMo, *Fondo Arciconfraternita di San Giovanni Battista della Morte*).

110 "Confessors and comforters should not take pains to find out about the offender when seeing him" (Giacinto Manara della Compagnia di Gesú, *Notti malinconiche nelle quali con occasione di assister a' condannati a morte, si propongono varie difficoltà spettanti a simile materia* [Bologna, 1658], 13).

111 Pompeo Serni, *Memorie a' fratelli della venerabile confraternita di S. Giovanni Decollato* (BCAL, ms Corsiniano 285, 38 A 14, c. 22r).

112 Ibid., c. 23v.

113 Ibid., c. 22r.

18. A CHARITY OF NOBLES AND THE POWERFUL

1 An overall picture of the developments that took place in the Middle Ages can be found in Anna Esposito, "Donne e confraternite," in *Studi confraternali. Orientamenti, problemi, testimonianze,* ed. Marina Gazzini (Florence: Firenze University Press, 2009), 53–78; for the following age, see Nicholas Terpstra, *Cultures of Charity: Women, Politics, and the Reform of Poor Relief in Renaissance Italy* (Cambridge, MA: Harvard University Press, 2013).

2 Nicholas Terpstra, who for many years has been an attentive scholar of the Bologna *conforteria,* analyzes the social composition of its "cohorts" in "Theory into Practice: Executions, Comforting, and Comforters in Renaissance Italy," in *The Art of Executing Well: Rituals of Execution in Renaissance Italy,* ed. Nicholas Terpstra (Kirksville, MO: Truman State University Press, 2008), 118–158.

3 In 1752, Count Baldassarre Carrati selected from the register of condemned a list of the *Giustiziati nobili bolognesi e nobili forestieri, sacerdoti e persone ragguardevoli* (BCA, ms B 790).

4 *Codice di leggi, e costituzioni per gli Stati di Sua Altezza Serenissima,* vol. 1 (Modena: Società Tipografica, 1771), bk. 4, heading 18.

5 *Direttorio ad uso della Conforteria di Ferrara,* 2nd ed. (Ferrara, 1757), 5–8.

6 See Chiara Traverso, *La Scuola di San Fantin o dei "Picai": Carità e giustizia a Venezia* (Venice: Marsilio, 2000), 64 and note.

7 See Mario Bendiscioli, "L'età della Riforma cattolica," in *Storia di Milano,* vol. 10: *L'età della Riforma cattolica* (Milan: Fondazione Treccani degli Alfieri, 1957), 400–401.

8 Marco Gambarucci, *Ricordi et avvertimenti per i sacrestani della compagnia della Misericordia della nazione fiorentina in Roma in occasione di giustizie, e liberazione de' prigioni,* BCAL, ms 285, cc. 126r–127v. I have not seen the illustrated copy held in the Vienna Hauptstadtarchiv, *Handschriften* no. 1082.

9   See Nicholas Terpstra, *Lay Confraternities and Civic Religion in Renaissance Bo-logna* (Cambridge: Cambridge University Press, 1995), 214–216.

10 *Capitoli per la conforteria concessi da' Serenissimi Dominanti ampliati, e confirmati dal serenissimo Sig. Duca Rinaldo Primo,* original copy recorded and signed by Borso Santagata on December 31, 1718 (ACMo, *Fondo Arciconfraternita di San Giovanni Battista della Morte*).

11 Ibid., 28–31. The exemplar in ACMo, together with a number of manuscript notes, also has a list updated to 1875, including many other names of nobles and churchmen.

12 For more about this, see the important study by Giovanni Romeo, *Aspettando il boia: Condannati a morte, confortatori e inquisitori nella Napoli della Controriforma* (Florence: Sansoni, 1993), chap. 5, "Per la storia dei Bianchi della Giustizia," 105ff., esp. 108–110.

13 The quotations are from Adriano Ceruti, "La chiesa di S. Giovanni alle Case rotte in Milano," *Archivio storico lombardo* 1, no. 1 (1874): 165.

14 Ibid., 169. The privilege of naming two condemned prisoners to pardon was granted by Charles II in 1675.

15 Carlo Verri, *Ricordi per essercitar il caritativo officio d'aiutar a christianamente morire quei meschini che sono dalla giustitia condannati a morte, con l'aggiunta di alcuni dubbii spettanti allo stato, e salvezza di detti Giustitiati dopo la loro morte* (Milan, 1672).

16 Ibid., 7.

17 See also the reproduction of some of these prints, from the private collection of Giancarlo Beltrame, in the appendix to Italo Mereu, *La pena di morte a Milano nel secolo di Beccaria* (Vicenza: Neri Pozza, 1988). Other eighteenth-century prints of the same kind are held in the Biblioteca Ambrosiana di Milano, ms L.128.sup., cc. 43*r*–46*r*.

18 Terpstra, "Theory into Practice."

19 ASDFe, *Fondo Arciconfraternita della Morte e Orazione di Ferrara,* busta 87, fasc. 27, cc. n. n.

20 Giacomo Brachet Contol, "La Confraternita di San Giovanni Battista Decollato o della Misericordia, cenni storici," in *Arte, pietà e morte nella Confraternita della Misericordia di Torino* (Turin: Arciconfraternita della Misericordia, 1978), 24.

21 Antonino Cutrera, *Cronologia dei giustiziati di Palermo 1541–1819* (Palermo: Scuola Tipografica Boccone del Povero, 1917), 18–19.

22 Ibid., 21–22.

23 See Simonetta Adorni Braccesi, *"Una città infetta": La repubblica di Lucca nella crisi religiosa del Cinquecento* (Florence: Olschki, 1994), 145–161.

24 This did not just regard the Protestant Reformation: see Edward Muir, *Ritual in Early Modern Europe* (Cambridge: Cambridge University Press, 1997), 176–179.

25 "Debet enim intelligi hoc dictum quoad forum paenitentiale et animae, videlicet quod non sint eis deneganda ecclesiastica sacramenta, si illa humiliter petant, non autem quod eorum vitae parcatur" (BAV, Vat. Lat. 5468, fols. 7*r*–10*v*).

26 "Bene vivat, qui bene mori desiderat" (Roberto Bellarmino, *De arte bene moriendi* [Antwerp, 1623], 2).

27 Ibid., 100.

28 This is shown by the episode that occurred in Venice in 1584, when an Augustinian friar was interrogated by the inquisitor for having denied that there was any hope of salvation for condemned prisoners. See my "Morire volentieri: Condannati a morte e sacramenti," in *Misericordie: Conversioni sotto il patibolo tra Medioevo ed età moderna,* ed. Adriano Prosperi (Pisa: Edizioni della Normale, 2007), 3–54, esp. 12–14.

29 *Monumenta infelicitatis sive mortes peccatorum pessimae ex variis probatisque auctoribus,* vol. 2 (Rome, 1664), 296–300.

30 No adequate bibliography exists for the richness of this literary genre, which spread throughout Europe in different forms in the Early Modern Age. A dossier of Italian texts is indicated in Giancarlo Baronti, "Serpi in seno: Figure e fantasmi di donne criminali nella letteratura di piazza," in *Il delitto narrato al popolo: Immagini di giustizia e stereotipi di criminalità in età moderna,* ed. Roberto De Romanis and Rosamaria Loretelli (Palermo: Sellerio, 1999), 199–218. The study by Willi Hirdt, *Italienischer Bänkelsang* (Frankfurt: Klostermann, 1979), deals with late nineteenth-century Italy.

31 Giovanni Briccio, *La sciagurata vita di Arrigo Gabertinga assassino di strada, il quale ha ammazzato un infinito numero di persone, con i suoi figliuoli, nel territorio di Trento, posta in ottava rima da Giovanni Briccio romano ad essempio dei tristi* (Milan, Genoa, Pisa, Florence, Todi, 1625) (the quote is from the copy in the Biblioteca Universitaria di Bologna).

32 *Il lacrimoso lamento che fece la signora Prudenza, anconitana, avanti, che fosse condota alla giusticia per havere avelenato il marito* (Bologna, 1636).

33 *Esempio miracoloso di un figliuolo ingrato al padre et alla madre: Opera utilissima, et degna d'esser intesa da i padri di fameglia, e da i figliuoli, et da ogn'uno* (Lyon, 1587; reprinted in Ferrara in the same year).

34 *Vita e morte di Bastiano, detto Mascella boia in Bologna, il quale è stato impiccato per diversi furti da lui commessi, di A. E. I. O. U.* (Bologna, 1619). The executioner was hung on April 13, 1619, "after having confessed and communicated," and having given instructions regarding his possessions, which he left to the "Mothers of the Corpus Domini of Bologna," though he asked them to do a charitable deed for a "Giulia fantina" (a daughter?) (BABo, ms B 4423, cc. n. n.: Mascella, who was illiterate, signed with a cross).

35 *Il lamento et morte di Benedetto Mangone capo di banditi nel Regno di Napoli con li crudelissimi assassinamenti, che lui faceva in Campagnia . . .* (Florence, 1605). The text did not escape the attention of Benedetto Croce, who mentioned a print in *Curiosità storiche* (Naples: Ricciardi, 1921), 127, and in "Aneddoti di storia civile e letteraria," *La Critica* 38 (1940): 184–185.

36 "Gl'angelici confratri stanno accorti | la passion gli stanno a ricordare, | dicendo non temer tormento, et morte, | che hoggi beato ti potrai chiamare, | pensa a gl'errori tuoi tenaci e forti | e quanti in precipizio ne fai stare, | rimira questo Dio nell'aspro legno | volse morir per darci il santo regno" (The angelic brothers are attentive, evoking the Passion and saying not to fear torments and death, as today you can call yourself blessed. Reflect on your persistent and powerful errors, and how many you have cast into the precipice. Look once again at this God in the harsh wood, who was willing to die to give us the holy kingdom) *(Il lamento et morte di Benedetto Mangone).*

37 Giovan Battista Del Tufo, *Ritratto o modello delle grandezze, delitie e meraviglie della nobilissima città di Napoli,* ed. Calogero Tagliareni (Naples: Agar, 1959); the passage about the work of the Whites is cited in Guido Panico, *Il carnefice e la piazza: Crudeltà di Stato e violenza popolare a Napoli in età moderna* (Naples: Edizioni scientifiche italiane, 1985), 15–16.

38 *Nuovo aviso venuto di Milano, dove s'intende la morte di un gentil'huomo principalissimo, il quale è stato giustitiato per haver commesso 120 homicidii, sotterrato un prete vivo, squartato un puttino, et altre cose inaudite . . . , tutte cose verissime, e di gran stupore* (Bologna, 1609). This text and the others mentioned above are drawn from the exemplars housed in the Biblioteca Universitaria di Bologna, which has a rich collection.

39 *Nuova, e vera relazione della grande giustizia seguita li 12 settembre 1745 nella città di Livorno dove s'intende la morte di tre persone, cioè Francesco Chiari fiorentino, Marc'Antonio Giuriani livornese tutti due impiccati, e Giacomo Lenzi fiorentino impiccato e squartato per aver commesse gran crudeltà barbaricamente, et intenderete tutti i loro crudelissimi misfatti, e quel che dissero quand'erano al patibolo* (Venice and Bologna, 1745). The booklet was part of a collection of texts of the same kind conserved in the collection of the *Conforteria* in the Biblioteca Arcivescovile di Bologna.

40 *Relazione della scelerata morte di Angiolo Secchiarolo detto Bigaratta da Ripe stato d'Urbino, condannato a morire nella forca li 11 del mese di giugno 1729 nella città d'Ancona* (Bologna, 1729), Biblioteca Arcivescovile di Bologna.

41 Michel Foucault, "Lives of Infamous Men," trans. Robert Hurley and others, in *Foucault: Essential Works of Foucault,* vol. 3 (London: Allen Lane / Penguin Press, 2001), 157–175, esp. 157.

19. THE VOICES OF THE CONDEMNED

1 If "on the day of judgment it was known that the person now was then blessed, the devils would laugh" (Giacinto Manara della Compagnia di Gesú, *Notti malinconiche nelle quali con occasione di assister a' condannati a morte, si propongono varie difficoltà spettanti a simile materia* [Bologna, 1658], 455).

2 *Libro di memorie dei giustiziati, 1461–1580,* BCSi, ms 381 (A.IX.46), c. 72r.

3   See Chapter 17.

4   Giuseppe Rondoni, "I 'giustiziati' a Firenze (dal secolo XV al secolo XVIII)," *Archivio storico italiano,* ser. 5, 28 (1901): 212–213.

5   BCA, *Libro di tutti li giustiziati in Bologna incominciando l'anno 1030 per sino al 1834 con i nomi e cognomi de' medemi,* libro primo, ms B 3159, 41.

6   See Maria Serena Mazzi, *"Gente a cui si fa notte innanzi sera": Esecuzioni e potere nella Ferrara estense* (Rome: Viella, 2003), 99.

7   BAMi, ms L.128.sup., c. 2v. If the body of the murder victim bled in a person's presence, it was considered proof of the latter's guilt.

8   This count was made by Matteo Benvenuti, "Come facevasi giustizia nello Stato di Milano dall'anno 1471 al 1763," *Archivio storico lombardo* 9 (1882): 148–185. On the basis of new research among the papers of the state archives in Milan, it has been calculated that the number of executions carried out between 1535 and 1706 is 1,767 (Giovanni Liva, "Aspetti dell'applicazione della pena di morte a Milano in epoca spagnola," *Archivio storico lombardo,* ser. 11, 6 [1989]: 162, 185). See also Stefano D'Amico, *Spanish Milan: A City within the Empire, 1535–1706* (New York: Palgrave Macmillan, 2012).

9   Benvenuti, "Come facevasi giustizia," 455–456, was still capable of commenting that one should not deny "the good faith of those judges," implicitly polemicizing with *La colonna infame* (The Infamous Column), Alessandro Manzoni's great work. It should be noted that the confraternity's list mentions the execution of an Antonio da Previso, hung on May 17, 1560, "for having greased door bars to spread the plague around Milan."

10 ASR, *Confraternita di S. Giovanni decollato (1497–1870),* busta 6, registro 10, *Giornale.*

11 Ibid., busta 6, registro 11, *Libro grande del Proveditore,* cc. 91v–92r. On Paleologo, see the excellent entry by Lech Szczucki for the *Dizionario storico dell'Inquisizione,* vol. 3 (Pisa: Edizioni della Normale, 2011), 1159–1161.

12 ASR, *Confraternita di S. Giovanni decollato,* busta 6, registro 11, c. 91v.

13 Ibid., busta 16, fasc. 33, *Testamenti de' giustiziati,* cc. 3r–v.

14 Ibid., busta 35, 131.

15 The long story is in Pietro Giacomo Bacci, *Vita di san Filippo Neri fiorentino* (Rome, 1678), 35–36.

16 ASR, *Confraternita di S. Giovanni decollato,* busta 6, registro 11, cc. 91v–92r.

17 Traiano Boccalini, *Comentarii di Traiano Boccalini romano sopra Cornelio Tacito, come sono stati lasciati dall'autore: Opera ancora non stampata & grandemente desiderata da tutti li virtuosi* (Geneva, 1677), 202. Still useful with regard to this episode is the old work by Giovanni Gozzadini, *Giovanni Pepoli e Sisto V. Un racconto storico* (Bologna: Zanichelli, 1879).

18 The names recorded in BABo, *Fondo Ospedali,* ms 65 (41.1), cc. 19r–20v, are those of Bernardino Brescaglia (Brascaglia) da Modena, Baldiserra veneziano (also called Baldassarre "bambinaro"), Martino Forni, and Silvio Lanzoni, burned alive because

they were "very obdurate Lutherans"; Pellegrino Righetti and Pietr'Antonio da Cervia, painter, Alessandro Panzacchi and Giorgio da Udine, Pietro Arrigoni and Sante Cingaro, hung. See Guido Dall'Olio, *Eretici e inquisitori nella Bologna del Cinquecento* (Bologna: Istituto per la storia di Bologna, 1999), 311 and passim.

19 Lionello Puppi, *Un trono di fuoco: Arte e martirio di un pittore eretico del Cinquecento* (Rome: Donzelli, 1995).

20 ASR, *Confraternita di S. Giovanni decollato,* busta 16, *Testamenti de iustitiati,* 160–161. On Paleario, the subject of an old diatribe between Catholics and members of the Reformed Churches, there is the study by the Waldensian historian Salvatore Caponetto, *Aonio Paleario (1503–1570) e la Riforma protestante in Toscana* (Turin: Claudiana, 1979), which was then followed by the massive and exhaustive work of Mons. Ernesto Gallina, *Aonio Paleario,* 3 vols., ed. Luigi Gulia (Sora: Centro di studi sorani, 1989).

21 See Caponetto, *Aonio Paleario,* 163. Mons. Gallina talks of the "sophisticated play" of the humanist, who ended up displaying an "ultimate two-facedness" (Gallina, *Aonio Paleario,* vol. 1, 737).

22 ASR, *Confraternita di S. Giovanni decollato,* registro 7, c. 134*v*. For another annotation, see ibid., busta 16, *Testamenti de iustitiati,* 124.

23 Letter of February 23, 1567 (ASMo, *Inquisizione,* s. Lettere, b. I, fasc. VIII).

24 ASR, *Confraternita di S. Giovanni decollato,* busta 8, registro 16, c. 68*v*. This and other cases were collected together and listed in Domenico Orano, *Liberi pensatori bruciati in Roma dal XVI al XVIII secolo: Da documenti inediti dell'Archivio di stato in Roma* (Rome: Tip. dell'unione cooperativa editrice, 1904). The list was corrected and added to following new research by Luigi Firpo, see Firpo, "Esecuzioni capitali in Roma (1567–1671)," in *Eresia e Riforma nell'Italia del Cinquecento, miscellanea I* (Florence: Sansoni; Chicago: Newberry Library, 1974), 307–342.

25 ASR, *Confraternita di S. Giovanni decollato,* busta 8, registro 16, c. 87*r*. See also Luigi Firpo, *Il processo di Giordano Bruno,* ed. Diego Quaglioni (Rome: Salerno, 1993), 347–348.

26 Firpo, "Esecuzioni capitali," 319.

27 From the diary of Abbot Placido Eustachio Ghezzi, which appeared in Alessandro Ademollo, "Le Giustizie a Roma dal 1674 al 1739 e dal 1796 al 1840," *Archivio della Società Romana di Storia Patria* 4 (1881): 429–534, esp. 449–450 and 517–518; 5 (1882): 305–364.

28 The anonymous report, included in the journal of memories of the Citone family (see Simona Foa and Abramo Alberto Piattelli, *Le Croniche della famiglia Citone* [Rome: Edizioni di Storia e Letteratura, 1988], 293ff.) has been published separately (Anonymous Friar, *La "giustizia" degli ebrei* [Rome: Carocci, 1987]) and inspired Paolo Benvenuti's film *Il confortorio.*

29 Marco Gambarucci, *Ricordi et avvertimenti per i sacrestani della compagnia della Misericordia della nazione fiorentina in Roma in occasione di giustizie, e liberazione de' prigioni,* BCAL, ms 285, cc. 124*v*–125*v*.

30   ASR, *Confraternita di S. Giovanni decollato,* busta 8, registro 16, c. 66*v.* Stendhal
     is known to have worked on the Roman chronicles of this and other cases (see the
     preface by Dominique Fernandez to Stendhal, *Chroniques italiennes* [Paris: Gal-
     limard, 1973]). The entry on Beatrice Cenci in *DBI* 23 (1979): 512–525, is by Luigi
     Caiani.

31   Giuseppe Civitale, *Historie di Lucca,* ed. Mario F. Leonardi (Rome: Istituto storico
     italiano per l'eta moderna e contemporanea, 1988), 555.

32   See Frank Lestringant, *Lumière des martyrs: Essai sur le martyre au siècle des
     Réformes* (Paris: Honoré Champion, 2004).

33   Niccolò Machiavelli, *The Discourses,* ed. Bernard Crick (Harmondsworth, UK:
     Penguin, 1970), II, 2.

34   ASCMo, *Vachetta per li iustitiati 1593–1826,* reg. e mem. diversi, Lucchi II 8, cc.
     n. n.

35   Giovanna Fiume, *La vecchia dell'aceto: Un processo per veneficio nella Palermo di fine
     Settecento* (Palermo: Gelka, 1990), 180.

36   BCSi, ms 381 (A.IX.46), cc. 71*r–v.*

37   Gambarucci, *Ricordi et avvertimenti,* c. 123*v.*

38   BABo, ms *Fondo Ospedali* 68 (43), c. 8*r.*

39   The executions of Caterina Trochi from Carmignano and Caterina Mutti from Se-
     ravezza took place, respectively, on July 1 and July 14 (see BNCFi, ms II. I. 138,
     *Nome cognome e tempo di quelli che hanno finito la loro vita con morte violenta, e
     sentenziata dalla Santa Giustizia,* n. 1907ff.). Cosimo III's memorandum is dated
     July 25 (see Adriano Prosperi, *Dare l'anima: Storia di un infanticidio* [Turin:
     Einaudi, 2005], 62 n.).

40   Gambarucci, *Ricordi et avvertimenti,* cc. 123*r–v.*

41   Ibid., c. 122*v.*

42   *Successo della morte di Livia e Madalena da Linara giustiziate in Ravenna sotto li
     29 novembre 1608 sabato, vigilia di Santo Andrea Apostolo, e giorno di Santo Saturnino
     martire, descritta da Bernardino Sacchi Confratello della Venerabile Compagnia della
     Morte d'essa città di Ravenna, e già confessore della Compagnia della Misericordia di
     Roma* (Biblioteca Comunale di Forlì, *Collezioni Piancastelli,* ms V / 60, autograph);
     see also Elide Casali, "Religione e 'Instruzione' cristiana," in *Storia di Ravenna,*
     vol. 4 (Venice: Marsilio, 1994), 417–460, esp. 450–451. In the Libro della Ven.
     Compagnia della Morte di Ravenna, conserved in ASRa, *Fondo Ospedale S. Maria
     delle Croci e altre opere pie,* primo deposito, vol. 54, the record of cases of those sen-
     tenced to execution begins from January 31, 1609. My thanks to Dante Bolognesi
     for his help and useful indications.

43   *Successo della morte di Livia e Madalena,* 33.

44   Ibid., 38.

45   Ibid., 60.

46   The child had not, therefore, been killed by his mother: ibid., 61–62.

47 According to Don Bernardino, it was the first time in which "in that place, and for that occasion, the condemned were deemed worthy of that gift and blessing (ibid., 63), which appears to be at odds with what we know about the granting of Communion to the condemned.

48 Ibid., 66–67.

49 Ibid., 68.

50 Ibid., 73.

51 Ibid., 78.

52 Ibid., 79.

53 See Benedetto Croce, *Canti politici del popolo napoletano* (Naples: G. M. Priore, 1892), 45.

54 The executioner's real name was probably Tommaso Paradiso. "Master Donato" was a name commonly used to denote an executioner.

55 ASR, *Confraternita di S. Giovanni decollato,* registro 35, 135–138. His was the last of the "personal files" produced by the confraternity (ibid., busta 18, fasc. n. 154).

56 Ibid., busta 16, *Testamenti,* 96.

57 Ibid., busta 35, *Testamenti,* 88.

58 "Raising my hands to the sky I thank the eternal Majesty of Jesus Christ our lord for everything that He wishes and desires, in the knowledge that his divine majesty does not wish or permit any thing if not with the highest and most infinite providence. I have therefore expressed contrition and confessed, and entrust myself in every way and for everything to his most holy arms" (ibid., busta 16, 6–9).

59 ASR, *Confraternita di S. Giovanni decollato,* busta 16, *Testamenti,* fasc. 33, cc. 160*v*–163*r*. For the modern ramifications of the Protestant and Catholic traditions, see note 20 above.

60 Aonio Paleario's text appears with some small differences in Caponetto, *Aonio Paleario,* 162–163.

61 Luigi Martini, *Il confortatorio di Mantova negli anni 1851, 52, 53 e 55* (Mantua: Benvenuti, 1867).

62 AABo, *Scuola dei confortatori,* 7, fasc. 114, cc. 55*v*–57*v*.

63 Giovanni [Juan de] Polanco, *Avvertimenti per confortare et aiutare coloro che son condannati a morte per giustizia* (Macerata, 1576), c. 10*v* (emphasis added).

64 ASDFe, *Fondo Arciconfraternita Morte e Orazione di Ferrara,* busta 87, fasc. 2, 1–5. My thanks to the archivist Don Enrico Peverada for his generous and invaluable assistance.

65 Ibid., 6–8.

66 Ibid., fasc. 2, 9.

67 Ibid., fasc. 3, cc. 3*r*–4*r*.

68 Ibid., busta 87, registro n. 27, 110–115.

69 Ibid., 107–108.

70 BABo, *Libro di confortaria . . . principiato l'anno 1597,* ms B 4423, cc. n. n.

71 The "*escolpazioni* and wishes" of the condemned are annotated in the *Libro della venerabile Compagnia della Morte di Ravenna nel quale saranno notati tutti quelli, che per via di giustizia dovranno morire, e parimente le scolpationi, e volontà loro per la salute dell'anime,* 1609–1673, held in ASRa, *Fondo Ospedale S. Maria delle Croci e altre opere pie,* primo deposito, vol. 54.

72 See Paolo Prodi, *Settimo non rubare: Furto e mercato nella storia dell'Occidente* (Bologna: il Mulino, 2009), 113 (but see the whole section at 113–115). In summing up his research, Prodi again advances the thesis "that the tradition of the Church has never considered that the confession of sins, with the consequent absolution, can cancel out the damage inflicted by a person on their fellow human being without adequate reparation for that wrong on a concrete and juridical level (Prodi, "Il sacramento della penitenza e la 'restitutio,'" in *Riti di passaggio, storie di giustizia: Per Adriano Prosperi,* vol. 3, ed. Vincenzo Lavenia and Gianna Paolin [Pisa: Edizioni della Normale, 2011], 117–126). The present work is part of a dialogue with Paolo Prodi that lasted many decades.

73 On this issue, see the fundamental work of Piero Fiorelli, *La tortura giudiziaria nel diritto comune,* 2 vols. (Milan: Giuffrè, 1953–1954). At the time, the basic reference text for the application of torture was that of Francesco Bruni, *Tractatus de indiciis et tortura* (Rome, 1543, reprinted many times), about which see the entry by Piero Fiorelli in *DBI* 14 (1972): 614–615.

74 "Ego semel Papiae vidi committi magnum errorem," wrote Giovanni Nevizzano in his *Sylva.* One victim of such an error was a servant accused of stealing some rings. These then turned up, but of course he had confessed. And, regarding the rule that the confession was to be ratified in a place where the instruments of torture could not be seen, Nevizzano added: "Praesumitur durare metus torturae in tali ratificatione et perseverantia confessionis (*Sylva nuptialis* [Lyon, 1526], 44).

75 Lorenzo Priori, *Prattica criminale secondo il rito delle leggi della Serenissima Republica di Venetia* (Venice, 1612). I quote from the Venice edition for Gasparo Girardi, 1738, 98–99.

76 *Escolpazioni fatte dalli giustiziati prima d'uscire dalla Cappella della Vicaria,* in ASDNa, *Archivio dei Bianchi della Giustizia,* reg. 373, c. 1r.

77 Ibid., c. 2r.

78 BABo, *Libro di confortaria . . . principiato l'anno 1597,* ms B 4423, cc. n. n.

79 Giovanni Romeo, *Aspettando il boia: Condannati a morte, confortatori e inquisitori nella Napoli della Controriforma* (Florence: Sansoni, 1993), 45, and 393 n. 51.

80 Ibid., 45–48.

81 ASDNa, *Archivio dei Bianchi della Giustizia,* fol. 373, *Escolpazioni fatte dalli giustiziati prima d'uscire dalla cappella della Vicaria,* vol. 1, 1587–1659, n. 18.

82 Ibid., n. 48.

83 Ibid., n. 49.

84 Ibid., n. 93 (document of October 25, 1656).

85 Ibid., n. 47.

86 On October 4, 1558, Paola Savonese, an eighteen-year-old Jew of Spanish origin, was redeemed from a man named Simonetto, a "seller of slaves," when it was discovered that she had been baptized in Saragozza (ibid., n. 431, *Escarcerazioni*, c. 1).

87 Don Garsia Mastrillo, *Decisiones Consistorii Sacrae regiae conscientiae Regni Siciliae [. . .] in quatuor partes distinctae, liber secundus (tertia editione aucta et expurgata)* (Palermo, 1620), 239–240.

88 Curia Arcivescovile di Napoli, Archivio dei Bianchi, n. 328, *Diario 1574–1696*, cc. n. n.

89 The documents that survived the dispersal of the archive have been gathered together in a recent edition: Maria Pia Di Bella, *La pura verità: Discarichi di coscienza intesi dai Bianchi 1541–1820* (Palermo: Sellerio, 1999).

90 Ibid., 85–86.

91 As stipulated in chap. 23 of the *Capitoli* of 1598 (ibid., 177).

20. COMPASSIONATE CRUELTY

1 A good example is the description found in the *Journal de Voyage,* published in Paris in 1730 by Father Labat (1663–1738). The account is so clear and effective that it was included in Alessandro Ademollo, *Le annotazioni di Mastro Titta carnefice romano: Supplizi e suppliziati; Giustizie eseguite da Gio. Batt. Bugatti e dal suo successore (1796–1870)* (Città di Castello: S. Lapi, 1886), 20–36. A modern edition can be found in Jean-Baptiste Labat, *La comédie ecclésiastique: Voyage en Espagne et en Italie,* ed. Albert t'Serstevens (Paris: B. Grasset, 1927).

2 "Il s'arresta pour voir ce spectacle," Montaigne's secretary noted (Michel de Montaigne, *Oeuvres complètes,* ed. Albert Thibaudet and Maurice Rat [Paris: Gallimard, 1962], 1210).

3 According to the Rome announcements of January 11 cited by Alessandro D'Ancona, *L'Italia alla fine del secolo XVI: Giornale del viaggio di Michele di Montaigne in Italia nel 1580 e 1581* (Città di Castello: Lapi, 1889), 232. The announcement of January 14 talks about a crowd of thirty thousand people.

4 See Giancarlo Angelozzi and Cesarina Casanova, *La giustizia criminale in una città di antico regime: Il tribunale del Torrone di Bologna (secc. XVI–XVII)* (Bologna: Clueb, 2008), 416–417.

5 From the minutes of the congregation on Sunday, March 28, 1568 (ASR, *Confraternita di S. Giovanni decollato [1497–1870],* fol. 3, registro 6, 139–140).

6 See Michel de Montaigne, *Les Essais,* ed. Pierre Villey (Paris: Presses Universitaires de France, 1962), 400–415. The *Oeuvres complètes,* ed. Thibaudet and Rat for Pléiade, to which we have referred, erroneously dates the passage relating to Catena to the 1580 edition (see p. 411). In English as *The Complete Essays,* trans. M. A. Screech (London: Penguin Books, 2003), 472–488, esp. 484.

7 ASR, *Confraternita di S. Giovanni decollato,* busta 6, registro 11, c. 2r.

8   ASR, *Libri dei testamenti,* registro 17, fasc. 34, cc. 88r–v. Among the names of the five witnesses to Catena's declaration of his last wishes were those of Averardo Serristori and Carlo Strozzi, members of two noble Florentine families. The governor of the company at the time was Amerigo Strozzi.

9   "Ces pauvres gens qu'on void sur un eschafaut, remplis d'une ardente devotion, y occupant tous leurs sens autant qu'ils peuvent, les oreilles aux instructions qu'on leur donne, les yeux et les mains tendues au ciel, la voix à des prières hautes . . . on les doibt louer de religion, mais non proprement de constance" (*Essais,* 3, chap. IV, "De la diversion"; p. 811 of the cited edition of the *Oeuvres complètes*); *Complete Essays,* 938.

10   See the foreword by Adriano Prosperi to Nicola Panichi, Renzo Ragghianti, and Alessandro Savorelli, eds., *Montaigne contemporaneo* (Pisa: Edizioni della Normale, 2011).

11   The depositions made by the young Galileo in the hearings regarding the legacy of Giovambattista Ricasoli are published in Galileo Galilei, *Opere,* Edizione nazionale, vol. 19 (Florence: Barbera, 1966), 44–108, esp. 49.

12   Thomas More, *Utopia,* ed. and with a revised translation by George M. Logan, 3rd ed. (New York: W. W. Norton, 2011), 22.

13   More's name also appears in the context of the comment on the fifth commandment: "Praeceptum Domini generaliter loquitur: 'Non occides' . . . Late Thomas Morus in tractatu De optimo reipublicae statu" (Giovanni Nevizzano da Asti, *Sylva nuptialis libri sex* [Lyon, 1526], 47).

14   Martino Azpilqueta Navarro, *Commentario resolutorio del furto notabile,* in *Manuale de' confessori nel quale si contiene la universale et particolar decisione di tutti i dubii, che nelle confessioni de' peccati sogliono occorrere* (Venice, 1572), 190–199. For more about Navarro and, in general, about the relationship between legal norms and moral conscience, see Vincenzo Lavenia, *L'infamia e il perdono: Tributi, pene e confessione nella teologia morale della prima età moderna* (Bologna: il Mulino, 2004).

15   "Crudeliter mortem inferunt": Iulius Clarus Alexandrinus, *Volumen, alias Liber Quintus: In quo omnium Criminum materia sub receptis sententiis copiosissime tractatur* (Venice, 1583), section "Homicidium." The importance of More's thinking is considered by Italo Mereu, *Storia del diritto penale nel '500: Studi e ricerche* (Naples: Morano, 1964), 180–197. Regarding the great criminal-law culture of the sixteenth century, Mario Sbriccoli's project for a comprehensive history of penal law to replace the work of Antonio Pertile sadly did not come to fruition, but a measure of his many analytic inquiries can be gained from a posthumous collection of essays (Mario Sbriccoli, *Storia del diritto penale e della giustizia: Scritti editi e inediti, 1972–2007,* 2 vols. (Milan: Giuffrè, 2009).

16   "Ut homo hominem, non iratus, non timens, tantum spectaturus, occidat" (Seneca, *Epistulae,* 90); Montaigne, *The Complete Essays,* "On cruelty," 484.

17   The censure can be found in Peter Godman, *The Saint as Censor: Robert Bellarmine between Inquisition and Index* (Leiden: Brill, 2000), 45–48, 339–342.

18 *Travel Journal,* in M. de Montaigne, *The Complete Works of Montaigne,* trans. Donald M. Frame (Stanford, CA: Stanford University Press, 1971), 955. In actual fact the document conserved in the archive of the Holy Office is more detailed than might appear from what Montaigne was charged with verbally. An incomplete, grammatically incorrect sentence signals that there were suspicions about Montaigne's whole position on the death penalty ("allega un fundamento dell'opinione di quei qui damnant punitione capitali ha…".: Godman, *The Saint as Censor,* 341).

21. THE FATE OF THE BODY

1 ASR, *Confraternita di S. Giovanni decollato (1497–1870),* busta 6, registro 11, c. 2r.

2 BNCFi, ms II. I. 138, fols. 175v–176r.

3 The episode dates to 1547. See Cosimo I de' Medici, *Lettere,* ed. Giorgio Spini (Florence: Vallecchi, 1940), 109.

4 ASR, *Confraternita di S. Giovanni decollato,* busta 8, reg. 16, c. 68r.

5 "Vestes, pannos et quaecumque indumenta," reads the privilege granted by Julius III to the Roman company, reaffirmed on June 10, 1576, by Gregory XIII for the confraternity in Bologna and confirmed once again by Benedict XIV in 1741 (printed copies in AABo, *Archivio consorziale del clero urbano,* IX A 1 and IX A 4).

6 In November 1626, the body of a thief who had killed himself in prison was brought here: see Giovan Battista Spaccini, *Cronaca di Modena,* vol. 1: *Anni 1588–1602,* ed. Albano Biondi, Rolando Bussi, and Carlo Giovannini (Modena: Panini, 1993), 37.

7 See Antonio Menniti Ippolito and Paolo Vian, eds., *The Protestant Cemetery in Rome: The "Parte antica"* (Rome: Unione Internazionale degli Istituti di Archeologia, Storia e Storia dell'Arte, 1989), 31–36 and passim.

8 Matteo Al Kalak and Marta Lucchi, *Oltre il patibolo: I fratelli della Morte di Modena tra giustizia e perdono* (Rome: Bulzoni, 2009), 200.

9 According to the records for 1726 (ASCMo, *Vachetta per li iustitiati 1593–1826,* 51). But in November 1598 the executioner was caught in the act of disinterring a hanged man to recover the noose (ASMo, *Inquisizione di Modena,* b. 9).

10 See Al Kalak and Lucchi, *Oltre il patibolo,* 48. The recording by notarial deed of the public ritual of the incineration of the ropes is reported in the *Vachetta per li iustitiati 1593–1826.*

11 The ritual of burning the nooses in Bologna is reported by Carlo Antonio Macchiavelli, *Rituale della sacra scuola della conforteria di Bologna ad uso delle conforterie pratiche della istessa città,* compiled on August 29, 1733, ms BABo, Aula 2° C. VII 13, n. 4850, 126.

12 Letter of the Compagnia di Santa Maria della Carità, June 1570 (ASGD, busta 18 C, *Registro copialettere,* cc. 66r–v).

13 [Edwin Sandys], *Relatione dello stato della religione: E con quali dissegni & arti è stata fabricata e maneggiata in diuersi stati di queste occidentali parti del mondo. Tradotta dall'Inglese del cavaliere Edoino Sandis in lingua volgare,* s. l. 1625, 6, 8.

14 See Richard J. Evans, *Rituals of Retribution: Capital Punishment in Germany, 1600–1987* (Oxford: Oxford University Press, 1996), chap. 2, "Rites of Blood," esp. 90–98.

15 Pliny, *Natural History,* vol. 8, ed. Jeffrey Henderson, trans. W. H. S. Jones (Cambridge, MA: Harvard University Press, 1963), bk. 28, 4. Specific instructions regarding the legal proof value of the appearance of the murdered person's blood in identifying the presence of the killer on the scene of the crime were given by Antonio Maria Cospi, *Il giudice criminalista dato in luce dal dottor Ottaviano Carlo Cospi* (Florence, 1643), 483–485.

16 Heinrich Kornmann, *Opera curiosa in tractatus sex distributa* (Frankfurt, 1696), 195–196, 206 (pt. 2, "De miraculis mortuorum"); Kornmann was taken to task by the physician of Chemnitz, L. Christian Friedrich Garmann, *De miraculo mortuorum* (Chemnitz, 1670).

17 For more on the idea of radical dampness, see Chiara Crisciani and Giovanna Ferrari, introduction to *Arnaldi de Villanova Opera Medica omnia,* vol. 2: *Tractatus de humido radicali,* ed. Michael R. McVaugh (Barcelona: Publicacions de la Universitat de Barcelona, 2010), 319–571. It is no coincidence that in her studies Giovanna Ferrari moved on from an investigation of capital punishment to Aristotelian theories about radical dampness. The connection between the "particular regimes and medicines" with which the physician can prolong life (ibid., 436) and the drinking of human blood, a vehicle of warmth and of the plasticity of organs, found ideal expression in executions.

18 Agostino Paravicini Bagliani, *Il corpo del papa* (Turin: Einaudi, 1994), 300–305.

19 The Roman episode is in Alessandro Ademollo, "Le Giustizie a Roma dal 1674 al 1739 e dal 1796 al 1840," *Archivio della Società Romana di Storia Patria* 4 (1881): 470. The two episodes, together with the passage from Pliny and other sources, are also cited in Giancarlo Baronti, "Pratiche terapeutiche spettacolari nel rito dell'esecuzione capitale," in *La piazza nella storia: Eventi, liturgie, rappresentazioni,* ed. Marina Vitale and Domenico Scarfoglio (Naples: Edizioni scientifiche italiane, 1995), 125–148.

20 Andrea Bernardi (Novacula), *Cronache forlivesi,* ed. Giuseppe Mazzatinti, 2 vols. (Bologna: R. Deputazione di storia patria, 1895), 1:263–264; the episode is reported, albeit with an inexact date and page number, by Lionello Puppi, *Lo splendore dei supplizi: Liturgia delle esecuzioni capitali e iconografia del martirio nell'arte europea dal XII al XIX secolo* (Milan: Bruno Alfieri, 1990), 42.

21 Bernardi, *Cronache forlivesi,* 2:170 (the event described took place on July 2, 1508).

22 Puppi, *Lo splendore dei supplizi,* makes reference to Domenico Bortolan, *Supplizi e prigioni* (Vicenza: G. Rumor, 1886).

23 *Tariffa da osservarsi da tutti i tribunali della Città, e Stato di Firenze nel pagare le spese, e mercedi, che appresso* (Florence, 1681), 7–8 (copy in the Bibliotheque Royale de Bruxelles, ms II, 290, 2651).

24 Even though on one occasion a Saxon lawyer was, after his death, found to be missing his tongue, according to the widely circulated collection of "exempla" from

the sermons of Caesarius of Heisterbach (*Die Wundergeschichten des Caesarius von Heisterbach,* ed. Alfons Hilka [Bonn: Peter Hanstein, 1933], no. 167, pp. 131–132).

25 BCA, ms B 1883, cc. 531*r*–532*v*.

26 As attested by a scholarly thesis discussed by Johann Landsberg in Jena (*Disputatio iuridica, de cadaveribus punitorum . . . quam . . . sub praesidio D. Adriani Beyeri Jenens: Publice defendendam suscipiet Joh Ernestus Landsberg Halberstadt; Anno 1659* [Jena, 1720], 22–23; a copy is in BAV, *Miscell.* F. 118, int. IV).

27 Giorgio Vasari, *Le Vite de' più eccellenti architetti, pittori, et scultori italiani, da Cimabue, insino a' tempi nostri* (1550 edition), ed. Luciano Bellosi and Aldo Rossi (Turin: Einaudi, 1986), 483. Daniela Bohde ("Skin and the Search for the Interior: The Representation of Flaying in the Art and Anatomy of the Cinquecento," in *Bodily Extremities, Preoccupations with the Human Body in Early Modern European Culture,* ed. Florike Egmond and Robert Zwijnenberg [Aldershot, UK: Ashgate, 2003], 10–47) reports the episode, subtly showing how the magic value that skin held for Cosini contrasts with the search for the inner truth of identity in the work of Michelangelo.

28 The source is cited in Romano Canosa and Isabella Colonnello, *Streghe maghi e sortileghi in Abruzzo tra Cinquecento e Settecento* (Pescara: Edizioni Menabo, 2002), 107.

22. PUBLIC ANATOMY

1 Peter Linebaugh, "The Tyburn Riot: Against the Surgeons," in *Albion's Fatal Tree: Crime and Society in Eighteenth-Century England,* ed. Douglas Hay, Peter Linebaugh, John G. Rule, E. P. Thompson, and Cal Winslow (London: Allen Lane, 1975), 65–117, esp. 69.

2 This is the most concrete and convincing observation made in an essay—more ambitious and suggestive than solid—by Florike Egmond: "Execution, Dissection, Pain and Infamy: A Morphological Investigation," in *Bodily Extremities: Preoccupations with the Human Body in Early Modern European Culture,* ed. Florike Egmond and Robert Zwijnenberg (Aldershot, UK: Ashgate, 2003), 92–127.

3 See Michele Medici, *Compendio storico della scuola anatomica di Bologna dal Rinascimento delle scienze e delle lettere a tutto il secolo XVIII* (Bologna: Tipografia governativa della Volpe e del Sassi, 1857), 36–37; the trial is reported on 427ff. Still useful with regard to the history of dissection is the study by Fielding H. Garrison, *An Introduction to the History of Medicine* (Philadelphia: Saunders, 1917; reprint London: Hafner, 1966). For more on ancient history and anatomy texts, see Heinrich von Staden, ed., *Herophilus: The Art of Medicine in Early Alexandria* (Cambridge: Cambridge University Press, 1989).

4 See Giovanni Ricci, *Il principe e la morte: Corpo, cuore, effigie nel Rinascimento* (Bologna: il Mulino, 1998).

5 Johann Landsberg, *Disputatio iuridica, de cadaveribus punitorum . . . quam . . . sub praesidio D. Adriani Beyeri Jenens: Publice defendendam suscipiet Joh Ernestus*

Landsberg Halberstadt; Anno 1659 (Jena, 1720), 22–23 (copy in BAV, *Miscell.* F. 118, int. IV).

6 See Giorgio Toni and Pericle Di Pietro, *L'insegnamento dell'Anatomia nello Studio modenese e l'Istituto di Anatomia Umana Normale* (Modena: Istituto di Anatomia Umana Normale, 1971). For more about Falloppia (or Falloppio), see the entry by Gabriella Belloni Speciale in *DBI* 44 (1994).

7 Ladislao Münster, "Le vedute di Andrea Vesalio sull'anatomia galenica e sul galenismo, espresse in occasione della sua prima Notomia pubblica di Bologna (gennaio 1540)," in *Atti della IV Biennale della Marca e dello Studio Firmano per gli studi storici dell'arte medica* (Fermo, 1961; Montegranaro, 1962), 157–171, esp. 160.

8 Andrea Carlino, *La fabbrica del corpo: Libri e dissezione nel Rinascimento* (Turin: Einaudi, 1994).

9 AABo, *Archivio consorziale del clero urbano,* IX D 1, 73.

10 One such case, in Bologna in 1712, is reported in my preface to Carlino, *La fabbrica del corpo,* xvii–xviii.

11 The connection is emphasized by David C. Humphrey, "Dissection and Discrimination: The Social Origins of Cadavers in America, 1760–1915," *Bulletin of New York Academy of Medicine* 49 (1973): 819–827. On the regulations of the medical colleges, see Raffaele Ciasca, ed., *Statuti dell'Arte dei medici e speziali* (Florence: Vallecchi, 1922), 280; Aldo Bottero, "I più antichi statuti del Collegio dei medici di Milano," *Archivio storico lombardo* 8 (1943), fasc. 1–4: 84–85; and, in general, see also Arturo Castiglioni, *Storia della medicina* (Milan: Mondadori, 1936), 295ff., 314ff.

12 ASFi, *Archivio Mediceo del principato,* Otto di Guardia, fol. 2603, c. 31; ibid., fol. 2298, cc. n. n.; a similar provision was made for a woman named Francesca di Meo from Scarperia, who was executed for murder.

13 *Statuta Almi Studii Pisani,* ms in ASPi, *Università* A.I.3, cc. 345v–346r. See Giovanni Targioni Tozzetti, *Notizie sulla storia delle scienze fisiche in Toscana cavate da un manoscritto inedito* (Florence: I. e R. Biblioteca Palatina, 1852), 218. Worth reading, in relation to the anatomy ritual in Pisa, is Grazia Tomasi, *Occasione mancata per un notomista pisano del Seicento* (Pisa: Igraf, 1981), and the extensive firsthand documentation analyzed by Luigi Lazzerini, "Le radici folkloriche dell'anatomia: Scienza e rituale all'inizio dell'età moderna," *Quaderni storici* 29, no. 85 (1994): 193–233.

14 In 1642 the anatomist Gian Battista Ruschi had to be content with dissecting a sheep, because the designated victim, a young man, had been pardoned, according to a playful and rather grotesque letter written by one of Ruschi's colleagues at the Studio in Pisa, which is reproduced, with a commentary, in Tomasi, *Occasione mancata.* An emulator of Baron Munchhausen ahead of his time, the young man, out of desperation, supposedly pulled his hair with such force that he rose "two *braccia* off the ground," causing "the company and all the guards" to flee. The triumph of

skulls and skeletons carved on the funeral monument erected to Giovanni Battista Ruschi in the church of San Frediano attests to the social ascent of anatomists in the university world during the seventeenth century.

15 On Falloppia, see Ladislao Münster, "La laurea di Gabriele Falloppio allo Studio di Ferrara (1552)," *Ferrara viva* 5, nos. 13–14 (1965): 181–206; for more about Mantua, see Gilberto Carra and Attilio Zanca, *Gli statuti del Collegio dei Medici di Mantova del 1559* (Mantua: Accademia Virgiliana di Mantova, 1977), 79–80.

16 See the important study by Giovanna Ferrari, "Public Anatomy Lessons and the Carnival: The Anatomy Theatre of Bologna," *Past and Present* 117, no. 1 (1987): 50–106.

17 See Adriano Prosperi, *Dare l'anima: Storia di un infanticidio* (Turin: Einaudi, 2005).

23. ART AND SPECTACLE AT THE SERVICE OF JUSTICE

1 H. L. A. Hart, *The Concept of Law*, 3rd ed. (Oxford: Oxford University Press, 2012), chap. 4, 50–78. My thanks to Pasqualino Masciarelli for drawing my attention to this.

2 See Gherardo Ortalli, *La peinture infamante du XIIIᵉ au XVIᵉ siècle* (Paris: Gérard Monfort, 1994). Original edition: *"Pingatur in Palatio": La pittura infamante nei secoli XIII–XVI* (Rome: Jouvence, 1979).

3 See Lionello Puppi, *Lo splendore dei supplizi: Liturgia delle esecuzioni capitali e iconografia del martirio nell'arte europea dal XII al XIX secolo* (Milan: Bruno Alfieri, 1990).

4 This is the solidly argued thesis of Mitchell B. Merback, *The Thief, the Cross and the Wheel: Pain and the Spectacle of Punishment in Medieval and Renaissance Europe* (Chicago: University of Chicago Press, 1999).

5 The term is used by Achim Timmermann, "The Poor-Sinner's Cross and the Pillory: Late Medieval Microarchitecture and Liturgies of Criminal Punishment" [2000], *Umění: Journal of the Institute for Art History of the Academy of Sciences of the Czech Republic* 55 (2007): 362–373. The microarchitectural piece erected in Venice, which is not covered by Timmermann, is mentioned in Chiara Traverso, *La Scuola di San Fantin o dei "Picai": Carità e giustizia a Venezia* (Venice: Marsilio, 2000), 46–47.

6 The merit for discovering this and conducting the first careful research belongs to Samuel Y. Edgerton Jr., who published his initial findings in a number of essays (commencing with "A Little-Known 'Purpose of Art' in the Italian Renaissance," *Art History* 2, no. 1 [1979]: 45–61), and then gathered together the results of his studies in *Pictures and Punishment: Art and Criminal Prosecution during the Florentine Renaissance* (Ithaca, NY: Cornell University Press, 1985). His exclusively Florentine perspective has been corrected by the important research of Massimo Ferretti, "Pitture per condannati a morte del Trecento bolognese," in *Misericordie: Conversioni sotto il patibolo tra Medioevo ed età moderna,* ed. Adriano Prosperi (Pisa:

Edizioni della Normale, 2007), 85–151 (an abbreviated form of this essay appeared in English as "In Your Face: Paintings for the Condemned in Renaissance Italy," in *The Art of Executing Well: Rituals of Execution in Renaissance Italy,* ed. Nicholas Terpstra [Kirksville, MO: Truman University Press, 2008], 79–97).

7   See the images reproduced in Edgerton, *Pictures and Punishment,* nos. 43 (p. 166) and 44 (p. 168), and the ones discovered and examined by Ferretti, "Pitture per condannati," especially the cases of the *tavolette* now in the Musée des Beaux Arts in Tours and the Staatsgalerie in Stuttgart (pp. 130–131, 136–137).

8   Ferretti, "Pitture per condannati," 114.

9   ". . . but it was destroyed by the fire two years later along with the entire church" (Giorgio Vasari, *The Lives of the Artists,* trans. Julia Conaway Bondanella and Peter Bondanella [Oxford: Oxford University Press, 1991], 497). The fire that destroyed the *tavoletta* in 1562 did not spare the confraternity's documents either, as Traverso notes in *La Scuola di San Fantin,* 100–101.

10 The parchment manuscript is now in the Fondazione Cini in Venice, as reported by Pietro Toesca (*Miniature di una collezione veneziana* [Venice: Hoepli, 1958], 44–52), who edited a complete reproduction (*Miniature di una collezione veneziana commentate da Pietro Toesca* [Venice: G. Mardersteig, 1958], 59–63, together with an illustrative apparatus); his proposed dating of the work to around 1450, on the basis of the characters' attire, was corrected by Roberto Longhi, who spoke of "a style to be located in the Verona-Bologna-Ferrara-Padua quadrilateral toward 1400–1420," *La Critica d'Arte* 5 (1940): 182. In dating the work nowadays, a distinction tends to be made between the first part, produced around 1430, and a second series of five drawings composed around 1480 by the miniaturist known as the Master of Pico (see Daniele Benati, "Il primo tempo di Ercole I: Da Cosmè Tura a Ercole de' Roberti," in *La miniatura a Ferrara dal tempo di Cosmè Tura all'eredità di Ercole de' Roberti,* exhibition catalogue, ed. Federica Toniolo [Modena: Panini, 1998], 225–267). For more about Ercole de' Roberti and the artistic patronage of the confraternity, see Adriano Franceschini, *Artisti a Ferrara in età umanistica e rinascimentale: Testimonianze archivistiche,* vol. 2 (Ferrara: Corbo, 1993–1997), pt. 2, 205 and passim.

11 See Adalgisa Lugli, *Guido Mazzoni e la rinascita della terracotta nel Quattrocento* (Turin: Allemandi, 1990), 321.

12 Mario Fanti, "Nuovi documenti e osservazioni sul 'Compianto' di Niccolò Dell'Arca e la sua antica collocazione in Santa Maria della Vita," in *Niccolò dell'Arca: seminario di studi,* ed. Grazia Agostini and Luisa Ciammitti (Bologna: Nuova Alfa, 1989), 59–83, esp. 59.

13 The statues were removed in 1488 and placed in the courtyard of the Palazzo di Re Enzo, where they can still be seen today; see Renzo Grandi, "La scultura in Bologna nell'età di Niccolò," in Agostini and Ciammitti, *Niccolò dell'Arca,* 25–43.

14 The source is *The Golden Legend* of Jacobus de Voragine.

15 Giorgio Vasari, *Le Vite de' piú eccellenti architetti, pittori, et scultori italiani, da Cimabue, insino a' tempi nostri* (1550 edition), ed. Luciano Bellosi and Aldo Rossi (Turin: Einaudi, 1986), 733. Vasari saw the work in this same place, and described it as "the death of Our Lady, with the Apostles in round figures and the Jew whose hands are left stuck to the coffin of the Virgin."

16 One of these is a "miracle of Saint Francis of Paola, who raised a child from the dead," by Lavinia Fontana (Carlo Cesare Malvasia, *Le pitture di Bologna,* ed. Giampietro Zanotti [Bologna, 1706], 260–264).

17 BNCFi, ms II. I. 138, fols. 179*v*–180*r.*

18 BNCFi, ms II. I. 138, fol. 175*v.*

19 See Marinella Mazzei Traina, ed., *L'Oratorio dell'Annunziata di Ferrara* (Ferrara: Ferrariae Decus, 2002). The contribution of Enrico Peverada, "Feste, musica e devozione presso la Compagnia della Morte ed Orazione: Antologia dai registri contabili (1486–1599)," 197–246, includes extensive documentation from accounts books, which provides important information about commissions given to painters and craftspeople.

20 See Giovanni Pierluigi Calessi, *Ricerche sull'Accademia della Morte di Ferrara* (Bologna: A.M.I.S., 1976). In addition to this study there is now the essay by Peverada, "Feste, musica e devozione," from which it emerges that organ music, accompanied by songs, was habitually played during the company's processions.

21 See Juliane Riepe, *Die Arciconfraternita di S. Maria della Morte in Bologna: Beiträge zur Geschichte des italienischen Oratoriums im 17. und 18. Jahrhundert* (Paderborn: Ferdinand Schoningh, 1998).

22 ASBo, *Ospedali.* S. Maria della Morte, Oratorio, Misc. 17 (840), Funzioni straordinarie (1533–1739).

23 For a full list of librettos, authors, and the circumstances of performances, see Laura Callegari, Gabriella Sartini, and Gabriele Bersani Berselli, eds., *La librettistica bolognese nei secoli XVII e XVIII: Catalogo ed indici* (Rome: Edizioni Torre d'Orfeo, 1989).

24 Adolfo Equini, *C. I. Frugoni alle corti dei Farnesi e dei Borboni di Parma,* vol. 1 (Palermo: Sandron, 1919), 29.

25 From the libretto of the *Oratorio* sung on Good Friday, 1761. ASBo, *Ospedali.* S. Maria della Morte, Oratorio, Misc. 17 (840), Funzioni straordinarie (1533–1739), vol. 4, D9.

24. CAPITAL PUNISHMENT AS A RITE OF PASSAGE

1 See Chapter 19, note 27.

2 Maria Antonietta Visceglia, *La città rituale: Roma e le sue cerimonie in età moderna* (Rome: Viella, 2002).

3 For example, Foucault's ideas are drawn on in the recent work of a scholar who has made significant contributions to our understanding of the history of the *conforteria* in Palermo: Maria Pia Di Bella, *Essai sur les supplices: L'état de victime* (Paris: Hermann, 2011).

4 Michel Foucault, *Discipline and Punish: The Birth of the Prison* [1975], trans. Alan Sheridan (London: Penguin Books, 1979), 60.

5 The source cited in relation to England is the celebrated *Inquiry* by Henry Fielding (ibid.).

6 Giovan Battista Spaccini, *Cronaca di Modena: Anni 1588–1602,* ed. Albano Biondi, Rolando Bussi, and Carlo Giovannini (Modena: Panini, 1993), 187.

7 As a "gracious madman called Messer Gianetto" shouted during the execution of a Piedmontese Waldensian: see Vincenzo Lavenia, "Eretici sentenziati e 'reincorporati,'" in *Misericordie: Conversioni sotto il patibolo tra Medioevo ed età moderna,* ed. Adriano Prosperi (Pisa: Edizioni della Normale, 2007), 153–154.

8 BABo, *Libro di confortaria . . . principiato l'anno 1597,* ms B 4423, cc. n. n.

9 Taken up by, among others, Peter Spierenburg, *The Spectacle of Suffering: Executions and the Evolution of Repression; From a Preindustrial Metropolis to the European Experience* (Cambridge: Cambridge University Press, 1984), with regard to capital punishment in Amsterdam; and Richard Van Dülmen, *Theatre of Horror: Crime and Punishment in Early Modern Germany,* trans. Elisabeth Neu (Cambridge: Polity Press, 1990), for Germany.

10 Richard J. Evans, *Rituals of Retribution: Capital Punishment in Germany, 1600–1987* (Oxford: Oxford University Press, 1996); and see also, for France, Pascal Bastien, *L'execution publique à Paris au XVIIIe siècle: Une histoire des rituels judiciaires* (Paris: Champ Vallon, 2006). On the rituality of executions in Rome, see now also Irene Fosi, "La justice et ses rites à Rome à l'époque moderne," in *Rites, justice, pouvoirs: France-Italie, XIVe–XIXe siècle,* ed. Lucien Faggion and Laure Verdon (Aix-Marseille: Université de Provence, 2013), 131–146.

11 Marino Sanudo, *I diarii,* vol. 8 (Venice, 1882; repr. Bologna: Forni, 1969), col. 353.

12 See also Sebastiano Guazzini, *Tractatus ad defensam inquisitorum, carceratorum, reorum* (Venice, 1649), 71–76.

13 The chronicler recounts that they said: "Stay with God, pray for us" (Sanudo, *I diarii,* vol. 17 [Venice, 1886; repr. Bologna: Forni, 1971], col. 77). The episode is mentioned by Chiara Traverso, *La Scuola di San Fantin o dei "Picai": Carità e giustizia a Venezia* (Venice: Marsilio, 2000), 50.

14 Robert Hertz, *Death and the Right Hand* [1960], trans. Rodney Needham and Claudia Needham (London: Routledge, 1960), 36. Attention is drawn to the liminal condition of the condemned, and the findings of anthropological studies from Van Gennep to Turner, in Filippo Fineschi, *Cristo e Giuda: Rituali di giustizia a Firenze in età moderna* (Florence: Alberto Bruschi, 1995), 200ff.

25. THE ARRIVAL OF THE JESUITS

1 Josephine von Henneberg, "An Unknown Portrait of St Ignatius Loyola," *Art Bulletin* 49, no. 159 (1967): 140–142. The proposal is considered "not convincing" by Jean S. Weisz, *Pittura e Misericordia: The Oratory of S. Giovanni Decollato in Rome* (Ann Arbor, MI: UMI Research Press, 1984), 38.

2   The appearance of Michelangelo's name in a commission of the archconfraternity dating to 1551 is reported by Jean S. Weisz in "Daniele da Volterra and the Oratory of S. Giovanni Decollato," *Burlington Magazine* 123, no. 939 (1981): 355.

3   There is no mention of this aspect of the Jesuits' work in Lance Gabriel Lazar, *Working in the Vineyard of the Lord: Jesuit Confraternities in Early Modern Italy* (Toronto: University of Toronto Press, 2005).

4   This is also the thesis of John Bossy, *Peace in the Post-Reformation* (Cambridge: Cambridge University Press, 1998).

5   *Opere pie le quali s'esercitano nel regio tribunale della Vicaria dalli RR. PP. della Compagnia di Giesú da vent'anni in qua,* undated manuscript report, but written around 1630 (ARSI, Neap. 78).

6   Gian Battista Scanaroli, *De visitatione carceratorum libri tres* (Rome, 1655) (from the dedication to Saint Jerome, patron of the Arciconfraternita della Carita).

7   See also the letter of Tommaso Romano, June 13, 1556, in *MHSI, Epistolae mixtae ex variis Europae locis ab anno 1537 ad 1556 scriptae, nunc primum a patribus Societatis Jesu in lucem editae,* vol. 5 (1555–1556) (Madrid: Avrial, 1901), 344–355.

8   See Jacques Chiffoleau's dense and fascinating treatment of wills in the Avignon area in *La comptabilité de l'au-delà: Les hommes, la mort et la religion dans la région d'Avignon à la fin du Moyen Âge* (Rome: École Française, 1980), 105ff.

9   See Roger Chartier, "Les arts de bien mourir, 1450–1600," *Annales ESC* 31 (1976): 51–76.

10 Juan de Mariana, *Controversia de manifestatione complicis,* 1588, ms in ARSI, Opp. NN. 305.

11 See Ronald Po-chia Hsia, *Social Discipline in the Reformation: Central Europe, 1550–1750* (London: Routledge, 1989); and also Richard J. Evans, *Rituals of Retribution: Capital Punishment in Germany, 1600–1987* (Oxford: Oxford University Press, 1996), 40.

12 Roberto Bellarmino, *De arte bene moriendi* (Antwerp, 1623), 2.

13 See James A. Sharpe, *Crime in Early Modern England, 1550–1750* (London: Longman, 1984), 154–163.

14 Bellarmino, *De arte bene moriendi,* 100.

15 Published in English in 1605, and in an Italian translation in Geneva in 1625 with the additions of Fra Paolo Sarpi (see Chapter 21, note 13); partially reproduced in Paolo Sarpi, *Opere,* ed. Gaetano Cozzi and Luisa Cozzi (Milan: Ricciardi, 1969), 295–330.

16 For the Lutherans, see Benjamin T. G. Mayes, *Counsel and Conscience: Lutheran Casuistry and Moral Reasoning after the Reformation* (Göttingen: Vandenhoecht und Ruprecht, 2011).

17 Pierre Hurtubise, *La casuistique dans tous ses états: De Martin de Azpilcueta à Alphonse de Liguori* (Ottawa: Novalis, 2005), 26.

18 Giacinto Manara, *Notti malinconiche nelle quali con occasione di assister a' condannati a morte, si propongono varie difficoltà spettanti a simile materia* (Bologna, 1658). The title of the text is the focus of an interesting exploration of the theme of comforting

in the seventeenth century by Isabella Rosoni, "Le notti malinconiche: Esecuzioni capitali e disciplinamento nell'Italia del XVII secolo," in *La notte: Ordine, sicurezza e disciplinamento in età moderna,* ed. Mario Sbriccoli (Florence: Ponte alle Grazie, 1991), 94–126.

19   Manara, *Notti malinconiche,* 6.

20   Ibid., 747. Here Manara explicitly evokes the theme of disdain for the world developed by Lothar of Segni, later Pope Innocent III.

21   Ibid., 4–5.

22   Ibid., 17–29.

23   Ibid., 111–112. Pius V's intervention calling for the elimination of the "abuse" of not permitting the condemned to receive the Eucharist, expressed in a message to the nunzio Gian Battista Castagna on January 25, 1568, is documented in José Ignacio Tellechea Idígoras, *El Papado y Felipe II: Colección de breves pontificios,* vol. 3: *1550–1598* (Madrid: Fundación Universitaria Española, 2002), 131. On the role played on this occasion by the bishop of Granada, Pedro Guerrero, see Adriano Prosperi, "Morire volentieri: Condannati a morte e sacramenti," in *Misericordie: Conversioni sotto il patibolo tra Medioevo ed età moderna,* ed. Adriano Prosperi (Pisa: Edizioni della Normale, 2007), 41–42.

24   Manara, *Notti malinconiche,* 135–137.

25   Ibid., 208–209.

26   Ibid., 287.

27   Ibid., 359.

28   See Enrica Guerra, *Una eterna condanna: La figura del carnefice nella società tardomedievale* (Milan: Franco Angeli, 2003). The definition of the *barattiere* (see ibid., 102–103) falls within the metamorphoses of barratry, recently and perceptively studied by Gherardo Ortalli, *Barattieri: Il gioco d'azzardo fra economia ed etica, secoli XIII–XV* (Bologna: il Mulino, 2012).

29   Manara, *Notti malinconiche,* 296. But the witchcraft described by Lucan in the *Pharsalia* offered the Jesuit the opportunity for a display of doctrine on the topic.

30   Manara, *Notti malinconiche,* 263.

31   Ibid., 422.

32   Ibid., 733.

33   Ibid., 718. Manara claims to have read the details recounted "in his trial and printed around then." For more on the circulation of information about the episode, see Ermanno Paccagnini's entry on Gian Giacomo Mora in *DBI* 76 (2012): 411–413.

26. LABORATORIES OF UNIFORMITY

1   *Constitutioni della Congregatione o Scuola de' confortatori della città di Bologna* (Bologna, 1640), 13, 16. The regulation remained substantially unchanged in the following edition of 1667. Two seventeenth-century copies of the constitutions are in AABo, *Archivio consorziale del clero urbano,* IX B 5–6.

2 Giovanni Battista Gargiaria, *Conforto de gli afflitti condannati a morte* (Piacenza, 1650). Carlo Antonio Macchiavelli, *Catalogo delli autori, e delle materie spettanti alla Conforteria* (Bologna, 1729), 8, records two printings in Piacenza, in 1650 and 1652, and two reprints in Bologna, in 1675 and 1676. On p. 15 there is also a list of the "cases proposed for the theoretical sessions" by Ovidio Montalbani between 1639 and 1669.

3 The notary was a Gian Battista Cavazza, who came from a long line of Bolognese notaries. In the postmortem inventories he drew up, there is, among the many documents regarding the school of comforters, a list of the works in Ovidio Montalbani's library, prepared on December 18, 1668 (ASBo, *Notarile,* G. B. Cavazza, vol. 15, cc. 634*r*–658*r*).

4 Gargiaria, *Conforto de gli afflitti,* 7.

5 Loose sheet (Bologna, 1641); copy in AABo, K.502.

6 "Dedit signum poenitentiae et conversionis ad fidem catholicam" (ASBo, *Tribunale criminale del Torrone, Vacchetta dei giustiziati,* Rubrica I, 1613–1641, unnumbered papers, but 127, 130). In the register of the executed, we read: "Assuero of the late Gio. Bisbiacini da Sartorix of Cologne, Lutheran, was hung from a pole in the marketplace and then burned as a Lutheran, as he had converted in the *conforteria,* and his ashes were buried" (BABo, ms *Fondo Ospedali,* 65 [41.1], *Condannati alla morte libro primo dall'anno 1540 a tutto l'anno 1787,* c. 41*r*).

7 See Vittorio Frajese, "Ateismo," in *Dizionario storico dell'Inquisizione,* vol. 1, ed. Adriano Prosperi, with the collaboration of Vincenzo Lavenia and John Tedeschi (Pisa: Edizioni della Normale, 2010), 114–118.

8 Mention is also made of "writings and booklets in his hand, of which there are around forty." He left these to the confessor and to doctors Gandolfi and Zoppio, "that they might use them as they wished"; there was also "a certain booklet bound with the coat of arms of the lord Count Ridolfo Campeggi," which he wanted "to be given to the above-mentioned lord count" (BABo, ms B 4423, cc. n. n.).

9 Ridolfo Campeggi, *Racconto degli eretici iconomiasti giustiziati in Bologna adí 28 novembre 1622* (Bologna, 1622).

10 See Carlo Ginzburg and Maurizio Ferrari, "La colombara ha aperto gli occhi," *Quaderni storici* 13, no. 38 (1978): 631–639; and Carlo Ginzburg, "The Dovecote Has Opened Its Eyes: Popular Conspiracy in Seventeenth-Century Italy," in *The Inquisition in Early Modern Europe: Studies on Sources and Methods,* ed. Gustav Henningsen and John Tedeschi (DeKalb: Northern Illinois University Press, 1986), 190–198. The case is mentioned in the context of a systematic analysis of Bolognese criminal sources by Giancarlo Angelozzi and Cesarina Casanova, *La giustizia criminale in una città di antico regime: Il tribunale del Torrone di Bologna (secc. XVI–XVII)* (Bologna: Clueb, 2008), 416.

11 On blasphemy and defamatory statements, see Adriano Prosperi, *Tribunali della coscienza: Inquisitori, confessori, missionari,* new ed. (Turin: Einaudi, 2007), 359.

12 ACMo, *Fondo Arciconfraternita di San Giovanni Battista della Morte*, Casi di Conforteria, libro A.

13 Prosperi, *Tribunali della coscienza*, 57.

14 *Quesiti proposti, e decisi nella Sacra Scuola de' confortatori di Bologna dall'abate Carl'Antonio Macchiavelli* (Bologna, 1745), 4.

15 Ibid., 5–7.

16 Ibid., 7–9.

17 Ibid., 10–11.

18 Ibid., 21.

19 Ibid., 23–24.

20 Ibid., 29–31.

21 Ibid., 32–34.

22 Ibid., 49–51.

23 From the *Libro del Provveditore*, reg. 7 (cited by Michele Di Sivo, "Archivio della Confraternita di S. Giovanni Decollato, 1497–1870," *Rivista storica del Lazio* 8, no. 12 [2000]: 18).

24 See Chapter 19.

25 The collection of preprinted modules compiled by members of the School is conserved in a chronologically ordered but unnumbered dossier in the collection of the Confraternity in the Biblioteca Arcivescovile di Bologna.

26 AABo, *Archivio consorziale del clero urbano, Conforteria dei condannati*, Libro del censore IX C 2, cc. 19r–22r.

27 *Nuova, e distinta relazione della giustizia seguita in Bologna li 20 giugno 1744 nella persona di Giovanni Menghi di Transinico dello Stato di Modona . . .* (Bologna, n.d.).

28 The page in the *Libro dei giustiziati* concerning this celebrated case was published in the *Catalogo illustrativo dei libri, documenti ed oggetti esposti dalle provincie dell'Emilia e delle Romagne nel Tempio del Risorgimento italiano, Esposizione regionale in Bologna*, compiled by Raffaele Belluzzi and Vittorio Fiorini (Bologna: Zamorani e Albertazzi, 1897), vol. 2, no. 2. More recently it has been reproduced by Maria Antonietta Terzoli, *Le prime lettere di Jacopo Ortis: Un giallo editoriale tra politica e censura* (Rome: Salerno, 2004), 11–12. The comforters' report is in AABo, *Archivio consorziale del clero urbano*, IX F 3.

27. DEVOTIONS FOR EXECUTED SOULS

1 See, for example, the one painted by the Genoese artist Orazio de Ferrari in 1654 for the parish church of Sestri Levante (reproduced in Fulvio Cervini, "L'immaginario della morte nelle confraternite della Liguria in età moderna," in *Confraternite, chiese e società*, ed. Liana Bertoldi Lenoci (Bari: Schena, 1994), 139.

2 *Capitoli della venerabile congregazione, e chiesa degl'agonizzanti di questa capitale rinnovati . . . 17 settembre 1783* (Palermo, 1839). My thanks to Tullio Viola for drawing my attention to this document.

3 Ibid., 6.

4 *Sacro ragguaglio a tutto il mondo della particolare institutione della Compagnia degl'Agonizanti canonicamente erreta nella chiesa di S. Isaia di Bologna l'anno 1627* (Bologna, 1635), c. 2r.

5 Ibid., 10.

6 *Esercizio di pietà nella Congregazione degli Agonizzanti in Bologna per la mattina di que' giorni, ne' quali si fa giustizia per implorare da Sua divina Maestà la salute dell'anima dei condannati a morte* (Bologna, 1723—the reproduction of a Rome edition published in 1701 on behalf of the Roman archconfraternity of the Natività degli Agonizzanti). I would like to thank Piero Bellettini, the director of the Biblioteca dell'Archiginnasio, for his help in this and other research.

7 A copy of the *Istruzione per quelli, che desiderano aggregarsi alla Pia unione,* printed in Bologna for Lorenzo Martelli in 1743, is housed in the Biblioteca Arcivescovile di Bologna.

8 [Girolamo Baruffaldi], *Direttorio ad uso della conforteria di Ferrara,* 2nd ed. (Ferrara, 1757), 72.

9 Voltaire, *Histoire de Charles XII,* critical edition, ed. Gunnar von Proschwitz (Oxford: Voltaire Foundation, 1996), 284–286, 229–230. A more detailed reconstruction of the episode can be found in Adriano Prosperi, "Il giurista mite: Johann Jacob Moser e l'infanticidio," in *Il costituzionalista riluttante: Scritti per Gustavo Zagrebelsky,* ed. Andrea Giorgis, Enrico Grosso, and Jörg Luther (Turin: Einaudi, 2016), 209–222.

10 Natalie Zemon Davis, "Ghosts, Kin, and Progeny: Some Features of Family Life in Early Modern France," *Daedalus* 106, no. 2 (1977): 87–114.

11 Giovanni Lorenzo Guadagno, *Thesoro della dottrina di Christo* (Venice, 1722), 277.

12 Paolo Segneri, *Il cristiano istruito nella sua legge,* vol. 2: *Ragionamento vigesimo* (Brescia: Pasini, 1823), 574–575 (the first edition was printed by Paolo Baglioni in Venice in 1687).

13 See Cervini, *L'immaginario della morte,* 125–143, esp. 138. In Liguria there were many confraternities dedicated to the devotion of a good death; at the time the Agonizzanti were encouraged by the Jesuits and Theatines. See Edoardo Grendi, "Le confraternite urbane nell'età moderna: L'esempio genovese," now in Grendi, *In altri termini: Etnografia e storia di una società di antico regime,* ed. Osvaldo Raggio and Angelo Torre (Milan: Feltrinelli, 2004), 75.

14 Giovanni Battista Manni da Modena, *Sacro trigesimo di varii discorsi per aiuto dell'anime del Purgatorio* (Bologna, 1673), 608.

15 Guadagno, *Thesoro della dottrina di Christo,* 307.

16 Archivio della Curia di Firenze, *Miscellanea s. Uffizio,* busta II–III, no. 73: costituto di Margherita q. Sebastiani de Cucchis dal Mugello, del 3 dicembre 1639. This section draws in part on a text I contributed to *Cultura d'élite e cultura popolare nell'arco alpino fra Cinque e Seicento,* ed. Ottavio Besomi and Carlo Caruso (Basel: Birkhauser Verlag, 1995), 29–34.

17 ASLu, *Cause delegate 15,* processo per stregoneria contro Polissena e Margherita, cc. n. n.

18 Denunciation presented to the Holy Office of Venice by Lucrezio Cilla on May 30, 1587; edited by Marisa Milani, it is reproduced in *Processi del S. Uffizio di Venezia contro ebrei e giudaizzanti (1587–1598),* vol. 8, ed. Pier Cesare Ioly Zorattini (Florence: Olschki, 1990), 177. For more on this case, see also Marisa Milani, "Indovini ebrei e streghe cristiane nella Venezia dell'ultimo '500," *Lares* 53, no. 2 (1987): 207–213.

19 Denunciation by Lucrezio Cilla, May 30, 1587, 179. In a Modenese variant of the same incantation, the ritual consisted of reciting (at the window, "by night, and looking at a fixed star," and holding a rope) the following formula three times: "Dio v'salva, stella crespa | la gratia ch'a v'domand non ve rencresca | a'v'domand el nod d'i tre appicca | el nod di tri squarta, | el nod d'i tre danna, | che dighin andar l cor del tal, che el debban batter e flagellar si forte | che per amor mie el sie congiont'alla morte." (May God save you, wrinkled star / do not be displeased by the blessing I ask of you / I ask for the knot of three hanged men, the knot of three quartered men, the knot of three damned men, who must go to his heart [that is, of the loved one], and beat and rent him so strongly that out of love for me he will be united [with me] until death.) Each time, a knot was to be made in the rope (cost. 16 luglio 1600 di Camilla da Novellara, in ASMo, *Inquisizione,* busta 12; I am indebted to Maria Pia Fantini for drawing my attention to this).

20 Testimony of Fulvia Brugnalesco, June 10, 1587. See Marisa Milani, *Streghe e diavoli nei processi del S. Uffizio: Venezia, 1554–1587* (Bassano del Grappa: Ghedina & Tassotti, 1994), 182.

21 Ibid., 220. From these documents it emerges that there was a widespread popular belief that the executed and those who died a violent death ended up in hell, a point emphasized by Chiara Traverso, *La Scuola di San Fantin o dei "Picai": Carità e giustizia a Venezia* (Venice: Marsilio, 2000), 76–77.

22 Giuseppe Pitre, *Usi e costumi credenze e pregiudizi del popolo siciliano,* vol. 4 (Florence: Barbera, 1952), 11–32.

23 Giuseppe Bonomo, *Scongiuri del popolo siciliano* (Palermo: Palumbo, 1978), 370–372.

24 Giovanna Fiume, *La vecchia dell'aceto: Un processo per veneficio nella Palermo di fine Settecento* (Palermo: Gelka, 1990), 270–271.

25 A Pugliese version gathered by Cosimo Luccarelli can be found on a blog about the folklore of Grottaglie and the ancient devotion of the townspeople for souls in purgatory (http://grottagliesitablog.wordpress.com/2009/10/31/). The souls of the executed—"ca ci sempri spierti sciati | pi mmuntagni e ppi mmarini" ("you, who always roam the mountains and seas")—are in threes: "Tre ssiti l'uccisi | tre ssiti l'ampisi | tre ssiti li tracullati." ("three killed, three hung, three beheaded").

26 "Something happened between the mid-sixteenth and mid-seventeenth centuries that transformed the way in which Italian Catholics saw the souls of executed criminals and plague victims" (Michael P. Carroll, *Veiled Threats: The Logic of Popular Catholicism in Italy* [Baltimore, MD: Johns Hopkins University Press, 1996], 150).

27 Aron Jakovlevič Gurevič, *Medieval Popular Culture: Problems of Belief and Perception,* trans. János M. Bak and Paul A. Hollingsworth (Cambridge: Cambridge University Press; Paris: Éditions de la Maison des Sciences de l'Homme, 1988), xv.

28 Marc Bloch, "La vie d'outre-tombe du roi Salomon," in *Mélanges Historiques,* vol. 2 (Paris: SEVPEN, 1963), 920–938.

29 See Jean-Claude Schmitt, *Religione, folklore e società nell'Occidente medievale* (Rome–Bari: Laterza, 1988), 198.

30 Giovanni Tassoni, *Arti e tradizioni popolari: Le inchieste napoleoniche sui costumi e le tradizioni del Regno italico* (Bellinzona: Casagrande, 1973), 159.

31 Ibid., 295, 304.

32 Ibid., 465.

33 Ibid., 134.

34 There are many examples in the illustrative material accompanying the article by Mimma Pasculli Ferrara, "La committenza Orsini della 'Ducal' chiesa del Purgatorio e del Monte del Suffragio delle anime dei Morti a Gravina di Puglia," in Lenoci, *Confraternite, chiese e società,* 529–602.

28. DYING WITHOUT TREMBLING

1 BAMi, ms L.128.sup., *Confraternita di san Gio. Battista Decollato in Milano, Giustiziati,* cc. 81r–86v. For more about the Sala case, see Angela Lischetti, "Vita e morte di Carlo Sala (1738–1775), ladro sacrilego e miscredente," in *Milano nella storia dell'età moderna,* ed. Carlo Capra and Claudio Donati (Milan: Franco Angeli, 1997), 122–138.

2 *Carteggio di Pietro e Alessandro Verri, dal 1766 al 1797,* vol. 7, ed. Emanuele Greppi and Alessandro Giulini (Milan: Cogliati, 1931), 253. On the Sala case, see Giovanni Biancardi, ed., *Un illustre impiccato: Lettere dell'autunno 1775* (Milan: il Muro di Tessa, 2007).

3 *Carteggio,* 252. Verri's prudence on religious matters had already found expression in his rewriting of the work of Beccaria (see Gianni Francioni's observations in Cesare Beccaria, *Dei delitti e delle pene,* Edizione Nazionale delle opera di Cesare Beccaria diretta da Luigi Firpo, vol. 1 [Milan: Mediobanca, 1984], 268–274).

4 *Viaggio a Parigi e a Londra (1766–1767): Carteggi di Pietro e Alessandro Verri,* ed. Gianmarco Gaspari (Milan: Adelphi, 1980), 250–256, letter dated January 25, 1767.

5 Ibid., 127–128.

6 AABo, *Archivio consorziale del clero urbano,* IX F 3, fol. 1.

7 Ibid., IX F 1.

8 On this image, see Luigi Firpo, "Le edizioni italiane dei *Delitti e delle pene*," in Beccaria, *Dei delitti e delle pene*, 1:419–420; a reproduction of the allegorical illustration is at 547.

9 The plates held in the Biblioteca Ambrosiana, ms L.128. sup. coincide at least in part with those of the Beltrame private collection reproduced in the appendix to Italo Mereu, *La pena di morte a Milano nel secolo di Beccaria* (Vicenza: Neri Pozza, 1988); see Chapter 32.

10 Adriano Ceruti, "La chiesa di S. Giovanni alle Case rotte in Milano," *Archivio storico lombardo* 1, no. 1 (1874): 182.

29. COMFORTING OF THE CONDEMNED IN CATHOLIC EUROPE

1 M. Bonus Merbesius, *Summa christiana seu orthodoxa morum disciplina*, vol. 2 (Paris, 1683), 339–341: "quaestio XVII: An reis ultimo supplicio afficiendis Eucharistia porrigi debeat."

2 See Pascal Bastien, "La parole du confesseur auprès des suppliciés (Paris, XVIIᵉ–XVIIIᵉ siècle)," *Revue historique* 307, no. 634 (2005): 283–308, esp. 286. Also from Sorbonne circles is a printed text of Pierre de Besse, published in Paris in 1624, and the testimony of a comforter: see Pascal Bastien, *L'execution publique à Paris au XVIIIᵉ siècle: Une histoire des rituels judiciaires* (Paris: Champ Vallon, 2006), 177–184.

3 "S'il leur eust declare l'attentat qu'il vouloit commettre contre le Roy s'estoit leur devoir se saisir de sa personne . . . d'autant qu'en ce qui concerne le public les prestres sont obliges de reveler le secret" (Bibliothèque Nationale, Paris, ms fr. 16 536, fols. 429r–442r: *Interrogatoire de Ravaillac par le President le P. Potier*, 17 mai 1610, see also fol. 534v).

4 As noted by Bastien, "La parole du confesseur," 289.

5 "Telle Cour a ordonne qu'apres l'execution . . . son corps sera imhue en terre saincte s'il le requiert" (in actual fact it was the Franciscans who collected the body and took it to their church). The citations are from Bibliothèque Nationale, Paris, ms fr. 16536, cc. 154r–163r; ibid., fol. 162r, the sentence of December 19, 1475. An edition of the trial proceedings has been promised by Yves Lallemand, the author of "Le procès pour trahison du connétable de Saint-Pol," in *Les procès politiques (XIVᵉ–XVIIᵉ siècle)*, ed. Yves-Marie Bercé (Rome: École Française de Rome, 2007), 145–155.

6 Jean Muret, *Ceremonies funebres de toutes les Nations* (Paris, 1675), 138–139; the passage is cited by Bastien, "La parole du confesseur," 300.

7 This is the view of Michel Bée, "Le spectacle de l'exécution dans la France d'Ancien Régime," *Annales ESC* 38 (1983): 843–862.

8 Bastien, "La parole du confesseur," 286.

9 Giovanni Lorenzo Berti, *Librorum de theologicis disciplinis t. VII, in quo plura traduntur, quae ad confirmationis, Eucharistiae, et poenitentiae pertinent sacramenta* (Rome, 1743), 383–385.

10   See Marc Venard, "Les confréries de pénitents au XVIᵉ siècle dans la province ecclésiastique d'Avignon," *Memoires de l'Academie de Vaucluse* 1 (1967): 55–79.

11   Undated letter from the 1620s, held in the Archives départementales du Rhône. All of the largely unpublished documentation relating to Cesare Lauro's initiative is cited here from Serena Bertuccelli, "L'assistenza ai prigionieri e ai condannati a morte: La Confraternita della Misericordia a Lione nei secoli XVII–XVIII" (degree thesis, University of Pisa, 1997–1998). For the draft of the plea to the pope: ibid., 30–31.

12   "Project de supplique à sa Sainteté"; ibid., 56.

13   See Alain Tallon, *La Compagnie du Saint-Sacrement (1629–1667)* (Paris: Cerf, 1990).

14   [Joseph Filère], *La consolation des prisonniers et des criminels condamnés à mort: Et le bonheur des âmes charitables qui les secourent en toutes les necessitez de l'esprit et du corps* . . . (Lyon, 1658), 88–102.

15   Ibid., 248.

16   See also the photographic reproduction of the document in the appendix to Serena Bertuccelli's thesis "L'assistenza," and likewise the 1639 statutes in French *(Règles et statuts de la confrérie des pénitents de la Miséricorde érigée à Lyon)* and the revised version of 1749.

17   "Christianae pietati magis conforme esse, ut vivifici Sacramenti participatio iis etiam, qui ob grave delictum sententia capitali damnati sunt, petentibus, et alioquin recte dispositis, non denegetur" (Pope Benedict XIV, *De Synodo dioecesana libri tredecim* [Venice, 1775], l. I, 186).

18   "Censemus, Episcoporum partes esse, hanc disciplinam in suis dioecesibus invehendam curare, ut delinquentibus ultimo supplicio afficiendis Eucharistia praebeatur, idque in Synodalibus constitutionibus inserere, auctore nimirum immortalis memoriae Pontifice S. Pio V" (ibid.).

19   "We do not wish to censure or to approve the conduct of others" (Benedict XIV, *Della Santa Messa,* vol. 1 [Venice, 1792], 197).

20   For the history of the issue in the Portuguese-speaking world, a fundamental work is Giuseppe Marcocci, "La salvezza dei condannati a morte: Giustizia, conversioni e sacramenti in Portogallo e nel suo impero, 1450–1700 circa," in *Misericordie: Conversioni sotto il patibolo tra Medioevo ed età moderna,* ed. Adriano Prosperi (Pisa: Edizioni della Normale, 2007), 189–255. The key reference work regarding the "disciplinary" development of the administration of justice is António Manuel Hespanha, "Da 'iustitia' à 'disciplina': Textos, poder e política penal no antigo regime," in *Justiça e litigiosidade; História e prospectiva* (Lisbon: Fundação Calouste Gulbenkian, 1993).

21   "Exclusão escatologica" is discussed in Ana Cristina Araújo, "Cerimónias de execução pública no Antigo Regime—escatologia e justiça," *Revista de História da Sociedade e da Cultura* 1 (2001): 169–211, esp. 182.

22 The bull "Hospitalium et aliorum piorum locorum," published in *Portugaliae Monumenta Misericordiarum,* 10 vols., ed. José Pedro Paiva (Lisbon: União das Misericórdias Portuguesas, 2013), 3:32.

23 Ibid., *Introdução,* 7–21.

24 Ibid., 385–393.

25 See Giuseppe Marcocci, "A evolução dos rituais da misericòrdias (1498–1910)," in Paiva, *Portugaliae Monumenta Misericordiarum,* 10:189–213.

26 A summary can be found in Isabel dos Guimarães Sá, *As Misericordias portuguesas de D. Manuel I a Pombal* (Lisbon: Libros Horizonte, 2001), 89–98.

27 Paiva, *Portugaliae Monumenta Misericordiarum,* 3:393.

28 Dos Guimarães Sá, *As Misericordias portuguesas,* 31.

29 The *Auto de Deus Padre e Justiça e Misericòrdia,* undated but 1508, is in Paiva, *Portugaliae Monumenta Misericordiarum,* 3:493–508.

30 "Hinc fit ut rarissime quis in hac praepotenti urbe vivens ad furcas ducatur, vel ad iustitiam puniendus" (ibid., 3:537; the epistle, dated February 21, 1500, and addressed to García Moniz, appeared in print in Lisbon in the same year).

31 Maria Inmaculada Rodríguez Flores, *El perdón real en Castilla (siglos XIII–XVIII)* (Salamanca: Universidad de Salamanca, 1971), 46–47. The same thing also went on in France at the time: see Claude Gauvard, *"De grâce especial": Crime, état et société en France à la fin du Moyen Age,* vol. 2 (Paris: Publications de la Sorbonne, 1991), 928–929.

32 Rodriguez Flores, *El perdón real,* 312.

33 Yosef Hayim Yerushalmi, *The Lisbon Massacre of 1506 and the Royal Image in the "Shebet Yehudah"* (Cincinnati: Hebrew Union College, 1976).

34 For the information presented below, see Marcocci, "La salvezza dei condannati a morte," 189–255 (with extensive literature), esp. 207.

35 This aspect is emphasized in Isabel dos Guimarães Sá and Maria Antónia Lopes, *História breve das misericórdias portuguesas* (Coimbra: Imprensa da Universidade de Coimbra, 2008), 54–55.

36 The passage from *Don Quijote de la Mancha* is cited by Michele Olivari, "La scienza del conforto del gesuita catalano Pere Gil," in Prosperi, *Misericordie,* 257–276, esp. 264.

37 José Ignacio Tellechea Idígoras, *El Papado y Felipe II: Colección de breves pontificios,* vol. 3: *1550–1598* (Madrid: Fundación Universitaria Española, 2002), 131 (see Chapter 25).

38 For more on the delays to executions caused by the resort to sacramental confession and appeals to the ecclesiastic authorities, see Giovanni Romeo, *Aspettando il boia: Condannati a morte, confortatori e inquisitori nella Napoli della Controriforma* (Florence: Sansoni, 1993).

39 See Francisco Tomás y Valiente, *El derecho penal de la monarquía absoluta (siglos XVI, XVII y XVIII)* (Madrid: Tecnis, 1969), 373.

40 Marcocci, "A evolução dos rituais da misericòrdias," 194–195.

41 *Ordenações Filipinas* (1603), Liv. 5, Tit. 137: *Das execuções das penas corporais.* See also Araújo, "Cerimónias de execução pública," 184–185.

42 See Marcocci, "La salvezza dei condannati a morte," 233–234, who refers to the work of Manuel de Sá, *Aphorismi confessariorum ex doctorum sententiis collecti* (Lyon, 1600), 194. According to Kornmann's treatise, the first edition of which was published at the beginning of the century, the Eucharist was granted in many cities in the empire but not in France or in Spain (Heinrich Kornmann, *Opera curiosa in tractatus sex distributa* [Frankfurt, 1696], 414–415, pt. 2, chap. 12: "An damnatis . . . danda sit Eucharistia").

43 Valiente, *El derecho penal,* 372.

44 See Ángel Rodríguez Sánchez, *Morir en Extremadura: La muerte en la horca a finales del Antiguo Régimen, 1792–1909* (Cáceres: Institución Cultural El Brocense de la Diputación Provincial, 1980), 35.

45 Marcocci, "La salvezza dei condannati a morte," 210.

46 See António Manuel Hespanha, *Da "iustitia" à "Disciplina": Textos, poder e política no antigo regime* (Coimbra: Faculdade de Direito de Coimbra, 1989).

47 Antonio da Gama, *De sacramentis praestandis ultimo supplicio damnatis, ac de testamentis, anatomia, et eorum sepultura* (Lisbon, 1559). I am indebted to Giuseppe Marcocci for drawing my attention to and making available this important treatise, which he studies in his essay "La salvezza dei condannati a morte."

48 "Villon's Epitaph," in *François Villon: Selected Poems,* trans. Peter Dale (London: Penguin Books, 1978), 219.

49 The first edition of the *Journal* of Versoris was edited by Gustave Fagniez and published in 1885; the abridged modern edition is the one cited here: *Journal d'un bourgeois de Paris sous François Ier: Le livre de raison de Maître Nicolas Versoris* (Paris: Union Generale d'éditions, 1963), 99.

50 Ibid., 178–180. The case of the heretic who refused confession is described at 99.

51 Antonio da Gama, *De sacramentis,* cc. 71r–77r.

52 Ibid., cc. 1r–2v; see Vincenzo Lavenia, "Eretici sentenziati e 'reincorporati,'" in Prosperi, *Misericordie,* 165.

53 Antonio da Gama, *De sacramentis,* c. 4v.

54 Erasmus, "Preparing for Death / De praeparatione ad mortem," trans. John N. Grant, in *Collected Works of Erasmus,* vol. 70, *Spritualia and Pastoralia,* ed. John O'Malley (Toronto: University of Toronto Press, 1998), 389–450, esp. 420.

55 Ibid., 433.

56 Antonino Pierozzi, *Medicina de l'anima tanto per quelli che sono amalati, quanto per quelli che sono sani* (Venice, 1544). The edition brought out in 1545 by the printer Vincenzo Valgrisi was enriched with "simulacra, stories, and figures of death"—the etchings of Hans Holbein. The book was prohibited in 1554 but continued to be reprinted clandestinely, and was still being sold in 1570 when Valgrisi was put on

trial by the Inquisition. For a systematic investigation into the diffusion of this literature, see Gunther Franz, *Huberinus, Rhegius, Holbein: Bibliographische und druckgeschichtliche Untersuchung der verbreitesten Trost und Erbauungsschriften des 16. Jahrhunderts* (Nieuwkoop: B. De Graaf, 1973).

57 Pierozzi, *Medicina de l'anima,* c. 38.

58 Veit Dietrich's diary of 1543 was referred to by the texts of instruction circulating at the time in Lutheran churches: see Peter Schuster, "Le rituel de la peine capitale dans les villes allemandes à la fin du Moyen Âge: Ruptures et continuités," in *Pratiques sociales et politiques judiciaires dans les villes de l'Occident à la fin du Moyen Âge,* ed. Jacques Chiffoleau, Claude Gauvard, and Andrea Zorzi (Rome: École Française de Rome, 2007), 707.

59 Joost Van Damhouder, *Praxis rerum criminalium: Opus absolutissimum* (Antwerp, 1601; anastatic reprint, Clark, NJ: Lawbook Exchange, 2005). The first edition came out in 1554. For more about Joost (also Joos and Jost) Damhouder (Bruges, 1507; Antwerp, 1581) and the plagiarism in his *Praxis,* see Robert Feenstra's entry on "Damhouder, Joos de," in *Juristen: Ein biographisches Lexicon; Von der Antike bis zum 20. Jahrhundert,* ed. Michael Stolleis (Munich: Beck, 2001), 159; and especially the essay by Jos Monballyu in *Lexicon zur Geschichte der Hexenverfolgung,* ed. Gudrun Gersmann, Katrin Moeller, and Jürgen-MichaelSchmidt, 2007, http:www .historicum.net, in which the author points out that Damhouder borrowed a long passage from Paolo Grillando's *Tractatus de sortilegiis,* and many others from Johannes Trithemius, Giovanni Francesco Ponzinibio, and Jakob Sprenger, to the extent that Damhouder's work is more than anything else a skillful compilation of different texts. Monballyu also produced the modern edition of the work most heavily plundered by Damhouder: Filips Wielant (1441–1520), *Verzameld Werk, I: Corte instructie in materie criminele* (Brussels: Paleis der Academiën, 1995). Monballyu looks carefully at Damhouder's chapter on witchcraft, where he describes one of his experiences as a judge: the story of a healer and presumed saint from Bruges, whom he tried and had tortured and shaved. After the discovery of a parchment scroll in her vagina, she was condemned to be burned alive in Middelburg.

30. "... Y PIDDIENDO A DIOS MISERICORDIA LO MATAN"

1 Jerome Xavier, *La ley y el Evangelio: Fuente de vida en que se declaran las cosas de la ley del Evangelio y se da razon de los principales misterios della y se impugnan las leys contrarias, especialmente la de Mahoma,* ARSI, Opp.N.N. 259, c. 226r (the copy sent to the superior general of the Society in Rome). Jerome Xavier, a relative of Saint Francis Xavier, entered the novitiate of Alcalá in 1568 and devoted his energies to converting the Indians, becoming superior of the professed house of Goa. He undertook a mission to the court of the Grand Mughal, during which the text cited above was probably written. There is a version in Persian dated 1596. After returning to Goa, he died there in 1617 (Carlos Sommervogel, *Bibliothèque de la Compagnie de Jésus,* new ed., vol. 8 [Brussels: O. Schepens; Paris: A. Picard, 1898],

coll. 1337–1340). Regarding Xavier, see also László Polgár, *Bibliographie sur l'histoire de la Compagnie de Jésus, 1901–1980,* vol. 3 (Rome: Institutum Historicum S. I., 1990), 732, who indicates a work I was unable to consult: Ángel Santos Hernández, *Jéronimo Xavier S. J., Apóstol del Gran Mogol y arzobispo electo de Cranganor, en la India, 1559–1617* (Pamplona: Gomez, 1958); but see also a number of preparatory essays by Santos: "Dos Javieres en la India," *Miscelánea Comillas* 18 (1952): 27–87; and "Un sobrinho de Javier en la Corte del Gran Mogol," *Missionalia Hispanica* 10 (1953): 417–493, and *Missionalia Hispanica* 11 (1954): 565–577.

2   The passage from the manuscript treatise *De sacris admirandis auditionibus* (in the Biblioteca Ambrosiana) is cited by José C. Sola, "El P. Juan Bautista Eliano: Un documento autobiográfico inédito," *Archivum Historicum Societatis Iesu* 4 (1935): 291–321.

3   See Giuseppe Marcocci, "La salvezza dei condannati a morte: Giustizia, conversioni e sacramenti in Portogallo e nel suo impero; 1450–1700 circa," in *Misericordie: Conversioni sotto il patibolo tra Medioevo ed età moderna,* ed. Adriano Prosperi (Pisa: Edizioni della Normale, 2007), 193–195.

4   In 1632 his works were placed on the Index, which also included the Italian version of the *Práctica* (see the entry for "Poza" by Jesús M. Escalera in *Diccionario histórico de la Compañia de Jesús,* vol. 4, ed. Charles E. O'Neill and Joaquín M. Domínguez (Rome: Institutum historicum S.I., 2001), 3209. "Il avait de grandes connaissances et aussi un entêtement que rien ne pouvait fléchir," noted Sommervogel (*Bibliothèque des écrivains de la Compagnie de Jésus,* vol. 6, 1895, coll. 1135–1142).

5   Pedro de León, *Compendio de algunas experiencias en los ministerios de que usa la Compañia de Jesús,* of which there also exists a partial edition: *Grandeza y miseria de Andalucía: Testimonio de una encrucijada histórica (1578–1616),* ed. Pedro Herrera Puga (Granada: Facultad de Teologia, 1981). I am indebted to Michele Olivari for drawing my attention to this work.

6   Ibid., 291.

7   Ibid., 394–600.

8   "Yo temblava de la cárcel, como de la misma muerte, y huía de ir a ver ajusticiados, porque me parecía que si fuese a ver alguno que me había de aparecer aquella noche" (ibid., 198).

9   Letter of Tommaso Romano, June 13, 1556, in *MHSI, Epistolae mixtae ex variis Europae locis ab anno 1537 ad 1556 scriptae, nunc primum a patribus Societatis Jesu in lucem editae,* vol. 5: 1555–1556 (Madrid: Avrial, 1901), 354–355.

10 "Padre, una palabra . . . Acúsome que todo cuanto le he dicho hasta ahora ha sido mentira" (De León, *Compendio,* 284).

11 Ibid., 286.

12 Ibid., 466–472.

13 Ibid., 472–475.

14 Ibid., 300–301.

15 Ibid., 297–298.

16 Ibid., 310–311.

17 The work was published in Barcelona in 1605: see Antonio Espino López and Francisco López Molina, "El arte de bien morir del jesuita Padre Pere Gil," in *Muerte, religiosidad y cultura popular: Siglos XIII–XVIII,* ed. Eliseo Serrano Martín (Zaragoza: Institucion "Fernando el Catolico," 1994), 321–342; see, on this subject, Michele Olivari, "La scienza del conforto del gesuita catalano Pere Gil," and Mario Prades Vilar, "Persuasión, Confesión y Expiación en el Modo de aiudar a ben morir als Qui per malaltia o per Justicia moren del jesuita padre Pere Gil," both in Prosperi, *Misericordie,* 257–276 and 277–321.

18 As emphasized by Espino López and López Molina, "El arte de bien morir," 325–327. Polanco's work had been translated and printed in Saragozza in 1577.

19 *Modo de aiudar a morir,* fol. 122v (see also Olivari, "La scienza del conforto," 262n).

20 López and Molina, "El arte de bien morir," 335n.

21 "Lo qui pateix ab culpa, pateix en la Creu del bon Lladr: Pero lo qui pateix sens culpa, pateix en la Creu de Christo," *Modo de aiudar a morir,* fols. 141rv; see also Prades Vilar, "Persuasión, Confesión y Expiación," 318.

22 See William Zammitt, *Kissing the Gallows: A Cultural History of Crime, Torture and Punishment in Malta, 1600–1798* (Saint John, Malta: BDL, 2016).

31. THE GERMAN WORLD, THE REFORMATION, AND THE NEW IMAGE OF THE EXECUTIONER

1 Uwe Israel, "Hinrichtung in spätmittelalterlichen Städten: Öffentlichkeit, Ritual, Kritik," in *Pratiques sociales et politiques judiciaires dans les villes de l'Occident à la fin du Moyen Âge,* ed. Jacques Chiffoleau, Claude Gauvard, and Andrea Zorzi (Rome: École Française de Rome, 2007), 661–687, esp. 673–678. See also, in the same volume, Peter Schuster, "Le rituel de la peine capitale dans les villes allemandes à la fin du Moyen Âge: Ruptures et continuités," 689–712.

2 Peter Schuster, *Eine Stadt vor Gericht: Recht ud Alltag im spätmittelalterlichen Konstanz* (Paderborn: Schoningh, 2000), 270.

3 This tradition includes Karl von Amira (*Die germanischen Todesstrafen: Untersuchungen zur Rechts- und Religionsgeschichte* [Munich: Verlag der Bayerischen Akademie der Wissenschaften, 1922]), and the man who followed in his footsteps, Hans von Hentig (*Die Strafe: Ursprung, Zweck, Psychologie* [Stuttgart: Deutsche Verlag-Anstalt, 1932; 2nd ed., Berlin: Springer, 1954–1955]). As Richard J. Evans observes in *Rituals of Retribution: Capital Punishment in Germany, 1600–1987* (Oxford: Oxford University Press, 1996), 5, they interpreted capital punishment in Germany as a "ritual propitiation of pre-Christian Gods."

4 According to Richard Martin Allen, "Crime and Punishment in Sixteenth-Century Reutlingen" (PhD diss., University of Virginia, 1980), 15, the study of crime carried out by comparing ordinances and official regulations with "actual practice" yields quantitative data that downplay the image of the cruelty of punishments.

5 For more on this, see Adriano Prosperi, *Giustizia bendata: Percorsi storici di un'immagine* (Turin: Einaudi, 2007), 37–67.

6 See the images from the Brandeburgische Halsgerichtsordnung, in Mitchell B. Merback, *The Thief, the Cross and the Wheel: Pain and the Spectacle of Punishment in Medieval and Renaissance Europe* (Chicago: University of Chicago Press, 1999), 131, no. 54. The image of the Praxis Criminalis is on p. 143, no. 57. See also nos. 45 and 46, p. 111.

7 See Christopher J. Kauffman, *Tamers of Death: The History of the Alexian Brothers from 1300 to 1789* (New York: Seabury Press, 1976), 169–210, esp. 204.

8 See Gustav Radbruch, ed., *Die peinliche Gerichtsordnung Kaiser Karls V. von 1532 Carolina* (Stuttgart: Reclam, 1960), art. 102, pp. 72–73. The old editions have etchings showing the penitent kneeling before the confessor.

9 *Lübecker Kirchenordnung von Johann Bugenhagen, 1531,* ed. Wolf-Dieter Hauschild (Lubeck: M. Schmidt-Romhild, 1981), 138; see also *Die evangelischen Kirchenordnungen des XVI. Jahrhunderts* (Leipzig: O. R. Reisland, 1902). In the church ordinance of Nuremberg (*Kirchenordnung wie es mit der Christenlichen Leer . . . , gehalten werden soll* [Nuremberg, 1557]), a brief final section deals with how to visit and console prisoners and those condemned to death—they were simply to be reminded to trust in the mercy ("Barmherzigkeit") of God (cc. CXXXV*rv*).

10 According to Hans von Hentig, *Vom Ursprung der Henkersmahlzeit* (Tübingen: J. C. B. Mohr, 1958), 99, this demonstrates that traditions of a Germanic ritual of human sacrifice lived on in the German ritual of capital punishment.

11 The crucifix had the Crucifixion on one side and the Madonna and Child, surrounded by saints, on the other: a reproduction is in Kauffman, *Tamers of Death,* 169.

12 As can be read in a criminal ordinance of 1717 (Richard Van Dülmen, *Theatre of Horror: Crime and Punishment in Early Modern Germany,* trans. Elisabeth Neu [Cambridge: Polity Press, 1990], 64).

13 Timothy J. Wengert, *Martin Luther's Ninety-Five Theses: With Introduction, Commentary, and Study Guide* (Minneapolis: Fortress Press, 2015), 18.

14 Martin Luther, *On Secular Authority,* in *Luther and Calvin on Secular Authority,* ed. and trans. Harro Höpfl (Cambridge: Cambridge University Press, 1991), 18.

15 Ibid., 15.

16 See Cesare Paoli, "'Manigoldo,'" *Archivio storico italiano* 28, no. 224 (1901): 300–306, who enriches with documentary sources the linguistic profile of the term *manigoldo* provided by Giulio Rezasco in his *Dizionario del linguaggio italiano storico e amministrativo* (Florence: Le Monnier, 1881).

17 *Memoria de' giustiziati in Firenze* (BNCFi, ms Magl. XXV. 159, cc. 6*r*–7*v*).

18 Tommaso Garzoni, *Piazza universale di tutte le professioni del mondo* (1585), ed. Giovan Battista Bronzini (Florence: Olschki, 1996), 919–920. The passage is cited, together with many others, in Giancarlo Baronti, *La morte in piazza: Opacità della*

giustizia, ambiguità del boia e trasparenza del patibolo in età moderna (Lecce: Argo, 2000), 111–142.

19 Giovanni Battista Gargiaria, *Conforto de gli afflitti condannati a morte* (Piacenza, 1650), 136–137.

20 Martin Luther, *On Secular Authority*, 15. The passages of sentences from Luther inserted into the regulations of the evangelical Churches (see *Die evangelische Kirchenordnungen des XVI. Jahrhunderts,* ed. Emil Sehling, vol. 11 [Tübingen, 1961], 131, 222) are emphasized by Schuster, "Le rituel de la peine capitale," 706.

21 See Wolfgang Stürmer, *Peccatum und Potestas: Der Sündenfall und die Entstehung der herrscherlichen Gewalt im mittelalterlichen Staatsdenken* (Sigmaringen: Thorbecke, 1987).

22 Jacob Döpler, *Theatrum poenarum, suppliciorum et executionum criminalium, oder Schau-Platz derer Leibes und Lebens-Straffen . . .* , vol. 1 (Leipzig, 1693), 457. The passage is also cited by Hans von Hentig in *Vom Ursprung des Henkermahlszeit,* 112–113.

23 "There is no better way in society to keep tight or retie the bond of general fellowship," he wrote in the introduction to the second part of the work, dealing with capital punishment ("Kein besser und kräfftiger Mittel in bürgerlicher Gesellschaft . . . durch welches das allgemeine Freundschaffts-Band könne erhalten oder wieder zusammen geknüpffet werden": Döpler, *Theatrum poenarum,* vol. 2, c. 2*v*).

24 See Joel F. Harrington, *The Faithful Executioner: Life and Death, Honour and Shame in the Turbulent Sixteenth Century* (London: Bodley Head, 2013), 169–184.

25 Sentences of this kind from Thomas Stieber's manual of Christian instructions (1574) are referred to in Schuster, "Le rituel de la peine capitale," 707–708.

26 John Calvin, *Institutes of the Christian Religion,* 2 vols., ed. John T. McNeill, trans. Ford Lewis Battles (Philadelphia: Westminster Press, 1960), bk. 3, chap. 12, p. 960 (the passage from Paul is Eph. 1:4).

27 Ibid., bk. 4, chap. 23, p. 1510.

28 For example, the executioner was allowed to receive Communion (see Evans, *Rituals of Retribution,* 58).

29 Giovanni Fontana, *La santità e la pietà trionfante: Parte prima: in cui s'espongono le vite in compendio d'alcuni santi et huomini piamente vissuti in ogni stato, posto, impiego, mestiero etc., coll'istruzione per vivere bene in essi* (Venice, 1716), 492.

30 See Alessandro Ademollo, *Le annotazioni di Mastro Titta carnefice romano: Supplizi e suppliziati; Giustizie eseguite da Gio. Batt. Bugatti e dal suo successore (1796–1870)* (Città di Castello: S. Lapi, 1886), 42.

31 For more on this reality, evoked in John Bossy, *Peace in the Post-Reformation* (Cambridge: Cambridge University Press, 1998), see the groundbreaking research of Osvaldo Raggio, *Faide e parentele: Lo stato genovese visto dalla Fontanabuona* (Turin: Einaudi, 1990). Sienese judicial sources form the basis for the research in Oscar Di Simplicio, *Peccato penitenza perdono, Siena, 1575–1800* (Milan: Franco Angeli, 1994). See also Ottavia Niccoli, *Perdonare: Idee, pratiche e rituali in Italia tra Cinque e Seicento* (Rome: Laterza, 2007).

32 Of fundamental importance is the *Thesaurus Consiliorum et decisionum* of Georg Dedekenn, published in Jena in 1671, about which see Benjamin T. G. Mayes, *Counsel and Conscience: Lutheran Casuistry and Moral Reasoning after the Reformation* (Göttingen: Vandenhoecht und Ruprecht, 2011), 30–31.

33 An overall picture of the situation in Germany at the beginning of the modern age is in Evans, *Rituals of Retribution,* chap. 1, "Theatres of Cruelty," 27–64.

34 In the cities of Frankfurt and Mecheln, the number of executed from 1401 to 1500 and from 1501 to 1700 was more than double that of the previous century and the subsequent century (Von Hentig, *Vom Ursprung des Henkermahlszeit,* 219).

35 See Bernard Vogler, "Attitudes devant la mort et cérémonies funèbres dans les églises protestantes rhénanes vers 1600," *Archives des sciences sociales des religions* 39 (1975): 139–146.

36 See the episodes gathered by Michel Bée, "Le spectacle de l'exécution dans la France d'Ancien Régime," *Annales ESC* 38 (1983): 843–862.

37 *Theatrum mortis humanae tripartitum* (Salzburg, 1682). For more on Valvasor (1641–1693), see Maria Bidovec, "Johann Weichard Valvasor: Polimata nonché avvincente narratore nella Carniola del Seicento," *eSamizdat* 2, no. 3 (2004): 77–83, www.esamizdat.it/bidovec_art_eS_2004_(II)_3.pdf.

38 The citation, from Senault's *L'homme criminel* (1644), appears in the fundamental work of Jean Delumeau, *Sin and Fear: The Emergence of a Western Guilt Culture, 13th–18th Centuries* [1983], trans. Eric Nicholson (New York: St. Martin's Press, 1990), 288.

39 In the Netherlands alone there were around 482 (see Université de Gand, *Bibliographie des martyrologes protestants néerlandais* [The Hague: Martinus Nijhoff, 1890], 13).

40 See David Nicholls, "Theatre of Martyrdom in the French Reformation," *Past and Present* 121, no. 1 (1988): 49–73.

41 See Michel Vovelle, *La mort et l'Occident de 1300 à nos jours* (Paris: Gallimard, 1983), 209.

42 See Peter Spierenburg, *The Spectacle of Suffering: Executions and the Evolution of Repression; From a Preindustrial Metropolis to the European Experience* (Cambridge: Cambridge University Press, 1984), 53.

43 The perceptive work of Rebecca Lemon, *Treason by Words: Literature, Law, and Rebellion in Shakespeare's England* (Ithaca, NY: Cornell University Press, 2006), highlights the echoes in *Macbeth.*

44 Ibid., 88.

32. PRINTING AND SCAFFOLD STORIES

1 Documents held in the collection *Conforteria, miscellanea stampati dall'anno 1733 al 1740* of the Biblioteca Arcivescovile di Bologna, *Archivio consorziale del clero urbano,* aula 2, C.VII 9, n. 4846, in the folder bearing the following heading, written in Carlo Antonio Macchiavelli's hand: "Printed miscellanea relating either directly

or indirectly to matters pertaining either to the Holy School or to the *Conforteria* of Bologna, gathered together in such form so as to draw on them readily for any need, a collection formerly begun in 1733 and then [continued] in 1740 . . . produced by Carlo Antonio Macchiavelli." In Florence, a similar ban imposed by the grand duke, dated September 10, 1608, issued instructions "not to admit anyone into the chapel, or other such places, at a time of execution" (Florence, Biblioteca Riccardiana, ms Riccardiano 3252, cc. 164–168).

2 A critical edition of the text of the lament, prepared by Francesco Novati, is in "La Raccolta di stampe popolari italiane della Biblioteca di Franc. Reina," *Lares: Bullettino della societa di etnografia italiana* 2, nos. 2–3 (1913): 155–160.

3 *Morte di Marzia Basile napolitana la quale fu decollata per la crudel morte data al suo marito per causa dell'amante, e la morte della sua serva, e di uno sbirro, che come complici del delitto furon impiccati.* The original is in the Fondazione Benedetto Croce, together with Croce's essay on the text, "Giovanni della Carriola e la sua 'Storia di Marzia Basile,'" *Napoli nobilissima,* ser. 2, vol. 2 (1921): 65–68 (later included in his *Nuove curiosità storiche* [Naples: Ricciardi, 1922], 93–106). Included in the dossier is a carefully prepared information sheet by Benedetto Croce and the text of the communication to Croce of an authentic copy of the documents held in the Archivio di Stato di Napoli, *Archivio dei Bianchi "S. Maria succurre miseris,"* regarding the case of Marzia Basilia. I wish to thank the Fondazione Croce for having allowed me to consult this material and reproduce the frontispiece of the booklet.

4 As emerges from the copy sent to Croce and from the volume of the *Archivio dei Bianchi,* "Capece Scrivano, 1602–1603," cc. 38*v*–39*r*.

5 *Morte di Marzia Basile,* c. n. n. The story of Marzia Basile is touched on by Guido Panico, *Il carnefice e la piazza: Crudeltà di Stato e violenza popolare a Napoli in età moderna* (Naples: Edizioni scientifiche italiane, 1985), 23.

6 "Who will ever resume, in Italy, the work on Italian popular prints, and the varied history and poetry they carry, that was conducted with erudite industriousness by Francesco Novati in the final years of his life?" (Croce, *Nuove curiosità storiche,* 93). The question remains pertinent.

7 *Maraviglioso et horribil caso occorso nella città di Bologna, di quattro scelerati, e sacrileghi heretici, ch'imbrattavano le sacre imagini dipinte per la detta città, scoperti per intercessione della Sacratissima Imagine del Santiss. Rosario, dove s'intende il processo di tutta la vita loro, et la sentenza, et giustitia esequita contro di loro li 28 novembre del 1623, composto per Al. Ghi. Et dispensato per Domenico Barbieri di Bologna* (Parma, Cremona, Brescia, Verona, and Bologna, 1623). I quote from the copy held in the Zanetti miscellany of the Biblioteca Universitaria di Bologna. Giving the author's name in an abbreviated form (hard for the modern reader to decipher) is unusual, and may have been due to the Inquisition's control over what had been a case of heresy.

8 As can be read in the *Relatione della giustitia seguita nelli banditi, et assassini nella città di Ravenna alli 25 d'ottobre 1614 . . .* (Ravenna and Bologna, 1614) and in other booklets from the same collection.

9 See Genevieve Bolleme, *La Bibliothèque bleue: La littérature populaire en France du XVIIᵉ au XIXᵉ siècle* (Paris: Julliard, 1971).

10 Gio. Battista Madalena da Brembio, *Gratie fatte dalla Sacratissima Vergine Maria del Carmine a' suoi devoti* (Ferrara, 1611), 14–15: the episode is illustrated with an interesting etching (a copy can be found in the Biblioteca Universitaria di Bologna, Tab. I.N.III.254, no. 10).

11 See Giancarlo Baronti, "Serpi in seno: Figure e fantasmi di donne criminali nella letteratura di piazza," in *Il delitto narrato al popolo: Immagini di giustizia e stereotipi di criminalità in età moderna,* ed. Roberto De Romanis and Rosamaria Loretelli (Palermo: Sellerio, 1999), 199–218, esp. 202–204.

12 One of Macchiavelli's responses, a *Risposta sopra un quesito proposto in conforteria,* printed in Venice in 1728, is in AABo, *Archivio consorziale del clero urbano,* IX A 3.

13 *Relazione della sentenza di morte eseguita nella città di Pavia li 23 marzo 1741 nelle persone di Gaspare Ceppi, Giuseppe Lochino, e Gio. Battista padre di esso Gaspare per barbaro omicidio, rubberie, ed incendio commessi la notte delli 13 ed il giorno delli 14 gennaio 1639* (Pavia, Ferrara, and Modena, 1741). The text is held in the previously cited collection of the Biblioteca Arcivescovile di Bologna (booklet no. 80), and was consulted many years ago at the Istituto per le Scienze religiose di Bologna.

14 See Chapter 28, note 9.

15 The notice, or *polizzotto,* is in the Biblioteca Arcivescovile di Bologna, part of a whole collection of such documents.

16 *Distinta relazione di quanto è successo in Abruzzo . . .* (Naples and Reggio Calabria, 1726); *Distinto ragguaglio del tremendo, e spaventevole spettacolo di giustizia fatto in Baviera . . .* (Milan, Piacenza, Parma, and Modena, 1732), BABo, nn. 68, 73.

17 *Nuova, e vera relazione della grande giustizia seguita li 12 settembre 1745 nella città di Livorno dove s'intende la morte di tre persone, cioè Francesco Chiari fiorentino, Marc'Antonio Giuriani livornese tutti due impiccati, e Giacomo Lenzi fiorentino impiccato e squartato per aver commesso gran crudeltà barbaricamente, ed intenderete tutti i loro crudelissimi misfatti, e quel che dissero quand'erano al patibolo* (Venice and Bologna, 1745), BABo, n. 114.

18 See the *Distinta relatione della solenne condanna fatta fare avanti la porta maggiore della Basilica Vaticana dal Supremo Tribunale della Sacra Inquisitione di Pavolo Antonio Galles da Ierace in Calabria per aver rubata la Sacra Pisside con le particole consagrate oltre li vasi dell'oglii sacri in Santa maria in Trastevere* (Rome, 1708).

19 *Relazione copiosa, distinta, e veridica, della nascita, vita, e morte oprobriosa, et infame di Domenico Spallaccini, impiccato, et abbrugiato in Roma nel dí 18 luglio 1711 in vigore della di lui condanna fatta dal supremo Tribunale della Santa Romana, et Universale Inquisizione* (Rome, 1711).

20 *Relazione distinta del ristretto del processo, e sentenza contro Silvestro Legni dalla città di Velletri, e Giovanni Vecchioli da Cisterna della detta Diocesi, e della loro abiura fatta pubblicamente nella Chiesa di S. Maria sopra Minerva li 25 gennaro 1719* (Rome, 1719). Their case is linked to that of three other atheists from Velletri sentenced to a harsh regime of imprisonment the following day, described in the *Relazione distinta del ritretto del processo, e sentenza contro Giulio Legni, Bonaventura Arigoni, e Bernardino Salviati tutti tre di Velletri, e della loro abiura fatta pubblicamente nella Chiesa di S. Maria sopra Minerva li 26 Gennaro 1719* (Rome, 1719); the booklet, like the three previous ones, is in the *Jesuiten* collection of the Hauptstadtarchiv of Munich.

21 As regards the story of the book "De tribus impostoribus" and the libertine and Spinozist circles of the seventeenth and eighteenth centuries, see Silvia Berti, *Anticristianesimo e libertà* (Naples: Istituto italiano per gli studi storici, 2012).

22 Antonino Mongitore, *L'atto pubblico di fede solennemente celebrato nella città di Palermo a 6 aprile 1724 dal tribunale del S. Uffizio di Sicilia* (Palermo, 1724), chap. 16, 101ff. The diary of Canon Mongitore was used as a source by Leonardo Sciascia for his *Recitazione della controversia liparitana dedicata ad A. D.,* in Mongitore, *Opere* (Milan: Adelphi, 2012).

23 This does not seem to have been taken sufficiently into consideration by those who emphasize the connection between law and punishment, such as Anne de Vaucher Gravili, *Loi et transgression: Les histoires tragiques au XVIIᵉ siècle* (Lecce: Milella, 1982).

24 William Perkins, *Epieikeia, or a Treatise of Christian Equity and Moderation* (Cambridge, 1604), on which see John Bossy, *Peace in the Post-Reformation* (Cambridge: Cambridge University Press, 1998), 93–94.

25 This is the case recorded in the seventeenth century by the pastor of Göppingen in Württemberg reported by David Warren Sabean, *Power in the Blood: Popular Culture and Village Discourse in Early Modern Germany* (Cambridge: Cambridge University Press, 1984), 38ff.

26 See Lacey Baldwin Smith, "English Treason Trials and Confessions in the Sixteenth Century," *Journal of the History of Ideas* 15, no. 4 (1954): 471–498.

27 See Sarah Covington, *The Trail of Martyrdom: Persecution and Resistance in Sixteenth-Century England* (Notre Dame, IN: University of Notre Dame Press, 2003).

28 Ibid., 196.

29 Leon Radzinowicz, *A History of English Criminal Law and Its Administration from 1750*, vol. 1 (London: Stevens and Sons, 1948), 49–79.

30 E. P. Thompson, *Whigs and Hunters: The Origin of the Black Act* (London: Allen Lane, 1975), 188–189.

31 "He will pardon all your sins" (*The Penitent Thief or a Narrative of two Women, fearing God, who visited in prison a Highwayman, Executed at Stafford, April 3rd 1773*

[London: R. Hawes, 1773]). The text is in Timothy Gorringe, *God's Just Vengeance: Crime, Violence and the Rhetoric of Salvation* (Cambridge: Cambridge University Press, 1996), 2–3.

32 See Peter Linebaugh, *The London Hanged: Crime and Civil Society in the Eighteenth Century* (Harmondsworth, UK: Penguin, 1991), 214–215. The passage is cited in Gorringe, *God's Just Vengeance*, 3–4.

33 One of the most celebrated works in this regard is the three-volume *Lives of the Most Remarkable Criminals* (London: John Osborn, 1735), republished by Arthur L. Hayward in 1874 and on other occasions thereafter (New York: Dodd, Mead and Co., 1927; London: Routledge, 2002). On the context and fortunes of this textual genre, a useful survey is Karl S. Gutke, *Last Words: Variations on a Theme in Cultural History* (Princeton, NJ: Princeton University Press, 1992), chap. 4, 98–154.

34 See Peter Linebaugh, "The Ordinary of Newgate and His 'Account,'" in *Crime in England, 1550–1800,* ed. J. S. Cockburn (London: Methuen, 1977), 247–269, esp. 255.

35 Rosamaria Loretelli, "Modelli e legittimazioni: La letteratura popolare racconta," in De Romanis and Loretelli, *Il delitto narrato al popolo,* 36–61, esp. 46.

36 On these texts, see James A. Sharpe, "'Last Dying Speeches': Religion, Ideology and Public Execution in Seventeenth-Century England," *Past and Present* 107 (1985): 144–167.

37 See Peter Linebaugh, "The Tyburn Riot: Against the Surgeons," in *Albion's Fatal Tree: Crime and Society in Eighteenth-Century England,* ed. Douglas Hay, Peter Linebaugh, John G. Rule, E. P. Thompson, and Cal Winslow (London: Allen Lane, 1975), 65–117, esp. 69–78. A picture of how justice functioned is offered by John Maurice Beattie, *Crime and the Courts in England, 1660–1800* (Oxford: Clarendon Press, 1986).

38 The distinction is made by E. P. Thompson, *The Making of the English Working Class* (Harmondsworth, UK: Penguin, 1963), 41.

39 Ibid., 663–664.

40 Gorringe, *God's Just Vengeance*, 4–6.

41 An important collection of studies about the origin and diffusion of this literary genre is Rudolf Lenz, *Leichenpredigten als Quelle historischer Wissenschaften* (Cologne: Böhlau Verlag, 1975).

42 Also underlined by James A. Sharpe, *Crime in Early Modern England, 1550–1750* (London: Longman, 1984), 150ff.

43 Ibid., 162–163.

44 See Adelisa Malena, "Imparzialità confessionale e conversione come 'rigenerazione' nel pietismo radicale: La *Historie der Wiedergebohrnen* di J. H. Reitz (1698–1753)," in *Les modes de la conversion confessionnelle à l'époque moderne,* ed. Maria-Cristina Pitassi and Daniela Solfaroli Camillocci (Florence: Olschki, 2010).

45 On autobiographic writing in Pietist circles in the eighteenth and nineteenth centuries, see Ulrike Gleixner, *Pietismus und Bürgertum: Eine historische Anthropologie der Frömmigkeit* (Göttingen: Vandenhoeck und Ruprecht, 2005), 123–208.

46 See Susanne Kord, *Murderesses in German Writing, 1720–1860: Heroines of Horror* (New York: Cambridge University Press, 2009).

47 For more on his biography and activity, see Reinhard Rürup, *Johann Jacob Moser, Pietismus und Reform* (Wiesbaden: F. Steiner, 1965). On his work as a collector and editor of stories about conversions before the scaffold, see Jonathan Strom, "Pietist Conversion Narratives and Confessional Identity," in *Conversion and the Politics of Religion in Early Modern Germany,* ed. David M. Luebke, Jared Poley, Daniel C. Ryan, and David Warren Sabean (New York: Berghahn Books, 2012).

48 [Johann Jacob Moser, ed.,] *Selige letzte Stunden einiger dem zeitlichen Tode übergebener Missethäter, mit einem Vorrede,* vol. 1 (Ebersdorf, 1740); 2nd ed., Jena, 1742, with the title *Selige letzte Stunden hingerichteter Personen.* A new edition of the collection, introduced by Moser, came out in Munich in 1752, and was later reprinted with additions in Stuttgart (Belser'sche Buchhandlung, 1861).

49 The case of Christian Friedrich Ritters appeared in the second edition of Moser's collection, ibid., 46–84; and also in a similar collection prepared by Ernst Gottlieb Woltersdorf, ed., *Der Schächer am Kreuz: Das ist, Vollständige Nachricht von der Bekehrung und seeligem Ende hingerichteter Missethäter,* vol. 1 (Budißin und Görlitz: Jacob Deinzer, 1761). I cite from the recent edition with commentary in a collection of Pietist texts: Manfred Jakubowski-Tiessen, ed., *Bekehrung unterm Galgen* (Leipzig: Evangelische Verlagsanstalt, 2011), 9–60 (I wish to thank Adelisa Malena for pointing this out to me).

50 Jakubowski-Tiessen, *Bekehrung unterm Galge,* 63–142.

51 Woltersdorf, *Der Schächer am Kreuz.*

52 Kord, *Murderesses in German Writing,* 196–197. In the extensive bibliography on this topic, mention must at least be made of Rainer Lächele, "Maleficanten und Pietisten auf dem Schafott: Historische Überlegungen zur Delinquentenseelsorge im 18. Jahrhundert," *Zeitschrift für Kirchengeschichte* 107, no. 2 (1996): 179–200.

53 The cases in Woltersdorf's collection are presented and commented on by Heinz D. Kittsteiner, *Die Entstehung des modernen Gewissens* (Frankfurt: Suhrkamp, 1995), 336–338.

54 The quotation is taken from Marzio Barbagli, *Congedarsi dal mondo: Il suicidio in Occidente e in Oriente* (Bologna: il Mulino, 2009), 87–90.

55 See Tyge Krogh, *A Lutheran Plague: Murdering to Die in the Eighteenth Century* (Leiden: Brill, 2012), appendix, 199–211. My thanks to Marzio Barbagli for drawing my attention to this book.

56 Ibid., 137–162, esp. 149.

57 See also the Italian version of his comment in Cesare Beccaria, *Dei delitti e delle pene,* vol. 1, Edizione Nazionale delle opera di Cesare Beccaria diretta da Luigi Firpo (Milan: Mediobanca, 1984), 597–624.

58 See the concluding chapter of Benjamin T. G. Mayes, *Counsel and Conscience: Lutheran Casuistry and Moral Reasoning after the Reformation* (Göttingen: Vandenhoeck und Ruprecht, 2011), 204ff. That a "modern conscience" was taking shape in Germany at the time is the thesis of Kittsteiner, *Der Entstehung.*

59 See Jacques Le Rider, "L'autobiographie en question: Herder, juge des *Confessions* de Rousseau," *Revue germanique internationale* 20 (2003): 83–100.

60 Michel Foucault, *Discipline and Punish: The Birth of the Prison,* 2nd ed., trans. Alan Sheridan (New York: Vintage Books, 1995), 30.

61 See Scott D. Seay, *Hanging between Heaven and Earth: Capital Crime, Execution Preaching, and Theology in Early New England* (DeKalb: Northern Illinois University Press, 2009), 26.

62 See Paul S. Boyer and Stephen Nissenbaum, *Salem Possessed: The Social Origins of Witchcraft* (Cambridge, MA: Harvard University Press, 1974).

63 "From magistrate to slave" (Seay, *Hanging between Heaven and Earth,* 27). A careful analysis of the production, sale, and circulation of crime literature as a form of American popular culture is offered by Daniel Cohen, *Pillars of Salt, Monuments of Grace: New England Crime Literature and the Origins of American Popular Culture, 1674–1860* (New York: Oxford University Press, 1993).

64 Seay, *Hanging between Heaven and Earth,* 114, 172.

65 Ibid., 38.

33. THE SLOW EPILOGUE OF COMFORTING IN NINETEENTH-CENTURY ITALY

1 As an anonymous commentator put it in *Civiltà cattolica,* quoted in Mario Pisani, *Cesare Beccaria e "l'Index Librorum Prohibitorum"* (Naples: Edizioni scientifiche italiane, 2013), 19 (Lazeri's assessment is in the appendix).

2 The decree is published in Eugenio Cappelli, *La Compagnia dei Neri* (Florence: Cappelli, 1927), 74.

3 Luigi Cibrario, *Storia di Torino,* vol. 2 (Turin: Alessandro Fontana, 1846), 11.

4 The letter was published by Benedetto Croce in *La rivoluzione napoletana del 1799: Biografie–racconti–ricerche,* Edizione nazionale delle opere di Benedetto Croce, ed. Cinzia Cassani (Naples: Bibliopolis, 1999), 218–221; the quotes from the registers of the Whites are taken from Attilio Simioni, *Le origini del risorgimento politico dell'Italia meridionale,* vol. 2 (Messina: Giuseppe Principato, 1925), 99–103, 150–152. On the medieval Christian tradition of the ancient theme of dying for one's country, see Ernst H. Kantorowicz, "*Pro patria mori* in Medieval Political Thought," *American Historical Review* 56, no. 3 (1951): 472–492.

5 The letter from the ministry of ecclesiastic affairs communicating the decree is dated March 9, 1820: see Antonino Cutrera, *Cronologia dei giustiziati di Palermo, 1541–1819* (Palermo: Scuola Tipografica Boccone del Povero, 1917), 23. It orders that the Company "is to be considered a wholly ecclesiastic congregation."

6 Ibid., 309–310.

7   Ibid., 312.

8   The ministerial letter of June 27, 1821, is held in ASDNa, *Archivio dei Bianchi della Giustizia,* filza 334, doc. n. 51; see also Antonio Illibato, *La Compagnia napoletana dei Bianchi della Giustizia: Note storico-critiche e inventario dell'archivio* (Naples: D'Auria, 2004), 115.

9   Illibato, *La Compagnia napoletana,* 20; emphasis in original.

10 For the Lucca confraternity of Sant Croce, suppressed in 1801, we have a land and property register, or *martilogio* (Archivio Arcivescovile di Lucca, *Archivio della commissione ecclesiastica,* ms 3079).

11 ASCMo, *Vachetta per li iustitiati 1593–1826,* 89. The ritual appears unchanged in the description of an execution in 1801: see Antonio Rovatti, *Dall'aquila imperiale al ritorno dei francesi,* ed. Gian Paolo Brizzi (Cinisello Balsamo: Pizzi, 1997), 219–220.

12 ACMo, *Fondo Arciconfraternita di San Giovanni Battista della Morte,* Partiti 1823–1829, cc. 35v–39r.

13 Luigi Martini, *Il confortatorio di Mantova negli anni 1851, 52, 53 e 55* (Mantua: Benvenuti, 1867).

14 The loose leaf sheet is in AABo, *Archivio consorziale del clero urbano,* IX A 8.

15 His name appears at the beginning of the "libro censorio 1724–1767" (*Archivio consorziale del clero urbano,* IX, C 1).

16 AABo, *Archivio consorziale del clero urbano,* IX F 4.

17 Ibid., IX F 10.

18 BCA, *Libro di tutti li giustiziati in Bologna incominciando l'anno 1030 per sino al 1834 con i nomi e cognomi de' medemi,* c. 159v.

19 AABo, *Archivio consorziale del clero urbano,* Scuola dei confortatori, Corrispondenza, cc. n. n.

20 BCA, *Libro di tutti li giustiziati,* c. 180r. For more on the story of Gaetano Prosperi, who had waged his own personal war against the new liberal state, see Claudio Evangelisti, *Lo Spirito: Il brigante del papa re* (Rastignano [Bologna]: Gruppo di studi Savena Setta Sambro, 2012), which includes an exhaustive apparatus of sources. My thanks to Roberto Finzi for drawing my attention to the work.

21 The text of the statutes was published in the appendix to the history of the confraternity pieced together on the basis of archive documents by Giovanni Battista Vermiglioli, *Nuova riforma delle costituzioni della venerabile Compagnia dei SS. Andrea e Bernardino in Perugia detta della giustizia con la storia del medesimo pio istituto* (Perugia: Bartelli, 1846), 57–79, esp. 78.

22 Isabella Rosoni, *Criminalità e giustizia penale nello Stato Pontificio del secolo XIX: Un caso di banditismo rurale* (Milan: Giuffrè, 1988), 223–232, esp. 225.

23 *Ipotesi de' propositi probabili a trattarsi nella conforteria del condannato Fabbri Mariano fratricida* (ASDFe, *Fondo Arciconfraternita della Morte e Orazione di Ferrara*).

24 *Sunto del direttorio di conforteria praticatosi fin ora e da conservarsene l'osservanza dalla Scuola e congregazione di conforteria della venerabile arciconfraternita della morte ed orazione in Ferrara* (1852). The booklet in 12° comprises 12 pages. The *Statuti della Ven. Archiconfraternita della Morte, ed Orazione prima approvati, e confermati l'anno 1590, e poi riformati l'anno 1698, e ristampati nell'anno del Santissimo Giubileo MDCCL* (Rome, 1750) is much larger.

25 *Sunto del direttorio,* 6–9.

26 Printed *quinterno* (five sheets of paper) dated May 1, 1853, bound inside the copy of eighteenth-century statutes conserved in ASDFe, *Fondo Arciconfraternita della Morte e Orazione di Ferrara.* On the definition of "dangerous classes," see Louis Chevalier, *Laboring Classes and Dangerous Classes in Paris during the First Half of the Nineteenth Century* [1958], trans. Frank Jellinek (Princeton, NJ: Princeton University Press, 1981). For more on Italian aspects and the role of the confraternities, see John Anthony Davis, *Conflict and Control: Law and Order in Nineteenth-Century Italy* (London: Macmillan, 1988), 40.

27 The exercise entitled "death penalty" is in ASDFe, *Archivio Arciconfraternita della Morte e Orazione,* cc. n. n.

28 In that year the governor Giorgio Massai wrote the foreword to a celebrative volume rich in documents and artistic reproductions: *Arciconfraternita di San Giovanni Decollato detta della Misericordia della nazione fiorentina in Roma, 1488–1988* (Rome: Palombi, 1988).

29 See David I. Kertzer, *The Kidnapping of Edgardo Mortara* (London: Picador, 1997).

30 ASR, *Confraternita di S. Giovanni decollato (1497–1870),* registro 35, 128–131.

31 Gaetano Sanvittore, *I misteri del processo Monti e Tognetti* (Milan: Cesare Cioffi, 1869), esp. 147–154.

32 "He declared great remorse for his wrongdoing, in the presence of brothers who acted as witnesses, and at the same time displayed the most beautiful and Christian sentiments that one can hear in the mouth of a Christian, toward his parents, relatives, and friends. It pleases us here to quote some passages from the original written in the hand of the brother Provveditore, Don Giovanni de' Principi Chigi, in lieu of the notary. He said that prayers should be offered to the same [relatives], that they might bless and not forget him, and he will not forget them. . . . He professes that he dies as a good Christian, resigned to the will of God, forgiving his fellow human beings for any offense he may have received, as he hopes that the Lord will forgive him his sins" (*Relazione degli ultimi giorni di Giuseppe Monti e di Gaetano Tognetti giustiziati in Roma il dì 24 novembre 1868, articolo estratto dal quad. 450 della Civiltà Cattolica con aggiunte* [Rome, 1868], 13–14).

33 ASR, *Confraternita di S. Giovanni decollato (1497–1870),* registro 35, 135–137 (see Chapter 19). Bellomo's name is the final one in the register of the executioner Vincenzo Balducci (see Alessandro Ademollo, *Le annotazioni di Mastro Titta carnefice*

romano: Supplizi e suppliziati. Giustizie eseguite da Gio. Batt. Bugatti e dal suo successore (1796–1870) [Città di Castello: S. Lapi, 1886], 79).

34 On the successful struggle to win over public opinion conducted by a fairly small group of professors and cultural figures, see Italo Mereu, *La morte come pena: Saggio sulla violenza legale* (Milan: Editori europei associati, 2000), 189.

35 Lucien Febvre, *The Problem of Unbelief in the Sixteenth Century: The Religion of Rabelais* [1947], trans. Beatrice Gottlieb (Cambridge, MA: Harvard University Press, 1982).

36 Helen Prejean, *Dead Man Walking* (New York: Random House, 1993).

37 Fyodor Dostoyevsky, *Crime and Punishment* [1866], trans. Jessie Coulson (Oxford: Oxford University Press, 2008), 152.

INDEX

Note: Page numbers in *italics* indicate figures; *pl.* indicates the color plates.